computer
sciences

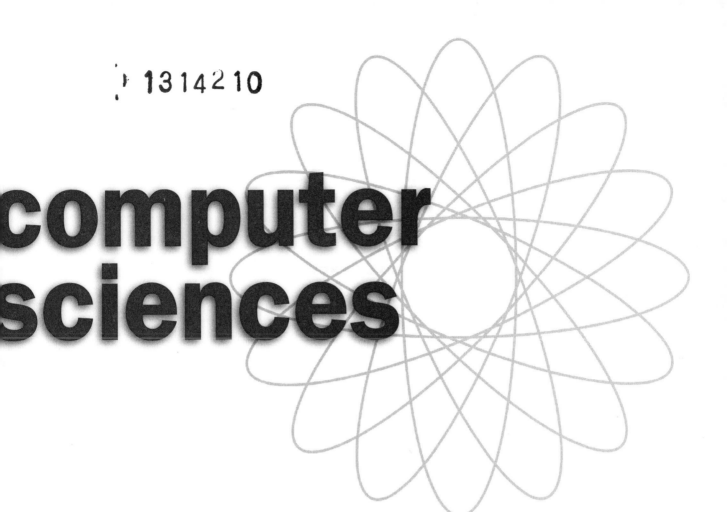

computer
sciences

VOLUME **4**
Electronic Universe

Roger R. Flynn, Editor in Chief

MACMILLAN
REFERENCE
USA™

THOMSON
───────
GALE

New York • Detroit • San Diego • San Francisco • Cleveland • New Haven, Conn. • Waterville, Maine • London • Munich

Macmillan Reference USA   Gale Group
300 Park Avenue South   27500 Drake Rd.
New York, NY 10010   Farmington Hills, MI 48331-3535

Library of Congress Cataloging-in-Publication Data
Computer sciences / Roger R. Flynn, editor in chief.
          p.   cm.
        Includes bibiographical references and index.
        ISBN 0-02-865566-4 (set: hardcover : alk. paper) —
        ISBN 0-02-865567-2 (Volume 1: Foundations: Ideas and People : alk. paper) —
        ISBN 0-02-865568-0 (Volume 2: Software and Hardware : alk. paper) —
        ISBN 0-02-865569-9 (Volume 3: Social Applications : alk. paper) —
        ISBN 0-02-865570-2 (Volume 4: Electronic Universe : alk. paper)
        1. Computer science. I. Flynn, Roger R., 1939-
QA76 .C572   2002
004—dc21

                                                    2002000754

Printed in the United States of America
1 2 3 4 5 6 7 8 9 10

Preface

The science of computing has come a long way since the late 1930s, when John Vincent Atanasoff and Clifford Berry began work on the first electronic digital computer. One marvels to see how the science has advanced from the days of Charles Babbage, who developed the Difference Engine in the 1820s, and, later proposed the Analytical Engine. Computer science was and continues to be an intriguing field filled with interesting stories, colorful personalities, and incredible innovations.

Ever since their invention, computers have had a profound impact on society and the ways in which humans conduct business and financial matters, fight wars and maintain peace, provide goods and services, predict events (e.g., earthquakes, the weather, global warming), monitor security and safety, and a host of other applications too numerous to mention. Plus, the personal computer revolution, beginning in the 1980s, has brought computers into many homes and schools. This has helped students find new ways to prepare reports, conduct research, and study using computerized methods. In the new millennium, the role that computers play in society continues to grow.

The World of Computer Science

In preparing this encyclopedia, I came across references to the early work on the IBM System/360 series of computers, which featured capacities of 65,000 to 16 million bytes (4 byte-words) of main storage and disk storage of several million to tens or hundreds of million bytes. At the same time, I opened the Sunday paper in February of 2002 and scanned the ads for personal computers, announcing memories of several hundred million bytes and disk storage of gigabytes. The cost of the 360 series ranged from fifty to several hundred thousand dollars to more than a million. Prices for the computers advertised in my Sunday paper ranged from several hundred dollars to a few thousand. The IBM 360 series was released in 1964. If a similar breakthrough occurred in education or automobile manufacturing (a factor of 1000, on the conservative side), a year in college would cost $20, as would a good model car! This, of course, is not the case.

However, computer hardware is not the entire story. Machines all need software, operating systems, applications software, and the like. While a person was hard pressed to get a line drawing or a bar chart on the screen 25 years ago, someone today has a choice of presentation software (slides or projections of the computer screen), desktop publishing, spreadsheets, and the like, much of which comes bundled with the system.

In fact, today one can purchase, for a few thousand dollars, more equipment and software than the Department of Information Science and

Telecommunications at my school (the University of Pittsburgh) or, for that matter, the entire university, could buy, when I first arrived in 1974. This is, indeed, an extraordinary era to have been a part of and witnessed. However, this does not happen in a vacuum. In this encyclopedia we aim to detail the people, activities, products, and growth of knowledge that have helped computer science evolve into what it is today.

Volume Breakdown

The organization of this encyclopedia reflects the history and application of the field. Our first volume in this series is dedicated to the history of computing. Its subtitle is *Foundations: Ideas and People.* The second volume describes *Software and Hardware,* while the third addresses *Social Applications.* The fourth is appropriately subtitled the *Electronic Universe* as it looks at such developments and inventions as the Internet, ubiquitous computing (embedded computing), and miniaturization.

While the intent is to give an exhaustive view of the field, no encyclopedia of this size, or, for that matter, ten times its size, could provide a complete rendering of the developments, events, people, and technology involved. Hence, the four volumes provide a representative selection of the people, places, and events involved. The encyclopedia was developed from a U.S. point of view, but we trust that the articles herein are not intentionally biased and, hopefully, do justice to innovations and contributions from elsewhere in the world. A brief look at each volume of the encyclopedia follows.

Volume 1

Volume I discusses the foundations of computer science, including computing history and some important innovators. Among the people are American inventor Herman Hollerith (1860–1929), the designer of punched card and punched card equipment; English mathematician Charles Babbage (1791–1871), the inventor of the Difference Engine and the proposed Analytical Engine, a precursor of the stored program computer; English noblewoman Ada Byron King, the Countess of Lovelace (1815–1852), the first "computer programmer"; American executive Thomas J. Watson Sr. (1874–1956), early chief of the IBM Corporation; and American mathematician Grace Hopper (1906–1992), who helped in the development of COBOL (COmmon Business Oriented Language) and developed one of its predecessors, FLOW-MATIC, and is the person who allegedly coined the term "computer bug."

Within Volume 1, various groups and organizations are discussed. These include the Association for Computing Machinery (ACM), which brings together people from around the globe to exchange ideas and advance computer science; the Institute of Electrical and Electronic Engineers (IEEE), which serves as the world's largest technical professional association, with more than 350,000 members; and the IBM Corporation, Apple Computer Inc., and the Microsoft Corporation, which all contributed to the start of the personal computer (PC) revolution. Among the more general articles the reader will find those concerning topics such as early pioneers, featuring primarily American and European scientists and their work; language generations, focusing on the evolution of computer languages; and computer generations, discussing early machines such as the ENIAC (Electronic

*Explore further in Hollerith, Herman; Babbage, Charles; Lovelace, Ada Byron King, Countess of; Watson, Thomas J., Sr; and Hopper, Grace.

*Explore further in Association for Computing Machinery; Institute of Electrical and Electronic Engineers (IEEE); IBM Corporation; Apple Computer, Inc.; Microsoft Corporation; Early Pioneers; Generations, Languages; and Generations, Computers.

Numerical Integrator and Computer) and the EDVAC (Electronic Discrete Variable Automatic Computer).

Finally, other articles of general interest in Volume 1 concern the history and workings of supercomputers; the development of the mouse; the question of computer security; the beginnings of the Internet; and the basics of digital and analog computing. The government's role is explained in articles on the U.S. Census Bureau and funding research projects. In addition, mathematical tools such as the binary number system and the slide rule as well as innovations such as France's Minitel are also featured.

*Explore further in Supercomputers; Mouse; Security; Internet; Digital Computing; Analog Computing; Census Bureau; Government Funding, Research; Binary Number System; Slide Rule; Minitel.

Volume 2

Volume 2 describes software and hardware. Articles cover topics from system analysis and design, which is the cornerstone of building a system, to operating systems, compilers, and parallel processing, which discuss some of the technical aspects of computing. Telecommunication subjects range from network design to wireless technology to ATM transmission, while application-oriented articles include pattern recognition, personal digital assistants (PDAs), and computer music. Essays concerning software products include object-oriented languages, client/server technology, invasive programs, and programming.

*Explore further in System Analysis; Systems Design; Operating Systems; Compilers; Parallel Processing; Network Design; Wireless Technology; ATM Transmission; Pattern Recognition; Personal Digital Assistants; Music, Computer; Object-Oriented Languages; Client/Server Systems; Invasive Programs; and Programming.

Among the people featured in Volume 2 are John Bardeen (1908–1991), Walter H. Brattain (1902–1987), and William B. Shockley (1910–1989), inventors of the transistor; English mathematician George Boole (1815–1864), developer of Boolean logic; and Alexander Graham Bell (1847–1922), inventor of the telephone. Rounding out Volume 2 are the technical aspects of hardware-related topics, including coding techniques, digital logic design, and cellular technology.

*Explore further in Bardeen, John, Brattain, Walter H., and Shockley, William B.; Boole, George; Boolean Algebra; Bell, Alexander Graham; Coding Techniques; Codes; Digital Logic Design; and Cellular Technology.

Volume 3

In Volume 3, the emphasis is on social applications. From fashion design to meteorology, the use of computers impacts our everyday lives. For example, computer technology has greatly influenced the study of biology, molecular biology, physics, and mathematics, not to mention the large role it plays in air traffic management and aircraft flight control, ATM machines and magnetic stripe cards for shopping and business. Businesses, large and small, have significantly benefited from applications that track product growth, costs, and the way products are managed. Volume 3 essays also explore the computer's role in medical image analysis and legal systems, while our use of computers in everyday life and our means of interacting with them are addressed in subjects such as library applications and speech recognition.

*Explore further in Fashion Design; Weather Forecasting; Biology; Molecular Biology; Physics; Mathematics; Aircraft Traffic Management; Aircraft Flight Control; ATM Machines; Magnetic Stripe Cards; Project Management; Economic Modeling; Process Control; Productivity Software; Integrated Software; Image Analysis: Medicine; Legal Systems; Library Applications; Speech Recognition.

Volume 3 addresses our aesthetic and intellectual pursuits in areas such as composing music, playing chess, and designing buildings. Yet the advancements of computer sciences go much further as described in articles about agriculture, geographic information systems, and astronomy. Among the people featured in the volume are American inventor Al Gross (1918–2001), the "father of wireless"; Hungarian mathematician Rózsa Péter (1905–1977), promoter of the study of recursive functions; and American author Isaac Asimov (1920–1992), famed science fiction writer who wrote extensively about robots.

*Explore further in Music Composition; Chess Playing; Architecture; Agriculture; Geographic Information Systems; Astronomy; Gross, Alfred J.; Péter, Rózsa; Asimov, Isaac.

Volume 4

✱Explore further in Internet: History; Internet: Applications; Internet: Backbone; Molecular Computing; Artificial Life; Mobile Computing; Cryptography; E-banking; E-books; E-commerce; E-journals and E-publishing; Information Access; Information Overload; Ethics; Copyright; and Patents.

Volume 4 delves into our interconnected, networked society. The Internet is explored in detail, including its history, applications, and backbone. Molecular computing and artificial life are discussed, as are mobile computing and encryption technology. The reader will find articles on electronic banking, books, commerce, publishing, as well as information access and overload. Ethical matters pertaining to the electronic universe are also addressed.

Volume 4 extends our aesthetic interest with articles on photography and the use of computers in art. Readers will learn more about how cybercafes keep friends and family connected as well as the type of social impact that computers have had on society. Data gathering, storage, and retrieval are investigated in topics such as data mining and data warehousing. Similarly, Java applets, JavaScript, agents, and Visual Basic are featured.

✱Explore further in Photography; Art; Cybercafe; Social Impact; Data Mining; Data Warehousing; Java Applets; JavaScript; Agents; Visual Basic.

Among the people highlighted in Volume 4 are Italian physicist Guglielmo Marconi (1874–1937), inventor of wireless communications; American engineer Claude E. Shannon (1916–2001), a pioneer of information theory; and Soviet mathematician Victor M. Glushkov (1923–1982), who advanced the science of cybernetics.

✱Explore further in Marconi, Guglielmo; Shannon, Claude E.; Glushkov, Victor M.

The Many Facets of Computer Science

Computer science has many interesting stories, many of which are told in this volume. Among them are the battle between John Atanasoff and John Mauchley and J. Presper Eckert Jr. over the patent to the electronic digital computer and regenerative memory, symbolized and embodied in the lawsuits between Sperry-Rand (Mauchley-Eckert) and Honeywell (Atanasoff) and Sperry-Rand (Mauchley-Eckert) and CDC (Atanasoff). The lawsuits are not covered here, but the principal actors are. And there is Thomas J. Watson's prediction, possibly apocryphal, of the need ("demand") for 50 computers worldwide! Plus, Ada Byron King, Countess of Lovelace, became famous for a reason other than being British poet Lord George Gordon Byron's daughter. And German inventor Konrad Zuse (1910–1995) saw his computers destroyed by the Allies during World War II, while Soviet mathematician Victor M. Glushkov (1923–1982) had an institute named after him and his work.

✱Explore further in Zuse, Konrad.

Scientific visualization is now a topic of interest, while data processing is passé. Nanocomputing has become a possibility, while mainframes are still in use and e-mail is commonplace in many parts of the world. It has been a great half-century or so (60 some years) for a fledgling field that began, possibly, with the Abacus!

✱Explore further in Data Processing; Nanocomputing; Mainframes; E-mail; Abacus.

Organization of the Material

Computer Sciences contains 286 entries that were newly commissioned for this work. More than 125 people contributed to this set, some from academia, some from industry, some independent consultants. Many contributors are from the United States, but other countries are represented including Australia, Canada, Great Britain, and Germany. In many cases, our contributors have written extensively on their subjects before, either in books or journal articles. Some even maintain their own web sites providing further information on their research topics.

Most entries in this set contain illustrations, either photos, graphs, charts, or tables. Many feature sidebars that enhance the topic at hand or give a glimpse into a topic of related interest. The entries—geared to high school students and general readers—include glossary definitions of unfamiliar terms to help the reader understand complex topics. These words are highlighted in the text and defined in the margins. In addition, each entry includes a bibliography of sources of further information as well as a list of related entries in the encyclopedia.

Additional resources are available in the set's front and back matter. These include a timeline on significant events in computing history, a timeline on significant dates in the history of programming and markup and scripting languages, and a glossary. An index is included in each volume—Volume 4 contains a cumulative index covering the entire *Computer Sciences* encyclopedia.

Acknowledgments and Thanks

We would like to thank Elizabeth Des Chenes and Hélène Potter, who made the project possible; Cindy Clendenon; and, especially, Kathleen Edgar, without whose work this would not have been possible. Also thanks to Stephen Murray for compiling the glossary. And, I personally would like to thank the project's two other editors, Ida M. Flynn and Ann McIver McHoes, for their dedicated work in getting these volumes out. And finally, thanks to our many contributors. They provided "many voices," and we hope you enjoy listening to them.

Roger R. Flynn
Editor in Chief

Measurements

Data Unit	Abbreviation	Equivalent (Data Storage)	Power of Ten
Byte	B	8 bits	1 byte
Kilobyte	K, KB	$2^{10} = 1,024$ bytes	1,000 (one thousand) bytes
Megabyte	M, MB	$2^{20} = 1,048,576$ bytes	1,000,000 (one million) bytes
Gigabyte	GB	$2^{30} = 1,073,741,824$ bytes	1,000,000,000 (one billion) bytes
Terabyte	TB	$2^{40} = 1,099,511,627,776$ bytes	1,000,000,000,000 (one trillion) bytes
Petabyte	PB	$2^{50} = 1,125,899,906,842,624$ bytes	1,000,000,000,000,000 (one quadrillion) bytes

Time	Abbreviation	Equivalent	Additional Information
femtosecond	fs, fsec	10^{-15} seconds	1 quadrillionth of a second
picosecond	ps, psec	10^{-12} seconds	1 trillionth of a second
nanosecond	ns, nsec	10^{-9} seconds	1 billionth of a second
microsecond	μs, μsec	10^{-6} seconds	1 millionth of a second
millisecond	ms, msec	10^{-3} seconds	1 thousandth of a second
second	s, sec	1/60 of a minute; 1/3,600 of an hour	1 sixtieth of a minute; 1 thirty-six hundredths of an hour
minute	m, min	60 seconds; 1/60 of an hour	1 sixtieth of an hour
hour	h, hr	60 minutes; 3,600 seconds	
day	d	24 hours; 1,440 minutes; 86,400 seconds	
year	y, yr	365 days; 8,760 hours	
1,000 hours		1.3888... months (1.4 months)	$1,000 \div (30 \text{ days} \times 24 \text{ hours})$
8,760 hours		1 year	365 days $\times$ 24 hours
1 million hours		114.15525... years	$1,000,000 \div 8,760$
1 billion hours		~114,200... years	$1,000 \times 114.15525...$
1 trillion hours		~114,200,000 years	$1,000 \times 114,200$

Length	Abbreviation	Equivalent	Additional Information
nanometer	nm	10^{-9} meters (1 billionth of a meter)	~ 4/100,000,000 of an inch; ~ 1/25,000,000 of an inch
micrometer	μm	10^{-6} meter (1 millionth of a meter)	~ 4/100,000 of an inch; ~ 1/25,000 of an inch
millimeter	mm	10^{-3} meter (1 thousandth of a meter)	~ 4/100 of an inch; ~ 1/25 of an inch (2/5 $\times$ 1/10)
centimeter	cm	10^{-2} meter (1 hundredth of a meter); 1/2.54 of an inch	~ 2/5 of an inch (1 inch = 2.54 centimeters, exactly)
meter	m	100 centimeters; 3.2808 feet	~ 3 1/3 feet or 1.1 yards
kilometer	km	1,000 meters; 0.6214 miles	~ 3/5 of a mile
mile	mi	5,280 feet; 1.6093 kilometers	1.6×10^3 meters

Volume	Abbreviation	Equivalent	Additional Information
microliter	μl	1/1,000,000 liter	1 millionth of a liter
milliliter	ml	1/1,000 liter; 1 cubic centimeter	1 thousandth of a liter
centiliter	cl	1/100 liter	1 hundredth of a liter
liter	l	100 centiliters; 1,000 milliliters; 1,000,000 microliters; 1.0567 quarts (liquid)	~ 1.06 quarts (liquid)

Base 2 (Binary)	Decimal (Base 10) Equivalent	Approximations to Powers of Ten
2^0	1	
2^1	2	
2^2	4	
2^3	8	
2^4	16	
2^5	32	
2^6	64	
2^7	128	10^2; 100; one hundred; 1 followed by 2 zeros
2^8	256	
2^9	512	
2^{10}	1,024	10^3; 1,000; one thousand; 1 followed by 3 zeros
2^{11}	2,048	
2^{12}	4,096	
2^{13}	8,192	
2^{14}	16,384	
2^{15}	32,768	
2^{16}	65,536	
2^{17}	131,072	
2^{18}	262,144	
2^{19}	524,288	
2^{20}	1,048,576	10^6; 1,000,000; one million; 1 followed by 6 zeros
2^{21}	2,097,152	
2^{22}	4,194,304	
2^{23}	8,388,608	
2^{24}	16,777,216	
2^{25}	33,554,432	
2^{26}	67,108,864	
2^{27}	134,217,728	
2^{28}	268,435,456	
2^{29}	536,870,912	
2^{30}	1,073,741,824	10^9; 1,000,000,000; one billion; 1 followed by 9 zeros
2^{31}	2,147,483,648	
2^{32}	4,294,967,296	
2^{33}	8,589,934,592	
2^{34}	17,179,869,184	
2^{35}	34,359,738,368	
2^{36}	68,719,476,736	
2^{37}	137,438,953,472	
2^{38}	274,877,906,944	
2^{39}	549,755,813,888	
2^{40}	1,099,511,627,776	10^{12}; 1,000,000,000,000; one trillion; 1 followed by 12 zeros
2^{50}	1,125,899,906,842,624	10^{15}; 1,000,000,000,000,000; one quadrillion; 1 followed by 15 zeros
2^{100}	1,267,650,600,228,229,401,496,703,205,376	10^{30}; 1 followed by 30 zeros
2^{-1}	1/2	
2^{-2}	1/4	
2^{-3}	1/8	
2^{-4}	1/16	
2^{-5}	1/32	
2^{-6}	1/64	
2^{-7}	1/128	1/100; 10^{-2}; 0.01; 1 hundredth
2^{-8}	1/256	
2^{-9}	1/512	
2^{-10}	1/1,024	1 /1000; 10^{-3}; 0.001; 1 thousandth

Base 16 (Hexadecimal)	Binary (Base 2) Equivalent	Decimal (Base 10) Equivalent	Approximations to Powers of Ten
16^0	2^0	1	
16^1	2^4	16	
16^2	2^8	256	2×10^2; 2 hundred
16^3	2^{12}	4,096	4×10^3; 4 thousand
16^4	2^{16}	65,536	65×10^3; 65 thousand
16^5	2^{20}	1,048,576	1×10^6; 1 million
16^6	2^{24}	16,777,216	
16^7	2^{28}	268,435,456	
16^8	2^{32}	4,294,967,296	4×10^9; 4 billion
16^9	2^{36}	68,719,476,736	68×10^9; 68 billion
16^{10}	2^{40}	1,099,511,627,776	1×10^{12}; 1 trillion
16^{-1}	2^{-4}	1/16	
16^{-2}	2^{-8}	1/256	
16^{-3}	2^{-12}	1/4,096	$1/4 \times 10^{-3}$; 1/4-thousandth
16^{-4}	2^{-16}	1/65,536	
16^{-5}	2^{-20}	1/1,048,576	10^{-6}; 1 millionth
16^{-8}	2^{-32}	1/4,294,967,296	$1/4 \times 10^{-9}$; 1/4-billionth
16^{-10}	2^{-40}	1/1,099,511,627,776	10^{-12}; 1 trillionth

Base 10 (Decimal)	Equivalent	Verbal Equivalent
10^0	1	
10^1	10	
10^2	100	1 hundred
10^3	1,000	1 thousand
10^4	10,000	
10^5	100,000	
10^6	1,000,000	1 million
10^7	10,000,000	
10^8	100,000,000	
10^9	1,000,000,000	1 billion
10^{10}	10,000,000,000	
10^{11}	100,000,000,000	
10^{12}	1,000,000,000,000	1 trillion
10^{15}	1,000,000,000,000,000	1 quadrillion
10^{-1}	1/10	1 tenth
10^{-2}	1/100	1 hundredth
10^{-3}	1/1,000	1 thousandth
10^{-6}	1/1,000,000	1 millionth
10^{-9}	1/1,000,000,000	1 billionth
10^{-12}	1/1,000,000,000,000	1 trillionth
10^{-15}	1/1,000,000,000,000,000	1 quadrillionth

Sizes of and Distance to Objects

Object	Equivalent	Additional Information
Diameter of Electron (classical)	5.6×10^{-13} centimeters	5.6×10^{-13} centimeters; roughly 10^{-12} centimeters
Mass of Electron	9.109×10^{-28} grams	roughly 10^{-27} grams (1 gram = 0.0353 ounce)
Diameter of Proton	10^{-15} meters	10^{-13} centimeters
Mass of Proton	1.67×10^{-24} grams	roughly 10^{-24} grams (about 1,836 times the mass of electron)
Diameter of Neutron	10^{-15} meters	10^{-13} centimeters
Mass of Neutron	1.673×10^{-24} grams	roughly 10^{-24} grams (about 1,838 times the mass of electron)
Diameter of Atom (Electron Cloud)	ranges from 1×10^{-10} to 5×10^{-10} meters;	$\sim 10^{-10}$ meters; $\sim 10^{-8}$ centimeters; $\sim 3.94 \times 10^{-9}$ inches (roughly 4 billionth of an inch across or 1/250 millionth of an inch across)
Diameter of Atomic Nucleus	10^{-14} meters	$\sim 10^{-12}$ centimeters (10,000 times smaller than an atom)
Atomic Mass (Atomic Mass Unit)	1.66×10^{-27} kilograms	One atomic mass unit (amu) is equal to 1.66×10^{-24} grams
Diameter of (standard) Pencil	6 millimeters (0.236 inches)	roughly 10^{-2} meters
Height (average) of Man and Woman	man: 1.75 meters (5 feet, 8 inches) woman: 1.63 meters (5 feet, 4 inches)	human height roughly 2×10^{0} meters; $1/804.66$ miles; 10^{-3} miles
Height of Mount Everest	8,850 meters (29,035 feet)	~ 5.5 miles; roughly 10^{4} meters
Radius (mean equatorial) of Earth	6,378.1 kilometers (3,960.8 miles)	$\sim 6,400$ kilometers (4,000 miles); roughly 6.4×10^{6} meters
Diameter (polar) of Earth	12,713.6 kilometers (7,895.1 miles)	$\sim 12,800$ kilometers (8,000 miles); roughly 1.28×10^{7} meters (Earth's diameter is twice the Earth's radius)
Circumference (based on mean equatorial radius) of Earth	40,075 kilometers (24,887 miles)	$\sim 40,000$ kilometers (25,000 miles) (about 8 times the width of the United States) (Circumference = $2 \times \pi \times$ Earth's radius)
Distance from Earth to Sun	149,600,000 kilometers (92,900,000 miles)	$\sim 93,000,000$ miles; ~ 8.3 light-minutes; roughly 10^{11} meters; roughly 10^{8} miles
Distance to Great Nebula in Andromeda Galaxy	2.7×10^{19} kilometers (1.7×10^{19} miles)	~ 2.9 million light-years; roughly 10^{22} meters; roughly 10^{19} miles

Timeline: Significant Events in the History of Computing

The history of computer sciences has been filled with many creative inventions and intriguing people. Here are some of the milestones and achievements in the field.

c300-500 BCE	The counting board, known as the ancient abacus, is used. (Babylonia)
CE 1200	The modern abacus is used. (China)
c1500	Leonardo da Vinci drafts a design for a calculator. (Italy)
1614	John Napier suggests the use of logarithms. (Scotland)
1617	John Napier produces calculating rods, called "Napier's Bones." (Scotland)
	Henry Briggs formulates the common logarithm, Base 10. (England)
1620	Edmund Gunter devises the "Line of Numbers," the precursor to slide rule. (England)
1623	Wilhelm Schickard conceives a design of a mechanical calculator. (Germany)
1632	William Oughtred originates the slide rule. (England)
1642	Blaise Pascal makes a mechanical calculator, which can add and subtract. (France)
1666	Sir Samuel Morland develops a multiplying calculator. (England)
1673	Gottfried von Leibniz proposes a general purpose calculating machine. (Germany)
1777	Charles Stanhope, 3rd Earl of Stanhope, Lord Mahon, invents a logic machine. (England)
1804	Joseph-Marie Jacquard mechanizes weaving with Jacquard's Loom, featuring punched cards. (France)
1820	Charles Xavier Thomas (Tomas de Colmar) creates a calculating machine, a prototype for the first commercially successful calculator. (France)
1822	Charles Babbage designs the Difference Engine. (England)
1834	Charles Babbage proposes the Analytical Engine. (England)
1838	Samuel Morse formulates the Morse Code. (United States)
1842	L. F. Menabrea publishes a description of Charles Babbage's Analytical Engine. (Published, Italy)

1843	Ada Byron King, Countess of Lovelace, writes a program for Babbage's Analytical Engine. (England)
1854	George Boole envisions the Laws of Thought. (Ireland)
1870	William Stanley Jevons produces a logic machine. (England)
1873	William Thomson, Lord Kelvin, devises the analog tide predictor. (Scotland)
	Christopher Sholes, Carlos Glidden, and Samuel W. Soule invent the Sholes and Glidden Typewriter; produced by E. Remington & Sons. (United States)
1875	Frank Stephen Baldwin constructs a pin wheel calculator. (United States)
1876	Alexander Graham Bell develops the telephone. (United States)
	Bell's rival, Elisha Gray, also produces the telephone. (United States)
1878	Swedish inventor Willgodt T. Odhner makes a pin wheel calculator. (Russia)
1884	Dorr Eugene Felt creates the key-driven calculator, the Comptometer. (United States)
	Paul Gottlieb Nipkow produces the Nipkow Disk, a mechanical television device. (Germany)
1886	Herman Hollerith develops his punched card machine, called the Tabulating Machine. (United States)
1892	William Seward Burroughs invents his Adding and Listing (printing) Machine. (United States)
1896	Herman Hollerith forms the Tabulating Machine Company. (United States)
1901	Guglielmo Marconi develops wireless telegraphy. (Italy)
1904	John Ambrose Fleming constructs the diode valve (vacuum tube). (England)
	Elmore Ambrose Sperry concocts the circular slide rule. (United States)
1906	Lee De Forest invents the triode vacuum tube (audion). (United States)
1908	Elmore Ambrose Sperry produces the gyrocompass. (United States)
1910	Sperry Gyroscope Company is established. (United States)
1912	Frank Baldwin and Jay Monroe found Monroe Calculating Machine Company. (United States)
1914	Leonardo Torres Quevado devises an electromechanical calculator, an electromechanical chess machine (End Move). (Spain)
	Thomas J. Watson Sr. joins the Computing-Tabulating-Recording Company (CTR) as General Manager. (United States)

1919	W. H. Eccles and F. W. Jordan develop the flip-flop (memory device). (England)
1922	Russian-born Vladimir Kosma Zworykin develops the iconoscope and kinescope (cathode ray tube), both used in electronic television for Westinghouse. (United States)
1924	The Computing-Tabulating-Recording Company (CTR), formed in 1911 by the merger of Herman Hollerith's Tabulating Machine Company with Computing Scale Company and the International Time Recording Company, becomes the IBM (International Business Machines) Corporation. (United States)
1927	The Remington Rand Corporation forms from the merger of Remington Typewriter Company, Rand Kardex Bureau, and others. (United States)
1929	Vladimir Kosma Zworykin develops color television for RCA. (United States)
1931	Vannevar Bush develops the Differential Analyzer (an analog machine). (United States)
1933	Wallace J. Eckert applies punched card machines to astronomical data. (United States)
1937	Alan M. Turing proposes a Theoretical Model of Computation. (England)
	George R. Stibitz crafts the Binary Adder. (United States)
1939	John V. Atanasoff devises the prototype of an electronic digital computer. (United States)
	William R. Hewlett and David Packard establish the Hewlett-Packard Company. (United States)
1940	Claude E. Shannon applies Boolean algebra to switching circuits. (United States)
	George R. Stibitz uses the complex number calculator to perform Remote Job Entry (RJE), Dartmouth to New York. (United States)
1941	Konrad Zuse formulates a general-purpose, program-controlled computer. (Germany)
1942	John V. Atanasoff and Clifford Berry unveil the Atanasoff-Berry Computer (ABC). (United States)
1944	The Colossus, an English calculating machine, is put into use at Bletchley Park. (England)
	Howard Aiken develops the Automatic Sequence Controlled Calculator (ASCC), the Harvard Mark I, which is the first American program-controlled computer. (United States)
	Grace Hopper allegedly coins the term "computer bug" while working on the Mark I. (United States)
1946	J. Presper Eckert Jr. and John W. Mauchly construct the ENIAC (Electronic Numerical Integrator and Computer),

the first American general-purpose electronic computer, at the Moore School, University of Pennsylvania. (United States)

J. Presper Eckert Jr. and John W. Mauchly form the Electronic Control Company, which later becomes the Eckert-Mauchly Computer Corporation. (United States)

1947   John Bardeen, Walter H. Brattain, and William B. Shockley invent the transistor at Bell Laboratories. (United States)

J. Presper Eckert Jr. and John W. Mauchly develop the EDVAC (Electronic Discrete Variable Automatic Computer), a stored-program computer. (United States)

1948   F. C. Williams, Tom Kilburn, and G. C. (Geoff) Tootill create a small scale, experimental, stored-program computer (nicknamed "Baby") at the University of Manchester; it serves as the prototype of Manchester Mark I. (England)

1949   F. C. Williams, Tom Kilburn, and G. C. (Geoff) Tootill design the Manchester Mark I at the University of Manchester. (England)

Maurice V. Wilkes develops the EDSAC (Electronic Delay Storage Automatic Calculator) at Cambridge University. (England)

Jay Wright Forrester invents three dimensional core memory at the Massachusetts Institute of Technology. (United States)

Jay Wright Forrester and Robert Everett construct the Whirlwind I, a digital, real-time computer at Massachusetts Institute of Technology. (United States)

1950   J. H. Wilkinson and Edward A. Newman design the Pilot ACE (Automatic Computing Engine) implementing the Turing proposal for a computing machine at the National Physical Laboratory (NPL). (England)

Remington Rand acquires the Eckert-Mauchly Computer Corporation. (United States)

1951   Engineering Research Associates develops the ERA 1101, an American commercial computer, for the U.S. Navy and National Security Agency (NSA). (United States)

The UNIVAC I (Universal Automatic Computer), an American commercial computer, is created by Remington Rand for the U.S. Census Bureau. (United States)

Ferranti Mark I, a British commercial computer, is unveiled. (England)

Lyons Tea Co. announces Lyons Electronic Office, a British commercial computer. (England)

1952   UNIVAC I predicts election results as Dwight D. Eisenhower sweeps the U.S. presidential race. (United States)

Remington Rand Model 409, an American commercial computer, is originated by Remington Rand for the Internal Revenue Service. (United States)

Remington Rand acquires Engineering Research Associates. (United States)

1953 The IBM 701, a scientific computer, is constructed. (United States)

1954 The IBM 650 EDPM, electronic data processing machine, a stored-program computer in a punched-card environment, is produced. (United States)

1955 Sperry Corp. and Remington Rand merge to form the Sperry Rand Corporation. (United States)

1957 Robert N. Noyce, Gordon E. Moore, and others found Fairchild Semiconductor Corporation. (United States)

Seymour Cray, William Norris, and others establish Control Data Corporation. (United States)

Kenneth Olsen and Harlan Anderson launch Digital Equipment Corporation (DEC). (United States)

1958 Jack Kilby at Texas Instruments invents the integrated circuit. (United States)

1959 Robert N. Noyce at Fairchild Semiconductor invents the integrated circuit. Distinct patents are awarded to both Texas Instruments and Fairchild Semiconductor, as both efforts are recognized. (United States)

1960 The first PDP-1 is sold by Digital Equipment Corporation, which uses some technology from the Whirlwind Project. (United States)

The UNIVAC 1100 series of computers is announced by Sperry Rand Corporation. (United States)

1961 The Burroughs B5000 series dual-processor, with virtual memory, is unveiled. (United States)

1964 The IBM/360 family of computers begins production. (United States)

The CDC 6600 is created by Control Data Corporation. (United States)

1965 The UNIVAC 1108 from Sperry Rand Corporation is constructed. (United States)

The PDP-8, the first minicomputer, is released by Digital Equipment Corporation. (United States)

1968 Robert N. Noyce and Gordon E. Moore found Intel Corporation. (United States)

1969 The U.S. Department of Defense (DoD) launches ARPANET, the beginning of the Internet. (United States)

1970 The PDP-11 series of computers from Digital Equipment Corporation is put into use.(United States)

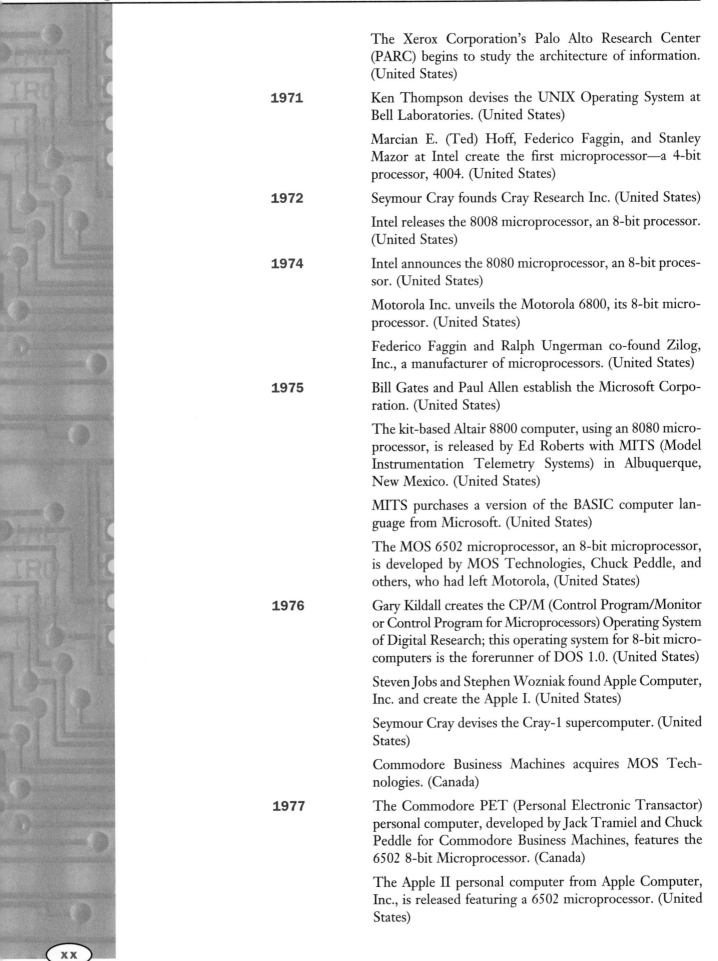

The Xerox Corporation's Palo Alto Research Center (PARC) begins to study the architecture of information. (United States)

1971   Ken Thompson devises the UNIX Operating System at Bell Laboratories. (United States)

Marcian E. (Ted) Hoff, Federico Faggin, and Stanley Mazor at Intel create the first microprocessor—a 4-bit processor, 4004. (United States)

1972   Seymour Cray founds Cray Research Inc. (United States)

Intel releases the 8008 microprocessor, an 8-bit processor. (United States)

1974   Intel announces the 8080 microprocessor, an 8-bit processor. (United States)

Motorola Inc. unveils the Motorola 6800, its 8-bit microprocessor. (United States)

Federico Faggin and Ralph Ungerman co-found Zilog, Inc., a manufacturer of microprocessors. (United States)

1975   Bill Gates and Paul Allen establish the Microsoft Corporation. (United States)

The kit-based Altair 8800 computer, using an 8080 microprocessor, is released by Ed Roberts with MITS (Model Instrumentation Telemetry Systems) in Albuquerque, New Mexico. (United States)

MITS purchases a version of the BASIC computer language from Microsoft. (United States)

The MOS 6502 microprocessor, an 8-bit microprocessor, is developed by MOS Technologies, Chuck Peddle, and others, who had left Motorola, (United States)

1976   Gary Kildall creates the CP/M (Control Program/Monitor or Control Program for Microprocessors) Operating System of Digital Research; this operating system for 8-bit microcomputers is the forerunner of DOS 1.0. (United States)

Steven Jobs and Stephen Wozniak found Apple Computer, Inc. and create the Apple I. (United States)

Seymour Cray devises the Cray-1 supercomputer. (United States)

Commodore Business Machines acquires MOS Technologies. (Canada)

1977   The Commodore PET (Personal Electronic Transactor) personal computer, developed by Jack Tramiel and Chuck Peddle for Commodore Business Machines, features the 6502 8-bit Microprocessor. (Canada)

The Apple II personal computer from Apple Computer, Inc., is released featuring a 6502 microprocessor. (United States)

The TRS-80 personal computer from Tandy Radio Shack, equipped with the Zilog Z80 8-bit microprocessor from Zilog, is unveiled. (United States)

1978   Intel announces the 8086 16-bit microprocessor. (United States)

Digital Equipment Corporation launches the VAX 11/780, a 4.3 billion byte computer with virtual memory. (United States)

1979   Intel presents the 8088 16-bit microprocessor. (United States)

Motorola Inc. crafts the MC 68000, Motorola 16-bit processor. (United States)

1980   Tim Patterson sells the rights to QDOS, an upgrade operating system of CP/M for 8088 and 8086 Intel microprocessors, 16-bit microprocessor, to Microsoft. (United States)

1981   The IBM Corporation announces the IBM Personal Computer featuring an 8088 microprocessor. (United States)

The Microsoft Operating System (MS-DOS) is put into use. (United States)

The Osborne I, developed by Adam Osborne and Lee Felsenstein with Osborne Computer Corporation, invent the first portable computer. (United States)

1982   Scott McNealy, Bill Joy, Andy Bechtolsheim, and Vinod Khosla found Sun Microsystems, Inc. (United States)

1984   The Macintosh PC from Apple Computer Inc., running with a Motorola 68000 microprocessor, revolutionizes the personal computer industry. (United States)

Richard Stallman begins the GNU Project, advocating the free use and distribution of software. (United States)

1985   The Free Software Foundation is formed to seek freedom of use and distribution of software. (United States)

Microsoft releases Windows 1.01. (United States)

1986   Sperry Rand and the Burroughs Corporation merge to form Unisys Corporation. (United States)

1989   SPARCstation I from Sun Microsystems is produced. (United States)

1991   Tim Berners-Lee begins the World Wide Web at CERN. (Switzerland)

Linus Torvalds builds the Linux Operating System. (Finland)

Paul Kunz develops the first web server outside of Europe, at the Stanford Linear Accelerator Center (SLAC). (United States)

1993	Marc Andreesen and Eric Bina create Mosaic, a web browser, at the National Center for Supercomputing Applications (NCSA), University of Illinois-Urbana Champaign. (United States)
1994	Marc Andreesen and James H. Clark form Mosaic Communications Corporation, later Netscape Communications Corporation. (United States)
	Netscape Navigator is launched by Netscape Communications Corporation. (United States)
1995	Java technology is announced by Sun Microsystems. (United States)
1996	World chess champion Garry Kasparov of Russia defeats Deep Blue, an IBM computer, in a man vs. computer chess matchup, four to two. (United States)
1997	IBM's Deep Blue defeats world chess champion Garry Kasparov in a rematch, 3.5 to 2.5. (United States)
	An injunction is filed against Microsoft to prohibit the company from requiring customers to accept Internet Explorer as their browser as a condition of using the Microsoft operating system Windows 95. (United States)
1998	America OnLine (AOL) acquires Netscape. (United States)
	Compaq Computer Corporation, a major producer of IBM compatible personal computers, buys Digital Equipment Corporation. (United States)
	America OnLine (AOL) and Sun form an alliance to produce Internet technology. (United States)
1999	Shawn Fanning writes code for Napster, a music file-sharing program. (United States)
	The Recording Industry Association of America (RIAA) files a lawsuit against Napster for facilitating copyright infringement. (United States)
2000	Zhores I. Alferov, Herbert Kroemer, and Jack Kilby share the Nobel Prize in Physics for contributions to information technology. Alferov, a Russian, and Kroemer, a German-born American, are acknowledged for their contributions to technology used in satellite communications and cellular telephones. Kilby, an American, is recognized for his work on the integrated circuit. (Sweden)

Timeline: The History of Programming, Markup and Scripting Languages

The history of computer sciences has been filled with many creative inventions and intriguing people. Here are some of the milestones and achievements in the field of computer programming and languages.

CE c800	al-Khowarizmi, Mohammed ibn-Musa develops a treatise on algebra, his name allegedly giving rise to the term algorithm.
1843	Ada Byron King, Countess of Lovelace, programs Charles Babbage's design of the Analytical Engine.
1945	Plankalkul is developed by Konrad Zuse.
1953	Sort-Merge Generator is created by Betty Holberton.
1957	FORTRAN is devised for IBM by John Backus and team of programmers.
	FLOW-MATIC is crafted for Remington-Rand's UNIVAC by Grace Hopper.
1958	LISP is produced by John McCarthy at Massachusetts Institute of Technology.
1960	ALGOL is the result of work done by the ALGOL Committee in the ALGOL 60 Report.
	COBOL is formulated by the CODASYL Committee, initiated by the the U.S. Department of Defense (DoD)
1961	JOSS is originated by the RAND Corporation.
	GPSS (General Purpose Simulation System) is invented by Geoffrey Gordon with IBM.
	RPG (Report Program Generator) is unveiled by IBM.
	APL (A Programming Language) is designed by Kenneth Iverson with IBM.
1963	SNOBOL is developed by David Farber, Ralph Griswold, and Ivan Polonsky at Bell Laboratories.
1964	BASIC is originated by John G. Kemeny and Thomas E. Kurtz at Dartmouth.
	PL/I is announced by IBM.
	Simula I is produced by Kristen Nygaard and Ole-Johan Dahl at the Norwegian Computing Center.
1967	Simula 67 is created by Kristen Nygaard and Ole-Johan Dahl at the Norwegian Computing Center.

	LOGO is devised by Seymour Papert at the MIT Artificial Intelligence Laboratory.
1971	Pascal is constructed by Niklaus Wirth at the Swiss Federal Institute of Technology (ETH) in Zurich.
1973	C developed by Dennis Ritchie at Bell Laboratories.
	Smalltalk is invented by Alan Kay at Xerox's PARC (Palo Alto Research Center).
1980	Ada is developed for the U.S. Department of Defense (DoD).
1985	C++ is created by Bjarne Stroustrup at Bell Laboratories.
1986	SGML (Standard Generalized Markup Language) is developed by the International Organization for Standardization (ISO).
1987	Perl is constructed by Larry Wall.
1991	Visual Basic is launched by the Microsoft Corporation.
	HTML (HyperText Markup Language) is originated by Tim Berners-Lee at CERN (Organization Europeene pour la Recherche Nucleaire).
1993	Mosaic is created by Marc Andreesen and Eric Bina for the National Center for Computing Applications (NCCA) at the University of Illinois-Urbana Champaign.
1995	Java is crafted by James Gosling of Sun Microsystems.
	A written specification of VRML (Virtual Reality Markup Language) is drafted by Mark Pesce, Tony Parisi, and Gavin Bell.
1996	Javascript is developed by Brendan Eich at Netscape Communications co-announced by Netscape and Sun Microsystems.
1997	VRML (Virtual Reality Modeling Language), developed by the Web3D Consortium, becomes an international standard.
1998	XML (Extensible Markup Language) is originated by a working group of the World Wide Web Consortium (W3C).

Contributors

Tom Abel
Penn State University, University Park, PA

Martyn Amos
University of Liverpool, United Kingdom

Richard Archer
Pittsburgh, PA

Pamela Willwerth Aue
Royal Oak, MI

Nancy J. Becker
St. John's University, New York

Mark Bedau
Reed College, Portland, OR

Pierfrancesco Bellini
University of Florence, Italy

Gary H. Bernstein
University of Notre Dame, Notre Dame, IN

Anne Bissonnette
Kent State University Museum, Kent, OH

Kevin W. Bowyer
University of Notre Dame, Notre Dame, IN

Stefan Brass
University of Giessen, Germany

Barbara Britton
Windsor Public Library, Windsor, Ontario, Canada

Kimberly Mann Bruch
San Diego Supercomputer Center, University of California, San Diego

Ivan Bruno
University of Florence, Italy

Dennis R. Buckmaster
Pennsylvania State University, University Park, PA

Dan Burk
University of Minnesota, Minneapolis, MN

Guoray Cai
Pennsylvania State University, University Park, PA

Shirley Campbell
University of Pittsburgh, Pittsburgh, PA

Siddharth Chandra
University of Pittsburgh, Pittsburgh, PA

J. Alex Chediak
University of California, Berkeley, CA

Kara K. Choquette
Xerox Corporation

John Cosgrove
Cosgrove Communications, Pittsburgh, PA

Cheryl L. Cramer
Digimarc Corporation, Tualatin, OR

Anthony Debons
University of Pittsburgh, Pittsburgh, PA

Salvatore Domenick Desiano
NASA Ames Research Center (QSS Group, Inc.)

Ken Doerbecker
Perfection Services, Inc.; WeirNet LLC; and FreeAir Networks, Inc.

Judi Ellis
KPMG, LLP, Pittsburgh, PA

Karen E. Esch
Karen Esch Associates, Pittsburgh, PA

Ming Fan
University of Notre Dame, Notre Dame, IN

Jim Fike
Ohio University, Athens, OH

Ida M. Flynn
University of Pittsburgh, Pittsburgh, PA

Roger R. Flynn
University of Pittsburgh, Pittsburgh, PA

H. Bruce Franklin
Rutgers University, Newark, NJ

Thomas J. Froehlich
Kent State University, Kent, OH

Chuck Gaidica
WDIV-TV, Detroit, MI

G. Christopher Hall
PricewaterhouseCoopers

Gary Hanson
Kent State University, Kent, OH

Karen Hartman
James Monroe Center Library, Mary Washington College, Fredericksburg, VA

Melissa J. Harvey
Carnegie Mellon University, Pittsburgh, PA

Albert D. Helfrick
Embry-Riddle Aeronautical University, Daytona Beach, FL

Stephen Hughes
University of Pittsburgh, Pittsburgh, PA

Bruce Jacob
University of Maryland, College Park, MD

Radhika Jain
Georgia State University, Atlanta, GA

Wesley Jamison
University of Pittsburgh at Greensburg

Sid Karin
San Diego Supercomputer Center, University of California, San Diego

Declan P. Kelly
Philips Research, The Netherlands

Betty Kirke
New York, NY

Mikko Kovalainen
University of Jyväskylä, Finland

Paul R. Kraus
Pittsburgh, PA

Prashant Krishnamurthy
University of Pittsburgh, Pittsburgh, PA

Marina Krol
Mount Sinai School of Medicine, New York, NY

Susan Landau
Sun Microsystems Inc., Mountain View, CA

Nicholas C. Laudato
University of Pittsburgh, Pittsburgh, Pennsylvania

George Lawton
Eutopian Enterprises

Cynthia Tumilty Lazzaro
Pinnacle Training Corp., Stoneham, MA

Joseph J. Lazzaro
Massachusetts Commission for the Blind, Boston, MA

John Leaney
University of Technology, Sydney, Australia

Robert Lembersky
Ann Taylor, Inc., New York, NY

Terri L. Lenox
Westminster College, New Wilmington, PA

Joyce H-S Li
University of Pittsburgh, Pittsburgh, PA

Michael R. Macedonia
USA STRICOM, Orlando, FL

Dirk E. Mahling
University of Pittsburgh, Pittsburgh, PA

Cynthia J. Martincic
St. Vincent College, Latrobe, PA

Michael J. McCarthy
Carnegie Mellon University, Pittsburgh, PA

Ann McIver McHoes
Carlow College, Pittsburgh PA

Genevieve McHoes
University of Maryland, College Park, MD

John McHugh
CERT™ Coordination Center, Software Engineering Institute, Carnegie Mellon University, Pittsburgh, PA

Donald M. McIver
Northrop Grumman Corporation, Baltimore, MD

Maurice McIver
Integrated Databases, Inc., Honolulu, HI

William J. McIver, Jr.
University at Albany, State University of New York

Trevor T. Moores
University of Nevada, Las Vegas

Christopher Morgan
Association for Computing Machinery, New York, NY

Bertha Kugelman Morimoto
University of Pittsburgh, Pittsburgh, PA

Tracy Mullen
NEC Research Inc., Princeton, NJ

Paul Munro
University of Pittsburgh, Pittsburgh, PA

Stephen Murray
University of Technology, Sydney, Australia

Carey Nachenberg
Symantec Corporation

John Nau
Xceed Consulting, Inc., Pittsburgh, PA

Paolo Nesi
University of Florence, Italy

Kai A. Olsen
Molde College and University of Bergen, Norway

Ipek Özkaya
Carnegie Mellon University, Pittsburgh, PA

Bob Patterson
Perfection Services, Inc.

Robert R. Perkoski
University of Pittsburgh, Pittsburgh, PA

Thomas A. Pollack
Duquesne University, Pittsburgh, PA

Guylaine M. Pollock
IEEE Computer Society; Sandia National Laboratories, Albuquerque, NM

Wolfgang Porod
University of Notre Dame, Notre Dame, IN

Anwer H. Puthawala
Park Avenue Associates in Radiology, P.C., Binghamton, NY

Mary McIver Puthawala
Binghamton, NY

Sudha Ram
University of Arizona, Tucson, AZ

Edie M. Rasmussen
University of Pittsburgh, Pittsburgh, PA

Robert D. Regan
Consultant, Pittsburgh, PA

Allen Renear
University of Illinois, Urbana-Champaign

Sarah K. Rich
Pennsylvania State University, University Park, PA

Mike Robinson
Sageforce Ltd., Kingston on Thames, Surrey, United Kingdom

Elke A. Rudensteiner
Worcester Polytechnic Institute, Worcester, MA

Frank R. Rusch
University of Illinois at Urbana-Champaign

William Sherman
National Center for Supercomputing Applications, University of Illinois at Urbana-Champaign

Marc Silverman
University of Pittsburgh, Pittsburgh, PA

Munindar P. Singh
North Carolina State University, Raleigh, NC

Cindy Smith
PricewaterhouseCoopers, Pittsburgh, PA

Barry Smyth
Smart Media Institute, University College, Dublin, Ireland

Amanda Spink
Pennsylvania State University, University Park, PA

Michael B. Spring
University of Pittsburgh, Pittsburgh, PA

Savitha Srinivasan
IBM Almaden Research Center, San Jose, CA

Igor Tarnopolsky
Westchester County Department of Laboratories and Research, Valhalla, NY

George A. Tarnow
Georgetown University, Washington, DC

Lucy A. Tedd
University of Wales, Aberystwyth, Wales, United Kingdom

Umesh Thakkar
National Center for Supercomputing Applications, University of Illinois at Urbana-Champaign

Richard A. Thompson
University of Pittsburgh, Pittsburgh, PA

James E. Tomayko
Carnegie Mellon University, Pittsburgh, PA

Christinger Tomer
University of Pittsburgh, Pittsburgh, PA

Upkar Varshney
Georgia State University, Atlanta, GA

Jonathan Vos Post
Webmaster <http://magicdragon.com>

Tom Wall
Duke University, Durham, NC

Brett A. Warneke
University of California, Berkeley, CA

Patricia S. Wehman
University of Pittsburgh, Pittsburgh, PA

Isaac Weiss
University of Maryland, College Park, MD

Martin B. Weiss
University of Pittsburgh, Pittsburgh, PA

Jeffrey C. Wingard
Leesburg, VA

Victor L. Winter
University of Nebraska at Omaha

Charles R. Woratschek
Robert Morris University, Moon Township, PA

Peter Y. Wu
University of Pittsburgh, Pittsburgh, PA

William J. Yurcik
Illinois State University, Normal, IL

Gregg R. Zegarelli
Zegarelli Law Group, P.C.

Table of Contents

VOLUME 1

PREFACE v

MEASUREMENTS xi

TIMELINE: SIGNIFICANT EVENTS IN
   THE HISTORY OF COMPUTING xv

TIMELINE: THE HISTORY OF
   PROGRAMMING, MARKUP AND
   SCRIPTING LANGUAGES xxiii

LIST OF CONTRIBUTORS xxv

A

Abacus 1

Analog Computing 2

Analytical Engine 5

Animation 8

Apple Computer, Inc. 15

Artificial Intelligence 18

Association for Computing
   Machinery 21

B

Babbage, Charles 24

Bell Labs 27

Binary Number System 29

C

Census Bureau 31

Computer Fraud and Abuse Act
   of 1986 34

Computer Scientists 38

D

Digital Computing 40

E

E-commerce 43

E-mail 47

Early Computers 50

Early Pioneers 58

Ergonomics 64

G

Games 67

Generations, Computers 71

Generations, Languages 75

Government Funding, Research 80

H

Hollerith, Herman 83

Hopper, Grace 84

Hypertext 87

I

IBM Corporation 88

Information Retrieval 92

Information Technology
   Standards 97

Institute of Electrical and
   Electronics Engineers (IEEE) 102

Integrated Circuits 104

Intel Corporation 107

Interactive Systems 109

Internet 115

J

Jacquard's Loom 117

K

Keyboard 119

L

Lovelace, Ada Byron King,
   Countess of 122

M

Mainframes 125

Memory 128

Microchip 131

Microcomputers 134

Microsoft Corporation 137
Minicomputers 139
Minitel 142
Mouse 145
Music 147

N

Napier's Bones 150
National Aeronautics and Space
   Administration (NASA) 151
Networks 154

O

Office Automation Systems 157
Optical Technology 160

P

Pascal, Blaise 164
Privacy 166

R

Robotics 169

S

Security 174
Simulation 178
Slide Rule 181
Supercomputers 182

T

Tabulating Machines 185
Telecommunications 189
Transistors 192
Turing, Alan M. 197
Turing Machine 199

V

Vacuum Tubes 201
Virtual Reality in Education 203
Viruses 206

W

Watson, Thomas J., Sr. 210
Window Interfaces 212
World Wide Web 218

X

Xerox Corporation 220

PHOTO AND ILLUSTRATION
   CREDITS 225
GLOSSARY 227
TOPIC OUTLINE 257
INDEX 267

VOLUME 2

A

Algol-60 Report 1
Algorithms 3
Assembly Language and Architecture 5
Asynchronous and Synchronous
   Transmission 8
ATM Transmission 10

B

Bardeen, John, Brattain, Walter H.,
   and Shockley, William B. 12
Bell, Alexander Graham 15
Boole, George 18
Boolean Algebra 20
Bridging Devices 24

C

Cache Memory 27
Cellular Technology 29
Central Processing Unit 32
Client/Server Technology 35
Codes 40
Coding Techniques 42
Communication Devices 45
Compatibility (Open Systems
   Design) 48
Compilers 50
Computer System Interfaces 52

D

Design Tools 55
Digital Logic Design 58
Display Devices 62
Document Processing 68

E

Eckert, J. Presper, Jr., and Mauchly,
   John W. 72

F

Fiber Optics 75

G

Game Controllers 79
Graphic Devices 81

H

Hypermedia and Multimedia 83

I

Information Systems 86
Input Devices 90
Invasive Programs 93

J

JPEG, MPEG 96

L

LISP 99
Logo 100

M

Markup Languages 104
Memory Devices 108
Morse, Samuel 112
Music, Computer 114

N

Network Design 117
Network Protocols 119
Network Topologies 122

O

Object-Oriented Languages 124
Operating Systems 128
Optical Character Recognition 132

P

Parallel Processing 134
Pattern Recognition 138
Personal Digital Assistants 141
Pointing Devices 144
Printing Devices 148
Procedural Languages 153
Programming 160

R

Reading Tools 163
Robots 166

S

Satellite Technology 169
Security Hardware 172
Security Software 174
Serial and Parallel Transmission 176
Simulators 178
Sound Devices 181
SQL 185
Storage Devices 187
System Analysis 191
Systems Design 195

T

Touch Screens 197
Transmission Media 200

V

Video Devices 203
Virtual Memory 205
Virtual Private Network 211
Virtual Reality 214
von Neumann, John 217

W

Wireless Technology 218

Z

Zuse, Konrad 221

PHOTO AND ILLUSTRATION
    CREDITS 225
GLOSSARY 227
TOPIC OUTLINE 257
INDEX 267

VOLUME 3

A

Accounting Software 1
Agriculture 3
Aircraft Flight Control 6
Aircraft Traffic Management 10
Airline Reservations 13
Architecture 16
Asimov, Isaac 19
Astronomy 21
ATM Machines 24

B

Biology 26

C

CAD/CAM, CA Engineering 29

Cell Phones 32

Chess Playing 35

Chip Manufacturing 38

Computer Assisted Instruction 41

Computer Professional 44

Computer Supported Cooperative
    Work (CSCW) 47

Computerized Manufacturing 50

Cormack, Allan, and Hounsfield,
    Godfrey Newbold 55

Cray, Seymour 57

D

Data Processing 59

Data Visualization 61

Database Management Software 64

Decision Support Systems 67

Desktop Publishing 70

Distance Learning 75

E

Economic Modeling 78

Educational Software 80

Embedded Technology (Ubiquitous
    Computing) 83

Expert Systems 87

F

Fashion Design 91

Film and Video Editing 94

G

Geographic Information Systems 99

Gross, Alfred J. 102

H

Hacking 104

Hewlett, William 107

Home System Software 109

I

Image Analysis: Medicine 114

Integrated Software 117

K

Kemeny, John G. 120

Knowledge-Based Systems 122

L

Laser Technology 125

Legal Systems 128

Library Applications 131

M

Magnetic Stripe Cards 134

Mathematics 137

Medical Systems 139

Molecular Biology 142

Music Composition 145

N

Navigation 148

Neural Networks 151

O

Open Source 155

Organick, Elliot 158

P

Péter, Rózsa 160

Physics 161

Process Control 164

Productivity Software 166

Project Management 170

R

Railroad Applications 173

S

Scientific Visualization 176

Security Applications 179

Software Piracy 182

Space Travel and Exploration 185

Speech Recognition 188

Spreadsheets 191

SQL: Databases 194

T

Technology of Desktop
    Publishing 196

Telephony 199

U

User Interfaces 202

W

Wang, An 206

Weather Forecasting 208

Word Processors 210

PHOTO AND ILLUSTRATION
    CREDITS 215

GLOSSARY 217

TOPIC OUTLINE 247

INDEX 257

VOLUME 4

A

Agents 1

Amdahl, Gene Myron 4

Art 6

Artificial Life 9

Assistive Computer Technology for
    Persons with Disabilities 11

Asynchronous Transfer Mode
    (ATM) 17

Authentication 21

B

Bandwidth 24

Browsers 27

C

Censorship: National, International 31

Chemistry 34

Computer Vision 37

Cookies 40

Copyright 43

Credit Online 46

Cryptography 49

Cybercafe 53

Cybernetics 55

D

Data Mining 58

Data Warehousing 63

Digital Images 65

Digital Libraries 68

Digital Signatures 71

E

E-banking 73

E-books 76

E-commerce: Economic and Social
    Aspects 78

E-journals and E-publishing 81

Electronic Campus 84

Electronic Markets 88

Entrepreneurs 92

Ethics 99

F

Feynman, Richard P. 102

Fiction, Computers in 104

Firewalls 107

FTP 110

G

Global Positioning Systems 112

Global Surveillance 115

Glushkov, Victor M. 119

Guru 120

H

Hackers 121

Home Entertainment 124

Human Factors: User Interfaces 127

I

Information Access 130

Information Overload 133

Information Theory 136

Internet: Applications 138

Internet: Backbone 142

Internet: History 146

Intranet 150

J

Java Applets 152

JavaScript 155

Journalism 159

M

Marconi, Guglielmo 163

Mobile Computing 164

Molecular Computing 167

N

Nanocomputing 169

Newell, Allen 172
Nyquist, Harry 174

P
Patents 176
Photography 178
Political Applications 181

R
Routing 185

S
Search Engines 188
Service Providers 191
Shannon, Claude E. 195
Simon, Herbert A. 197
Social Impact 198

T
TCP/IP 202
Telnet 204

U
Urban Myths 206

V
Visual Basic 208

PHOTO AND ILLUSTRATION
    CREDITS 213

GLOSSARY 215

TOPIC OUTLINE 245

INDEX 255

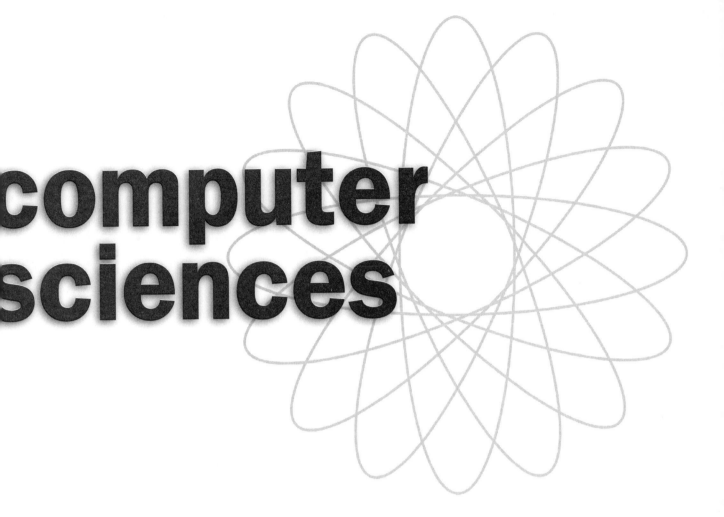

computer sciences

Agents

People have long dreamed of automated slaves that would do their every bidding, someone to run errands and do chores. Finally, with advances in computing and communications, some of those dreams are turning into reality. Whereas robotic slaves are still in development, software assistants are becoming quite popular. These are better known as agents, often called intelligent software agents.

Software agents have been studied since the 1950s—the early days of computer science. However, interest in agents began to climb with the expansion of personal computing and **local area networks (LANs)** in the 1980s, and then increased dramatically after the popularization of the Internet from 1995 onward.

local area networks (LANs) high-speed computer networks designed for users who are located near each other

Types of Agents

There are five main kinds of agents. The most well-known are personal assistants. These are often incorporated in desktop software products. Personal assistants try to understand what task a user is trying to perform and then help the user in performing that task. They might advise the user about the actions he or she might take to improve the quality of his or her work. A simple example is the Microsoft Clippy, who shows up when one starts an application program, such as Microsoft Word, and offers help on Word features that might be needed. Although some popular software assistants have a visual presence as a cartoon character, this is not necessary. An assistant may simply place text on a screen or interact through voice.

The second kind of agent is an information aggregating agent. These are used for searching for information or products on the web. The user can ask an agent to find the cheapest airline ticket from, say, Raleigh to the Bahamas, and the agent comes back with a set of options. These agents gather information from several sources on the web, but generally do not update it. They often combine with personal assistants that "learn" a user's preferences through the requests a user makes.

The third category of agents exists within information systems, typically of large enterprises. These software agents help correctly link and update information across related databases that often have subtle differences in meaning. For example, the payroll database in a company records salaries for all workers who are currently being paid, and the benefits database

The Active Buddy software agent lives up to its name by retrieving information for users on various topics.

records health insurance premiums for current and former workers who are receiving health benefits. Such databases are designed to function independently, but people may need to receive interrelated information from them. For example, a manager might query for total monthly labor expenditures, which depend closely on the salaries and the health premiums paid out. However, if the manager queries for a list of permanent employees, neither database has the information. The payroll database includes temporary employees; the benefits database includes retirees. A possible solution is the set of workers who are listed in both databases. Software agents that can understand the information in the underlying "dumb" databases can prevent erroneous or misleading results from being computed. However, creating these agents is not an easy task and it gets more complex when the task requires that information be consistently updated in several places.

The fourth kind of agent functions within complex **distributed systems**. Such agents are used to manage computer networks by keeping track of the status of various hosts and routers, monitoring traffic patterns, and attempting to detect security threats. They can analyze data transmissions that either do not fit the normal usage profile, or those that fit the profile

distributed systems
computer systems comprised of many individual computers that are interconnected and act in concert to complete operations

of an attack, and take action to either stop an attack or alert a system administrator of a possible breach in security.

The fifth kind of agent provides services for the management and actions of a distributed system. These services include directories so that a software agent may find other agents and resources such as databases and web sites. The agent-location services can be more complex than a directory and may help find agents and provide additional support for negotiation among the agents. A practical agent system will typically include assistants for the various users, several agents to do the required work, and at least one directory or broker agent.

Connectivity and Communication

In most cases, an agent needs network connectivity to communicate with other agents or access remote resources. Only assistants for local applications like Microsoft's Clippy can function without connectivity. Occasionally, one will see references to mobile agents, whose executing code moves from one computer to another. Although this is an interesting idea, it raises security concerns. A malicious agent running on one's computer could wreak havoc on one's data and use the computer to launch attacks on others. Moreover, in all practical applications, the effect of mobility can be achieved by having stationary agents reside on different computers and communicate securely with one another. For this reason, mobile agents are not used in practical applications.

There is no magic in computing. Ultimately, an agent is a software program, not completely unlike other programs. What makes agents interesting is that they provide programming abstractions that help users deal with complexity. Agents are programs that exhibit intelligence and autonomy, and can communicate with other programs. Unlike conventional programs, which must be explicitly invoked, agents can act proactively. Of these, the ability to communicate is central.

When these features are present, they enable the modular engineering of distributed systems. We create an agent for each major player in the system and set up the rules or protocols through which the agents can communicate and, presto, we have a distributed system. Virtually all serious applications of agents involve creating a multiagent system.

For example, designing an **enterprise information system** from scratch is practically impossible, especially because real-life enterprises split and merge quite often. But when we build the components as agents, they can be composed together with the agents of different divisions or even different enterprises. Likewise, it is generally impossible to allocate resources centrally in a manner that will satisfy everyone competing for them. Often, a reasonable solution is to create a market for the given resource and let each interested party field its agents in that market. For example, agents can help people bid in auctions. Although present-day agents are simple, computational markets and agents for them are fast becoming a common feature of the business landscape, specifically, for trading in **commodities** such as electrical power.

The power of software agents comes from their human-like traits of reasoning, acting autonomously, and communicating. Therefore, the study of agents not only incorporates traditional computing ideas of program-

> ### "AGENTS ON THE WEB"
>
> The Internet is host to a column about agents called "Agents on the Web." It appears in the *IEEE Internet Computing Online* magazine at <http://computer.org/internet>.

enterprise information system a system of client and server computers that can be used to manage all of the tasks required to manage and run a large organization

commodities raw materials or services which are marketed prior to being used

ming languages, objects, and concurrency, but also develops computational variants of cognitive, economic, ethical, legal, organizational, and social constructs. The science of agents is inherently interdisciplinary and one of the most exciting branches of computing. SEE ALSO Ergonomics; Interactive Systems.

Munindar P. Singh

Bibliography

Bigus, Joseph, and Jennifer Bigus. *Constructing Intelligent Agents Using Java*, 2nd ed. New York: John Wiley & Sons, 2001.

Huhns, Michael N., and Munindar P. Singh, eds. *Readings in Agents*. San Mateo, CA: Morgan Kaufmann, 1998.

Amdahl, Gene Myron
American Computer Designer and Entrepreneur
1922–

Gene Myron Amdahl was born November 16, 1922, in Flandreau, South Dakota. He received a bachelor's degree in engineering physics from South Dakota State University in 1948 and a doctorate in theoretical physics from the University of Wisconsin in 1952. His major contributions to the field of computer science are in the design of computers and the founding of computer-related companies.

Prior to attending college, Amdahl served two years in the U.S. Navy during World War II, learning electronics and taking a computer programming course. This served him well academically and in his later entrepreneurial efforts. Amdahl's doctoral dissertation was on "The Logical Design of an Intermediate Speed Digital Computer." The computer itself was called the Wisconsin Integrally Synchronized Computer (WISC). Amdahl's design was implemented by successive classes of students at the University of Wisconsin.

Amdahl worked at IBM from 1952 to 1955 and was a lead designer in the redesign of the IBM 701, which was later marketed as the IBM 704. After determining that he would not be made the manager of the IBM Stretch Project, a project aimed at developing advanced computer technology and a **supercomputer** at IBM, Amdahl left the company for several years. He returned to IBM in 1960 after working at Ramo Wooldridge and Aeronautic, Inc., and he became a leader in the design of the IBM System/360 series of computers.

Amdahl was made an IBM fellow in 1965, which meant he was able to pursue his own research projects. In 1969 he became the director of IBM's Advanced Computing Systems Laboratory in Menlo Park, California. IBM subsequently closed this laboratory on Amdahl's recommendation, and in 1970 he left IBM and formed the Amdahl Corporation, a **mainframe computer** manufacturer in direct competition with IBM.

Amdahl computers could run the same software as the IBM series of computers, but they were priced more economically. They were, in a sense, IBM "clones" in the mainframe computer market. A similar phenomenon later occurred in the personal computer market, when several manufactur-

Gene Amdahl.

supercomputer a very high performance computer, usually comprised of many processors and used for modeling and simulation of complex phenomena, like meteorology

mainframe computer large computer used by businesses and government agencies to process massive amounts of data; generally faster and more powerful than desktop computers but usually requiring specialized software

ers "cloned" or imitated the IBM personal computer. The cloning was done on the processors to run the software and on the peripherals as well, creating "plug-to-plug" compatible systems.

The first Amdahl computer was not shipped until 1975, but in subsequent years (1976–1978), the company was quite competitive, with between one and several hundred million dollars of product shipping per year. In 1979 Amdahl lost control of the company to Japanese investors, Fujitsu, Ltd., who were still running it as of 2002.

Amdahl resigned as chairman of Amdahl Corporation in 1979, becoming chair emeritus, then left the company in 1980. That year he founded the Trilogy Systems Corporation with $230 million in start-up money. His intent was to develop a high performance computing system with large scale integration (several hundred functions on a chip), fault tolerant wafer-scale chips, and a high performance **central processing unit (CPU)**.

When Trilogy Systems encountered manufacturing problems, Amdahl acquired Elxsi, Ltd. to obtain computer systems, and subsequently became its chairman. In 1987 he founded Andor Systems to develop computers to compete with IBM's smaller mainframes. However, this company, too, suffered manufacturing problems, and IBM came out with its own midsize computer, employing some of the same technology that Andor had developed. Hoping to remain a viable company, Andor turned to the manufacturing of peripheral systems and finally a data backup system, but by the mid-1990s, the company was forced to declare bankruptcy.

In 1996, at the age of seventy-four, Amdahl helped found Commercial Data Servers, a company intended to produce IBM-compatible, PC-based mainframes. By 1998 people and companies worldwide had become concerned about what would happen to their computerized data as computer systems rolled over from the year 1999 to the year 2000. The so-called Y2K problem caused uncertainty because traditionally only two digits had been used to identify the year in many applications, and programmers could not predict what would happen to time-sensitive systems when the year "99," for 1999, was followed by the year "00," for 2000 (not 1900). Commercial Data Servers developed the CDS2000E Enterprise Server to test applications for Year 2000 compliance, and provided it without affecting ongoing operations. It set the computer's clock ahead to simulate the start of 2000 and tested the software for problems. Many companies used this product to test their systems, rewrite programs, and adjust data storage accordingly. Few systems worldwide actually experienced any major Y2K problems. Amdahl eventually retired from Commercial Data Servers.

In 1987 Amdahl received the Eckert-Mauchly Award, bestowed jointly by the Association for Computing Machinery (ACM) and the Institute of Electrical and Electronic Engineers (IEEE) Computer Society for "outstanding innovations in computer architecture, including pipelining, instruction lookahead, and cache memory." He also won the Computer Entrepreneur Award from the IEEE Computer Society in 1989, which is awarded to managers and leaders responsible for the growth of some segment of the computer industry whose efforts occurred at least fifteen years before the award and whose effects in the industry are easily recognizable. SEE ALSO GENERATIONS: COMPUTERS; IBM CORPORATION; MAINFRAMES; SUPERCOMPUTERS.

Roger R. Flynn

IBM 360 SERIES

The IBM 360 series of computers (System/360) was one of the first families of computers. The plan was to provide a wide range of computers, in price and performance, which were compatible with one another in what was termed "upward compatibility." This meant that programs written on lower priced, less powerful models could be run on the more expensive, more powerful models. Customers could, for the first time, upgrade the power of their computing systems without having to rewrite programs for a new system. The concept proved extremely popular and was adopted by other computer manufacturers of the mid-1960s. Upward compatibility remains an industry standard.

central processing unit (CPU) the part of a computer that performs computations and controls and coordinates other parts of the computer

Bibliography

Bashe, Charles J., et al. *IBM's Early Computers*. Cambridge, MA: MIT Press, 1986.

Lee, J. A. N. *Computer Pioneers*. Los Alamitos, CA: Computer Society Press, 1995.

Art

It would be difficult to exaggerate the impact of computers on the study and production of art. Not since the invention of photography has the art world been so radically transformed by a new technology.

Computers have changed methods of making art. Programs such as Adobe Photoshop, for example, can imitate the effects of watercolor, pastels, and paint through digital techniques and with greater flexibility than more traditional media such as oil or charcoal, because virtually every mark can be easily reversed or erased. Further, images produced with a program like Photoshop are much more transportable than images in traditional media because a digital image can be sent through e-mail or posted on a web site with ease.

There have been, however, some concerns about the alienating effects that such new technology might have on art and artists alike. With the production of images through traditional media such as oil paint, artists are able to leave physical marks on a surface such as canvas. Such imagery allows the presence of the artist to be recorded directly through brushstrokes or other gestures. With the mediating power of computer imagery, all artistic choices are filtered through a program. Thus the direct relationship between the artist and his or her medium is compromised. Further, with digital images certain non-visual pleasures that accompany artistic production—the smell and feel of paint, for example—are lost. Other changes might be architectural and environmental, as artists occupy computer labs rather than the romanticized environment of the studio.

Nevertheless, many contemporary artists enjoy the new possibilities computers offer, far beyond the intended capabilities of image-producing software. Some artists use computer parts as sculptural elements. Janet Zweig, for example, sometimes produces kinetic (moving) sculpture with computer fragments to explore the ways in which new technologies change the way one understands processes of thought. In *Mind over Matter* (1993), Zweig programmed a computer to generate all combinations of three sentences: "I think therefore I am" (Rene Decartes); "I am what I am" (Popeye); and "I think I can" (the little engine that could). The resulting **permutations** of sentences (such as "I think I can think") make it seem as if the computer truly contemplates its own existence. Further, a dot matrix printer scrolls the resulting sentences out into a hanging basket. The basket is balanced by a hanging rock that rises as the paper-filled basket slowly descends. The computer's "thoughts" thus achieve a weighty presence and seem to have an affect on the world (the rock)—though not according to computers' usual methods of "working."

Other artists create web sites. Mark Napier's now canonical web site <www.potatoland.org>, for example, offers a number of digital works that comment upon the notion of waste in cyberspace. At the site, one can visit Napier's "Digital Landfill," an ever-changing site to which people can con-

permutations significant changes or rearrangement

RESTORING A MASTERPIECE

Dirt, dust, and candle smoke covered the frescoes on the ceiling of the Sistine Chapel in Rome for centuries. To make the needed repairs, a team of art restorers worked on the frescoes for fifteen years to remove the age-old grime. Using sophisticated photographic equipment, spectrometers, and computers, the group located the areas needing the most work. Once the restoration was complete, the ceiling showed the brilliant colors and depictions created by Michelangelo in the 15th century. To ensure the long-lasting effects of the restoration work, a special air filtering system, like that used by NASA on the space shuttle, was installed to monitor the amount of humidity and dust.

tribute e-mail messages or other computer-generated documents that they wish to delete. One can then visit Napier's site to see how this "digital" land-fill changes from day to day. The work is all the more interesting when one thinks about the ways in which "waste" works in a cyber environment. One usually thinks of waste as a pile of unpleasant refuse taking up physical space on the margins of a community. In some ways this conceptualization of waste persists in cyberspace, as people delete files by moving them to the "trash can" or "cleaning up" their hard drives. But with cyberspace, the marginal location of a "landfill" changes. Because all web sites are basically equal, the junkyard is just as likely to be next door to more "pristine" sites.

Other artists use computers to produce digital photography. Jason Salavon's *Top Grossing Film of All Time, 1 × 1* (2000) reduces each individual frame of the film *Titanic* down to one average color. Salavon then places each small frame in order from beginning to end in a rectangle. The resulting image references computer **pixilation**, and supposedly allows the viewer to "see" the entire movie all in one shot.

pixilation the process of generating animation, frame by frame

John Haddock's digital photography addresses the imagery of computer games. His *Lorraine Motel* (2000) shows the assassination of Dr. Martin Luther King Jr. as pictured according to the conventions of computer games like SimCity, and thus comments on the ways in which technology for children is intertwined with images of violence and social upheaval.

Digital images are transforming attitudes regarding the collection and exhibition of works of art. Once an image is digitally produced and posted on a web site, virtually anyone with a modem can gain access to that image and use it in whatever fashion one chooses. Images are evermore accessible, as major museums now offer web sites cataloging their collections. Some museums have adopted this development directly. The Alternative Museum, for example, once occupied a building in Manhattan's Soho district. Now it only exists in cyberspace at <http://www.alternativemuseum.org/>. The museum specializes in contemporary digital projects, web sites, digital photography, links to scholarly sites, and chat rooms.

This widespread distribution of images seems to democratize the art world. More people have access to images, while museums maintain less control over reproductions of images in their collections. Further, artists are increasingly producing "digital" works of art outright. Such images are not reproductions, but rather works of art in and of themselves. To download such an image from a web site is, therefore, to possess the work—thus more people can gain access to "original" works (or to works that challenge the very distinction between "original" and "reproduction"). Such images may allow some to bypass institutions like galleries, auction houses, and museums that usually control traffic in art sales. These changes in the distribution and ownership of images have raised legal issues regarding copyright privileges.

Computers also facilitate art and art history research. Computerized databases such as *Art Abstracts* and *The Bibliography of the History of Art* can help a researcher locate books and articles that have been written on art in the past several decades. Another online resource, <www.artincontext.org>, can also help researchers locate information on artists, galleries, current exhibitions, and reproductions of works of art. Even more impressive, the Getty Institute of California offers one of the most complete collections of databases and other digital research facilities in all of cyberspace. Its site offers art-specific dictionaries, auction catalogs, and catalogs of archival holdings in the collection.

Such sites are only the beginning. Every day research institutes post new information on the web. Scanned primary documents, finders' aids, and more sophisticated research engines are making art history research more accessible and efficient. This process, however, is still incomplete. Although computers are tremendous tools for researching works of art, they are no replacement for physical trips to museums and research libraries. SEE ALSO DIGITAL IMAGES; FASHION DESIGN; GRAPHIC DEVICES.

Sarah K. Rich

Bibliography

Benjamin, Walter. "The Work of Art in the Age of Mechanical Reproduction." In *Illuminations*, Hannah Arendt, ed. New York: Schocken Press, 1968.

Drucker, Johanna, ed. "Digital Reflections: The Dialogue of Art and Technology." *Art Journal* 59, no. 4 (Winter 2000).

Druckery, Timothy, ed. *Electronic Culture: Technology and Visual Representation*. New York: Aperture, 1996.

Leeson, Lynn Hershman. *Clicking In: Hot Links to a Digital Culture*. Seattle, WA: Bay Press, 1996.

Lunenfeld, Peter, ed. *The Digital Dialectic: New Essays on New Media*. Cambridge, MA: MIT Press, 1999.

Schor, Mira. "Painting as Manual." *Wet: On Painting, Feminism, and Art Culture.* Durham: Duke University Press, 1997.

Internet Resources

J. Paul Getty Institute Databases. <http://www.getty.edu/research/tools/>

Artificial Life

Artificial life (also known as "ALife") is an interdisciplinary study of life and lifelike processes by means of computer simulation and other methods. The goals of this activity include understanding and creating life and lifelike systems, and developing practical devices inspired by living systems. The study of artificial life aims to understand how life arises from non-life, to determine the potentials and limits of living systems, and to explain how life is connected to mind, machines, and culture.

The American computer scientist Christopher Langton coined the phrase "artificial life" in 1987, when he organized the first scientific conference explicitly devoted to this field. Before there were artificial life conferences, the simulation and synthesis of lifelike systems occurred in isolated pockets scattered across a variety of disciplines. The Hungarian-born physicist and mathematician John von Neumann (1903–1957) created the first artificial life model (without referring to it as such) in the 1940s. He produced a self-reproducing, computation-universal entity using **cellular automata**. Von Neumann was pursuing many of the questions that still drive artificial life today, such as understanding the spontaneous generation and evolution of complex adaptive structures.

Rather than modeling some existing living system, artificial life models are often intended to generate wholly new—and typically extremely simple—instances of lifelike phenomena. The simplest example of such a system is the so-called Game of Life devised by the British mathematician John Conway in the 1960s before the field of artificial life was conceived. Conway was trying to create a simple system that could generate complex self-organized structures.

The Game of Life is a two-state, two-dimensional cellular automaton. It takes place on a rectangular grid of cells, similar to a huge checkerboard. Time advances step by step. A cell's state at a given time is determined by the states of its eight neighboring cells according to the following simple "birth-death" rule: a "dead" cell becomes "alive" if and only if exactly three neighbors were just "alive," and a "living" cell "dies" if and only if fewer than two, or more than three, neighbors were just "alive." When all of the cells in the system are simultaneously updated again and again, a rich variety of complicated behavior is created and a complex zoo of dynamic structures can be identified and classified (blinkers, gliders, glider guns, logic switching circuits, etc.). It is even possible to construct a universal **Turing machine** in the Game of Life, by cunningly arranging the initial configuration of living cells. In such constructions, gliders perform a role of passing signals. Analyzing the computational potential of cellular automata on the basis of glider interactions has become a major direction in research. Like living systems, Conway's Game of Life exhibits a vivid hierarchy of dynamical self-organized structures. Its self-organization is not

cellular automata a collection or array of objects that are programmed identically to interact with one another

Turing machine a proposed type of computing machine that takes inputs off paper tape and then moves through a sequence of states under the control of an algorithm; identified by Alan Turing (1912-1954)

CELLULAR AUTOMATON

Cellular Automaton is a regular spatial lattice of "cells," each of which can be in any one of a finite number of states. The states of all the cells in the lattice are updated simultaneously and the state of the entire lattice advances in discrete time steps. The state of each cell in the lattice is updated according to a local rule that may depend on the state of the cell and its neighbors at the previous time step. Each cell in a cellular automaton could be considered to be a finite state machine which takes its neighbors' states as input and outputs its own state. The best known example is John Conway's Game of Life.

At New Mexico's Los Alamos National Laboratory, theoretical mathematician Steen Rasmussen works on an artificial life simulation.

artificial intelligence (AI) a branch of computer science dealing with creating computer hardware and software to mimic the way people think and perform practical tasks

a representation of processes in the real world, but a wholly novel instance of this phenomenon.

To understand the interesting properties of living systems, von Neumann and Conway each used a constructive method. They created simple and abstract models that exhibited the kind of behavior they wanted to understand. Contemporary artificial life employs the same constructive methodology, often through the creation of computer models of living systems. This computer methodology has several virtues. Expressing a model in computer code requires precision and clarity, and it ensures that the mechanisms invoked in the model are feasible.

Artificial life is similar to **artificial intelligence (AI)**. Both fields study natural phenomena through computational models, and most naturally occurring intelligent systems are, in fact, alive. Despite these similarities, AI and artificial life typically employ different modeling strategies. In most traditional artificial intelligence systems, events occur one by one (serially). A complicated, centralized controller typically makes decisions based on global information about all aspects of the system, and the controller's decisions have the potential to affect directly any aspect of the whole system.

This centralized, top-down architecture is quite unlike the structure of many natural living systems that exhibit complex autonomous behavior. Such systems are often parallel, distributed networks of relatively simple low-level "agents," and they all simultaneously interact with each other. Each agent's decisions are based on information about only its own local situation, which they affect.

In similar fashion, artificial life characteristically constructs massively parallel, bottom-up-specified systems of simple local agents. One repeats the simultaneous low-level interactions among the agents, and then observes what aggregate behavior emerges. These are sometimes called "agent-based" or "individual-based" models, because the system's global behavior arises out of the local interactions among a large collection of "agents" or "individuals." This kind of bottom-up architecture with a population of autonomous agents that follow simple local rules is also characteristic of the connectionist (parallel, distributed processing, **neural networks**) movement that swept through AI and cognitive science in the 1980s. In fact, the agents in many artificial life models are themselves controlled internally by simple neural networks.

Computer simulation in artificial life plays the role that observation and experiment play in more conventional science. The complex self-organizing behavior of Conway's Game of Life would never have been discovered without computer simulations of thousands of generations for millions of sites. Simulation of large-scale complex systems is the single most crucial development that has enabled the field of artificial life to flourish.

Living systems exhibit a variety of useful properties such as robustness, flexibility, and automatic adaptability. Some artificial life research aims to go beyond mere simulation by constructing novel physical devices that exhibit and exploit lifelike properties. Some of this engineering activity also has a theoretical motivation on the grounds that a full appreciation of life's distinctive properties can come only by creating and studying real physical devices. This engineering activity includes the construction of evolving hardware, in which biologically-inspired adaptive processes control the configuration of micro-electronic circuitry. Another example is biologically inspired robots, such as those robotic controllers automatically designed by evolutionary **algorithms**. SEE ALSO ARTIFICIAL INTELLIGENCE; BIOLOGY; COMPUTER VISION; NEURAL NETWORKS; ROBOTICS.

Mark A. Bedau

> **THE TURING MACHINE**
>
> Alan Turing's famous machine is an abstract automaton that can be in any one of a number of states and that is capable of moving back and forth on an infinitely long tape of instructions (customarily zeros and ones), reading and writing instructions on each segment of tape as it moves. A Turing machine's state at a given time is a finite function of both the machine's current state and the information on the currently scanned section of tape. A universal Turing machine is a Turing machine capable of executing any algorithm.

neural networks pattern recognition systems whose structure and operation are loosely inspired by analogy to neurons in the human brain

algorithms rules or procedures used to solve mathematical problems—most often described as sequences of steps

Bibliography

Bedau, Mark A., et al. "Open Problems in Artificial Life." *Artificial Life* 6 (2000): 363–376.

Berlekamp, Elwyn R., John H. Conway, and Richard K. Guy. *Winning Ways for Your Mathematical Plays*, vol. 2: *Games in Particular*. New York: Academic Press, 1982.

Boden, Margaret, ed. *The Philosophy of Artificial Life*. Oxford: Oxford University Press, 1996.

Kauffman, Stuart A. *At Home in the Universe: The Search for the Laws of Self-Organization and Complexity*. New York: Oxford University Press, 1995.

Levy, Steven. *Artificial Life: The Quest for a New Creation*. New York: Pantheon, 1992.

Assistive Computer Technology for Persons with Disabilities

The personal computer (PC) can be the backbone of independence for millions of individuals with sensory, physical, and learning disabilities. Com-

central processing unit the part of a computer that performs computations and controls and coordinates other parts of the computer

puters and information technology can be modified with alternative input, alternative output, and other assistive technology to empower consumers who have disabilities. Computer vendors support persons with disabilities by incorporating accessibility utilities into operating systems such as Microsoft Windows, Apple Macintosh, and UNIX. PCs equipped with assistive technology permit individuals to function independently at school, work, and home, and allow access to great quantities of information from diverse sources such as compact disks, networks, electronic mail, instant messaging, the World Wide Web, and other Internet resources. For the purposes of this discussion, the term "assistive technology" will be used to describe any hardware device or software program that permits individuals with disabilities to operate PCs and access information technology independently. Moreover, this article uses the definition of disability as outlined in the Americans with Disabilities Act in the United States, and the Disabilities Discrimination Act in the United Kingdom—any permanent condition that impairs a major life function such as seeing, hearing, walking, or speaking.

Personal Computer Platforms

Since their advent in the early 1980s, PCs have become a vital tool for business and education applications, and are now common in many homes. Personal computer platforms are a combination of hardware and software, working together in synergy. The hardware is the physical structure of the system, and software is the set of instructions that control the hardware. PC hardware consists of several fundamental components, including the **central processing unit,** memory units, disk drive storage, keyboard, and video monitor or screen.

For persons with disabilities, the keyboard, mouse, and monitor are of prime concern. PCs employ input devices like keyboards and mice for entering information and for controlling the system. Output devices, like monitors and printers, display processed information. Adapting PCs for use by persons with disabilities involves the modification of these standard input and output devices with assistive hardware or software. For example, adapting a computer's output systems to use speech or Braille printouts can make the computer accessible for persons with visual disabilities.

Technology for Persons with Vision Impairments

The video monitor is a standard output device for PCs. By its nature, the monitor relies on the visual sense to convey information. For persons with vision-related disabilities, the monitor can present a significant barrier, depending on the nature of the vision loss. The output of a standard computer printer is also fundamentally inaccessible for persons with vision impairments. Several assistive technologies that can help compensate for visual impairments include video magnification, screen readers, Braille displays and printers, and optical character recognition systems.

Magnification software enlarges text and graphics displayed on PC monitors. Magnification programs are widely used by persons with poor vision or who have difficulty reading. They focus a larger image on the retina, making text and graphics more visible. Most magnification programs can magnify either the whole screen, or just a select region of the screen. Some basic magnification utilities magnify just the mouse pointer or cursor. Most comprehensive packages allow the user to change the screen contrast and font or adjust the magnification in steps. Some programs provide speech output and magnification at the same time. Magnification software can enlarge the output from commercial applications such as word processors, databases, spreadsheets, browsers, e-mail, and other applications. Some magnification programs can also display books, magazines, and other printed materials magnified on the monitor using an external camera or scanner.

Screen readers are software programs that provide either speech or Braille output, and are commonly employed by persons who are blind or visually impaired. Screen readers require a computer **sound card** and speakers to provide voice output. For Braille output, a screen reader requires a Braille display. Braille displays connect to the PC and contain a row of mechanical Braille dots that pop up and down under computer control. The user employs arrow keys to scroll text for reading. Braille displays allow vision-impaired users to control the operating system and application programs.

For persons with vision impairments, the printed word can present a formidable barrier to independence. **Optical character recognition** (OCR) software can help overcome this barrier. OCR software requires a flatbed or handheld scanner to be connected to the host PC in order to function.

OCR systems are used to scan printed materials directly into the PC to accommodate many types of disabilities. Once scanned, the text can be read using a screen reader, magnification software, or Braille display or printer. OCR software can also help users with learning disabilities scan and format information in ways that help them process the information. In addition, the technology empowers those with motor-related disabilities to process and access information.

sound card a plug-in card for a computer that contains hardware devices for sound processing, conversion, and generation

optical character recognition the science and engineering of creating programs that can recognize and interpret printed characters

Technology for Persons with Motor Impairments

For persons with motor-related disabilities, the computer keyboard and mouse can present a significant barrier. There is a wide range of assistive technology available to compensate users who have motor disabilities. Several common input modifications include adapted keyboards, on-screen keyboards, alternative communication programs, and voice recognition.

Keyboard adaptations designed to assist users who have difficulty using the standard keyboard come in many different forms. Models exist that can be used with one hand, or with another part of the body. There are adapted keyboards that allow the keys to be rearranged to suit the user's needs. Some models allow the keyboard to be adjusted for the most suitable ergonomic fit. These can be adjusted to lay flat on the desk in the traditional manner or they can be used in a vertical configuration, if that best suits a user's preferences and needs.

On-screen keyboards are software programs that display a pictorial representation of a standard keyboard on the computer screen. The on-screen keyboard can be configured to scan through the keys one at a time through software. When the desired key is highlighted, a user can select the key by striking an adapted switch connected to the computer. Adapted switches come in many configurations; they can be controlled by breath, by hand, or by another part of the body. Some adapted switches can also be activated using voice commands.

Many motor disabilities can impact one's ability to speak, so alternative communications systems have been developed to assist persons with communications tasks at home, school, or in the workplace. Alternative communications systems range from picture boards to notebook computers equipped with speech synthesis systems capable of an unlimited vocabulary. Such systems can be used to communicate with friends, family members, and co-workers, and for tasks such as delivering presentations.

Voice recognition and dictation systems are powerful assistive technologies that allow persons with disabilities to control a computer and dictate documents verbally using spoken commands. Voice recognition software requires a computer with a sound card and a microphone to accept verbal input. Voice recognition software must be trained by the user to recognize the speaker's voice accurately, a process that takes about an hour. The software stores recorded voice patterns from the training process, and matches these stored templates against the incoming verbal command stream from the microphone. Voice recognition can be used for applications such as e-mail, web browsing, and word processing.

Technology for Persons with Hearing Impairments

Numerous forms of adaptive and non-assistive technologies are available to increase independence and quality of life for individuals who are deaf or hard of hearing. For persons with hearing-related disabilities, access to the spoken word can often present a significant barrier. Assistive technology to support users with hearing-related disabilities focuses on accessing the spoken word at home, in the classroom, or at the work site. Technologies to assist the hearing-impaired include such systems as TTYs, amplification systems, and applications like e-mail and instant messaging.

TTYs, or text telephones, allow people to type messages back and forth over the telephone. These devices allow individuals to send text messages using a keyboard and printer or visual display. They access the telephone system using standard connectors, and can be used for home, school, or business applications. There are also portable TTYs that can be used in a mobile environment.

Amplification systems increase the volume and clarity of the spoken word, making it more accessible for persons with limited hearing ability. These devices range from hearing aids that fit inside the ear to assistive listening devices that can be carried in a pocket or purse and used for large gatherings.

Users can also adjust the speaker volume on most computer platforms to increase access for persons who are deaf or hard of hearing. If the speaker volume is adjusted to zero, this causes the visual display to flash and alert the user to the presence of audio output.

Non-assistive computer programs like electronic mail and instant messaging empower individuals with hearing-related impairments to communicate over the Internet. The widespread availability of electronic mail contributes greatly to the independence of persons with hearing impairments. Instant messaging allows for expanded communication in much the same manner as electronic mail does, with an immediacy similar to that of a telephone conversation, and its wide availability to all computer users, regardless of disability, makes it attractive as a means of communication.

THE TTY

TTY technology helps people with hearing and speech impairments communicate by telephone. Short for "Teletypewriter for the Deaf," the device is also referred to as a "text telephone" because the TTY permits users to send and receive text messages.

Noted scientist Stephen Hawking, author of *A Brief History of Time*, uses a computer-enabled synthesizer to replace his voice, which he lost due to illness in 1985.

Technology for Persons with Learning Disabilities

The term "learning disabilities" covers many impairments that impact the ability to process information. Technologies to assist persons with learning disabilities include speech systems that read printed material aloud, digital assistants to maintain schedules and lists of tasks, software to correct spelling, and task management software to guide users through the successful completion of projects. Many of these are standard productivity software programs used in business and education.

The Internet

The Internet is a vast network of computers that spans the globe. This important network allows persons with disabilities to share and exchange information in an accessible form. The Internet supports applications like e-mail, instant messaging, and the World Wide Web. PCs connected to the Internet, or a private Intranet, can be adapted with a wide variety of technologies to allow access to applications such as e-mail, web browsers, and online databases. The Internet and Intranets empower persons with disabilities to access information using speech, Braille, magnification, or some other form of assistive technology. The Internet increases independence for people with mobility issues to interact, work, and socialize. Assistive software can be loaded onto a network to allow that software to be shared by all users belonging to the network.

Assistive Technology and Computer Operating Systems

Accessibility utilities are being integrated into computer operating systems such as Windows, Macintosh, and UNIX. While these accessibility utilities differ from one platform to another, most operating systems include utilities to magnify text and graphics, convert text into synthesized speech, and help users control the keyboard and mouse functions. Operating systems are growing more compatible with assistive technology in general, and this is evidenced by Microsoft's Active Accessibility, which helps assistive technologies work together with the operating system and application programs.

Future Technology

Legislation such as the Americans with Disabilities Act in the United States and the Disabilities Discrimination Act in the United Kingdom is fostering the development of assistive technology for persons with disabilities. Section 508 of the Rehabilitation Act in the United States is helping to make the World Wide Web more accessible as well. The development of computer platforms of increasing speed and power also contributes to the ongoing evolution of assistive technology. As computers get more powerful, assistive technology also increases in capacity and potential, driven by the advancement of microprocessor-based technology. The increasing miniaturization of powerful computer components will lead to assistive technologies that are more portable, lightweight, and cost effective, allowing for increased independence and improving the overall quality of life for persons with disabilities. SEE ALSO HUMAN FACTORS: USER INTERFACES; INPUT DEVICES; INTERNET: APPLICATIONS; ROBOTICS.

Joseph J. Lazzaro

Bibliography

Cunningham, Carmela, and Norman Coombs. *Information Access and Adaptive Technology*. New York: Oryx Press, 1997.

Lazzaro, Joseph J. *Adapting PCs for Disabilities*. Reading, MA: Addison Wesley, 1995.

———. *Adaptive Technologies for Learning and Work Environments*, 2nd ed. American Library Association, 2001.

Internet Resources

"Abledata, Your Source for Assistive Technology Information." Assistive Technology Online Databases. <http://www.abledata.com>

"Assistive Technology." Boston University web site. <http://www.bu.edu/assist_tech/index.html>

"IBM Accessibility Center." IBM web site. <http://www.ibm.com/able>

Microsoft Accessibility web site. <http://www.microsoft.com/enable>

"People with Special Needs." Apple Computer Inc. web site. <http://www.apple.com/disability>

Rehabilitation Engineering and Assistive Technology Society of North America. <http://www.resna.org>

"Web Accessibility Initiative (WAI) Home Page." World Wide Web Consortium. <http://www.w3.org/wai>

Asynchronous Transfer Mode (ATM)

The physical infrastructure supporting data communications has improved its ability to transmit data quickly with advances such as optical fibers. As this physical capacity increases, there is a need to utilize effectively the **bandwidth** to carry a variety of traffic (voice, video, data) in an efficient manner. Traditionally, circuit switching is used to support the real-time delivery needed for voice and video. **Packet switching** is used to support intermittently heavy data traffic. Asynchronous Transfer Mode (ATM) has emerged as a technology that efficiently utilizes the bandwidth while carrying one or more traffic types. ATM is a high-speed packet switching technology that is capable of supporting both real-time voice and video and the kind of data traffic that has peaks and plateaus in its transmission.

ATM uses fixed size packets (called cells) to reduce processing and switching delays. The cell size is kept small, at 53 bytes, to allow for fast preparation and transmission. ATM allows different users to request varying amounts of resources to support the desired quality of transmission. It supports several traffic classes with differing quality-of service-requirements.

A user requests a connection to another user with a desired quality of service. The ATM switches use **signaling protocols** to communicate with one another about the availability of resources needed for the requested connection. ATM allocates bandwidth dynamically, so if some users are not transmitting their cells for some time, lower priority traffic with higher tolerance for delays can be transmitted.

History of ATM

ATM has grown out of the need for a worldwide standard to allow interoperability of information, regardless of the end-system or type of information. There have been separate methods used for the transmission of information among users on a **local area network (LAN)**, versus users on a **wide area network (WAN)**. This has added to the complexity of networking as users' needs for connectivity expand from the LAN to metropolitan, national, and finally worldwide connectivity.

Today separate networks are being used to carry voice, data, and video information due to their different characteristics. Data traffic tends to be "bursty"—not needing to communicate for an extended period of time and then needing to communicate large quantities of information as fast as possible. Voice and video, on the other hand, tend to be more even in the amount of information required, but are very sensitive to when and in what order the information arrives. With ATM, separate networks are not required. ATM is the only standards-based technology that has been designed from the beginning to accommodate the simultaneous transmission of data, voice, and video. Although some technologies today are scalable in terms of one of the factors (size or bit-rate or number of users), only ATM is truly "scalable" in terms of bit-rate, network size, and number of users.

bandwidth a measure of the frequency component of a signal or the capacity of a communication channel to carry signals

packet switching an operation used in digital communications systems whereby packets (collections) of data are dispatched to receivers based on addresses contained in the packets

signaling protocols protocols used in the management of integrated data networks that convey a mix of audio, video, and data packets

local area network (LAN) a high-speed computer network that is designed for users who are located near each other

wide area network (WAN) an interconnected network of computers that spans upward from several buildings to whole cities or entire countries and across countries

ATM Cells

An ATM cell is 53 bytes long with a 5-byte header possessing information for control and signaling, and 48 bytes of data payload. Having fixed-size cells may reduce queuing delays for high priority cells. Because one knows the size of a cell beforehand, it becomes easier to implement the switching mechanism in hardware for efficient switching. The header information is generated in the ATM Layer, while the ATM Adaptation Layer (AAL) breaks the entire message into 48-byte data chunks. The cell header contains fields to help deal with congestion, maintenance, and error control problems. It is broken up into the following fields:

- Generic Flow Control (GFC), a mechanism used to alleviate short-term overload conditions in the network. It is intended to provide efficient and equal utilization of the link between all the users.

- Virtual Path Identifier (VPI), which allows for more virtual paths to be supported within the network.

- Virtual Channel Identifier (VCI), which functions as a service access point as it is used for routing to and from the end user.

- Payload Type (PT), which is used to distinguish between user information and connection-associated layer management information.

- Cell Loss Priority (CLP), which is used to provide guidance to the network to discard the cell in case of congestion.

- Header Error Control (HEC), which contains the information that can be used by the physical layer for error detection or correction. It is calculated from the first 32 bits of the header.

VCI/VPI Connections

The entire ATM network is based on virtual connections set up by the switches upon initialization of a call. Virtual Channel Identifiers (VCI) and Virtual Path Identifiers (VPI) are used to identify these virtual connections. They are used to route information from one switch to another. VCI and VPI are not addresses; they are explicitly assigned to each segment within a network.

A Virtual Channel Connection (VCC) is set up between two end users through the network and used for full-duplex flow of cells. They are also used for user-network exchange (control signaling) and network-network exchange (network management and routing). The VCI label identifies a VCC between two ATM switches and may change at intermediate nodes within a route.

Virtual channels having the same endpoints are often grouped together to form a Virtual Path Connection (VPC). This grouping of channels makes the task of network management easier without losing flexibility. Usually many virtual channels share a physical link at the same time, allowing asynchronous interweaving of cells from multiple connections. VPI connections share a common path through the network and thus network management actions need to be applied to only a single virtual path as opposed to all of the individual virtual channels.

Layers and Their Functions

ATM is a layered architecture allowing multiple services—voice, data, and video—to be carried over the network. It consists of three layers: the physical layer, the ATM layer, and the ATM adaptation layer. Layers are as shown in Figure 1 and their functionality is summarized in Figure 2.

Physical Layer. The physical layer of ATM is similar to layer 1 of the **Open Systems Interconnections (OSI)** model and performs bit level functions. It defines electrical characteristics and network interfaces. It is further divided into two layers: Physical Medium (PM) and Transmission Convergence (TC) sub-layer.

The PM sublayer contains physical medium (e.g. optical fiber, coaxial, or twisted pair) dependent functions and provides bit transmission capability including bit alignment.

The TC sublayer performs five primary functions as shown in Figure 2. The lowest function is the generation and recovery of the transmission frame. Transmission frame adaptation adapts the cell flow according to the used payload structure of the transmission system in the sending direction, and extracts the cell flow from the transmission frame in the receiving direction.

The cell delineation function enables the receiver to recover the cell boundaries. The Header Error Control (HEC) sequence generation is done in the transmit direction and its value is recalculated and compared with the received value. Cell rate decoupling inserts the idle cells in the transmitting direction in order to adapt the rate of the ATM cells to the payload capacity of the transmission system. It suppresses all idle cells in the receiving direction. Only assigned and unassigned cells are passed to the ATM layer.

ATM Layer. The ATM layer is next above the physical layer. The ATM layer takes the data to be sent and adds the 5-byte header information. It performs the following four actions:

- Cell header generation/extraction, which adds the appropriate ATM cell header to the received cell information field from the upper layer in the transmit direction. It does the opposite in the receive direction.

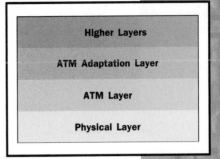

Figure 1. ATM architecture.

Open Systems Interconnections (OSI) a communications standard developed by the International Organization for Standardization (ISO) to facilitate compatible network systems

Upper layer functions	upper layers	
Convergence	CS	AAL
Segmentation & Reassembly	SAR	
Generic Flow Control Cell header generation/extraction Cell VPI/VCI Translation Cell multiplex and de-multiplex		ATM
Cell rate Decoupling HEC generation & verification Cell delineation Transmission frame adaptation Transmission frame generation & recovery	TC	Physical Layer
Bit timing Physical Medium	PM	

Figure 2. ATM functionality.

multiplexes operations in ATM communications whereby data cells are blended into one continuous stream at the transmitter and then separated again at the receiver

- Cell multiplex and demultiplex function, which **multiplexes** cells from individual virtual channels and virtual paths into one resulting cell stream in the transmit direction. It divides the arriving cell stream into individual cell flows to VCs or VPs in the receive direction.

- VPI and VCI translation, which is performed at the ATM switching and/or cross-connect nodes.

- Generic Flow Control (GFC), which supports control of the ATM traffic flow in a customer network.

ATM Adaptation Layer. The AAL performs the adaptation of OSI higher layer protocols, as most applications cannot deal directly with cells. The Adaptation Layer assures the appropriate service characteristics, and divides all types of data into the 48-byte payload that will make up the ATM cell. AAL is further divided into two sublayers: Segmentation and Reassembly (SAR) and Convergence Sublayer (CS).

The SAR sublayer performs segmentation of the higher layer information into a size suitable for the payload of the ATM cells of a virtual connection and, at the receiving side, it reassembles the contents of the cells of a virtual connection into data units to be delivered to the higher layers. The CS sublayer performs functions like message identification and time/clock recovery.

Key Benefits of ATM

ATM offers significant benefits to users and those who design and maintain communications networks. Because network transport functions can be separated into those related to an individual logical connection (virtual connection) and those related to a group of logical connections (virtual path), ATM simplifies network management. ATM also allows for the integration of networks, improving efficiency and manageability and providing a single network for carrying voice, data, and video.

ATM increases network performance and reliability because the network is required to deal with fewer aggregated entities. There is also less processing needed and it takes less time to add new virtual channels because capacity is reserved beforehand on a virtual path connection. Finally, ATM offers a high degree of infrastructure compatibility. Because ATM is not based on a specific type of physical transport, it can be transported over twisted pair, coaxial, and fiber optic cables. SEE ALSO INTERNET; NETWORK DESIGN; NETWORKS; WORLD WIDE WEB.

Radhika Jain and Upkar Varshney

Bibliography

Stallings, William. "Asynchronous Transfer Mode (ATM)." *Data and Computer Communications*, 5th ed. Upper Saddle River, NJ: Prentice Hall, 1997.

Internet Resources

"Asynchronous Transfer Mode (ATM) Switching." Cisco Connection Online. <http://www.cisco.com/univercd/cc/td/doc/cisintwk/ito_doc/atm.htm>

ATM Technology: The Foundation for Broadband Networks. <http://www.atmforum .com>

Authentication

Authentication is the process of verifying the identity of something or someone, often for security purposes, through some unique characteristic. Although the term has a specific meaning in the context of computer use, authentication is something people do on a regular basis. An object may be identified to an expert as an "authentic" antique by its manufacturer's mark or signature. An individual will be "authenticated" to family and friends by face recognition, or in the case of speaking, voice recognition. So for instance, in a telephone call to a friend, the caller is granted access to information that the call recipient regards as appropriate based on the recipient's recognition of the caller's voice. This is a basic form of authentication. In the computer world, authentication is the process by which a user (a person or a device) is granted access to a computer, a computer network, an application, or another form of information that is contained in or protected by a device or software.

Authentication can take numerous forms, and can require several factors. There are one-, two-, and three-factor authentication methods. A factor is a single representation of a user's identity. For example, in two-factor authentication, a user is required to provide two pieces of information in order to be verified by the requestor. The most common method of two-factor authentication is the use of a user identification name or account, and a password. The more factors that are involved, the higher the reliability of the verification process.

To be permitted access to a computer, a database, or a web site, for example, a user must provide unique credentials in response to a query from a device or requesting resource. This unique information could be a user identifier (userid or ID) and password combination, as mentioned earlier. It could also be a one-time use password or passcode, a token to be read by a special reader or application, or a biometric device used to read biological information that is obviously unique to the user, such as a fingerprint or **retinal scan**.

In the case of userid and password combinations, the resource being asked to provide access requires that the user present an ID and password that is supposed to be unique to that individual or user. This information has been previously stored in a database or other application, and is generally **encrypted** for added security. When requesting access to the resource, the user provides this combination of ID and password so that it can be compared to the combination that was previously stored. If they match, then access is granted. If not, the user may be prompted several times for the correct information. Access will not be granted until the correct combination is entered. Access can be blocked indefinitely if the number of failed attempts exceeds a predetermined amount. The purpose of this is to reduce the possibility of access by a non-authorized user who guesses at enough possible combinations to manage an accidental match.

A one-time use passcode or password requires some form of synchronization between the user and resource. For example, a computer system or application performs the duty of generating a passcode at a predetermined interval. The user has a token or other device that also generates the same password or passcode at precisely the same time. When users request

FACIAL SCANS

In the wake of the terrorist attacks on September 11, 2001, in the United States, airport security personnel tested out new technologies designed to improve safety measures. One of the methods was a facial recognition system, which scans people's faces and digitally compares the images against those of suspected terrorists. The technology, however, is not new. Some casinos use such devices to identify people who have been known to cheat.

retinal scan a scan of the retina of the eye, which contains a unique pattern for each individual, in order to identify (or authenticate) someone

encrypted coded, usually for purposes of security or privacy

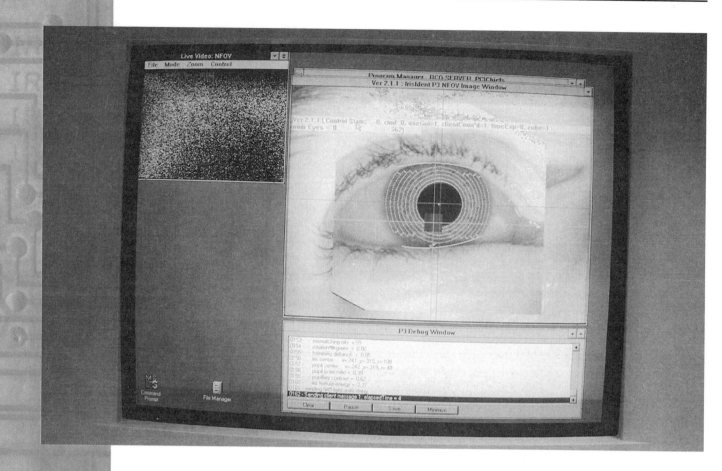

In order to authenticate employees, some companies use an iris identification scan. This system generates a bar code in order to identify people.

access, they must present the generated password or passcode. This passcode or password is generally valid for a predetermined period of time that usually varies from 30 seconds up to 30 minutes. A security benefit with this method is that the passcode is continually changing and one code is valid only within a limited and specific period of time.

A biometric scanner works differently. It may or may not require a userid. Instead, users, via some device, have a small portion of their bodies scanned—most commonly a fingerprint. This information has been previously recorded, as in the case of the userid/password combination described earlier. The requested resource then compares this information with what is on file. This information can be stored in itself or on another resource, and it is generally encrypted for added security. This form of authentication makes it more difficult for someone to impersonate or masquerade as an authorized user by attempting to pass along credentials belonging to someone else. Biometric devices can be expensive. One of the primary hurdles in their widespread use is arguably the societal fear of having a system or organization that possesses biometric data, such as fingerprints.

Another method of authentication involves the use of a token, which is a device or file that contains information permanently stored on or in it. For example, a typical Automated Teller Machine (ATM) requires the use of a card. The card stores the user's account number, along with other information. In addition to using an ATM card to initiate the transaction—neither a driver's license nor a credit card would work, for example—one must also be authenticated by the machine with the use of a personal iden-

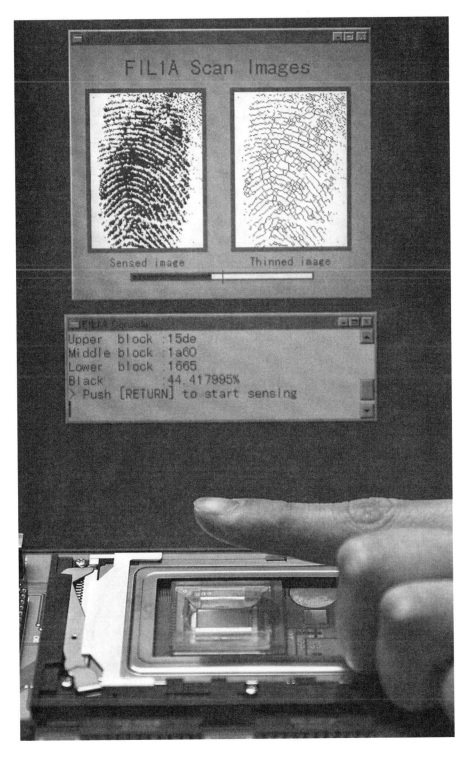

Fingerprint scans are another way to authenticate someone's identity. Researchers at Japan's Nippon Telephone and Telegraph Corporation developed the first microchip that can identify fingerprints.

tification number (PIN). Without the PIN, the user's ATM card will not provide the desired results, and without the card, the PIN is insufficient to identify the user with the bank's computers.

Another form of a token is a digital certificate. This is a file that contains information pertaining to a user or resource. It is stored on a computer or in an application, and it "invisibly" allows a user authorized access to something like an account, web site, or another computer. Digital certificates are becoming more popular as a form of user authentication for web site access or usage. An organization called Certificate Authority (CA) issues a certificate and, in doing so, verifies the identity of the owner. CAs can issue certificates to individuals, computers, or other CAs. Certificates are usually issued for a specific period of time, after which they expire; however, they can generally be renewed.

Authentication can be accomplished by various means. The most widely used method is by using the operating system of the resource a user wishes to access. Virtually all operating systems are able to require users to verify their identity through authentication mechanisms. Organizations such as large companies and the government may elect to install additional software programs with more advanced authentication mechanisms built in. This adds another layer of security to the authentication process. SEE ALSO E-COMMERCE; NETWORKS; SECURITY.

G. Christopher Hall

Bibliography

Oppliger, Rolf. *Authentication Systems for Secure Networks.* Artech House Inc., 1996.

Smith, Richard E. *Authentication: From Passwords to Public Keys.* Reading, MA: Addison-Wesley, 2001.

Bandwidth

Communication channels are classified as analog or digital. Bandwidth refers to the *data throughput capacity* of any communication channel. As bandwidth increases, more information per unit of time can pass through the channel. A simple analogy compares a communication channel to a water pipe. The larger the pipe, the more water can flow through it at a faster rate, just as a high capacity communication channel allows more data to flow at a higher rate than is possible with a lower capacity channel.

In addition to describing the capacity of a communication channel, the term "bandwidth" is frequently, and somewhat confusingly, applied to information transport requirements. For example, it might be specified that a broadcast signal requires a channel with a bandwidth of six MHz to transmit a television signal without loss or distortion. Bandwidth limitations arise from the physical properties of matter and energy. Every physical transmission medium has a finite bandwidth. The bandwidth of any given medium determines its communications efficiency for voice, data, graphics, or full motion video.

Widespread use of the Internet has increased public awareness of telecommunications bandwidth because both consumers and service providers are interested in optimizing the speed of Internet access and the speed with which web pages appear on computer screens.

Analog Signals

sine wave a wave traced by a point on the circumference of a circle when the point starts at height zero (amplitude zero) and goes through one full revolution

Natural signals such as those associated with voice, music, or vision, are analog in nature. Analog signals are represented by a **sine wave**, and analog channel capacities are measured in hertz (Hz) or cycles per second. Analog signals vary in amplitude (signal strength) or frequency (signal pitch or tone). Analog bandwidth is calculated by finding the difference between the minimum and maximum amplitudes or frequencies found on the particular communication channel.

For example, the bandwidth allocation of a telephone voice grade channel, which is classified as **narrowband**, is normally about 4,000 Hz, but the voice channel actually uses frequencies from 300 to 3,400 Hz, yielding a bandwidth that is 3,100 Hz wide. The additional space or guardbands on each side of the voice channel serve to prevent signal overlap with adjacent channels and are also used for transmitting call management information.

Digital Signals

Signals in computing environments are digital. Digital signals are described as discrete, or discontinuous, because they are transmitted in small, separate units called bits. Digital channel capacities are measured in either bits per second (bps) or signal changes per second, which is known as the baud rate. Although these terms are frequently used interchangeably, bits per second and baud rate are technically not the same. Baud rate is an actual measure of the number of signal changes that occur per second rather than the number of bits actually transmitted per second. Prefixes used in the measurement of data transmission speeds include kilo (thousands), mega (millions), giga (thousands of millions), and tera (thousands of giga). To describe digital transmission capabilities in bits per second, notations such as Kbps, Mbps, Gbps, and Tbps are common.

The telephone system has been in a gradual transition from an analog to a digital network. In order to transmit a digital signal over a conventional analog telephone line, a modem is needed to *modulate* the signal of the sender and *demodulate* the signal for the receiver. The term **modem** is an abbreviation of *modulate-demodulate*. Although the core capacity of the telephone network has experienced an explosion in available bandwidth, local access to homes and businesses, referred to as the local loop in the telephone network, frequently is limited to analog modem connections. Digital transmission is popular because it is a reliable, high-speed service that eliminates the need for modems.

Broadband Communications

Financial and other business activities, software downloads, video conferencing, and distance education have created a need for greater bandwidth. The term broadband is used to refer to hardware and media that can support a wide bandwidth. Coaxial cable and microwave transmission are classified as broadband. Coaxial cable, used for cable television, has a bandwidth of 500,000,000 Hz, or 500 megahertz, and microwave transmission has a bandwidth of 10,000 Hz.

The capacity potential of broadband devices is considerably greater than that of narrowband technology, resulting in greater data transmission speeds and faster download speeds, which are important to Internet users. Data transmission speeds range from a low of 14,400 bps on a low speed modem to more than ten gigabits per second on a **fiber optic** cable. On the assumption that 50,000 bits represents a page of data, it takes 3.5 seconds to transmit the page at 14,400 bps, but only 8/10 of a second at 64,000 bps. If a page of graphics contains one million bits per page, it

narrowband a general term in communication systems pertaining to a signal that has a small collection of differing frequency components (as opposed to broadband which has many frequency components)

modem a contraction of MOdulator DEModulator; a device which converts digital signals into signals suitable for transmission over analog channels, like telephone lines

fiber optic refers to a transmission technology using long, thin strands of glass fiber; internal reflections in the fibers assure that light entering one end is transmitted to the other end with only small losses in intensity; used widely in transmitting digital information

Bundles of wires make up coaxial cables, which are used for cable television. Such cables have a bandwidth of 500 megahertz.

takes more than a minute to transmit the page at 14,400 bps, compared to 16 seconds at 64 Kbps. Full motion video requires an enormous bandwidth of 12 Mbps.

Upload versus Download Bandwidth

Internet Service Providers (ISPs) commercial enterprises which offer paying subscribers access to the Internet (usually via modem) for a fee

Among **Internet Service Providers (ISPs)** and broadband cable or satellite links, there is considerable difference in upstream, or upload, bandwidth and downstream, or download, bandwidth. Upstream transmission occurs when one sends information to an ISP whereas downstream transmission occurs when information is received from an ISP. For example, a broadband cable modem connection might transmit upstream at one Mbps and downstream at ten Mbps.

Typical media used to connect to the Internet, along with upstream and downstream bandwidths include: T3 leased lines, T1 leased lines, cable modems, asymmetric digital subscribe lines (ADSLs), integrated services digital networks (ISDNs), and dial-up modems. As noted in Gary P. Schneider and James T. Perry's book *Electronic Commerce*, T3 leased lines provide the fastest speeds (44,700 kbps for both upstream and downstream speeds) while the rates for T1 leased lines are 1,544 kbps, ISDNs are 128 kbps, and dial-up modems are 56 kbps. ADSL upstream and downstream speeds are 640 and 9,000 kbps, respectively, while cable modem speeds are 768 kbps upstream and 10,000 kbps downstream.

Each of the connections has advantages and disadvantages. As the speed of the medium increases in the broadband media beginning with T1 lines, costs increase substantially. Although classified as broadband, cable modems are considered optimal in price and performance for the home user.

History of Bandwidth Research

Researchers have studied the effects of bandwidth on network traffic since the 1920s. Research objectives have always focused on the development of encoding techniques and technology enhancements that allow more bits to be transmitted per unit of time. In 1933 Harry Nyquist discovered a fundamental relationship between the bandwidth of a transmission system and the maximum number of bits per second that can be transmitted over that system. The Nyquist Intersymbol Interference Theorem allows one to calculate a theoretical maximum rate at which data can be sent. Nyquist's Theorem encourages data communications professionals to devise innovative coding schemes that will facilitate the maximum transmission of data per unit of time.

In 1948, noting that Nyquist's Theorem establishes an absolute maximum not achievable in practice, Claude Shannon of Bell Labs provided refinements to the theorem to account for the average amount of inherent noise or interference found on the transmission line. Shannon's Theorem can be summarized as saying that the laws of physics limit the speed of data transmission in a system and cannot be overcome by innovative coding schemes. SEE ALSO FIBER OPTICS; NETWORKS; SHANNON, CLAUDE E.; TELECOMMUNICATIONS.

Thomas A. Pollack

Bibliography

Comer, Douglas E. *Computer Networks and Internets.* Upper Saddle River, NJ: Prentice Hall, 2001.

Frenzel, Carroll W. *Management of Information Technology.* New York: Course Technology, 1999.

Lucas, Henry C., Jr. *Information Technology for Management.* New York: McGraw-Hill, 2000.

Rosenbush, Steve. "Broadband: 'What Happened?'" *Business Week,* June 11, 2001, pp. 38-41.

Schneider, Gary P., and James T. Perry. *Electronic Commerce.* Canada: Course Technology, 2001.

Browsers

A browser is a computer program that allows a computer to display information from the Internet. It also provides a way for the user to access and navigate through this information space.

A browser can also be thought of as a **client**, sending requests to Web servers using **Hypertext Transfer Protocol (HTTP)**. Whenever a browser is started, or a user clicks on a hyperlink, or a Uniform Resource Locator (URL) is typed in, the browser sends a message to a web server (based on the address indicated by the URL) to have a file transferred. The browser interprets the information in the file so that it can be viewed in the browser window, or if necessary, through another program. The information dis-

client a program or computer often managed by a human user, that makes requests to another computer for information

Hypertext Transfer Protocol (HTTP) a simple connectionless communications protocol developed for the electronic transfer (serving) of HTML documents

27

played may be text or images. The browser interprets information written in **Hypertext Markup Language (HTML)** and displays this information in the browser window.

Files that have sounds or animation may require different programs to enable the information to be heard or seen. Most capabilities are built into the browser but sometimes the computer needs special equipment or programs. To hear sounds, for example, the computer needs a sound card, speakers, and software that enable the sounds to be heard. Some other files need a type of program called a **plug-in** in order to be viewed. For example, to read files written in Portable Document Format (PDF), users need to download the Adobe Acrobat program to their computers so the documents can be displayed in the browser window.

Browser Features

More than 100 different browsers exist, and most of them are available to download from the Internet for free; however, not all of them are usable on all computer platforms. There are specialized browsers, for example, that are designed to work only on devices such as **personal digital assistants (PDAs)** (e.g., Palm Pilots). Others only work on Macintosh computers, Windows operating systems, or UNIX computers.

The two most popular browsers are Netscape Navigator and Microsoft Internet Explorer. Both work on Macintosh and Windows platforms, in addition to others. Online services such as America Online and CompuServe have offered their own browsers for some time, but now most online services offer Netscape and Internet Explorer as well.

Most browsers share similar characteristics and elements, and employ many of the same options and techniques. In addition to providing ways for the user to navigate between web pages, browsers also generally allow a user to search for words in an individual web page. A browser also keeps a history of the web pages the user has already visited, and allows the user to organize what has been accessed. Users may save locations of web pages for easy future retrieval. Netscape's Bookmarks and Internet Explorer's Favorites organize URLs into files and save them indefinitely.

A browser allows the user to move between web pages by going back and forward, and features a scrolling device so that the user can move up and down a web page. Most browsers display the title of the current web page being viewed at the very top of the browser window. Browsers have menus with several elements available that can help the user manage the information found on the web. There are options such as saving a web page, sending a page, printing a page, and more. In addition, there are options that allow the user to copy text and other information from the current web page and paste it in other applications. Also included is the ability to search a web page for a word or phrase.

A web browser also provides a way for the user to view the HTML source of the current web page. This is a useful function for web page developers who want to know how a particular page was constructed and which HTML tags and elements were used in its design. The user may also view the vital information about a page, including the date the page was modified or updated, and whether it is a secure document for private transac-

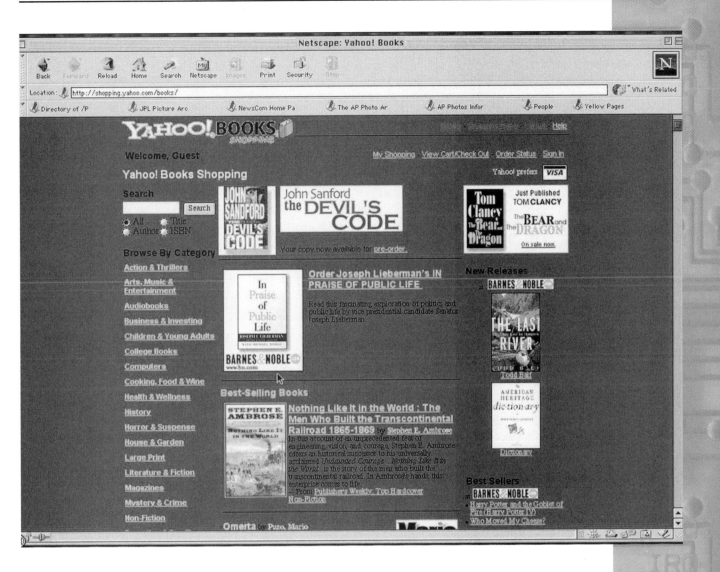

tions. The option to reload a web page is also provided, as is the option to stop loading a page. Stopping is a useful option when a page is taking a long time to load.

History of Browsers

The browser as it is known today owes its development to Tim Berners-Lee, director of the World Wide Web Consortium (W3C) and a researcher at the Laboratory for Computer Science at the Massachusetts Institute of Technology. It was while working at CERN, the European Particle Physics Laboratory near Geneva, Switzerland, in the 1980s and early 1990s, that Berners-Lee developed the groundwork for the World Wide Web.

Crucial to the web's development was Berners-Lee's work in defining Hypertext Transfer Protocol (HTTP), a set of rules that enable a web page to be browsed using hypertext, and the language computers use to communicate with each other over the Internet. Hypertext, a term coined by Ted Nelson in 1965, and a concept invented by Vannevar Bush in 1945, is defined as a way of presenting information non-sequentially. It includes hyperlinks, or selections of text or images, that when activated by a point-and-click with a mouse, take the user to other related text or images.

Browsers, such as Netscape and Internet Explorer, help computer users navigate through the vast offerings of the web. Buttons along the top of the screen allow the user to travel back and forth between viewed screens, return to a preselected home page, and print screens, among other functions.

HYPERTEXT AND HYPERLINKS

Hypertext is information organized so that it can be connected to other related information in a non-sequential way. The information is linked together by hyperlinks. By clicking on hyperlinks, users can choose various paths through the hypertext material.

A hyperlink is a word, phrase, image, or region of an image, often highlighted, that can be selected from a web page. Each hyperlink represents another web page, a location in the current web page, an image or multimedia file, or some other resource on the World Wide Web. When a user clicks on a hyperlink, the browser sends a message to the web server that holds the resource to send it to the user's browser window.

graphical user interface (GUI) an interface that allows computers to be operated through pictures (icons) and mouse-clicks, rather than through text and typing

As the information linked to can include images and sounds as well as text, the term is more aptly named hypermedia.

Berners-Lee completed his work on the first World Wide Web browser in 1990 on a NeXT machine, a personal computer developed by Steve Jobs, founder of Apple Computer. Special features of the NeXT platform made it easier for him to try his idea of programming a hypertext client program on it, and combining it with the Internet.

While there were several hypertext projects being worked on in several countries at the time, none of the projects fit Berners-Lee's vision of what he wanted this system to look like, so he developed his own. He wrote the code for HTTP and invented the Universal Resource Identifier (URI), the scheme for document addresses. The most common type of URI is the URL. The browser he developed was called WorldWideWeb. He later renamed the browser Nexus so as not to confuse it with the World Wide Web itself. He also wrote Hypertext Markup Language (HTML) that contains the rules for formatting pages with hypertext links, or hyperlinks.

The problem with the WorldWideWeb browser was that it only ran on the NeXT computer. Browser clients were needed for use on PCs, Macintosh computers, and UNIX platforms. Universities in Europe and the United States were urged to take on browser creation projects. In 1992 students at Helsinki University developed a browser called Erwise that ran on a UNIX machine. At about the same time, Pei Wei, a student at the University of California, Berkeley, created Viola-WWW, a web browser for UNIX computers that was able to display HTML with graphics, load animations, and download small, embedded applications. Viola-WWW was a precursor to the popular software Hot Java, which was not in use until a few years later.

Mosaic, developed by Marc Andreessen and Eric Bina at the National Center for Supercomputing Applications (NCSA) at the University of Illinois at Urbana-Champaign, was the first widely distributed browser that was compatible with several platforms. It was also the first web browser with a **graphical user interface (GUI)**. It was released in 1993 as free, downloadable software on the Internet.

Mosaic introduced the Internet and the World Wide Web to a wide audience. The graphical interface made the web appear more exciting and made the information more accessible to people. Lynx, a text-only browser, was developed at the University of Kansas at around the same time. Lynx is still used by people who are not able to use graphical browsers due to their computers' limitations. It is also useful for users who want to view information only in text format, or those who are visually impaired and find that Lynx is ideal for use with Braille or screen reading software.

Many of the features of Mosaic were integrated into a new browser developed by Netscape Communications, a company formed with Andreessen and other people from the NCSA. In October 1994 Netscape released the first version of its browser, called Mozilla, as a beta, or test version. The commercial version, Netscape Navigator 1.0, was released in December of 1994 as a free, downloadable software package on the Internet. In August 1995 Microsoft released Windows 95 and the Internet Explorer browser. In the spring of 1998 Microsoft provided the Windows 98 operating system along with Internet Explorer 4.0, which came as an integral part of the operating system. Netscape Navigator and Microsoft Internet Explorer continue to compete with each other as the dominant software options in the web browser market.

Browser Development

The World Wide Web Consortium and other developers continue to try to create speech recognition software that will allow users to interact with the Internet using spoken words. People with visual impairments or those who access the web in situations where their eyes and hands are occupied, will find these browsers helpful. Also possible are browsers that talk back to the user. Other browser developments will include the full support of Extensible Markup Language (XML) and Resource Description Framework (RDF), both of which advance the organization of web information in a structured way. Browser programmers will continue to work on projects that increase the browser's capability to improve human-computer information processing in the complexity of the web environment. SEE ALSO BAND-WIDTH; INTERNET; INTERNET: APPLICATIONS; WORLD WIDE WEB.

Karen Hartman

Bibliography

Ackermann, Ernest, and Karen Hartman. *Internet and Web Essentials: What You Need to Know.* Wilsonville, OR: Franklin, Beedle, and Associates, 2001.

Berners-Lee, Tim, with Mark Fischetti. *Weaving the Web: The Original Design and Ultimate Destiny of the World Wide Web.* New York: Harper Collins, 2000.

Head, Milena, Norm Archer, and Yufei Yuan. "World Wide Web Navigation Aid." *International Journal of Human-Computer Studies* 53 (2000): 301–330.

Mintz, Bridget. "Graphics on the Internet." *Computer Graphics World* 23, no. 10 (2000): 32–44.

Internet Resources

Berners-Lee, Tim. "WorldWideWeb, The First Web Client." World Wide Web Consortium. <http://www.w3.org/People/Berners-Lee/WorldWideWeb.html>

BrowserWatch. 2001. <http://browserwatch.internet.com>

Censorship: National, International

Censorship is a practice that limits public access to materials, including printed text, photographs and art, music and video, or other multimedia, based on the value judgments or prejudices of the censoring individuals or groups. According to psychologist Sara Fine, censorship is essentially a defense mechanism triggered by fear of threats of some sort. Whether this fear is based on a real threat, an exaggeration of some actual danger, or an unconscious reaction to some dark, hidden impulse is irrelevant. Thus, just about any material can be censored. Materials most likely to be censored in the United States are those that deal with sex and sexuality, challenge the authority of adults, or differ from the censor's beliefs and traditions.

Librarian Lester Asheim points out that censorship is different from *selection*, which is the process of deciding which resources to include in a museum or library collection, for example, in that censorship favors the control of thought whereas selection favors the liberty of thought. Censorship's

---

approach to materials is negative, seeking vulnerable characteristics within or outside the work, and often without considering the work as a whole. Selection's approach is positive, seeking the merits of the work by examining the entire document. Censorship seeks to protect others from images, ideas, or language deemed by the censor to be negative in some way, whereas selection seeks to protect people's right to read, view, or otherwise experience the material in question. Censors trust only their own intelligence; selectors have faith in the reader's intelligence. In sum, censorship is authoritarian while selection is democratic.

The primary argument against censorship is that it infringes on the First Amendment to the U.S. Constitution which reads: "Congress shall make no law respecting an establishment of religion, or prohibiting the free exercise thereof; or abridging the freedom of speech, or of the press, or the right of the people peaceably to assemble, and to petition the government for a redress of grievances."

While some citizens are strongly against censorship of any kind, believing it is undemocratic, others advocate some censorship on the Internet for several reasons. Chief among them are web sites featuring adult or child pornography as well as those with racist or hate speech. Many of the concerned people are parents who do not want their kids exposed to such material, which they believe is easily accessible via the Internet. They fear their children might stumble onto such sites while innocently surfing the web.

Censorship and Computers

As it pertains to the world of computing—and to the Internet, in particular—censorship may be accomplished by the use of filtering or blocking software. There are several types of filtering software available: keyword blocking, host or site blocking, and **protocol** blocking. These filters are generally promoted as ways to limit children's access to "adult materials" available via the Internet. Parents, schools, and public libraries are the target customers for filtering software.

protocol an agreed understanding for the sub-operations that make up a transaction, usually found in the specification of inter-computer communications

Keyword blocking indiscriminately targets individual words or strings of words to be blocked; the vocabulary usually consists of taboo words related to parts of the body, sex, etc. Thus, web sites or pages with information about breast cancer, penile erectile dysfunction, and Essex county might be blocked out and rendered inaccessible.

Host blocking targets specific Internet sites for blocking; the block could include the entire site or only files on that site. Host blocking sometimes results in the politically motivated exclusion of sites dealing with women's issues (e.g., the site of the National Organization for Women), feminism, or the environment.

file transfer protocol (FTP) a communications protocol used to transfer files

Protocol filtering blocks entire domains, such as Usenet, which hosts a variety of pornographic chat groups, and **file transfer protocol (FTP)**, which could theoretically retrieve materials from blocked sites. This, of course, also limits user access to chat groups and other resources that would not otherwise be censored.

Examples of commercial filtering products are CyberPatrol, CyberSitter, NetNanny, SafeSurf, SurfWatch, and WebSENSE. These filters have their own web sites and most have test software that can be downloaded. In

each case, vendors determine the blocking language and decide which sites should be blocked. However, each offers a password that can turn off the system, and various options for custom configuration of categories.

Censorship Abroad

There are constitutional guarantees and a strong commitment to the full exercise of free speech in the United States. However, this is not the case in many countries of the world. The international organization, Human Rights Watch, issued a report on the global attack on free speech on the Internet. In the document's summary, the threat is clearly stated: "Governments around the world, claiming they want to protect children, thwart terrorists and silence racist and hate mongers, are rushing to eradicate freedom of expression on the Internet, the international 'network of networks,' touted as the Information Superhighway."

In China users and **Internet Service Providers (ISPs)** are required to register with authorities. Vietnam and Saudi Arabia permit only a single,

Hate speech on the Internet raises concerns about censorship and whether such sites should be banned from the web. Some groups counter racist material by monitoring such sites and promoting their own message of anti-hate.

Internet Service Providers (ISPs) commercial enterprises which offer paying subscribers access to the Internet (usually via modem) for a fee

government-controlled gateway for Internet service; Germany has severed access to particular host computers or Internet sites; and Singapore requires political and religious content providers to register with the state so that the government may regulate the Internet as if it were a broadcast medium like television. These are just a few examples of the ways in which Internet-based communication and content are monitored, regulated, and often censored worldwide.

Conclusion

Should cyberspace receive the full freedom of speech and press that is accorded to print materials, or are there valid arguments for increased restrictions? One might ask: Is a teen more likely to take up smoking because he or she sees pictures of celebrities on the Internet with cigarettes in hand? Is a child more likely to find lewd pictures on the Internet than in a bookstore or library? These are the types of questions that need to be raised when considering whether the risks of offensive texts or images on the Internet are greater than those from printed materials, and whether they are worth weakening the freedom of speech that is important to protecting political, religious, and personal freedom in the United States. SEE ALSO INTERNET; INTERNET: APPLICATIONS; PRIVACY; SECURITY; WORLD WIDE WEB.

Joyce H-S Li

Bibliography

Asheim, Lester. "Not Censorship but Selection." *Wilson Library Bulletin* 28 (1953): 63–67.

———. "Selection and Censorship: A Reappraisal." *Wilson Library Bulletin* 58 (1983): 180–184.

Burress, Lee. *Battle of the Books: Literary Censorship in the Public Schools, 1950–1985.* Metuchen, NJ: Scarecrow, 1989.

Fine, Sara. "How the Mind of a Censor Works: The Psychology of Censorship." *School Library Journal* 42 (1996): 23–27.

Godwin, Mike. *Cyber Rights: Defending Free Speech in the Digital Age.* New York: Random House, 1998.

"Silencing the Net: The Threat to Freedom of Expression On-line." *Human Rights Watch* 8 (May 1996).

Wallace, Jonathan, and Mark Mangan. *Sex, Laws, and Cyberspace: Freedom and Censorship on the Frontiers of the Online Revolution.* New York: Henry Holt, 1996.

Internet Resources

Index on Censorship: The International Magazine for Free Expression. <http://www.oneworld.org/index_oc/index.html>

Chemistry

The field of chemistry requires the use of computers in a multitude of ways. Primarily, computers are useful for storing vast amounts of data for the researcher or student to use. From facts about the periodic table to displaying 3-D models of molecules for easy visualization, computers are vital in the chemistry lab.

Equally important, many aspects of chemistry are explained in mathematical terms, and mathematicians have applied the laws of physics to much

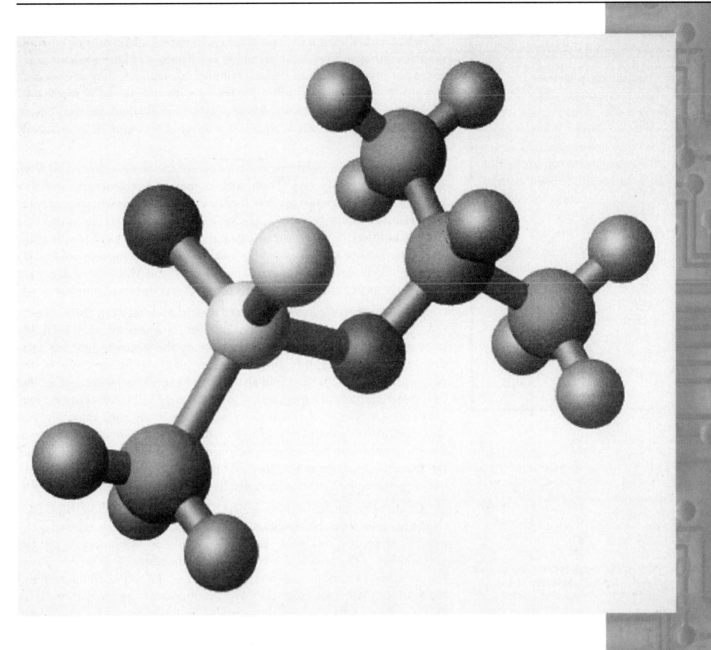

Chemists use computer-generated molecular models, such as this rendition of the poisonous nerve agent SARIN, to analyze the molecule's structure and function.

of chemistry. The result of this work is a diversity of equations that define chemical properties and predict chemical reactions. Because of these equations, for example, one can figure out the volume and density of gases. Equations are also used to calculate atmospheric pressures or to figure out the molecular weight of a solute (dissolved substance) in a solvent.

Typically, chemistry software applications include a multitude of equations. Some equations are quite complex. Using an equation engine, much like a search engine, allows the user to search for equations and bring them to the desktop in a format that allows for the insertion of values. Because the chemist does not need to recopy complex equations and constants, equation engines save time as well as decrease the chance of errors. Computers then allow the easy and accurate processing of this information.

Computers are so necessary in chemistry that some colleges and universities require chemistry majors to take courses in computer science. The chemist must gain proficiency in using word processors and constructing

CHEMOMETRICS

Chemometrics, an advanced field of chemistry, utilizes the application of mathematics and statistics to clinical information. One example of chemometrics is pyrolysis mass spectrometry, in which an unidentified material is fixed to a metal strip and heated to a specific temperature. At this temperature, the electrostatic bonds holding the atoms together break. Using the light components given off by the atoms, the mass spectrometer creates a chemical profile, or chemical fingerprint. With these statistics, the chemist is able to identify the material.

mass spectrometers instruments that can identify elemental particles in a sample by examining the frequencies of the particles that comprise the sample

polypeptide the product of many amino acid molecules bonded together

molecular modeling a technique that uses high performance computer graphics to represent the structure of chemical compounds

spreadsheets for presentations. Statistics, statistical methods, and scientific graphing are also important elements in chemistry. Many students learn computer programming to become comfortable with a variety of operating systems. Familiarity with utility programs, networking, and network software is essential. Some knowledge of graphic design allows for the demonstration and manipulation of chemical principles, for example, in molecular modeling.

More and more instruments for chemists are being designed to work seamlessly with computers. Tools such as **mass spectrometers** are being interfaced with computers to allow for fast and accurate presentation of complex data. A thorough knowledge of computer architecture allows the chemist to interface these instruments if such interfacing is not readily available. The field of chemistry is also ideally suited to computer assisted instruction. Some universities, such as the University of Massachusetts, market general chemistry courses on CD-ROM (compact disc-read only memory).

Not only are computers helpful as a resource but they can also cut costs, time, and errors in the classroom. For instance, biochemistry students might want to participate in an experiment to study the structure-function relationship of a **polypeptide** (including the study of the structure of the polypeptide using an amino acid analyzer and peptide sequencer). The cost of conducting such an experiment—approximately $200,000—can be a major drawback. The time constraints, even if the study runs smoothly, can also exceed the limits of a single semester course. Computer simulation, however, can make the process much easier and more cost effective. Also, the student's attention can be focused on a specific point of interest instead of being distracted by the endless details involved in the actual experiment.

Computational chemistry is similar to **molecular modeling**. Both consist of the interactive combination of visualization and computational techniques. Molecular modeling keeps the emphasis of the work on the visualization of the molecule. Computational chemistry concentrates on the computational techniques. A fine illustration of the use of computers and the Internet with molecular (DNA) modeling was constructed by James Watson of Clare College and Francis Crik of Gonville and Caius College, in Cambridge, England.

Chemists, like scientists in other fields, are growing increasingly dependent upon the Internet. The World Wide Web, and especially e-mail, allows instant mass communication between teachers and students, as well as the isolated chemist and his or her colleagues. Online professional journals are becoming more common, allowing scientists to review literature more easily. The first online chemistry conference was held in 1993 by the American Chemical Society. Online classes are being offered more frequently. The Internet also allows scientists to collaborate on projects with each other without necessarily working in the same building, or even the same continent. The Internet makes it far easier for individuals to participate in professional organizations.

Database management is essential to chemistry. Many databases evolve too quickly and are too extensive to be maintained by a single chemist. The National Institutes of Health (NIH) is a major supplier of resources for molecular modeling for researchers. The Center for Molecular Modeling is part of the Division of Computational Bioscience, Center for Informational Technology. At this web site, computational chemists work with researchers on the relationships between structure and function of molecules. This allows researchers to develop a greater understanding of chemical interactions, enzyme production, ion bonds, and other properties of molecules.

The Internet is also a wonderful resource for students and educators of chemistry. Web resources include tutorials and reference sites for almost all fields and levels of chemistry students, from high school and college. One site, the Schlumberger SEED, or the Science Excellence in Educational Development web site, promotes the science and technology to students by introducing lab experiments, providing science news, offering help to teachers, and hosting a question and answer forum. This site offers another forum for one-on-one communication between future scientists and those actively working in the field.

Some chemists have decided that the computer and Internet can allow them to make chemistry entertaining. For example, John P. Selegue and F. James Holler of the University of Kentucky have put their research and technical skills to use by composing a web page that explores the use of the elements of the periodic table (even molybdenum) throughout the history of comic books. This site was one of the winners of the 2001 Scientific American's Sci/Tech Web Awards. SEE ALSO COMPUTER ASSISTED INSTRUCTION; MOLECULAR BIOLOGY; PHYSICS; SCIENTIFIC VISUALIZATION.

Mary McIver Puthawala

Internet Resources

The Chemistry Place. Needham, MA: Peregrine Publishers, Inc. <http://www.chemplace.com>

Schlumberger SEED, The Science Education Web Site. <http://www.slb.com/seed/>

Selegue, John P., and F. James Holler. *The Comic Book Periodic Table of the Elements*. <http://www.uky.edu/Projects/Chemcomics/>

Watson, James, and Francis Crik. *DNA and RNA Structures*. <http://www.ch.cam.ac.uk/SGTL/Structures/nucleic/>

Zielinski, Theresa Julia, and Mary L. Swift. "What Every Chemist Should Know About Computers, II." *The Chemical Educator* 2, no.3 (1996). <http://link.springer-ny.com/link/service/journals/00897/sbibs/s0002003/spapers/23tjz897.htm>

Computer Vision

Computer vision is a technical capability that enables a computer to recognize or understand the content of a picture. **Robotics** is a field that is particularly affected by the development of computer vision. A robot with vision capability will be much more effective in its workspace than one that is unsighted. Robots with vision can be programmed to respond to unstructured or random changes. For example, imagine that a robot is needed to pick up and use bolts that are lying loose in a box. The bolts can be at any orientation with respect to the gripper and only a sighted robot will have the ability to adapt to this random configuration. A robot with no vision system would have to be pre-programmed by somebody to know exactly where every bolt was lying in the box—not a very cost-effective solution.

robotics the science and engineering of building electromechanical machines to replace human laborers

photosensitive a term for describing any material that will change its properties in some way if subjected to visible light, such as photographic film

isosceles triangle a triangle that has two sides of equivalent length (and therefore two angles of the same size)

ultrasonic the transmission and reception of sound waves that are at frequencies higher than those audible to humans

radar the acronym for RAdio Direction And Ranging; a technique developed in the 1930s that uses frequency shifts in reflected radio waves to measure distance and speed of a target

Human vision, which is what one would normally expect a computer to be able to mimic, is actually a more complex process than most people might imagine it is. The human eye is composed of a lens that is flexible. Muscles around the periphery of the lens can stretch the lens so that it becomes thinner and its focal length increases, or the muscles can compress the lens so that it becomes thicker and its focal length decreases. These adjustments all take place "automatically" as far as we are concerned; we make no conscious effort to adjust the focal length of the lenses of our eyes. Instead, whether we look at distant objects or those close to us, the eye is automatically adjusted to focus accordingly. A vision system connected to a computer cannot function this way; the machine must be designed and programmed to distinguish between far and near objects and then have the capacity to adjust its focus accordingly.

As well as managing lens adjustment, the human eye has an intricately structured light sensitive "film" at the back of the eye called the retina. The retina is **photosensitive**, so it collects the focused light and converts it into signals that are dispatched to the brain. The light-sensitive elements are classified as either cones or rods. There are approximately six to seven million cones in the retina, mostly grouped around its center. The cones are responsive to variations in the wavelength of the light that reaches them—this means they are the receptors of color. The cones can also sense a variation in light intensity and as such are the principle enablers of daylight vision.

The function of rods is slightly different. There are about 130 million of them and they are predominantly found around the periphery of the retina. Rods are really only sensitive to the amount of light and tend to be more useful in assisting with night vision. The rods and cones are connected by minute nerve endings that all tend to gather at one point on the retina, where the optic nerve connects the eye and the brain. Arranging for a computer to incorporate a device that could act in a way that is anything like a retina is challenging.

The fact that humans have two eyes that are forward-facing makes it possible, with the help of the brain, to perceive depth. The two lines of sight between each eye and one object in focus, together with the line between the two eyes, form an **isosceles triangle**. The height of the triangle provides a perception of the distance between the plane that contains the eyes, and the object itself. A computer vision system attempting to simulate human vision would also have to try to deal with distance perception. It is possible, though, that distance measurement might be attained in other ways in a computer system; for example, a computer's sensory system could be augmented with extra facilities that use **ultrasonic** or **radar** techniques.

Components of Computer Vision

A computer vision system requires one or more television cameras that are capable of digitizing an image so that these can be stored in memory. A processor will then be commanded to analyze the information by identifying and defining any objects that may be significant. It then deals with primary objects differently than it does with objects from the scene or background. There are several commonly used camera types, but in all cases they operate by transferring an image into horizontal scan lines that make up a picture. In most cases the cameras and the central processor will be assisted by two other elements: a "frame-grabber" and an "image pre-processor."

The frame-grabber is a special device that can take an image from the camera, digitize it if it has not already been digitized, and make it available as one object to the remainder of the system. The digitizing is necessary since the computer only handles digital data and many cameras will produce only **analog** images. The digitized images tend to be rather large blocks of data. Each individual **pixel** in the image will have parameters for brightness, and perhaps color, associated with it. Thousands of these are found in just one static picture, and as soon as either the scene or the camera position changes, some or all of the data associated with the pixels changes and must therefore be updated.

In order to help with the management of these large amounts of data, the pre-processor assists by discarding parts of the image that are not considered useful, thereby reducing the image size and the computational effort involved in dealing with the image. It does this by various means, but one common way is to group together collections of pixels that have almost the same color or brightness values and changing them so that they are all the same. This obviously distorts the original image, but it can be a successful optimization technique if none of the important image information is lost. Unfortunately, it is difficult to guarantee that all the important information will always be safeguarded.

Steps of Computer Vision

Once an image has been captured by the camera and set up for further operations by the pre-processor, then the real business of computer vision can begin. One of the important results of the pre-processing operations is known as "edge-detection." Here, the pre-processor identifies areas of the image that possess regions of clearly differing light intensity. This is the first step in providing the vision system with a way of recognizing objects.

The next step is called "image segmentation." Segmentation is an operation whereby the vision system tries to identify particular shapes or regions by differentiating them from their backgrounds. It does this by choosing an intensity threshold level and organizing the image so that all pixels darker than this level are sectioned off from all those that are lighter. This breaks the image up into segments that will correspond directly to the main features and objects in the field of view. The difficulty is in selecting the most suitable threshold level; normally there will be a way to adjust the threshold so that the most satisfactory segmentation results can be produced.

Image segmentation can be artificially enhanced, if the environment is conducive to it, by intentionally selecting bland and uniform backgrounds that contrast in color and brightness with objects in the foreground. Image segmentation can also be carried out using attributes of the image other than light intensity such as color or texture.

After segmentation has been completed, the next step is image extraction and recognition. Segmentation permits regions of the image to be isolated, but getting the computer system to recognize what it is looking at requires further effort. This operation requires "training" the computer system to be aware of certain specific objects and shapes that it is expected

analog a quantity (often an electrical signal) that is continuous in time and amplitude

pixel a single picture element on a video screen; one of the individual dots making up a picture on a video screen or digital image

to encounter. This is easier to do if one limits the nature of the working environment of the machine. The computer can be given data sets of standard objects called "templates" and then can be asked to ascertain similarities among these templates and the segments of the images that it captures. It uses statistical techniques to attempt to determine what types of objects it is looking at, based on the templates that it has been given.

Computer vision is important in manufacturing and other industry areas that use robotic technology, but it is also being developed to assist with **pattern recognition** and provide support to visually impaired people. SEE ALSO ARTIFICIAL INTELLIGENCE; OPTICAL TECHNOLOGY; PATTERN RECOGNITION; ROBOTICS.

Stephen Murray

Bibliography

Malcolm, Douglas R., Jr. *Robotics: An Introduction.* Belmont, CA: Breton, Wadsworth Inc., 1985.

McCormick, Ernest J., and Mark S. Sanders. *Human Factors in Engineering and Design,* 5th ed. Singapore: McGraw-Hill, 1986.

Pugh, Alan, ed. *Robot Vision.* United Kingdom: IFS Publications Ltd., 1983.

Sanz, Jorge L. C. ed. *Advances in Machine Vision.* New York: Springer-Verlag, Inc., 1989.

Shahinpoor, Mohsen, *A Robot Engineering Textbook.* New York: Harper and Row, 1987.

Snyder, Wesley E. *Industrial Robots: Computer Interfacing and Control.* Englewood Cliffs, NJ: Prentice-Hall, 1985.

Cookies

In the World Wide Web, a computer "cookie" is a small piece of data that a web server sends to an Internet user's computer along with the requested web page. The web browser is supposed to save the cookie and send it together with all future requests to the same server (or group of servers). Although there are privacy and security concerns that cause some Internet users to block cookies, there is no danger that cookies will damage data on a user's computer or server; cookies cannot contain viruses since they are not executable files.

When a user clicks on a hyperlink, the browser sends a request to the web server specified in the **Uniform Resource Locator (URL)** underlying the hyperlink. The formal **syntax** for such requests and the corresponding answer (response) is regulated by the **Hypertext Transfer Protocol (HTTP)**. For performance reasons, HTTP was designed to be "stateless"— which means that each request is treated in isolation. After a web server answers a request, the connection between the browser and the server is closed within seconds. The HTTP protocol has no notion of a session (with logon and logoff). For some Internet activity this is a serious limitation; therefore, cookies were invented by Netscape as an extension to the HTTP protocol.

What Does a Cookie Do?

Cookies identify and track users of web sites. For instance, in an online shop, a user navigates through a number of pages to fill a "shopping basket." The

pattern recognition a process used by some artificial-intelligence systems to identify a variety of patterns, including visual patterns, information patterns buried in a noisy signal, and word patterns imbedded in text

Uniform Resource Locator (URL) a reference to a document or a document container using the Hypertext Transfer Protocol (HTTP); consists of a hostname and path to the document

syntax a set of rules that a computing language incorporates regarding structure, punctuation, and formatting

Hypertext Transfer Protocol (HTTP) a simple connectionless communications protocol developed for the electronic transfer (serving) of HTML documents

Some web sites send cookies (small pieces of recorded data) to be stored on the user's computer to be activated the next time the user enters those sites. Other sites, like many online banking services, will not send cookies due to privacy concerns.

web server tracks user activity by means of cookies. The very first time a user enters an online shop, the web server notices that no identifying cookie was received with the request for web page access. Therefore, the web server generates a new unique number and sends it in a cookie, along with the response. In future requests from that user to the same server, the browser will automatically include the cookie, which will alert the server that the user is continuing with his/her shopping session. The contents of the shopping basket are stored on the web site's server, indexed by the cookie. When the user purchases something from the shopping basket, thus identifying him or herself by name and address, that information, along with the number of the cookie, is stored on the server.

Personalized web pages also depend on cookies: Some online shops make special offers to returning customers based on their previous buying behavior or suggest new products that are similar to previous purchases. Other web sites allow their users to customize the appearance or contents of the page as it appears on their computer screen.

Search engines can use cookies to track users and build up a list of search terms the user has entered previously. This information can be used to display advertisements to the user, related to his or her interests. Normally, the search engine will not know the name and address of the user, only the unique number linked to the user's computer.

Cookie Concerns

Advertisements on web pages are often managed by specialized agencies, rather than by the companies that operate the web servers. Such agencies can send cookies alongside the images containing the advertisement. Agencies that manage advertisements on a relatively large subset of the World Wide Web can build up quite a detailed profile of interests for users. As long as they do not know the names and addresses of the users, this might be acceptable. However, through collaboration with online shops, the information of the shop and the advertising agency can be brought together. Technically, the shop refers to images stored on the web server of the advertising agency. In the URLs referencing the images, the unique identifications of users in the shop are included. The server of the advertising agency then gets its own cookies together with the name and address information from the online shop.

Because of such possible privacy problems, web browsers allow users some options to switch cookies off. If a user so chooses, the browser will simply throw away the cookies sent by a server and will not include them in future requests. However, some online shops will not work without cookies. Other shops add the unique number to the hypertext links embedded in the pages. This works only as long as the user stays within the shop; subsequent visits appear as being from a new user.

Internet Explorer stores cookies in "C:\WINDOWS\COOKIES" or "C:\WINDOWS\Temporary Internet Files." Netscape stores cookies in a file called "cookies" or "cookies.txt." A text editor like Wordpad will show the name of the cookie, the contents of the cookie, and the domain of the originating web server plus some additional data (e.g. expiration time). The same server can define several cookies. It is possible for users to delete cookies (the browser must be closed first), but if a user returns later to a web site for which cookies have been deleted, the site's server will not recognize personalized options.

Some cookies contain passwords. This is a security risk, especially if different people have access to the same computer. In addition, the cookie and history folders on a PC give a good picture of the kind of web pages that were viewed by previous users of that PC. SEE ALSO INTERNET; INTERNET: APPLICATIONS; PRIVACY; SECURITY; WORLD WIDE WEB.

Stefan Brass

PRIVACY THREAT

In the communication between web browsers and web servers, cookies are used to link together several page requests to one session. They are useful because otherwise each time a user clicks on a web link, the page request is treated in isolation. However, cookies endanger the privacy of the web server.

Bibliography

Kristol, David M. "HTTP Cookies: Standards, Privacy, and Politics." *ACM Transactions on Internet Technology* 1, no. 2 (2001): 151–198.

Ladd, Eric, Jim O'Donnell, et al. *Using HTML 4, XML, and Java 1.2, Platinum Edition.* Indianapolis, IN: Que, 1999.

Internet Resources

"The Cookies Page." *Electronic Privacy Information Center (EPIC).* <http://www.epic.org/privacy/internet/cookies/>

Kristol, D., and L. Montuilli. *HTTP State Management Mechanism.* October 2000. Request for Comments (RFC) 2965. <http://www.rfc-editor.org/rfc/rfc2965.text>

"Persistent Client State, HTTP Cookies" (Preliminary Specification). Netscape Support Documentation, 1999. <http://www.netscape.com/newsref/std/cookie_spec.html>

Whalen, David. "The Unofficial Cookie FAQ." *Cookie Central.* <http://www.cookiecentral.com/faq/>

Copyright

Copyright includes not only the right to make copies of a work—called the right of reproduction—it also includes several other rights, including the right to distribute, adapt, publicly perform, and publicly display a work. By allowing authors to control reproduction and other uses of their creative works for a period of time, copyright allows authors to make money by charging for such uses during the copyright term. This in turn creates a financial incentive for authors to invest time and effort to produce new works for the benefit of everybody.

In the United States, the period of copyright control lasts for different periods of time, depending upon who the author may be. The copyright term for a work created by a natural person is the lifetime of the author plus seventy years. The copyright term for a work created by a corporation, through its employees, is 120 years from the date of creation or 95 years from the date of publication. After a copyright expires, the work falls into the public domain for anyone to use.

The proliferation of computer technology poses a problem for copyright owners. Computer technology typically functions by reproducing copies of something in memory devices: when a computer file, such as a digitized music file, is digitally transmitted or even loaded into memory to run, copies are being made. Computers therefore make reproduction and distribution of digitized works cheap and easy, and the technology to do so has become widely available at a low cost.

This is good news for information consumers, because the cost of access to creative works becomes minimal; nearly everyone can afford access. But this is bad news for information producers, because they make no money from virtually free, unauthorized digital copies, and so they have less incentive to produce the works in the first instance. Copyright law, which provides artists and authors the legal right to prohibit unauthorized digital reproduction, is more difficult to enforce when the technology to make such reproductions is widespread. Much of the public controversy over copyright and the Internet, such as the debate over the Napster peer-to-peer music trading service during 2000, revolves around this clash between the interests of information consumers and those of information producers.

Some digital copying has been justified on the basis of "fair use," which is a limited user right that allows unauthorized use of portions of a copyrighted work for certain select purposes. The fair use privilege is especially

Lars Ulrich (center), member of the heavy metal band Metallica, speaks to Napster CEO Hank Barry as the Byrds' Roger McGuinn listens. Ulrich spoke against the unauthorized distribution of Metallica's music through Napster at a Senate Judiciary Committee meeting convened in July 2000. Metallica sued Napster for allegedly encouraging music piracy earlier that year.

important in allowing study, scholarship, commentary, and criticism of copyrighted works. For example, quoting a few lines of a book in a book review would be a classic example of fair use. Without the fair use privilege, copying the lines out of the book would constitute infringement, and could not be done without the permission of the copyright owner.

In the United States, the standard for fair use is extremely flexible, depending upon the circumstances of the use: in some instances, using an entire work without permission might be a fair use, while in other instances, fair use might permit the use of only a small portion. However, the fair use privilege is not unlimited, and many instances of unauthorized digital copying exceed the privilege. Other countries recognize a much more narrow user right of "fair dealing," which allows a few specific unauthorized uses of a copyrighted work, such as for news reporting. Fair dealing would permit even less latitude for unauthorized digital copying.

Establishing Copyright

Such controversies are likely to be widespread because the majority of creative works, including those found in digital format on the Internet or elsewhere, are likely to be copyrighted. Unlike patents for inventions, which must be applied for and approved, copyrights arise spontaneously when the work is fixed. As soon as pen is set to paper, or brush to canvas, or fingers to keyboard, the resulting work is automatically copyrighted. No application or registration is necessary. The work may be registered with the Copyright Office if the author wishes, but this is optional.

There are benefits for choosing to register the work. In particular, the copyright cannot be enforced in a U.S. court unless it has been registered. There are also benefits to placing a copyright notice on the work, but an author need not do so. This presents a problem for consumers who wish to use a work, as it may be copyrighted even though there is no notice of copyright attached to the work. Because copyright arises automatically, it is likely that any given work is copyrighted unless the work is old enough for the copyright to have expired, or unless it falls into a category of uncopyrightable subject matter.

What Is Covered? What Is Not?

Copyright has traditionally covered literary works, such as books, plays, and poems; musical works; sound recordings; pictorial and graphic works, such as paintings, drawings, cartoons, and photographs; and audiovisual works, such as motion pictures and graphic animation. Court decisions and international treaties have recognized that these types of works are protected by copyright, whether they are in digital format or in hardcopy. Additionally, in the United States since 1978, copyright covers computer software, which is considered a kind of literary work. Most other countries around the world have also added software to the list of copyrightable works. Copyright also covers the original selection and arrangement of collections or compilations of information, including databases. Thus, a great deal of the content found in digitized formats falls within the subject matter of copyright.

Copyright does not cover facts, short phrases or words, ideas, processes, or "unfixed" works. For example, an improvisational theater performance or musical "jam session" will not be covered by copyright if it is not recorded because if it is unrecorded, the work is unfixed. Similarly, a measurement or a law of nature cannot be copyrighted because they are facts that did not originate from an author, but which simply exist as part of the world. Business names or book titles usually are not copyrightable because they are short phrases or words. Recipes and game rules usually are not copyrightable because they simply describe processes. Thus, the copyright on a work such as a computer program extends to the original expression of the program—the software code—but not to the underlying computer functions or processes.

The fundamental premise of copyright law is the distinction between a copy and the work. The work is the abstract, **intangible**, intellectual work that is embodied in a **tangible** copy. Works may be embodied in paper, canvas, stone, celluloid film, computer memory devices, or almost any other kind of material. Copyright grants authors the right to control the underlying work but does not necessarily grant the copyright holder rights in a particular copy. This contrast is perhaps best illustrated in copyright's "First Sale" doctrine. The purchaser of a particular copy does not by virtue of the purchase gain rights in the work. The copyright in the work still rests with the author or copyright owner, so the purchaser of the copy is still precluded from, for example, reproducing the work by creating additional copies embodying the work. But the purchaser does generally have the right to dispose of his copy as he wishes, by reselling it, giving it away, or even

HIGH-TECH FAILURE

The Semiconductor Chip Protection Act, or SCPA, is similar to copyright. The law applies only to the design of semiconductor chips, which include microprocessors, computer memory, and other electronic devices at the heart of computer hardware. Their circuits are designed into "masks" that are used in manufacturing. The SCPA prohibits unauthorized copying of the masks while allowing competitors to examine chips to learn how they work. SCPA is generally regarded as a failure. The technology of semiconductor chips has changed so fast that the statute is no longer relevant to the industry it was intended to protect. Many commentators see this as an example of the danger of enacting laws for a specific technology.

intangible a concept to which it is difficult to apply any form of analysis; something which is not perceived by the sense of touch

tangible of a nature that is real, as opposed to something that is imaginary or abstract

destroying it. The copyright owner may, of course, also sell the copyright to the work, but that is a different matter from selling copies of the work. And here again, digital technology has changed the interpretation and implementation of copyright protection. When the purchaser or owner of a traditional hardcopy embodiment of a copyrighted work, such as a sound recording, gave away or sold the copy, no new copies were created; the purchased unit itself passed from one person to another. In contrast, transfer of ownership of a digital work usually means no physical object is handed over; instead, a digital copy is rendered to the recipient.

International Copyright and Computer Technology

The international nature of the Internet poses certain challenges for copyright law. As in the case of patents, there is no international copyright or universally recognized copyright; copyright laws differ from nation to nation. When digitized works are transmitted from one country to another, it may be very difficult to determine which country's copyright law should apply. This situation is not as problematic as it could be because many nations have signed an international treaty, the Berne Convention, which sets minimum standards for copyright protection. It also requires nations to accord the citizens of other signatory nations the same rights that it gives to its own citizens. Additionally, the standards of the Berne Convention have been adopted as part of the series of **intellectual property** treaties accompanying membership in the World Trade Organization. Consequently, the basics of copyright are similar among most nations, although variations are possible.

Owners of copyrighted works may also use technological measures to prevent unauthorized uses of their works in digital form. These may include software or hardware devices that prevent reproduction or use of the protected content unless a password or other access code is obtained from the owner of the content. Many countries have adopted laws making it illegal to disable, tamper with, or "hack" around such content management devices. SEE ALSO INTERNET: APPLICATIONS; PATENTS; SECURITY; WORLD WIDE WEB.

Dan Burk

intellectual property the acknowledgement that an individual's creativity and innovation can be owned in the same way as physical property

Bibliography

Davis, Randall. "The Digital Dilemma." *Communications of the ACM*, 44, no. 2 (2001) 77–83.

Miller, Arthur R., and Michael H. Davis. *Intellectual Property in a Nutshell.* St. Paul, MN: West Publishing, 2000.

Credit Online

Credit online can have two meanings. It refers to services that provide online credit verification on companies that conduct business over the Internet. It can also refer to online credit card applications and obtaining credit reports for individuals.

With the enormous growth of the Internet and electronic commerce, online credit, or trust, has become an increasingly important issue. Although the Internet offers tremendous new opportunities in business and other areas, there are also great uncertainties and risks in the online world. Does an

Despite concerns about the safety of using credit cards for online purchases, e-commerce sales grew by 20 percent in 2001.

online store have a good credit history? Can you trust the store to send you the product you are ordering and paying for in advance? Those questions center on the notion of credit and what that means.

Credit can be defined as a belief and a confidence in the reliability of the other party. We can check the credit of an individual or a company by assessing the party's past behavior. We can also try to infer a party's credit by examining its ability to meet its obligations. For example, we can look at a company's financial information—such as assets, earnings, and stock price—to have a better understanding of the company's trustworthiness.

In the world of the Internet, consumers often deal with a distant party that can be identified only by an Internet address. An online business must have a good reputation in order for consumers to have confidence in doing business with the company. Credit between long-term business partners can develop through past business experiences. Among strangers, however, trust is much more difficult to build because strangers lack known past histories. Given these factors, the temptation for someone to cheat over the Internet could outweigh the incentive to cooperate. Two types of credit systems can help consumers overcome these concerns.

Building Online Trust

An Internet reputation system allows a customer to verify a company's credit even though the customer has never interacted with the firm before. At eBay, the largest person-to-person online auction site, although the company offers limited insurance and buyers and sellers have to accept significant risks, the overall rate of fraud remains astonishingly low. eBay attributes this to its reputation system. After a transaction is complete, buyers have the opportunity to rate the seller and leave comments. The reputation system at eBay serves as a credit system for its customers. Before purchasing an item,

ONLINE FRAUD

According to MSNBC, research companies that conduct studies about credit card fraud disagree regarding the extent of the problem. While some analysts cite the occurrence of online credit card theft as about 3.5 times higher than non-Internet credit card fraud, others claim the rate to be about 10 times greater.

Hypertext Markup Language (HTML) an encoding scheme for text data that uses special tags in the text to signify properties to the viewing program (browser) like links to other documents or document parts

a new buyer can check the seller's credit by examining its ratings from past customers. Such reputation systems are not limited to eBay and other auction sites, however. For example, Bizrate.com rates online retailers by asking consumers to complete a survey after each purchase.

Online credit can also be established through third-party endorsement and assurance. Usually, the third party has a good reputation and is highly trusted in society. For example, the Better Business Bureau (BBB) offers two programs to endorse companies that have met the BBB's standard. The reliability program confirms that a company is a member of a local Better Business Bureau, that it has been reviewed to meet truth-in-advertisement guidelines, and that it follows good customer service practices. The privacy program can confirm that a company stands behind its online privacy policy and has met the program requirements regarding the handling of personal information that is provided through its web site. The BBB gives qualifying companies a seal of endorsement. The seal can then be displayed on the qualifying company's web site, encouraging users to check BBB information on the company.

Companies such as eBay and the BBB that provide online credit services utilize the Internet and World Wide Web to collect information on online merchants and make the credit information available on the Internet. For example, customers at eBay can easily submit comments on a particular seller online. eBay then collects the comments electronically, saves them in a database, and makes the compiled information available to all potential buyers. In order to get a BBB seal of endorsement, companies can go to the BBB web site and apply electronically. Consumers can also use the Internet to file complaints with the BBB if they are unsatisfied with the service of a company.

For these online credit systems, the Internet is the interface through which consumers can access credit information and submit comments or complaints. The information is written in **Hypertext Markup Language (HTML)** so that web browsers can display the multimedia information consistently. Companies that provide credit information use web servers, database management systems, and web software programs written in Java, C++, VBScript, or other programming languages to build such applications.

Credit Cards and Credit Reports Online

Consumers can also apply for credit cards online and obtain their credit reports over the Internet. Banks and credit companies such as Citibank and American Express allow customers to apply for credit cards online and receive an instant response. This is made possible because individual credit information is stored electronically in large databases, and financial companies can access the information and make quick decisions. Companies such as QSpace.com provide credit reports to individuals over the Internet. In the United States, companies such as Equifax maintain consumer and commercial credit information on file. However, errors sometimes occur in these credit profiles, which may cause problems for the affected individuals. By checking their credit profiles, consumers can manage their own credit by correcting credit reporting errors and finding out how to improve their credit rating, if necessary.

Security is a major concern for both online credit card application and access to credit profiles because sensitive personal information is involved. The transmission of private information is protected using Secure Socket Layer (SSL), an encryption technology that allows the web browser to encrypt or scramble data automatically before they are sent through the Internet. SEE ALSO E-COMMERCE; PRIVACY; SECURITY.

Ming Fan

Bibliography

Fukuyama, Francis. *Trust: The Social Virtues and the Creation of Prosperity.* New York: Free Press, 1995.

Kalakota, Ravi, and Andrew B. Whinston. *Electronic Commerce: A Manager's Guide.* Reading, PA: Addison-Wesley Longman, 1997.

Seligman, Adam B. *The Problem of Trust.* Princeton, NJ: Princeton University Press, 1997.

Cryptography

Cryptography, the science of encoding communications so that only the intended recipient can understand them, is ancient. In almost every civilization, cryptography appeared almost as soon as there was writing. For example, in 1500 B.C.E. a Mesopotamian scribe, using **cuneiform** signs that had different syllabic interpretations (akin to spelling "sh" as "ti," as in nation), disguised a formula for pottery glazes. According to the Greek historian Herodotus, in the fifth century B.C.E. a Greek at the Persian court used steganography, or hiding one message within another, to send a letter urging revolt against the Persians. In the fourth century B.C.E. the Spartans developed a transposition **algorithm** that relied on wrapping a sheet of papyrus around a wooden staff; in the same period, the Indian political classic the *Arthasastra* urged **cryptanalysis** as a means of obtaining intelligence. In the fifteenth century C.E., the Arabic encyclopedia, the *Subh al-a 'sha*, included a sophisticated discussion of cryptanalysis using frequency distributions.

cuneiform in the shape of a wedge

algorithm a rule or procedure used to solve a mathematical problem—most often described as a sequence of steps

cryptanalysis the act of attempting to discover the algorithm used to encrypt a message

The increasing use of digitized information and the rise of the Internet has made cryptography a daily tool for millions of people today. People use cryptography when they purchase an item via the World Wide Web, when they call on a European (GSM) cell phone, or when they make a withdrawal from a bank machine. Cryptography provides confidentiality (assurance that an eavesdropper will not be able to understand the communication), authenticity (proof of the message's origin), and integrity (guarantee that the message has not been tampered with in transit). Modern communications—phone, fax, or e-mail—are frequently in digital form (0's and 1's), and the unencrypted string of bits, or plaintext, is transformed into ciphertext by an encryption algorithm.

There are two parts to any encryption system: the algorithm for doing the transformation and a secret piece of information that specifies the particular transformation (called the key). (In the Spartan system described earlier, the key is the width of the wooden staff. If someone were to intercept an encrypted message, unless the interceptor had a staff of the correct width, all the spy would see would be a confused jumble of letters.) Each user has a personal key. This private chunk of information enables many people to use the same cryptosystem, yet each individual's communications are con-

Cryptography plays an important role in government, business, and military communications. Here, a soldier uses a cryptograph machine in Afghanistan while checking a code book for further information.

cipher a code or encryption method

cryptanalyst a person or agent who attempts to discover the algorithm used to encrypt a message

fidential. In modern cryptography the encryption algorithm is public and all secrecy resides in the key. Researchers can study the cryptosystem, and if they are unable to break the system, this helps establish confidence in the algorithm's security.

In theory an eavesdropper should be unable to determine significant information from an intercepted ciphertext. The Caesar **cipher**, developed by the Roman general Julius Caesar (c. 100–44 B.C.E., shifts each letter three to the right ("a" is encrypted as "D," "b" becomes "E," "z" becomes "C," and so on), and fails this test. Indeed, systems which replace letters of the alphabet by others in a fixed way—called simple substitution ciphers—do not produce random-looking output. As any Scrabble player knows, letters do not appear equally often in English text. For example, "e" occurs 13 percent of the time, "t" 9 percent, and so on. If "W" crops up as 13 percent of the ciphertext, it is a likely bet that W is substituting for e. The complex patterns of a language provide grist for the **cryptanalyst**, who studies such characteristics as the frequency of each letter's appearance at the beginning and end of a word and the frequency of occurrence of pairs of letters, triples, etc. If a message is encrypted under a simple substitution cipher, a trained cryptanalyst can usually crack the message with only twenty-five letters of the ciphertext.

The development of polyalphabetic ciphers in fifteenth- and sixteenth-century Europe signified a major advancement in encryption. These ciphers employ several substitution alphabets and the key is a codeword that indicates which alphabet to use for each letter of the plaintext. Both polyalphabetic ciphers and transposition ciphers, in which the letters of the plaintext trade positions with one another, also fall prey to frequency analysis.

Despite its fame, for 4,000 years cryptography remained relatively unimportant in the context of wartime communications. The advent of radio changed that. Radio technology gave military commanders an unparalleled means to communicate with their troops, but this ability to command at a distance came at a cost: transmissions could be easily intercepted. Encrypted versions of a general's orders, troops' positions, and location and speed of ships at sea were available for friend and foe alike, and cryptanalysis became a critical wartime tool. However, errors made by cipher clerks were cryptography's greatest weakness. A single error, by substantially simplying the breaking of a cryptosystem, could endanger all communications encrypted under that system. This led to the development of automatic cryptography, a part of the mechanized warfare that characterized World War I.

American Gilbert Vernam developed encryption done directly on the telegraph wire, eliminating error-prone cipher clerks. This was done using "one-time" pads, a string of bits that is added, bit by bit, to the numeric version of the message, giving a completely secure cryptosystem. One-time pads can be used only once; if a key is ever reused, the system becomes highly vulnerable. The constant need for fresh keys, therefore, eliminates much of the advantage of one-time pads.

After the war inventors designed automated polyalphabetic substitution systems. Instead of looking up the substitutions in a paper table, they could be found by electric currents passing through wires. Rotor machines, in which the plaintext and ciphertext alphabets are on opposite sides of an insulated disk and wires connect each letter on one side to a letter on the other, were simultaneously developed in Europe and the United States. A single rotor is a simple substitution cipher. Automation can provide more. After encrypting a single letter, the rotor can shift, so that the letters of the plaintext alphabet are connected to new letters of the ciphertext alphabet. More rotors can be added and these can shift at different intervals. Such a system provides far more complex encryption than simple polyalphabetic substitution. These were also the principles behind the most famous rotor machine, the Enigma, used by the Germans during World War II. The Allies' ability to decode the Japanese cryptosystem Purple and the German Enigma dispatches during World War II played crucial roles in the battles of the Pacific and control of the Atlantic. The Colossus, a precursor of the first electronic, general-purpose computer, was built by the British during the war to decode German communications.

While substitution and transposition used by themselves result in weak cryptosystems, combining them properly with the key can result in a strong system. These were the operations used in the design of the U.S. Data Encryption Standard (DES), an algorithm with a 56-bit key that became a U.S. cryptography standard in 1977. With the exception of web-browser encryption and relatively insecure cable-TV signal encryption, DES was the most widely used cryptosystem in the world in the late 1990s. It was used for electronic funds transfer, for the protection of civilian satellite communications, and—with a small variation—for protecting passwords on computer systems.

FOOLING THE ENEMY

Unlike the Germans' infamous Engima code, one of the most successful codes used during World War II was not produced by a machine. Instead, it was developed and implemented by Navajo Indians serving in the U.S. Marines. Based on the ancient language of the Navajo, the code was unbreakable because so few people in the world then knew or understood the language. The contributions of the servicemen, now referred to as the "Navajo Code Talkers," were vital in keeping the enemy unaware of the activities and plans of American forces during the war.

For a cryptosystem to be secure, the difficulty of breaking it should be roughly the time it takes to do an exhaustive search of the keys. In the case of DES, this would be the time it takes to perform 2^{56} DES encryptions. By 1998, however, the speed of computing had caught up with DES, and a $250,000 computer built by the Electronic Frontier Foundation decrypted a DES-encoded message in 56 hours. In 2001 the National Institute of Standards and Technology, whose predecessor (the National Bureau of Standards) certified DES, chose a successor: the Advanced Encryption Standard algorithm Rijndael (pronounced "Rhine Dahl"). This algorithm, which works in three key lengths (128, 192, and 256 bits), was developed by two Belgian researchers. Used even at its shortest key length, a message encrypted by Rijndael is expected to remain secure for many billions of years.

DES and Rijndael are "symmetric," or "private-key," systems; the same key is used for encryption and decryption and is known to both sender and receiver. But electronic commerce requires a different solution. What happens when a shopper tries to buy an item from an Internet merchant? The parties may not share a private key. How can the customer securely transmit credit information? The answer is public-key cryptography.

Public-Key Cryptography

Public-key cryptography operates on the seemingly paradoxical idea that one can publish the encryption algorithm and the key, and yet decryption remains computationally unfeasible for anyone but the correct recipient of the message. The concept, invented by Whitfield Diffie and Martin Hellman in 1975, relies on the existence of mathematical functions that are fast to compute but which take an extremely long time to invert. Multiplication and factoring are one such pair. Using processors available in 2001, the product of two 200-digit primes can be determined in under a second. Even with the world's fastest computers in 2002, factoring a 400-digit integer is estimated to take trillions of years. The well-known public-key algorithm RSA, named after its inventors Ronald Rivest, Adi Shamir, and Leonard Adleman, relies on the difficulty of factoring for its security.

Public-key cryptography is sometimes called "two-key" cryptography, since the public encryption key is different from the decryption key. By enabling two parties communicating over an insecure network to establish a private piece of information, public-key cryptography simplifies the problem of key distribution. Public-key systems run much slower than private-key ones, and so they are primarily used to establish an encryption key. This key is then used by a private-key system to encode the communication. Public-key cryptography also enables **digital signatures**, which verify the identity of the sender of an electronic document.

digital signatures identifiers used to authenticate the senders of electronic messages or the signers of electronic documents

Although cryptography has been studied and used for thousands of years by mathematicians, politicians, linguists, and lovers, it became the province of national security in the half century following World War I. And while humans have always sought to keep information from prying eyes, the Information Age has intensified that need. Despite controversy, cryptography has returned from being a tool used solely by governments to one that is used by ordinary people, everyday. SEE ALSO Internet: Applications; Security; World Wide Web.

Susan Landau

Bibliography

Buchmann, Johannes. *Introduction to Cryptography.* New York: Springer Verlag, 2000.

Dam, Kenneth, and Herbert Lin. *Cryptography's Role in Securing the Information Society.* Washington, DC: National Academy Press, 1996.

Diffie, Whitfield, and Susan Landau. *Privacy on the Line: The Politics of Wiretapping and Encryption.* Cambridge, MA: MIT Press, 1998.

Kahn, David. *The Codebreakers: The Story of Secret Writing.* New York: Macmillan Company, 1967.

Schneier, Bruce. *Applied Cryptography.* New York: John Wiley and Sons, 1996.

Sinkov, Abraham. *Elementary Cryptanalysis: A Mathematical Approach.* Washington, DC: Mathematical Association of America, New Mathematical Library, 1966.

Cybercafe

Cybercafes, also called Internet cafes, are places where people can pay by the minute to access the Internet. By combining two modern essentials, coffee and the Internet, cybercafes have merged the need for public computer access with the age-old practice of meeting socially in cafes. At a cybercafe, people can meet to chat with friends in the room or sip beverages at a terminal while chatting with friends long-distance over the Internet.

Cyberia, one of the oldest Internet cafe's in existence, is located in London. It was one of the first to coin the term "cybercafe." In the early 1990s fewer than 100 cybercafes existed, but that number quickly grew to an estimated 1,500 worldwide by 1997. By 2001 there were an estimated 3,400 cybercafes in 160 countries. They have proved popular with a wide range of patrons, including vacationers accessing e-mail, travelers using online banking services, students creating class assignments, and researchers browsing international databases.

Types of cybercafes vary, but—according to the International Association for Cybercafes—the only requirement is that the establishment offers public access to computers. Some cybercafes provide a sparse selection of snacks and vending machine drinks, while others are renowned coffeehouses, bistros, or bars that offer a full menu as well as access to computers. Most cybercafes prefer a relaxed atmosphere to draw customers. Almost all cybercafes host a web page where anyone can learn more about the services provided by the cafe they are visiting.

Cybercafes collect payment in a variety of ways. At some, customers are timed by the minute and then asked to bring their tab to a cashier when they are done. At others, users pay in advance for a certain amount of time, using the computer until the screen goes blank. Popular in the United States are coin-operated terminals that add a certain number of minutes with each coin inserted. Many cybercafes are connected through a network to other cybercafes around the world and offer their customers e-mail addresses from their domain. Most also provide a selection of desktop computer brands with a choice of keyboard layouts to support a variety of popular international languages. Others feature telephone connections for laptop computers as well as printers, scanners, web cameras, microphones, and other peripheral devices.

Because cafes are popular in Europe, the largest number of cybercafes can be found throughout that continent. Cybercafes are extremely useful

CYBERIA

London's Cyberia Internet cafe opened its doors in 1994. It offers food, coffee, and tea along with access to the Internet and e-mail. Cyberia also provides photocopying, fax, scanning, and CD burning services. Other Cyberia locations include Bangkok, Thailand, and Dublin, Ireland.

Friends gather at a cybercafe to talk, eat, surf the Internet, check e-mail, and chat with others via cyberspace.

in countries where domestic Internet service is commonly slow and expensive. In many parts of the world, the average person goes to a cybercafe to use a computer instead of buying and installing one in the home, although the precise reason for frequenting the establishment varies from place to place.

- In the United Kingdom, cybercafes take the form of Internet-equipped pubs that allow patrons to enjoy a pint while using a computer.

- In Bosnia-Herzegovina, many customers are drawn to cybercafes for the arcade-like atmosphere provided through computer gaming.

- In France, many students go to cybercafes to type and print school papers. However, most French students do not to use cybercafe computers to explore the Internet, preferring instead to use their Minitel console at home for those tasks. Minitel is a countrywide network that preceded the Internet, electronically connecting most French homes, businesses, cultural organizations, and government offices.

- In Malaysia, one political party set up a cybercafe in each of its 100 territorial divisions to encourage party members to master the new technology. In the capital of Kuala Lumpur, a cybercafe was set up in a police training center to help officers and their families learn to use the Internet and multimedia applications.

- In Japan, where computers are widely available and inexpensive to own, cybercafes are frequented primarily by out-of-town tourists or visitors away from home.

- In Mexico, where international telephone calls can be very expensive, cybercafes offer Mexicans and visitors a cheap way to communicate long-distance.

- In Colorado, one cybercafe even promotes jazz concerts and gourmet dishes while offering Internet access as an added convenience.

Cybercafes also appeal to businesses marketing new products. They are especially valuable for software developers because customers can familiarize themselves with new software before choosing to buy it. Most cybercafes that are promoting a software program will also have a resident expert on hand for quick answers. For this reason, many companies offer promotional deals to cybercafes in the hope of attracting a wider consumer audience. Many cybercafe owners also take advantage of their computer expertise by offering classes or seminars in computer or software use.

The cybercafe is evolving from a meeting place to a learning center, where members of many communities can use new technologies as they expand their horizons. SEE ALSO EMBEDDED TECHNOLOGY (UBIQUITOUS COMPUTING); HOME ENTERTAINMENT; HOME SYSTEM SOFTWARE; INTEGRATED SOFTWARE; WORLD WIDE WEB.

Genevieve McHoes and Ann McIver McHoes

Bibliography

"Cybercafes Offer Both Types of Java." *Database* 20, no. 6 (1997): 38 (1).

Internet Resources

Cyber Cafe Guide version 13.0. <http://www.cyberiacafe.net/cyberia/guide/ccafe.htm>

The International Association of Cybercafes. <http://www.theiac.org/>

Cybernetics

The term *cybernetics* is much misused in the popular media. Often used to convey notions of high-technology, **robotics**, and even computer networks like the Internet, in reality, cybernetics refers to the study of communications and control in animal and machine.

Great mathematicians of the past such as Wilhelm Leibniz (1646–1716) and Blaise Pascal (1623–1662) had been interested in the nature of computing machinery long before these machines had ever been realized. They concerned themselves with philosophizing over what special peculiarities might be present in machines that had the ability to compute. In the mid-1930s Alan Turing (1912–1954) developed the idea of an abstract machine (later to become known as the **"Turing Machine"**). Turing machines introduced the possibility of solving problems by mechanical processes that involved a machine stepping through a sequence of states under the guidance of a controlling element of some sort. This laid the fundamental groundwork that was then developed by Norbert Wiener (1894–1964) into what has become cybernetics.

robotics the science and engineering of building electromechanical machines to replace human laborers

Turing machine a proposed type of computing machine that takes inputs off paper tape and then moves through a sequence of states under the control of an algorithm; identified by Alan Turing (1912-1954)

Norbert Wiener, pictured here, determined the need to define a new branch of science, cybernetics, that would consider what a machine *does* versus *how* a machine does it.

In 1948 Wiener concluded that a new branch of science needed to be developed. This field would draw from the realms of communication, automatic control, and statistical mechanics. He chose the word cybernetics, deriving it from the Greek word for "steersman" which underlines one of the essential ingredients of this field—that of governance or control. He defined cybernetics to be "control and communication in the animal and the machine." What really makes cybernetics stand apart from other fields in science and engineering is that it focuses on what machines do rather than the details of how they actually do it.

Classically, the study of a particular piece of conventional mechanical machinery—for example, a typewriter—would not be considered complete until all of the intricacies of the physics of movement of the constituent parts had been accounted for. This constitutes a **Newtonian view** of systems—one that commences with a perspective of Newtonian mechanics and builds from there. Cybernetics, on the other hand, accentuates the behav-

Newtonian view an approach to the study of mechanics that obeys the rules of Newtonian physics, as opposed to relativistic mechanics; named after Sir Isaac Newton (1642–1727)

ior and function of the machine as a whole. The result of this stance is that cybernetics is not restricted to dealing with mechanical or perhaps electrical machines only; instead it applies to anything that might possibly be viewed in some way as a machine—including organisms. That is, cybernetics looks at all the elements that are common denominators in that class of entities that might describe as machines. Wiener concluded that for a system to be classed as cybernetic, communication between parts of a system was a necessary characteristic, as was feedback from one part to another. The presence of feedback means that a cybernetic system is able to measure or perceive a quantity of some sort, then compare this to a required or desired value, and then instigate some strategy or behavior that affects change in that quantity. This is as much true of a heater and thermostat used to regulate temperature in a house, as it is of a bird that seeks refuge in a bird bath on a hot day.

Historically, the human body, in particular the human brain, has been viewed by many as a type of machine. This perception was generated by people who were hopeful of finding a way of modeling human behavior in the same way that they could model human-made machines—an approach with which they were comfortable. Much effort was directed toward understanding the operation of the human brain in this light.

Throughout the nineteenth and early twentieth centuries, significant advances were made in understanding the physiology of the human brain. Research into the structure of the cerebral cortex, the discovery of the brain as the center of perception, and the identification of neurones and synapses were all contributors to the conclusion that the brain is the regulator, controller, and seat of behavior of the human species. Because these ideas are fundamental to cybernetics, the human brain and the notion of intelligence are also considered as subjects that are within the realm of the cybernetic field. As a consequence, a great deal of research has been carried out in the areas of biological control theory, **neural modeling**, **artificial intelligence (AI)**, cognitive perception, and **chaos theory** from a perspective that resulted from the development of cybernetics.

With respect to computer systems, cybernetics has been prominent in two areas. The first is artificial intelligence, where computer **algorithms** have been developed that attempt to exhibit some traits of intelligent behavior—initially by playing games and later by processing speech and carrying out complex image and pattern manipulation operations. The second is in robotics, which frequently encompasses artificial intelligence and other cybernetic areas such as communication and automatic control using feedback. Early robotic systems were nothing more than complex servo-mechanisms that carried out manual tasks in place of a human laborer; however, the modern cybernetic approach is to attempt to construct robots that can communicate and be guided toward acting together as a team to achieve a collective goal. This has generated interest in a new type of adaptive machine that has the capacity to re-organize its strategies and behavior if its environment or mission changes.

Finally, beyond a computing context, cybernetics offers some advantages in our understanding of nature. First, it permits a unified approach to studying and understanding machine-like systems. This results from the distinct way in which the cybernetic viewpoint of systems is formulated; it is

HUMAN PLUS MACHINE

Researchers at British Telecommunications are embarking on a radical project called "Soul Catcher." The goal of this project, led by Peter Cochrane, is to develop a computer that can be implanted into the human brain in order to support memory and computational skills. The work is complex and introduces ethical as well as technological problems.

neural modeling the mathematical study and the construction of elements that mimic the behavior of the brain cell (neuron)

artificial intelligence (AI) a branch of computer science dealing with creating computer hardware and software to mimic the way people think and perform practical tasks

chaos theory a branch of mathematics dealing with differential equations having solutions which are very sensitive to initial conditions

algorithms rules or procedures used to solve mathematical problems—most often described as sequences of steps

not restricted to particular machine or system types. For example, we can draw a correspondence between an electro-mechanical system like a collection of servo-motors and linkages that give a robot locomotion, and a biological system like the nervous and musculo-skeletal systems of a caterpillar. One is not required to undertake greatly differing analyses to gain an appreciation of both. Secondly, it offers a manageable way of dealing with the most predominant type of system—one that is highly complex, non-linear, and changes over time. SEE ALSO ARTIFICIAL INTELLIGENCE; ROBOTICS; SPACE TRAVEL AND EXPLORATION.

Stephen Murray

Bibliography

Arbib, Michael A. *Brains, Machines, and Mathematics*, 2nd ed. New York: Springer-Verlag, 1987.

Ashby, W. Ross. *An Introduction to Cybernetics*. London: Chapman and Hall Ltd., 1971.

Caianiello, E. R., and G. Musso, eds. *Cybernetic Systems: Recognition, Learning, Self-Organisation*. Letchworth: Research Studies Press Ltd., 1984.

Glorioso, Robert M. *Engineering Cybernetics*. Englewood Cliffs: Prentice-Hall Inc., 1975.

Wiener, Norbert. *Cybernetics or Control and Communication in the Animal and the Machine*, 2nd ed. Cambridge: MIT Press, 1961.

Data Mining

Data mining is the process of discovering potentially useful, interesting, and previously unknown patterns from a large collection of data. The process is similar to discovering ores buried deep underground and mining them to extract the metal. The term "knowledge discovery" is sometimes used to describe this process of converting data to information and then to knowledge.

Data, Information, and Knowledge

Data are any facts, numbers, or text that can be processed by a computer. Many organizations accumulate vast and growing amounts of data in a variety of formats and databases. These data may be loosely grouped into three categories: operational or transactional data, such as company sales, costs, inventory, payroll, and accounting; non-operational data, such as industry sales, forecast data, and macro-economic data; and metadata, which is data about the data themselves, such as elements related to a database's design or query protocol.

The patterns, associations, and relationships among all these data can provide information. For example, analysis of retail point-of-sale transaction data can yield information on which products are selling and when. Information can then be converted into knowledge about historical patterns and future trends. For example, summary information on retail supermarket sales can be analyzed in light of promotional efforts to provide knowledge of consumer buying behavior. Thus, a manufacturer or retailer could determine which items to combine with promotional efforts for the best sales or profit results.

Applications of Data Mining

Data mining is used today by companies with a strong consumer focus, such as retail, financial, communication, and marketing organizations. Data mining enables these companies to identify relationships among "internal" factors such as price, product positioning, or staff skills, and "external" factors such as economic indicators, competition, and customer **demographics**. It enables them to determine what impact these relationships may have on sales, customer satisfaction, and corporate profits. Finally, it enables them to "drill down" into summary information to view detailed transactional data and to find ways to apply this knowledge to improving business.

With data mining, a retailer can use point-of-sale records of customer purchases to send targeted promotions based on an individual's purchase history. By mining demographic data from comment or warranty cards, retailers can develop products and promotions to appeal to specific customer segments. For example, Blockbuster Entertainment can mine its VHS/DVD rental history database to recommend rentals to individual customers, and American Express can suggest products to its cardholders based on an analysis of their monthly expenditures.

Many large, national stores track customer purchase preferences at checkout stations. They assemble the information into large databases to track purchase patterns and to make offers to customers in anticipation of future visits.

demographics the study of the statistical data pertaining to a population

terabytes one million million (one trillion, or 10^{12}) bytes

artificial intelligence (AI) a branch of computer science dealing with creating computer hardware and software to mimic the way people think and perform practical tasks

data reduction technique an approach to simplifying data, e.g. summarization

Data mining has many applications in science and medicine. Astronomers use data mining to identify quasars from **terabytes** of satellite data, as well as to identify stars in other galaxies. It can also be used to predict how a cancer patient will respond to radiation or other therapy. With more accurate predictions about the effectiveness of expensive medical treatment, the cost of health care can be reduced while the quality and effectiveness of treatment can be improved.

The data mining process is interactive and iterative, and many decisions are made by the user. Data mining is not an automatic process. It does not simply happen by pushing a button. Data mining requires an understanding of the decision-maker's intentions and objectives, the nature and scope of the application, as well as the limitations of data mining methods. Data mining is research. It is a process that requires one to develop knowledge about every task at hand, to research possibilities and options, to apply the best data mining methods, and to communicate the results in a comprehensible form. Armed with solid information, researchers can apply their creativity and judgment to make better decisions and get better results. A variety of software systems are available today that will handle the technical details so that people can focus on making the decisions. Most of these systems employ a variety of techniques that can be used in several combinations. Advanced techniques yield higher quality information than simpler ones. They automate the stages of information gathering to enhance the decision-making process through speed and easily understood results.

Techniques for Data Mining

Just as a carpenter uses many tools to build a sturdy house, a good analyst employs more than one technique to transform data into information. Most data miners go beyond the basics of reporting and OLAP (On-Line Analytical Processing, also known as multi-dimensional reporting) to take a multi-method approach that includes a variety of advanced techniques. Some of these are statistical techniques while others are based on **artificial intelligence (AI)**.

Cluster Analysis. Cluster analysis is a **data reduction technique** that groups together either variables or cases based on similar data characteristics. This technique is useful for finding customer segments based on characteristics such as demographic and financial information or purchase behavior. For example, suppose a bank wants to find segments of customers based on the types of accounts they open. A cluster analysis may result in several groups of customers. The bank might then look for differences in types of accounts opened and behavior, especially attrition, between the segments. They might then treat the segments differently based on these characteristics.

Linear Regression. Linear regression is a method that fits a straight line through data. If the line is upward sloping, it means that an independent variable such as the size of a sales force has a positive effect on a dependent variable such as revenue. If the line is downward sloping, there is a negative effect. The steeper the slope, the more effect the independent variable has on the dependent variable.

Correlation. Correlation is a measure of the relationship between two variables. For example, a high correlation between purchases of certain products such as cheese and crackers indicates that these products are likely to be purchased together. Correlations may be either positive or negative. A positive correlation indicates that a high level of one variable will be accompanied by a high value of the correlated variable. A negative correlation indicates that a high level of one variable will be accompanied by a low value of the correlated variable.

Positive correlations are useful for finding products that tend to be purchased together. Negative correlations can be useful for diversifying across markets in a company's strategic portfolio. For example, an energy company might have interest in both natural gas and fuel oil since price changes and the degree of substitutability might have an impact on demand for one resource over the other. Correlation analysis can help a company develop a portfolio of markets in order to absorb such environmental changes in individual markets.

Factor Analysis.   Factor analysis is a data reduction technique. This technique detects underlying factors, also called "latent variables," and provides models for these factors based on variables in the data. For example, suppose you have a market research survey that asks the importance of nine product attributes. Also suppose that you find three underlying factors. The variables that "load" highly on these factors can offer some insight about what these factors might be. For example, if three attributes such as technical support, customer service, and availability of training courses all load highly on one factor, we might call this factor "service." This technique can be very helpful in finding important underlying characteristics that might not be easily observed but which might be found as manifestations of variables that can be observed.

Another good application of factor analysis is to group together products based on similarity of buying patterns. Factor analysis can help a business locate opportunities for cross-selling and bundling. For example, factor analysis might indicate four distinct groups of products in a company. With these product groupings, a marketer can now design packages of products or attempt to cross-sell products to customers in each group who may not currently be purchasing other products in the product group.

Decision Trees.   Decision trees separate data into sets of rules that are likely to have different effects on a target variable. For example, we might want to find the characteristics of a person likely to respond to a direct mail piece. These characteristics can be translated into a set of rules. Imagine that you are responsible for a direct mail effort designed to sell a new investment service. To maximize your profits, you want to identify household segments that, based on previous promotions, are most likely to respond to a similar promotion. Typically, this is done by looking for combinations of demographic variables that best distinguish those households who responded to the previous promotion from those who did not.

This process gives important clues as to who will best respond to the new promotion and allows a company to maximize its direct marketing effectiveness by mailing only to those people who are most likely to respond, increasing overall response rates and increasing sales at the same time. Decision trees are also a good tool for analyzing attrition (churn), finding cross-selling opportunities, performing promotions analysis, analyzing credit risk or bankruptcy, and detecting fraud.

Neural Networks. **Neural networks** mimic the human brain and can "learn" from examples to find patterns in data or to classify data. The advantage is that it is not necessary to have any specific model in mind when running the analysis. Also, neural networks can find interaction effects (such as effects from the combination of age and gender) which must be explicitly specified in regression. The disadvantage is that it is harder to interpret the resultant model with its layers of weights and arcane transformations. Neural networks are therefore useful in predicting a target variable when the data are highly non-linear with interactions, but they are not very useful when these relationships in the data need to be explained. They are considered good tools for such applications as forecasting, credit scoring, response model scoring, and risk analysis.

Association Models. Association models examine the extent to which values of one field depend on, or are predicted by, values of another field. Association discovery finds rules about items that appear together in an event such as a purchase transaction. The rules have user-stipulated support, confidence, and length. The rules find things that "go together." These models are often referred to as Market Basket Analysis when they are applied to retail industries to study the buying patterns of their customers.

The Future of Data Mining

One of the key issues raised by data mining technology is not a business or technological one, but a social one. It is concern about individual privacy. Data mining makes it possible to analyze routine business transactions and glean a significant amount of information about individuals' buying habits and preferences.

Another issue is that of data integrity. Clearly, data analysis can only be as good as the data that is being analyzed. A key implementation challenge is integrating conflicting or redundant data from different sources. For example, a bank may maintain credit card accounts on several different databases. The address (or even the name) of a single cardholder may be different in each. Software must translate data from one system to another and select the address most recently entered.

Finally, there is the issue of cost. While system hardware costs have dropped dramatically within the past five years, data mining and data warehousing tend to be self-reinforcing. The more powerful the data mining queries, the greater the usefulness of the information being gleaned from the data, and the greater the pressure to increase the amount of data being collected and maintained. The result is increased pressure for faster, more powerful data mining queries. These more efficient data mining systems often cost more than their predecessors. SEE ALSO DATABASE MANAGEMENT SOFTWARE; DATA WAREHOUSING; E-COMMERCE; ELECTRONIC MARKETS; PRIVACY.

Sudha Ram

Bibliography

Berthold, Michael, and David J. Hand, eds. *Intelligent Data Analysis: An Introduction.* Germany: Springer-Verlag, 1999.

Fayyad, Usama, et al. *Advances in Knowledge Discovery and Data Mining.* Boston, MA: MIT Press, 1996.

Han, Jiawei, and Micheline Kamber. *Data Mining: Concepts and Techniques*. San Diego, CA: Academic Press, 2001.

Internet Resources

"DB2 Intelligent Miner for Data." *IBM's Intelligent Miner*. IBM web site. <http://www-4.ibm.com/software/data/iminer/fordata/about.html>

Hinke, Thomas H. "Knowledge Discovery and Data Mining Web References." *Computer Science Department Web Site*. University of Alabama Huntsville. <http://www.cs.uah.edu/~thinke/Mining/mineproj.html>

Data Warehousing

With the advent of the information age, the amount of digital information that is recorded and stored has been increasing at a tremendous rate. Common data formats for storage include commercial **relational database** engines, often interconnected via an **intranet**, and more recently World Wide Web sites connected via the Internet. The interconnectivity of these data sources offers the opportunity to access a vast amount of information spread over numerous data sources. Modern applications that could benefit from this wealth of digital information abound, and they range over diverse domains such as business intelligence (e.g., trade-market analysis or online web access monitoring), leisure (e.g., travel and weather), science (e.g., integration of diagnoses from nurses, doctors, and specialists about patients), libraries (e.g., multimedia online resources like museums and art collections), and education (e.g., lecture notes, syllabi, exams, and transparencies from different web sites). The one common element among all these applications is the fact that they must make use of data of multiple types and origins in order to function most effectively. This need emphasizes the demand for suitable integration tools that allow such applications to make effective use of diverse data sets by supporting the browsing and querying of tailored information subsets.

In contrast to the on-demand approach to information integration, where applications requests are processed on-the-fly, the approach of tailored information repository construction, commonly referred to as data warehousing, represents a viable solution alternative. In data warehousing, there is an initial setup phase during which relevant information is extracted from different networked data sources, transformed and cleansed as necessary, fused with information from other sources, and then loaded into a centralized data store, called the data warehouse. Thereafter, queries posed against the environment can be directly evaluated against the pre-computed data warehouse store without requiring any further interaction and resultant processing delay.

Data warehousing offers higher availability and better query performance than the on-demand approach because all data can be retrieved directly from one single dedicated site. Thus, it is a suitable choice when high-performance query processing and data analysis are critical. This approach is also desirable when the data sources are expensive to access or even sometimes become unavailable, when the network exhibits high delays or is unreliable, or when integration tasks such as query translation or information fusion are too complex and ineffective to be executed on-the-fly.

However, such a static snapshot of the data kept in a data warehouse is not sufficient for many real-time applications, such as investment

relational database a collection of records that permits logical and business relationships to be developed between themselves and their contents

intranet an interconnected network of computers that operates in the same way as the Internet, but which is restricted in size to a company or organization

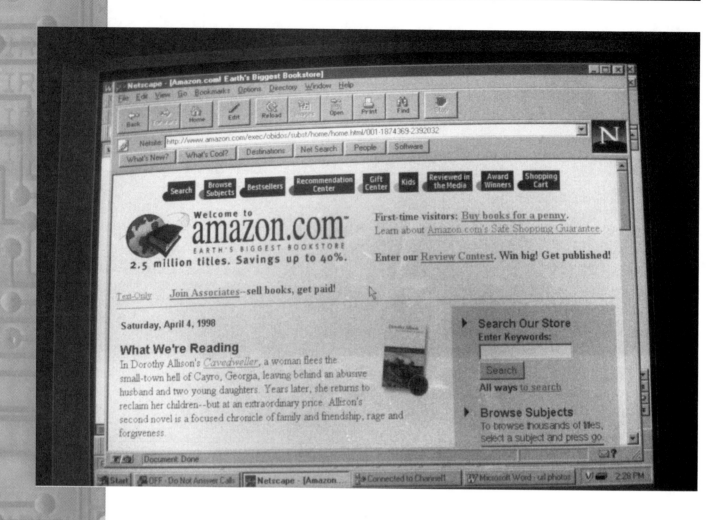

Amazon.com is a huge data warehouse, bringing together information on books, movies, music, and other products. Included in this warehouse are titles, authors/artists, release dates, reviews, buyer preferences, and the like, not to mention customer transactions.

paradigm an example, pattern, or way of thinking

advising. Hence updates made to the data in individual sources must be reflected in the data warehouse store. This can be accomplished by a complete reload of the data warehouse store on some periodic schedule, say once a day during the off-peak business time. Given the size of many modern data warehouses, such a reload is often too time consuming and hence not practically feasible. This has led to the development of strategies for incremental database maintenance, a process whereby a data warehouse is updated more efficiently with information that is fed into an existing database.

Many types of systems benefit from such a data warehousing **paradigm**. The first category includes monolithic systems, where one organization controls both the single data source providing the data feed as well as the back-end data warehouse store. An online purchasing store such as Amazon.com has, for example, the web-based front end that handles high-performance transactions by customers, whereas the underlying data warehouse serves as a container of all transactions logged over time for offline analysis. The second category includes distributed yet closed environments composed of a small number of independent data sources controlled by trusted owners with a joint cooperative goal. An example would be a hospital information system that attempts to integrate the data sources maintained by different units such as the personnel department, the pharmacy, and the registration system. Large-scale open environments such as the World Wide Web represent the third category where unrelated sources come and go at unpredictable times and the construction of temporary data warehouses for new purposes are common.

These data warehousing systems often feature a multi-tier architecture. The individual data sources in a networked environment are at the bottom tier. These sources often are heterogeneous, meaning that they are modeled by diverse data models and each support different query interfaces and search engines. This may include legacy systems, proprietary application programmer interfaces, traditional relational database servers, or even new technology such as web sites, **SGML** or **XML** web documents, news wires, and multimedia sites. Due to the heterogeneity of the data sources, there is typically some wrapper software associated with each data source that allows for smoother communication between the queries and processes associated with both the new data and the data warehousing system.

The software tools in the middle tier, collectively referred to as the data warehouse management system, are dedicated to diverse integration services. These software tools offer services beyond those common to a traditional database engine. For example, there may be tools for filtering and cleansing information extracted from individual data sources, for intelligently fusing information from multiple sources into one integrated chunk of knowledge, or for incrementally keeping the data warehouse up-to-date under source changes.

Finally, the actual data warehouse store is (at least logically) a centralized database repository that must support complex analysis queries at high levels of performance. In current systems, such a data warehouse store is built using standard relational database servers due to the maturity of this technology. Such complex decision and analysis query support on databases is commonly referred to as online analytic processing. Depending on the requirements of the application, additional data analysis services may be built on top of the integrated data warehouse store. This may include graphical display systems, statistics and modeling packages, and even sophisticated data mining tools that enable some form of discovery of interesting trends or patterns in the data. SEE ALSO DATA MINING; DATABASE MANAGEMENT SOFTWARE; E-COMMERCE.

Elke A. Rundensteiner

SGML the acronym for Standard Generalized Markup Language, an international standard for structuring electronic documents

XML the acronym for eXtensible Markup Language; a method of applying structure to data so that documents can be represented

Bibliography

Bulletin of the Technical Committee on Data Engineering, Special Issue: Materialized Views and Data Warehousing, 18, no. 2 (1995): 2.

Chaudhuri, Surajit, and Umeshwar Dayal. *An Overview of Data Warehousing and OLAP Technology*. (ACM Special Interest Group on Management of Data) ACM SIGMOD Record 26 (1997): 65-74.

Rundensteiner, Elke A., Andreas Koeller, and Xin Zhang. "Maintaining Data Warehouses over Changing Information Sources." *Communications of the ACM* 43, no. 6-(2000): 57-62.

Digital Images

A digital image is a representation of a real image as a set of numbers that can be stored and handled by a digital computer. In order to translate the

This digital camcorder, unveiled by Matsushita in 2001, features a 200,000-pixel color LCD screen. The camera can store up to 180 still images, which can be transferred to a PC.

pixels single picture elements on a video screen; the individual dots making up a picture on a video screen or digital image

image into numbers, it is divided into small areas called **pixels** (picture elements). For each pixel, the imaging device records a number, or a small set of numbers, that describe some property of this pixel, such as its brightness (the intensity of the light) or its color. The numbers are arranged in an array of rows and columns that correspond to the vertical and horizontal positions of the pixels in the image.

Digital images have several basic characteristics. One is the *type* of the image. For example, a black and white image records only the intensity of the light falling on the pixels. A color image can have three colors, normally RGB (Red, Green, Blue) or four colors, CMYK (Cyan, Magenta, Yellow, blacK). RGB images are usually used in computer monitors and scanners, while CMYK images are used in color printers. There are also non-optical images such as ultrasound or X-ray in which the intensity of sound or X-rays is recorded. In range images, the distance of the pixel from the observer is recorded. *Resolution* is expressed in the number of pixels per inch (ppi). A higher resolution gives a more detailed image. A computer monitor typically has a resolution of 100 ppi, while a printer has a resolution ranging from 300 ppi to more than 1440 ppi. This is why an image looks much better in print than on a monitor.

The *color depth* (of a color image) or "bits per pixel" is the number of **bits** in the numbers that describe the brightness or the color. More bits make it possible to record more shades of gray or more colors. For example, an RGB image with 8 bits per color has a total of 24 bits per pixel ("true color"). Each bit can represent two possible colors so we get a total of 16,777,216 possible colors. A typical **GIF image** on a web page has 8 bits for all colors combined for a total of 256 colors. However, it is a much smaller image than a 24 bit one so it downloads more quickly. A fax image has only one bit or two "colors," black and white. The *format* of the image gives more details about how the numbers are arranged in the image file, including what kind of compression is used, if any. Among the most popular of the dozens of formats available are TIFF, GIF, JPEG, PNG, and Post-Script.

Digital images tend to produce big files and are often compressed to make the files smaller. *Compression* takes advantage of the fact that many nearby pixels in the image have similar colors or brightness. Instead of recording each pixel separately, one can record that, for example, "the 100 pixels around a certain position are all white." Compression methods vary in their efficiency and speed. The GIF method has good compression for 8 bit pictures, while the **JPEG** is **lossy**, i.e. it causes some image degradation. JPEG's advantage is speed, so it is suitable for motion pictures.

One of the advantages of digital images over traditional ones is the ability to transfer them electronically almost instantaneously and convert them easily from one medium to another such as from a web page to a computer screen to a printer. A bigger advantage is the ability to change them according to one's needs. There are several programs available now which give a user the ability to do that, including Photoshop, Photopaint, and the Gimp. With such a program, a user can change the colors and brightness of an image, delete unwanted visible objects, move others, and merge objects from several images, among many other operations. In this way a user can retouch family photos or even create new images. Other software, such as word processors and desktop publishing programs, can easily combine digital images with text to produce books or magazines much more efficiently than with traditional methods.

A very promising use of digital images is automatic object recognition. In this application, a computer can automatically recognize an object shown in the image and identify it by name. One of the most important uses of this is in **robotics**. A robot can be equipped with digital cameras that can serve as its "eyes" and produce images. If the robot could recognize an object in these images, then it could make use of it. For instance, in a factory environment, the robot could use a screwdriver in the assembly of products. For this task, it has to recognize both the screwdriver and the various parts of the product. At home a robot could recognize objects to be cleaned. Other promising applications are in medicine, for example, in finding tumors in X-ray images. Security equipment could recognize the faces of people approaching a building. Automated drivers could drive a car without human intervention or drive a vehicle in inhospitable environments such as on the planet Mars or in a battlefield.

bits the plural of bit, which is a single binary digit, 1 or 0—a contraction of Binary digIT; the smallest unit for storing data in a computer

GIF image the acronym for Graphic Interchange Format where a static image is represented by binary bits in a data file

JPEG (Joint Photographic Experts Group) organization that developed a standard for encoding image data in a compressed format to save space

lossy a nonreversible way of compressing digital images; making images take up less space by permanently removing parts that cannot be easily seen anyway

robotics the science and engineering of building electromechanical machines to replace human laborers

To recognize an object, the computer has to compare the image to a database of objects in its memory. This is a simple task for humans but it has proven to be very difficult to do automatically. One reason is that an object rarely produces the same image of itself. An object can be seen from many different viewpoints and under different lighting conditions, and each such variation will produce an image that looks different to the computer. The object itself can also change; for instance, a smiling face looks different from a serious face of the same person. Because of these difficulties, research in this field has been rather slow, but there are already successes in limited areas such as inspection of products on assembly lines, fingerprint identification by the FBI, and optical character recognition (OCR). OCR is now used by the U.S. Postal Service to read printed addresses and automatically direct the letters to their destination, and by scanning software to convert printed text to computer readable text. SEE ALSO ART; DIGITAL LIBRARIES; FASHION DESIGN; OPTICAL TECHNOLOGY; PHOTOGRAPHY.

Isaac Weiss

Bibliography

Baxes, Gregory H. *Digital Image Processing: Principles and Applications.* New York: John Wiley and Sons, 1994.

Davies, Adrian. *The Digital Imaging A-Z.* Boston: Focal Press, 1998.

Kasai, Akira, and Russell Sparkman. *Essentials of Digital Photography.* Translated by Elisabeth Hurley. Indianapolis, IN: New Riders Publishing, 1997.

Price, Lisa, and Jonathan Price. *Fun with Imaging: The Official Hewlett-Packard Guide.* Foster City, CA: IDG Books Worldwide, 1999.

Digital Libraries

The term "digital library" was coined relatively recently and is used to describe distributed access to collections of digital information. The terms "electronic library" and "virtual library" are sometimes also used. However, there is still considerable debate about the definition of a digital library because the term may mean different things to different groups. For example, sometimes it is used to refer to the content or collection of materials ("a digital library of historic photographs"), whereas at other times it refers to the institution or service provided ("the digital library provided electronic reference").

A unique characteristic of a digital library is that it is a collection of material organized for access by the users of the electronic documents. The material is in digital form and may consist of or incorporate various media, such as photographs, video, sound recordings, as well as text and page images. Access is provided through search engines that search the actual text of the materials, or more formal cataloging such as **Library of Congress Classification** or Subject Headings. Bibliographic and descriptive information about the contents is usually referred to as **metadata**, making the information accessible for use. Once users locate information in the form of digital documents, they are able to view or download them.

The users for whom the digital library is intended are a defined community or group of communities. They may be scattered around the world, or may be in the same geographical location but wish to access the infor-

Library of Congress Classification the scheme by which the Library of Congress organizes classes of books and documents

metadata data about data, such as the date and time created

mation from off-site. Therefore, another key aspect of the digital library is that it can be accessed remotely, usually through a web browser. In general, the information contained in the World Wide Web is not considered to be a digital library (though it is sometimes referred to as such) because it lacks the characteristics of a collection organized for a specific purpose.

Because the development of digital libraries is a relatively new undertaking, research and development is being conducted even as new digital library projects are being launched. A number of organizations have taken a leadership role in integrating research and practice. For example, the National Science Foundation, along with other government bodies, funded a series of Digital Library Initiatives in order to help create a number of large- and medium-sized digital library projects with a research focus. The Association for Computing Machinery (ACM) and Institute of Electrical and Electronics Engineers (IEEE) sponsor the Joint Conference on Digital Libraries which brings together researchers and practitioners. The Institute of Museum and Library Services, a federal agency, provides funding for digital library projects at various levels. The Digital Library Federation is a consortium of libraries and organizations that attempt to identify standards and "best practices," coordinate research and development in the field, and initiate cooperative projects <http://www.diglib.org/dlfhomepage.htm>.

Advantages of the Digital Library

The digital library increases access to information in a number of ways. First, in many cases, the digital library allows documents to be searched based on content that is automatically indexed. This is true not only for text but also to some extent for images, video, and sound because content-based retrieval techniques have been developed to index digital characteristics such as image color and texture. Documents that have not received formal cataloging may still be located in a digital library, and even if cataloging information is available, the content-based information provides extra ways to search it. Once the relevant material has been found, access is again improved because the material can be viewed online, or even downloaded and viewed or printed at the user's location. This means that scholars need not travel to a distant library, or request an interlibrary loan. Instead, they have instantaneous access to the information at their desktop. Access is also improved because in many cases, through the medium of the World Wide Web, the information in the digital library is available not just to the local population, but to anyone who wishes to use it.

An additional advantage of the digital library is that because the digital information can be viewed and copied without access to the original document, it prevents wear and tear on library materials. This is particularly important when the original is valuable or fragile. The digital library, however, is not primarily concerned with preserving the original document because digitization changes the format of the document and the digital form itself may be difficult to preserve.

Types of Digital Libraries

There are many different types of digital libraries, ranging from simple collections to large-scale projects. The national libraries in many countries have been leaders in developing digital libraries of historical materials. In the

IMPACT OF DIGITAL LIBRARIES

Digital libraries, which provide widespread access to collections of electronic materials, are changing popular and scholarly use of textual and multimedia information. Their continued growth depends on the solution of technological problems, particularly the development of standards, as well as underlying legal, social, and economic questions.

King Juan Carlos of Spain and the U.S. Librarian of Congress James Billington jointly click a mouse to launch a collaborative digital project between the National Library of Spain and the Library of Congress on February 24, 2000. Early travel maps and logs of Spanish explorers are among the items to be digitized and made available via the Internet.

United States, for example, the Library of Congress has an ongoing digital library project called "American Memory," which includes many historically important and interesting collections of photographs, sound recordings, and video. The materials are cataloged in ways similar to the library's physical collections in Washington, D.C., but, unlike those collections, they are available for viewing and downloading by anyone with a web browser and an Internet connection. The digital collection includes everything from baseball cards to Civil War photographs to video clips of Coca-Cola advertisements.

University and college libraries and many public libraries around the world are also undertaking digital library projects to make their materials more readily and widely available. The libraries of ten University of California campuses have initiated a "co-library," the California Digital Library, which provides access to faculty and students around the state. Materials include reference material such as encyclopedias and dictionaries, electronic journals, databases, and a "digital archive" of important manuscripts, photographs, and works of art held in libraries, museums, archives, and other institutions across California.

Technological Issues

The enabling technologies for digital libraries are economical storage of large quantities of data, high-speed connectivity and networking, and technologies related to digitizing, indexing, retrieving, and using multimedia. As digital libraries evolve, many technological issues remain to be solved. Desirable characteristics of digital libraries are scalability, interoperability, and sustainability—they need to be able to grow, to interact with other digital libraries, and to continue to function as organizations and technologies change.

Builders of digital libraries consider the identification of standards important to ensure the smooth development and growth of their products. For example, standard formats are needed for digitization so digital products can be universally distributed and read. For content, metadata standards are needed for cataloging, and encoding standards for indicating. Because digital libraries are often federations of individual sites, standards for digital library architecture are also important. Often, an open architecture is specified, in which the digital library is considered to be a set of services and functions, with a specific **protocol** specifying what the **interface** to that function will be.

Social, Legal, and Economic Issues

In this new field, many questions related to social, legal, and economic issues need to be addressed. For instance, should digital materials be free? If not, what is an appropriate pricing model? Who owns digital materials? How does the copyright law in place for non-digital materials apply to digital images, sound, and text? How can **intellectual property** rights be protected, for example, through **digital watermarks**? Is there a digital divide—do some people have the means and skills to access the digital library while others do not? How can privacy and security be ensured? These questions, like those of developing standards, are still open to research and debate. SEE ALSO DATA MINING; DATABASE MANAGEMENT SOFTWARE; INFORMATION TECHNOLOGY STANDARDS; LIBRARY APPLICATIONS.

Edie Rasmussen

protocol an agreed understanding for the sub-operations that make up a transaction, usually found in the specification of inter-computer communications

interface a boundary or border between two or more objects or systems; also a point of access

intellectual property the acknowledgement that an individual's creativity and innovation can be owned in the same way as physical property

digital watermarks special data structures permanently embedded into a program or other file type, which contain information about the author and the program

Bibliography

Arms, W. Y. *Digital Libraries.* Cambridge, MA: MIT Press, 2000.

Borgman, C. L. *From Gutenberg to the Global Information Infrastructure: Access to Information in the Networked World.* Cambridge, MA: MIT Press, 2000.

Lesk, M. *Practical Digital Libraries.* San Francisco, CA: Morgan-Kaufman, 1997.

Digital Signatures

A digital signature is an identifier that can be used to authenticate the sender of an electronic message (e-mail) or the signer of an electronic document. This technology can also be used to ensure the integrity of the message or document (that no alterations have been made since it was signed) as well as to date/time-stamp the document at signing. Finally, the signatory cannot easily repudiate or refuse to acknowledge his digital signature, nor can the document be easily forged.

Due to these criteria, a digital signature can be trusted and used like a written signature. On October 1, 2000, the Electronic Signatures in Global and National Commerce Act (known as the E-Signature Act) became effective in the United States. This act basically states that a signature cannot

WHAT IS A DIGITAL SIGNATURE?

A digital signature can be trusted and used like a written signature. Not all electronic signatures, however, are digital signatures.

be denied simply because it is electronic, and an electronic signature must be considered as legally valid as a written signature. Not all electronic signatures, however, are digital signatures, so it is worth noting the following electronic signature examples that are *not* digital signatures:

- a biometric identifier;

- a written signature on a document that has been scanned into an electronic file; or

- a signature on a document that has been faxed (transmitted by facsimile).

cryptographic pertaining to the science of understanding the application of codes and cyphers

encrypted coded, usually for purposes of security or privacy

So what *is* a digital signature? A digital signature uses **cryptographic** technology to create an electronic identifier, but it can be used with any message, whether the message is **encrypted** or not. Thus, digital signatures can accompany an unencrypted or an encrypted message. For example, the Computer Emergency Response Team (CERT) broadcasts messages of computer vulnerabilities in clear text (unencrypted) to everyone on its mailing list. To allow its recipients to verify that these messages come from the CERT and are not spoofed (counterfeited into looking like messages from CERT) or modified in transit, the CERT signs all of its messages with its digital signature. Yet a government employee protecting classified information or a company employee protecting trade secrets would not only digitally sign his document but would encrypt the base message as well.

public key infrastructures (PKIs) the supporting programs and protocols that act together to enable public key encryption/decryption

Many different software packages can be used to create a digital signature, from freeware to PC-based, shrink-wrapped software to large server-based systems, also known as **public key infrastructures (PKIs)**. The process for sending a digitally signed unencrypted message is the same regardless of the package used as follows. A user creates a digital signature with a private key that he keeps to himself. He then attaches this signature to a document and sends it to others. His private key is mathematically linked to a public key that he posts on a public key server. He then tells the recipient(s) where his public key is stored. The recipient can then retrieve the sender's public key and reverse the process to determine the authenticity of the document.

The process for sending a digitally signed encrypted message is similar. In this case, the sender must retrieve the recipient's public key from a public key server. She then uses it to encrypt the message and send it to the recipient. The recipient then uses her own private key to decrypt the document, and the sender can be sure that only the recipient can read it.

Although there are many advantages to using digital signatures, several problems also exist:

- Anyone can create a public/private key pair and contact the recipient, claiming to be the sender. Without knowing the sender by voice or another method, there is no way to guarantee that the owner of the key is indeed the person sending the document.

malicious code program instructions that are intended to carry out malicious or hostile actions, for example, deleting a user's files

- If someone other than the owner of the computer has had physical or logical access to the computer that houses the encryption software, **malicious code** could be inserted into this software to enable other actions, such as collecting the owner's private key and mailing it to the author of the code.

- A computer may legitimately have a person's digital signature resident on it, but if that computer is stolen or used by another and the private key guessed, then a document created on that computer may not have been "signed" by the digital signature's owner.

In other words, the integrity of a digital signature can be compromised if someone gains improper access to the computer that runs the encryption software.

Regardless of the problems, digital signatures have great potential. However, for electronic business to reach its full potential, the end user must feel secure in either signing or receiving a document electronically. Digital signature technology has the potential to create that level of trust. SEE ALSO AUTHENTICATION; COOKIES; SECURITY.

Cindy Smith

Internet Resources

American Bar Association's Digital Signature Guidelines. <http://www.abanet.org/scitech/ec/isc/dsgfree.html>

Computer Emergency Response Team (CERT). <http://www.cert.org>

Electronic Signatures in Global and National Commerce Act. <http://www.ecommerce.gov/ecomnews/ElectronicSignatures_s761.pdf>

"Digital Signatures." *Software Industry Issues.* <http://www.softwareindustry.org/issues/1digsig.html>

E-banking

Traditional banks offer many services to their customers, including accepting customer money deposits, providing various banking services to customers, and making loans to individuals and companies. Compared with traditional channels of offering banking services through physical branches, e-banking uses the Internet to deliver traditional banking services to their customers, such as opening accounts, transferring funds, and electronic bill payment.

E-banking can be offered in two main ways. First, an existing bank with physical offices can also establish an online site and offer e-banking services to its customers in addition to the regular channel. For example, Citibank is a leader in e-banking, offering walk-in, face-to-face banking at its branches throughout many parts of the world as well as e-banking services through the World Wide Web. Citibank customers can access their bank accounts through the Internet, and in addition to the core e-banking services such as account balance inquiry, funds transfer, and electronic bill payment, Citibank also provides premium services including financial calculators, on-line stock quotes, brokerage services, and insurance.

E-banking from banks like Citibank complements those banks' physical presence. Generally, e-banking is provided without extra cost to customers. Customers are attracted by the convenience of e-banking through the Internet, and in turn, banks can operate more efficiently when customers perform transactions by themselves rather than going to a branch and dealing with a branch representative.

In addition to traditional banks that have both a physical and online presence, there are several e-banks that exist only on the Internet, allowing users to work with a "virtual" bank. NetBank is such an Internet-only bank. Without physical branches, NetBank can cut operating costs and can potentially offer higher deposit rates to its customers and waive many fees normally charged by a bank with a large network of physical branches. The challenge for Internet-only banks is to provide quality customer services without physical offices. One way in which NetBank is dealing with this issue is via an agreement with the MAC ATM Network (automated teller machine network), thus providing its customers access to nearly 18,000 ATMs across the United States. NetBank customers can deposit and withdraw funds from their NetBank accounts through these ATMs, and in addition, customers can also deposit and receive funds through wire transfer.

E-banking services are delivered to customers through the Internet and the web using **Hypertext Markup Language (HTML)**. In order to use e-banking services, customers need Internet access and web browser software. Multimedia information in HTML format from online banks can be displayed in web browsers. The heart of the e-banking application is the computer system, which includes web servers, database management systems, and web application programs that can generate dynamic HTML pages.

Bank customers' account and transaction information is stored in a database, a specialized software that can store and process large amounts of data in high speed. The function of the web server is to interact with online customers and deliver information to users through the Internet. When the web server receives a request such as an account inquiry from an online customer, it requires an external web application program to process the request. C++, Visual Basic, VBScript, and Java are some of the languages that can be used to develop web application programs to process customer requests, interact with the database, and generate dynamic responses. Then, the web server will forward the response HTML files to e-banking customers. Several banks, such as NationsBank, also use state-of-the-art imaging systems, allowing customers to view images of checks and invoices over the Internet.

One of the main concerns of e-banking is security. Without great confidence in security, customers are unwilling to use a public network, such as the Internet, to view their financial information online and conduct financial transactions. Some of the security threats include invasion of individuals' privacy and theft of confidential information. Banks with e-banking service offer several methods to ensure a high level of security: (1) identification and authentication, (2) encryption, and (3) **firewalls**. First, the identification of an online bank takes the form of a known Uniform Resource Locator (URL) or Internet address, while a customer is generally identified by his or her login ID and password to ensure only **authenticated** customers can access their accounts. Second, messages between customers and online banks are all **encrypted** so that a hacker cannot view the message even if the message is intercepted over the Internet. The particular encryption standard adopted by most browsers is called Secure Socket Layer (SSL). It is built in the web browser program and users do not have to take any extra steps to set up the program. Third, banks have built firewalls, which are software or hardware barriers between the corporate network and the external Internet,

Hypertext Markup Language (HTML) an encoding scheme for text data that uses special tags in the text to signify properties to the viewing program (browser) like links to other documents or document parts

firewalls special purpose network computers or software that are used to ensure that no access is permitted to a sub-network unless authenticated and authorized

authenticated verifying that users are who they say they are and that they are allowed access to certain systems

encrypted coded, usually for purposes of security or privacy

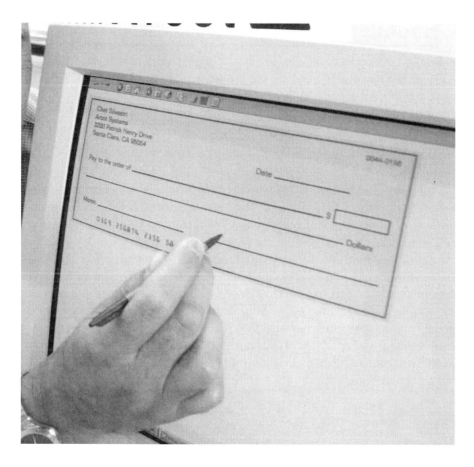

On October 1, 2000, the electronic signatures bill took effect, recognizing documents signed online as legal. Some banks plan to begin using electronic checks as soon as they can work out various security measures.

to protect the servers and bank databases from outside intruders. For example, Wells Fargo Bank connected to the Internet only after it had installed a firewall and made sure the firewall was sufficiently impenetrable.

The range of e-banking services is likely to increase in the future. Some banks plan to introduce electronic money and electronic checks. Electronic money can be stored in computers or **smart cards** and consumers can use the electronic money to purchase small value items over the Internet. Electronic checks will look similar to paper checks, but they can be sent from buyers to sellers over the Internet, electronically endorsed by the seller, and forwarded to the seller's bank for electronic collection from the buyer's bank. Further, banks seek to offer their customers more products and services such as insurance, mortgage, financial planning, and brokerage. This will not only deliver more value to the customers but also help banks to grow business and revenues. SEE ALSO E-COMMERCE; PRIVACY; SECURITY; WORLD WIDE WEB.

Ming Fan

smart cards credit-card style cards that have a microcomputer embedded within them; they carry more information to assist the owner or user

Bibliography

Furst, Karen, William W. Lang, and Daniel E. Nolle. "Special Studies on Technology and Banking." *Office of the Comptroller of the Currency Quarterly Journal* 19, no. 2 (2000): 29–48.

Kalakota, Ravi, and Andrew B. Whinston. *Electronic Commerce: A Manager's Guide.* Reading, MA: Addison-Wesley Longman, 1997.

Wenninger, John. "The Emerging Role of Banks in E-Commerce." *Federal Reserve Bank of New York Current Issues* 6, no. 3 (2000): 1–6.

E-books

E-books, or electronic books, are books stored in digital format that are created, delivered, and read by electronic methods. This means that the book's text may be available on CD-ROM through a computer or **encrypted** and delivered through a handheld device. The term "e-book" is also used to refer to a dedicated handheld device used to read electronically based text, although these devices should more properly be referred to as e-book readers.

The availability and delivery of the text of books in electronic format is not new. Project Gutenberg (www.gutenberg.net/) has been providing the text of public domain books free over the Internet since 1971. Computerized texts have several advantages. Compared to a print volume, a computer can store much more text. Computerized text is also much easier to search, and **hyperlinks** can move the reader easily throughout the text, or from one text to another. Most people, however, continue to prefer reading from a printed page. They dislike scrolling down a screen rather than flipping pages, and they also find reading text on a conventional computer monitor tiring. These preferences have resulted in numerous attempts to try to create an electronic reading experience that mimics that of reading a printed book.

The technology to accomplish this is still in a state of flux. Although everyone involved with e-books agrees that there should be unified stan-

encrypted coded, usually for purposes of security or privacy

hyperlinks connections between electronic documents that permit automatic browsing transfer at the point of the link

E-book readers, designed to mimic the format of a printed and bound text, have the capacity to bring works—both popular and obscure—to readers.

dards, these had yet to be developed as of fall 2001. There are two major software developments that hope to become the standard for e-text, one **ASCII** based and the other **PDF** (portable document format—Adobe) based.

A recent development is the handheld e-book reader. This is a device created specifically for reading electronic text. Several different versions of these readers have been created, each one about the size of a large paperback book, weighing about the same as a hardcover book. Because they store text digitally, these readers can hold numerous books worth of text. They use touch-screen technology, provide built-in dictionaries, have the capability to highlight text and store notes made by the reader, and also offer keyword searching. Pages can be bookmarked for easy reference, and battery life is more than sufficient for the reading of a complete book. Other options include varying font sizes and adjustable screen backlighting to meet users' needs. Two differing models of these readers were sold—one by Rocket eBooks and another by SoftBooks. Both companies have now merged, and the new company, Gemstar, has licensed RCA to sell two different and upgraded readers. This merger highlighted one of the new technology's drawbacks: until a standard is derived, earlier technologies face becoming obsolete quickly. Another drawback is cost. At this point, readers are seen as expensive toys rather than as an essential part of everyday living. Present readers also need to develop an improved capability for dealing with color, graphics, and multimedia.

Improved dedicated readers are undoubtedly coming in the future. Another possibility being developed rapidly is special reading software for smaller (handheld) computers. Despite the evolving state of the technology, it is clear that e-books are here to stay. The advantages of being able to access books in digital format are too great to ignore. Students will be able to access all their textbooks on one small device. Users of reference books will want the advantages of having a text that never goes out of date. Travelers will enjoy having only one small device to carry, rather than multiple books.

Although e-books are mainly copies of print-based texts as of this writing, they are likely to become more interactive in the future. Hyperlinks for scholars and researchers may be added or multimedia effects may enhance the experience of recreational reading. Multimedia CD-ROMs to help teach children to read already incorporate both text and interactive elements.

E-books are now being offered for sale commercially. The cost of digitally producing a book should be cheaper, as there is less physical **overhead**. Publishers appear to see the field of digital publishing as one more way they can reach readers. Both publishers and authors have started to experiment with different ways of selling books online. The most well known example of this is Stephen King's novella *Riding the Bullet*, which was only published electronically. This can be considered the first e-book bestseller as more than 50,000 copies were downloaded. The announcement of several prestigious awards for e-books in 2000 also signals that they have become part of our culture. SEE ALSO ASSISTIVE COMPUTER TECHNOLOGY FOR PERSONS WITH DISABILITIES; DIGITAL LIBRARIES; WORLD WIDE WEB.

Barbara Britton

ASCII an acronym that stands for American Standard Code for Information Interchange; assigns a unique 8-bit binary number to every letter of the alphabet, the digits (0 to 9), and most keyboard symbols

PDF the acronym for Portable Document Format, developed by Adobe Corporation to facilitate the storage and transfer of electronic documents

overhead the expense or cost involved in carrying out a particular operation

WAITING FOR THE E-BOOK REVOLUTION

E-book sales are off to a slow start, even though such books save paper, not to mention book shelf space, and could bring many more titles in reach of consumers than traditional booksellers can. So why the slow start? Because many people have yet to acquire an e-book player. However, some industry experts project that sales will dramatically increase as e-book player technology improves and costs decrease.

Bibliography

Day, Rebecca. "Reading the Future." *Popular Mechanics* 178, no. 4 (2001): 82–86.

Hawkins, Donald T. "Electronic Books: A Major Publishing Revolution, Part 1." *Online* 24, no. 4 (2000): 14–26.

———. "Electronic Books: A Major Publishing Revolution, Part 2." *Online* 24, no. 5 (2000): 18–30.

Internet Resources

Ormes, Sarah. "It's the End of the World as We Know It (and I Feel Fine) or How I Learned to Stop Worrying and Love the E-Book." *Ariadne* 26 (2001). <http://www.ariadne.ac.uk/issue26/e-book/>

E-commerce: Economic and Social Aspects

E-commerce is technology-enabled buying and selling that occurs over telecommunications networks such as the Internet. As in physical marketplaces, these exchanges can occur between businesses, between a business and a consumer, or even between consumers. E-commerce has grown dramatically since the late 1990s. This transition from traditional physical marketplaces to technology-enabled ones has important economic and social implications.

One significant economic effect is the reduction of transaction costs compared to traditional commerce. In the 1930s economist Ronald Coase defined transaction costs as the costs associated with organizing

James Walker (left) and Elena Kholodenko were among three dozen students who developed a web site as part of their master of science degrees in electronic commerce from Carnegie Mellon University in 2000. They were in the first class to be awarded this degree.

a transaction, starting with searching for a product, then negotiating for a price, and finally making the exchange. E-commerce reduces transaction costs by removing many of the geographic and time barriers that buyers and sellers previously faced. Customers who had to drive to a physical store location during business hours, park, and manually do comparison shopping before buying, can now do this for many products online, anytime, with the help of comparison shopping sites such as MySimon. For information products, such as digital music, which can be both bought and delivered online, e-commerce also reduces the product delivery cost.

For businesses, the potential cost savings are even greater. Most industries are organized into supply chains that integrate supply and demand requirements across manufacturers, suppliers, warehouses, and stores so that merchandise shows up on time and at the right location. Business rules provide the glue that binds the various producers together by specifying company policies on pricing, payment, returns, and other contractual information. By automating business rules using technologies such as **XML**, e-commerce platforms provide fast, synchronized exchange of supply and demand information between supply chain members thereby reducing both labor and inventory costs, as well as increasing customer satisfaction. Joint work between and within companies is also fostered by Internet-based technologies that allow easy communication across different time zones and collaboration using communal web sites.

XML the acronym for eXtensible Markup Language; a method of applying structure to data so that documents can be represented

Privacy

Internet technologies also have an effect on social issues, such as privacy. Physical and technological barriers to gathering personal information about consumers are rapidly disappearing. While companies have always gathered and resold information about their customers' purchasing habits, the Internet simplifies this process and allows new types of information to be collected. DoubleClick, a market research firm, compiles information not only about customer purchasing habits but also about their web browsing behavior across multiple stores and information sites.

Privacy issues exist concerning who owns and controls the use of this information and how it may be gathered. During 2001, the U.S. Congress reviewed at least fifty privacy-related bills, many of which had to do with whether consumers must opt in or opt out of such information gathering. In the private sector, major companies such as the IBM Corporation endorse using clearly posted privacy policies on web sites that detail where and how personal information can be used.

On the positive side, companies generally collect customer information to provide more personalized service and to speed up online transactions. Amazon.com's recommendation services combine information about a customer's past purchases with those of other customers with similar interests. Companies such as Soundscan and Bookscan gather previously unavailable music and book sales transaction data. Since these data detail not only how much merchandise was sold, but also where and to which demographic groups, marketing campaigns can use these data to target their focus and promote products to niche markets.

digital certificates certificates used in authentication that contain encrypted digital identification information

authenticate to ensure that an object or entity is in fact what it purports to be; verification of identity

firewalls special purpose network computers or software that are used to ensure that no access is permitted to a sub-network unless authenticated and authorized

dot.com a common term used to describe an Internet-based commercial company or organization

infrastructure the foundation or permanent installation necessary for a structure or system to operate

TRAVELOCITY.COM

Many travelers are turning to online vendors in the hope of getting discounted or bargain rates. One of the e-businesses specializing in travel is Travelocity.com. As of early 2002, the company had sold more that 19 million airline tickets to online buyers since its founding in 1996. Headquartered in Fort Worth, Texas, Travelocity.com provides reservation services for 700 airlines, 50 car rental companies, and 50,000 hotels. This e-commerce company also offers tour packages and travel magazines, as well as luggage and other sundries—articles that a traveler might need while on vacation or a business trip.

Security

While privacy addresses the customers' control over the confidentiality of their transaction information, security considers how such transactions can be protected from assault or corruption. Customers must be confident that credit card numbers will remain secure before providing them on the Internet. While credit card theft and other types of financial fraud have always been possible, the potential for thieves to use the Internet to steal credit card numbers on a wholesale basis has been a big concern. To reduce this possibility, companies use **digital certificates** to **authenticate** that they are who they claim to be, and not some fraudulent site stealing customer credit card numbers. Certificate authorities, such as VeriSign, act as trusted third parties to issue digital certificates to companies. Using industry-standard Secure Sockets Layer (SSL) technology, digital certificates employ encryption-based protocols to protect the integrity of customer data exchanged online. Once the transaction data resides on the merchant site, **firewalls** can be used to restrict Internet access.

Finding the Niche

E-commerce businesses may be completely online enterprises, such as Travelocity which sells airline tickets and other travel services, or they may comprise a mixture of online and traditional business, wherein the Internet adds another channel for reaching the consumer. In the early days of the Internet economy, many so-called **"dot.com"** startups commanded astronomical stock prices without posting real profits. For a brief period, investors were willing to support e-commerce ventures without the usual need to be convinced of the soundness of a particular business plan. Vast amounts of money were poured into the rapid creation of web-based businesses and services.

One of the more spectacular dot.com failures was WebVan, the biggest online grocer, which went through $1.2 billion of funding during 18 months of business before closing in July 2001. Much of WebVan's money went into building a new distribution **infrastructure**. According to industry analysts, the company tried to grow too rapidly, outpacing consumer interest in the service it wanted to provide. The company's assumption was that large numbers of customers, dissatisfied with certain aspects of in-store shopping, would change their buying habits and switch to purchasing groceries through an online service. The kind of market surveys and analysis usually required by investors before they fund a new enterprise was overlooked during the rush to fund Internet-based companies such as WebVan that offered an appealing idea.

By contrast, traditional grocers, avoiding a purely Internet-based strategy, have more slowly entered the realm of e-commerce by combining traditional grocery stores and distribution methods with Internet order-taking capabilities. Other traditional retailers that rely on a solid existing distribution infrastructure, such as Land's End, have capitalized on the Internet's new sales channels while minimizing new distribution costs.

Although the business-to-consumer sector was hardest hit by the Internet-bust, business-to-business trading hubs also faced a high failure rate. One well-known example was the Chemdex marketplace for the chemicals industry. Such independent marketplaces generally start out lacking brand name and existing supplier-buyer relationships, both of which cost time and money to acquire, and often end up running out of money (and the ability to raise more money) before they can turn a profit.

However, some traditional businesses do face rigorous e-commerce competition, and some fully web-based businesses have become profitable, creating new market categories in the process. In the travel industry, travel agents serve as intermediaries between the airlines and customers. As more online services such as Travelocity and Orbitz are available to connect customers with the products and services they want, the Internet often effectively disintermediates travel agents, creating new competition. The fully web-based online auction site eBay, which effectively launched the online auction market, is an example of a successful "dot.com" enterprise.

Finding the right mixture of on-and-offline commerce is always a challenge. As is the case in traditional business ventures, the experience gained by the successes and failures of one generation of entrepreneurs can serve as case studies for the e-commerce leaders of the future. SEE ALSO E-COMMERCE; INTERNET: APPLICATIONS; PRIVACY; SECURITY; WORLD WIDE WEB.

Tracy Mullen

Bibliography

Brown, Keith. *The Interactive Marketplace: Business-to-Business Strategies for Delivering Just-in-Time, Mass-Customized Products.* New York: McGraw-Hill Professional Publishing, 2001.

Camp, L. Jean. *Trust and Risk in Internet Commerce.* Cambridge, MA: MIT Press, 2000.

Tedeschi, Bob. "Divining the Nature of Business." *New York Times*, October 2, 2000.

Internet Resources

Mendelson, Haim. "Don't Bury E-Commerce." *Stanford Business School.* <http://www.gsb.stanford.edu/news/mendelson_ecommerce.html>

E-journals and E-publishing

Electronic journal (e-journal) publishing on the World Wide Web is a flourishing field, providing users with online access to various journals. However, there is still a lack of standardization among publishers, and users need to be aware that most journals are still published in print, therefore titles available on the web often cover only a small percentage of a journal's back issues. Despite that challenge, the ease of use and universal acceptance of the web has ushered in e-publishing with a flurry.

E-journals have numerous benefits compared to their print versions. For example, most e-journals can be accessed twenty-four hours a day, seven days a week, making it unnecessary for users to visit libraries in order to make copies of articles. E-journals eliminate the need to track down missing hardcopies or wait for a group of issues to be bound together at the bindery to preserve them for later use. Another benefit is that many e-publishers allow users to download most articles. E-journals are also often an enhanced version of their print counterparts, with embedded links that add value to the journal. Some publishers make particular articles of an e-journal available electronically before the entire issue is available. One of

applet a program component that requires extra support at run time from a browser or run-time environment in order to execute

dynamic links logical connections between two objects that can be modified if the objects themselves move or change state

Uniform Resource Locators (URLs) references to documents or document containers using the Hypertext Transfer Protocol (HTTP); consists of hostnames and paths to the documents

servers computers that do not deal directly with human users, but instead handle requests from other computers for services to be performed

Internet Protocol (IP) a method of organizing information transfer between computers; the IP was specifically designed to offer low-level support to TCP (transmission control protocol)

authentication the act of ensuring that an object or entity is in fact what it is intended to be; verification of identity

SPARC

The Scholarly Publishing and Academic Resources Coalition (SPARC) was founded to offer an affordable alternative to the high-priced scientific and high-tech journals on the marketplace. By publishing the latest scientific discoveries and research findings through print and online articles, SPARC helps meet the needs of the library market, as well as the scientific, technical, and medical fields.

the most important benefits is that multiple users at one location can access the same article at the same time.

Many libraries are making tough choices to save shelf space and labor costs by canceling their print subscriptions and subscribing to electronic versions only. However, they are finding that they rarely save money with this approach because many publishers require libraries to subscribe to the print version in order to access the electronic version. This often adds between 30 and 50 percent of the cost of the print version alone, if not more. Also, some publishers may force a library that wants both print and electronic access to choose one or the other—they may not allow both options.

Regardless of these problems, e-journals continue to offer several advantages. For example, whereas print journals are limited to traditional static text and two-dimensional graphics, e-journals can include sound, video, Java **applets**, or other multimedia options. References in articles can be dynamically linked to other works, if they are online as well. Articles can also list **dynamic links** to various examples and other sources, rather than just being limited to the standard citations or two-dimensional images seen in the print versions.

There are two primary criticisms of e-journals: their instability in the publishing market and the lack of a permanent archive (backlog) for many journals. Common complaints include **Uniform Resource Locators (URLs)** that change frequently and **servers** that crash. Also, many publishers and vendors show little concern over the need to maintain a consistent archive of issues that are made available on the web. This is a matter of great concern to libraries, especially if they choose to cancel print subscriptions in favor of access to e-journals. Libraries need to ensure that all years of a title are available to its patrons.

Relationship to Traditional Research

Many scholarly journals are available as e-journals. In fact, some scholarly e-journals that have a significant impact on their respective fields are available for free. Attitudes toward papers published in e-journals are gradually changing, making them more accepted. At the same time, scholars continue to have concerns about how to view e-journals in the peer review process, the integrity of publishing in e-journals, and the use of such publications for tenure and promotion decisions. This process is evolving and changing, largely due to a movement underway between various scientific societies and universities to transform and have an impact on scholarly publishing. Leading this movement is an initiative called "Scholarly Publishing and Academic Resources Coalition (SPARC)" <http://www.arl.org/sparc/> with the goal of "returning science to scientists."

Authentication and Verification

There are primarily two methods for accessing e-journals: by password and by **Internet Protocol (IP)** authentication. Passwords work well for people with individual subscriptions, but in a library setting, it becomes cumbersome to keep patrons apprised of password information. Therefore, although passwords are an effective way to provide users with access when they are using the journals from off-site, IP **authentication** is the most efficient way for an institution to provide access to its e-journals for users who want to access the information while on-site. If organizations use the IP authentication method, they have to inform the publisher of all the possible IP addresses for their institution. IP authentication works by providing the user with a certificate or token that certifies their identity within an organization. When the identity of the user is verified, the user is either passed on to the publisher's server or to a server that acts as a proxy. This method can sometimes be expensive and complex, and there is a need for an organization to maintain a local server with an access control list of eligible users. Another challenge is that some publishers limit the number of simultaneous users, which can present its own set of problems.

Another type of authentication technique built upon public keys and certificates for establishing a user's identity is X.509. A user is required to provide an encrypted **certificate** with personal information about his or her identity. This certificate is then paired with the user's **public key information** that can be seen by other servers. Certificates can be created with special software or received from third party organizations known as certification authorities. Certificates are sent by a web browser and authentication is handled by a server that accepts these certificates with an access control list of eligible users.

Kerberos is also an authentication scheme based on **encrypted** credentials. It was created at Massachusetts Institute of Technology (MIT) and is freely available. Kerberos uses hidden tickets that can be used over open networks for authentication. A central server with account information authenticates each ticket and then passes the user through to the resources on that server. Kerberos was developed with an important emphasis on security and uses a strong cryptography **protocol** that can be used on insecure networks.

Proxy Servers

Proxy servers are important for organizations with a dispersed group of users. An example would be a university whose faculty and students travel worldwide for conferences, internships, and other events. These people may need access to their university library's e-journals while off-campus, and proxy servers provide them with this common means of access.

A proxy server works by masking remote users with the accepted IP address needed to access an e-journal restricted by an IP address. Users configure their browsers to access a proxy server and are prompted to authenticate themselves when they link to an e-journal. Authentication may require a user's name, social security number, student identification number, or other unique piece of information that will identify a user. The most attractive feature of the proxy server is that a user can access a restricted resource from any location. The most important problem with a proxy server, however, is that some publishers refuse access to their e-journals by a proxy server. Also, if all users are funneled through a proxy server, it may create a bottleneck, especially if the proxy server goes down.

Technology and Software

The primary formats used for e-journals are HTML, Adobe Acrobat **PDF**, Catchword's RealPage, and SGML. PDF has become somewhat of a

certificate a unique electronic document that is used to assist authentication

public key information certain status and identification information that pertains to a particular public key (i.e., a key available for public use in encryption)

encrypted having used a mathematical process to disguise the content of messages transmitted

protocol an agreed understanding for the sub-operations that make up a transaction; usually found in the specification of inter-computer communications

PDF the acronym for Portable Document Format, developed by Adobe Corporation to facilitate the storage and transfer of electronic documents

standard for many e-journals because it is readily available, flexible, and inexpensive. But there has been little agreement between publishers regarding the different formats.

Organizations

For computer sciences, some of the key organizations that publish e-journals are as follows.

- ACM (Association for Computing Machinery) Digital Library: <http://www.acm.org/dl/>
- American Mathematical Society Journals: <http://www.ams.org/mathscinet/searchjournals>
- Cambridge Journals Online: <http://journals.cambridge.org/>
- Elsevier Science Direct: <http://www.sciencedirect.com/web-editions/>
- IDEAL: <http://www.apnet.com/www/ap/aboutid.htm>
- IEEE Xplore: <http://www.ieee.org/ieeexplore/>
- JSTOR: <http://www.jstor.org/>
- Kluwer Online: <http://www.wkap.nl/journal/>
- MIT Journals Online: <http://www-mitpress.mit.edu/>
- Oxford University Press Journals: <http://www3.oup.co.uk/jnls/online/>
- Springer LINK: <http://link.springer-ny.com/>
- Wiley InterScience: <http://www.interscience.wiley.com/>

SEE ALSO DESKTOP PUBLISHING; DOCUMENT PROCESSING; EDUCATIONAL SOFTWARE.

Melissa J. Harvey

Internet Resources

E-Journals.Org. World Wide Web Virtual Library. <http://www.e-journals.org/>

Gibson, Craig. "Electronic Journals: New Resources, Traditional Research Habits?" *Inventio* 1, no. 2 (2000). <http://www.doiiit.gmu.edu/Archives/spring00/cgibson.html>

Journal of Electronic Publishing. University of Michigan Press. <http://www.press.umich.edu:80/jep/>

Public Library of Science. <http://www.publiclibraryofscience.org/>

Electronic Campus

The traditional classroom lecture, supplemented with blackboard and chalk, has stood for centuries as the prevailing model for formal instruction. The term "lecture" is based on the Latin *lectura*, meaning "a reading," and classroom design has traditionally reflected the format where lecturers read from texts or notes held before them on a lectern. Educational institutions are now replacing blackboards and lecterns with hardware and software solu-

tions that provide rich multimedia support for instructional presentations and help engage students in active learning experiences.

Early attempts to supplement the classroom lecture experience involved adding equipment such as 16mm film and 35mm slide projectors to allow students to view previously prepared images. The film projectors were difficult to run, often requiring an equipment operator and the purchase or rental of expensive films, but had the advantage of offering high quality images and sound. Similarly, 35mm slides were difficult and time-consuming to create, but offered excellent viewing quality.

The technology that had the greatest impact in the classroom from the 1950s through the 1990s was borrowed from the bowling alley—the overhead projector. The overhead projector allowed the instructor to prepare a presentation in advance, print it on clear transparencies, and project it onto a screen. More importantly, it allowed the instructor to be spontaneous and write notes, draw illustrations, or scribble equations with a grease pencil and save them for future classes. The overhead projector became, and still is in many places, an indispensable classroom aid, particularly in large classrooms where the chalkboard cannot be seen from a distance.

Large classrooms present other problems as well, particularly with audio. Program audio from films, audiotapes, and videocassettes must be amplified and broadcast over a system of speakers. Typically, instructors in large lecture halls must have their voices amplified through audio reinforcement, captured by a microphone. **Wireless lavaliere microphones**

Electronic classrooms, like this one located in Benedum Hall in the School of Engineering at the University of Pittsburgh, provide students with an interactive approach to learning.

wireless lavaliere microphones small microphones worn around speakers' necks which attach to their shirts

85

fiber optic transmission technology using long, thin strands of glass fiber; internal reflections in the fiber assure that light entering one end is transmitted to the other end with only small losses in intensity; used widely in transmitting digital information

microcomputers computers that are small enough to be used and managed by one person alone; often called personal computers

liquid crystal display (LCD) a type of crystal that changes its level of transparency when subjected to an electric current; used as an output device on a computer

infrastructure the foundation or permanent installation necessary for a structure or system to operate

lumens a unit of measure of light intensity

digitizes converts analog information into a digital form for processing by a computer

free instructors from the confines of the lectern and allow them to walk around the room while their voices are still picked up by the audio system.

With the advent of videocassette recorders (VCRs), videotapes replaced films in the classroom except in special circumstances requiring large, high quality displays. The video display unit was typically a standard television monitor, heavy and limited in size, but with the advantage of being viewable in normally lit rooms. Some institutions experimented with video distribution networks that allowed video to be distributed from a centralized source, such as a media center, to the classroom, using **fiber optic** cable. As VCRs reached commodity prices, however, most institutions found it more cost-effective to build individual VCRs and monitors into classrooms. Some institutions combine the two forms of technology. This allows for centralized distribution of announcements or special presentations, as well as for classroom-level use and control of videotaped material.

When **microcomputers** became popular, instructors sought the ability to display the contents of their computer screens to the entire class. In the 1980s, **liquid crystal display (LCD)** units became available that could be placed on top of overhead projectors, building on existing **infrastructure** the foundation or permanent installation necessary for a structure or system to operate. Although early models had limited screen resolution and required the room to be darkened, making it difficult for students to take notes, this new capability provided instructors with several clear advantages. It reduced the need for preparing overhead transparencies and allowed live demonstrations of computer-related content. The wide availability of network access further increased their value.

By the end of the twentieth century, LCD projection technology had evolved to allow a single projector to display both data and video material adequately. By 2001 projectors could output in excess of 4,000 **lumens**, sufficient for viewing under normal classroom lighting conditions. The wide availability of quality display technology now allows virtually all material to be viewed digitally in many schools and institutions.

Components of the Electronic Classroom

Today's general-purpose electronic classrooms, sometimes referred to as "smart" classrooms, typically provide at least one LCD data/video projector and offer the ability to connect to a wide range of source input devices, including built-in or portable microcomputers equipped with network communications ports, videocassette recorders, DVD (digital video disc) and/or laser disc players, audiocassette decks, and document cameras. The document camera **digitizes** two- and three-dimensional objects placed on its stand and displays an image via an LCD projector. This setup provides all of the functionality associated with the old overhead projectors and also allows the digitized images to be transmitted to remote sites or recorded.

Smaller classrooms can utilize a touch-sensitive display panel, such as Smart Technologies' SmartBoard, that acts as either a rear or front projector screen and allows the instructor to make annotations on a presentation or create new images spontaneously. These images can be retained for subsequent printing, posted to a class web page, or edited for future use. The end result provides the instructor with virtually unlimited whiteboard space and an electronic recording of the class displays.

In the classroom, as in most other areas, necessity often proves to be the mother of invention. Innovators at the University of Pittsburgh combined technologies to address two related problems: allowing instructors who use wheelchairs to make use of SmartBoard-like capabilities and providing a means for students in large lecture halls to view the instructors' ad hoc notes, drawings, and illustrations. The solution pairs a small, touch-sensitive LCD panel with a laptop computer and an LCD projector. The LCD panel doubles as graphics tablet and preview screen, allowing the instructor to stand or sit, facing the class, and make drawings and annotations that the entire class can view on the large projection screen.

Assistive computer technologies provide more teaching options.

The needs of some academic disciplines often require more specialized classroom designs, including:

- Electronic tally systems, providing hardware and/or software solutions to allow the class to respond electronically to the instructor's questions and view the results on the classroom display equipment.

- Computers at every seat, or ports and power outlets to allow the connection of networked laptops. Many institutions are moving to wireless networks to accomplish this goal.

- Hardware or software to network the monitors, keyboards, and mouse inputs from the classroom microcomputers. This setup allows the instructor, from the console, to redirect and control any individual computer display so the entire class can see the example.

- Interactive Television (ITV) capabilities, which use **video compression algorithms** to create two-way audio, video, and data interactions between similarly equipped classrooms. Such facilities use Integrated Services Digital Network (ISDN), Asynchronous Transfer Mode (ATM), or other **high-bandwidth** network connections to provide **real-time** support for distance education programs between the instructor and students at one or more remote sites.

Classroom technology continues to evolve at a rapid pace. For example, networked LCD projectors can now display content stored in web pages, allowing an instructor to make presentations without having a local microcomputer. Tomorrow's classroom will be an exciting place for learning with and about technology. SEE ALSO DISTANCE LEARNING; E-BOOKS; EDUCATIONAL SOFTWARE; TELECOMMUNICATIONS.

Nicholas C. Laudato

video compression algorithms special algorithms applied to remove certain unnecessary parts of video images in an attempt to reduce their storage size

high-bandwidth a communication channel that permits many signals of differing frequencies to be transmitted simultaneously

real-time a system, often computer based, that ensures the rates at which it inputs, processes, and outputs information meet the timing requirements of another system

Bibliography

Neff, Raymond K. *The Classroom of the Future, Realizing the Potential of Information Resources: Information, Technology, and Services.* Proceedings of the 1995 CAUSE Annual Conference, 1995. <http://www.educause.edu/ir/library/text/CNC9548.txt>

Electronic Markets

Markets are a fundamental feature of modern capitalism and have a long history behind them. During the Middle Ages in England, for example, fairs and markets were organized by individuals under a franchise from the king. Organizers of these markets not only provided the physical facilities for the markets, but were also responsible for security and settlement of disputes in the trading. Throughout history, some traditional markets have diminished in importance while new ones have gained in importance. For example, stock and **commodities** markets, previously not significant, now play a vital role in the world economy. Regardless of changes, the fundamental functions of markets remain the same: to match buyers and sellers, enforce contracts, and provide a price mechanism to guide the trade.

Electronic markets are markets connected through modern communications networks and powered by high-speed computers. In an electronic marketplace, buyers and sellers do not have to be in the same physical lo-

commodities raw materials or services that are marketed prior to being used

cation in order to interact. A classic example of electronic markets is the Nasdaq stock market. Nasdaq was launched in the 1970s, long before the widespread use of the Internet, and it does not have an exchange floor. Essentially, Nasdaq is a huge electronic network connecting investors, brokers, and dealers, allowing various parties to exchange information and buy and sell securities. With the explosive development of the Internet, electronic markets will play a more important role in people's everyday lives. The World Wide Web has become the universal **interface** for electronic markets. People can use the web to access various electronic markets virtually from anywhere at any time. Ordinary investors can use the Internet to conduct online trading through online brokerage firms, and customers can bid for various products at online auction houses such as eBay.

Consider the development of electronic markets in the financial world. In just a few years, online trading has fundamentally changed the dynamics of investment. Before the advent of web-based technologies, an investor who wanted to place an order with a broker had to either walk to the local office of the broker or call by phone. Then, some time later, a second call was necessary to get a confirmation of the transaction. As of 2002, a growing number of brokerage firms offer Internet-based services that contrast sharply with the traditional scenario. Online investors can log onto the web site of

A trader at the Chicago Mercantile Exchange uses a computer to monitor transactions.

interface a boundary or border between two or more objects or systems; also a point of access

the brokerage firm using a web browser. The following are some of the typical functions of the online trading application offered by most online brokers to investors:

- Place buy and sell orders and receive electronic confirmations as soon as the order is executed;
- Check account balances;
- Receive real-time price updates;
- View historic account activities;
- Track the portfolio performance on a real-time basis.

Online trading is not only flexible and easy to use, it also incurs lower costs. Online brokerage firms are able to charge customers lower commission fees since they no longer have to employ a large staff to field phone calls from customers. The savings in overhead costs from replacing human brokers with Internet-based communication systems are passed on to investors in the form of lower fees.

The popularity of online trading has resulted in a new category of traders known as day traders. Some individual investors use online brokers to make dozens of trades per day, many times on the same security. Even though day trading can be profitable, it involves high risks and has significant tax issues to day traders. While all the trading gains are subject to federal income tax, investors can only claim a loss of a maximum of $3,000 per year.

New Avenues

Electronic markets have had an impact that reaches far beyond the financial world. Entrepreneurs have created new markets to better match buyers and sellers, and they have also introduced innovative products for trading. Two examples, eBay and the catastrophe insurance market, illustrate such recent developments.

eBay. eBay is the world's leading online person-to-person auction market. Individual buyers and sellers can register at eBay and exchange products and services. Founded in 1995, eBay had more than 29 million registered users in 2001, and many businesses use eBay to sell their products as well. eBay has created a worldwide central marketplace that lists millions of items such as computers, antiques, coins, and furniture. Such a large-scale market has never existed before, and without the Internet, it would have been impossible to create such a market.

Although there are several other auction sites on the Internet, eBay is by far the most successful. Since the beginning, eBay tried to be the dominant player in the online market environment. It has taken full advantage of the network effect in electronic markets. Without geographical barriers in the Internet, buyers and sellers would like to visit the dominant market because it is the place where sellers will find the most buyers and buyers will find the most sellers. The network effect is simple: more buyers and sellers will attract even more buyers and sellers to the same market. By providing a central marketplace, eBay has lowered the costs of trading for millions of buyers and sellers.

DIGITAL CASH

Digital cash is simply a series of bits and bytes. In order to use digital cash, users first need to purchase some digital cash tokens from digital cash providers. The digital cash provider maintains a central database to keep track of the digital cash tokens that have been issued. Once a token is spent, the token is deleted from the database to prevent it from being duplicated.

Catastrophe Insurance. Another successful online offering is the catastrophe insurance market, showing how electronic markets can bring innovative products for trading and fundamentally change the way existing companies do businesses. Risk and insurance are integral parts of modern-day life. Insurance companies provide protection against loss in value of human capital, physical property, and financial assets. However, almost any insurance company is limited in the amount of insurance it can write on any one risk. The law of averages makes it safer to insure a large number of small risks than to insure a few large risks. For example, a catastrophe as big as Hurricane Andrew, which devastated Florida in 1992, can easily bankrupt an insurance company. Therefore, insurance companies have to seek ways to reduce large risks.

A catastrophe insurance market tries to share risks between insurance companies and other institutions. Risk is the product that is traded in a catastrophe market. The process to convert risks to tradable products is called securitization, which transforms **illiquid** assets into liquid financial securities in a financial market. Securitizing insurance risk enables institutions and individuals who are not in the insurance business to participate in the insurance market. Currently, the products that are openly traded include Cat (catastrophe) bonds and Cat options.

The Catastrophe Risk Exchange (CATEX) is a New Jersey-based electronic market that allows property and casualty insurers, reinsurers, and brokers to swap or trade risk exposure to natural disasters. Developed in reaction to events such as Hurricane Andrew and the Northridge Earthquake, the exchange is designed to allow insurers to protect themselves against severe losses by geographically distributing risk and diversifying across different perils through an electronic marketplace. Trading operations on CATEX started in 1996. In 1998 CATEX was launched over the Internet. Meanwhile, CATEX began evolving from the initial swap exchange to a more complete insurance market, which supported the reinsurance transactions of marine, energy, and political risk.

Growth of Electronic Banking

Rapid growth in electronic market applications requires a secure and efficient electronic banking and payment services. If one buys shares of a company listed on a stock exchange, she has to send in her payment within three days of the date of purchase. She can either send a check by express mail or make a bank transfer. Both options are relatively expensive. Many brokers require that she maintain sufficient funds with them to cover the cost of any such purchase, but there can be situations when she would prefer not to leave money sitting idle in her brokerage account. Payment systems that allow the investor to make payments directly out of her bank account would be far superior in a number of ways.

Individuals can have better control over the movement of cash in and out of their accounts. Today's check-based systems are also considerably more expensive than most electronic payment systems under development. Though many banks do not directly charge customers for use of checks, they do recover it in other ways, typically by paying low interest rates on checking accounts. Safer and more efficient payment systems such as digital check, digital wallets, or electronic money are still in the experimental stage. The bottom

---

DIGITAL WALLETS

Digital wallet is a software component that a user can install on his or her computer. A user can store credit card, digital cash, and other personal information in the digital wallet. Every time the user shops at merchants who accept digital wallets, he or she does not need to enter personal information again. The digital wallet automatically fills in the payment information and allows the user to perform shopping effortlessly.

illiquid lacking in liquid assets; or something that is not easily transferable into currency

DIGITAL CHECKS

A digital check is simply the electronic version of a paper check and works the same way that a paper check works. When a customer pays a merchant with a digital check, the check information, including the check's routing number, account number, and check number, is sent to the clearing network and the transaction is settled electronically. Digital checks can be processed more quickly and at less cost compared to paper checks.

line is that the trend is toward electronic payment and real-time settlement of transactions. Electronic payment systems being designed for electronic markets will allow transactions to be settled on a real-time basis as soon as the transaction is executed, or at least on the same day. Faster settlement will lower the risks of default by the counter-party in the transaction. SEE ALSO E-BANKING; INTERNET: APPLICATIONS; WORLD WIDE WEB.

Ming Fan

Bibliography

Fan, Ming, et al. *Electronic Commerce and the Revolution in Financial Markets.* Stamford, CT: Thomson Learning, 2002.

Fan, Ming, Jan Stallaert, and Andrew B. Whinston. "The Internet and the Future of Financial Markets." *Communications of the ACM* 43, no. 11 (2000): 83-88.

North, Douglass C. *Institutions, Institutional Change, and Economic Performance.* Cambridge: Cambridge University Press, 1990.

Entrepreneurs

In general, entrepreneurs are enthusiastic and bright risk takers who are willing to take a chance and create new markets. In the computer industry, some have become very wealthy, very fast. During the last half of the twentieth century, the vision and daring of computer entrepreneurs generated one of the most extensive technological revolutions ever.

This article contains, in alphabetical order, brief biographical sketches of ten of those entrepreneurs and their contributions: Tim Berners-Lee, Jeff Bezos, Bill Gates, Steven Jobs, Mitchell Kapor, Sandra Kurtzig, Pamela Lopker, Pierre Omidyar, John W. Thompson, and Jerry Yang.

Tim Berners-Lee

Hypertext Markup Language (HTML) an encoding scheme for text data that uses special tags in the text to signify properties to the viewing program (browser) like links to other documents or document parts

Hypertext Transfer Protocol (HTTP) a simple connectionless communications protocol developed for the electronic transfer (serving) of HTML documents

Uniform Resource Locator (URL) a reference to a document or a document container using the Hypertext Transfer Protocol (HTTP); consists of a hostname and path to the document

Tim Berners-Lee was born in England in 1955, graduated from Oxford University with a degree in physics, and is generally acknowledged as the originator of the World Wide Web. During his adolescence, he was influenced by Arthur C. Clarke's short story "Dial F for Frankenstein." This possibly influenced his later vision that the web could truly seem alive.

While consulting at CERN (the European Organization for Nuclear Research), he created a program called Enquire to master CERN's intricate information system and his own mental associations of information. With this program, he could enter several words in a document, and when the words were clicked, the program would lead him to related documents that provided more information. This is a form of hypertext, a term coined by Ted Nelson in the 1960s to describe text connected by links.

In collaboration with colleagues, Berners-Lee developed the three cornerstones of the web: the language for encoding documents—**Hypertext Markup Language (HTML)**; the system for transmitting documents—**Hypertext Transfer Protocol (HTTP)**; and the scheme for addressing documents—**Uniform Resource Locator (URL)**.

Berners-Lee runs the nonprofit World Wide Web Consortium (W3C) that helps set technical standards for the web. Its members come from in-

dustry, such as Microsoft, Sun, Apple, and IBM, some universities, and some government research centers, both from the United States and elsewhere, for example, CERN. As of December 2001, W3C had more than 500 members. As director of W3C, he brings members together to negotiate agreement on technical standards. In May 1998, Berners-Lee was awarded one of the prestigious MacArthur "genius" fellowships, freeing him to do just about whatever he wanted for a few years.

Director of the World Wide Web Consortium, British computer entrepreneur Tim Berners-Lee (b. 1955–) made easy access to the Internet a possibility. He maintains a web site detailing his life and career: <http://www.w3.org/People/Berners-Lee/>.

Jeff Bezos

Jeff Preston Bezos was born in New Mexico in 1964. He was raised by his mother and his stepfather, Mike Bezos, who had emigrated from Cuba. Bezos became famous for using the Internet as the basis for the Seattle-based bookseller Amazon.com.

After graduating from Princeton summa cum laude in electrical engineering and computer science in 1986, he joined FITEL, a high-tech start-up company in New York; two years later, he moved to Bankers Trust Company to develop their computer systems, becoming their youngest vice-president in 1990. He then worked at D. E. Shaw & Co., an investment firm. It was there that he got the idea to start an online company based on the Internet.

In 1994 Bezos left Wall Street to establish Amazon.com. He had no experience in the book-selling business, but, after some research, realized that books were small-price commodities that were easy and relatively inexpensive to ship and well-suited for online commerce. More than three million book titles are in print at any one time throughout the world; more than one million of those are in English. However, even the largest bookstore cannot stock more than 200,000 books, and a catalog for such a large volume of books is too large for a mail-order house to distribute. Bezos had identified a strategic opportunity for selling online.

Amazon.com has continued to extend its product line offerings, which now include a variety of consumer goods, including electronics, software, art and collectibles, housewares, and toys. In December 1999 *Time* magazine chose Bezos as its Person of the Year.

Bill Gates

As a teenager, William H. Gates (born in 1955 in Seattle, Washington) was a devoted hacker. He knew how to make computers work and make money. Together with his friend, Paul Allen, he designed a scheduling program for their school, Lakeside School, in Seattle. Later, the two designed a program to perform traffic analysis that reportedly earned their company, Traf-O-Data, $20,000.

Gates entered Harvard in 1973, and while there was impressed by an article that Allen had shown him in *Popular Electronics* about the MITS Altair home computer. He recognized that these computers would need software and that much money could be made writing such programs. He and Allen developed a full-featured BASIC language interpreter that required only 4KB of memory. BASIC made the Altair an instant hit; in 1975, Allen and Gates formed Microsoft Corporation. Much to the disappointment of his parents, Gates dropped out of Harvard to pursue his software development dreams.

Gates's biggest break came when the IBM Corporation decided to enter the personal computer business. He convinced IBM that his small company could write an original operating system that would take advantage of the disk drives and other peripherals that IBM had planned.

By 1998, Gates had turned Microsoft into the largest and most dominant computer software company ever. By the end of fiscal year 2000, Microsoft had revenues of $22.96 billion and employed more than 39,000 people in 60 countries.

Steven Jobs

Orphaned shortly after his birth in California in 1955, Steven Paul Jobs was adopted by Paul and Clara Jobs in Mountain View, California, and was raised there and in Los Altos, California. His interest in electronics started in high school. In order to build his projects, he had to beg for parts, going as far as asking William Hewlett, president of Hewlett-Packard, for the parts he needed to build a computer device. His boldness landed him a summer job at Hewlett-Packard where he befriended electronics wizard Stephen Wozniak.

THE GATES FOUNDATION

Improving health care in developing nations throughout the world is one of the main goals of the Gates Foundation, begun by Bill and Melinda Gates. Headed by Gates' dad, retired attorney Bill Gates, Sr., the foundation had assets of $24 billion as of early 2002. Among the group's goals is to help poor countries, which carry the burden of 90 percent of disease but have few health care resources to combat it. The foundation seeks to provide medications to fight easily curable diseases, make vaccinations for measles and other childhood diseases readily available, and improve conditions and thereby significantly lessen infant and maternal mortality rates. They seek to make quality heath care a basic human right.

Through his company, Microsoft Corporation, Bill Gates followed his dream to make personal computers readily available and easily used by the general public. Helping start the PC revolution, Gates became one of the world's richest people along the way.

Jobs was thirteen and Wozniak eighteen when they met. They built the prototype of the Apple I in Jobs's garage, and together founded Apple Computer in 1976. They sold their first computers to a local electronics store, one of the first "computer stores." Wozniak eventually left Hewlett-Packard to work at Apple full time.

From the day it opened for business in 1976, Apple prospered, first with the Apple I, and then the Apple II. The introduction of the VisiCalc spreadsheet introduced Apple products to the business world, and in 1982 Jobs made the cover of *Time* magazine.

When sales of Apple computers dropped off after the introduction of the IBM-PC, Jobs set to work on the design of a new computer, the affordable and hugely successful Apple Macintosh. Jobs left Apple in September 1985, in a dispute over management, to found a new company, NeXT, Inc, which built workstations for university and business environments. However, despite a revenue of $60 million in 1996, NeXT was unsuccessful as a hardware company and was sold to Apple later that year for $400 million. Jobs later returned to Apple and became its chairman.

Mitchell Kapor

Mitch Kapor was born in Brooklyn in 1950 and raised in Freeport, New York, on Long Island. He graduated from Yale University in 1971 with a B.A. in psychology. Kapor spent several years doing odd jobs until 1978, when he became interested in personal computers and purchased an Apple II. Kapor became a serious programmer and created VisiPlot, an application that would plot and graph the results of a spreadsheet, and VisiTrend. Before long, Kapor's royalty checks were running into the six-figure range.

In 1982 Kapor and Jonathan Sachs went on to establish Lotus Corporation to make and market his multipurpose Lotus 1-2-3, a program that combined some of the best features of a then well known and widely used spreadsheet program, VisiCalc, with graphics and database management capabilities.

Lotus 1-2-3 was designed to work on IBM's sixteen-bit processor rather than on the eight-bit processor, which was the standard for other microcomputers. Kapor felt that this new processor would soon become the standard throughout the personal computer industry, giving his program a head start. By the summer of 1986 Kapor left Lotus, and in 1987 he established ON Technology; he later founded Kapor Enterprises, Inc. Lotus was sold to IBM in 1997.

Sandra Kurtzig

Sandra Kurtzig was born in Chicago in 1946. She received a bachelor's degree from UCLA in 1967 and later a master's degree from Stanford University. In 1971 she used $2,000 to found a software company, ASK Computer Systems, Inc., which went public in 1974.

ASK started as a part-time contract software programming business based in her second bedroom. She received $1,200 from her first client, a telecommunications equipment manufacturer that needed programs to track inventory, bills of material, and purchase orders. ASK grew into a company that had $450 million in annual sales in 1992.

Kurtzig could not convince venture capitalists in **Silicon Valley** to invest in her company, so she launched it on her earnings alone. At one point she needed a computer to run a manufacturing program under development. She managed to gain access to a Hewlett-Packard facility where her colleagues could test the program during off hours. It was here that they developed computer software that was packaged with Hewlett-Packard computers.

In 1994 ASK was purchased by Computer Associates, a software company founded by Charles Wang, Judy Cedeno, and Russ Artzt; Wang and Artzt attended Queens College, in New York, at the same time. The company is based in Long Island, New York, but is a worldwide enterprise.

Kurtzig later became chairperson of the board of E-benefits, a San Francisco insurance and human resources service provider, founded in 1996 by one of her sons. ASK stands for Arie (the name of her ex-husband), Sandy, and Kurtzig.

Silicon Valley an area in California near San Francisco, which has been the home location of many of the most significant information technology orientated companies and universities

Pamela Lopker

In 1979 Pamela Lopker founded QAD Inc., a software company which employed more than 1,200 people in 21 countries at last report. Their major product, MFG/PRO, is a software system that helps manufacturing firms track their products from sale order, to manufacturing, to delivery.

These enterprise resource planning (ERP) programs are used by a variety of companies—such as Avon, Coca-Cola, Lucent, and Sun Microsystems—to deliver large quantities of products manufactured and distributed from more than 5,100 sites in some 80 countries.

QAD's 2006 Project was set up by Lopker in 1995. Its goal is to provide an introduction to the Internet to elementary school students in the Santa Barbara South Coast area. In 1998 Lopker was named "Entrepreneur of the Year" for the Los Angeles area. She was also named to the WITI (Women in Technology International) Hall of Fame in 1997.

Pierre Omidyar

Pierre Omidyar is the founder of eBay, the online marketplace where anyone, according to its mission, can buy or sell just about anything. Omidyar was born in Paris in 1968 and lived there until he was six when his family emigrated to the United States. He admits that his interest in computers started in high school and continued in college. He graduated with a bachelor of science in computer science from Tufts University in 1988.

The auction web site eBay, founded in 1995, was not his first venture; in 1991 he was the co-founder of Ink Development Corp., one of the pioneers in online shopping. It was bought by Microsoft in 1996 under the name of eShop.

Omidyar also worked as a developer for Claris, a subsidiary of Apple Computer, and, while he was launching eBay, he was working for General Magic, Inc., a mobile telecommunications company. Omidyar started eBay hoping to provide people with a democratic opportunity to trade goods, and to fulfill the wishes of his wife-to-be to find people who collected and wanted to trade Pez candy dispensers.

By the end of 1999 eBay had a market value of $20 billion and had close to 29.7 million registered users. Currently Omidyar lives in France and spends most of his time on philanthropic projects.

John W. Thompson

John W. Thompson received a bachelor's degree in business administration from Florida A&M University and a master's degree in management science from MIT's Sloan School of Management. Upon graduation he joined the IBM Corporation, where he spent twenty-eight successful years, advancing to general manager of IBM Americas, a 30,000 employee division, where his major responsibilities were in sales and support of IBM's products and services.

In 1999 he left IBM to join Symantec, a world leader of Internet security technology. As chief executive officer of Symantec, Thompson transformed the company from a publisher of software products to a principal provider of Internet security products aimed at individuals as well as large businesses.

Probably, the company's most well known product is their Norton line of security systems, which includes Norton Internet Security 2001, Norton AntiVirus 2001, Norton Personal Firewall 2001, Norton SystemWorks 2001, and Norton Utilities 2001. However, it also provides much needed security to most of the leading corporations.

Jerry Yang

Jerry Yang, born in Taiwan in 1968, emigrated to the United States with his mother when he was ten. He graduated from Stanford in 1990 with a bachelor of science and a master of science degree in electrical engineering in four years. There he met and formed a close friendship with David Filo, who had also earned a master's in electrical engineering at Stanford.

Yang and Filo entered the doctorate program at Stanford and, after Filo discovered Mosaic, they became addicted to surfing the World Wide Web. Their addiction developed into a list of links to their favorite web sites, which was stored on Yang's home page and was called *Jerry's Guide to the World Wide Web*.

Knowledge of *Jerry's Guide* spread fast and his site began to experience thousands of hits every day. Yang and Filo quickly realized that the guide had market potential and decided to form a company to promote it. The name Yahoo! is a take off on the UNIX program YACC, "Yet Another Compiler Compiler," and stands for "Yet Another Hierarchical Officious Oracle." The "hierarchical" comes from its categorization scheme of web sites. Yahoo! is one of the few search engines that use the intelligence of human labor to categorize the sites found.

Yahoo! went public in 1996, and in 2001 it was the leading online media company, with more global unique visitors than AOL or Microsoft networks, and, together with them, formed the top three in the United States.

Epilogue

The list of entrepreneurs is never-ending. Others that merit special mention are: Daniel Bricklin and Robert Frankston (VisiCalc), Nolan Bushnell (Atari), Steve Case (AOL), Larry Ellison (Oracle), and Ross Perot (EDS). Who knows, maybe your name will be added to the list. SEE ALSO DISTANCE LEARNING; E-COMMERCE; EDUCATIONAL SOFTWARE; INTERNET: APPLICATIONS.

Ida M. Flynn

YAHOO'S DAVID FILO

Born in 1966 in Wisconsin, David Filo grew up in Louisiana in an "alternative community" (a commune-like atmosphere) with six other families. He received his B.A. from Tulane University in New Orleans before relocating to California to attend Stanford University. At Stanford, Filo met Jerry Yang and the pair went on to create Yahoo. In time the pair's "road map" to the Internet, called *Jerry's Guide to the World Wide Web*, was renamed *Jerry and David's Guide to the World Wide Web*. Yang has received more notoriety for Yahoo because he has served as its spokesperson while Filo has preferred to stay behind the scenes.

Bibliography

Jager, Rama D., and Rafael Ortiz. *In the Company of Giants: Candid Conversations with the Visionaries of the Digital World.* New York: McGraw-Hill, 1997.

Kurtzig, Sandra L., with Tom Parker. *CEO: Building a $400 Million Company from the Ground Up.* New York: W. W. Norton & Co., 1991.

Lee, J. A. N. *Computer Pioneers.* Los Alamitos, CA: IEEE Computer Society Press, 1995.

Wright, Robert. "The Man Who Invented the Web." *Time* 149, no. 20 (1997): 64–68.

Internet Resources

"About QAD." QAD.com web site. <http://www.qad.com/company/>

"Bill Gates' Web Site: Biography." Microsoft.com. <http://www.microsoft.com/billgates/bio.asp>

"CEO News and Views; John W. Thompson, CEO and Chairman, Symantec Corporation." Symantec.com. <http://www.symantec.com/corporate/ceo.html>

Cohen, Adam. "Coffee with Pierre." *Time.* December 27, 1999. <http://www.time.com/time/poy/pierre.html>

"First Lady of Software: Sandra Kurtzig." Entrepreneur.com web site. <http://www.entrepreneur.com/Magazines/MA_SegArticle/0,1539,233034-6,00.html>

"Jeff Bezos Biography." *Entrepreneur.* <http://www.annonline.com/interviews/970106/biography.html>

"Jerry Yang." *Tallahasee Democrat Online.* <http://www.tdo.com/local/graphics/1pyang/html/1.htm>

"Jerry Yang and David Filo." Stanford University School of Engineering web site. <http://soe.stanford.edu/AR95-96/jerry.html>

"Mitchell Kapor Biography." Kapor Enterprises, Inc. <http://www.kapor.com/homepages/mkapor/bio0701.htm>

Moran, Susan. "The Candyman, Pierre Omidyar." *Business 2.0.* June 1999. <http://www.business2.com/articles/mag/0,1640,13015,FF.html>

"Pamela Meyer Lopker." Women in Technology International web site. <http://www.witi.org/center/witimuseum/halloffame/1997/plopker.shtml>

"Pierre Omidyar Biography." *The Industry Standard* web site. <http://www.thestandard.com/people/profile/0,1923,1646,00.html>

Ramo, Joshua Cooper. "Person of the Year: Jeff Bezos." *Time.* <http://www.time.com/time/poy/index.html>

"Steve Jobs and Steve Wosniak: The Personal Computer." Lemelson-MIT Prize Program web site. <http://web.mit.edu/invent/www/inventorsI-Q/apple.html>

"Steve Paul Jobs." Virginia Polytechnic Institute and State University. <http://ei.cs.vt.edu/~history/Jobs.html>

Ethics

Education for professionals in the computing disciplines includes, but is not limited to, degree tracks called computer science, computer engineering, software engineering, information systems, and information technology. Major professional organizations for the computing disciplines include the Association for Computing Machinery (ACM), the Institute of Electrical and Electronics Engineers Computer Society (IEEE-CS), and the Association for Information Technology Professionals (AITP). Each of these professional organizations has published a code of ethics. The complete, current versions of these codes can generally be found on the organizations' web sites. These codes are designed to establish a framework for judging the ethical quality of professional behavior, and anyone who aspires to be a professional in the computing disciplines should be aware of them.

One important general principle contained in these codes is that a professional has a responsibility to society as a whole. For example, the AITP standards of conduct lists six items under the heading of "obligation to society." These include informing the public about computing technology, ensuring that work products are used in socially responsible ways, and making information public when it is relevant to a situation of public concern. The ACM code and the joint ACM/IEEE-CS Software Engineering Code of Ethics each include similar concerns. This overall obligation to society is the foundation for a responsibility to "blow the whistle" if one's company engages in illegal or unethical activities.

Motion Picture Association of America President Jack Valenti addressed lawmakers in 2001 to discuss the problem of copyright violation, noting that the film *Gladiator,* appearing on screen next to him, was illegally downloaded off the Internet.

intellectual property
the acknowledgement that an individual's creativity and innovation can be owned in the same way as physical property

Rights and Responsibilities

Another important general principle is to respect **intellectual property** laws and ensure that credit is fairly assigned for the results of intellectual work. For example, the "General Moral Imperatives" in the ACM code of ethics contains the statements "Honor property rights, including patents and copyrights" and "Give proper credit for intellectual property." The "honoring" of existing intellectual property laws can be a controversial issue. Sharing, or facilitating the sharing of, copyrighted digital audio and video files on the World Wide Web is certainly a violation of existing copyright laws. Some users of the World Wide Web believe strongly in the right to such activity. However, the codes clearly label this behavior as unethical. Existing copyright law also labels it as illegal! Many computing professionals who do not agree with existing copyright law suggest that the more appropriate action is to change copyright laws.

The codes of ethics also touch on general principles regarding software development. These are most fully detailed in the joint ACM/IEEE-CS Software Engineering Code of Ethics. Two elements listed under the "Product" section of this code are the following: (1) "Ensure that specifications for software on which you work have been well documented, satisfy the users' requirements and have the appropriate approvals." (2) "Ensure adequate testing, debugging, and review of software and related documents on which you work." One classic case study of failures in software design, implementation, and testing is that of the Therac-25 radiation therapy machine. Several patients died as a direct result of software failures in this system. Concern about the quality of software development, especially software for safety-critical systems, is one of the factors behind the movement to license software engineers.

In general, a code of ethics cannot be used as a means to avoid serious thought and judgment. In particular, codes should not be used to search for "proof text" for a desired conclusion. Consider the situation of a technician who accidentally discovers that his or her manager has used an office computer to collect a large amount of pornography downloaded from the web. The question is whether the technician should report the pornography or keep it private. One element of the AITP standards of conduct states "Protect the privacy and confidentiality of all information entrusted to me." But other elements of the same code state "Take appropriate action in regard to any illegal or unethical practices that come to my attention" and "Protect the proper interest of my employer at all times."

So if people use the code to search for justification for what they already want to do, they will likely find it. Instead, the correct approach is to look at the code of ethics and the particular situation as a whole, and to make a judgment based on careful consideration of all the relevant facts. In this example, the use of a company-owned computer to collect pornography for personal enjoyment seems to be outside the bounds of acceptable professional behavior, making it something that should be reported to upper management.

Social Issues

There are several important and controversial social issues at the forefront of ethics and computing. One issue involves missile defense systems. In 1983 U.S. President Ronald Reagan proposed a "Star Wars" missile defense system that would protect the United States from attack by the Soviet Union. The goal of the proposed system was to use space-based sensors to detect missiles launched by the Soviet Union, to track the missiles on their way toward the United States, and to direct anti-missile weapons to destroy the missiles before they hit the United States. This proposal was eventually abandoned. In 2001 U.S. President George W. Bush renewed the call for a scaled-down version of the system to meet the perceived threats of the time. Computer programs designed to operate a missile defense system are an extreme example of safety-critical software, and concerns about specifications and testing raise important ethical issues.

Many experts argue that it is not possible to create missile defense software that would have a high reliability of working. One reason for this is that identifying the software specifications requires knowing how the enemy will choose to attack. Therefore, it is difficult to know the specifications with any certainty. Another reason is that it is difficult to envision how the software could be realistically tested. As a result of these and other concerns, many programmers and designers feel that working on such software would go against the values embedded in the code of ethics governing their profession.

Another issue at the cutting edge of ethics and computing is freedom of speech. The first amendment to the U.S. Constitution provides a general protection against the government regulating the speech of its citizens. The United States has perhaps the strongest protections for freedom of speech of any country. For instance, some "hate speech" web sites that are legal in the United States would be illegal in Canada, England, France, Germany, and other countries. But it is still unclear how to enforce national laws in cyberspace, and perhaps the free speech tradition as it is known in the United States is not the only workable alternative. Some people argue that traditional free speech rights in the United States should be restricted in the modern world of cyberspace.

The introduction and use of computing technology continues to raise important ethical and social concerns. The professional societies have developed codes of ethics to help provide a framework for ethical decision-making in the computing disciplines. It is the responsibility of each individual computing professional to be aware of and to integrate a code of ethics into their professional behavior. SEE ALSO E-COMMERCE; PRIVACY; SECURITY; WORLD WIDE WEB.

Kevin W. Bowyer

Bibliography

Bowyer, Kevin W. *Ethics and Computing: Living Responsibly in a Computerized World.* New York: IEEE Press, 2001.

Leveson, Nancy G., and Clark S. Turner. "An Investigation of the Therac-25 Accidents." *IEEE Computer* 26, no. 7 (1993): 18–41.

Parnas, David L. "Software Aspects of Strategic Defense Systems." *Communications of the ACM* 28 (1985): 1326–1335.

Internet Resources

Association for Computing Machinery. <http://www.acm.org/>

Association of Information Technology Professionals. <http://www.aitp.org/>

Electronic Frontier Foundation. <http://www.eff.org/>

IEEE Computer Society. <http://www.computer.org/>

Feynman, Richard P.

American Physicist
1918–1988

Richard P. Feynman was born in 1918 in Far Rockaway, New York. He graduated with a bachelor of science degree from Massachusetts Institute of Technology in 1935, and he received a Ph.D. in physics from Princeton University in 1942. It was during this time that he began working on the **Manhattan Project** at New Mexico's Los Alamos Scientific Laboratory, which resulted in the development of the first atomic bomb. While working on this team, he had his first experience with computers.

The project required many implosion calculations, which had to be done quickly and correctly. At the start, the group used Marchand hand calculators, but the devices kept breaking down and were very cumbersome. To speed up the process, one of the group's members, Stanley Frankel, decided to order some IBM business machines—adding machines called tabulators, for listing sums, and a multiplier, which used cards for input. This scheme would have worked out just fine if Frankel had not succumbed to the "disease" that afflicts many who work extensively with computers. Feynman described it in these words, as noted in *Surely You're Joking, Mr. Feynman!* "It's a very serious disease and it interferes completely with the work. The trouble with computers is you *play* with them. They are so wonderful. You

Manhattan Project the U.S. project designed to create the world's first atomic bomb

have these switches—if it's an even number you do this, if it's an odd number you do that—and pretty soon you can do more and more elaborate things if you are clever enough, on one machine."

After a while Frankel spent less time doing his job and more time playing with the computers. Those who have worked with computers have probably experienced the feeling of delight in being able to do just one more thing with the computer; hence, they can understand the "disease." However, this situation was delaying the final results, so Feynman was put in charge of the group that worked with the computers. To speed things up and meet deadlines, he devised a way to work out two problems in parallel. His group also realized that errors made in one of the program cycles would affect nearby data values, so they used smaller sets of data to test the program and correct the errors as they occurred, making the work go faster. Feynman never contracted the computer disease.

Feynman was known for his irreverent nature and general disregard for official rules and regulations. During his years with the Manhattan Project, he learned how to break into filing cabinets where classified information was stored. Although he never took any of the secret documents, he left behind notes and evidence that made it clear to those responsible for the files that someone had managed to bypass their security efforts.

After Los Alamos, Feynman never worked with the military again, but taught physics at Cornell University where he worked on reconstructing and restating quantum mechanics and electrodynamics in terms of particles. In 1951 he left Cornell for the California Institute of Technology, where he continued to teach until shortly before his death.

Feynman received the Albert Einstein Award in 1954, and the Lawrence Award in 1962. In 1965 he was one of three scientists to receive the Nobel Prize for work done on the theory of quantum electrodynamics. His contributions to the field included simplification of the rules of calculation and a diagrammatic approach to analyzing atomic interactions, both of which became standard tools of theoretical analysis.

In addition to his work in teaching and research, Feynman was an author. *The Feynman Lectures on Physics*, published in 1963, remained a favorite textbook for physics students for more than three decades. A writer in *The Economist* magazine called it "one of the best physics texts, as well as the most readable." In 1985 his popular book, *Surely You're Joking, Mr. Feynman!*, began a 15-week run on the *New York Times* list of bestselling nonfiction titles. In 1986 he wrote *QED: The Strange Theory of Light and Matter* to introduce the theory of quantum electrodynamics to a general, nonacademic audience.

His fame in the scientific and academic world as a teacher, theoretician, and author expanded when in 1986 he was appointed to the President's Commission on the Space Shuttle Challenger Accident. Feynman's impatience with the bureaucracy of the hearings process led him to offer a simple, but dramatic illustration of the effect of cold on the ill-fated space shuttle's **O-rings**, which were supposed to seal the joints of the shuttle's rocket booster segments. During televised testimony, he used ice and water to show that a piece of the O-ring material would rapidly harden when submerged in low temperatures. Typical of his direct approach to

Richard Feynman.

O-rings 37-foot rubber circles (rings) that seal the joints between the space shuttle's rocket booster segments

THE MANHATTAN PROJECT

Beginning in June 1942 during World War II, the United States' Manhattan Project brought together scientists and military experts to create the world's first atomic bomb. The project began following concerns that the Nazis were close to creating effective atomic weapons of mass destruction. Led by Gen. Leslie Groves and J. Robert Oppenheimer, the Manhattan Project successfully detonated the first atomic bomb at the Trinity test site in New Mexico in July 1945.

explaining the properties and behavior of physical matter, this simple experiment crystallized a key point of the commission's investigative conclusions.

Feynman, who is remembered by students and peers as a man who was curious about everything and light-hearted in his dealings with others, died on February 15, 1988 of abdominal cancer. His legacy includes his innovative approach to problem solving and his ability and desire to make the study of complex science accessible to students and the general public alike. SEE ALSO PHYSICS; PROGRAMMING.

Ida M. Flynn

Bibliography

Chandler, David L. "Richard Feynman, Nobel Laureate in Physics; Probed Shuttle Disaster." *The Boston Globe*, 17 February, 1988.

Feynman, Richard P. *Surely You're Joking, Mr. Feynman!* New York: Bantam Books, 1985.

Lee, J. A. N. *Computer Pioneers*. Los Alamitos, CA: IEEE Computer Society Press, 1995.

Fiction, Computers in

Computers appeared in fiction centuries before they materialized as working devices, helping to inspire the creation of real computers and also warning of their dangers. The first fictional computer appears in Jonathan Swift's 1726 satire *Gulliver's Travels* and has all words of a language on "Bits" turned by wires and cranks. Scribes make hard copy by recording any sequence of words that seems to make sense, thus showing the absurdity of valuing machine-generated texts more than human thought.

Actual mechanical automata, common in the eighteenth century, suggested the possibility of lifelike creatures with mechanical brains. An influential fictional **automaton** of the early nineteenth century was Olympia, who slavishly dotes on her human lover in E. T. A. Hoffman's story "The Sandman" (1816). There is a direct connection between Olympia and the slavish women constructed by computer scientists to replace their uppity wives in Ira Levin's novel (1972) and film (1975) *The Stepford Wives*.

By the early twentieth century, the standard fictional computer was the brain of a robot, usually conceptualized as a metal man. The archetype was Tik-Tok, the "Thought-Creating, Perfect Talking Mechanical Man" equipped with "Improved Combination Steel Brains" in L. Frank Baum's *Ozma of Oz* (1907) and *Tik-Tok of Oz* (1914). When asked whether he is alive, Tik-Tok responds: "No, I am only a machine. But I can think and speak and act."

The most influential shaper of robot fiction was Isaac Asimov (1920–1992), who conceived of all-purpose mechanical beings with "positronic brains" governed by his Three Laws of Robotics, first articulated in his 1942 story "Runabout." According to these "Laws," all robots' brains were preprogrammed to guarantee that they would never harm humans, would obey orders, and would protect themselves, in that order.

The tendency to conceive of thinking machines as humanoid in appearance was dominant until the advent of the first actual electronic digital

automaton an object or being that has a behavior that can be modeled or explained completely by using automata theory

ROBOTIC MAYHEM

In the 1973 movie *Westworld*, vacationers arrive at a new futuristic amusement park where they can live out their fantasies as gunslingers. During their stay, guests live in a recreated Old West town and fight humanlike robots, dressed as outlaws, who are programmed to lose. Then, one day, the robots begin to malfunction and start killing their human challengers. In the end it is every man and robot for himself as the battle between human and machine is waged.

computers in the 1940s, huge machines that did not look at all like people. But some fiction did project computers based on the evolving automated mechanisms of industry. For example, George Parsons Lathrop's 1879 story "In the Deep of Time" imagines vast automated future factories run by a person at a keyboard. Jules Verne (1828–1905) prophesied, in his 1863 manuscript *Paris in the Twentieth Century*, giant "calculating machines" resembling huge pianos operated by a "keyboard" and hooked to "facsimile" machines; banks used the most advanced models of these computers to coordinate the activities of this hypercapitalist future.

To some, the evolution of machines seemed menacing. E. M. Forster's novella "The Machine Stops" (1909) imagines a future Earth run by a global computer that caters to every physical human need (except sex) through its automated appendages. Living in a mechanical environment, people rarely come into contact with each other because they communicate as individuals and chat groups through the machine's Internet.

By the 1930s, fiction about human overdependence on computers or the replacement of humans by intelligent machines was quite commonplace. Examples include: Edmond Hamilton's "The Metal Giants" (1926) featuring an atom-powered metal brain that constructs a rampaging army of 300-foot-tall robots; S. Fowler Wright's "Automata" (1929), in which machines take over all human activities and then eliminate our species; and Lionel Britton's 1930 play "The Brain" where an enormous mechanical brain ends up as the only form of intelligence left on a doomed Earth.

The computers created during World War II and its aftermath invited an avalanche of fictional computers. Because the supercomputers of the 1940s and 1950s were gigantic, their fictional descendants were commonly imagined as colossal masses of panels, buttons, switches, relays, and **vacuum tubes**.

Some fictional computers were global and malevolent. The computer in D. F. Jones's 1966 novel *Colossus* (filmed in 1970 as *Colossus—The Forbin Project*) takes over the world. In Harlan Ellison's 1967 story "I Have No Mouth, and I Must Scream," the American, Russian, and Chinese **supercomputers** waging thermonuclear war merge into a single conscious entity that destroys the entire human race except for five people it saves to torture forever.

Two memorable 1960s visions of computers came in masterpieces of film director Stanley Kubrick. In *Dr. Strangelove; Or How I Learned to Stop Worrying and Love the Bomb* (1964), civilization ends because a U.S. atomic attack activates a computerized Soviet doomsday weapon. The most memorable character in *2001: A Space Odyssey* (1968) is HAL, the spaceship's psychotic supercomputer.

As computers have become commonplace features of everyday life, their cultural representations have spread from science fiction into other literature and film. Indeed, fiction about normal existence, at least in industrial societies, could exclude computers no more than it could ignore automobiles, telephones, airplanes, and television. This has been especially true for movies. When functioning as more than background in non-science-fiction movies, computers are often presented as a menacing power of the all-seeing bureaucratic state, as in *Enemy of the State* (1998). The main character

vacuum tubes electronic devices constructed of sealed glass tubes containing metal elements in a vacuum; used to control electrical signals

supercomputers very high performance computers, usually comprised of many processors and used for modeling and simulation of complex phenomena, like meteorology

FANTASTIC VOYAGE

In 1966 movie audiences experienced a high tech medical approach to treating an injured man in the film *Fantastic Voyage*. The patient—an important scientist—is so severely injured that traditional medical methods cannot save him. So a team of doctors and scientists are shrunk to microscopic size and sent into the man's body to repair the damage. However, the team encounters unexpected danger when the scientist's immune system kicks in and tries to destroy the crew, thinking they represent a threat rather than a cure.

in *The Net* (1995), a lonely computer hacker, has her actual identity deleted from all records by the computers of government conspirators.

Computer games had become a familiar fictional topic by the early 1980s. After it was revealed that malfunctions of an Air Force supercomputer had, on numerous actual occasions, almost precipitated global thermonuclear war, the 1983 movie *WarGames* portrayed a teenaged boy who nearly causes the apocalypse by playing what he thinks is a game with an Air Force computer programmed for "Global Thermonuclear War."

The possibilities of organic computers are explored in fiction from the mid-1980s on. For example, in Greg Bear's *Blood Music* (1985), medical biochips accidentally convert DNA molecules into living computers that transmute the human species into the **progenitor** of "an intelligent plague" designed to reshape some of the fundamental principles of the universe. During the 1980s, computers also became central in the science fiction known as cyberpunk, especially the work of William Gibson, where action often takes place in cyberspace and some characters even metamorphose into beings who exist solely as cyber phenomena.

The concept of existing in cyberspace became widespread. In *Tron* (1982), one of the first commercial films to depend on computer animation, a video-game designer is sucked inside a computer, where he becomes a character in a computer game. In the *Max Headroom* movie (1985) and TV series (1987–1988), a reporter continues his career after being uploaded to become a computerized character. The 1999 hit movie *The Matrix* focused old and new images into a nightmare vision of a future where the only human function is supplying energy for computers, which have created a virtual reality where humans imagine they live real lives. SEE ALSO ASIMOV, ISAAC; ROBOTICS; SCIENTIFIC VISUALIZATION; WORLD WIDE WEB.

H. Bruce Franklin

Bibliography

Asimov, Isaac, Patricia S. Warrick, and Martin Greenberg, eds. *Machines That Think.* New York: Holt, Rinehart, and Winston, 1984.

Conklin, Groff, ed. *Science-Fiction Thinking Machines.* New York: Vanguard, 1954.

Porush, David. *The Soft Machine: Cybernetic Fiction.* New York: Methuen, 1985.

Warrick, Patricia. *The Cybernetic Imagination in Science Fiction.* Cambridge, MA: MIT Press, 1980.

Firewalls

In computer terms, a firewall is a boundary system that sits between two networks and enforces a security policy that determines what information is allowed to pass between them. The networks in question are typically a corporate, or private, **local area network (LAN)** and the public Internet. The security policy can be very simple, allowing most communication to pass through, or can be very complex, allowing only specifically designated traffic from specifically designated hosts to cross the boundary.

A firewall acts like a security guard that monitors all incoming and outgoing traffic and makes decisions about whether or not certain traffic is allowed. These decisions are based on the security policy. Under the simplest, least restrictive security policy, everything is allowed except that which is explicitly denied. Under the most complex, most restrictive policy, everything is denied except that which is explicitly allowed. What this means in practical terms is that a firewall may be relatively simple to configure and manage, or it can be very complex and time-consuming to maintain.

Firewalls can be implemented at the *network, transport,* or *application* layers of the **TCP/IP Protocol Suite**. The level of sophistication that a security policy can enforce depends on the layer at which the firewall is implemented. The TCP/IP protocol suite, sometimes referred to as the DoD (Department of Defense) model, divides the network into four layers. From the bottom up, they are the *physical* or *hardware* layer, which describes the way networks are connected together; the *network* layer, which defines the addresses of the network and its hosts (computers that are part of the network, whether workstations or servers) and manages the routing of packets between networks; the *transport* layer, which provides end-to-end communication between services and establishes the reliability of the connection between networks and hosts; and the *application* layer, which is responsible for the actual services provided by a network such as e-mail, authentication method, and file transfer capability.

Network Layer Firewalls

At the network layer, a firewall controls access by examining the addresses or ports that the data packet is coming from or going to. This is the most

local area network (LAN) a high-speed computer network that is designed for users who are located near each other

TCP/IP Protocol Suite Transmission Control Protocol/Internet Protocol; a range of functions that can be used to facilitate applications working on the Internet

ADDRESSES FOR SECURITY AND IDENTITY

A computer offering a service to the network is like an apartment building. The building itself has only one street address; in the case of the network server, that would be the IP address. But each apartment inside has a number that differentiates it from the others. In this analogy, each service offered by the server has a specific number, as each apartment does. In the case of the network server, that number is called a port ID.

A computer user's face is reflected on his computer screen as he waits to see if the "Code Red" Internet worm will strike his computer in 2001. Programmers study viruses, worms, and other invasive programs to create firewalls to protect computer systems from damage caused by hackers, including creators of malicious programs.

basic type of firewall and is called a *packet filtering firewall*. Not only can packets be filtered based on the IP address of a host, they can also be filtered based on the port number of the service desired. For example, a security policy for a packet filtering firewall might be configured to allow all incoming packets from any address only if they are destined for SMTP (Simple Mail Transfer Protocol) port 25, which is the service that processes e-mail. This would allow the network to accept incoming e-mail from anywhere on the Internet. But anyone trying to access the FTP (File Transfer Service) that operates on port 21 would be denied.

On the other hand, if it was determined that a network called "spam-me.com" was sending unwanted e-mail, the security association could be extended to deny any incoming packets from that specific network, while still allowing SMTP traffic from all other networks. At this layer, the firewall does no analysis of the data contained in the packets, nor does it provide any ability to hide the addresses of the internal systems on outgoing packets. A packet filtering firewall is the least effective of all the types of firewalls available.

Transport Layer Firewalls

For firewalls at the transport layer, the decisions made by the security policy can be more complex and therefore offer more security. Sometimes referred to as circuit level or proxy firewalls, these types of firewalls can verify the source and destination of the communicating devices before opening the connection. After that initial verification, it is assumed that all further communication is allowed until the session is closed.

With this type of firewall, the addresses for the internal or private network can be hidden behind the address of the device providing the proxy service. The result is that only the address of the firewall is made public, preventing unauthorized individuals or hosts from knowing too much about the private network. The hiding of the internal addresses is called Network Address Translation (NAT) and is the feature most commonly implemented on firewalls at this level. This type of firewall can also provide proxy port IDs for network services, so that on the private network, common service destination ports can be changed but the sources trying to communicate with those services are unaware of the change.

As an example, incoming e-mail destined for the firewall's IP address and Port 25 is transparently routed to a host with a different IP address that may even have the SMTP service assigned to a port other than Port 25. This effectively hides the e-mail server so intruders can not find it. But even if they do discover the address of the mail server, they would still need to discover the port number to which the service has moved. This makes the job of attacking the mail server much more difficult.

Application Layer Firewalls

Firewalls that operate at the application layer offer the most security of all possible configurations. Sometimes called Stateful Packet Filtering firewalls, these devices can perform an analysis on the contents of an individual data packet in order to do a more thorough job determining what is to be allowed or denied. For example, if the firewall allowed incoming **Hypertext Transfer Protocol (HTTP)** packets to be passed to the network, a malicious user could hide a Trojan Horse in a web page. A Trojan Horse is a malicious program hidden inside of a program that the network accepts as harmless. In this case, it could be an **applet** embedded in a web page. When the web page reaches its destination, the applet is released and causes harm to the network or host. A simple Packet Filtering Firewall would let the packet in because it appears to be on the allowed list but the Stateful Packet Filtering Firewall would look inside the packet and see that there is an embedded application and choose to deny that packet entry to the network.

Hypertext Transfer Protocol (HTTP) a simple connectionless communications protocol developed for the electronic transfer (serving) of HTML documents

applet a program component that requires extra support at run time from a browser or run-time environment in order to execute

Regardless of which layer the firewall functions at, the actual firewall can be either a software solution or a dedicated appliance. There is typically degradation in performance when running a firewall as software on a computer that runs other applications. Also, the firewall is typically exposed to the Internet so the computer and its other applications will be exposed as well. Dedicated appliances generally offer the most secure solution as a firewall, and provide the best performance. But they are more costly and can be more complicated to configure. Software or hardware, application, transport or network layer, no matter the type or level of implementation, a firewall is a necessary part of today's networking technology to provide a measure of security and privacy for data and the people who use it. SEE ALSO E-COMMERCE; SECURITY; SECURITY SOFTWARE; WORLD WIDE WEB.

Cynthia Tumilty Lazzaro

Bibliography

Blacharski, Dan. *Network Security in a Mixed Environment.* Foster City, CA: IDG Books Worldwide, Inc., 1998.

Strebe, Matthew, and Charles Perkins. *Firewalls 24seven*, 2nd ed. San Francisco: Sybex Books, 2002.

Internet Resources

Smith, Gary. "A Brief Taxonomy of Firewalls." SANS Institute. May 2001. <http://rr.sans.org/firewall/taxonomy.php>

Tyson, Jeff. "How Firewalls Work." *Marshall Brain's How Stuff Works.* <http://www.howstuffworks.com/firewall.htm>

FTP

File transfer protocol (FTP) is an Internet-standard application for transferring files. FTP was first developed in 1971 as part of the U.S. Department of Defense's ARPANET **protocols** and thus predates both **TCP** and **Internet Protocol (IP)**. It is currently documented for use with TCP in RFC 959.

The objectives of FTP are to promote file-sharing between different file systems, to promote use of remote computers across the Internet, and to allow effective file transfer. Although the World Wide Web became the major application for transferring files in 1995, FTP can still be used with most web browsers, and many organizations still maintain an FTP repository for public and/or restricted access. The convention for public FTP access is popularly referred to as anonymous FTP because the username is "anonymous."

FTP transmits copies of files between two computers. It allows users to upload and download file copies between local and remote computers. FTP is an elastic application that is sensitive but adjustable to traffic fluctuations over the Internet. User expectation of file transfer delay is not only proportional to file size but also sensitive to changes caused by Internet traffic load.

Protocol

FTP is an interactive, connection-oriented client/server protocol that relies on TCP for transferring files. After a user invokes an FTP application, he or she receives a prompt that signals the application is ready for user commands. A username and password are requested by the remote FTP server in order to determine ownership and limit file system access. After successful **authentication**, the local FTP client accepts user requests.

After receiving each request from the client, the remote FTP server responds by interacting with its local file system to execute each request as if it had been locally generated. Throughout each session, the remote FTP server maintains state information on each control connection and restricts file system access according to defined security permissions. Normally a single client can support multiple users and an FTP server can respond to multiple clients concurrently, but keeping track of each session can significantly constrain the total number of simultaneous sessions.

protocols agreed understanding for the sub-operations that make up transactions; usually found in the specification of inter-computer communications

TCP the acronym for Transmission Control Protocol; a fundamental protocol used in the networks that support the Internet (ARPANET)

Internet Protocol (IP) a method of organizing information transfer between computers; the IP was specifically designed to offer low-level support to TCP (Transmission Control Protocol)

authentication the act of ensuring that an object or entity is in fact what it is intended to be; verification of identity

Technique

Different FTP packages have different commands available, and even those with similar names may operate differently. To access an FTP site, users must know three pieces of information: the remote computer domain name, the file system path location of desired file(s) (folders/directories and/or sub-folders/subdirectories), and the name of the file(s) to be transmitted. The general command for initiating an FTP session to a specific remote computer is FTP *remote_computer_domain_name_or_IP_address*. If FTP is already executing, OPEN *remote_computer_domain_name_or_IP_address* can be used. This opens an FTP control connection dedicated to sending commands and receiving responses for the entire session.

A separate data transfer connection is needed for each file transfer. Two parallel connections are necessary: a first connection for control information, and a second connection for the actual data transfer. Although one control connection exists for an entire session, many data connections come and go. The local FTP client does not pass user keystrokes directly to the remote FTP server but instead interprets user input. Only if a user command requires interaction with the remote FTP server does the local FTP client send an FTP request to the remote FTP server. Because FTP uses a separate control connection, it is said to send its control information **out-of-band**, which provides extra functionality. For example, a client can abort a transfer while FTP is executing.

After a file transfer connection begins, files are transferred over the data connection without the overhead of any headers or control information at the application layer. When an end-of-file condition indicates a file transfer has finished, the control connection is used to signal completion and to accept new FTP commands. Because the server does not tell the client how much data to expect in advance, the file can grow during transfer. An FTP session between a local/remote pair of computers is closed with a BYE (CLOSE) command, and the FTP application is terminated with a QUIT command.

The two most common FTP commands are GET (or RETRieve) and PUT (or STORe). The GET command downloads, or copies, a file from a remote computer to a local computer. The FTP server locates the file that the user requested and uses TCP to send a copy of the file across the Internet to the client. As the client program receives data, it writes the data into a file on the user's local disk. The PUT command uploads a file from a local computer to a remote computer in a reversal of the GET command. Other FTP commands address the additional complexity introduced by file systems. For instance, data representation can be text (ASCII characters) or binary (nontext). FTP assumes that data transfers are text transfers unless the TYPE command is used to change the transfer mode to binary. FTP has the following commands for file system navigation: cd (move down a directory), cdup (move up a directory), dir (show contents of present directory), ls (show contents of present directory), and pwd (present working directory).

FTP accommodates diversity—it can be used to transfer a copy of a file between any arbitrary pair of computers. It hides the details of individual computer systems from users by providing a common set of services similar

FTP VS. TELNET

Telnet, a TCP application for remote login, was developed between 1969 and 1971 and was the first application developed for packet-switching. Telnet, like FTP, is also a message transfer protocol. A telnet connection is a TCP connection used to transmit data with interspersed (in-band) control information. Rather than being limited to transferring files, a telnet login session appears to the user as a virtual terminal directly attached to a remote computer. However, telnet does not directly provide file system interaction between local and remote computers.

out-of-band pertaining to elements or objects that are external to the limits of a certain local area network (LAN)

to those found on most operating systems, such as list directory, create new files, read an existing file, and delete files. SEE ALSO DISTANCE LEARNING; ELECTRONIC CAMPUS; TELECOMMUNICATIONS.

William J. Yurcik

Bibliography

Comer, Douglas E. *The Internet Book: Everything You Need to Know About Computer Networking and How the Internet Works*, 3rd ed. Upper Saddle River, NJ: Prentice Hall, 2000.

Internet Resources

Postel, Jon, and Joyce Reynolds. "File Transfer Protocol (FTP)." *IETF, RFC 959 (superceding RFC 765).* <http://www.ietf.org/rfc/rfc959.txt>

Global Positioning Systems

The Global Positioning System (GPS) is undoubtedly one of the most practical of all satellite projects. It provides navigation and location information to other satellites, commercial airliners, cruise ships, land surveyors, map makers, bicyclists, and hikers. GPS is based on a very simple theoretical principle that is complex to achieve practically.

The basic principle behind GPS is the measurement of distance—in this case, the distance between satellites and receivers on the ground. The satellites transmit a radio message. Their distance from the receiver can be easily calculated using the speed at which the message travels (the speed of light) and the time it takes to complete its travel. By comparing the time the signal was sent and received, the distance from the satellite can be calculated as: Distance = Speed (C) × Time Difference. If the satellite were directly overhead, the time for the signal to travel to the receiver would be 0.6 seconds. However, the real world's dynamic satellite orbits, ionospheric distortion of the radio signal, and inaccuracies in timing measurements complicate the realization of this simple principle.

GPS Components

In order to achieve accurate, real-world measurements, the GPS is composed of three segments: space, control, and user. The space segment consists of GPS satellites in orbit around the Earth. The control segment is made up of ground stations that monitor the satellites. The user segment is comprised of the receivers used to make the measurements.

Space Segment. The space segment is a constellation of twenty-four NAVigation Satellite Timing and Ranging (NAVSTAR) satellites orbiting the Earth in circular orbits at 20,278 kilometers (12,600 miles). The constellation is composed of six orbital planes, each tilted 55 degrees with respect to the equator. Each orbital plane has four satellites spaced 60 degrees apart so that a minimum of five satellites are viewable from any location on the Earth. Although the constellation is comprised of twenty-four satellites, there are currently twenty-nine satellites in orbit (five are spares). The most recent satellite was launched on January 30, 2001.

Each satellite transmits precise time, position, and orbit information. In order to minimize or eliminate ionospheric distortion, the satellites trans-

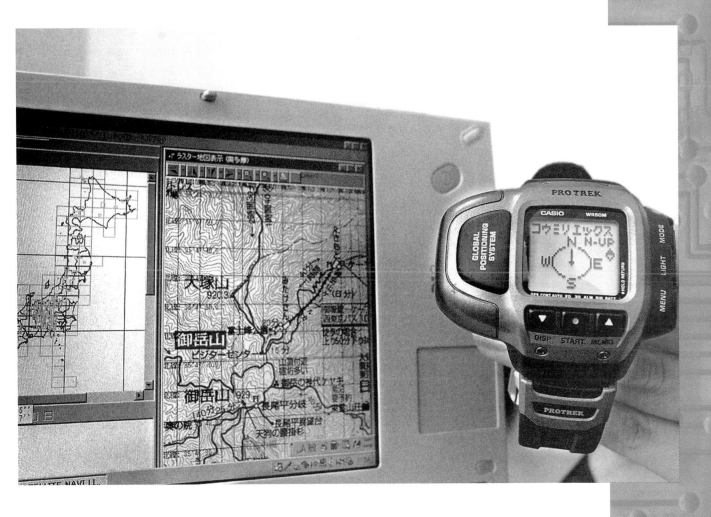

mit two signals with binary codes at different frequencies. The binary signals use a pseudo-random code (i.e., a binary signal with random noise-like properties), which obviates the need for great power or large antennas.

Control Segment.   The control segment, consisting of a master control station in Colorado Springs, Colorado, and four additional ground stations around the world, keeps the space segment operational and accurate. This segment, properly known as the Operational Control System (OCS), is a vital part of the GPS system but is basically invisible to the GPS user. The control segment constantly measures and calculates detailed orbits, monitors satellite clock accuracy, and assesses the health status of all satellites to determine if any repositioning is required. Updated satellite orbital **(ephemeris)** information, clock information, and routine maintenance commands are transmitted once or twice a day to the satellites from uplink antennas at three of the ground stations.

User Segment.   The user segment consists of users and their receivers. The GPS receiver contains a processor that calculates the location based on the satellite signals. The user does not transmit anything to the satellite and the satellite does not know the user is there. There is no limit to the number of users who can use the system at any time.

The GPS receiver detects and converts the signals transmitted by the satellites into useful information. It measures the time it takes for the signal to reach the receiver. This information is used together with satellite

In 2000 Casio Computer launched its GPS wristwatch, which weighs 84 grams (3 ounces). The watch is capable of receiving transmissions from twenty-seven GPS satellites.

ephemeris a record showing positions of astronomical objects and artificial satellites in a time ordered sequence

ionosphere a region of the upper atmosphere (above about 60,000 meters or 196,850 feet) where the air molecules are affected by the sun's radiation and influence electromagnetic wave propagation

ephemeris data to compute position in three dimensions. In a perfect world, spherical trigonometry would require only three measurements to locate a point in three-dimensional space. However, four or more measurements are used in the GPS to eliminate any timing error. Dimensions are computed in Earth-Centered, Earth-Fixed X, Y, and Z coordinates. Position in XYZ is converted in the receiver to geodetic latitude, longitude, and elevation.

It should be noted that GPS signals are very weak, subject to atmospheric distortion, subject to signal bounce and diffusion, and difficult to access in dense forests and dense urban environments.

GPS Measurements

A simple hand-held receiver can provide a measurement of location that is accurate to approximately 50 meters (164 feet). However, this is not accurate enough for many applications such as mapmaking and surveying. More complex, and expensive, receivers and alternative measurement techniques can be used to improve locational accuracies to less than 1 meter (3.3 feet), and even to the centimeter (0.4 inch) range.

One of the most common techniques for achieving improved accuracies is differential GPS measurements. This is a method of eliminating errors in a GPS receiver to make the output more accurate. This technique is based on the principle that most of the errors seen by GPS receivers in a local area are common errors such as clock deviation or changing radio propagation conditions in the **ionosphere**. In the differential approach, two receivers are employed, with one called a base station placed at a location for which the coordinates are known and accepted. The base station constantly monitors the difference between the known coordinates and the GPS-calculated coordinates to provide a measure of the error.

There are two ways of utilizing the base station data. In post processing, data at the base station and the surveying receiver, or rover, are recorded and processed together at a later time. In real-time processing, data are transmitted from the base station to the rover and the error is calculated in real time.

Many commercial, private, and government base stations have data that can be used in either post processing or real-time processing. Commercial satellite services also provide correction signals for real-time processing of data.

A discussion of GPS would not be complete without mentioning GLOSNASS, which is made up of twenty-four satellites, eight in each of three orbital planes. GLOSNASS was deployed by the Russian Federation and is a system that has much in common with the NAVSTAR GPS. SEE ALSO DATABASE MANAGEMENT SOFTWARE; GEOGRAPHIC INFORMATION SYSTEMS; TELECOMMUNICATIONS.

Robert D. Regan

Internet Resources

Dana, Peter H. *Global Positioning System Overview*. Department of Geography, University of Texas. <http://www.colorado.edu/geography/gcraft/notes/gps/gps.html>

GPS Elements. The Aerospace Corporation. <http://www.aero.org/publications/GPSPRIMER/GPSElements.html>

Time Services Department, U.S. Naval Observatory, Washington, D.C. *Current GPS Constellation*. <http://tycho.usno.navy.mil/gpscurr.html>

Global Surveillance

It has repeatedly been written that "information is power." Throughout history, the fate of nations has repeatedly hinged on the quality and timeliness of intelligence gathering and analysis. During a military or economic confrontation, knowing the capability of a friend or foe often means the difference between success and failure. Even during peacetime, global surveillance systems are utilized for verification purposes, preventing potentially dangerous conflicts.

The Space Age and Surveillance: A New Era

The onward march of technology has continued to drive intelligence gathering and surveillance. With the advent of the electronics and aerospace industries, the technology of intelligence gathering and analysis encountered significant change during the twentieth century. Declassified imagery and technology is now trickling down to private citizens and organizations outside the government.

The Space Age dawned in 1957, when the former Soviet Union launched Sputnik, the first artificial object to be placed in orbit around Earth. Since then, space has played a dominant role in global communication and surveillance. Space lets us see the planet in its entirety, or zoom in to examine select portions of the globe. Because of its numerous advantages, space has been accurately nicknamed the new "High Ground."

Space reconnaissance satellites are small, unmanned spacecraft fitted with cameras, sensors, radio receivers, and small rocket motors for maneuvering.

The extent of destruction at the Pentagon in Washington, D.C., after a hijacked plane slammed into it on September 11, 2001, is clearly visible from this satellite image. It was taken by Space Imaging's IKONOS satellite, which travels 28,164 kilometers (17,500 miles) per hour and at a distance of 681 kilometers (423 miles) above the Earth.

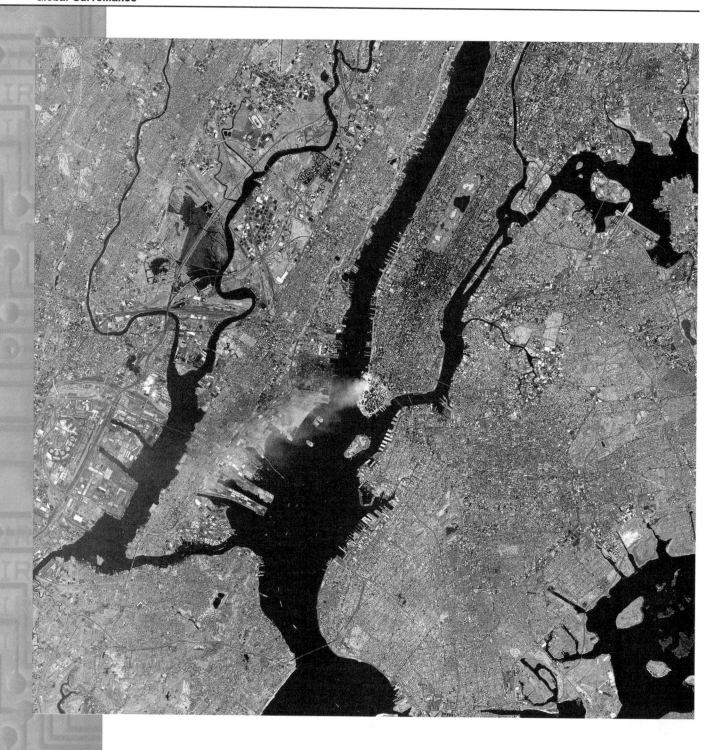

The devastation of New York City, following the collapse of the twin towers of the World Trade Center on September 11, 2001, is seen via the Landsat 7 satellite. This image was taken September 12, more than 24 hours after the tragedy.

They are generally launched into orbit atop a rocket booster or via one of the U.S. space shuttles. Once they are in orbit, they activate cameras, sensors, and receivers to begin their mission. Flight controllers on the ground can program the satellite to perform specific surveillance tasks, or to change the orbit to satisfy the requirements of the mission.

The National Reconnaissance Office (NRO) is responsible for designing, building, and flying space satellites for the U.S. Department of Defense (DoD) and the Central Intelligence Agency (CIA). The NRO was declassified in 1992, making 800,000 satellite reconnaissance photos available to the National Archives and placing them in the public domain.

Satellites are designed and built to accomplish specific missions including communications, weather forecasting, photographic reconnaissance, remote sensing, and signals intelligence. There are two basic types of satellites: those that perform their mission in Low Earth Orbit (LEO) and those that operate in the higher geo-stationary orbit (GSO). Low Earth Orbit is the region of space from about 322 to 805 kilometers (200 miles to 500 miles) above the Earth's surface. Geo-stationary orbit is much higher, and is located at an altitude of 36,210 kilometers (22,500 miles) above Earth. Satellites in GSO always remain over the same point on the ground, and take 24 hours for one orbit, while those in LEO move from horizon to horizon as they orbit once every 90 minutes. For this reason, satellites in geo-stationary orbit can be permanently "parked" over a city or other fixed point on the surface. Satellites in LEO do not stay over one point all the time, and are much closer to the planet. Satellites in LEO are able to photograph very detailed images of the surface, as well as closely intercept other forms of signal intelligence.

Geographic Information Systems

Maps have long been a vital tool for exploring the globe and its physical resources. Geographic Information Systems (GIS) have their roots in traditional map making, but they offer a much higher degree of analysis and efficiency for the user. GIS systems are electronic databases containing maps of the Earth's surface, and are capable of providing advanced imagery and other information. GIS systems receive data from aircraft or space satellites. Because the electronic maps can be searched and sorted to provide solutions to questions and to solve real world problems, they are useful in many different disciplines.

GIS systems can display data in a wide variety of formats according to user needs. Maps containing diverse data can be superimposed to show trends or to assist with prediction making. A time component can also be added to the information to determine future cause and effects. GIS systems can thus provide information for a diverse assortment of users: resource managers, development planners, environmentalists, and even emergency response personnel.

Recently declassified photographic intelligence from orbiting space satellites has been used to show the changes over time to the Antarctic ice flow. Using satellite imagery taken over multiple decades, scientists have been able to determine the patterns of ice flow on a continental scale. The declassified photographs have shown that the Antarctic ice is flowing at a different rate than had previously been assumed.

The Global Positioning System

The Global Positioning System (GPS) is an important technology that aids a wide variety of users. The system consists of a string of Earth-orbiting satellites that beam signals to ground-based receivers. The receivers translate the signals into exact time and location coordinates, showing the position of the user on the ground. The system was first developed for the U.S. military, but a civilian version is also available. The civilian GPS system is somewhat less accurate than the military version. Applications for GPS systems include navigation, scientific research, vehicle tracking, precision farming, map making, and the creation of travel aids for visually impaired persons.

CCTV Systems

Closed Circuit Television (CCTV) systems are used for a variety of security and surveillance-related applications. CCTV systems consist of video cameras that connect to video monitoring or recording equipment. These systems transmit images in real time to remote video monitors or recorders. Some CCTV systems are equipped with microphones, allowing them to transmit audio in addition to the video signal. CCTV systems are used by civil governments to oversee traffic and for security monitoring of public spaces. Home and business owners employ CCTV systems to monitor private property. CCTV systems can operate in a wireless mode, and can be monitored and controlled over standard computer networks or the Internet.

Surveillance and American Society

The power gained from global surveillance technology was once the private domain of rich and powerful governments, but now much of the technology belongs to private citizens as well. Consumer-oriented surveillance equipment empowers groups of users including automobile drivers, boaters, pilots, scientists, students, environmentalists, hobbyists, farmers, engineers, and persons with disabilities. Declassified reconnaissance photographs have helped environmentalists and scientists uncover the truth about the planet's ecology and biosphere. Surveillance technology permits the identification of threats from potential adversaries to prevent conflicts before they occur.

Civil libertarians claim that surveillance technology may impede personal privacy, and many are concerned that the technology may be turned on the civilian population by a tyrannical regime. However, members of the intelligence community maintain that surveillance technology is vital for national security.

In the classic novel *1984*, author George Orwell described a tyrannical government run by "Big Brother" that routinely spied on its citizens, forcing personal freedom to fall by the wayside, reminding some critics of the following statement by Benjamin Franklin on freedom: "They that can give up essential liberty to obtain a little temporary safety deserve neither liberty nor safety." Democratic societies such as the United States will continue to struggle to use surveillance technology to ensure domestic security while guarding against the possibility that such technology could be used to eliminate the very personal freedoms they wish to protect. SEE ALSO GEOGRAPHIC INFORMATION SYSTEMS; GLOBAL POSITIONING SYSTEMS; PRIVACY; SECURITY.

Joseph J. Lazzaro

Bibliography

Bamford, James. *The Puzzle Palace*. New York: Penguin Books, 1983.

Clarke, Arthur C. "Extra-terrestrial Relays." *Wireless World*, October (1945): 305–308.

Orwell, George. *1984*. New York: New American Library Classics, 1990.

Internet Resources

Central Intelligence Agency. <http://www.cia.gov>

National Reconnaissance Office. <http://www.nro.gov>

National Security Agency. <http://www.nsa.gov>

Glushkov, Victor M.

Soviet Mathematician and Computer Engineer
1923–1982

Victor M. Glushkov was a pioneer in **cybernetics**, computer engineering, and mathematics. He initially made his reputation as the first mathematician to solve the fifth generalized problem of Hilbert but is better known as the force behind the U.S.S.R.'s Institute of Cybernetics that was of primary importance to the application of computers in the Soviet Union. Glushkov is a holder of the Silver-Core award of the International Federation for Information Processing (IFIP). He issued more than 800 papers including thirty monographs, many of which have been translated into other languages.

Glushkov was born on August 24, 1923, in Rostov on the river Don. He attended and graduated from Rostov University (1947 to 1948) and Novocherkassk Polytechnic Institute (1943 to 1948). He started his career as a teacher at the Ural Timber-Technology Institute (Sverdlovsk) while performing research under two leading Soviet algebraists, S. N. Chernikov and A. S. Kurosh. In 1955 he received his Ph.D. from Moscow State University with a dissertation titled "Topological Locally Nilpotent Group." In 1956 Victor went to Kiev to become the head of the Computer Engineering Laboratory of the Institute of Mathematics of the National Academy of Sciences that became the basis for the Computer Center of the Academy of Sciences of Ukraine in 1957.

In 1961 the Computing Center became the Institute of Cybernetics of the Ukrainian Academy of Sciences and Glushkov became its director. His tenure lasted until his death. Under the leadership of Glushkov, the institute gained an international reputation for computer science research and the training of scientists (100 professors and 600 doctors of science under Glushkov). The year 1962 marked the release of Glushkov's classic book, *Synthesis of Computing Automata*, which he followed with *Introduction to Cybernetics* in 1964. Ten years later, Glushkov edited a compilation of all leading Soviet cybernetic scientists in the notable *Encyclopedia of Cybernetics*. When he died on January 30, 1982, after a long illness, he left behind a foundation that would eventually lead to the "informatization of Soviet society."

A scientist with a wide range of interests and talents, he was elected in 1961 as a member of the Ukrainian Academy of Sciences, and in 1962 he became the vice president of the same organization. In 1964 Glushkov was honored with the Lenin Prize for a series of contributions on discrete **automata theory** and was elected a member of the Academy of Science of the U.S.S.R. In 1966 a team of designers headed by Glushkov was awarded the first state prize for the development of principles for the construction of small computers incorporating structural high-level languages for engineering calculations. In 1969, for achievements in the advancement of science and training of scientists, Glushkov was granted the title of "Hero of Socialist Labor," and the Institute of Cybernetics was awarded the Order of Lenin. In 1977 Glushkov and colleagues were awarded the U.S.S.R. State Prize for a series of contributions to the methods of computer-aided design of computers.

cybernetics a unified approach to understanding the behavior of machines and animals developed by Norbert Wiener (1894-1964)

automata theory the analytical (mathematical) treatment and study of automated systems

---

INSTITUTE OF CYBERNETICS

The Institute of Cybernetics, under the direction of Glushkov, was the leading organization in the field. Journals published by the Institute of Cybernetics and started under Glushkov's leadership have had consistently high ratings among computer scientists. Titles include *Automatica, Cybernetics* (1965, called *Cybernetics and Systems Analysis* from 1991), and *UsiM* (1972).

pattern recognition a process used by some artificial-intelligence systems to identify a variety of patterns, including visual patterns, information patterns buried in a noisy signal, and word patterns imbedded in text

robotic pertaining to the field of robotics, which is the science and engineering of building electromechanical machines to replace human laborers

When computer science was a young discipline, Glushkov envisioned the use of a computer as more than just a calculator. He visualized the simulation of "brain-like" structures, evolutionary computing, automatic theorem proving, **pattern recognition**, and the first **robotic** systems. He developed technologies for the design and construction of computer components, including the joint design of computer hardware and software.

Glushkov was the first to formulate and document the concepts of computer design on the basis of automated algebraic models. He designed several special programming languages, such as ANALYTIC, for the translation of algebraic expressions on a computer. The personal computer MIR, a predecessor of present-day personal computers, was developed and mass produced under Glushkov. He is also associated with the publication of many books, journals, and scientific papers on cybernetics and computer science. The latter years of Glushkov's life were dominated by work on the Statewide Automated System or Data Collection and Processing (OGAS), which was designed to automate the management of the state economy. SEE ALSO CYBERNETICS.

William J. Yurcik

Bibliography

Lee, J. A. N., ed. *International Biographical Dictionary of Computer Pioneers.* Chicago: Fitzroy Dearborn Publishers, 1995.

Zemanek, Heinz. "Eloge: Victor Mikhaylovich Glushkov." *IEEE Annals of the History of Computing* 4, no. 2 (1982): 100–101.

Internet Resources

Glushkov Institute of Cybernetics. <http://www.icyb.kiev.ua/>

Guru

Guru is a Hindi word that refers to a teacher or a religious and spiritual guide. Similarly, modern usage of the word in the West usually refers to a wise person—maybe a teacher—with knowledge and expertise about a particular subject, and its usage was made common first in computer circles. Gurus are typically people who are easy to get in touch with and are interested in sharing their knowledge with others.

One of the early gurus in computer science was Jackson Granholm, who in 1962 coined the term "kludge." This word initially referred to a poorly planned combination of parts put together while designing a computer. Therefore, a kludge is a machine that contains several features that are annoying to users and, in retrospect, are aspects that the designer wishes had been done differently. The term now encompasses programs, documentation, and even computing centers, so that the new definition describes systems that were hastily planned, patched together, and have proven themselves to be unreliable.

Another early computer guru was H. R. J. Grosch, who, while working for the IBM Corporation in the 1950s, introduced Grosch's Law, which states that organizations can reduce the overall cost of their hardware if they strengthen their computing power because this will reduce the cost of performing computing functions. This means that the more powerful a com-

Linus Torvalds (1970–) envisioned a freely available operating system while a student in Finland. Linux made him a cult hero.

puter system is, the lower its costs will be per unit of performance. So, if one spends twice as much on a new computer, one would anticipate its performance to be four times greater.

A third early guru was Gordon Moore, former chairman of the board of Intel, and the person who formulated Moore's Law in 1965 shortly after patenting the **integrated circuit**. His hypothesis, which states that transistor densities on a single chip will double every eighteen months, has proven to be very accurate over the years. Moore's Law has had an impact on costs and overall system performance, as well as in increased microprocessor speeds.

Some current computer gurus include:

- Peter J. Denning. His work on virtual memory systems helped make virtual memory a permanent part of modern operating systems.

- James Gosling, creator of Java and developer of Sun's NeWS windowing system. He was also the principal investigator on the Andrew project while earning his Ph.D. in computer science from Carnegie Mellon University.

- Tim Berners-Lee, originator of the World Wide Web. Together with colleagues, he developed **Hypertext Markup Language (HTML)**, the language used for web documents; **Hypertext Transfer Protocol (HTTP)**; and the **Uniform Resource Locator (URL)** used to find anything on the web.

- Linus Torvalds. He developed Linux, an operating system originally designed to maximize the capabilities of the Intel 80386 microprocessor. Later, Linux became widely adopted in industry and educational markets around the world because of its power and flexibility.

More recently, the word "guru" has appeared in numerous web sites covering a wide range of topics, from computer-related sites to supermarket shopping. A recent search for the word brought out 190 different web sites, and the numbers are growing daily. Can all these sites be populated with knowledgeable people who are interested in sharing their knowledge? Are they manned by people who claim to be experts but are not? How is one to know for sure? While doing online research, one has to be wise and take the time to validate the sources of information. SEE ALSO Hacking; Invasive Programs; Procedural Languages; Programming; Security.

Ida M. Flynn

Bibliography

Lee, J. A. N. *Computer Pioneers*. Los Alamitos, CA: IEEE Computer Society Press, 1995.

Hackers

Hacking emerged with the invention of computers. The term "hacker" has a variety of definitions. Among computer professionals, it is applied to someone who is proficient at software programming, debugging systems, or identifying vulnerabilities in a given computer, software application, or computer network. These are valuable skills for computer programmers and technicians.

GURU OR WIZARD?

Gurus are not necessarily programmers, and so, as a rule, they are not considered to be "wizards." However, gurus usually are significant users of specific operating systems, user interfaces, or application software.

---

integrated circuit a circuit with the transistors, resistors, and other circuit elements etched into the surface of a single chip of semiconducting material, usually silicon

Hypertext Markup Language (HTML) an encoding scheme for text data that uses special tags in the text to signify properties to the viewing program (browser) like links to other documents or document parts

Hypertext Transfer Protocol (HTTP) a simple connectionless communications protocol developed for the electronic transfer (serving) of HTML documents

Uniform Resource Locator (URL) a reference to a document or a document container using the Hypertext Transfer Protocol (HTTP); consists of a hostname and path to the document

Considered the world's most notorious hacker, Kevin Mitnick signed a plea agreement in 1999 that confirmed his involvement in breaking into the computer systems of major corporations, including Motorola and Sun Microsystems. He eluded authorities for several years before his arrest in 1995. Held without bail for nearly five years, Mitnick was eventually released from prison in January of 2000. The terms of his parole stipulate that he cannot use a computer until January of 2003. Mitnick's story is detailed in several books and on the Internet at <www.kevinmitnick.com>.

However "hacker" has taken on a negative meaning among the public and in the media. Outside the computer industry, the term is now generally used to describe a person with these skills who decides to apply them toward a damaging or illegal purpose.

The United States has two definitions of illegal hacking. First of all, it is illegal to have in one's possession the password to a computer or network without permission to possess that password. Secondly, it is a felony to "enter" a computer or network system without permission. If damage is caused in that system, the hacker is liable for additional legal charges.

The people who hack and the hacker organizations to which they may belong are as varied as their goals. Some hackers break into computer systems for bragging rights, causing no intentional damage. Others hack for political gain or protest. Still others release devastating codes called viruses, worms, or **Trojan horses**. Many of these codes self-replicate and "infect" other computers, sometimes causing billions of dollars in damage worldwide. Hackers also have a variety of terms to describe themselves and classify what they do.

Types of Hackers

"Phreakers" are hackers who specialize in telephone networks. This was the first kind of hacker, as telephones used one of the first automated systems. Early phreakers developed a device called a Blue Box to use when placing free telephone calls, sometimes using several telephone lines and telephone numbers around the world. With the emergence of analog cellular phones, phreakers could hack literally from thin air. When a victim used his or her cell phone, phreakers intercepted the message along with the caller's identification code. The phreakers then supplied additional cell phones with the stolen identification code. The subsequent telephone bills went to the surprised victim. Digital cell phones make this practice impossible for phreakers.

Those who lack skills for hacking but attempt to access technology or information belonging to others are called "Wannabes" or "Script Kiddies." Some experts say most of the world's hackers fall into this category. "Elite" hackers have proven their hacking abilities. "Black Hat" hackers reserve their skills for their own illegal profit.

"White Hat" hackers work legally. "Ethical" hackers are hired to break into computer networks to help improve security. In the past, many considered hiring ethical hackers to be a high-risk technique for companies, calling for strict supervision and solid insurance policies. By 2002, however, it was often considered a vital part of computer security.

Another category of hackers, "Warez Dudez," target software. They copy, or "pirate," existing software, removing copy-preventing safeguards if necessary. An estimated 50 percent of software worldwide is illegally manufactured. Many times, hackers install their own viruses on pirated software before distribution.

Finally, criminal hackers, called "Crackers," use hacking to complement their other illegal activities.

Consequences of Hacking

As computer technology becomes more complex and intricate, hackers need more specialized knowledge, experience, equipment, and money. The computers that hackers target do too.

With the growing dependence upon computer information systems and automation, many in the hacking world are increasingly drawn to corporate networks to engage in corporate espionage. In one study, 85 percent of businesses surveyed admitted that hackers had penetrated their computer

Trojan horses potentially destructive computer programs that masquerade as something benign; named after the wooden horse employed by the Acheans to conquer Troy

security systems during the previous year, causing damage measured in hundreds of millions of dollars. Many times these businesses bear the cost quietly without prosecuting the hacker for fear of causing customer loss of confidence. However, they have the option of suing for damages in civil court without the publicity inherent in taking action in the criminal court system. Many do.

Successful hacking depends upon experience and knowledge. Because of this, experts warn that devastating damage is increasingly likely to be caused by disgruntled and former employees. In many high-tech firms, dismissed employees are immediately escorted from the building upon termination and their computer system access codes are promptly changed. Companies that spend few, if any, resources to strengthen computer security, such as small businesses, and those lax about keeping discharged employees away from their business computer systems are vulnerable.

According to the Federal Bureau of Investigation (FBI), at least 122 countries employ hackers to engage in international espionage. Experts speculate that the United States also uses hackers to advance its knowledge of other countries. Various branches of the U.S. government devote increasing portions of their budgets to defend against hackers; national security concerns include terrorist hackers.

Any networked or online computer can be the target of hackers. Without adequate security measures, any computerized network—including those that power Wall Street, banks and credit institutions, health institutions, educational institutions, air traffic control networks, power supply grids, traffic light systems, or municipal water supply systems—can become a prime target for domestic or international hackers. SEE ALSO GURU; HACKING; PRIVACY; SECURITY; WORLD WIDE WEB.

Mary McIver Puthawala

Bibliography

Freedman, David H., and Charles C. Mann. *At Large: The Strange Case of the World's Biggest Internet Invasion.* New York: Simon and Schuster, 1997.

Schwartau, Winn. *CyberShock: Surviving Hackers, Phreakers, Identity Thieves, Internet Terrorist and Weapons of Mass Disruption.* New York: Thunder Mouth Press, 2000.

Home Entertainment

Home entertainment is the application of technology and the arts for private amusement and enjoyment. The proliferation of the microprocessor and digital media has produced a wide variety of innovative technologies for home entertainment. Digital entertainment systems now found in many homes include portable compact disc (CD) players for listening to music, digital versatile disc (DVD) players for movies and music videos, digital cameras, and game consoles.

People also increasingly use personal computers networked to the Internet for games and chats. Electronic "toys" such as the Sony AIBO robotic dog, high definition television (HDTV), music keyboards and synthesizers, and digital video recorders such as the Philips TiVo are becoming increasingly popular sources of home entertainment as well.

Early Entertainment

The revolution in home entertainment technologies is a relatively new phenomenon. For centuries, most entertainment was almost exclusively a luxury for the wealthy or conducted in public. A major expansion of the traditional public arts such as plays and development of new forms of art such as opera followed the Renaissance period in Europe (c. 1350–1600). Prior to the development of electricity, the most advanced technology used in performances was musical instruments such as the pipe organ and the piano (from which the modern concept of the computerized electronic keyboard is derived).

The use of modern technology for home entertainment is a product of the Industrial Revolution (c. 1730–1850) and extends back to the nineteenth century with the mass production of mechanical music boxes. These often-elaborate devices presaged the use of the computer as an entertainment component, with the use of punched holes in metal to program musical notes. Following mechanical music boxes, Hollerith cards, which were first used

Computers can even offer companionship as evidenced in this robot dog. Running a 16-bit central processing unit, it is able to learn simple words like a human infant.

punched card a paper card with punched holes which give instructions to a computer in order to encode program instructions and data; now obsolete

vacuum tube an electronic device constructed of a sealed glass tube containing metal elements in a vacuum; used to control electrical signals

transistor a contraction of TRANSfer resISTOR; semiconductor device, invented by John Bardeen, Walter Brattain, and William Shockley, which has three terminals; can be used for switching and amplifying electrical signals

by the U.S. Census in 1890, were invented and were the precursor to the IBM **punched card**.

Advent of Electricity

With the growth of the middle class in Europe and the United States beginning in the late 1800s, and the concurrent invention of electrical devices such as motors, new forms of entertainment for the home were developed. For example, Thomas A. Edison (1847–1931) was a prolific inventor of entertainment systems such as the phonograph and the first movie projection system.

However, the first electronic system for home entertainment was the radio. Invented in 1895 by Guglielmo Marconi (1874–1937), the radio became a mass medium through the efforts of David Sarnoff at RCA. The first musical broadcast was from the stage of the Metropolitan Opera in 1910. The key component of the radio—a **vacuum tube** amplifier—spurred the creation of the first digital computers. For example, the ENIAC (Electronic Numerical Integrator and Analyzer Computer) developed by the University of Pennsylvania during World War II was composed of thousands of vacuum tubes. Similarly, the **transistor**, invented at Bell Laboratories, saw its first application in small AM radios. It was later incorporated into computers.

Television was an extension of broadcast radio technology. Like radio and the phonograph, television is now being totally transformed by the digital era. In fact, high definition televisions (HDTVs) are essentially personal computers that are capable of receiving digital broadcasts.

Video Games and Beyond

Following television, the invention of the video game in the early 1970s was the next great home entertainment system and the beginning of the digital era in the home. Game consoles were, in effect, the first home computers. Founded by Nolan Bushnell, Atari produced the first hit video game in 1972. The game, Pong, used simple black and white graphics to represent a virtual Ping Pong (or table tennis) game. Atari also created the first console system for the home in 1975.

Game consoles rapidly grew more sophisticated and popular with the introduction of 2-dimensional and 3-dimensional graphics, digital sound, and a variety of input devices such as joysticks and game pads. Computer games also advanced modern graphics techniques such as texturing. Later, more sophisticated game consoles included Nintendo 64 (developed with computer manufacturer SGI) and the Sega Dreamcast. None has been as successful as the Sony Playstation I, of which more than 90 million have been sold since the product's introduction in 1995. The Playstation I took advantage of a digital storage medium, the compact disc (CD), which has become the standard for music recording.

The relationship between entertainment and computing technologies is such that large-scale production tends to drive down the cost of manufacturing new systems and spur further advances. The convergence of entertainment with digital technology has given rise to many exciting possibilities, including the ability to obtain digital music in the form of the Fraunhofer-developed MPEG Layer 3 (or MP3) and streaming video on the World Wide Web. In fact, many people use their personal computers for entertainment at home and work. It also has established the development of new consumer devices such as MP3 players and writeable CD and DVD players for recording music. The Philips TiVo television recorder is essentially a computer that records video to a hard disk.

This new ability to make accurate reproductions of digital media has caused major controversies in copyright law and rules regarding **encryption** and stenographic techniques such as **digital watermarks**. SEE ALSO BELL LABS; COMPUTER VISION; COPYRIGHT; GAME CONTROLLERS; GAMES; GRAPHIC DEVICES; HOLLERITH, HERMAN; HOME SYSTEM SOFTWARE; MARCONI, GUGLIELMO; ROBOTICS; VACUUM TUBES.

Michael R. Macedonia

encryption also known as encoding; a mathematical process that disguises the content of messages transmitted

digital watermarks special data structures permanently embedded into a program or other file type, which contain information about the author and the program

Bibliography

Macedonia, Michael R. "Why Digital Entertainment Drives the Need for Speed." *IEEE Computer* 33, no. 2 (2000): 124–127.

Herz, J. C. *Joystick Nation: How Computer Games Ate Our Quarters, Won Our Hearts, and Rewired Our Minds.* Boston: Little, Brown, 1997.

Human Factors: User Interfaces

Every computer system has an interface that consists of software and hardware, which are needed for users interacting with the system. User interfaces allow people to input commands to the computer, read the computer's output, structure information, and complete certain tasks that may be related to business, education, government, medical, military, industrial, scientific, or home environments. Different types of interfaces allow users to perform a multitude of tasks on a computer, such as creating documents, searching the Internet, or sending and receiving e-mail messages. A user interface may enable a user to enter, locate, manipulate, analyze, monitor, or retrieve information.

Effective user interfaces are extremely important. Many users find computer interfaces difficult to use, and a user's ability to perform tasks on a computer is directly related to the effectiveness of the computer interface. Human-computer interactions should be structured and presented to ease learning, minimize errors, and facilitate use. A poorly designed interface display may lead to user mistakes, non-use of the computer system, and low user satisfaction. In general, interface design needs to answer questions about when, what, and how a user completes a task. User interface designers consider issues such as human memory, color perception, and task complexity to define the display requirements for a computer interface.

Computer games, such as Nintendo and Red Alert, are very popular with people of all ages. Popular computer games include sophisticated interfaces using multimedia effects such as color and sound. Many schools use software programs in the classroom to teach skills and make lessons more interesting for students. The importance of a well-designed user interface is more important than ever as the number of people using computer systems has dramatically increased over the last decade, fueled by the dramatic increase of the Internet on home computers.

REALISM IN MULTIMEDIA

Some computer games use multimedia presentations that are so realistic, they are used to simulate the real experience. Take Microsoft's Flight Simulator game, for example. It has been used in pilot training programs at flight schools. The game helps students learn how to conduct flight safety checks as well as how to operate navigational tools. A new edition of the game underwent alterations, however, after the terrorist attack on New York City's World Trade Center in 2001. Microsoft removed images of the WTC from its simulator game.

Computer games, such as Red Alert 2, feature elaborate interfaces that allow players to engage in real-time strategy (RTS) situations, complete with colorful graphics and sound. In Red Alert 2, for example, players participate in a massive battle between the United States and Soviet Union. The game's user-friendly interface allows players to perform multiple actions (e.g., deploying troops, building barracks, defending positions) simultaneously, greatly speeding the pace of the game.

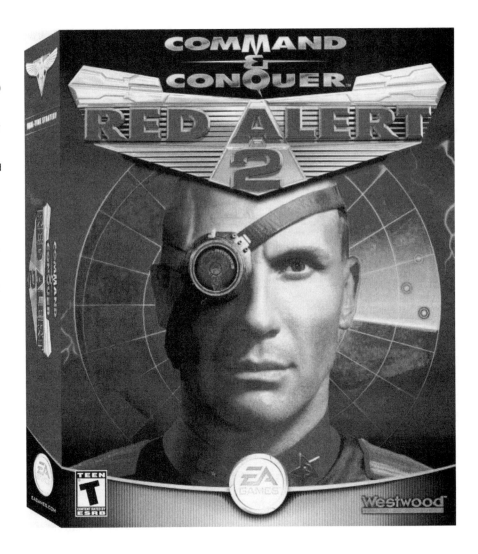

Types of Displays

Humans interact with different computer interface displays, such as command line interfaces, menus, natural language, form-fill and spreadsheets, WIMP (windows, icons, menus, and pointers) interfaces, and three-dimensional interfaces. Displays vary in format, type, size, color, and content. Users find color displays attractive, which makes computer software easier to use.

Command line interfaces allow users to give instructions to the computer using commands and keywords. Most online search engines use command line interfaces. Menu-driven interfaces provide the user with a set of options from which to choose. For example, an automated teller machine (ATM) displays a list of options that allow users to deposit and withdraw money and check account balances. Natural language interfaces allow users to communicate with the computer through spoken or written sentences. For example, the Internet search engine "Ask Jeeves" allows users to ask questions when searching for information.

Fill-in forms or spreadsheets present users with a form to complete with numbers or words. For example, to book an airline ticket via the Travelocity web site, a user must complete a form by providing destination and travel details. WIMP interfaces combine various display types and allow users to complete multiple tasks at the same time, click on icons (or pictures), and use their mouse as a pointer. For example, Microsoft Windows allows users to use many software programs at the same time.

Three-dimensional (3D) interfaces are used in **virtual reality (VR)**. For example, computer games often use 3D interfaces and helmet-mounted displays. As the power of personal computer systems increases, the use of 3D interfaces becomes more practical. New types of heads-up displays can project information or images on the windscreen of a car or airplane.

virtual reality (VR) the use of elaborate input/output devices to create the illusion that the user is in a different environment

Agents, Direct Manipulation

Computer interfaces may include software agents that perform tasks for users. Agents may perform tasks directly specified by a user, or watch and learn from a user's actions and perform tasks without the user present. For example, an e-mail agent may filter a user's e-mail. Direct manipulation means that specific tasks are represented as pictures to make the task easier for the interface user. For example, to print a document in the word processing package Word, the user can click on a printer graphic to initiate printing.

Software

Software is the sequence of instructions in one or more programming languages or software tools that enable a computer application to automate a task. Computing languages, such as C++ or Java, are used by software engineers to create different types of interfaces with different features, depending on the task for which the interface was designed. Each software program provides users with an interface that allows them to complete a particular task or set of tasks. For example, a word processing interface that allows users to create and modify documents has different features than a web search engine interface. Better software design and software tutorials can make computer interfaces easier to use.

Hardware

Hardware refers to the type of computer used to interact with a software program such as a micro or personal computer. Computer hardware includes the keyboard, mouse, joysticks, and other devices that allow the user to interact with the computer system. New technologies such as speech input, touch screens, and 3D displays increase interface usability. Computers are also getting smaller and more powerful. Portable wireless computers allow users to access the Internet from any location at anytime.

The hardware used in any given system has a significant impact on the user interface that can be designed. For example, the limited screen resolution and processing power available on a wireless telephone limits its ability to perform the intensive 3D graphics that are available on a typical home computer. Improved computer hardware and software can allow users to complete tasks more quickly and effectively, reduce user errors, and minimize the training time and skill needed to use a computer. Specially designed user interfaces are helping younger, blind, elderly, and disabled people use computers. Better interface designs can continue to reduce the potential health risks of prolonged computer use. The interfaces of the future will take users into a 3-dimensional world of virtual reality sight, sound, smell, and touch. SEE ALSO ASSISTIVE COMPUTER TECHNOLOGY FOR PERSONS WITH DISABILITIES; ERGONOMICS; GRAPHIC DEVICES; INTERACTIVE SYSTEMS.

Amanda Spink

Bibliography

Dix, Alan, Janet Findlay, Gregory Abowd, and Russell Beale. *Human-Computer Interaction*, 2nd ed. London: Prentice Hall, 1997.

Neilsen, Jakob. *Designing Web Usability*. Indianapolis: New Riders Publishing, 2000.

Shneiderman, Ben. *Designing the User Interface: Strategies for Effective Human-Computer Interaction*. Reading, MA: Addison Wesley Longman, 1998.

Information Access

Information access is the ability to identify, retrieve, and use information effectively. Access to information is vital to social, political, and economic advancement. Traditionally, information has been disseminated in a variety of formats that have been widely accessible, often through public libraries. Many individuals also relied on other people and the media for information. However, advances in computer technology have revolutionized information access, making vast stores of business, education, health, government, and entertainment information accessible on the World Wide Web. Yet, despite technology's dramatic impact on the extent and availability of digital information, many people do not have access to these resources.

The Digital Divide

The gap between those who have technological access, and those who do not, is known as the "digital divide." It is attributed to constraints imposed by educational attainment, socioeconomic status, gender, age, disability, and geography as well as limits experienced by particular ethnic and racial groups. The disparity between the digital information "haves" and "have-nots" is reflected in access, content, literacy, and training, and remains a persistent international problem. Resolution of inequitable access is particularly important for developing nations because they cannot build and maintain economic independence without adequate information.

In the United States, the October 2000 Department of Commerce document, "Falling Through the Net: Toward Digital Inclusion," reported increases overall in Internet access and use. However, the digital divide continues in some sectors of the American population, particularly among blacks, Hispanics, and Native Americans, individuals with disabilities, people fifty years of age or older, and single-parent households. For many, the cost of computer ownership and **Internet Service Provider (ISP)** connections creates significant barriers and high-speed, broadband connections via cable, **digital subscriber line (DSL)**, or satellite remain beyond reach. Geography is also a difficult constraint with many rural areas still not wired for Internet access. In some rural communities, the only access method is through large ISPs that do not have local access telephone numbers, making the cost of using the Internet prohibitive.

Effective use of information content requires a complex set of competencies. With the uneven quality of web resources, as well as the absence of a consistent organizational structure, locating relevant and reliable information can be difficult and time-consuming. Search and meta-search engines as well as hierarchical subject indexes and portals were developed to improve access to specific information. Virtual reference desks, some with

Internet Service Provider (ISP) a commercial enterprise which offers paying subscribers access to the Internet (usually via modem) for a fee

digital subscriber line (DSL) a technology that permits high speed voice and data communications over public telephone networks; it requires the use of a DSL modem

access to experts through AskA services, were opened. However, search precision remains problematic because, even when used in combination, search engines neither examine the entire web nor return all types of files equally.

Most information on the Internet is in English and its use requires basic reading proficiency. This narrow orientation limits the accessibility of web resources for many in a multilingual world as well as for the illiterate and readers with limited skills. Optimal use of the Internet also requires competency in navigation and searching; without appropriate instruction, these skills can be difficult to master. Adequate training is crucial because even the most poorly constructed search will generally produce some results. The challenge then is not only connecting to the Internet or retrieving information, but also effectively evaluating the results.

The Internet makes information easily accessible around the globe. At an e-Expo in 2000 in Thailand, a Buddhist monk and a teenager test out free Internet stations.

Modes of Access

Most people connect to the Internet from home, work, or public access sites like libraries, schools, and community centers using personal computers, e-mail stations, interactive digital televisions, game stations, or web kiosks. However, even more flexible options are beginning to emerge, including web-enabled cellular telephones and handheld **personal digital assistants (PDAs)**. Because cost is a barrier to access for many, the increasing affordability and wider distribution of cell phones and PDAs may help bridge the digital divide.

personal digital assistants (PDAs) small scale hand-held computers that can be used in place of diaries and appointment books

Applications

The need for improved access has led to the development and refinement of applications. Web browsers, like Netscape and Microsoft Explorer, use graphical interfaces with embedded hyperlinks for navigation, making the underlying commands transparent to the user. With these applications, the Internet became more accessible and it emerged as a global information source. Scholarly, scientific, and everyday research was transformed by access to full-text documents as well as by the digitization of primary sources. Text translation applications minimized language barriers and text-to-speech technology improved access for the visually impaired. Educational opportunities were extended to new audiences and business access to management information and market intelligence was improved.

Asynchronous applications, like e-mail, bulletin boards, and listservs as well as real-time or synchronous applications, like instant messaging, chat rooms, and video conferencing, altered communication patterns and changed the flow of information substantially. The gap between limited local information and highly specialized but distant resources was dramatically narrowed, particularly in agriculture and healthcare. With geographical information systems (GIS), maps could be individualized and produced on demand. Combining **XML** applications with **Global Positioning Systems (GPS)** led to the development of virtual advisors with a voice interface that provides drivers with personalized traffic and news reports, e-mail, stock market, and sports news. Intelligent agents and push technology mine and filter user-specified data from the web and push it out directly to desktops. Driven by these still-evolving applications, the web has become crucial to the flow of information.

Impact on Society

Digital information access has affected virtually every aspect of modern life by opening new communication pathways and fostering greater individual participation in society. Technological access has changed everyday activities like banking, shopping, and travel as well as business, education, and the economy. The Internet has not only eased traditional boundaries and opened access to global resources, it has also generated new questions as society struggles to adapt to rapid and often autonomous information access.

Copyright laws developed for earlier publication mediums have been difficult to adapt to electronic publishing and **intellectual property** rights have been jeopardized by the cut and paste functions of word processors. As different constituencies try to balance First Amendment rights with the desire to protect children from inappropriate material, legal questions related to filtering and censorship have emerged. Without the government's role in regulating the Internet clearly defined, resolution of these and other emerging issues has been difficult.

Although technology has opened exciting new avenues of "information access," the full benefits of these advances will remain elusive until the digital divide is closed. Until that is accomplished, many individuals and communities will be barred from participation in an increasingly technological world. As United Nations Secretary-General Kofi Annan noted in his World Telecommunications Day remarks on May 17, 2001, addressing access to

XML the acronym for eXtensible Markup Language; a method of applying structure to data so that documents can be represented

Global Positioning System (GPS) a method of locating a point on the Earth's surface that uses received signals transmitted from satellites to accurately calculate position

intellectual property the acknowledgement that an individual's creativity and innovation can be owned in the same way as physical property

technological information resources is a worldwide problem that will require international commitment and efforts to resolve. SEE ALSO DIGITAL LIBRARIES; DISTANCE LEARNING; HOME ENTERTAINMENT; HOME SYSTEM SOFTWARE.

Nancy J. Becker

Bibliography

Brown, John Seely, and Paul Duguid. *The Social Life of Information*. Boston: Harvard Business School Press, 2000.

Head, Alison J. *Design Wise: A Guide for Evaluating the Interface Design of Information Resources*. Medford, NJ: Information Today, 1999.

Mates, Barbara T. *Adaptive Technology for the Internet: Making Electronic Resources Accessible to All*. Chicago: American Library Association, 2000.

Wresch, William. *Disconnected: Haves and Have-Nots in the Information Age*. New Brunswick, NJ: Rutgers University Press, 1996.

Internet Resources

Annan, Kofi. World Communications Day May 17, 2001 Message. <http://www.powerup.org/world_telecom.shtml>

Digital Divide Network: Knowledge to Help Everyone Succeed in the Digital Age. Benton Foundation. <http://www.digitaldividenetwork.org/>

Falling through the Net. U.S. Department of Commerce. <http://www.digitaldivide.gov/>

Information Overload

The world's total yearly production of digital information content amounts to 1.5 billion gigabytes of storage, or 250 megabytes of information for every individual on the planet. Locating key strategic information, such as the latest market predictions for the telecommunications sector, is as easy as accessing the bus timetable for one's local area, at least in theory. However, defects are beginning to appear in this digital fabric, highlighting the problem of "information overload" in everyday life.

Information overload, a great contributor to which is the Internet, refers to the difficulty that users experience in trying to locate and process useful information quickly and easily. The ability to create new information content has far outstripped the ability to process and search it. Moreover, changes in how individuals access information are exacerbating the problem.

In the early stages of the online information age, PC-based Internet access was the primary way of interacting with online information sources. Today there are mobile computing devices such as **personal digital assistants (PDAs)** and cellular phones. These devices are designed to help people access and manage information. While they provide greater access to online information, they also suffer from significant limitations such as small screen-sizes. A typical cell phone screen is up to 200 times smaller than a standard PC monitor. This imposes limits on one's ability to locate and display the right information quickly at the right time, and therefore the information overload problem itself becomes even more acute.✳ Because these access devices are becoming the norm rather than the exception, there is a need to make the next generation of information retrieval tools capable of actively reducing information overload.

personal digital assistants (PDAs) small scale hand-held computers that can be used in place of diaries and appointment books

✳**Information overload exists when users are presented with large quantities of information without the necessary tools to locate relevant information quickly and easily.**

Advances in technology make rapidly increasing amounts of data available to consumers electronically, leading to information overload. Even fishermen can get digital help with the handheld pocket fish finder.

Traditionally, the search engine has been the primary tool for information retrieval. Search engines operate by maintaining a comprehensive index of available information. Typically an index represents an information item (such as a web page or a document) in terms of a set of relevant index terms. For example, words that occur frequently in a web page, but that are relatively rare in the web as a whole, are likely to be chosen as relevant index terms for the page.

When an end-user submits query terms to a search engine, they are compared against index terms for relevant items in the search engine index. An overall relevancy score for each information item is computed according to how many of the user's query terms occur in its index, and how important these terms are for that item. The relevant items are then ranked according to their relevancy score before being presented to the user.

Of course there are no guarantees that users will select the same terms for their queries as the search engine has used for its index. This "vocabulary mismatch" problem greatly limits the effectiveness of search engines. In addition, many search engines are incapable of resolving latent ambiguities in query terms. For example, does the query term "jaguar" refer to the cat or the car?

The usefulness of search engines in general is measured by their precision and recall characteristics. Ideally, search engines should have both high precision and high recall.

Precision refers to the proportion of retrieved items that are actually relevant to the user's query. Search engines tend to return very large result lists and many of these results may have been selected because of spurious matches with the query. For example, a user looking for information about Jaguar cars may submit "jaguar" as a query only to be overloaded with irrelevant pages about wild cats among the relevant car-related pages. In this case, precision is low.

The recall of a search engine refers to the proportion of relevant items that are actually retrieved in a search. For example, the "jaguar" search may miss many relevant web pages that focus on the famous E-Type sports car (manufactured by Jaguar in the 1960s) but that fail to mention Jaguar explicitly. In this case, recall is low.

If search engines are limited in their ability to solve the information overload problem by their low precision and recall characteristics, then what does the future hold? What new technologies will provide a solution? One answer lies with recent **artificial intelligence (AI)** research in the area of personalization. One of the fundamental problems with current search engine technologies is their inability to recognize the motivations and preferences of individual users when carrying out a search. Two users submitting the same query will receive the same results, irrespective of their individual preferences. Personalization✳ techniques look at ways of learning about the preferences of individual users over time, by monitoring their online interactions for example, and then use this information to better direct their searches.

For example, a personalization system can learn that a user is interested in cars by noting that the term "automobile" tends to occur frequently in web pages that they visit, and this can be used as an additional query term every time that user searches for information. Thus, the user's "jaguar" query becomes "jaguar automobile" and the search engine is better able to filter out the irrelevant wildlife pages that would otherwise be retrieved.

Personalized information services hold great promise when it comes to relieving the problem of information overload. There are technologies today that are capable of automatically and accurately learning about the information needs and preferences of individual users, and of using this information to guide searches. For example, PTV (www.ptv.ie) is a personalized television listings service based in Dublin, Ireland, that actively learns about the viewing preferences of users (channel, show, and viewing time preferences, for example) in order to compile personalized television guides for them. PTV solves the information overload in the television listings space for PC, PDA, and cellular phone users.

Information overload is a significant problem but personalization techniques provide a real solution at the technology level. However, personalization techniques must also provide a solution at the user level. Due care must be taken to recognize and respect the impact that these new technologies will have on end-users. By their very nature, personalization techniques are designed to learn about the preferences of users automatically—preferences that users may not be willing to reveal to others. Steps are being taken today to define standards for regulating the collection and usage of private user information. With these standards in place, the large-scale deployment of personalization technology may usher in a new information age free from the gridlock of information overload. SEE

artificial intelligence (AI) a branch of computer science dealing with creating computer hardware and software to mimic the way people think and perform practical tasks

✳**Personalization is the ability of an information service to adapt its information automatically for the needs of an individual user.**

ALSO DIGITAL LIBRARIES; ERGONOMICS; HUMAN FACTORS: USER INTERFACES; INFORMATION ACCESS; INFORMATION RETRIEVAL; WORLD WIDE WEB.

Barry Smyth

Bibliography

Baeza-Yates, Ricardo, and Berthier Ribeiro-Neto. *Modern Information Retrieval.* New York: Addison-Wesley, 1999.

Perkowitz, Mike, and Oren Etzioni. "Adaptive Web Sites." *Communications of the ACM* 43, no. 8 (2000): 152–158.

Smyth, Barry, and Paul Cotter. "A Personalized TV Listings Service." *Communications of the ACM* 43, no. 8 (2000): 107–111.

Internet Resources

"The Platform for Privacy Preferences 1.0 (P3P1.0) Specification." *World Wide Web Consortium.* <http://www.w3.org/TR/P3P>

Information Theory

"Information" is a term used universally in fields associated with computing technology. It is often loosely applied when no other term seems to be readily at hand; examples of this are terms such as "information technology," "information systems," and "information retrieval." It surprises most people when they discover that the term "information" actually has a very real meaning in an engineering context. It does not mean the same thing as "knowledge" or "data," but is instead intertwined with elements of communication systems theory.

When computing systems are connected together, it is necessary to consider how they might exchange data and work cooperatively. This introduces the notion that messages can be formulated by computing machines and be dispatched to other machines that receive them and then deal with their contents. All of the issues that are involved with these transmission and reception operations constitute what is known as "information theory."

A communication channel is a connective structure of some sort that supports the exchange of messages. Examples are wired interconnections such as **ethernets** or perhaps **fiber optic** cables, or even wireless communications such as microwave links. These are all paths over which digital information can be transmitted.

Noise and Errors

Information theory has to do with how messages are sent via communication channels. When this field was first being studied, the common consensus was that it would be impossible to get digital machines to make exchanges in a way that was guaranteed to be error-free. This is because all the components used to construct computing machines are imperfect; they tend to distort the electrical signals they process as a side effect of their operation.

The components add extra electrical signals called "noise." In this instance, the term "noise" does not necessarily refer to something that can be heard. Instead, "noise" is used to describe the corruption of electrical signals, which makes them harder for devices in the computer system to understand correctly. This signal corruption might appear as extra voltage levels in the signal, or some signals may be completely missing.

ethernets a networking technology for mini and microcomputer systems consisting of network interface cards and interconnecting coaxial cables; invented in the 1970s by Xerox corporation

fiber optic refers to a transmission technology using long, thin strands of glass fiber; internal reflections in the fiber assure that light entering one end is transmitted to the other end with only small losses in intensity; used widely in transmitting digital information

Because communication channels inherently contain noise, exchanged messages are always being damaged in one way or another. When a particular message is dispatched from one machine to another, there is a chance that it might be distorted by imperfections in the channel and therefore not correctly interpreted by the recipient. Channel noise cannot be entirely eliminated. For this reason, early information theorists believed that it was a reality that messages transmitted digitally would not arrive at their destinations in exactly the way that the senders had sent them.

Information Defined

This pessimistic outlook all changed in 1947 with the publication of Claude Shannon's seminal study of information theory. He proposed that even in the presence of noise (which it had been agreed was unavoidable), it was possible to ensure error-free transmission. This effectively heralded the era of a new field of computing science and engineering: that of information theory. "Information" was granted a precise definition. It was related to the inverse of the probability of the content of a message. For example, if a person was told in a message that "tomorrow, the sky will be blue," that person would conclude that there was not much in that message that he or she had not already expected. In other words, there was not much information in that message, because it essentially reaffirmed an expectation. There is not much information in that message, because the probability of the outcome is high. Conversely, if one were told in a message that "tomorrow, the sky will be green," then he or she would be greatly surprised. There is more information in this second message purely by virtue of the fact that the probability of this event is so much lower. The information pertaining to a particular event is inversely proportional to the logarithm of the probability of the event actually taking place.

Information = log (1/p) where p is the probability of an event within the message.

Shannon's work led to a new field of engineering. Quantities such as the capacity of a channel to transmit information could be evaluated. This provided telecommunications specialists with a way of knowing just how many messages could be simultaneously transmitted over a channel without loss.

Encoding

In addition to this, ways of representing, or encoding, information during transmission from one place to another were explored; some approaches were better than others. Encoding simply means that some pieces of information that are normally represented by particular symbols are converted to another collection of symbols that might better suit their reliable transfer. For example, text messages are often represented by collections of alphabetic characters when created and read, but they are then converted into another form, such as **ASCII** codes, for transmission over a communication channel. At the receiving end, the codes are converted back into text again.

The advantage these conversions offer is that some ways of representing information are more robust to the effects of noise in information channels than others, and perhaps more efficient, as well. So, the extra expense involved in carrying out these encoding and decoding operations is offset by the reliability they offer.

ASCII an acronym that stands for American Standard Code for Information Interchange; assigns a unique 8-bit binary number to every letter of the alphabet, the digits (0 to 9), and most keyboard symbols

Information theory has become a mature field of engineering and computer science. It has enhanced the reliability of computer-based networks at all levels, from small **local area networks (LANs)** to the Internet, and it has done so in a way that is unobtrusive, so that users are unaware of its presence. In addition to this, information theory has also assisted in the development of techniques for encoding digital information and sending this over analog communication channels that were not designed for handling computer-based transmissions, such as the public telephone networks. It is important to remember that these contributions of information theory to modern computing began with the ability to define information mathematically, and the work Claude Shannon did to understand communication channels and encoding schemes. SEE ALSO CYBERNETICS; NETWORKS; SHANNON, CLAUDE E.

Stephen Murray

Bibliography

Lathi, Bhagwandas P. *Modern Digital and Analog Communication Systems*, 2nd ed. Orlando, FL: Holt, Rinehart and Winston, 1989.

Proakis, John G. *Digital Communications*, 3rd ed. New York: McGraw-Hill, 1995.

Shanmugam, K. Sam. *Digital and Analog Communication Systems*. New York: John Wiley & Sons, 1985.

Sklar, Bernard. *Digital Communications, Fundamentals and Applications*. Englewood Cliffs, NJ: Prentice Hall, 1988.

Internet: Applications

The Internet has many important applications. Of the various services available via the Internet, the three most important are e-mail, web browsing, and **peer-to-peer services**. E-mail, also known as electronic mail, is the most widely used and successful of Internet applications. Web browsing is the application that had the greatest influence in dramatic expansion of the Internet and its use during the 1990s. Peer-to-peer networking is the newest of these three Internet applications, and also the most controversial, because its uses have created problems related to the access and use of copyrighted materials.

E-Mail

Whether judged by volume, popularity, or impact, e-mail has been and continues to be the principal Internet application. This is despite the fact that the underlying technologies have not been altered significantly since the early 1980s. In recent years, the continuing rapid growth in the use and volume of e-mail has been fueled by two factors. The first is the increasing numbers of **Internet Service Providers (ISPs)** offering this service, and secondly, because the number of physical devices capable of supporting e-mail has grown to include highly portable devices such as **personal digital assistants (PDAs)** and cellular telephones.

The volume of e-mail also continues to increase because there are more users, and because users now have the ability to attach documents of various types to e-mail messages. While this has long been possible, the formulation of Multipurpose Internet Mail Extensions (MIME) and its adoption by software developers has made it much easier to send and receive attachments, including word-processed documents, spreadsheets, and

---

local area networks (LANs) high-speed computer networks that are designed for users who are located near each other

peer-to-peer services the ways in which computers on the same logical level can interoperate in a structured network hierarchy

Internet Service Providers (ISPs) commercial enterprises which offer paying subscribers access to the Internet (usually via modem) for a fee

personal digital assistants (PDAs) small scale hand-held computers that can be used in place of diaries and appointment books

In Moscow, Russia, computer users can check their e-mail at Cafemax, a facility that features some 300 terminals connected to the Internet.

graphics. The result is that the volume of traffic generated by e-mail, as measured in terms of the number of data **packets** moving across the network, has increased dramatically in recent years, contributing significantly to network congestion.

E-mail has become an important part of personal communications for hundreds of millions of people, many of whom have replaced it for letters or telephone calls. In business, e-mail has become an important advertising medium, particularly in instances where the demand for products and services is time sensitive. For example, tickets for an upcoming sporting event are marketed by sending fans an e-mail message with information about availability and prices of the tickets. In addition, e-mail serves, less obviously,

packets collections of digital data elements that are part of a complete message or signal; packets contain their destination addresses to enable reassembly of the message or signal

as the basis for some of the more important collaborative applications that have been developed, most notably Lotus Notes.

In the near future, voice-driven applications will play a much larger role on the Internet, and e-mail is sure to be one of the areas in which voice-driven applications will emerge most rapidly. E-mail and voice mail will be integrated, and in the process it seems likely that new models for Internet-based messaging will emerge.

Synchronous communication, in the form of the highly popular "instant messaging," may be a precursor of the messaging models of the near future. Currently epitomized by AOL Instant Messenger and Microsoft's Windows Messenger, instant messaging applications generally allow users to share various types of files (including images, sounds, **URLs**), stream content, and use the Internet as a medium for telephony, as well as exchanging messages with other users in real time and participating in online chat rooms.

Web Browsing

The web browser is another Internet application of critical importance. Unlike e-mail, which was developed and then standardized in the early, non-commercial days of the Internet, the web browser was developed in a highly commercialized environment dominated by such corporations as Microsoft and Netscape, and heavily influenced by the World Wide Web Consortium (W3C). While Microsoft and Netscape have played the most obvious parts in the development of the web browser, particularly from the public perspective, the highly influential role of the W3C may be the most significant in the long term.

Founded in 1994 by Tim Berners-Lee, the original architect of the web, the goal of the W3C has been to develop interoperable technologies that lead the web to its full potential as a forum for communication, collaboration, and commerce. What the W3C has been able to do successfully is to develop and promote the adoption of new, open standards for web-based documents. These standards have been designed to make web documents more expressive (Cascading Stylesheets), to provide standardized labeling so that users have a more explicit sense of the content of documents (Platform for Internet Content Selection, or PICS), and to create the basis for more interactive designs (the Extensible Markup Language, or **XML**). Looking ahead, a principal goal of the W3C is to develop capabilities that are in accordance with Berners-Lee's belief that the web should be a highly collaborative information space.

Microsoft and Netscape dominate the market for web browsers, with Microsoft's Internet Explorer holding about three-quarters of the market, and Netscape holding all but a small fraction of the balance. During the first few years of web growth, the competition between Microsoft and Netscape for the browser market was fierce, and both companies invested heavily in the development of their respective browsers. Changes in business conditions toward the end of the 1990s and growing interest in new models of networked information exchange caused each company to focus less intensely on the development of web browsers, resulting in a marked slowing of their development and an increasing disparity between the standards being developed by W3C and the support offered by Internet Explorer or Netscape Navigator.

URLs (Uniform Resource Locators) references to documents or document containers using the Hypertext Transfer Protocol; each consists of a hostname and path to the document

BROWSER LITIGATION

In January of 2002 Netscape Communications, owned by AOL Time Warner, filed suit against Microsoft, which produces Internet Explorer (IE). Netscape alleged that Microsoft engaged in illegal activities (e.g., unfair competition practices) to gain the vast share of the browser market. Once the most-used browser, Netscape claimed that Microsoft violated anti-trust laws when it made IE an integral part of its Windows operating system. According to *USA Today*, some 92 percent of personal computers run Microsoft's Windows operating system as of 2002.

XML the acronym for eXtensible Markup Language; a method of applying structure to data so that documents can be represented

Now, the future of the web browser may be short-lived, as standards developers and programmers elaborate the basis for network-aware applications that eliminate the need for the all-purpose browser. It is expected that as **protocols** such as XML and the Simple Object Access Protocol (SOAP) grow more sophisticated in design and functionality, an end user's interactions with the web will be framed largely by desktop applications called in the services of specific types of documents called from remote sources.

protocols agreed understanding for the sub-operations that make up transactions; usually found in the specification of inter-computer communications

The open source model has important implications for the future development of web browsers. Because open source versions of Netscape have been developed on a modular basis, and because the source code is available with few constraints on its use, new or improved services can be added quickly and with relative ease. In addition, open source development has accelerated efforts to integrate web browsers and file managers. These efforts, which are aimed at reducing functional distinctions between local and network-accessible resources, may be viewed as an important element in the development of the "seamless" information space that Berners-Lee envisions for the future of the web.

Peer-To-Peer Computing

One of the fastest growing, most controversial, and potentially most important areas of Internet applications is peer-to-peer (P2P) networking. Peer-to-peer networking is based on the sharing of physical resources, such as hard drives, processing cycles, and individual files among computers and other intelligent devices. Unlike client-server networking, where some computers are dedicated to serving other computers, each computer in peer-to-peer networking has equivalent capabilities and responsibilities.

Internet-based peer-to-peer applications position the desktop at the center of a computing matrix, usually on the basis of "cross-network" protocols such as the Simple Object Access Protocol (SOAP) or XML-RPC (Remote Procedure Calling), thus enabling users to participate in the Internet more interactively.

There are two basic P2P models in use today. The first model is based on a central host computer that coordinates the exchange of files by indexing the files available across a network of peer computers. This model has been highly controversial because it has been employed widely to support the unlicensed exchange of commercial sound recordings, software, and other copyrighted materials. Under the second model, which may prove ultimately to be far more important, peer-to-peer applications aggregate and use otherwise idle resources residing on low-end devices to support high-demand computations. For example, a specially designed screensaver running on a networked computer may be employed to process astronomical or medical data.

The Future

The remarkable developments during the late 1990s and early 2000s suggest that making accurate predictions about the next generation of Internet applications is difficult, if not impossible. Two aspects of the future of the Internet that one can be certain of, however, are that network

bandwidth a measure
of the frequency compo-
nent of a signal or the
capacity of a communi-
cation channel to carry
signals

bandwidth will be much greater, and that greater bandwidth and its management will be critical factors in the development and deployment of new
applications. What will greater bandwidth yield? In the long run, it is difficult to know, but in the short term it seems reasonable to expect new
communication models, videoconferencing, increasingly powerful tools for
collaborative work across local and wide area networks, and the emergence
of the network as a computational service of unprecedented power. SEE
ALSO ANIMATION; FILM AND VIDEO EDITING; GRAPHIC DEVICES; MUSIC
COMPOSITION.

Christinger Tomer

Bibliography

Berners-Lee, Tim, and Mark Fischetti. *Weaving the Web: The Original Design and Ultimate Destiny of the World Wide Web.* San Francisco: HarperCollins, 1999.

Loshin, Pete, and Paul Hoffman. *Essential E-Mail Standards: RFCs and Protocols Made
Practical.* New York: Wiley, 1999.

Oram, Andy, ed. *Peer-to-Peer: Harnessing the Power of Disruptive Technologies.* Sebastopol, CA: O'Reilly & Associates, 2001.

Raymond, Eric S. *The Cathedral & the Bazaar: Musings on Linux and Open Source by
an Accidental Revolutionary.* Sebastopol, CA: O'Reilly & Associates, 2000-2001.

Internet Resources

About the World Wide Web Consortium. <http://www.w3.org/Consortium/>

Internet: Backbone

The first Internet backbone was invented to assist in the attempt to share
supercomputers. The U.S. government realized that supercomputing was
crucial to advances in science, defense, and economic competitiveness but
the budget for research was insufficient to provide supercomputers for all
scientists who needed them. Thus, the first Internet backbone, called the
NSFNET because it was funded by the U.S. National Science Foundation
(NSF), linked six supercomputing centers (University of California-San
Diego, National Center for Atmospheric Research, National Center for Supercomputing Applications at the University of Illinois, Pittsburgh Supercomputing Center, Cornell University, and the John von Neumann
Supercomputing Center/Princeton) and their associated regional networks
in the United States in order to provide supercomputer access to scientists.
Today, a single government-managed Internet backbone has been transformed into a multitude of different backbones, most of which are private
commercial enterprises.

supercomputers very
high performance com-
puters, usually com-
prised of many
processors and used for
modeling and simulation
of complex phenomena,
like meteorology

Backbone Basics

A backbone is a high-speed **wide area network (WAN)** connecting lower
speed networks. A country typically has several backbones linking all of its
Internet Service Providers (ISPs). In the United States, these backbones are
linked in a small number of interconnection points. Finally, national backbones interconnect in a mesh with other countries, usually with international trunk lines via land, undersea, or satellite.

The current Internet is a loose connection of **TCP/IP networks** organized into a multilevel hierarchy using a wide variety of technologies. At

**wide area network
(WAN)** an intercon-
nected network of com-
puters that spans
upward from several
buildings to whole cities
or entire countries and
across countries

TCP/IP networks interconnected computer
networks that use
Transmission Control
Protocol/Internet Proto-
col

the lowest level, computers are connected to each other, and to a router, in a **local area network (LAN)**. Routers can be connected together into campus, metropolitan, or regional networks. Non-backbone ISPs exist solely to provide Internet access to consumers. For Internet connectivity, at some point all non-backbone networks must connect to a backbone ISP (the highest level). It is typical for a large corporation to connect with one or more backbone ISPs. Backbone and non-backbone ISPs exchange traffic at what is generally called peering points. Federal agencies have always shared the cost of common infrastructure such as peering points for interagency traffic—the Federal Internet Exchanges (FIX-E and FIX-W) were built for this purpose and have served as models for the Network Access Points (NAPs) and **"*IX"** facilities that are prominent features of today's Internet.

Technology

In the NSFNET, each interconnected supercomputing site had an LSI-11 microcomputer called a fuzzball. These fuzzballs were running TCP/IP and were connected with 56 Kbps leased lines. NSFNET was an immediate success and was overloaded from the day it started. NSFNET version 2 leased 448 Kbps fiber optic channels and IBM RS/4000s were used as routers. In 1990 NSFNET version 3 was upgraded to T1 lines (1.544 Mbps). Later that same year, NSFNET upgraded to T3 lines (45 Mbps). European backbone networks (e.g., EBONE) had a similar evolution from 2 Mbps to 34 Mbps. Current speeds of Internet backbones are based on **SONET** framing speeds in the **gbps** range.

Because peering points handle large volumes of traffic, they are typically complex high-speed switching networks within themselves although concentrated in a small geographical area (single building). Commonly, peering points use ATM switching technology at the core to provide traffic quality-of-service management, with IP running on top.

Transmission Mechanisms

The Internet can be viewed as a collection of sub-networks or Autonomous Systems (ASes) that are controlled by a single administrative authority. These ASes are interconnected together by routers with high-speed lines. Routing within an AS (interior routing) does not have to be coordinated with other ASes. Two routers that exchange routing information are exterior routers if they belong to two different ASes. For scalability, each AS designates a small number of exterior routers. The protocol that exterior routers use to advertise routing information to other ASes is called the Exterior Gateway Protocol (EGP).

From the point of view of an exterior router, the Internet consists of other exterior routers and the lines connecting them; two exterior routers are considered connected if they share a common network, and all networks can be grouped into three categories: (1) stub networks (all traffic goes to end computer systems); (2) transit networks (all traffic goes to other ASes); and (3) multiconnected networks (traffic goes to both end computer systems and selectively to other ASes).

Routers in the NSFNET Internet backbone exchanged routing information periodically—once a single backbone router learned a route, all

local area network (LAN) a high-speed computer network that is designed for users who are located near each other

*IX short for "Internet Exchange"; the asterisk indicates that there are different possible types of Internet Exchanges—the two most common are the Commercial Internet Exchange (CIX) and the Federal Internet Exchange (FIX)

SONET the acronym for Synchronous Optical NETwork, a published standard for networks based on fiber optic communications technology

gbps the acronym for gigabits per second; a binary data transfer rate that corresponds to a thousand million (billion, or 10^9) bits per second

backbone routers learned about it. When the single Internet backbone became multiple backbones, the Internet transitioned from a core backbone routing architecture to a peer backbone routing architecture with interconnections at several points. While the desired goal is shortest-path routing, peer routing uses route aggregation between exterior routers as opposed to individual routes for individual computers, which may not result in shortest paths. Also, peer backbones must agree to keep routes consistent among all exterior routers or routing loops will develop (circular routes).

History

The U.S. Department of Defense funded research on interconnecting computers in networks using packet switching that eventually culminated in a wide area network called ARPANET. ARPANET was the network (there were no other networks to connect to) that linked Advanced Research Projects Agency (ARPA) researchers working on central Internet ideas like TCP/IP. Although ARPANET was successful, it was restricted to sites that received funding from ARPA. However, many other universities were interested in forming networks using packet switching, even if they did not receive ARPA funding. This led to the construction of a series of backbone networks, some based on protocols other than TCP/IP (e.g., SNA, DECNET), before the NSFNET linked isolated regional TCP/IP networks into an Internet backbone:

- BITNET—academic IBM mainframe computers;
- CSNET—NSF/Computer Science Community;
- EARN—European Academic and Research Network;
- ESNET—U.S. Department of Energy Network;
- FIDONET—dial-in E-mail Network;
- JANET—U.K. Joint Academic Network;
- HEPNET—U.S. Department of Energy (High Energy Physicists);
- MFENET—U.S. Department of Energy (Magnetic Fusion Energy);
- NASA Science Internet—U.S. National Aeronautics and Space Administration;
- SPAN—NASA Space Scientists (DECnet);
- USAN—NSF Satellite Academic Network;
- USENET—based on AT&T's UNIX built-in UUCP communication protocols.

From 1985 to 1988, regional TCP/IP networks were formed around government institutions and universities, most supported with government funding. In 1988 these NSF regional and mid-level TCP/IP networks were interconnected via a backbone funded by NSF (also supported by donations from IBM, MCI, and MERIT). Given Internet growth in capacity demand, NSF realized it could not pay for managing a network forever so it did three things.

First, in 1992 it encouraged IBM, MERIT, and MCI to form a non-profit company, Advanced Networks and Services (ANS), which built the first private Internet backbone called ANSNET.

FOCUS ON ESNET

Operated by the U.S. Department of Energy, ESNET is short for the Energy Sciences Network. The goal of the high-speed network is to provide a link for collaboration between DOE scientists, researchers, and other staff throughout the country and abroad. Begun in 1976, ESNET was able to connect to more than 100 other networks by 2002.

Second, to ease transition and make sure regional networks could still communicate, NSF funded four different network operators to establish Network Access Points (NAPs): PacBell (San Francisco), Ameritech (Chicago), MFS (Washington, D.C.), and Sprint (Pennsauken, NJ). Every new Internet backbone provider had to connect to all four NAPs if it wanted to receive NSF funding. This arrangement meant that regional networks would have a choice of potential new Internet backbone providers to transmit traffic between NAPs. Other NAPs have also emerged: Metropolitan Area Exchange (MAE)-East, MAE-West, and Commercial Internet Exchange (CIX).

Third, NSF enforced an "Acceptable Use Policy" on the NSFNET, which prohibited usage "not in support of Research and Education." The predictable (and intended) result was stimulation of other commercial backbone networks in addition to ANSNET such as UUNET and PSINET.

NSF's privatization policy culminated in 1995 with the defunding of the NSFNET backbone. The funds previously earmarked for the NSFNET were competitively redistributed to regional networks to buy Internet backbone connectivity from the numerous new private Internet backbone networks that had emerged.

At about the same time in the mid-1990s, a European Internet backbone formed, EBONE, consisting of twenty-five networks interconnecting regions of Europe. Each country in Europe has one or more national networks, each of which is approximately comparable to an NSF regional network.

Technical Issues

As a result of having multiple backbones for Internet traffic, different agreements have evolved for handling traffic between networks at NAPs. The most common agreements between backbones take two forms: (1) Peering—exchanging traffic at no cost; and (2) Transit—exchanging traffic where one backbone pays another for delivery. As a result of increased congestion at NAPs, most backbones have begun to interconnect directly with one another outside of NAPs in what has come to be known as private peering. At one point it was estimated that 80 percent of Internet traffic was exchanged via private peering. Many backbones have taken a hybrid approach—peering with some backbones and paying for transit on other backbones. Those few backbones that interconnect solely by peering and do not need to purchase transit from any other backbones are referred to as top-tier backbones. Because of the proprietary and dynamic nature of this information, it is difficult to state with accuracy the exact number of top-tier backbones, but the following have been reported as such: Cable & Wireless, WorldCom, Sprint, AT&T, and Genuity (formerly GTE Internetworking).

Recently, there has been a call for regulation of backbone interconnection agreements since larger backbones have started to refuse to peer with smaller backbones. There is no accepted convention that governs when it is beneficial for two backbones to peer. While intuition would suggest equal size, there are many measures of backbone size—geographic coverage, transmission capacity, traffic volume, and number of customers—it is unlikely that any two backbones would match on many of these metrics. There is a growing consensus that Internet backbone interconnection agreements are complex contracts with private costs and benefits that can only be decided upon by the participating backbones. SEE ALSO INTERNET; EMBEDDED TECHNOLOGY (UBIQUITOUS COMPUTING); WORLD WIDE WEB.

William Yurcik

Bibliography

Comer, Douglas E. *The Internet Book: Everything You Need to Know About Computer Networking and How the Internet Works*, 3rd ed. Upper Saddle River, NJ: Prentice Hall, 2000.

Internet: History

In tracing the history of the Internet, it is useful to begin at its conceptual foundation. The Internet is an example of a type of network called a **packet-switched network**. These networks differ from telephone networks in a number of important ways. Technological differences aside, one significant difference between these networks is that packet-switched networks are designed to support a wide variety of applications, whereas the telephone network was designed to support one application (voice communications) optimally, though a few other applications are possible as well.

Intellectually, the origin of the Internet can be traced back to the early to mid-1960s, when Leonard Kleinrock, Joseph Licklider, Paul Baran, Lawrence Rogers, and others developed the ideas and theories underpinning these general purpose packet-switched networks. By 1967 some early experiments with using packet-switching technologies were taking place at the National Physical Laboratory in England. In 1969 the U.S. Defense Department's Advanced Research Projects Agency (ARPA) funded a larger scale network project. The initial network interconnected the University of California-Los Angeles, Stanford Research Institute, University of California-Santa Barbara, and the University of Utah. Researchers at these institutions began to develop the software needed to make the network operate, and, by the end of 1969, were able to send some data packets over the network. But the capabilities were very rudimentary, and much work remained to be done.

In the early 1970s, the network software, which caused the computers in the network nodes to perform basic packet-switching functions, was standardized into the **Network Control Protocol (NCP)**, and new sites were added. By 1971 there were 15 locations (nodes) on the network, serving 23 host computers. As the basic network software was being developed, so were the (initially rudimentary) applications that would use the network. One of the early applications was electronic mail; in fact, the use of the now standard "@" sign for e-mail was begun in 1972.

While the primary focus had remained on constructing packet-switched networks, Robert Kahn posed the "Internet problem"—namely how to get autonomous networks to exchange information—in 1972. The idea that a network could support (and even encourage) heterogeneity would ultimately be of great importance to the success of the Internet over technologies that were unable to provide this support easily.

The network continued to grow as well. By 1973, the first international site was introduced, which was to the University College in London via

packet-switched network a network that is based upon digital communications systems whereby packets of data are dispatched to receivers based on addresses that they contain

Network Control Protocol (NCP) a host-to-host protocol originally developed in the early 1970s to support the Internet, which was then a research project

Computer scientist Leonard Kleinrock helped develop the technological foundation for the Internet known as packet switching. Celebrating the 30th anniversary of the Internet on September 2, 1999, Kleinrock stands near the first network switch, noting that his watch has more microprocessing power.

Norway; in addition, the ARPANET supported approximately 2,000 users. The genesis of today's computer environment was also being developed at this time, with the basic theory of the *Ethernet* **local area network (LAN)**, which is today the dominant local networking system, and the modern computer workstation. The *Alto* workstation was developed at Xerox's Palo Alto Research Center (PARC) and had a **graphical user interface (GUI)** with icons and a mouse. While nobody could predict the extent to which these technologies would come to dominate computing, they, together with Kahn's statement of the Internet problem, would combine to form the Internet as it is known today.

By 1974, enough had been learned about techniques for implementing packet-switching technology that a second generation protocol and the associated network software could be proposed. This was called the

local area network (LAN) a high-speed computer network that is designed for users who are located near each other

graphical user interface (GUI) an interface that allows computers to be operated through pictures (icons) and mouse-clicks, rather than through text and typing

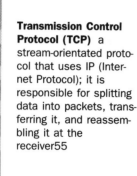

Transmission Control Protocol (TCP) a stream-orientated protocol that uses IP (Internet Protocol); it is responsible for splitting data into packets, transferring it, and reassembling it at the receiver55

EXPRESSING EMOTION

Emoticons, or "emotion icons," were created to help people express their state of mind in e-mails. On occasion, the tone of an e-mail can be misunderstood because the receiver cannot see the sender's facial expressions. Without such visual cues, a humorous statement can be misconstrued as a serious or sarcastic comment. The smiley face :) and the frowning face :(and the winking face ;) are the most popular emoticons. However, e-mail senders continue to devise other creative ways to express emotions, including =8-o for "fright" and :-$ for "put your money where your mouth is" and :*) for being "drunk."

---

supercomputer a very high performance computer, usually comprised of many processors and used for modeling and simulation of complex phenomena, like meteorology

---

Transmission Control Protocol (TCP). This proposal included what users today understand as TCP and IP. The initial tests of TCP did not take place until 1975. By this time, commercial packet-switching services (though not based on NCP or TCP) had come into being, and the possibilities that these networks afforded began to be imagined. In fact, in 1976 Queen Elizabeth II sent an e-mail.

TCP continued to be developed during this time, and, in 1978, TCP and IP were divided into separate components so that their functions could be improved. Other notable events of the late 1970s included the development of the first Multi-User Domain (MUD), the proliferation of mailing lists, and the emergence of emoticons. By this time the utility of electronic mail was more widely recognized. To extend this capability beyond the domain of the ARPANET, new networks were formed. They included CSNET, BITNET (because it is time network), and FIDONET. Each of these networks used different network protocols, had different organizational forms, and reached different users. CSNET was targeted at university computer science departments and received funding from the National Science Foundation. BITNET was targeted at a more diverse academic audience, and was organized cooperatively so that each member paid for its connection to the nearest node, and agreed to transport others' traffic. FIDONET was built upon message forwarding over dialup telephone lines and was generally used by home computer users and hobbyists.

Though Kahn had articulated the Internet problem in 1972, and work on TCP had begun in 1978, it was not until 1982 that the conversion from NCP to TCP/IP took place (the crossover took place on January 1, 1983), and the notion of the Internet was first defined as a set of interconnected networks. The conversion to TCP/IP was bolstered when the U.S. Department of Defense declared TCP/IP to be the standard for its computer networking applications. Other events of the early and mid 1980s include:

- Increased international expansion.

- The introduction of the Domain Name System (DNS), with the now familiar .com, .org, .edu names.

- Gateways between ARPANET, CSNET, and BITNET.

- The involvement of the National Science Foundation (NSF) in the funding of the Internet backbone segments (NSFNET) reaching between the five university **supercomputer** centers they funded (Princeton, Pittsburgh, San Diego, Cornell, and Urbana-Champaign). This would be the demise of CSNET and BITNET, because it became easy for networks to be directly connected.

- Network news was developed.

By the late 1980s, commercial interest in computer networking was growing. This was prohibited by the NSF's Acceptable Use Policy, so limited private networks (such as UUNET) began emerging. This was also the time of the first "bug," the Internet worm that disrupted many of the hosts attached to the network. The worm incident prompted the establishment of the Computer Emergency Response Team (CERT) at Carnegie Mellon University. By the end of the decade, there were more than 100,000 computers attached to the network.

It was also during this time that the utility of the Internet as an information resource began to emerge. Many researchers made their reports available via anonymous **File Transfer Protocol (FTP).** However, the problem of locating reports of interest brought the techniques of information storage and retrieval from the library and information science community to the Internet. The first tool for locating reports was *Archie*. Released in 1990, Archie was an index and search tool for anonymous FTP sites that researchers could use to locate information more efficiently. The next step was more interactive information content, which was embodied in *Gopher* for textual information, released in 1991; soon thereafter, an index of Gopher sites, called *Veronica*, was released in 1992. As useful as Gopher was, it was still limited. The hypertext-based WorldWideWeb (WWW) was initially released in 1991 by Tim Berners-Lee, which provided a framework for integrated information content. Despite this, no compelling interface for the web existed until Mosaic was released in 1993. Even without the web, the number of computers connected to the Internet increased by an order of magnitude (to 1 million) in only three years.

The promise of the Internet was not lost on commercial users. In the early 1990s, private network service providers (for example, PSINET) emerged to carry commercial traffic. These service providers created the Commercial Internet Exchange (CIX) to exchange traffic among themselves so that a user of any commercial network could contact a user of any other commercial network. The NSF came under increasing pressure to privatize the NSFNET. This was finally accomplished in 1994. The NSF continued to support next generation Internet research through projects such as the very high-speed Backbone Network Service (vBNS). With the removal of the restrictive Acceptable Use Policy of the NSF, commercial Internet ventures flourished with the introduction of streaming audio in 1995, Internet banking, and the like.

The growth explosion that followed privatization had a large impact on the broader telecommunications sector of the United States and world economies. Many traditional carriers were developing an Internet strategy, and the idea of "convergence" was central to these plans. In short, convergence refers to the notion that, as content (such as text, audio, image, and video) was digitized, any underlying network technology could be used for transport. This meant that IP carriers could easily invade the traditional "turf" of telephone companies, and other communication providers. This idea of convergence was one of the underlying forces behind the passage of the Telecommunications Act of 1996, which redefined the regulatory structure of the telecommunications industry. In essence this legislation attempted to create a policy convergence framework that could mirror the technological convergence that was going on in the industry. While notions of convergence are still relevant today, the hype and anticipation of the mid-1990s has cooled considerably.

The emergence of the Internet placed substantial pressure on existing legal structures as well. The Electronic Frontier Foundation (EFF) was founded in 1990 by Mitchell Kapor to explore these questions. As commercial interests became significant (following the Internet's privatization), issues such as trademarks, cryptography, copyright, and privacy became important legal as well as public policy issues. While there has been substantial evolution in this

File Transfer Protocol (FTP) a communications protocol used to transfer files

MAKING INTERNET HISTORY

As of 2001, South Dakota was the most "wired" state in America. Its drive to embrace technology has brought more computers into the classroom, which has increased students' exposure to information as well as the types of information available worldwide. In the state, there is one computer for approximately every 3.5 pupils.

regard over the last decade, substantial open questions remain. SEE ALSO BELL LABS; GOVERNMENT FUNDING: RESEARCH; INTERNET: BACKBONE; TELECOMMUNICATIONS; TELEPHONY.

Martin Weiss

Internet Resources

Leiner, Barry M., Vinton G. Cerf, David D. Clark, Robert E. Kahn, Leonard Kleinrock, Daniel C. Lynch, Jon Postel, Lawrence G. Roberts, and Stephen Wolff. "A Brief History of the Internet." <http://www.isoc.org/internet/history/brief.shtml>

"Life on the Internet." <http://www.pbs.org/internet/>

Intranet

One of the most desirable features of the Internet is the ability to access information from anywhere, independent of geographical location. However, there are valid reasons why a corporation may not want to grant worldwide access to its internal business information. This has led to Internet-like services restricted to inside a company that is referred to as an intranet. Intranets have been called a **paradigm** shift in internal business operations because of the potential networking efficiencies (dynamic online corporate information instantly accessible) and the standard, universal computer interface for all employees within an organization.

An intranet is an enterprise network (spanning geographical boundaries to connect different types of computers in various parts of an organization) that provides users with Internet application tools (i.e., web browsers) to access organizational information. Note that an intranet is an internal network to link organizational members to organizational information that is completely controlled by the organization. If any Internet connection does exist (one does not have to exist), a **firewall** prevents outside computers anywhere on the Internet from accessing computers on the intranet.

Uses and Applications

Intranets are popular for several reasons: (1) the infrastructure is often already in place in terms of computers, software, and connectivity for any networks with Internet access; (2) they work, allowing all organizational members instant and uniform access to broadcast organizational information, internal databases, and internal collaboration; (3) they scale well because the technology is the same as that used in the Internet; and (4) intranets are secure from the Internet. Due to the popularity of the World Wide Web, most intranets are implementations of an enterprise network providing access to web server(s).

In the web context, to create an intranet requires the following: (1) establishing a web server, requiring hardware and software; (2) establishing web server access by building a TCP/IP (Transmission Control Protocol/Internet Protocol) network—TCP/IP is the protocol suite that provides interoperability on the Internet; (3) loading client web browsers on each user's computer; and (4) creating a web homepage document using HTML (hypertext markup language) or an HTML editor. A big advantage of using an intranet is that most employees are already familiar with using the Internet and web so little extra training is needed.

paradigm an example, pattern, or way of thinking

firewall a special purpose network computer or software that is used to ensure that no access is permitted to a sub-network unless authenticated and authorized

---

SPEEDY ALTERNATIVE

At many large companies, staff announcements made via paper memo are a thing of the past. Instead, organizations post information via their own Intranets on topics ranging from employee activities, cafe lunch menus, services offered by various departments, and benefits information. Such notices can be added or updated quickly and distributed to staff en masse with the push of a button.

Security

Protection for an intranet connected to the Internet is provided by a fire-wall—a computer or group of computer systems that enforces an access control policy by blocking traffic or permitting traffic. Typically, a firewall is one computer that sits between the intranet and the Internet filtering **packets** according to various criteria. Firewalls simplify security management because network security can be consolidated on firewall systems rather than being distributed on systems all over an internal network. Firewalls thus offer a convenient point where logging and auditing functions can provide summaries about traffic flows passing through, traces of inbound and outbound connections, attempts to break through, and alarms for attacks as they occur. Without a firewall, protection defaults to individual computer security mechanisms implemented on each intranet computer device. Before implementing an intranet relying on a firewall, an organization must inventory all its traffic routing since a firewall cannot filter packets that are not routed through it.

A web-based intranet allows an organization to control information by tracking aggregate web traffic and individual user traffic. Emerging intranet products are developing methods to infer user information from web server request log information in files that can be used with **relational databases** for specific queries. Other products track web page users's access, the paths users follow through webpages, and the amount of e-mail an individual user sends and receives. It has already become common commercial practice for companies to keep track of search topics requested by an individual user

In 2001 technicians tested the security of the new Navy Marine Corps Intranet (NMCI), which was designed for use at the Norfolk Naval Base in Norfolk, Virginia.

packets collections of digital data elements that are part of a complete message or signal; packets contain their destination addresses to enable reassembly of the message or signal

relational databases collections of records that permit logical and business relationships to be developed between themselves and their contents and compile databases that allow tailored information designed for individual users.

Examples

Most companies today implement some form of intranet for internal operations. For example, KPMG, a management consulting firm, moved all of its information assets to an intranet called KWorld. The success of Cisco Systems has been largely attributed to its innovative corporate intranet. Even while selling systems using a non-interoperable proprietary protocol (Systems Network Architecture—SNA), IBM was also widely credited with having the largest TCP/IP corporate intranet. The People's Republic of China (PRC) is attempting to build a national intranet to take advantage of established Internet connectivity while limiting access to information forbidden by Chinese Internet regulations—if successfully implemented it would be the largest intranet in the world. SEE ALSO INTERNET; NETWORK DESIGN; NETWORKS; TELECOMMUNICATIONS.

William Yurcik

Bibliography

Comer, Douglas E. *The Internet Book: Everything You Need to Know About Computer Networking and How the Internet Works.* 3rd ed. Prentice Hall, 2000.

Java Applets

An applet is a small program that is embedded inside another application. Applets are not intended to run on their own. A Java applet is an applet written in the Java programming language. They are most commonly embedded in web pages to run in the environment of a web browser. Web pages are written in **Hypertext Markup Language (HTML)**. The web browser interprets the HTML source in order to render the pages on a display screen. Without using Java applets, HTML is quite limited in functionality, particularly in **graphical user interfaces (GUIs)** and multimedia. A Java applet is like a window application running within the embedding web page. It can provide much more sophisticated features in graphical user interfaces for interaction, as well as other functionalities such as animation and special effects.

The web browser must be equipped with the Java Virtual Machine (JVM) to handle web pages embedded with Java applets. The JVM is a Java interpreter that makes it possible to run compiled Java code; it enables the browser to run Java applets when rendering the embedding web page. The HTML source uses the <APPLET> tag to embed a Java applet in the web page. The parameters of the <APPLET> tag can specify the width and height of the window in the web page for the applet, and also refer to the file for the compiled code of the Java applet. The file usually would have the ".class" extension in the file name. This extension in the naming convention indicates that it is a file for compiled Java code. The following illustrates a simple HTML source sequence to embed a Java applet in the file myapplet.class.

```
<APPLET height = 100 width = 200 code = "myApplet.class">
</APPLET>
```

Hypertext Markup Language (HTML) an encoding scheme for text data that uses special tags in the text to signify properties to the viewing program (browser) like links to other documents or document parts (header)

graphical user interfaces (GUIs) interfaces that allow computers to be operated through pictures (icons) and mouse-clicks, rather than through text and typing

In the preceding <APPLET> tag, the parameters height and width instruct the browser to reserve a window in the web page, 100 **pixels** high and 200 pixels wide, as screen real estate for the applet. The compiled code of the Java applet is in the file myApplet.class, specified for the parameter code. To render the web page, the browser accesses the file for the applet code, and runs the JVM to execute the applet. The </APPLET> tag closes the scope of the <APPLET> tag, as required in the **syntax** of HTML.

A Java applet is different from a regular Java application program in that it is not started with its main method. Instead, the first time the browser renders the web page, the JVM loads the applet code from the file specified. To run the applet, it invokes the **init method** first and then the start method. Thereafter, whenever the browser leaves the web page, the JVM invokes the stop method; and subsequently whenever the browser returns to the page, it invokes the start method again. The start and stop methods are then repeated as many times as the browser would enter and leave the web page. Before the browser unloads the applet from its cache memory, the JVM then invokes the destroy method. For every instance of a Java applet embedded in a web page, the init method is always the first to be invoked, and is invoked only once. Thereafter, the start and stop methods may be invoked as many times as needed. The destroy method is also invoked only once and is always the last method invoked before the applet is unloaded from the cache (such as when the browser terminates).

The init method is designed for the applet to acquire and set up resources for use. For example, if a person would like a web page to play music whenever the browser opens the page, he or she will use the init method to acquire the audio channels for use, and set up the audio file for playback. The person will then use the start method to begin playback of the audio file. Whenever the browser leaves to go to another page, the stop method will stop playback and mark the position of the music playback. When the browser returns to the web page, the start method can then resume music playback at the place where it left off at the previous stop method. The destroy method releases the resources acquired, since it is the last method invoked. These four methods are often called the life cycle methods of a Java applet; the method declarations are listed:

```
public void init(void);

public void start(void);

public void stop(void);

public void destroy(void);
```

The parameters height and width in the <APPLET> tag assign an applet screen real estate in the web page for graphical display. Whenever it becomes necessary to refresh or update the display, the JVM of the browser invokes the paint method of the applet:

```
public void paint(Graphics g);
```

The parameter "g" is the Graphics object for the window in the embedding web page of dimensions specified by the height and width in the <APPLET> tag. The paint method can use it to draw the content for display in the web page.

pixels single picture elements on a video screen; the individual dots making up a picture on a video screen or digital image

syntax a set of rules that a computing language incorporates regarding structure, punctuation, and formatting

init method a special function in an object oriented program that is automatically called to initialize the elements of an object when it is created

---

HELP FOR BEGINNERS

Programs exist to help people without Java or HTML knowledge create applets to spruce up their home pages. Such programs claim that users can create "cool" effects for their web sites in just a matter of minutes.

A Java applet must support all these methods: init, start, stop, destroy, and paint in order to function properly. The Java class library provides the Applet class with default implementation for all five methods. One can make use of inheritance in object-oriented programming when he or she derives an applet class from Applet; the applet will then inherit these methods from the base class Applet. One has to implement the methods in the applet class only when he or she needs to override the default implementation.

A simple Java applet, myApplet, will illustrate the functionality. The complete HTML source of the web page, embedding the applet using the <APPLET> tag, follows:

```
<HTML>
<HEAD><TITLE>myApplet</TITLE></HEAD>
<BODY><H1>My Applet</H1>
<HR><APPLET CODE="myApplet.class" WIDTH=200
HEIGHT=50> </APPLET><HR>
</BODY>
</HTML>
```

The web page shows the heading "My Applet" and the window for the applet. The complete source program for the Java applet follows:

```java
// myApplet.java - a simple Java applet example.
//
import java.applet.*; // to use class Applet
import java.awt.*;    // to use Color

public class myApplet extends Applet
{
    int count = 0;
    Color spectrum[] = new Color[3];
    // init: to set up resources of 3 colors.
    public void init()
    {
        spectrum[0] = Color.blue;
        spectrum[1] = Color.red;
        spectrum[2] = Color.green;
    }
    // start: to increment count for next color.
    public void start()
    {
        count = count + 1;
    }
    // paint: to update content of display.
  public void paint(Graphics g)
    {
        g.setColor(spectrum[count%3]); // Change color.
        g.drawString("Applet DEMO: "+count,10,20);
    }
}
```

The applet keeps a count of how many times the start method has been invoked. The applet paints the text string "Applet DEMO" followed by the count. The color of the text rotates in the sequence of blue, red, and green:

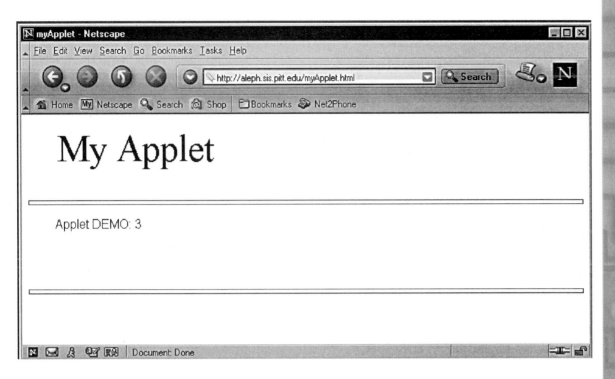

Figure 1.

every time the browser leaves and then returns to the page, the color changes, because the start method increments the count. Figure 1 shows the web page with the browser returning the third time. SEE ALSO INTERNET; OBJECT-ORIENTED LANGUAGES; PROCEDURAL LANGUAGES; PROGRAMMING; WORLD WIDE WEB.

Peter Y. Wu

Bibliography

Coad, Peter, Mark Mayfield, and Jonathan Kern. *Java Design: Building Better Apps and Applets, 2/e,* 2nd ed. Upper Saddle River, NJ: Yourdon Press, 1999.

Gottleber, Timothy T. *Excellent HTML with an Introduction to Java Applets.* Boston: Irwin/McGraw-Hill, 1998.

JavaScript

JavaScript is a programming language designed specifically for electronic documents on the World Wide Web. Documents on the web are written in **Hypertext Markup Language (HTML)**. JavaScript programs are embedded within HTML to add dynamic interactivity to web documents.

JavaScript may look like the programming language Java, but it is not Java. As a scripting language, JavaScript is intended to take web page designers a step beyond HTML without the complexity of a full programming language. A simple JavaScript program can add interesting interactive functions to a web page. JavaScript is also suitable for the development of large and elaborate user **interfaces** in web documents. Good programming skills are necessary to master it, and sophisticated tools are becoming available for JavaScript development.

JavaScript is not **compiled**. Embedded within HTML, JavaScript is interpreted by the web browser. A JavaScript program can control document

Hypertext Markup Language (HTML) an encoding scheme for text data that uses special tags in the text to signify properties to the viewing program (browser) like links to other documents or document parts

interfaces boundaries or borders between two or more objects or systems; also points of access

compiled a program that is translated from human-readable code to binary code that a central processing unit (CPU) can understand

content and its appearance, interacting with the HTML source code and the browser functions. It makes use of the user interface mechanisms already in HTML to interact with users of the web document. It can manipulate embedded images, but cannot produce graphical displays. It should not read or write files, except in using **cookies** as permitted by the web browser. It can access other web documents using the **Uniform Resource Locator (URL)**, but it cannot make network connections on its own.

The following is an example of the JavaScript program embedded in an HTML document. JavaScript program code is embedded between the <SCRIPT> and the </SCRIPT> tags.

cookies small text files that web sites can place on a computer's hard drive to collect information about a user's browsing activities or to activate an online shopping cart to keep track of purchases

Uniform Resource Locator (URL) a reference to a document or a document container using the Hypertext Transfer Protocol (HTTP); consists of a hostname and path to the document

```
<HTML><HEAD>
<TITLE>Java Script Example One</TITLE>
</HEAD><BODY>
<HR>
<H3>JavaScript Example: HELLO</H3>
<HR>
<SCRIPT LANGUAGE=JavaScript>
    //
    // Ask for the user's name to greet. (Default name is Peter.)
    //
    var name = prompt ("Tell me your name, please.","Peter") ;
    //
    // Set name to STRANGER if user refuses to enter a name.
    //
    if (name == null) name = "STRANGER" ;
    //
    // Generate greeting with the name, in different styles.
    //
    var greeting = "Hello " + name + "!";
    document.write(greeting.bold()+"<BR>");
    document.write(greeting.italics()+"<BR>");
    document.write(greeting.toUpperCase()+"<BR>");
</SCRIPT>
</BODY></HTML>
```

The HTML document makes use of the <SCRIPT> tag to include a JavaScript program. When the browser opens up the document, it interprets the JavaScript program. The short program uses the browser's prompt function to prompt the user to enter a name, and then generates the content of the page with the name that is entered.

In the JavaScript source program, the double slash "//" indicates a program comment until the end of line. The keyword *var* declares variable for use. The variables declared in the program are name and greeting. Any text included within a pair of double quotes (or single quotes) is a text string. Using the plus sign (+) between text strings **concatenates** them to form a longer string. The program calls the prompt function provided by the browser to first pop up a dialog box to prompt the user. The first argument of the function call is the text string to describe the information being requested. The second argument is the default text entry initially placed in the pop-up dialog box. Figure 1 illustrates the pop-up dialog box when the browser opens up the HTML document.

concatenates the joining together of two elements or objects; for example, words are formed by concatenating letters

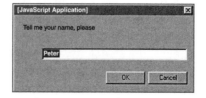

Figure 1. Pop-up dialog box.

The user can then type in an entry and click "OK," or refuse to supply an entry and cancel. The variable name in the JavaScript program will then pick up the entry. If no entry is supplied, the variable name becomes null, having no value. The next line in the program then checks to see if "name" has a value; if it does not have a value it is set to STRANGER. The next line in the program goes on to form the greeting string in the variable greeting. Because addition concatenates the strings, if the name entered is "Quincy," the variable greeting would have the string "Hello Quincy!" The next three lines then generate the document content with the greeting string in different styles. The function document.write( ) takes the string argument, and generates that as content in the HTML document. Note the different styles generated using the functions on the string—bold, italics, regular type setting to uppercase. Appropriate HTML source code is generated accordingly. The following illustrates the web page generated, with Peter as the name entered.

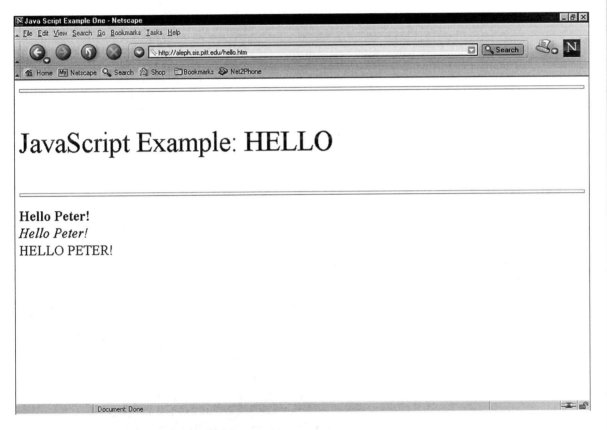

Figure 2. Web page generated using JavaScript.

Unlike Java, JavaScript is a loosely typed language. It means that variables used in the program do not have a definite type: a variable can take up any type of content, and they are all declared with the keyword "var." For example, a variable may take a text string as content, but the same variable can also take an integer number and use it in a calculation. Like many other programming languages, JavaScript also has control structures such as functions, conditional (if) statements and loop (while) statements, as well as data structures such as arrays.

JavaScript is an object-based language: A JavaScript program can create and use objects of existing types provided for it, but cannot create new types of objects. Therefore, it is not an object-oriented programming language like Java. A significant design point in JavaScript is its access to the Document

Object Model (DOM) used in the web browser. The DOM is the data structure in the web browser used to manage the documents viewed and used on the browser. When the browser is running, it has a window open for viewing of documents. Each document in turn comprises its content, links, anchors, images, and other components. All these are objects available to the JavaScript programs running in the browser. In the earlier program example, document.write( ) invokes the write( ) method in the current document object, generating content in the document as HTML source.

Along with the DOM, the web browser in use also generates events. An event occurs when the user interacts with the user interfaces on the web page presented by the web browser. For example, when the user clicks the mouse button with the mouse cursor over a radio button on the web page, it generates the onClick event. The HTML source can specify in the value of the onClick parameter in the <INPUT> tag, to call a JavaScript function. The specific event will therefore invoke the JavaScript function as an event handler to perform the necessary processing. The following is an illustrative example.

```
<HTML><HEAD>
<TITLE>JavaScript Example Two</TITLE>
<SCRIPT LANGUAGE=JavaScript>
function onButton()
{
                    var thisBox = document.myForm.radio1;
                    if (thisBox.checked == true)
                    {
                        document.myForm.radio2.checked = false;
                        document.bgColor='white';
                        alert("Thanks!");
                    }
}
function offButton()
{
                    var thisBox = document.myForm.radio2;
                    if (thisBox.checked == true)
                    {
                        document.myForm.radio1.checked = false;
                        document.bgClor='black';
                        alert("Hey! Turn the lights back ON!");
                    }
}
</SCRIPT>
</HEAD><BODY>
<HR>
<H3>JavaScript Example: LIGHT</H3>
<HR>
<P>Please feel free to try the buttons.
They turn ON and OFF the lights on the page,
using JavaScript functions as event handlers.<BR>
<FORM NAME=myForm>
<INPUT TYPE=radio NAME=radio1 onClick="onButton();" CHECKED>
Light ON<BR>
<INPUT TYPE=radio NAME=radio2 onClick="offButton();">
Light OFF<BR>
</FORM>
</BODY></HTML>
```

Note in the preceding HTML source how the event onClick also names a parameter for the <INPUT> tag, and the value of the parameter makes a call to the JavaScript function. The JavaScript functions can also use the name of the components to alter its state. The following shows the web page rendered by a browser opening up the HTML document. The radio buttons provide for user interaction to change the background color of the document, using JavaScript functions as event handlers.

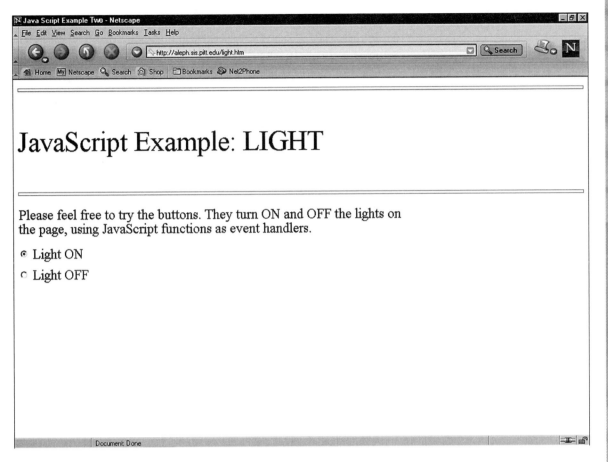

Figure 3. Web page rendered by a browser opening up the HTML document.

Since its inception, JavaScript has already gone through four releases at the time of this writing, the latest being JavaScript 1.3. JavaScript is still developing. There can be compatibility problems such that the same JavaScript program may behave differently with different web browsers and different browser versions. The European Computer Manufacturers' Association (ECMA) and the International Organization for Standardization (ISO) have adopted ECMAScript, which is based on JavaScript, as a standard. The adopted standard will surely help to resolve the compatibility problems. SEE ALSO INTERNET; OBJECT-ORIENTED LANGUAGES; PROCEDURAL LANGUAGES; PROGRAMMING; WORLD WIDE WEB.

Peter Y. Wu

Bibliography

Flanagan, David. *JavaScript: The Definitive Guide*, 4th ed. Cambridge, MA: O'Reilly & Associates, 2001.

Goodman, Danny. *JavaScript Bible*, 4th ed. New York: Hungry Minds, 2001.

Journalism

Since the early 1950s, computers have played a major role in journalism and mass communication. As early as 1956, computers were used to analyze political polling data and national election returns.

In the beginning, only the largest media organizations could afford computer-based technology. Today, computers are present in virtually every newsroom in the country. Journalists use computer technology in three major areas: (a) gathering information to be used in news stories; (b) producing newspaper and magazine articles and television or radio newscasts; and (c) distributing news stories and programs to the general public. Prior to the introduction of computers in journalism, news deadlines had to be set early enough for the material to be produced, published or recorded, and disseminated in a timely manner. The use of computers in journalism now allows the very latest news to appear in print or on the air—as well as in online form via the Internet.

Computers Enter the Newsroom

Newspapers began using computers in the early 1970s. These were large **mainframe** machines designed specifically to be used for copyediting and typesetting to produce the actual newspaper pages. Initially, computers were not used to gather the news, whether for print or for broadcast use.

mainframe large computer used by businesses and government agencies to process massive amounts of data; generally faster and more powerful than desktop computers but usually requiring specialized software

Computers first appeared in television newsrooms in the early 1980s. As was the case in print journalism, the first television news computers were proprietary machines that, unlike today's personal computers, were designed to perform a single function. One of the first proprietary television newsroom computers was manufactured by Dynatech Newstar. It allowed broadcast reporters to write scripts and read wire stories. Later versions of the program added the ability for newscast producers to organize newscasts and create detailed rundowns of the news program's content.

In the late 1980s, the computer systems shifted from proprietary hardware and software to personal desktop computers as PCs and Macintosh computers became more powerful. Today, virtually all newspaper, television, and radio news content is produced using computer terminals or notebook computers. These computers connect the newsroom with other parts of the media production process. Page layout software—such as Quark Express, Adobe PageMaker, and InDesign—has streamlined the production of newspapers by making it possible for entire pages to be created easily on the desktop. In television, computers can transmit production information, including on-screen graphics and closed-captioning text, directly to the control room for use on the air.

In the mid-1990s, desktop computers became powerful enough to handle the creation of multimedia products such as pictures, graphics, video, and sounds. Just as desktop publishing changed the way page layouts were created, programs like Adobe Photoshop changed the way in which media companies created graphics and pictures. Prior to the use of computers, newspapers used traditional photographic film and chemicals in "wet" darkrooms to create pictures. By the early 2000s, many newspapers used digital cameras to capture photographs and "digital" darkrooms to process them.

Digital Graphics and Audio

In television, the first computer-based graphics and video editing systems appeared in the early 1990s. Like other computer applications, the first systems were based on propriety hardware and were extremely expensive. It was not uncommon for a television graphics computer hardware and application to cost more than $250,000. Early computer-based, or non-linear, video editing programs were equally expensive. Now, programs such as Apple Final Cut Pro and Adobe Premiere are affordable for many hobbyists, as well as television stations and video production companies.

Non-linear video editing is replacing traditional tape-to-tape editing in which scenes were physically recorded from one videotape recorder to another. With computer-based editing, the pictures can be assembled electronically on a computer screen. Some television stations, such as the Gannett Corporation's WKYC in Cleveland, Ohio, are instituting an all-digital workflow. Video for news stories is converted to a digital format as soon as the reporter gets back to the station after covering an event. The digital video is then available to everyone in the news production process (reporters, photographers, editors, producers, and promotions department) via networked desktop computers. This speeds up the production process and makes it possible for last minute changes to be made in the news programs.

Computers are also used by radio stations to create digital audio. News reporters can edit interviews with newsmakers and add commentary from reporters without having to splice the audiotape physically or record it from one tape recorder to another.

Computer Assisted Reporting

Journalists also use computers to gather information for stories. The term for this function is "computer assisted reporting." For example, reporters can sift through complicated databases, such as census information supplied by the U.S. government to gather specific information about individual communities. Computer assisted reporting can help journalists to spot trends in a community, such as an increase in cancer rates among a certain segment of the population or a decrease in the number of young people who are planning to attend college. Computer assisted reporting can also be used to examine and investigate police statistics, such as the number of traffic citations that have been issued to public officials for which the fines were never paid.

The Internet provides a major source of information for journalists, particularly when they are working on a breaking story. For example, there are several aviation-related web sites that reporters can turn to for current and background information after a major airplane crash. These web sites can help reporters collect technical information about the type of airplane involved and its maintenance history. Many sites are also available to help reporters gather scientific, geographical, historical, and health-related information.

News Online

The latest use of computers in journalism is to disseminate information via sites on the World Wide Web. Most major newspapers, television networks, local television stations, and major radio stations have web sites that feature news content. It is possible to "read" almost any newspaper in the world if it is available on the Internet. Newspaper and television companies have tried several business models to make money with their web sites. In early tests, however, most journalism web sites have not been profitable. Surveys indicate that most people are, as yet, unwilling to pay for web-based news

A VITAL NEWS TOOL

According to Bruce Garrison, professor of journalism at the University of Miami in Coral Gables, Florida, journalists' dependence on computers for news gathering and connecting to the World Wide Web is now almost 100 percent. Of course, as with any other general source of news or background data, reporters must be cautious not to use web sites that may contain unreliable information.

Many people turn to electronic newspapers to learn the events of the day. The biggest advantage of e-newspapers over their print counterparts is that they can be updated frequently with the latest details of a story.

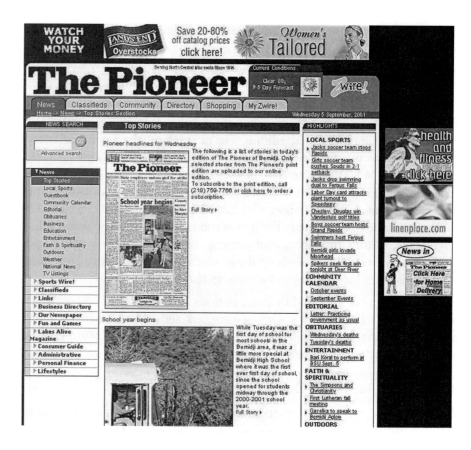

content. Many media web sites rely on on-screen advertising for their revenue. In most cases, however, the advertising revenue does not support the cost of producing the web material.

The Future

It is difficult to determine what effect computers will have on journalism in the future. A generation ago, only large newspaper companies had the economic muscle to publish a daily newspaper. Today, anyone with a page layout program and access to the World Wide Web can reach readers around the world. Likewise, the high cost of video production used to mean that only television stations and networks could afford to produce programs. The development of affordable desktop video has changed that, too. As Internet **bandwidth** increases, more and more companies will be able to produce their own video programs and distribute them over the World Wide Web. This is a far cry from those early mainframe computers used on election night in 1956. SEE ALSO ARCHITECTURE; DESKTOP PUBLISHING; DOCUMENT PROCESSING.

Gary Hanson

bandwidth a measure of the frequency component of a signal or the capacity of a communication channel to carry signals

Internet Resources

Himowitz, Mike. "Computer-Assisted Reporting." <http://www.clark.net/pub/mikeh/car.htm>

JournalismNet. <http://www.journalismnet.com>

"Today in Journalism." Poynter Institute for Media Studies. <http://www.poynter.org/>

Marconi, Guglielmo

Italian Physicist
1874–1937

Known as the father of radio, Guglielmo Marconi was born April 25, 1874 in Bologna, Italy. He was the younger son of an Italian landowner, Giuseppe Marconi, and Anne Jameson, whose father was the founder of the Jameson Irish whiskey distillery. As a youngster, Marconi spent the winter months in England or Florence, Italy, with his mother, brother, and English relatives. Schooling for the Marconi brothers was divided between their mother, who taught them English and religion, and a tutor, who provided instruction in Italian and other subjects. Perhaps through teaching her sons, Anne Marconi became aware her son's intellectual abilities and his determination to solve problems on his own. She supported Marconi's efforts throughout her life. He began exploring the properties of electricity at a young age by reading scientific publications and duplicating and modifying experiments. This exploration continued throughout his life resulting in the foundational work he did in the field of wireless technology and telecommunications.

Guglielmo Marconi.

Marconi attended primary and secondary schools. He was not noted for his scholarship. Instead of attending university, arrangements were made for him to study with Vincenzo Rosa, a professor of electrophysics. These sessions introduced Marconi to the work of Heinrich Hertz, James Clerk Maxwell, Oliver Joseph Lodge, and others conducting experiments to explain electromagnetic waves. Marconi approached the field with the idea of using these waves for wireless communication. His greatest contribution was applying theoretical and basic discoveries to develop useful applications. To test his ideas, Marconi built the necessary equipment from materials around the estate. His experiments were conducted in a laboratory at his home. The first hurdle to overcome was increasing the distance that a wireless transmission could travel. Marconi achieved greater distances by increasing the range of the transmitters, by improving the sensitivity of the receivers, and by using antennas. His standard message for testing equipment became the three-dot Morse code for the letter "S."

Once his messages were traveling more than a mile across the family estate, it was time to seek funding from the Italian government. His request was denied. The next logical place to apply was England because wireless telegraphy would benefit the country's naval and maritime activities. Also, his English relatives could and would help. In 1896, at age twenty-two, Marconi set out for England. He first applied for an English patent, then met with Sir William Peerce, chief engineer of the English Postal and Telegraph Services. Recognizing the value and potential of Marconi's work, Peerce became an advocate and close friend. Ship-to-ship and ship-to-shore wireless telegraphy was operational the following year and Marconi founded his first company, Wireless Telegraph and Signal Company Limited.

The next hurdle to overcome was sending a message across the Atlantic Ocean. The widely held theory was that the curvature of the Earth made the transmission impossible. Marconi enlisted the expertise of John Fleming to solve the technical problems related to his continuing experiments to transmit across the Atlantic. The first transatlantic transmission from Cornwall, England, to Newfoundland, Canada, occurred in 1901 proving that the curvature of the Earth did not limit transmissions. He solved the problem of messages going to multiple receivers by using different transmission frequencies and setting the sender and receiver to the same frequency. Marconi continued exploring the possibilities of radio waves for uses beyond telecommunications and is credited with proposing the use of microwaves as a form of physical therapy.

Marconi's approach to patents and business was very conservative. When applying for patents or support for his work, he would explain the function of his invention or outline the improvements over previous methods but did not include a full disclosure of the design until a patent was granted. He followed the same procedures when demonstrating his equipment. This method protected his work from others and allowed him more fully to realize the monetary value of his systems. Many honors were bestowed on him, including the Nobel Prize for Physics in 1909, which he shared with Karl Ferdinand Braun who modified Marconi's transmitters to increase their range and usefulness. Marconi's business empire stretched across Europe and the United States, and one result of his international reputation was his appointment to represent Italy at the Paris Peace Conference after World War I. (Marconi had served in the Italian Army and Navy during World War I.) He continued being productive until a few years before his death from a heart condition. Marconi died in Rome on July 20, 1937. SEE ALSO GEOGRAPHIC INFORMATION SYSTEMS; TELECOMMUNICATION; WIRELESS TECHNOLOGY.

Bertha Kugelman Morimoto

Bibliography

Masini, Giancarlo. *Marconi.* New York: Marsilio Publishers, 1995.

Mobile Computing

paradigm an example, pattern, or way of thinking

infrastructure the foundation or permanent installation necessary for a structure or system to operate

As the Internet becomes increasingly popular, a new **paradigm** is being developed in networked computing known as *nomadic computing* or *mobile computing*. Mobile computing aims to provide a network **infrastructure** and corresponding terminal capability to perform all desktop-like computing functions seamlessly at any place or time, even while the terminal is moving. This means that anytime and anywhere, a user would be able to browse the web, check e-mail, play digital music, and perform all other computing activities without having to be behind a desktop at home or work. At its best, mobile computing would allow a user to have access to a consistent working environment.

Practically, mobile computing is a challenge for several reasons. For anytime, anywhere functionality, the user must be able to carry the mobile computing device. The computing device must be small, light, and at the same time be capable of performing the complex tasks of a desktop computer. Anytime, anywhere access to a network will also require wireless connectivity as the user cannot be tied to a place where a wired connection is available. Both of these requirements are quite challenging to fulfill.

Currently, small lightweight devices operating on battery power are resource constrained. The display cannot be large, bright, or complex as this affects size and power consumption. For the same reason, the processing power, memory, storage space, and communication ports are limited or non-

existent. Ideally, mobile computing devices would be **dumb terminals** with all the services and computation performed by a powerful **server** computer on a network. In such a scenario, the mobile computing device would simply be a display for the information transferred from the server. However, current wireless connectivity is neither **ubiquitous** nor uniform. Data rates on wireless connections can range between 9.6 kbps in outdoor areas with wide coverage to 11 mbps in indoor areas with local coverage. This means that a user may not be always connected, and if the user is connected, the connections could be very slow or quite fast.

One solution to the problem of dynamic connection quality and disconnections is for the mobile computing device to download the information when there is good connectivity and then be able to work offline. The mobile computer must be sophisticated enough to store the information and process it offline. However, this approach is contradictory to the requirement that mobile computing devices be simple and dumb. As the flow of information is over wireless connections, security also becomes an issue and is especially challenging due to the size and resources of the device. There is consequently a tradeoff between the form factor of the device and the ability of the device to provide the user with a rich set of services.

Advances in technology have reduced many of these limitations, and mobile computing is closer to reality than ever before. Mobile computing devices are becoming smaller, lighter, and more powerful than their predecessors. They also come in various types and connectivity options. Two

The portability of laptops allows people to perform various computing activities while away from home. For example, a researcher can instantly report findings while studying the ancient Step Pyramid in Egypt.

dumb terminals keyboards and screens connected to a distant computer without any processing capability

server a computer that does not deal directly with human users, but instead handles requests from other computers for services to be performed

ubiquitous to be commonly available everywhere

Global Positioning System (GPS) a method of locating a point on the Earth's surface that uses received signals transmitted from satellites to accurately calculate position

local area networks (LANs) high speed computer networks that are designed for users who are located near each other

personal area networking the interconnectivity of personal productivity devices like computers, mobile telephones, and personal organizers

simputers simple to use computers that take on the functionality of personal computers, but are mobile and act as personal assistants and information organizers

WHAT IS MP3?

MP3 is a compressed audio format that was derived from the MPEG video format in the late 1980s. Files in MP3 format are not exactly small—approximately 1 megabyte per minute of CD-quality sound. However, they are a small fraction of the size of audio files found on commercially available compact discs, yet for most users the sound quality is comparable. Because of the small file size, MP3s are easily downloaded and managed by users with modest computer power and may be loaded into small portable devices that listeners can enjoy anywhere.

prominent classes of mobile computing devices today are those that use the PalmOS and the PocketPC operating systems. The former class of devices holds a dominant share of the market whereas the latter is growing in market size and is especially popular with executives in business organizations. Often referred to as palmtop computers or handheld computers, these devices are capable of simple word processing, spreadsheet applications, web browsing, calendar notations, and address management. There are low-end handheld computers with monochromatic displays, low resolution, limited memory, and somewhat bulky sizes. Higher-end devices are extremely thin, have a high-resolution, and can include color displays.

Because the size of handheld computers is expected to be small, but they are required to perform many tasks, manufacturers have adopted an "expansion slot" approach. Essentially, a handheld computer is equipped with a slot where a variety of attachments can be connected. Attachments could include memory cards for storage, a **Global Positioning System (GPS)** receiver for determining the user's location, a digital camera, an MP3 player for digital music, or modules for network connectivity—wired or wireless. Some of the attachments have their own power supply, increasing the size/weight of the handheld computer, but because they can be used only when needed, it eliminates the necessity of having all capabilities available in the handheld computer at the same time. The expansion slots of one device may not match that of a device from another vendor. For example, PocketPC devices have standard Type II PC card slots or flash card slots. But PalmOS devices have different slots like the larger Springboard module or postage stamp-sized secure digital/multimedia card slots.

Wireless connectivity for handheld computers also comes in several varieties. Most handheld computers come with built-in infrared ports that can be used to exchange information with a network or another computer at short range. Many of them can connect to wireless **local area networks (LANs)** based on the IEEE 802.11 standard. They can also connect to wireless services like Mobitex and the cellular digital packet data (CDPD) networks that provide service over larger areas spanning cities and along highways, although at a lower data rate. Some cellular telephone service providers are also making cell phone modules available for attachment to the expansion slots of handhelds computers. Bluetooth, a new wireless standard for **personal area networking**, is also available for some handheld computers.

Recently, the free Linux operating system has been modified to run on handheld computers of different types. Some manufacturers are also adopting Linux for their handheld computers. As this operating system carries no licensing fee, it could further reduce the cost of handheld computers. In developing countries like India, voice activated Linux-based **simputers** have been developed for mass usage in rural areas where the computing infrastructure is limited. Device integration, such as the integration of cell phones and handheld computers, is also occurring. Location aware mobile computing—in which a person is able to obtain information on local restaurants, theaters, coffee-shops, maps, driving directions, traffic, weather, news, tourist attractions, and the like on a handheld computer—is also becoming prominent. SEE ALSO Embedded Technology (Ubiquitous Computing); Geographic Information Systems; Wireless Technology.

Prashant Krishnamurthy

Bibliography

Dhawan, Chander. *Mobile Computing: A Systems Integrator's Handbook.* New York: Mc-Graw-Hill, 1997.

Roth, Cliff. *Mobile Computing for Dummies.* Foster City, CA: IDG Books, 1997.

Molecular Computing

Molecular computing is the science of using individual molecules to build computer programs. Instead of running software on a traditional computer, some scientists are now trying to replace the **silicon chip** with test tubes, liquids, and even living cells due to a concern about the limits of miniaturization—a real and pressing problem that threatens the future advancement of computers.

To get an idea of how small computers have already become, think of a standard processor chip and imagine this: if the chip circuit were magnified such that the individual components were the size of office buildings, and the interconnections between them were the size of streets and avenues, then the entire circuit at this scale would stretch from London to San Francisco. Very impressive, but can it continue? The answer is "no."

When it comes to creating smaller and smaller computers, existing technology—white-suited technicians in clean-rooms making silicon chips—will eventually hit a very solid wall imposed by the realities of physics. Once circuits are miniaturized down to the atomic level, components begin to interfere with one another, and the whole chip becomes useless. It is for this reason that some people are investigating alternatives to **silicon** to build the computers of the future.

Scientists in the field of **nanocomputing** are investigating several different possibilities, including the use of biological molecules. It seems that deoxyribonucleic acid (DNA), the very stuff of life, may hold the key. A tiny, almost invisible drop of water can contain trillions of molecules of DNA. Nature has information storage down to a fine art: a human body contains countless copies of the genetic sequence that makes a person who he or she is, and yet one single copy of that sequence would occupy a large encyclopedia if it were printed out.

Moreover, when scientists manipulate solutions of DNA, they operate on trillions of strands simultaneously. This massive parallel processing, combined with the incredible degree of miniaturization offered by DNA, leads scientists to believe it could form one of the main components of twenty-first-century computers.

The personal computer or laptop stores information in the form of bits, each of which may take the value one or zero. A computer software program is nothing more than a string of ones and zeroes, which is interpreted by the computer processor. DNA molecules are similar in that they are simply strings of, not ones and zeroes, but As, Gs, Cs, and Ts (this is how the 1997 film *Gattaca*, starring Ethan Hawke and Jude Law, got its name). The human genetic sequence can be thought of as "software," which is then interpreted by human "hardware"—the various processes that guide development from a single cell to a fully functioning human being.

silicon chip a common term for a semiconductor integrated circuit device

silicon a chemical element with symbol Si; the most abundant element in the Earth's crust and the most commonly used semiconductor material

nanocomputing the science and engineering of building mechanical machines at the atomic level

---

"BUNNY SUITS"

Employees involved in manufacturing microchips don special white suits reminiscent of those worn by crews handling hazardous materials or medical personnel dealing with highly contagious diseases. Sometimes called "bunny suits," the protective clothing worn in microchip processing plants is necessary to keep hair, skin, and dust particles from getting into the tiny microchips. One speck of dust could cause the microchip to malfunction, so precautions are taken to keep the environment free of such particles. In addition, employees must remove makeup, wear gloves and cover their shoes with booties, and go through an air shower before entering the work area.

Scientists Hendrik Schon and Zhenan Bao at Bell Labs work to perfect molecular-sized organic transistors. The transistor is so small that 10 million of them can fit on the head of a pin.

The key to using DNA to compute is that it can be manufactured in the laboratory. A request for a particular sequence (say, AGTTCA) can be given to a technician, and, after a short wait, a machine produces countless copies of the same short DNA sequence, ready for use. So how can DNA be used to solve a computing problem?

The problem of "coloring" has a long history. Given a map of the mainland United States, each state can be colored one of four colors such that no two states sharing a border are colored the same. However, what happens if there are only three colors, say, red, green, and blue? Will it still be possible to not color two adjacent states the same? This problem is easy to describe, but fiendishly difficult to solve once the map gets only moderately large.

The first thing to do is to generate all possible ways to color the map, each way represented by a single long sequence of DNA. This is done by mixing together trillions of copies of smaller sequences each encoding, say, "color Michigan green," "color Wisconsin blue," or "color Michigan red" as a distinct sequence of bases. If the sequence encoding is right, these sequences stick together to form larger sequences, where each state is represented only once. Of course, most of these longer sequences encode undesirable colorings, for example, where both California and Nevada (which are, of course, neighbors) are colored green.

However, if enough DNA is used, a correct coloring is probably in there somewhere; it is the needle in a very large haystack. The next step is to remove from the test tube all of the undesirable colorings—the equivalent of the "hay." For each state border, any sequences that color two neighboring states the same is removed. This is done by adding extra DNA sequences and a dash of chemicals to the tube. This process is repeated for each border until all that is left is the "needle"—a sequence encoding a correct coloring of the map.

Of course, biological operations work on geological time scales compared to twenty-first-century **supercomputers**. The power of the DNA computer lies in its massive parallel processing capability; when a chemical is added to the test tube it acts on every strand simultaneously. Because the average tube holds trillions of strands, that is a lot of computing going on at once.

Some scientists are going one stage further and re-engineering the genetic programs of living cells. The machinery of life that controls the development of cells can now be re-programmed to give the cells simple, human-defined "decision-making" capabilities. By replacing specific sequences within their genetic code, it may soon be possible to engineer cells to act as microbial "robots" that seek out disease or deliver drugs at the point of infection. Of course, these various developments may take decades to bear fruit, and some may never get beyond the concept stage. What is clear, however, is that the fusion of computers and biology will provide some of the most exciting scientific breakthroughs of the twenty-first century. SEE ALSO MEDICAL SYSTEMS; MOLECULAR BIOLOGY; NANOCOMPUTING.

Martyn Amos

supercomputers very high performance computers, usually comprised of many processors and used for modeling and simulation of complex phenomena, like meteorology

Bibliography

Adleman, Leonard M. "Computing with DNA." *Scientific American* (August 1998): 54–61.

———. "Molecular Computation of Solutions to Combinatorial Problems." *Science* 266 (1994): 1021–1024.

Nanocomputing

Nanocomputing describes computing that uses extremely small, or nanoscale, devices (one nanometer [nm] is one billionth of a meter). In 2001, state-of-the-art electronic devices could be as small as about 100 nm, which is about the same size as a virus. The **integrated circuits** (IC) industry, however, looks to the future to determine the smallest electronic devices possible within the limits of computing technology.

Until the mid-1990s, the term "nanoscale" generally denoted circuit features smaller than 100 nm. As the IC industry started to build commercial devices at such size scales since the beginning of the 2000s, the term "nanocomputing" has been reserved for device features well below 50 nm to even the size of individual molecules, which are only a few nm. Scientists and engineers are only beginning to conceive new ways to approach computing using extremely small devices and individual molecules.

integrated circuits circuits with the transistors, resistors, and other circuit elements etched into the surface of single chips of semiconducting material, usually silicon

All computers must operate by basic physical processes. Contemporary digital computers use currents and voltages in tens of millions of complementary metal oxide semiconductor (CMOS) **transistors** covering a few square centimeters of silicon. If device dimensions could be scaled down by a factor of 10 or even 100, then circuit functionality would increase 100 to 10,000 times.

Furthermore, if such a new device or computer architecture were to be developed, this might lead to millionfold increases in computing power. Such circuits would consume far less power per function, increasing battery life and shrinking boxes and fans necessary to cool circuits. Also, they would be remarkably fast and able to perform calculations that are not yet possible on any computer. Benefits of significantly faster computers include more accuracy in predicting weather patterns, recognizing complex figures in images, and developing **artificial intelligence (AI)**. Potentially, **single-chip** memories containing thousands of **gigabytes** of data will be developed, capable of holding entire libraries of books, music, or movies.

Modern transistors are engineering marvels, requiring hundreds of careful processing steps performed in ultraclean environments. Today's transistors operate with **microampere** currents and only a few thousand electrons generating the signals, but as they are scaled down, fewer electrons are available to create the large voltage swings required of them. This compels scientists and engineers to seek new physical phenomena that will allow information processing to occur using other mechanisms than those currently employed for transistor action.

Future nanocomputers could be evolutionary, scaled-down versions of today's computers, working in essentially the same ways and with similar but nanoscale devices. Or they may be revolutionary, being based on some new device or molecular structure not yet developed. Research on nanodevices is aimed at learning the physical properties of very small structures and then determining how these can be used to perform some kind of computing functions.

Current nanocomputing research involves the study of very small electronic devices and molecules, their fabrication, and architectures that can benefit from their inherent electrical properties. Nanostructures that have been studied include semiconductor quantum dots, single electron structures, and various molecules. Very small particles of material confine electrons in ways that large ones do not, so that the **quantum mechanical** nature of the electrons becomes important.

Quantum dots behave like artificial atoms and molecules in that the electrons inside of them can have only certain values of energy, which can be used to represent logic information robustly. Another area is that of "single electron devices," which, as the name implies, represent information by the behavior of only one, single electron. The ultimate scaled-down electronic devices are individual molecules on the size scale of a nm.

Chemists can synthesize molecules easily and in large quantities; these can be made to act as switches or charge containers of almost any desirable shape and size. One molecule that has attracted considerable interest is that of the common deoxyribonucleic acid (DNA), best known from biology. Ideas for attaching smaller molecules, called "functional groups," to the mol-

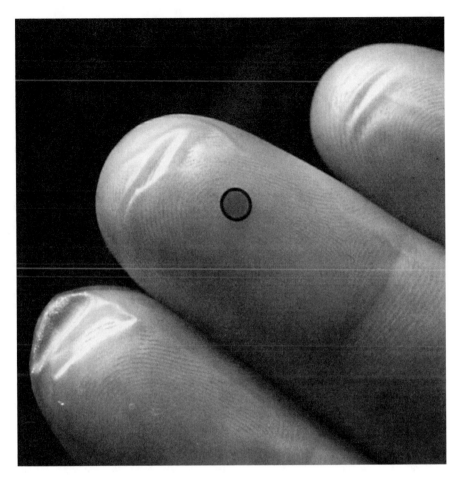

As the size of computer chips gets smaller and smaller, companies continue to invest research dollars to reduce the size. The near future of nanocomputing could bring powerful computers that are smaller than the head of a pin.

ecules and creating larger arrays of DNA for computing are under investigation. These are but a few of the many approaches being considered.

In addition to discovering new devices on the nanoscale, it is critically important to devise new ways to interconnect these devices for useful applications. One potential architecture is called **cellular neural networks (CNN)** in which devices are connected to neighbors, and as inputs are provided at the edge, the interconnects cause a change in the devices to sweep like a wave across the array, providing an output at the other edge.

An extension of the CNN concept is that of **quantum-dot cellular automata (QCA)**. This architecture uses arrangements of single electrons that communicate with each other by Coulomb repulsion over large arrays. The arrangement of electrons at the edges provides the computational output. The electron arrangements of QCA are controlled by an external clock and operate according to the rules of **Boolean logic**.

Another potential architecture is that of "crossbar switching" in which molecules are placed at the intersections of nanometer-scale wires. These molecules provide coupling between the wires and provide computing functionality.

The fabrication of these nanoscale systems is also a critical area of investigation. Current ICs are manufactured in a parallel process in which short wavelength light exposes an entire IC in one flash, taking only a fraction of a second. Serial processes, in which each device is exposed separately,

cellular neural networks (CNN) a neural network topology that uses multi-dimensional array structures comprised of cells that work together in localized groups

quantum-dot cellular automata (QCA) the theory of automata as applied to quantum dot architectures, which are a proposed approach for the development of computers at nanotechnology scales

Boolean logic a system, developed by George Boole, which treats abstract objects (such as sets or classes) as algebraic quantities; Boole applied his mathematical system to the study of classical logic

are too slow as of early 2002 to expose billions of devices in a reasonable amount of time. Serial processes that are capable of attaining nanometer, but not molecular, resolution include using beams of electrons or ions to write patterns on an IC. Atomic resolution can be achieved by using currents from very sharp tips, a process called scanning probe lithography, to write on surfaces one atom at a time, but this technique is too slow for manufacturing unless thousands of tips can be used in parallel.

It is reasonable to search for nanoscale particles, such as molecules, that do not require difficult fabrication steps. An alternative to the direct patterning of nanoscale system components is that of self assembly, a process in which small particles or molecules arrange themselves. Regardless of the method used to create arrays of nanostructures, organizing the nanodevices into useful architectures, getting data in and out, and performing computing are problems that have not yet been solved.

In summary, nanocomputing technology has the potential for revolutionizing the way that computers are used. However, in order to achieve this goal, major progress in device technology, computer architectures, and IC processing must first be accomplished. It may take decades before revolutionary nanocomputing technology becomes commercially feasible. SEE ALSO ARTIFICIAL LIFE; CENTRAL PROCESSING UNIT; GENERATIONS, COMPUTERS; MOLECULAR COMPUTING; NEURAL NETWORKS.

Gary H. Bernstein and Wolfgang Porod

Bibliography

"The Future of Microelectronics." *Nature* 406 (2000): 1021–1054.

Coontz, Robert, and Phil Szurami, eds. "Issues in Nanotechnology." *Science* 290, no. 5496 (2000): 1523–1558.

Turton, Richard. *The Quantum Dot: A Journey into the Future of Microelectronics.* New York: Oxford University Press, 1996.

Internet Resources

MITRE's Nanoelectronics and Nanocomputing Homepage. <http://www.mitre.org/research/nanotech/>

National Nanotechnology Initiative. <http://www.nsf.gov/home/crssprgm/nano/nni.htm>

Newell, Allen

American Scientist and Mathematician
1927–1992

A scientist and mathematician, Allen Newell is best remembered for his work and research on **artificial intelligence (AI)**. Some of his most well known initiatives include the Logic Theorem Machine, a mechanical device that would be used to create new theorems, as well as the SOAR project, a research initiative that attempted to implement cognitive or rule-based computer simulations.

Newell was born in San Francisco, California, on March 19, 1927, the son of Dr. Robert R. Newell, a distinguished professor of radiology at Stanford Medical School, and Jeanette Le Valley Newell. He attended Lowell High School—the intellectual high school of San Francisco—where he was inspired academically and fell in love (at age sixteen) with fellow student

artificial intelligence (AI) a branch of computer science dealing with creating computer hardware and software to mimic the way people think and perform practical tasks

Noel McKenna. Newell and McKenna married at age twenty and remained married for forty-five years.

Newell had no intention of following a scientific career upon graduation from high school. However, after working a summer in a shipyard, he enlisted in the U.S. Navy, and it was during his tenure in the navy that he became interested in scientific enterprise. He was serving on a ship that carried scientific observers to the Bikini atoll (island) to study the effect of nuclear tests, and Newell was assigned the task of mapping the radiation distribution over the atolls. Newell discovered how exciting science could be, and thereafter, he characterized himself simply as a scientist.

Newell received his bachelor of science degree in physics from Stanford University in 1949, spent a year at Princeton doing graduate work in mathematics, and obtained a Ph.D. from Carnegie Institute of Technology (now Carnegie Mellon University) in industrial administration in 1957.

Newell's primary interest, like that of his colleague Herbert A. Simon (1916–2001), was in understanding human intelligence and cognition. He developed the SOAR project with students and colleagues, including John E. Laird, a professor at the University of Michigan, and Paul S. Rosenbloom, a professor at the University of Southern California, and others. Essentially, SOAR was a rule-based computer simulation or emulation of a cognitive system that was capable of learning and solving problems. The rules are defined by such structures as "If . . . then . . .," similar to structures that are thought by some to govern human behavior.

Like Simon, Newell was primarily interested in organizations and their behavior, but he soon moved toward individual cognition. He and Simon had met while Newell was working for the RAND Corporation in Santa Monica, California. It was Simon who influenced Newell to come to Carnegie Tech to obtain a doctorate. Simon and Newell collaborated, and Newell continued to work for RAND in Pittsburgh, as a one-man "office" until he became part of the Carnegie Institute faculty in 1961.

Newell's interest in human learning and thinking was also spurred by Oliver Selfridge, an artificial intelligence researcher, who created theories on **pattern recognition**, that is, the recognition of letters and other patterns. This led Newell to think of computing as a symbolic manipulation, rather than an arithmetic one, and led him to write a chess playing program c. 1955, which was then implemented by himself, Simon, and John Clifford Shaw in 1956.

Newell also collaborated with Simon and Shaw on the Logic Theorem Machine, a program to find or develop theorems. The theorems were discovered by working backward from the theorem to the **axioms** in an inductive method of discovery, looking for patterns or regularity in the data. This was an interest that would last his entire life. Newell was also a member of the initial Dartmouth conference, considered to be the first conference in artificial intelligence, along with Simon, Marvin Minsky, John McCarthy, and others.

Newell won the A. M. Turing Award with Simon in 1975. He was also the recipient of the first Award for Research Excellence from the International Joint Conference on Artificial Intelligence and was elected the first president of the American Association for Artificial Intelligence.

Allen Newell.

pattern recognition a process used by some artificial-intelligence systems to identify a variety of patterns, including visual patterns, information patterns buried in a noisy signal, and word patterns imbedded in text

axioms statements that are taken to be true; the foundation of a theory

NEWELL AND SIMON

Due to Newell's long association with Herbert A. Simon, it is easy to lose track of Newell as an independent researcher. Yet, although his early career was heavily influenced and entwined with that of Simon, he conducted independent work both during and after his early association with Simon. In fact, after the 1970s and until his death, Newell mostly communicated with Simon via weekly chats, but did little direct collaboration.

With Stuart Card and Thomas Moran, Newell also participated in some of the early research in Human Computer Interaction. This involved the GOMS system of Goals, Operators, Methods, and Selection, a structure for studying human behavior with the computer (and other machines, e.g., calculators) as well as the performance of any task. He also developed the mechanism, with Simon, of "talking out loud" to study the way people solve problems, and the pair was instrumental in developing means-end analysis, a way of explaining how people solve problems that is based on the theory that people notice a discrepancy between their current state and some goal state and employ some operator or operation to remove or overcome the difference.

With Shaw and Simon, Newell developed the information processing languages (IPL-I through IPL-V), which, although not as popular as LISP, were early languages for artificial intelligence. He later took a lead in the effort to develop OPS5 (and other OPS languages), a rule-based language for building artificial systems such as expert systems. His final project, ongoing after his death, was, however, the SOAR system. This was a system that purported to give an architecture of cognition, meant to explore the nature of a unified theory of cognition, a "mental" architecture. SEE ALSO ARTIFICIAL INTELLIGENCE; DECISION SUPPORT SYSTEMS; SIMON, HERBERT A.

Roger R. Flynn

Bibliography

Card, Stuart K., Thomas P. Moran, and Allen Newell. *The Psychology of Human-Computer Interaction.* Hillsdale, NJ: Erlbaum, 1983.

Rosenbloom, Paul S., John E. Laird, Allen Newell, and Robert McCarl. "A Preliminary Analysis of the Soar Architecture as a Basis for General Intelligence." *Artificial Intelligence* 47, nos. 1–3 (1991): 289–325.

Internet Resources

Simon, Herbert A. *Biographical Memories.* <http://www.nap.edu/readingroom/books/biomems/anewell.html>

Nyquist, Harry

Swedish-born American Electrical Engineer
1889–1976

Harry Nyquist was an electrical engineer who was affiliated with AT&T from 1917 to 1954 as a researcher and inventor. His practical contributions to the computer science industry include improvements to long distance telephone circuits and picture transmission systems. His theoretical accomplishments in telecommunications laid the groundwork for **T1 digital circuitry**.

Nyquist was born on February 7, 1889, in Nilsby, Sweden. His family name was originally Jonsson. His parents, Lars and Kataerina Jonsson, had problems receiving their mail in Sweden because other men in the area were also named Lars Jonsson. A common local solution to such problems was for one family to change its name; thus, his family became the Nyquists. Although they were not wealthy and education was not free, the Nyquists managed to send all eight of their children to school for at least six years. Nyquist

T1 digital circuitry a type of digital network technology that can handle separate voice and/or digital communications lines

was a promising student who was encouraged to become a teacher. Since his family could not afford the extensive education necessary for a teaching degree, Nyquist, at age fourteen, decided to emigrate to the United States. For the next four years he worked at the construction site of a chemical factory in Sweden to qualify as an employable emigrant and to earn passage money.

In 1907 Nyquist arrived in the Unites States, and by 1912 he entered the University of North Dakota. He earned a bachelor of science degree in electrical engineering two years later, and his master's in 1915. Nyquist left North Dakota for Yale University to pursue a doctorate in physics, which he completed in 1917.

Upon graduation from Yale, Nyquist went to work for AT&T, where he remained until he retired in 1954. Nyquist started in the research department of AT&T. In the mid-1920s AT&T established Bell Laboratories as a research facility for studying theoretical and practical aspects of communication. Nyquist became a researcher with Bell Labs.

At that time Nyquist worked on telegraphy problems related to linear circuits—circuits that transmit electromagnetic signals in a fashion that allows the sending of multiple messages at different frequencies at the same time and allows two signals to travel in opposite directions at the same time. His observations were that the line speed of transmission was proportional to the width of the frequencies used. Nyquist published this theory in 1924 in the paper "Certain Factors Affecting Telegraph Speed." In his 1928 publication, "Certain Topics in Telegraph Transmission Theory," Nyquist presented the principles for converting **analog** signals, (i.e., voice or music) to digital signals, binary 0's and 1's, and back to analog, without loss of the signal's meaning.

analog a quantity (often an electrical signal) that is continuous in time and amplitude

The theorem that he offered was that a sample of twice the highest signal frequency rate captures the signal perfectly thereby making it possible to reconstruct the original signal. This work laid the foundation for many advances in telecommunications. Claude Shannon (1916–2001) incorporated this work in his development of **information theory**. It was not until the **transistor** was invented in 1947 that sampling, encoding, and transmitting of signals could be done fast enough to develop commercial communications systems that converted analog to digital signals. Today's T1 circuits, which carry digital signals converted from analog voice signals, are designed around the requirements of Nyquist's sampling theorem.

information theory a branch of mathematics and engineering that deals with the encoding, transmission, reception, and decoding of information

In addition, Nyquist expanded on J. B. Johnson's studies of thermal noise by providing a mathematical explanation which has become critically important for communications systems. His 1934 discovery of how to determine when negative feedback amplifiers are stable helped control artillery using electromechanical feedback systems during World War II.

transistor a contraction of TRANSfer resISTOR; semiconductor device, invented by John Bardeen, Walter Brattain, and William Shockley, which has three terminals; can be used for switching and amplifying electrical signals

Nyquist developed a method to transmit pictures—a crude but working facsimile (fax) machine—in which a photographic transparency was scanned, the scanned data was converted to electric signals in proportion to the intensity of shades and tones of the image, and these signals were sent over telephone lines to a photographic negative film. The film was developed using standard darkroom techniques. Today's fax machines work on the same principles.

Nyquist's thirty-seven-year career at Bell Laboratories included contributions to long distance telephone technology as well as the development of communication systems to transmit pictures. His accomplishments ranged from the theoretic to the technical and practical. In 1960 the Institute of Electrical and Electronics Engineers (IEEE) awarded Nyquist its medal of honor for significant contributions to the field of electronic engineering.

After retiring from Bell Laboratories in 1954, Nyquist served as a government consultant on military communications. He died on April 4, 1976, in Harlingen, Texas, at the age of eighty-seven. SEE ALSO BANDWIDTH; SHANNON, CLAUDE E.; TELECOMMUNICATIONS.

Bertha Kugelman Morimoto

Internet Resources

"Harry Nyquist." <http://www.geocities.com/bioelectrochemistry/nyquist.htm>

Verstraete, A. A. "Nyquist's Theorem In-Depth." <http://www.smeal.psu.edu/misweb/datacomm/id/id_nyqui.html>

intellectual property the acknowledgement that an individual's creativity and innovation can be owned in the same way as physical property

copyrights the legal rules and regulations concerning the copying and redistribution of documents

trademark rights a trademark is a name, symbol, or phrase that identifies a trading organization and is owned by that organization

Patents

Patents have become an important form of **intellectual property** protection for computer software and informational media, supplementing and sometimes replacing copyright protection. Patents are exclusive rights granted by the federal government to the inventors of new and useful machines, articles, substances, or processes. The patent right is offered in return for full disclosure by inventors as to how to make and use their patented invention.

The holder of a patent has the right to prevent others from making, using, selling, offering to sell, or importing the invention, and he or she can sue for damages if any of these exclusive rights is violated. However, because the patent right is extensive and nearly absolute, patents are granted only for very significant advances in technology: the invention cannot have been obvious to those of skill in that technology.

As a consequence, unlike other forms of intellectual property protection, such as **copyrights** and **trademark rights**, patent rights do not arise spontaneously. In the United States, patents are only issued after an administrative application procedure in the United States Patent Office. The inventor must submit an application that fully describes and explains the invention as well as sets out the limits of technology being claimed. This description will form the basis for the published patent once the application is approved. If the patent is granted, a full description of the invention and its use is published by the government in the patent. These published patent disclosures form a fund of knowledge for the public.

The term of the exclusive right lasts for twenty years from the date that the application is filed, and at the end of the patent term, the invention passes into the public domain; that is, anyone may freely use it. Should the Patent Office grant a patent improperly, the patent may be invalidated by a challenge in court.

As in the case of most intellectual property, including copyright and trademarks, there is no such thing as a worldwide patent. Successful appli-

Open Port Technology chairperson Randy Storch displays his company's patent to create least cost routing technology for Internet messages.

cations to the United States Patent Office will result in a patent that is good only in the United States. If inventors desire patent protection in other countries, they must apply for a patent in the patent office of each country where a patent is wanted. The expense of so many patent applications may be prohibitive, so inventors must frequently be selective as to the countries in which they wish to apply. The countries in which an inventor chooses to apply will be determined by long-range business plans; usually, inventors will choose to apply for patents in the countries where they are most likely to license their inventions.

Because patent law covers processes, and computer software constitutes a type of process, patent law might seem a natural form of intellectual property protection for software inventions. However, software and related inventions were nearly excluded from patent protection altogether. Patent protection does not extend to natural "discoveries," as it does to manufactured inventions. Thus, laws of nature and mathematical formulae are typically not considered patentable.

During the early 1980s, the U.S. Supreme Court issued two opinions denying patent protection to computer programs on the grounds that a software **algorithm** is like a mathematical formula, and therefore unpatentable. The court soon modified this position to hold that computer programs are not patentable by themselves, but only in association with a tangible machine or tangible output. During the next twenty years, this position grad-

TRADE SECRETS VS. PATENT PROTECTION

An alternative to patent protection is trade secrecy protection. Trade secrets can include software, databases, or any type of valuable information that is not generally known but which gives the owner a business advantage. The owner of a trade secret must take reasonable steps to keep the information confidential, such as locking away important documents, or passwords protecting computer files. The law prevents competitors from obtaining trade secrets through theft, bribery, espionage, or hiring away a business' employees. Competitors are permitted to discover independently a trade secret through their own efforts, or to reverse engineer a trade secret by examining a product in order to learn how it works. Employees of technology firms are frequently required to sign confidentiality agreements promising to keep their employers' valuable information secret.

algorithm a rule or procedure used to solve a mathematical problem—most often described as a sequence of steps

ually evolved in lower courts to a position that software would be patentable if it produced a "useful result."

The United States Patent Office began routinely accepting patent applications claiming software inventions first as new and useful processes, or as articles of manufacture when associated with some hardware or tangible media. This acceptance of software as patentable subject matter resulted in the explosive proliferation of software patents during the 1990s and early twenty-first century, both in the United States and abroad.

The acceptance of software patents by U.S. courts opened the door to widespread patenting of other types of processes or methods related to digital media. Because the standard for patentability is a "useful result," many processes involving computers now come under patent protection. Such processes need not be internal to the computer's operation, but may involve activity and interface with the user. Such patentable processes might include web-based methods for instruction, electronic commerce, and informational display. Some of these method patents have been controversial because critics view them as being too obvious to deserve patent protection. SEE ALSO COPYRIGHT.

Dan L. Burk

Bibliography

Davis, Randall. "The Digital Dilemma." *Communications of the ACM* 44, no. 2 (2001): 77–83.

Miller, Arthur R., and Michael H. Davis. *Intellectual Property in a Nutshell*, 3rd ed. St. Paul, MN: West Publishing, 2000.

Photography

The digital imaging technologies commonly used today evolved from technologies created by the National Aeronautics and Space Administration (NASA) and the Jet Propulsion Laboratory in the early 1960s. Government scientists were looking for a way to transmit imaging data more accurately from outer space to Earth. The analog (wave) technologies used at the time were prone to **degradation** during transmission. The scientists devised a way to digitize the images taken by satellites and rocket mounted cameras. By turning the analog transmission into a digital code, the scientists solved the problems of image degradation. The imaging data could be sent long distances without a loss of quality, thus rendering a more accurate view of distant galactic sights.

degradation the reduction in quality or performance of a system

The newly invented digital technologies were too expensive for the general public, but they were commonly used by governments, scientists, and corporations for **topographic**, atmospheric, military, medical, and astronomic purposes. The invention of the microchip, a small yet powerful processor, in the early 1980s enabled the creation of smaller, more affordable digital imaging equipment and the personal computer for the home and small business. The first commercial digital camera appeared in 1981 with the release of the Sony Mavica.

topographic pertaining to the features of a terrain or surface

Most digital cameras look similar to and share many common functions of 35mm cameras. Digital cameras have lenses, bodies, and flashes along with controls for focus and zoom like traditional cameras. Several manufacturers created a digital back that integrated existing analog cameras with the new digital technologies. Digital backs are mounted onto the back of analog cameras. The sensory mechanism of the digital back takes the place of the film and fits into position on the same plane as the film.

Unlike their film-based predecessors, digital cameras use disks instead of film for storage, and they often have controls for image playback, in-camera special effects, and image editing. These special digital controls enable the photographer to access the picture instantly and decide upon the quality of the image. The image can then either be saved or deleted. These editing functions are enabled by the digital camera's memory (RAM).

The most fundamental difference between digital and analog photography is the way an image is captured. Film-based photographic systems use light sensitive materials, usually a **silver halide**, to record physically the impression of light bouncing off a subject. A digital camera converts the light bouncing off the subject into a mathematical model that can be read and reconstructed to approximate the original scene.

An image is transformed from analog to digital in the camera using an electronic grid of chips that sense, map, and quantify light. The information from the grid is then sent and converted to digital code by processors. The digital camera's lens projects an analog image onto the grid, and each small square of the grid records the intensity, color, and location of the light. The unit of measure for digital pieces of information is a **pixel**. The color information is established using three filters: red, green, and blue. The camera does not sense color; it measures the gradations of intensity between the three filters. The processor then converts the information into a code. The light striking each pixel is given a numeric value: 0 for true black through 255 for true white. The numeric value then becomes part of the **binary number system** (bit code), a code of 0s and 1s eight bits long. This code is what a computer reads, processes, and reconstructs as a photographic image.

The large file size of digital images often makes them hard to process and transmit. To reduce the file size, digital camera images are often converted and stored as **JPEG** files. JPEGs are a standardized, compressed file type. Through compression and standardization, file sizes are reduced and made more convenient to store and transmit. They are also formatted in a uniform way that makes digital imaging with personal computers more feasible.

Digital cameras for personal use often have relatively poor image quality and small file sizes. A common resolution for a digital photograph is 72 dpi (dots per inch) with pixel dimensions of 640 × 480. To determine the measurements of a digital image, divide the dimensions (the number of pixels) by the resolution (the number of pixels in an inch). The standard resolution for computer screen based images, like the ones on web pages, is 72 dpi. Digital cameras with higher resolution are available, but because of their expense, they are used mainly for professional or scientific purposes.

The proliferation of digital photography is tied to advances in personal computers and business applications. Many people have taken up digital photography because of the expansion of affordable personal computers into the

silver halide a photosensitive product that has been used in traditional cameras to record an image

pixel a single picture element on a video screen; one of the individual dots making up a picture on a video screen or digital image

binary number system a number system in which each place represents a power of 2 larger than the place on its right (base-2)

JPEG (Joint Photographic Experts Group), an organization that developed a standard for encoding image data in a compressed format to save space

Computerized photography opens up endless possibilities to alter images via computer. Here, author K. A. Applegate morphs into a lion.

home. A computer set up for digital imaging often includes a color monitor, a color printer, a disk drive (compatible with the camera's), a program for image editing, a negative scanner, and a flatbed scanner.

Flatbed scanners have a flat glass bed where an image can be placed, scanned, digitized, and opened in a computer program. The scanner contains a laser-equipped carriage; the laser goes over the length of the bed, scanning the image line by line. The laser beam then reflects information back to the sensors, which convert the information much like a digital camera. A negative scanner works similarly but comes with a guide for the insertion of negatives and transparencies. A drum scanner is used for high quality, professional scanning. With drum scanners the image is placed inside a cylinder that rotates at high speeds while the laser tracks across the image.

Scanners come with software for limited editing in the scanning phase. The image scanned can commonly be adjusted for scale, media, contrast, and color balance. The scanned image is then usually opened in a more sophisticated program. The measure of scanner quality is the bit depth. Digital imaging software uses **interpolation** to scale images. Interpolation is a method for resampling images to adjust scale. The intensity and value of a group of pixels is established, then that group of pixels is transformed into one pixel with an average value. Extreme shifts in the scale of digital images can result in the loss of image quality; over-interpolation can create blurry, jagged, or pixilated images.

Once loaded on the computer's storage drive, and opened in an image editing program, digital photographs become easily manageable. Images can be edited, montaged, distorted, or completely fabricated while retaining the believability of traditional photographs. Many image-editing programs allow the user to adjust the scale, color balance, contrast, and levels of an image. More complicated programs allow the user to manipulate the image further by adding special effects, filters, and text, copying and pasting other images, painting and drawing, and converting file types. The most common editing program is Adobe PhotoShop, which has become the standard in publishing, design, and academia. Once digital images are edited with the computer, they can be printed, sent via e-mail attachment, opened in other programs, or used to create web pages. SEE ALSO ART; DESKTOP PUBLISHING; FASHION DESIGN; JOURNALISM; WORLD WIDE WEB.

Jim Fike

interpolation estimating data values between points where the points are known, but the values in between are not and are therefore estimated

Bibliography

Aaland, Mikkel. *Digital Photography*. New York: Random House, 1992.

Breslow, Norman. *Basic Digital Photography*. Boston: Butterworth-Heinemann, 1992.

Busch, David M. *Digital Photography*. New York: MIS Press, 1995.

Horenstein, Henry, and Hart Russell. *Photography*. Upper Saddle River, NJ: Prentice-Hall, 2001.

Political Applications

Computers have revolutionized the manner in which the political process is conducted in at least four areas: (1) computerization of political information; (2) international communication and communication between politicians and their constituencies; (3) political data processing; and (4) political events simulation.

Computerization of Political Information

The computerization of political information is linked to the computerization of libraries, archives, and museums and to the dissemination via the Internet of documents published by governments, non-profit organizations, and special interest "think tanks." Public libraries equipped with computers allow patrons to seek books and articles in periodicals, newspapers, and web sites on any given political subject. Through these resources, the general public can stay informed about local, regional, state, national, and global political issues. A museum's inventory, including articles pertaining to historical and political events, is usually kept in a computerized database where it can be searched directly by visitors. Also, many museum exhibits now display searchable information on computer monitors for patrons to use.

The Internet has had a significant impact on the degree of political information available to the general public. Prior to the advent of the Internet, political document archives were not easily accessible to ordinary citizens. Now, many web sites allow people to peruse documents acquired via the **Freedom of Information Act (FOIA)**. Current documents are often available through the Internet immediately after they have been issued, as happened during former U.S. President Bill Clinton's impeachment proceedings. In addition, most politically oriented non-profit organizations and think tanks have web sites where their presentations of political issues can be reviewed by citizens. These Internet resources enhance the democratic process because they offer all citizens the opportunity to become much more knowledgeable about a wide range of political issues.

Freedom of Information Act (FOIA) permits individuals to gain access to records and documents that are in the possession of the government

Politics and Computerized Communication

Widespread computer use affects the direct communication of political messages as well. Political campaigns now rely on computerized mailing lists, and Internet exposure is a major media consideration in political campaigning. Education of voters and the promotion of ideas and mutual understanding take place through e-mail, chat rooms, and instant messaging. Computerization is even responsible for improving the quality of presentation at public political discussions through the use of computer-generated slides, charts, graphs, maps, and other print and video materials.

Direct Mail. Political campaigns have long used direct mail to communicate with potential voters. The purpose of direct mailing is to influence opinion or solicit donations. Computers allow for the use of mailing lists and the production of computer letters that are targeted to specific constituent interests. This is accomplished by creating specialized letters and mailing databases based on personal characteristics such as the recipients' place of residence, financial status, religion, political affiliation, race, gender, educational background, ethnicity, or sexual orientation.

The Internet. Political communication now utilizes the Internet as well. Almost all elected officials have web sites of their own. Computers have made politicians more accessible by allowing their constituents to communicate with their elected officials via e-mail. Even the informal structures of the Internet, including chat rooms and instant messaging programs, have become part of the political process of promoting ideas and encouraging mutual understanding. For example, people from different countries engaged in chat room discussions about mutually important issues are less likely to support war efforts between their countries than people who have had little or no contact, either in person or by computer, with people from other countries. It is one thing to feel menace from an unknown "them," but people who know the views of somebody from the opposite side look differently at any potential conflict between their countries.

Political Materials. Political presentation materials, whether print or electronic, have been influenced by computerization as well. Television and Internet coverage of political discussions—debates between candidates, for example—require sleek visual presentations. Software tools, including desktop publishing and video presentation programs, help politicians present their views in attractive formats.

Political Data Processing

Political data processing includes the outlining of voting districts; the statistical analysis of polling results, voting results, and census results; voting and vote counting; and campaign-related data processing.

District Boundaries.   Non-partisan computer models are available to help with the logistical outlining of voting districts. Some computer models attempt to create an equally proportioned electorate in each district. Other models use the organization of districts on existing legislative boundaries and then connect them to other districts to achieve population parity. Although different software models take political logistics into consideration at varying degrees, all of them must recognize political boundaries such as towns and counties and geographical boundaries such as mountains and bodies of water.

Polling and Statistical Analysis.   Many companies, the most prominent among them being the Gallup Organization, conduct polls on various political topics and analyze their results. In most cases their predictions are quite accurate. The results of public opinion polls and questionnaires help politicians determine how to react to the information learned through polls. Candidates may change aspects of their campaigns depending on perceived strengths and weaknesses that may be defined geographically or demographically. Using computerized statistical models, strategists can also identify issues that may influence voters with particular political allegiances or those who are considered "independent" or "undecided."

The Internet provides an ideal medium for polling, from the perspective of access to potential respondents. It is inexpensive when compared with other methods, so more and more polls are conducted online. Their results are widely used in numerous political campaigns, although methodology and accuracy rates vary widely.

Since the 1952 presidential elections, computers have been used to perform a statistical analysis that uses a small sampling to predict the total outcome of an election. Television networks and the Internet have increasingly used computers to project election outcomes, although inaccurate early predictions following the presidential election of 2000 caused elected officials and media representatives to consider whether or not the desire to publicize early outcome predictions can skew the election process itself.

The computerized statistical analysis of census results started with **punched cards** more than a hundred years ago and has moved on to using modern computer technology. Census analysis is important for politicians because it can show demographic trends.

Voting and Vote Counting.   Computerized vote counting is common throughout the United States. Computerized votes are often tallied from cards on which voters fill in an oval or a square with a pen or pencil to represent their vote. Computerized voting machines are also available.

Internet technologies are sophisticated enough that they can now be used in the voting process, allowing people to vote online rather than in polling booths. Before online voting will become widespread in the United States, however, certain technological precautions will be needed to establish a voter's identity and prevent election fraud.

punched cards paper cards with punched holes which give instructions to a computer in order to encode program instructions and data; now obsolete

THE HANGING CHAD

Punched cards and the ability of tabulating machines to record accurate voting results came into question during the 2000 U.S. presidential election, which ultimately saw Vice President Al Gore lose to Texas Governor George W. Bush. The race came down to who would get the electoral votes in Florida. The race was so close that people's attention turned to those stacks of ballots that were not counted because the voter failed to punch through the holes on the card cleanly. Such failed punches were called a "hanging chad" or a "pregnant chad." Efforts were made to review punched cards manually and see if a determination could be made regarding the voters' intent. Ultimately, the problems associated with hanging chads led some election officials to consider alternative voting methods, including computer touch-screen ballots.

An elections worker uses a tabulating machine to count absentee ballots during the tight U.S. presidential election in 2000 between Vice President Al Gore and Texas Governor George W. Bush.

artificial intelligence (AI) a branch of computer science dealing with creating computer hardware and software to mimic the way people think and perform practical tasks

expert system a computer system that uses a collection of rules to exhibit behavior which mimics the behavior of a human expert in some area

Campaign Administration. Computer programs are also useful to politicians from an administrative perspective. They are useful in campaign scheduling and in calculating the distribution and allocation of funds.

Political Event Simulation

The simulation of political events is being done using both deterministic models and **artificial intelligence (AI)**. A deterministic model usually consists of a set of differential equations. The solutions of these equations supposedly mimic the development of real-life political events. AI is a branch of programming that attempts to emulate reasoning and perception exercised by human beings. Many mathematical methods are used to produce this emulation.

An example of using AI to model political events is an **expert system**. At the creation of such a system, political experts are interviewed. Based on the results of these interviews, a set of rules is established. This set constitutes a computerized model. The model can be applied to the evaluation of a new political situation. Whether deterministic models or artificial intelligence are used, simulation results should be interpreted with caution. However, it is a nice tool to have to analyze some of the possible outcomes of a political event.

SEE ALSO BABBAGE, CHARLES; GOVERNMENT FUNDING, RESEARCH; INTERNET; NATIONAL AERONAUTICS AND SPACE ADMINISTRATION (NASA).

Robert Lembersky and George A. Tarnow

Bibliography

Garson, G. David, ed. *Information Technology and Computer Applications in Public Administration: Issues and Trends.* Hershey, PA: Idea Group Publishing, 1999.

Hudson, Valerie M., ed. *Artificial Intelligence and International Politics.* Boulder, CO: Westview Press, 1991.

Patterson, David A. *Personal Computer Applications in the Social Services.* Upper Saddle River, NJ: Prentice Hall, 1999.

Tsagarousianou, Rosa, Damian Tambini, and Cathy Bryan, eds. *Cyberdemocracy: Technology, Cities and Civic Networks.* London: Routledge, 1998.

Routing

Computer networks allow messages to be exchanged between computers in different parts of the world. These messages may contain e-mails, requests for web pages, or the contents of a web page. When traveling from the source computer to the destination computer, messages typically pass through a number of other computers on the network. Routing is the function of choosing which computers a message should pass through on its way from source to destination. Some computers in the network, called routers, exist only to route messages onward in the network. Routing must be performed in large networks such as the Internet as well as in smaller networks such as within a university.

When a message is received from the network, the computer that receives the message—unless it is the intended recipient—must perform a routing action. Routing the message means choosing which of the connected computers should receive the forwarded message.

Each message includes the address of its intended destination, and this address is used to choose the route of the message. To route a message, the computer does not need to know anything about where the destination computer is. It merely needs to know in which direction to send the message. This is similar to the way addresses are used on normal letters. If U.S. Postal Service workers receive a letter for someone in France, they will probably not know anything about the exact location of the person that is to receive the letter. Despite this, the U.S. Postal Service can still route the letter by simply forwarding the letter to France. Then the French postal network takes care of routing the letter to its final destination.

In a global network such as the Internet, there are many possible routes for a message to take between a source and destination computer. The overwhelming number of possibilities makes routing messages very complicated. Also, the structure of the network is not fixed; computers or connections may be temporarily unavailable, in which case a route must be chosen to bypass the unavailable part of the network.

It is best to route the messages as directly as possible. One option is to choose the route so that the message passes through the minimum number of computers on its way from its source to destination. It is also possible to take into account other factors, such as the speed of the connections between

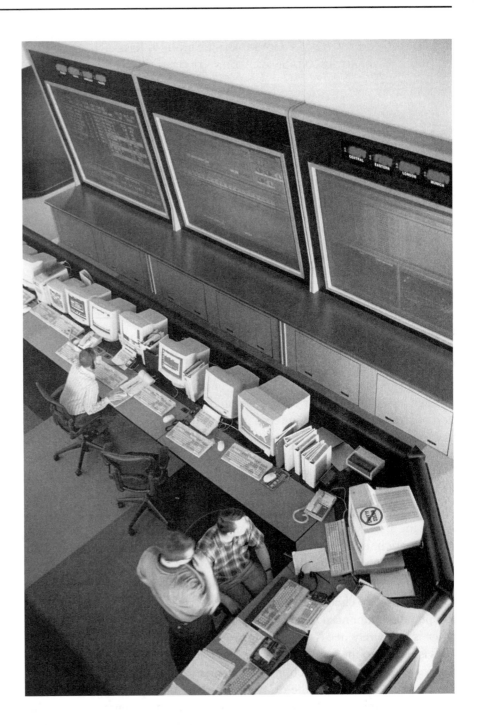

At CompuServe headquarters in Ohio, technicians monitor network traffic flow. Millions of messages are routed through service providers on the Internet each day.

computers on the route. By choosing a route with faster connections, the message will reach its destination faster, even though it may pass through more computers on its way. Another factor to consider when routing is the current state of the network. If parts of the network become overloaded, then messages routed through these parts of the network will suffer delays. Routing messages around the overloaded parts of the network will speed up the delivery of the messages and avoid adding to an already overloaded network.

Static Routing

The simplest approach to routing is static routing. In this case each computer on the network has a fixed routing table. When a message is received, the computer checks the address of the message against the routing table and then forwards the message to whichever computer is indicated by the routing table. The routing table may include alternative entries to deal with the case where part of the network is currently unavailable.

Static routing requires very little processing power, which is considered an advantage. However, this simple solution has the disadvantage that it cannot adapt to current situations in the network. For example, parts of the network may become overloaded if too many messages are being transmitted. With static routing, no change will be made to the routing **algorithm** to take into account the overloading. It is possible to adapt to such an overload situation and route messages away from the overloaded part of the network with what is known as dynamic routing.

algorithm a rule or procedure used to solve a mathematical problem—most often described as a sequence of steps

Dynamic Routing

In the simplest form of dynamic routing, each computer can adapt its routing based on its current situation. Thus, none of the computers knows about the overall state of the network; each computer adapts its routing based solely on its own situation. Messages are put in a **queue** before being transmitted. If the queue for a connection grows too big, this indicates that the connection is becoming overloaded. The computer can adapt its routing to avoid, where possible, the connections with large queues. This approach allows the computer to balance the load on its connections but the computer has no knowledge of the state of the rest of the network. Therefore, although the computer can prevent its own outgoing connections from becoming overloaded, it may still be sending messages to overloaded parts of the network.

queue the ordering of elements or objects such that they are processed in turn; first-in, first-out

A second form of dynamic routing is where computers share information about their current state with each other. This gives each computer a better understanding of the overall situation in the network so it can route messages away from overloaded parts of the network. One approach is for each computer to send information about the state of its connections to all directly connected computers. Each computer combines the incoming status information with its own current state to generate status messages, which are then sent to connected computers. This allows each computer to build up a picture of which parts of the network are overloaded, allowing it to route messages away from the overloaded parts of the network. With this solution, it is critical to find a balance between sending too many status messages, which themselves may cause overloading, and too few status messages, in which case the network may adapt too slowly to an overload situation.

The choice of routing strategy will depend on the network. Static routing may be suitable for small local networks, but for a large global network, such as the Internet, dynamic routing is necessary to avoid overloading parts of the network. SEE ALSO ASYNCHRONOUS TRANSFER MODE (ATM); BANDWIDTH; NETWORK DESIGN; NETWORKS.

Declan P. Kelly

Bibliography

Sportack, Mark A. *IP Routing Fundamentals*. New York: Macmillan, 1998.

Tannenbaum, Andrew S. *Computer Networks*. Upper Saddle River, NJ: Prentice Hall, 1996.

Search Engines

A search engine is an information retrieval system that allows someone to search the vast collection of resources on the Internet and the World Wide Web. All major search engines are similar in that keywords, phrases, or in some instances, questions, are entered in a search form. After clicking on the search command button, the database returns a collection of hyperlinks to resources that contain the search terms. These hyperlinks are listed in some sort of order, usually from most relevant to least relevant, or by how important the web pages are, depending on the search engine used. Search engines are composed of computer programs that create databases automatically. They should not be confused with human-built directories, such as Yahoo!, which depend on people for development and maintenance.

Search Engine Basics

Search engines have three components. The first part is a computer program called a *spider* or *robot*, which gathers information on the Internet. The **spider** retrieves hyperlinks attached to documents. It starts with an existing database and follows the existing **hyperlinks** to gather new and updated resources to add to the list. If a web page does not contain hyperlinks to other web pages, the search engine cannot find it. Other types of resources that most spiders are unable to locate include files that are not written in **Hypertext Markup Language (HTML)**, and from specialized databases that require the user to fill out a search form. Spiders automatically do this gathering of documents at intervals that differ from service to service.

Second, resources collected by the spider are loaded into a database that indexes them using a formula that is unique to each. The index contains a copy of every web page the spider finds. People can also submit web pages to this database in case the spider either fails to access it quickly enough, or if there are no links on the pages. While most search engines claim to index the entire World Wide Web, none actually do. Although spiders have many different ways of collecting information from web pages, the major search engines all claim to index the entire text of each web document in their databases. This is called **full-text indexing**. Some search engines may not index common words such as: and, a, I, to. These are called *stop words*.

The third part of the search engine is software that allows users to enter keywords in search forms using some type of *search expression*, with **syntax** that is supported by the search engine. The search results are then listed in order according to a ranking **algorithm**. Some search engines list results by *relevancy*, while others list them by how many web pages link to them, thereby showing the most important, or popular, web pages first, and others group results together by subject. Many search engines employ a combination of these.

Search Features

It is important to understand the different search features available before beginning to use a search engine as each engine has its own way of interpreting and manipulating search expressions. Because a search can retrieve many documents, it is common to have a number of hits, but only a few that are relevant to the query submitted. This is called **low precision/high**

spider a computer program that travels the Internet to locate web documents and FTP (File Transfer Protocol) resources, then indexes the documents in a database, which are then searched using software the search engine provides

hyperlinks connections between electronic documents that permit automatic browsing transfer at the point of the link

Hypertext Markup Language (HTML) an encoding scheme for text data that uses special tags in the text to signify properties to the viewing program (browser) like links to other documents or document parts (header)

full-text indexing a search engine feature in which every word in a document, significant or insignificant, is indexed and retrievable through a search

syntax a set of rules that a computing language incorporates regarding structure, punctuation, and formatting

algorithm a rule or procedure used to solve a mathematical problem—most often described as a sequence of steps

low precision/high recall a phenomenon that occurs during a search when a large set of results are retrieved, including many relevant and irrelevant documents

recall. On the other hand, a searcher may be satisfied with having very precise search results, even if a very small set of hits is returned. This is defined as **high precision/low recall**. Ideally, the search engine would retrieve all of the relevant documents that are needed. This would be described as **high precision/high recall**. Search engines support many search features, though not all engines support each one. If they do support certain features, they may use different syntax in expressing them. Before using a search feature, the user should always check the search engine's help pages to understand how the feature is expressed, if it is supported at all. Some examples of search syntax and features used by search engines are: Boolean operators (and, or, not), implied Boolean operators (+ and −), phrase searching, natural language searching, proximity searching, truncation, and **field searching**.

Types of Search Engines

Search engines can be divided into three basic types: general or major search engines, meta-search engines, and specialty search engines. Each of the major search engines attempts to do the same thing—index as much of the web as possible—so they handle a huge amount of data. Due to this tremendous amount of information, it is common for documents of little useful content to be picked up, making the quality of the ranking scheme used very important. In most first-generation search engines, such as AltaVista and HotBot, results are ranked by *relevancy*. Relevancy is determined by algorithms that usually count how many times the keywords typed in the search form appear in the documents that exist in the database. Second-generation tools such as Vivisimo, Google, and Direct Hit, use ranking algorithms that use techniques such as grouping and sorting results, importance or popularity of web sites, and human judgment from prior searches. *Meta-search engines* are tools that search more than one search engine or directory at once, compiling the results and consolidating them into an overall list.

Examples of meta-search engines are Metacrawler, Vivisimo, and Search.com. One drawback of meta-search engines is that they do not include all of the search engines possible, and they are unpredictable in how they handle complex searches. They can be useful for obscure searches.

Specialty search engines, or specialized databases, are search tools that focus on particular subjects, or types of file format (e.g. images or music files). These databases can be time savers because their databases are much smaller and focused on a particular subject area, or type of resource. For example, if a certain legal opinion is needed, a searcher would achieve greater success with FindLaw <http://www.findlaw.com> rather than spending the time in a major search engine such as AltaVista looking through perhaps hundreds of results.

Difficulties and Benefits of Major Search Engines

Search engines send their spiders to crawl the web periodically, so there may be infrequent updates and new sites may not be immediately added. Specialty search engines may be better for very current, dynamically changing information, such as fast-breaking news stories. There is evidence that the major search engines realize this problem and are starting to team with specialty services that provide recent news. For example,

---

high precision/low recall a phenomenon that occurs when a search yields a small set of hits; although each one may be highly relevant to the search topic, some relevant documents are missed

high precision/high recall a phenomenon that occurs during a search when all the relevant documents are retrieved with no unwanted ones

field searching a strategy in which a search is limited to a particular field; in a search engine, a search may be limited to a particular domain name or date, narrowing the scope of searchable items and helping to eliminate the chance of retrieving irrelevant data

---

BOOLEAN OPERATORS

Boolean operators help expand or narrow the scope of a search. A search for rivers OR lakes returns documents with either word in them. A search for rivers AND lakes returns documents with both words in them. A search for rivers AND lakes NOT swamps returns documents that mention both rivers and lakes but omits those that also mention swamps. Implied Boolean Operators are characters such as + and −, which can be used to require or prohibit a word or phrase as part of a search expression. The + acts somewhat like AND, and the − acts as NOT would in a Boolean expression. For example, the Boolean expression rivers AND lakes NOT swamps may be expressed as +rivers +lakes −swamps.

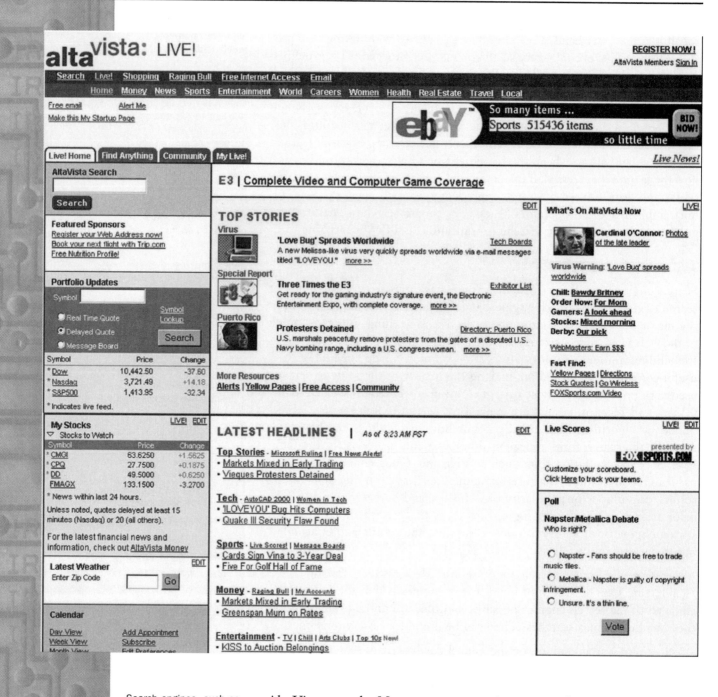

Search engines, such as Alta Vista, give users the means to search the Internet using keywords and phrases, yet also provide links to news, sports stories, stock quotes, and other information.

AltaVista uses the Moreover news service to provide users with news stories. Another difficulty is that according to a 1999 study by Steve Lawrence and C. Lee Giles, only 16 percent of the web is indexed. Besides content that cannot be gathered by search engine spiders, such as dynamically generated web pages, and pages that contain no hyperlinks, and certain file types, there is also evidence that commercial sites are more often indexed than non-commercial sites. This part of the web that is hidden from the major search engines is often referred to as the *invisible web*.

Another difficulty is that information found in major search engines has not been evaluated. The responsibility is placed upon the individual to evaluate what is found. These drawbacks should not detract from the benefits of these major search tools, however. Many general or major search engines, realizing the added benefit of human-managed information, include *directories* such as the Open Directory Project, in conjunction with the computerized indexes. And some directories, such as Yahoo!, employ search engines to search the web when their directories fail to provide the resources needed by the searcher. The usefulness of being able to search for obscure topics, multi-faceted subjects, specific web pages and sites, in addition to information from specific dates, languages, news stories, images, and more, makes search engines necessary tools for the searcher to learn and use.

Popular Search Engines

Some of the most popular search engines include:

- AltaVista. <http://altavista.com>
- All the Web. <http://alltheweb.com>
- Direct Hit. <http://www.directhit.com>
- Google. <http://www.google.com>
- Lycos. <http://www.lycos.com>
- MetaCrawler. <http://www.metacrawler.com>
- MSN. <http://search.msn.com>
- Search.com. <http://www.search.com>
- Vivisimo. <http://vivisimo.com>

SEE ALSO INFORMATION ACCESS; INFORMATION OVERLOAD; INFORMATION RETRIEVAL; WORLD WIDE WEB.

Karen Hartman

Bibliography

Ackermann, Ernest, and Karen Hartman. *Internet and Web Essentials: What You Need to Know.* Wilsonville, OR: Franklin, Beedle, and Associates, 2001.

Cohen, Laura. "Searching the Web: The Human Element Emerges." *Choice Supplement* 37 (2000): 17-30.

King, David. "Specialized Search Engines: Alternatives to the Big Guys." *Online* 24, no. 3 (2000): 67-74.

Lawrence, Steve, and C. Lee Giles. "Accessibility and Distribution of Information on the Web." *Nature* 400, no. 6740 (1999): 107-109.

Snow, Bonnie. "The Internet's Hidden Content and How to Find It." *Online* 24, no. 3 (2000): 61-66.

Internet Resources

Lawrence, Steve, and C. Lee Giles. "Accessibility and Distribution of Information on the Web." <http://www.wwwmetrics.com/>

Sullivan, Danny. "How Search Engines Work." *SearchEngineWatch.com.* <http://searchenginewatch.com/webmasters/work.html>

———. "Search Engine Features for Searchers." *SearchEngineWatch.com.* <http://searchenginewatch.com/facts/ataglance.html>

Service Providers

Telecommunications service providers are the companies at the heart of the telecommunications industry. They provide people with the means to communicate with one another by telephone, mobile phone, and the Internet.

DIRECTORIES

A directory is a topical list of Internet resources, arranged hierarchically. Directories differ from search engines in one major way—the human element is involved in collecting and updating the information included.

Telecommunications service providers also make available cable or satellite access for television and computer connectivity. Service providers are constantly trying to locate and build solutions that will tie organizations and individuals together no matter what their locations.

Early Telecommunications Service Providers

telegraph a communication channel that uses cables to convey encoded low bandwidth electrical signals

The first identifiable telecommunications service provider was the **telegraph** office of the late 1800s. Telegraph offices were typically owned or operated by the U.S. federal government in conjunction with local and state authorities. They provided the first end-to-end connectivity of wiring to enable instantaneous communication between two distant points. These simple telegraph offices created the foundation for modern day commercial telecommunication organizations.

One of the most notable service providers, Bell Telephone Company, dominated American communications for decades. This organization became the leader in wiring the country with telephone service and providing dial tone, call connectivity, phone services (e.g., call accounting and consolidated billing), telephone equipment, and simple yet expensive connectivity for a large number of private corporations that were starving for connectivity to tie their slowly evolving information technology infrastructures together. Bell Telephone remained dominant until its final breakup in 1980. The U.S. government determined that its grasp on the telecommunications industry was monopolistic in nature, obstructing competition and innovation.

Deregulation of Telecommunications

deregulation the lowering of restrictions, rules, or regulations pertaining to an activity or operation (often commercial)

bandwidth a measure of the frequency component of a signal or the capacity of a communication channel to carry signals

infrastructure the foundation or permanent installation necessary for a structure or system to operate

fiber optics transmission technology using long, thin strands of glass fiber; internal reflections in the fibers assure that light entering one end is transmitted to the other end with only small losses in intensity; used widely in transmitting digital information

The breakup of Bell Telephone was a first step in opening the industry to competition for all telecommunications systems of the United States, but there was still work to be done. By 1995, despite government intervention, there were still a finite number of service providers trying to compete in a heavily regulated industry. However, the type and number of innovations needed to propel the world into the twenty-first century were emerging far too slowly to handle the needs of the customers and the organizations they operated. At that time, the Internet was ready to explode in popularity, and the speed of connectivity was an issue and concern that slowed its deployment. Without further **deregulation**, the telecommunications infrastructure did not respond quickly enough to the demands for change.

The U.S. Communications Acts of 1995 and 1996 were designed to address this concern. These acts have set the stage for the continuing technology revolution still being experienced today. These changes have not come without consequences, and there have been many casualties along the way. The acts opened up new avenues of competition and innovation within traditionally regulated telecommunication markets. It quickly became possible to purchase **bandwidth**, or the speed of connectivity, from the lowest-cost provider despite customer location. The only limitation was that remote or rural areas of the country did not have the cabling **infrastructure** to tie it all together, but even that is changing as the cost of running cable has drastically dropped. The wide adoption of **fiber optics** as a medium to transfer data is making it possible for even the most remote schools and communities to become connected to the global digital world.

Types of Service Providers

There are many service providers of varying types. There are the traditional **Internet Service Providers (ISPs)** that provide basic access to the Internet and traditional telecommunication providers fighting with large multinational companies for access to local telephone customers in order to provide them with their needed long distance and local telephone service. "Tier 1" service providers (e.g., PSI.net, ATT.net, and UUNET) provide **uplinks** for smaller ISPs, providing local high speed **digital subscriber line (DSL)** service or cable modem service to residential and small business customers.

There are Application Service Providers (ASPs) that are connected to the T1 service providers. The ASPs provide **collocation** services for web sites, web-enabled application servers, and managed private networking for telecommuters who need to be connected to their corporate employers' networks. There are storage service providers whose sole competency is providing high-speed inexpensive storage to corporations, in addition to managed service providers whose core competency is not easily distinguishable as they provide many of the same services noted earlier. This list is not exhaustive by any means and the types of service providers change daily. This list grows almost as fast as the imaginations of the entrepreneurs behind this revolution.

Economic Realities

As a result of deregulation, companies that thought they could provide these types of complex services, and perhaps had an ingenious twist on how to provide it, could enter the market; these efforts met with varying degrees of success. In the stock rush of 1999 and 2000, even technology-driven dreamers with only a mediocre idea could obtain funding. Often it was a requirement to take more money than was needed. The monies were handed out by profit-driven venture capitalists who rushed into a strong stock market hoping to create mind-boggling degrees of wealth overnight.

Many of the venture capitalists and their well-funded entrepreneurs succeeded; however, many core business principles that helped to build traditional, solid companies of the 1980s and 1990s were overlooked in the effort to join the technology bandwagon quickly. In the stock market struggles that began at the end of 2000, most of the poor financial performance was linked with failures of the **dot.coms**, but the telecommunications industry has also been partially to blame.

Some of the casualties include DSL providers that offer fast connectivity to hundreds of thousands of customers and businesses. The customers, once connected, become dependent on the DSL provider and susceptible to connection interruptions or infrastructure collapses. Unfortunately, several large DSL providers in the market have failed. The companies providing service often carry tremendous debt and must experience continued growth in order to cover payments and expenses. Some of these companies have disappeared virtually overnight, leaving their customers scrambling to find ways to reconnect their business-essential and home-use communication lines. Competition, economic conditions, and market realities shake out the least fit of these service providers; in the end, the strongest few will survive.

Internet Service Providers (ISPs) commercial enterprises which offer paying subscribers access to the Internet (usually via modem) for a fee

uplinks connections from a client machine to a large network; frequently when information is being sent to a communications satellite

digital subscriber line (DSL) a technology that permits high speed voice and data communications over public telephone networks; it requires the use of a DSL modem

collocation the act of placing elements or objects in a specific order

INSTANT MESSAGING

How do teens stay connected in the e-universe? Some turn to instant messaging services provided by ISPs such as America Online. The service allows users to create buddy lists, which will then tell users if their "buddies" are online and presumably available to exchange messages. Cellular phone technology helps teens check their buddy list even while they are away from their home computers.

dot.coms a common term used to describe Internet-based commercial companies or organizations

193

Many Internet service providers employ technicians to resolve their customers' service problems twenty-four-hours a day.

Service Providers in the Future

As the telecommunications industry moves forward, new options are becoming available that will change the way people do business and interact with their environments. Throughout the past decade, many companies have begun to build fiber-optic rings within major metropolitan areas. These are typically near most of the major business districts in these population centers. Efforts are underway to connect these high-speed rings across a national fiber-optic backbone. These rings of connectivity are completely unregulated in the traditional sense. It is expected that they will provide the infrastructure that will help revive the industry and replicate the robust growth and innovation of the early Bell Telephone era.

Since the speeds available via fiber optics are unlimited relative to current technical capabilities, it is easy to comprehend how speed of light communications will once again change the vision and direction of telecommunications. Visionary entrepreneurs will develop ways to take advantage of this speed and push the costs of connectivity lower than they are now. These new service providers will make every effort to combine the best of all of the previous providers, providing unparalleled layers and levels of connectivity. Telecommunications service providers, having evolved from telegraph systems to fiber optics throughout the years, continue to be the core of the telecommunications revolution. SEE ALSO INTERNET; IN-TERNET: BACKBONE; TELECOMMUNICATIONS; WORLD WIDE WEB.

John Nau

Bibliography

Collins, Daniel. *Carrier Grade Voice Over IP.* New York: McGraw-Hill, 2001.

Green, James Harry. *The Irwin Handbook of Telecommunications Management.* Chicago: Irwin Professional Publishing, 1996.

Halabi, Sam (Bassam), and Danny McPherson. *Internet Routing Architecture.* Indianapolis, IN: Cisco Press, 2000.

Internet Resources

Cisco Connection Online. Cisco Systems, Inc. <http://www.cisco.com>

Carrier-Class IP Telephony Solutions. Nuera Communications, Inc. <http://www.nuera .com>

Shannon, Claude E.

American Mathematician and Electrical Engineer
1916–2001

An American mathematician and electrical engineer, Claude E. Shannon has been called the father of **information theory**. His early work had a significant impact on the early development of digital computer technology, and later in the twentieth century, his theories about communication contributed to the rapid evolution of telecommunications capabilities.

Shannon was born in Gaylord, Michigan, on April 30, 1916. As a child, he became interested in engineering and problem solving. These characteristics were revealed in such pastimes as the creation of a fully functioning telegraph system between his home and that of a friend who lived a half-mile away. In the fall of 1932, Shannon entered the University of Michigan, intending to major in electrical engineering. During his undergraduate years, he developed a keen interest in mathematics as well. In 1936 he completed his bachelor's degree with majors in both subjects.

Shortly after graduation, Shannon accepted a job at the Massachusetts Institute of Technology (MIT), where he earned two master's degrees, one in mathematics and one in electrical engineering, as well as a doctorate in mathematics. In this first job, Shannon worked with an early analog computer built by Vannevar Bush, who was also the vice president of MIT. The machine, called a differential analyzer, was a mechanical system based on electrical relay circuits. Shannon applied the principles of **Boolean algebra** and symbolic logic, which he studied as an undergraduate, to the problem of describing the way the differential analyzer's relay circuits worked.

In 1937 Shannon submitted a master's thesis on the subject. Titled "A Symbolic Analysis of Relay and Switching Circuits," the paper has been called "one of the most influential master's theses ever written," because in it, Shannon laid the logical foundation for building digital circuitry. All contemporary computer systems are based on Shannon's symbolic explanation of the behavior of relay circuits.

By 1940 Shannon had completed his graduate studies at MIT and joined Bell Laboratories as a researcher studying the electronic transmission of

Claude E. Shannon.

information theory a branch of mathematics and engineering that deals with the encoding, transmission, reception, and decoding of information

Boolean algebra a system developed by George Boole that deals with the theorems of undefined symbols and axioms concerning those symbols

information. During World War II, Shannon's energies were directed toward the interception and transmission of codes and other military applications of electronic technologies that were being developed to assist in the war effort. He became acquainted with Alan Turing, a British pioneer of computer technology, and others whose work would contribute to the mid-twentieth century evolution of the computer as a business tool.

Shannon's interest in understanding the electronic communication of information led him to focus on this subject in his research. In 1949 he issued *The Mathematical Theory of Communication*, a work that formed the foundation for the field of inquiry known as information theory. Shannon proposed that data could be broken into small components called "bits" to be transmitted electronically. The ideas Shannon proposed found their application during the last quarter of the twentieth century when telecommunications technology had advanced enough to demonstrate aspects of Shannon's theory that could not be supported by the technology of **vacuum tubes**. Shannon's information theory continues to shape the development of electronic communications media, from consumer products such as compact disks and home computers to business and scientific endeavors including the exploration of outer space with unmanned vehicles.

In the 1950s Shannon explored the frontiers of **artificial intelligence (AI)**, building chess-playing computers and a maze-running mechanical mouse. He was convinced that computers could be designed and programmed to function in ways similar to the human brain. By the late 1950s Shannon was teaching at MIT in addition to conducting research at the Bell Labs. From 1958 to 1978, he served full-time as MIT's Donner Professor of Science. He won many awards during his career as an academic, and he directly influenced a generation of electrical engineers involved in the cutting edge of computer development.

After his retirement in 1978, Shannon continued to invent gadgets and explore emerging applications of electronic technology. In addition to lecturing and publishing occasionally, he enjoyed mastering early computer games like Pac-Man, and indulged his interest in inventing by creating such contraptions as a two-seated unicycle. In fact, he was known to have mastered the skill of riding a unicycle, which was a gift from his wife, while juggling multiple objects.

Shannon married Mary Elizabeth Moore, a Bell Labs co-worker, in 1949. Together they eventually raised three children. Shannon died on February 24, 2001, following a long struggle with Alzheimer's disease.

Although Claude Shannon is not a household name, his life's work influences people worldwide daily through technology that is commonplace today, including fax machines, Internet instant messaging, and satellite, radio or television transmissions. Although his original ideas predated the technical ability to implement them, the mathematical theories he used to describe the hypothetical dissemination of information through digital electronic means are at the foundation of virtually every form of modern digital communications technology. SEE ALSO BANDWIDTH; BELL LABS; INTERNET; TELECOMMUNICATIONS.

Pamela Willwerth Aue

vacuum tubes electronic devices constructed of sealed glass tubes containing metal elements in a vacuum; used to control electrical signals

artificial intelligence (AI) a branch of computer science dealing with creating computer hardware and software to mimic the way people think and perform practical tasks

Bibliography

"Computing Before Silicon." *Technology Review* 103, no. 3 (2000): 120.

Internet Resources

"Biography of Claude Elwood Shannon." *AT&T Labs Research*. <http://www.research.att.com/~njas/doc/shannonbio.html>

"Claude Shannon 1916–2001." *AT&T Labs—Research*. <http://www.research.att.com/~njas/doc/ces5.html>

"Michigan Greats—Claude Shannon." *UM Research*. <http://www.research.umich.edu/research/news/michigangreats/shannon.html>

Simon, Herbert A.

American Professor of Computer Science and Psychology
1916–2001

Herbert A. Simon combined the study of social and behavioral science with the disciplines of mathematics, physics, and economics in a career that included a longtime focus on the science of decision-making in organizations. Of particular note is his analysis of decision-making and problem-solving, but he was also interested in **artificial intelligence (AI)** and the use of the computer to study intelligence and cognition, both in problem-solving, such as the discovery of theorems, and in game playing, such as chess.

Simon was born in Milwaukee, Wisconsin, on June 15, 1916. His father was an electrical engineer and his mother an accomplished pianist. He enrolled at the University of Chicago in 1933 and graduated in 1936 with a degree in political science. He received his doctorate through the University of Chicago in 1943 while heading a research group at the University of California, Berkeley, between 1939 and 1942. He taught at the Illinois Institute of Technology from 1942 to 1949, and he engaged in research with colleagues at the University of Chicago and the Cowles Commission for Research in Economics. His next professional post was at the Carnegie Institute of Technology (now Carnegie Mellon University), where he helped build the Graduate School of Industrial Administration.

Simon's career in Pittsburgh as an academic, researcher, and author spanned more than fifty years. He was well respected by colleagues and students. He believed that the approach of the "hard" sciences, such as physics and mathematics, could be applied to the behavioral sciences, both in economics and political science, his first field of study, and the behavioral sciences, primarily psychology and cognitive science.

One of Simon's earliest books, published in 1947, was *Administrative Behavior*. The book was an expansion of his doctoral dissertation, which began his studies of rationality. Later publications include *Models of Man* (1957), *The Sciences of the Artificial* (1969), *Human Problem Solving*, with Allen Newell (1972), and *Models of Discovery* (1977), among others. In 1991 he published an autobiography, *Models of My Life*.

Simon firmly believed that the computer could and should aid in the study of human cognition and, ultimately, that what the computer could do in terms of cognition was "think." He considered the computer to be a lab-

Herbert A. Simon.

artificial intelligence (AI) a branch of computer science dealing with creating computer hardware and software to mimic the way people think and perform practical tasks

A PREDICTION AHEAD OF ITS TIME

In 1957 Herbert Simon predicted that a computer would beat a grand master in chess in ten years. Although, as he noted, he was off by a factor of 4 (40 years), he did correctly anticipate this potential complexity of computing technology, if not the timeframe within which it would be achieved.

oratory for epistemology, the study of knowledge or truth, as well as a tool for investigating the human mind. In 1954 Simon began using computers to model problem-solving.

Simon developed what he termed the theory of "satisficing," that is, the making of decisions on the basis of a satisfactory rather than optimal (absolute best) solution. This is a technique familiar to anyone who has done even such a routine task as develop a schedule of college courses for a term. One must make choices that meet certain requirements for one's degree, balancing other factors such as personal preferences for times of classes, subjects one is interested in, distance to and from classes, and cost to create a satisfactory, albeit possibly imperfect, schedule.

Simon studied "bounded rationality," the theory of making rational decisions under constraints such as a lack of knowledge, computational difficulty, and personal and social circumstances. The decisions are rational, but not in the sense of an all-knowing, infallible optimizer. This leads to finding acceptable, but not necessarily optimal, solutions to problems.

From 1966 until his death on February 9, 2001, Simon was Richard King Mellon University Professor of Computer Science and Psychology. He won the Nobel Prize in Economics in 1978 for "pioneering research into the decision-making process within economic organizations." He was awarded the National Medal of Science in 1986 and the A.M. Turing Award by the Association of Computing Machinery (ACM) in 1975, with Allen Newell (1927–1992). He collaborated with Newell and Clifford Shaw to write a computer program, the Logic Theorist, or the Logic Theorem Machine, designed to find logical proofs. Together, the three also collaborated on a software program designed to play chess as a human, not an expert. He was involved in several computer projects to study human cognition and form models of human learning, problem solving, and "thinking" using computer programs. SEE ALSO Artificial Intelligence; Chess Playing; Decision Support Systems; Newell, Allen.

Roger R. Flynn

Bibliography

Newell, Allen, and Herbert A. Simon. *Human Problem Solving*. Englewood Cliffs, NJ: Prentice-Hall, 1972.

Simon, Herbert A. *Models of My Life*. New York: Basic Books, 1991.

Internet Resources

Simon, Herbert A. *Autobiography*. The Nobel E-Museum. <http://www.nobel.se/economics/laureates/1978/simon-autobio.html>

Social Impact

Computing technologies, like most other forms of technology, are not socially neutral. They affect and are themselves affected by society. Computers have changed the way people relate to one another and their living environment, as well as how humans organize their work, their communities, and their time. Society, in turn, has influenced the development of computers through the needs people have for processing information. The study of these relationships has come to be known as "social informatics."

Computing technology has evolved as a means of solving specific problems in human society. The earliest kinds of computational devices were the mechanical calculators developed by Blaise Pascal (1623–1662) in 1645 and Gottfried Leibniz (1646–1716) in 1694 for solving the navigational and scientific problems that began to arise as Europe entered a new and heightened period of scientific development and international commerce. In 1801 Joseph-Marie Jacquard (1752–1834) invented perhaps the first type of programmed machine, called Jacquard's Loom, in order to automate the weaving of cloth with patterns. Jacquard was motivated by the desire of capitalists in the early Industrial Age who wanted to reduce the cost of producing their goods through mass production in factories.

The twentieth century saw the development of scientific research and engineering applications that required increasingly complex computations. Urgent military needs created by World War II spurred the development of the first electronic computers; the devices in use today are the descendants of these room-sized early efforts to streamline military planning and calculation. The needs and desires of society have subsequently influenced the development of a vast array of computing technologies, including **supercomputers**, graphics processors, games, digital video and audio, mobile computing devices, and telephones.

In the twenty-first century, computers are used in almost every facet of society, including (but not limited to) agriculture, architecture, art, commerce and global trade, communication, education, governance, law, music, politics, science, transportation, and writing. In general, computing technologies have been applied to almost every situation falling into one of two categories. The first category covers applications that require the organization, storage, and retrieval of large amounts of information such as library catalogs or bank records. The second category includes applications that require the coordination of complex processes, like the control of machinery involved in the manufacture of cars or the printing of books and newspapers.

Impact of Computers on Work

One of the ways that computers have made an impact on society is in how people have organized themselves in workplace groups in relationship to computers. The earliest computers were developed to perform specific tasks in science, engineering, or warfare that had previously been done by hand. Soon general-purpose computers could automate almost any information processing task required to manage an organization, such as payroll processing and record management. However, since early generation computers were relatively expensive, all of an organization's information processing tasks were typically centralized around the one large computer it could afford. Departments and people in such organizations would likewise be organized in a centralized fashion to facilitate their access to the computer. Companies with centralized information processing, for example, usually had most of their administrative offices in the same geographic location as their computer resources.

SOCIAL INFORMATICS

Social informatics is a multidisciplinary field of study that examines the social and organizational roles and impacts of information and communication technologies. It examines many issues, including: impacts of computerization on work, the usefulness and usability of computer hardware and software, security and privacy, law, information needs and uses, and technological risks. For more information about this field, see the following web site: <http://www.albany.edu/~mciver/SI>.

---

supercomputers very high performance computers, usually comprised of many processors and used for modeling and simulation of complex phenomena, like meteorology

minicomputers computers midway in size between a desktop computer and a mainframe computer; most modern desktops are much more powerful than the older minicomputers

Subsequent developments in computing technology changed the way companies organized people who perform similar tasks. The advent of computer networking and lower cost **minicomputers** enabled entire organizations that were once centralized around a single computer to rearrange themselves into geographically dispersed divisions. The integration of telecommunications with computing allowed people in remote places such as branch offices to use computers located in distant parts of their organization. This decentralization continued with the advent of the personal computer. PCs provided a low-cost way for large organizations to transform themselves further by redistributing information processing responsibilities to small departments and individuals in many locations.

Not only have computers changed the way in which workplaces structure their tasks and workers, they have also dramatically changed the work itself. Computer-aided manufacturing (CAM) was first introduced in the 1950s with numerically controlled machines. These and other forms of computer-based automation have been associated with the loss of jobs and certain skills, and the need to master new skills. Since the middle of the twentieth century, computer-controlled devices have gradually eliminated certain types of jobs and the need for people to perform particular skills. As a consequence, workers have had to learn new skills in order to continue working in environments that increasingly depend on computers.

One major result has been the shift of some economies, such as that of the United States, from manufacturing to service jobs. Entirely new categories of jobs have been created to support and implement computer technology. In addition, the ease of networking computers has led businesses to relocate jobs to remote locations. For example, a number of companies now hire computer programmers who are located in other countries, such as India, in order to save on labor costs. Within the United States, increasing numbers of companies allow employees to work from their homes or work centers away from the corporate headquarters. These so-called telecommuters are able to communicate with their employers and deliver their work using the Internet.

The advent of e-mail, the World Wide Web, and other Internet technologies has perhaps made the most significant impact on the social fabric of American society. People can now communicate with others in remote places, easily, affordably, and often anonymously. They can search for, share, and transfer more information, and more quickly, than ever before. People distributed across remote locations can organize themselves into "virtual communities" based on shared interests, regardless of their geographic locations. The Internet has also changed the way both education and entertainment can be delivered into private homes and public spaces.

Effects of the Computer Age

Psychologists have long been interested in observing and analyzing the way humans interact with computers. Research in human-computer interaction has studied how people read and process information presented to them on computer screens, the types of input errors people are most likely to make when using different computer systems, and the effectiveness of various kinds

of input devices such as keyboards, mice, and light pens. Psychological issues have also been identified in how people behave toward other people when they use computing technologies such as e-mail and how they behave toward computers. Studies have shown, for example, that people use the anonymity that e-mail and other Internet technologies afford to construct alternate identities for themselves. Other studies indicate that people often apply the same rules of social behavior, such as politeness, toward computers as they would to other people.

The impact of computers on lifestyles has largely paralleled the impact of computing on social organization, work, and personal communication. The effect has become more pronounced as personal computing devices become increasingly more commonplace in American society. In particular, computers coupled with telecommunications technologies enable many people to live and work more independently and remotely than ever before. Individuals using personal computers can publish books, make airline reservations, and hold meetings to share information with any number of people across the globe. Some observers view these developments positively, while others are concerned that the widespread use of computers has led to lifestyles that contain increasing amounts of work. SEE ALSO E-commerce; Embedded Technology (Ubiquitous Computing); Ethics; Human Factors: User Interfaces; Internet; Jacquard's Loom; Privacy.

William J. McIver, Jr.

As technology advances, robots are taking over tasks, like welding automotive parts, that were once performed by humans. The loss of such assembly line jobs has forced former car builders to explore new career possibilities.

Bibliography

Greenbaum, Joan. *Windows on the Workplace: Computers, Jobs and the Organization of Office Work in the Late Twentieth Century.* New York: Cornerstone Books/Monthly Review Press, 1995.

Kling, Rob. "Learning about Information Technologies and Social Change: The Contribution of Social Informatics." *The Information Society* 16, no. 3 (2000): 217–232.

Landauer, Thomas K. *The Trouble with Computers: Usefulness, Usability, and Productivity.* Cambridge, MA: MIT Press, 1995.

Reeves, Byron, and Clifford Nass. *The Media Equation: How People Treat Computers, Television, and New Media Like Real People and Places.* Cambridge: Cambridge University Press, 1996.

Stern, Nancy, and Robert A. Stern. *Computers in Society.* Englewood Cliffs, NJ: Prentice-Hall, 1983.

Turkle, Sherry. *Life on the Screen: Identity in the Age of the Internet.* New York: Simon & Schuster, 1995.

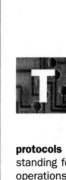

protocols agreed understanding for the sub-operations that make up transactions; usually found in the specification of inter-computer communications

TCP/IP

How do computer networks operate and why has the Internet been successful? A large part of the answer to both of these questions is what is known as the Transmission Control Protocol/Internet Protocol suite of computer communication **protocols**, more commonly referred to as TCP/IP. As late as the mid-1980s, there were many "islands" of computer networks that could not communicate with each other. These networks were limited in size and speed, and the technologies on which they were based used closed proprietary standards, meaning that they could not communicate with each other. TCP/IP has changed everything; what exists now is a fast, worldwide, and single network based on open standards: the Internet.

TCP/IP is the defining interoperability protocol for connecting computers to one another upon which the Internet is built. The creators of the TCP/IP protocol suite recognized that the task of communications is too complex and too diverse to be accomplished by a single layer. Thus, the functionality required for network interoperability is divided into separate layers that depend on each other.

The Transmission Control Protocol (TCP) and the Internet Protocol (IP) are the two primary protocols of this layered suite, at the transport and network layers respectively. The TCP protocol is implemented in end computer systems at the edge of the network while the IP protocol is implemented in intermediate network devices within the core of the network. Together, TCP/IP provides an end-to-end architecture for the Internet based on the principle that "intelligence" should be placed in end computer system applications, while the network should remain as simple as possible given the broad range of possible applications that the network might support. Many have credited the TCP/IP end-to-end architecture with subsequent Internet innovations, including the World Wide Web, because new applications can be easily implemented in an end computer system without the need to change the network infrastructure.

Protocols

A communications protocol is an agreement that specifies a common set of language (semantics), grammar (syntax), and timing (synchronization) for the exchange of information between computers. TCP is a communications protocol, not a piece of software; there are many different software implementations of the TCP protocol but only one TCP protocol itself, which has endured despite many challenges. TCP is a connection-oriented protocol that specifies the format of the data and reciprocal acknowledgments that any two computers must exchange to achieve a reliable transfer. TCP identifies a connection by a pair of endpoints. Each endpoint consists of an identifier in the format "IP number, TCP port number." Thus, a given TCP port number can be shared by multiple connections. TCP assumes little about its underlying communication system, so it can be used with a large variety of **packet-switching** systems including the Internet Protocol.

Within the Internet, the basic unit of data is an IP packet and the basic mechanism of transfer is packet-switching. Routing refers to the **algorithm** for choosing a path over which to send packets. A computer with multiple network connections (a router) examines the IP address field within the packet header and matches it to a table (IP routing table). Conceptually, three possible things could happen: (1) a match is made in the routing table and the packet is sent out to the specified router interface where it may be delayed behind other packets; (2) no match is made in the routing table so the packet is sent out via the default router interface where it may be delayed behind other packets; or (3) the router is so loaded down that packets have nowhere to go (match or no match) and thus the packet is lost (bit bucket).

IP routing is referred to as an "unreliable" (packets may be lost, duplicated, delayed, or delivered out-of-sequence), "best-effort" (not guaranteed due to varying levels of Internet traffic), or "connectionless" (each packet is handled independently) packet-delivery system. However, TCP matched with IP makes the Internet reliable. All computers that connect to the Internet run IP software and most of them also run TCP software. TCP handles the problems IP does not handle without duplicating the work IP does well. In fact, it is because TCP and IP work together so well that the entire set of protocols that the Internet uses is known as the TCP/IP protocol suite. It is not a coincidence that they work together; TCP and IP were designed simultaneously to work with and complement each other in 1974 by computer scientists Vinton Cerf and Robert Kahn. The original TCP/IP protocol suite was based on successful software implementations in the ARPANET, Packet Radio, and Packet Satellite networks so there was never any question of it not working as intended.

TCP/IP as a Standard

Open system standards like TCP/IP provide the agreed upon rules for communication between computers, independent of any vendor's proprietary product. TCP/IP was adopted as a U.S. Department of Defense (DoD) standard in 1980. The interoperability of the TCP/IP standard has allowed applications to be built at higher layers of abstraction without being burdened by the details of individual, lower-layer implementations.

ARPA Roots of TCP/IP and the Internet

TCP/IP is the direct result of protocol research and development conducted on experimental packet-switched networks. In the 1970s the U.S.

packet-switching an operation used in digital communications systems whereby packets (collections) of data are dispatched to receivers based on addresses that the packets contain

algorithm a rule or procedure used to solve a mathematical problem—most often described as a sequence of steps

Computer scientist Vinton Cerf (shown here in 2000) worked with Robert Kahn to develop TCP and IP technologies in 1974.

Department of Defense Advanced Research Project Agency (ARPA) funded three separate grants to implement TCP/IP, which led to three independent implementations within a short time. This is important because independent implementations are a basic requirement for an Internet standard. At the same time, ARPA funded a project to develop a portable operating system, which eventually converged with UNIX. The University of California-Berkeley released an especially popular version of this ARPA-funded UNIX (Berkeley Software Distribution, or BSD, UNIX) which also incorporated TCP/IP. Because its development was publicly funded, it was available for free. As universities found that they had TCP/IP functionality at their disposal via BSD UNIX, many began to form regional networks that eventually converged into the one large network that is now known as the Internet. SEE ALSO Babbage, Charles; Government Funding: Research; Internet; National Aeronautics and Space Administration (NASA).

William J. Yurcik

Bibliography

Cerf, Vinton G., and Robert E. Kahn. "A Protocol for Packet Network Interconnection." *IEEE Transactions on Communication Technology* COM-22 (1974): 627–641.

Comer, Douglas E. *The Internet Book: Everything You Need to Know About Computer Networking and How the Internet Works*, 3rd ed. Upper Saddle River, NJ: Prentice Hall, 2000.

Telnet

Telnet was officially adopted as a widely accepted computer communications protocol in May 1983. It was created and implemented to allow servers and PCs to communicate through the creation of a widely deployed communication **interface** where commands that were issued by the host computer were sent across a link as simple, clear text. Communication links of the time were typically very slow. The servers receiving the telnet transmission would execute the commands, summarize the results, and transmit them back across the same slow link to the host.

interface a boundary or border between two or more objects or systems; also a point of access

bandwidth a measure of the frequency component of a signal or the capacity of a communication channel to carry signals

In the early days of computer networking, **bandwidth** was afforded only at a premium. Its deployment was difficult, which required specialized skills. Telnet was able to minimize the impact and cost associated with this problem. Telnet allowed network managers to control devices remotely, and to run some simple applications across what could be hundreds or even thousands of miles without consuming all bandwidth on the network, or access points.

broadband access a term given to denote high bandwidth services

Even today, with the advent of **broadband access**, telnet has its place as a tool to be exploited in controlling one's digital assets. At the heart of all major and medium sized networks, one will likely find a router designed to join different networks together. These devices are provided an address so that all devices in the network for communication between the network and or the Internet can reach them. This address can also be reached via telnet. This simple fact makes telnet a very powerful protocol that can be used to troubleshoot, configure, and deploy new equipment on a network. In fact, telnet is the most widely used tool for the managing of all equipment in a given network.

Telnet Concerns

All switches, routers, and **translational bridges** built by such companies as Cisco, Marconi, Extreme Networks, and so on, come with a Command Line Interface (CLI). The CLI is a text-driven interface that is very obscure; it can be quite intimidating for first time users as they attempt to manage and configure a device. This is in stark contrast to a **graphical user interface (GUI)** that is intuitive and simple to use. The downside of a GUI is that it can often saturate a wide area link, and consume all available bandwidth, thus causing bottlenecks for users that can cost a great deal of money. The CLI is still widely used, however, and it is the perfect fit for managing a device or series of devices. Unfortunately for management, this method does not scale well as telnet can only access one device at a time. Thus, in a network of several hundred devices, the CLI with telnet access would not be a manageable condition, and would require a more robust management application to handle such a sizeable network.

There are other concerns about using the telnet protocol; for one, it is not secure. Text transferred to and from server devices and hosts is typically clear text. Even passwords for configuration of major devices are submitted across the wire unencrypted. This creates a serious management problem. When deploying the telnet protocol, a company's network manager must take care to secure unencrypted data from users outside the company network, as well as from internal employees, with whom the majority of all security violations originate. Typically, the best line of defense is to not allow the protocol to traverse the networks, thus making it impossible to breach the system with telnet. However, this results in the inability to utilize telnet for network configuration and management, which forces the purchase of expensive management applications. The decision to deploy or not to deploy telnet is a complicated management choice.

FTP

The File Transfer Protocol (FTP) was developed around the same time as telnet, and allowed for succinct transfer of files between servers and hosts and for the deployment of early remote storage solutions. This was particularly welcome in the early days of the Internet because bandwidth was at a premium. FTP would address this limitation and allow data to be transferred more efficiently.

Early implementers were also delighted with the option for remote storage of data because PC storage capabilities were still limited while user needs were growing. FTP and its usage are based on a simple command line utility. In addition, because FTP was a standard, it guaranteed that dissimilar systems and networks could interact with reasonable robustness and little variance in configuration.

FTP is still widely used today. Any user who gets an account with an ISP will likely be supplied space for a personal web site. To access this secured space, the user will typically utilize an FTP program for the downloading and uploading of HTML pages and graphical content for the web site. The application most commonly used is a GUI-based FTP application called Cute FTP. Cute FTP is a free **shareware** application that can be downloaded from many sites on the Internet.

translational bridges special network devices that convert low-level protocols from one type to another

graphical user interface (GUI) an interface that allows computers to be operated through pictures (icons) and mouse-clicks, rather than through text and typing

shareware a software distribution technique, whereby the author shares copies of his programs at no cost, in the expectation that users will later pay a fee of some sort

NET CONGESTION

FTP is also used in most of the world's major web sites and it can cause system usage congestion. The once-unregulated Napster music service, which facilitated free downloads of copyrighted music, provides an example of this. The massive downloads of music files were performed typically via FTP. This created a problem for many organizations. FTP is meant to alleviate bandwidth usage limitations, but left unto itself it will consume whatever bandwidth is available. When employees of corporations spent hours downloading music from Napster, they were taxing corporate networks that were already carrying heavy data traffic. FTP continues to be used because it is simple and easily deployed. It will continue to pose a bandwidth concern when its use is widespread.

FTP and telnet can be powerful tools for manipulating the web, in part because they require little networking knowledge to use them effectively and efficiently. From a technical perspective, telnet and FTP utilize a series of handshakes and negotiation parameters. The handshake is like the drone of a modem or fax machine as it attempts to connect with a compatible device somewhere in cyberspace. These handshakes and negotiation parameters are specified in Requests for Comments number 854 for telnet, and number 354 for FTP, respectively. The technical details of their implementation are extensive and beyond the scope of this text. Fortunately, understanding the technical aspects is not a prerequisite to using telnet or FTP because anyone who accesses the Internet will likely, at some time, make use of these protocols. SEE ALSO E-COMMERCE; FTP; INTERNET; TCP/IP.

John Nau

Internet Resources

Cisco Connection Online. Cisco Systems, Inc. <http://www.cisco.com>

"STD/STD8." Telnet Protocol Specifications. *Internet RFC/STD/FYI/BCP Archives.* <http://www.faqs.org/rfcs/std/std8.html>

"Telnet and FTP." Heart of the Web. <http://www.heartoftheweb.net/ftp_&_telnet.htm>

Urban Myths

An urban myth, also known as an urban legend, is a fictional tale that circulates widely, is told and retold with differing details, and is supposedly true. Urban myths are present in all media, including oral, print, and electronic. There is no single source from which these stories are derived or one method by which they are generated. For instance, some are deliberately manufactured **hoaxes** created to cause alarm and concern, while others are created by people who have encountered a humorous or remarkable story and wish to retell it in a personalized way. Urban myths can be created for entertainment and illustration of a point or are created by people who do not remember the exact details of a story that they have heard or read.

hoaxes false claims or assertions, sometimes made unlawfully in order to extort money

History of Urban Myths

It is not known who coined the phrase "urban myth," but the phenomenon has been studied as a serious form of folklore since the 1930s. Seminal studies of urban myths include Alexander Woollcott's monograph *While Rome Burns* (1934) and Marie Bonaparte's study of "The Corpse in the Car" legend that appeared in the psychiatric journal *American Imago* (1941).

American folklorists began to collect "urban belief tales" as they were then called in the 1940s and 1950s. Notable works from this period include Richard K. Beardsley and Rosalie Hankey's studies on "The Vanishing Hitchhiker" (1942-43); Ernest Baughman's article on "The Fatal Initiation" (1945); J. Russell Reaver's article on "The Poison Dress" (1952); B. A. Botkin's book *Sidewalks of America* (1954); and Richard M. Dorson's textbook *American Folklore* (1959).

In 1968 a groundbreaking urban myth publication appeared: the journal *Indiana Folklore*, produced by Indiana University's Folklore Institute, which is now part of the university's Department of Folklore and Ethnomusicology. For a number of years thereafter, folklorists turned their focus to analyzing the history, variety, persistence, and widespread acceptance as literal truth of urban myths.

To this day, studies of urban myths continue to flourish. There are international conferences on modern legends such as those held at the Centre for English Cultural Tradition and Language at the University of Sheffield. The International Society for Folk Narrative Research holds annual meetings and publishes a newsletter, *FOAFtale* (Friend of a Friend Tale) *News*, and an annual journal, *Contemporary Legend.* An indication of the popularity of urban myth studies is that 1,116 items were listed in Gillian Bennett and Paul Smith's compilation *Contemporary Legend: A Folklore Bibliography* (1993).

Computer-Related Urban Myths

The following are just a few examples of urban myths that have a computer connection.

- Early attempts at computer translation of text from one human language to another produced hilarious results. For instance, John Steinbeck's novel *Grapes of Wrath* became *Angry Raisins.* The adage "Out of sight, out of mind" became "Blind and insane" and "The spirit was willing, but the flesh is weak" became "The vodka was good, but the meat was rotten."

- A photo e-mail claiming to be the last picture taken from the top of the World Trade Center in New York City just seconds before a hijacked airplane (seen in the background) slammed into the building on September 11, 2001.

- Internet Service Providers will donate 1 cent toward "Brian's" (or any child who is currently hospitalized) operation for every person who forwards this e-mail.

- NASA scientists discovered a "missing day" in time that corresponds to Biblical accounts of the Sun's standstill in the sky (i.e., Joshua 10:12-13, and 2 Kings 20:8-11).

None of these myths are true, but all of them have been shared among friends and strangers, often via the Internet, as if they were fact.

Urban myths have been around since the beginning of humankind's history, for they almost certainly developed out of every culture's oral traditions. The Internet is merely another medium by which these myths are transmitted to people who have not yet been exposed to such tales. At best, Urban Myths disseminated via the Internet can be considered as junk e-mail. At worst, they can be libelous (e.g., Marlboro/Snapple/Troop clothing is owned by the Ku Klux Klan) and a danger to people's lives (e.g., taking 20 aspirins after unprotected sex will halt pregnancies). Unfortunately, there is no technical solution to this problem. Like gossip and rumors, urban myths are a part of life and have to be tolerated. To combat urban legends, various web sites have been established to help people determine fact from fiction. These include: <http://www.snopes2.com> and <http://www.truthorfiction.com/>. SEE ALSO HACKER; HACKING.

Joyce H-S Li

URBAN MYTHS TODAY

Computers have become the primary means by which urban myths and other pieces of misinformation are disseminated—including everything from "stupid computer user" stories to virus warning hoaxes.

Bibliography

Brunvand, Jan Harold. *The Truth Never Stands in the Way of a Good Story*. Urbana: University of Illinois Press, 2000.

Dundes, Alan. *Sometimes the Dragon Wins: Yet More Urban Folklore from the Paperwork Empire*. Syracuse, NY: Syracuse University Press, 1996.

Genge, Ngaire. *Urban Legends: The As-Complete-As-One-Could-Be Guide to Modern Myths*. New York: Three Rivers Press, 2000.

Roeper, Richard. *Urban Legends: The Truth Behind All Those Deliciously Entertaining Myths That Are Absolutely, Positively, 100 Percent Not True*. Franklin Lakes, NJ: Career Press, 1999.

Internet Resources

Mikkelson, Barbara, and David P. Mikkelson. *Urban Legends Reference Pages*. <http://www.snopes2.com>

Visual Basic

Visual Basic is one of the most widely used programming languages in the world. The major reason for its popularity is that it allows programmers to create Windows applications quickly and easily.

The origins of Visual Basic are found in a programming language created in 1964 by John Kemeny and Thomas Kurtz. BASIC (Beginners All-purpose Symbolic Instruction Code) was originally an interpreted language that was designed to simplify the programming process and make programming more accessible to the world at large. Using that philosophy, Microsoft integrated a BASIC interpreter into its operating system MS-DOS. Despite its wide distribution and relative simplicity, BASIC was not able to compete with faster, compiled languages such as C or C++. Thus, BASIC was commonly used for trivial or educational purposes, whereas "real" applications were usually developed in other languages.

graphical user interfaces (GUIs) interfaces that allow computers to be operated through pictures (icons) and mouse-clicks, rather than through text and typing

In the late 1980s, Microsoft Windows and other **graphical user interfaces (GUIs)** were still in their infancy. Most PCs were still using text-based operating systems. As people began to realize the benefits of graphical operating systems, Microsoft Windows gained popularity. Unfortunately, creating Windows-based programs was exceedingly difficult. Extensive code had to be written to define precisely what the interface would look like as well as how a user would interact with it.

syntax a set of rules that a computing language incorporates regarding structure, punctuation, and formatting

To overcome this problem, Microsoft revived BASIC in 1991 by introducing Visual Basic 1.0. Using BASIC's heritage of simplicity and its general **syntax**, this new development tool gave programmers an easy way to create Windows applications. In the years since, Microsoft has continued to improve Visual Basic by releasing newer versions. These improvements include not only enhancements to the development environment but also modernization of the core BASIC language as well. These renovations include making BASIC object oriented and fully event driven, and overcoming the limitations of being interpreted, allowing programmers to generate a **compiled executable code**.

compiled executable code the binary code that a central processing unit (CPU) can understand; the product of the compilation process

Using Visual Basic

The process of creating a program in Visual Basic can be clearly described in three stages: (1) Draw the interface on the screen by adding controls. (2)

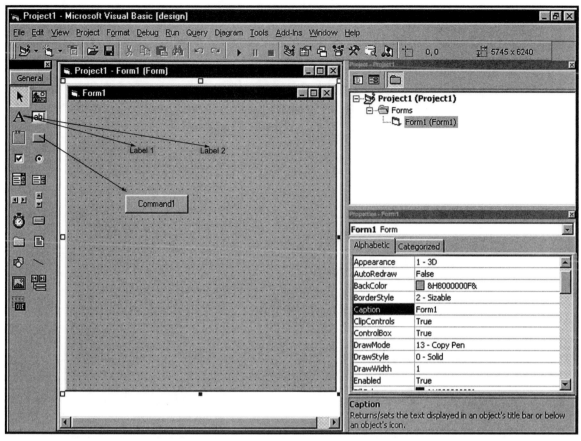

Figure 1. The addition of two text labels and one button to the workspace.

Define important characteristics of the controls. (3) Write code to determine how a control will react to user actions.

In the first step, the programmer creates the interface using an on-screen drawing tool. Windows controls, such as buttons and input boxes, are added to a workspace using an application similar to Paint (the standard Windows drawing utility). Almost all of the standard Windows interface components are available by default. More advanced controls, such as status bars, can also be added. The arrows in Figure 1 show the results of adding two text labels and a button to the workspace.

Every control has a set of characteristics that make it unique. For example, buttons have properties such as name (how the program will refer to it) and caption (the text that will be used to label it). In the second step, the programmer sets the initial values for the control in order to customize the appearance and behavior of the controls. As seen in Figure 2 (see page 210), the text on the button has been changed to "Click Me" by altering a property of the button.

In addition to the properties, every type of control has different ways that the user can interact with it. For example, buttons are clicked, or text is entered into an input box. These are known as events. Whenever an event occurs, the program must respond appropriately. The programmer is responsible for empowering the controls by providing a specific set of instructions regarding how the system should respond to the events. This usually comes in the form of doing some calculation and then updating the

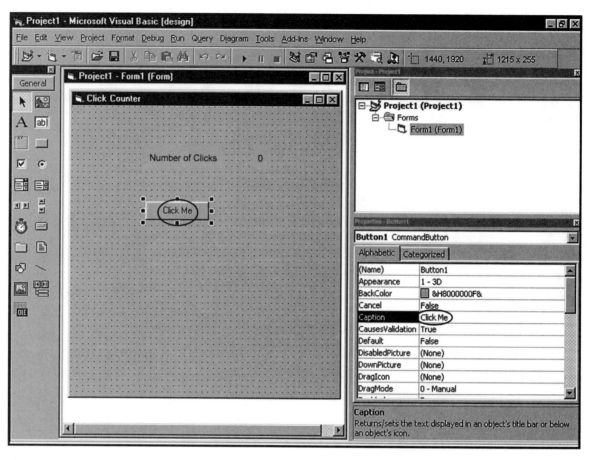

Figure 2. Altering a property of the button to "Click Me."

properties of other controls on the screen to reflect the current state of the system. Figure 3 shows some actual code. In the example, when the button is pressed, the program produces a label that keeps track of the number of times the button is pressed.

At this stage, the program must be run to evaluate that it is working properly. Figure 4 shows a screen shot of the program after the button has been pressed three times. While testing the program, the programmer has the ability to examine the inner workings of the program and even change the program while it is running. After the programmer is certain that the application functions properly, Visual Basic compiles the code into a working executable program that can be distributed to other users.

In addition to creating new programs and applications, Microsoft has also extended portions of Visual Basic to existing applications. Large-scale, popular applications like Microsoft Word, Excel, and Access contain a limited subset of Visual Basic capabilities known as Visual Basic for Applications (VBA). Often used as a macro-language, VBA can be used to control parts of existing applications. This is a very useful feature for automating repetitive tasks or for customizing existing applications to meet a user's personal needs.

Another variation of Visual Basic offers an alternative to JavaScript. Visual Basic Scripting Edition, or VBScript, can be embedded into HTML pages and distributed over the Internet. VBScript can be very useful for making dynamic web pages or for validating user input before it is submitted.

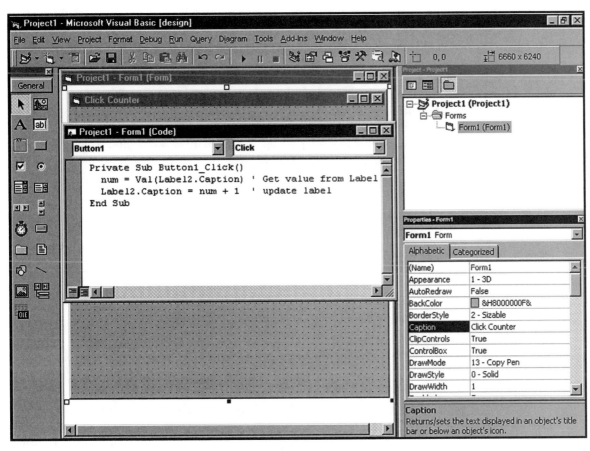

Figure 3. Display of actual code.

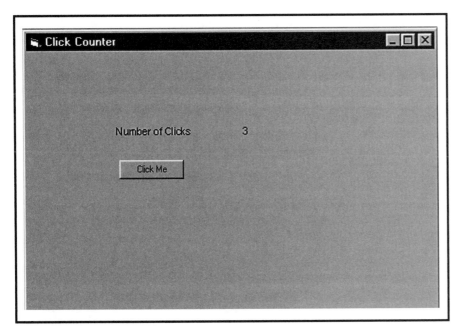

Figure 4. Screen shot after the button is pressed three times.

Both of these dialects of Visual Basic follow essentially the same syntax rules as the full-programming edition. Although some variation exists, this allows programmers to extend their existing skills without needing to learn something completely new.

Like its text ancestor, Visual Basic has greatly simplified the task of programming and enjoys widespread distribution. Unfortunately, to some degree, it has also inherited the stigma of being a second-rate programming language. This conception actually arises from the trade-off between ease-of-use and control. Visual Basic attempts to shield programmers from some of the details associated with what occurs at lower levels of the computer. This restricts the programmer to generalized, high-level functions. Alternative languages, such as C++ grants programmers more control over how processing occurs, and thus they can optimize the code to the specific task at hand. If sub-second optimizations are critical to the success of the program, Visual Basic may not be adequate. However, most applications to be run by businesses will not benefit from such minute speed-ups and programmers will find that the simplified development makes Visual Basic very appealing. SEE ALSO JAVA APPLETS; JAVASCRIPT; PROCEDURAL LANGUAGES; PROGRAMMING.

Stephen Hughes

Bibliography

Overland, Brian R. *Visual Basic in Plain English.* Foster City, CA: IDG Books World-Wide, 1999.

Perry, Greg M. *Sams Teach Yourself Visual Basic 6 in 21 Days.* Indianapolis, IN: Sams, 1998.

Schneider, David I. *An Introduction to Programming Using Visual Basic 6.0.* Upper Saddle River, NJ: Prentice-Hall, 1998.

Photo and Illustration Credits

The illustrations and tables featured in Computer Sciences *were created by GGS Information Services. The photographs appearing in the text were reproduced by permission of the following sources:*

Volume 1

Gale Research: **1**; AP/Wide World Photos, Inc.: **4, 35, 39, 44, 60, 82, 91, 136, 148, 190, 209, 219**; Courtesy of the Library of Congress: **6, 25, 52, 58, 83, 98, 103, 126, 150, 193, 211**; Kobal Collection/Warner Bros.: **9**; Kobal Collection: **11**; Archive Photos/Reuters/Sell: **16**; National Audubon Society Collection/Photo Researchers, Inc.: **19**; CORBIS/Bettmann: **22, 41, 73, 86, 165, 201, 221**; AT&T Archives: **28**; U.S. Census Bureau: **33**; Elena Rooraid/Photo Edit: **48**; Photo Edit: **66**; IBM Corporate Archives: **70, 163**; Colin Braley/Reuters/Getty Images: **94**; Adam Hart-Davis/National Audubon Society Collection/Photo Researchers, Inc.: **105**; Michael S. Yamashita/CORBIS: **110**; Reuters NewMedia Inc./CORBIS: **116**; UPI/CORBIS-Bettmann: **118, 176**; Associated Press/AP: **121**; Doris Langley Moore Collection: **122**; Astrid & Hanns-Frieder Michler/Photo Researchers, Inc.: **133**; Microsoft Corporation: **139**; Ted Spiegel/CORBIS: **140**; Prestige/Getty Images: **143**; Richard T. Nowitz/CORBIS: **146**; U.S. National Aeronautics and Space Administration (NASA): **152**; Robert Cattan/Index Stock Imagery/PictureQuest: **156**; Dave Bartruff/Stock, Boston Inc./PictureQuest: **159**; Courtesy Carnegie Mellon University Field Robotics Center/NASA: **172**; Roger Ressmeyer/CORBIS: **179, 184**; Hulton-Deutsch Collection/CORBIS: **187**; Granger Collection, Ltd.: **197**; Larry Chan/Reuters/Getty Images: **204**; Microsoft programs: 213, 214, 215, 216, 217.

Volume 2

Thomas E. Kurtz: **2**; Courtesy of the Library of Congress: **4, 18, 99, 112**; CORBIS/Bettmann: **13**; U.S. National Aeronautics and Space Administration (NASA): **16**; Roger Ressmeyer/CORBIS: **25, 92, 115, 118, 150, 179, 215**; A/P Wide World Photos, Inc.: **31, 36, 40, 65, 73, 89, 110, 133, 136, 143, 161, 165, 167, 171, 199, 205, 212, 221**; UPI/CORBIS-Bettmann: **34, 169, 217, 219**; Courtesy of BT Archives: **46**; CORBIS: **53**; Andrew Syred/National Audubon Society Collection/Photo Researchers, Inc.: **62**; Richard Pasley/Stock, Boston Inc./PictureQuest: **70**; Bob Krist/CORBIS: **77**; Patrik Giardino/CORBIS: **79**; Rob Crandall/Stock, Boston Inc./PictureQuest: **84**; Mario Tama/Getty Images: **94**; AFP/CORBIS: **98**; Custom Medical Stock Photo: **140**; William McCoy/Rainbow/PictureQuest: **147**; Courtesy of Niklaus Wirth: **157**; Reuters NewMedia Inc./CORBIS: **175**; Paul Almasy/CORBIS: **188**; Detlev Van Ravenswaay/Picture Press/CORBIS-Bettmann: **193**; James Marshall/CORBIS: **203**.

Volume 3

Bill Lai/Rainbow/PictureQuest: **2**; Agricultural Research Service/USDA: **5**; Carlos Lopez-Barillas/Getty Images: **8**; A/P Wide World Photos, Inc.: **11, 19, 28, 39, 89, 102, 106, 111, 118, 131**; Laima Druskis/Stock, Boston Inc./PictureQuest: **13**; Bojan Brecelj/CORBIS: **17**; JLM Visuals: **23**; Mediafocus: **24**; Ed Kashi/Phototake NYC: **30**; Reuters NewMedia Inc./CORBIS: **34**; Royalty Free/CORBIS: **42**; Srulik Haramaty/Phototake NYC: **46**; Mark

Antman/Phototake, NYC: **52**; CORBIS/Bettmann: **55, 206, 211**; Hulton-Deutsch Collection/CORBIS: **56**; Walter A. Lyons: **60, 210**; Smith & Santori/Gale Group: **62**; Darren McCollester/Getty Images: **69**; Richard Palsey/Stock, Boston Inc./PictureQuest: **73**; Ed Kashi/CORBIS: **79**; Index Stock Imagery: **81**; AFP/CORBIS: **85**; Montes De Oca & Associates: **92**; Millard Berry: **95**; Courtesy of NASA/JPL/NIMA/Visible Earth: **100**; Courtesy of the Library of Congress: **108, 124**; Nehau Kulyk/Photo Researchers, Inc.: **116**; CORBIS: **122**; U.S. Department of Education/National Audubon Society Collection/Photo Researchers, Inc.: **125**; Bob Rowan/Progressive Image/CORBIS: **133**; Bill Ross/CORBIS: **137**; Geoff Tompkincon/National Audubon Society Collection/Photo Researchers, Inc.: **141**; Clive Freeman/Photo Researchers, Inc.: **143**; Roger Ressmeyer/CORBIS: **150**; Free Software Foundation: **157**; Kenneth Eward/BioGrafx/National Audubon Society Collection/Photo Researchers, Inc.: **163**; Steven McBride/Picturesque/PictureQuest: **168**; Michael S. Yamashita/CORBIS: **175**; Photo Researchers, Inc.: **178**; Chris Hondros/Getty Images: **181**; David Silverman/Getty Images: **183**; U.S. National Aeronautics and Space Administration (NASA): **188**; Jim Sugar Photography/CORBIS: **200**; Leif Skoogfors/CORBIS: **205**.

Volume 4

A/P Wide World Photos, Inc.: **2, 15, 23, 29, 33, 41, 44, 59, 75, 100, 147, 151, 162, 168, 177, 180, 184, 186, 190, 195, 197, 201,** **203**; Gene M. Amdahl: **4**; Vittoriano Rastelli/CORBIS: **7**; Jim Sugar Photography/CORBIS: **10**; NNS: **22**; John Maher/Stock, Boston Inc./PictureQuest: **26**; Kenneth Eward/Photo Researchers, Inc.: **35**; Steve Chenn/CORBIS: **47**; Christopher Morris/Black Star Publishing/PictureQuest: **50**; Jonathan Elderfield/Getty Images: **54**; Courtesy of the Library of Congress: **56, 103, 163**; Amy Ritterbush/Stock, Boston Inc./PictureQuest: **64**; AFP/CORBIS: **66, 113, 125, 131, 134**; Reuters NewMedia Inc./CORBIS: **70, 89, 108, 120, 194**; Shahn Kermani/Getty Images: **76**; Associated Press/AP: **78, 93, 95**; Patricia Nagle/Center for Instructional Development and Distance Education/University of Pittsburgh: **85**; Alec Sarkas/Center for Instructional Development and Distance Education/University of Pittsburgh: **87**; Kobal Collection/MGM/UA: **106**; Space Imaging: **115**; Courtesy of USGS Landsat 7 Team at the Eros Data Center and NASA's Visible Earth: **116**; Reuters/News and Observer-Jim/Archive Photos, Inc.: **122**; Reuters/Getty Images: **128**; Oleg Nikishin/Getty Images: **139**; Netscape Communicator browser window (c) 1999 Netscape Communications Corporation—used with permission (Netscape Communications has not authorized, sponsored, endorsed, or approved this publication and is not responsible for its content): **155, 156, 157, 159**; YBSHY/CORBIS: **165**; James King-Holmes/Science Photo Library/The National Audubon Society Collection/Photo Researchers, Inc.: **171**; Carnegie Mellon University: **173**; Microsoft Visual Basic program: 209, 210, 211.

Glossary

abacus: an ancient counting device that probably originated in Babylon around 2,400 B.C.E.

acuity: sharpness or keenness, especially when used to describe vision

address bus: a collection of electrical signals used to transmit the address of a memory location or input/output port in a computer

aerodynamics: the science and engineering of systems that are capable of flight

agents: systems (software programs and/or computing machines) that can act on behalf of another, or on behalf of a human

aggregate: a numerical summation of multiple individual scores

ailerons: control surfaces on the trailing edges of the wings of an aircraft—used to manage roll control

ALGOL: a language developed by the ALGOL committee for scientific applications—acronym for ALGOrithmic Language

algorithm: a rule or procedure used to solve a mathematical problem—most often described as a sequence of steps

all-points-addressable mode: a technique for organizing graphics devices where all points (pixels) on the screen are individually accessible to a running program

alpha beta pruning: a technique that under certain conditions offers an optimal way to search through data structures called "trees"

alphanumeric: a character set which is the union of the set of alphabetic characters and the set of single digit numbers

ambient: pertaining to the surrounding atmosphere or environment

ambiguity: the quality of doubtfulness or uncertainty; often subject to multiple interpretations

amortized: phasing out something in until it is gradually extinguished, like a mortgage loan

amplitude: the size or magnitude of an electrical signal

analog: a quantity (often an electrical signal) that is continuous in time and amplitude

analogous: a relationship of logical similarity between two or more objects

analytic simulation: modeling of systems by using mathematical equations (often differential equations) and programming a computer with them to simulate the behavior of the real system

Analytical Engine: Charles Babbage's vision of a programmable mechanical computer

animatronics: the animation (movement) of something by the use of electronic motors, drives, and controls

anthropomorphic: having human form, or generally resembling human appearance

anti-aliasing: introducing shades of gray or other intermediate shades around an image to make the edge appear to be smoother

applet: a program component that requires extra support at run time from a browser or run-time environment in order to execute

approximation: an estimate

arc tangent: the circular trigonometric function that is the inverse of the tangent function; values range from $-\Pi/2$ to $\Pi/2$

artificial intelligence (AI): a branch of computer science dealing with creating computer hardware and software to mimic the way people think and perform practical tasks

ASCII: an acronym that stands for American Standard Code for Information Interchange; assigns a unique 8-bit binary number to every letter of the alphabet, the digits (0 to 9), and most keyboard symbols

assembler: a program that translates human-readable assembly language programs to machine-readable instructions

assembly language: the natural language of a central processing unit (CPU); often classed as a low-level language

asynchronous: events that have no systematic relationship to one another in time

attenuation: the reduction in magnitude (size or amplitude) of a signal that makes a signal weaker

authentication: the act of ensuring that an object or entity is what it is intended to be

automata theory: the analytical (mathematical) treatment and study of automated systems

automaton: an object or being that has a behavior that can be modeled or explained completely by using automata theory

autonomous: self governing, or being able to exist independently

autonomy: the capability of acting in a self-governing manner; being able to exist independently or with some degree of independence

axioms: statements that are taken to be true, the foundation of a theory

Bakelite: an insulating material used in synthetic goods, including plastics and resins

ballistics: the science and engineering of the motion of projectiles of various types, including bullets, bombs, and rockets

bandwidth: a measure of the frequency component of a signal or the capacity of a communication channel to carry signals

bar code: a graphical number representation system where alphanumeric characters are represented by vertical black and white lines of varying width

base-2: a number system in which each place represents a power of 2 larger than the place to its right (binary)

base-8: a number system in which each place represents a power of 8 larger than the place to its right (octal)

base-10: a number system in which each place represents a power of 10 larger than the place to its right (decimal)

base-16: a number system in which each place represents a power of 16 larger than the place to its right (hexadecimal)

batch processing: an approach to computer utilization that queues non-interactive programs and runs them one after another

Bayesian networks: structures that describe systems in which there is a degree of uncertainty; used in automated decision making

Bernoulli numbers: the sums of powers of consecutive integers; named after Swiss mathematician Jacques Bernoulli (1654-1705)

binary: existing in only two states, such as "on" or "off," "one" or "zero"

binary code: a representation of information that permits only two states, such as "on" or "off," "one" or "zero"

binary coded decimal (BCD): an ANSI/ISO standard encoding of the digits 0 to 9 using 4 binary bits; the encoding only uses 10 of the available 16 4-bit combinations

binary digit: a single bit, 1 or 0

binary number system: a number system in which each place represents a power of 2 larger than the place on its right (base-2)

binary system: a machine or abstraction that uses binary codes

binomial theorem: a theorem giving the procedure by which a binomial expression may be raised to any power without using successive multiplications

bit: a single binary digit, 1 or 0—a contraction of Binary digIT; the smallest unit for storing data in a computer

bit mapped display: a computer display that uses a table of binary bits in memory to represent the image that is projected onto the screen

bit maps: images comprised of bit descriptions of the image, in black and white or color, such that the colors can be represented by the two values of a binary bit

bit rate: the rate at which binary bits can be processed or transferred per unit time, in a system (often a computer communications system)

bit serial mode: a method of transferring binary bits one after another in a sequence or serial stream

bitstream: a serialized collection of bits; usually used in transfer of bits from one system to another

Boolean algebra: a system developed by George Boole that deals with the theorems of undefined symbols and axioms concerning those symbols

Boolean logic: a system, developed by George Boole, which treats abstract objects (such as sets or classes) as algebraic quantities; Boole applied his mathematical system to the study of classical logic

Boolean operators: fundamental logical operations (for example "and" and "or") expressed in a mathematical form

broadband access: a term given to denote high bandwidth services

browsers: programs that permits a user to view and navigate through documents, most often hypertext documents

bugs: errors in program source code

bus: a group of related signals that form an interconnecting pathway between two or more electronic devices

bus topology: a particular arrangement of buses that constitutes a designed set of pathways for information transfer within a computer

byte: a group of eight binary digits; represents a single character of text

C: a programming language developed for the UNIX operating system; it is designed to run on most machines and with most operating systems

cache: a small sample of a larger set of objects, stored in a way that makes them accessible

calculus: a method of dealing mathematically with variables that may be changing continuously with respect to each other

Callback modems: security techniques that collect telephone numbers from authorized users on calls and then dial the users to establish the connections

capacitates: fundamental electrical components used for storing electrical charges

capacitor: a fundamental electrical component used for storing an electrical charge

carpal tunnel syndrome: a repetitive stress injury that can lead to pain, numbness, tingling, and loss of muscle control in the hands and wrists

cartography: map making

cathode ray tube (CRT): a glass enclosure that projecting a beam of electrons onto the back of a screen

cellular automata: a collection or array of objects that are programmed identically to interact with one another

cellular neural networks (CNN): a neural network topology that uses multidimensional array structures comprised of cells that work together in localized groups

central processing unit (CPU): the part of a computer that performs computations and controls and coordinates other parts of the computer

certificate: a unique electronic document that is used to assist authentication

chaos theory: a branch of mathematics dealing with differential equations having solutions which are very sensitive to initial conditions

checksum: a number that is derived from adding together parts of an electronic message before it is dispatched; it can be used at the receiver to check against message corruption

chromatic dispersion: the natural distortion of pulses of light as they move through an optical network; it results in data corruption

cipher: a code or encryption method

client: a program or computer often managed by a human user, that makes requests to another computer for information

client/server technology: computer systems that are structured using clients (usually human driven computers) to access information stored (often remotely) on other computers known as servers

coaxial cable: a cable with an inner conducting core, a dielectric material and an outer sheath that is designed for high frequency signal transmission

cognitive: pertaining to the concepts of knowing or perceiving

collocation: the act of placing elements or objects in a specific order

commodity: raw material or service marketed prior to being used

compiled: a program that is translated from human-readable code to binary code that a central processing unit (CPU) can understand

compiled executable code: the binary code that a central processing unit (CPU) can understand; the product of the compilation process

compilers: programs that translate human-readable high-level computer languages to machine-readable code

computer-aided design (CAD): the use of computers to replace traditional drawing instruments and tools for engineering or architectural design

computer-assisted tomography: the use of computers in assisting with the management of X-ray images

computer peripheral: a device that is connected to a computer to support its operation; for example, a keyboard or a disk drive unit

concatenates: the joining together of two elements or objects; for example, words are formed by concatenating letters

concentric circles: circles that have coincident centers

conceptualization: a creative process that is directed at envisaging a structure or collection of relationships within components of a complex system

concurrency control: the management and coordination of several actions that occur simultaneously; for example, several computer programs running at once

concurrent: pertaining to simultaneous activities, for example simultaneous execution of many computer programs

configuration files: special disk files containing information that can be used to tell running programs about system settings

cookie: a small text file that a web site can place on a computer's hard drive to collect information about a user's browsing activities or to activate an online shopping cart to keep track of purchases

copyrights: the legal rules and regulations concerning the copying and redistribution of documents

cosine: a trigonometric function of an angle, defined as the ratio of the length of the adjacent side of a right-angled triangle divided by the length of its hypotenuse

counterfeiting: the act of knowingly producing non-genuine objects, especially in relation to currency

crawls: severe weather warnings that are broadcast on the bottom of TV screens

cross-platform: pertaining to a program that can run on many different computer types (often called hardware platforms)

CRT: the acronym for cathode ray tube, which is a glass enclosure that projects images by directing a beam of electrons onto the back of a screen

cryptanalysis: the act of attempting to discover the algorithm used to encrypt a message

cryptanalyst: a person or agent who attempts to discover the algorithm used to encrypt a message

cryptography: the science of understanding codes and ciphers and their application

cryptosystem: a system or mechanism that is used to automate the processes of encryption and decryption

cuneiform: in the shape of a wedge

cybercafe: a shop, cafe, or meeting place where users can rent a computer for a short time to access the Internet

cybernetics: a unified approach to understanding the behavior of machines and animals developed by Norbert Wiener (1894-1964)

cycloids: pertaining to circles, in either a static way or in a way that involves movement

dark fiber: a fiber optic network that exists but is not actively in service, hence the darkness

data mining: a technique of automatically obtaining information from databases that is normally hidden or not obvious

data partitioning: a technique applied to databases (but not restricted to them) which organizes data objects into related groups

data reduction technique: an approach to simplifying data, e.g. summarization

data warehousing: to implement an informational database used to store shared data

de facto: as is

de jure: strictly according to the law

debug: the act of trying to trace, identify, and then remove errors in program source code

decimal system: a number system in which each place represents a power of 10 larger than the place to its right (base-10)

decision trees: classifiers in which a sequence of tests are made to decide the class label to assign to an unknown data item; the sequence of tests can be visualized as having a tree structure

deformations: mechanical systems where a structure is physically misshapen, e.g., dented

degrade: to reduce quality or performance of a system

delimiters: special symbols that mark the beginnings and/or endings of other groups of symbols (for example to mark out comments in program source code)

demographics: the study of the statistical data pertaining to a population

densities: measures of the density of a material; defined as the mass of a sample of material, divided by its volume

deregulation: the lowering of restrictions, rules, or regulations pertaining to an activity or operation (often commercial)

die: the silicon chip that is the heart of integrated circuit fabrication; the die is encased in a ceramic or plastic package to make the completed integrated circuit (IC)

dielectric: a material that exhibits insulating properties, as opposed to conducting properties

Difference Engine: a mechanical calculator designed by Charles Babbage that automated the production of mathematical tables by using the method of differences

differential analyzer: a computer constructed in the early 1930s by Vannevar Bush at Massachusetts Institute of Technology (MIT); it solved differential equations by mechanical integration

digital: a quantity that can exist only at distinct levels, not having values in between these levels (for example, binary)

digital certificates: certificates used in authentication that contain encrypted digital identification information

digital divide: imaginary line separating those who can access digital information from those who cannot

digital library: distributed access to collections of digital information

digital signature: identifier used to authenticate the sender of an electronic message or the signer of an electronic document

digital subscriber line (DSL): a technology that permits high-speed voice and data communications over public telephone networks; it requires the use of a DSL modem

digital subscriber loop (DSL): the enabling of high-speed digital data transfer over standard telephone cables and systems in conjunction with normal telephone speech data

digital watermarks: special data structures permanently embedded into a program or other file type, which contain information about the author and the program

digitizes: converts analog information into a digital form for processing by a computer

diode: a semiconductor device that forces current flow in a conductor to be in one direction only, also known as a rectifier

diode tube: an obsolete form of diode that was made of metal elements in a sealed and evacuated glass tube

direction buttons: buttons on a program with a graphical user interface that provide a way of navigating through information or documents

discrete: composed of distinct elements

disintermediation: a change in business practice whereby consumers elect to cut out intermediary agencies and deal directly with a provider or vendor

distance learning: the form of education where the instructor and students are separated by either location or time (or both), usually mediated by some electronic communication mechanism

distributed denial of service (DDoS): an attack in which large numbers of messages are directed to send network traffic to a target computer, overloading it or its network connection; typically, the attacking computers have been subverted

distributed systems: computer systems comprised of many individual computers that are interconnected and act in concert to complete operations

documentation: literature in a human-readable form that is referred to in support of using a computer or computer system

domain: a region in which a particular element or object exists or has influence; (math) the inputs to a function or relation

doping: a step used in the production of semiconductor materials where charged particles are embedded into the device so as to tailor its operational characteristics

dot.com: a common term used to describe an Internet-based commercial company or organization

dragged: to have been moved by the application of an external pulling force; quite often occurring in graphical user interfaces when objects are moved with a mouse

DRAM: the acronym for Dynamic Random Access Memory; high density, low cost and low speed memory devices used in most computer systems

driver: a special program that manages the sequential execution of several other programs; a part of an operating system that handles input/output devices

drop-down menu: a menu on a program with a graphical user interface that produces a vertical list of items when activated

dumb terminal: a keyboard and screen connected to a distant computer without any processing capability

duplex: simultaneous two-directional communication over a single communication channel

dynamic: changing; possessing volatility

dynamic links: logical connections between two objects that can be modified if the objects themselves move or change state

e-books: short for electronic books; books available for downloading onto an e-book reader

EBCDIC: the acronym for Extended Binary Coded Decimal Interchange Code, which assigns a unique 8-bit binary number to every letter of the alphabet, the digits (0-9), and most keyboard symbols

egress: to move out of an object, system, or environment

electromagnetic: a piece of metal that becomes magnetic only when electricity is applied to it; in general, the more electricity applied to metal, the stronger its magnetism

electromagnetic relays: switches that have a high current carrying capacity, which are opened and closed by an electromagnet

electromagnetic spectrum: a range of frequencies over which electromagnetic radiation can be generated, transmitted, and received

embedded computers: computers that do not have human user orientated I/O devices; they are directly contained within other machines

embedded systems: another term for "embedded computers"; computers that do not have human user orientated input/output devices; they are directly contained within other machines

emoticons: symbols or key combinations used in electronic correspondence to convey emotions

enciphered: encrypted or encoded; a mathematical process that disguises the content of messages transmitted

encryption: also known as encoding; a mathematical process that disguises the content of messages transmitted

end-effector: the end piece of a robotic arm that can receive various types of grippers and tools

end users: computer users

enterprise information system: a system of client and server computers that can be used to manage all of the tasks required to manage and run a large organization

entropy: a measure of the state of disorder or randomness in a system

ephemeris: a record showing positions of astronomical objects and artificial satellites in a time-ordered sequence

ergonomic: being of suitable geometry and structure to permit effective or optimal human user interaction with machines

esoteric: relating to a specialized field of endeavor that is characterized by its restricted size

ether: a highly volatile liquid solvent; also, the far regions of outer space

ethernets: a networking technology for mini and microcomputer systems consisting of network interface cards and interconnecting coaxial cables; invented in the 1970s by Xerox Corporation

Euclidean geometry: the study of points, lines, angles, polygons, and curves confined to a plane

expert system: a computer system that uses a collection of rules to exhibit behavior which mimics the behavior of a human expert in some area

fiber optics: transmission technology using long, thin strands of glass fiber; internal reflections in the fiber assure that light entering one end is transmitted to the other end with only small losses in intensity; used widely in transmitting digital information

field searching: a strategy in which a search is limited to a particular field; in a search engine, a search may be limited to a particular domain name or date, narrowing the scope of searchable items and helping to eliminate the chance of retrieving irrelevant data

file transfer protocol (FTP): a communications protocol used to transfer files

filter queries: queries used to select subsets from a data collection, e.g., all documents with a creation date later than 01/01/2000

firewall: a special purpose network computer or software that is used to ensure that no access is permitted to a sub-network unless authenticated and authorized

firing tables: precalculated tables that can give an artillery gunner the correct allowances for wind conditions and distance by dictating the elevation and deflection of a gun

floating point operations: numerical operations involving real numbers where in achieving a result, the number of digits to the left or right of the decimal point can change

flowcharts: techniques for graphically describing the sequencing and structure of program source code

fluid dynamics: the science and engineering of the motion of gases and liquids

Freedom of Information Act (FOIA): permits individuals to gain access to records and documents that are in the possession of the government

freon: hydrocarbon-based gases used as refrigerants and as pressurants in aerosols

frequency bands: ranges of signal frequencies that are of particular interest in a given application

frequency modulation: a technique whereby a signal is transformed so that it is represented by another signal with a frequency that varies in a way related to the original signal

full-text indexing: a search engine feature in which every word in a document, significant or insignificant, is indexed and retrievable through a search

fuzzy logic: models human reasoning by permitting elements to have partial membership to a set; derived from fuzzy set theory

gallium arsenide: a chemical used in the production of semiconductor devices; chemical symbol GaAs

gates: fundamental building blocks of digital and computer-based electric circuits that perform logical operations; for example logical AND, logical OR

Gaussian classifiers: classifiers constructed on the assumption that the feature values of data will follow a Gaussian distribution

gbps: acronym for gigabits per second; a binary data transfer rate that corresponds to a thousand million (billion, or 109) bits per second

geometric: relating to the principles of geometry, a branch of mathematics related to the properties and relationships of points, lines, angles, surfaces, planes, and solids

germanium: a chemical often used as a high performance semiconductor material; chemical symbol Ge

GIF animation: a technique using Graphic Interchange Format where many images are overlaid on one another and cycled through a sequence to produce an animation

GIF image: the acronym for Graphic Interchange Format where a static image is represented by binary bits in a data file

gigabit networking: the construction and use of a computer network that is capable of transferring information at rates in the gigahertz range

gigabytes: units of measure equivalent to a thousand million (billion, or 109) bytes

gigahertz (GHz): a unit or measure of frequency, equivalent to a thousand million (billion, or 109) hertz, or cycles per second

Global Positioning System (GPS): a method of locating a point on the Earth's surface that uses received signals transmitted from satellites to calculate position accurately

granularity: a description of the level of precision that can be achieved in making measurements of a quantity; for example coarse granularity means inexpensive but imprecise measurements

graphical user interface (GUI): an interface that allows computers to be operated through pictures (icons) and mouse-clicks, rather than through text and typing

groupware: a software technology common in client/server systems whereby many users can access and process data at the same time

gyros: a contraction of gyroscopes; a mechanical device that uses one or more spinning discs which resist changes to their position in space

half tones: black and white dots of certain sizes, which provide a perception of shades of gray

ham radio: a legal (or licensed) amateur radio

haptic: pertaining to the sense of touch

Harvard Cyclotron: a specialized machine (cyclotron) developed in 1948 at Harvard University; it is used to carry out experiments in sub-atomic physics and medicine

head-mounted displays (HMD): helmets worn by a virtual reality (VR) participant that include speakers and screens for each eye, which display three-dimensional images

hertz (Hz): a unit of measurement of frequency, equal to one cycle per second; named in honor of German physicist Heinrich Hertz (1857-1894)

heuristic: a procedure that serves to guide investigation but that has not been proven

hexadecimal: a number system in which each place represents a power of 16 larger than the place to its right (base-16)

high-bandwidth: a communication channel that permits many signals of differing frequencies to be transmitted simultaneously

high precision/high recall: a phenomenon that occurs during a search when all the relevant documents are retrieved with no unwanted ones

high precision/low recall: a phenomenon that occurs when a search yields a small set of hits; although each one may be highly relevant to the search topic, some relevant documents are missed

high-speed data links: digital communications systems that permit digital data to be reliably transferred at high speed

hoaxes: false claims or assertions, sometimes made unlawfully in order to extort money

holistic: looking at the entire system, rather than just its parts

hydraulic: motion being powered by a pressurized liquid (such as water or oil), supplied through tubes or pipes

hydrologic: relating to water

hyperlinks: connections between electronic documents that permit automatic browsing transfer at the point of the link

Hypertext Markup Language (HTML): an encoding scheme for text data that uses special tags in the text to signify properties to the viewing program (browser) like links to other documents or document parts

Hypertext Transfer Protocol (HTTP): a simple connectionless communications protocol developed for the electronic transfer (serving) of HTML documents

I/O: the acronym for input/output; used to describe devices that can accept input data to a computer and to other devices that can produce output

I/O devices: devices that can accept "input" data to a computer and to other devices that can produce "output"

icon: a small image that is used to signify a program or operation to a user

illiquid: lacking in liquid assets; or something that is not easily transferable into currency

ImmersaDesks: large 4 x 5 foot screens that allow for stereoscopic visualization; the 3-D computer graphics create the illusion of a virtual environment

ImmersaWalls: large-scale, flat screen visualization environments that include passive and active multi-projector displays of 3-D images

immersive: involved in something totally

in-band: pertaining to elements or objects that are within the limits of a certain local area network (LAN)

inference: a suggestion or implication of something based on other known related facts and conclusions

information theory: a branch of mathematics and engineering that deals with the encoding, transmission, reception, and decoding of information

infrared (IR) waves: radiation in a band of the electromagnetic spectrum within the infrared range

infrastructure: the foundation or permanent installation necessary for a structure or system to operate

ingot: a formed block of metal (often cast) used to facilitate bulk handling and transportation

ingress: the act of entering a system or object

init method: a special function in an object oriented program that is automatically called to initialize the elements of an object when it is created

input/output (I/O): used to describe devices that can accept input data to a computer and to other devices that can produce output

intangible: a concept to which it is difficult to apply any form of analysis; something which is not perceived by the sense of touch

integrated circuit: a circuit with the transistors, resistors, and other circuit elements etched into the surface of a single chip of semiconducting material, usually silicon

integrated modem: a modem device that is built into a computer, rather than being attached as a separate peripheral

intellectual property: the acknowledgement that an individual's creativity and innovation can be owned in the same way as physical property

interconnectivity: the ability of more than one physical computer to operate with one or more other physical computers; interconnectivity is usually accomplished by means of network wiring, cable, or telephone lines

interface: a boundary or border between two or more objects or systems; also a point of access

Internet Protocol (IP): a method of organizing information transfer between computers; the IP was specifically designed to offer low-level support to Transmission Control Protocol (TCP)

Internet Service Provider (ISP): a commercial enterprise which offers paying subscribers access to the Internet (usually via modem) for a fee

interpolation: estimating data values between known points but the values in between are not and are therefore estimated

intranet: an interconnected network of computers that operates like the Internet, but is restricted in size to a company or organization

ionosphere: a region of the upper atmosphere (above about 60,000 meters or 196,850 feet) where the air molecules are affected by the sun's radiation and influence electromagnetic wave propagation

isosceles triangle: a triangle that has two sides of equivalent length (and therefore two angles of the same size)

iterative: a procedure that involves repetitive operations before being completed

Jacquard's Loom: a weaving loom, developed by Joseph-Marie Jacquard (1752-1834), controlled by punched cards; identified as one of the earliest examples of programming automation

Java applets: applets written in the Java programming language and executed with the support of a Java Virtual Machine (JVM) or a Java enabled browser

joysticks: the main controlling levers of small aircraft; models of these can be connected to computers to facilitate playing interactive games

JPEG (Joint Photographic Experts Group): organization that developed a standard for encoding image data in a compressed format to save space

k-nearest neighbors: a classifier that assigns a class label for an unknown data item by looking at the class labels of the nearest items in the training data

Kbps: a measure of digital data transfer per unit time—one thousand (kilo, K) bits per second

keywords: words that are significant in some context or topic (often used in searching)

kilohertz (kHz): a unit or measure of frequency, equivalent to a thousand (or 103) hertz, or cycles per second

kinematics: a branch of physics and mechanical engineering that involves the study of moving bodies and particles

kinetics: a branch of physics or chemistry concerned with the rate of change in chemical or physical systems

labeled data: a data item whose class assignment is known independent of the classifier being constructed

lambda calculus: important in the development of programming languages, a specialized logic using substitutions that was developed by Alonzo Church (1903-1995)

LEDs: the acronym for Light Emitting Diode; a diode that emits light when passing a current and used as an indicating lamp

lexical analyzer: a portion of a compiler that is responsible for checking the program source code produced by a programmer for proper words and symbols

Library of Congress Classification: the scheme by which the Library of Congress organizes classes of books and documents

light emitting diode (LED): a discrete electronic component that emits visible light when permitting current to flow in a certain direction; often used as an indicating lamp

linear: pertaining to a type of system that has a relationship between its outputs and its inputs that can be graphed as a straight line

Linux operating system: an open source UNIX operating system that was originally created by Linus Torvalds in the early 1990s

liquid crystal display (LCD): a type of crystal that changes its level of transparency when subjected to an electric current; used as an output device on a computer

local area network (LAN): a high-speed computer network that is designed for users who are located near each other

logarithm: the power to which a certain number called the base is to be raised to produce a particular number

logic: a branch of philosophy and mathematics that uses provable rules to apply deductive reasoning

lossy: a nonreversible way of compressing digital images; making images take up less space by permanently removing parts that cannot be easily seen anyway

low precision/high recall: a phenomenon that occurs during a search when a large set of results are retrieved, including many relevant and irrelevant documents

lumens: a unit of measure of light intensity

magnetic tape: a way of storing programs and data from computers; tapes are generally slow and prone to deterioration over time but are inexpensive

mainframe: large computer used by businesses and government agencies to process massive amounts of data; generally faster and more powerful than desktop computers but usually requiring specialized software

malicious code: program instructions that are intended to carry out malicious or hostile actions; e.g., deleting a user's files

mammogram: an X-ray image of the breast, used to detect signs of possible cancer

Manhattan Project: the U.S. project designed to create the world's first atomic bomb

mass spectrometers: instruments that can identify elemental particles in a sample by examining the frequencies of the particles that comprise the sample

mass spectrometry: the process of identifying the compounds or elemental particles within a substance

megahertz (MHz): a unit or measure of frequency, equivalent to a million (or 106) hertz, or cycles per second

memex: a device that can be used to store personal information, notes, and records that permits managed access at high speed; a hypothetical creation of Vannevar Bush

menu label: the text or icon on a menu item in a program with a graphical user interface

metadata: data about data, such as the date and time created

meteorologists: people who have studied the science of weather and weather forecasting

metropolitan area network (MAN): a high-speed interconnected network of computers spanning entire cities

microampere: a unit of measure of electrical current that is one-millionth (10-6) amperes

microchip: a common term for a semiconductor integrated circuit device

microcomputer: a computer that is small enough to be used and managed by one person alone; often called a personal computer

microprocessor: the principle element in a computer; the component that understands how to carry out operations under the direction of the running program (CPU)

millisecond: a time measurement indicating one-thousandth (or 10-3) of a second

milliwatt: a power measurement indicating one-thousandth (or 10-3) of a watt

minicomputers: computers midway in size between a desktop computer and a mainframe computer; most modern desktops are much more powerful than the older minicomputers

minimax algorithm: an approach to developing an optimal solution to a game or contest where two opposing systems are aiming at mutually exclusive goals

Minitel: network used in France that preceded the Internet, connecting most French homes, businesses, cultural organizations, and government offices

mnemonic: a device or process that aids one's memory

modalities: classifications of the truth of a logical proposition or statement, or characteristics of an object or entity

modem: the contraction of MOdulator DEModulator; a device which converts digital signals into signals suitable for transmission over analog channels, like telephone lines

modulation: a technique whereby signals are translated to analog so that the resultant signal can be more easily transmitted and received by other elements in a communication system

modules: a generic term that is applied to small elements or components that can be used in combination to build an operational system

molecular modeling: a technique that uses high performance computer graphics to represent the structure of chemical compounds

motherboard: the part of the computer that holds vital hardware, such as the processors, memory, expansion slots, and circuitry

MPEG (Motion Picture Coding Experts Group): an encoding scheme for data files that contain motion pictures—it is lossy in the same way as JPEG (Joint Photographic Experts Group) encoding

multiplexes: operations in ATM communications whereby data cells are blended into one continuous stream at the transmitter and then separated again at the receiver

multiplexor: a complex device that acts as a multi-way switch for analog or digital signals

multitasking: the ability of a computer system to execute more than one program at the same time; also known as multiprogramming

mylar: a synthetic film, invented by the DuPont corporation, used in photographic printing and production processes, as well as disks and tapes

nanocomputing: the science and engineering of building mechanical machines at the atomic level

nanometers: one-thousand-millionth (one billionth, or 10-9) of a meter

nanosecond: one-thousand-millionth (one billionth, or 10-9) of a second

nanotechnology: the design and construction of machines at the atomic or molecular level

narrowband: a general term in communication systems pertaining to a signal that has a small collection of differing frequency components (as opposed to broadband which has many frequency components)

National Computer Security Center (NCSC): a branch of the National Security Agency responsible for evaluating secure computing systems; the Trusted Computer Systems Evaluation Criteria (TCSEC) were developed by the NCSC

Network Control Protocol (NCP): a host-to-host protocol originally developed in the early 1970s to support the Internet, which was then a research project

network packet switching: the act of routing and transferring packets (or small sections) of a carrier signal that conveys digital information

neural modeling: the mathematical study and the construction of elements that mimic the behavior of the brain cell (neuron)

neural networks: pattern recognition systems whose structure and operation are loosely inspired by analogy to neurons in the human brain

Newtonian view: an approach to the study of mechanics that obeys the rules of Newtonian physics, as opposed to relativistic mechanics; named after Sir Isaac Newton (1642-1727)

nonlinear: a system that has relationships between outputs and inputs which cannot be expressed in the form of a straight line

O-rings: 37-foot rubber circles (rings) that seal the joints between the space shuttle's rocket booster segments

OEM: the acronym for Original Equipment Manufacturer; a manufacturer of computer components

offline: the mode of operation of a computer that applies when it is completely disconnected from other computers and peripherals (like printers)

Open Systems Interconnections (OSI): a communications standard developed by the International Organization for Standardization (ISO) to facilitate compatible network systems

operands: when a computer is executing instructions in a program, the elements on which it performs the instructions are known as the operands

operating system: a set of programs which control all the hardware of a computer and provide user and device input/output functions

optical character recognition: the science and engineering of creating programs that can recognize and interpret printed characters

optical computing: a proposed computing technology which would operate on particles of light, rather than electric currents

optophone: a system that uses artificial intelligence techniques to convert images of text into audible sound

orthogonal: elements or objects that are perpendicular to one another; in a logical sense this means that changes in one have no effect on the other

oscillator: an electronic component that produces a precise waveform of a fixed known frequency; this can be used as a time base (clock) signal to other devices

oscilloscopes: measuring instruments for electrical circuitry; connected to circuits under test using probes on leads and having small screens that display the signal waveforms

out-of-band: pertaining to elements or objects that are external to the limits of a certain local area network (LAN)

overhead: the expense or cost involved in carrying out a particular operation

packet-switched network: a network based on digital communications systems whereby packets of data are dispatched to receivers based on addresses that they contain

packet-switching: an operation used in digital communications systems whereby packets (collections) of data are dispatched to receivers based on addresses contained in the packets

packets: collections of digital data elements that are part of a complete message or signal; packets contain their destination addresses to enable reassembly of the message or signal

paradigm: an example, pattern, or way of thinking

parallel debugging: specialized approaches to locating and correcting errors in computer programs that are to be executed on parallel computing machine architectures

parallel processing: the presence of more than one central processing unit (CPU) in a computer, which enables the true execution of more than one program

parametric: modeling a system using variables or parameters that can be observed to change as the system operates

parity: a method of introducing error checking on binary data by adding a redundant bit and using that to enable consistency checks

pattern recognition: a process used by some artificial-intelligence systems to identify a variety of patterns, including visual patterns, information patterns buried in a noisy signal, and word patterns imbedded in text

PDF: the acronym for Portable Document Format, developed by Adobe Corporation to facilitate the storage and transfer of electronic documents

peer-to-peer services: the ways in which computers on the same logical level can interoperate in a structured network hierarchy

permutations: significant changes or rearrangement

personal area networking: the interconnectivity of personal productivity devices like computers, mobile telephones, and personal organizers

personal digital assistants (PDA): small-scale hand-held computers that can be used in place of diaries and appointment books

phosphor: a coating applied to the back of a glass screen on a cathode ray tube (CRT) that emits light when a beam of electrons strikes its surface

photolithography: the process of transferring an image from a film to a metal surface for etching, often used in the production of printed circuit boards

photonic switching: the technology that is centered on routing and managing optical packets of digital data

photons: the smallest fundamental units of electromagnetic radiation in the visible spectrum—light

photosensitive: describes any material that will change its properties in some way if subjected to visible light, such as photographic film

picoseconds: one-millionth of a millionth of a second (one-trillionth, or 10-12)

piezoelectric crystal: an electronic component that when subjected to a current will produce a waveform signal at a precise rate, which can then be used as a clock signal in a computer

PIN (personal identification number): a password, usually numeric, used in conjunction with a cryptographic token, smart card, or bank card, to ensure that only an authorized user can activate an account governed by the token or card

ping sweeps: technique that identifies properties belonging to a server computer, by sending it collections of "ping" packets and examining the responses from the server

piracy: the unlawful copying and redistribution of computer software, ignoring the copyright and ownership rights of the publisher

pixel: a single picture element on a video screen; one of the individual dots making up a picture on a video screen or digital image

pixilation: the process of generating animation, frame by frame

plug-in: a term used to describe the way that hardware and software modules can be added to a computer system, if they possess interfaces that have been built to a documented standard

pneumatic: powered by pressurized air, supplied through tubes or pipes

polarity: the positive (+) or negative (−) state of an object, which dictates how it will react to forces such as magnetism or electricity

polarizer: a translucent sheet that permits only plane-polarized light to pass through, blocking all other light

polygon: a many-sided, closed, geometrical figure

polynomial: an expression with more than one term

polypeptide: the product of many amino acid molecules bonded together

population inversion: used in quantum mechanics to describe when the number of atoms at higher energy levels is greater than the number at lower energy levels—a condition needed for photons (light) to be emitted

port: logical input/output points on computers that exist in a network

port scans: operations whereby ports are probed so that information about their status can be collected

potentiometer: an element in an electrical circuit that resists current flow (a resistor) but the value of the resistance can be mechanically adjusted (a variable resistor)

predicate calculus: a branch of logic that uses individuals and predicates, or elements and classes, and the existential and universal quantifiers, all and some, to represent statements

privatized: to convert a service traditionally offered by a government or public agency into a service provided by a private corporation or other private entity

progenitor: the direct parent of something or someone

propositional calculus: a branch of logic that uses expressions such as "If ... then ..." to make statements and deductions

proprietary: a process or technology developed and owned by an individual or company, and not published openly

proprietary software: software created by an individual or company that is sold under a license that dictates use and distribution

protocol: an agreed understanding for the sub-operations that make up a transaction, usually found in the specification of inter-computer communications

prototype: a working model or experimental investigation of proposed systems under development

pseudocode: a language-neutral, structural description of the algorithms that are to be used in a program

public key information: certain status and identification information that pertains to a particular public key (i.e., a key available for public use in encryption)

public key infrastructure (PKI): the supporting programs and protocols that act together to enable public key encryption/decryption

punched card: a paper card with punched holes which give instructions to a computer in order to encode program instructions and data

quadtrees: data structures resembling trees, which have four branches at every node (rather than two as with a binary tree); used in the construction of complex databases

quality-of-service (QoS): a set of performance criteria that a system is designed to guarantee and support as a minimum

quantification: to quantify (or measure) something

quantum-dot cellular automata (QCA): the theory of automata as applied to quantum dot architectures, which are a proposed approach for the development of computers at nanotechnology scales

quantum mechanical: something influenced by the set of rules that govern the energy and wave behavior of subatomic particles on the scale of sizes that are comparable to the particles themselves

queue: the ordering of elements or objects such that they are processed in turn; first-in, first-out

radar: the acronym for RAdio Direction And Ranging; a technique developed in the 1930s that uses frequency shifts in reflected radio waves to measure distance and speed of a target

radio telescopes: telescopes used for astronomical observation that operate on collecting electromagnetic radiation in frequency bands above the visible spectrum

random access memory (RAM): a type of memory device that supports the nonpermanent storage of programs and data; so called because various locations can be accessed in any order (as if at random), rather than in a sequence (like a tape memory device)

raster: a line traced out by a beam of electrons as they strike a cathode ray tube (CRT)

raster scan pattern: a sequence of raster lines drawn on a cathode ray tube such that an image or text can be made to appear

read only memory (ROM): a type of memory device that supports permanent storage of programs

real-time: a system, often computer based, that ensures the rates at which it inputs, processes, and outputs information meet the timing requirements of another system

recursive: operations expressed and implemented in a way that requires them to invoke themselves

relational database: a collection of records that permits logical and business relationships to be developed between themselves and their contents

relay contact systems: systems constructed to carry out logic functions, implemented in relays (electromechanical switches) rather than semiconductor devices

resistors: electrical components that slow the flow of current

retinal scan: a scan of the retina of the eye, which contains a unique pattern for each individual, in order to identify (or authenticate) someone

robotics: the science and engineering of building electromechanical machines that aim to serve as replacements for human laborers

routers: network devices that direct packets to the next network device or to the final destination

routing: the operation that involves collecting and forwarding packets of information by way of address

satellite: an object that orbits a planet

scalar: a quantity that has magnitude (size) only; there is no associated direction or bearing

scalar processor: a processor designed for high-speed computation of scalar values

schematic: a diagrammatic representation of a system, showing logical structure without regard to physical constraints

scripting languages: modern high-level programming languages that are interpreted rather than compiled; they are usually cross-platform and support rapid application development

Secure Sockets Layer (SSL): a technology that supports encryption, authentication, and other facilities and is built into standard UNIX communication protocols (sockets over TCP/IP)

semantics: the study of how words acquire meaning and how those meanings change over time

semiconductor: solid material that possesses electrical conductivity characteristics that are similar to those of metals under certain conditions, but can also exhibit insulating qualities under other conditions

semiconductor diode laser: a diode that emits electromagnetic radiation at wavelengths above about 630 nanometers, creating a laser beam for industrial applications

sensors: devices that can record and transmit data regarding the altitude, flight path, attitude, etc., so that they can enter into the system's calculations

sequentially: operations occurring in order, one after another

server: a computer that does not deal directly with human users, but instead handles requests from other computers for services to be performed

SGML: the acronym for Standard Generalized Markup Language, an international standard for structuring electronic documents

shadow mask: a metal sheet behind the glass screen of a cathode ray tube (CRT) that ensures the correct color phosphor elements are struck by the electron beams

shareware: a software distribution technique, whereby the author shares copies of his programs at no cost, in the expectation that users will later pay a fee of some sort

Sherman Antitrust Act: the act of the U.S. Congress in 1890 that is the foundation for all American anti-monopoly laws

signaling protocols: protocols used in the management of integrated data networks that convey a mix of audio, video, and data packets

SIGs: short for "Special Interest Group," SIGs concentrate their energies on specific categories of computer science, such as programming languages or computer architecture

silica: silicon oxide; found in sand and some forms of rock

silicon: a chemical element with symbol Si; the most abundant element in the Earth's crust and the most commonly used semiconductor material

silicon chip: a common term for a semiconductor integrated circuit device

Silicon Valley: an area in California near San Francisco, which has been the home location of many of the most significant information technology orientated companies and universities

silver halide: a photosensitive product that has been used in traditional cameras to record an image

simplex: uni-directional communication over a single communication channel

simputers: simple to use computers that take on the functionality of personal computers, but are mobile and act as personal assistants and information organizers

sine wave: a wave traced by a point on the circumference of a circle when the point starts at height zero (amplitude zero) and goes through one full revolution

single-chip: a computer system that is constructed so that it contains just one integrated circuit device

slide rule: invented by Scotsman John Napier (1550-1617), it permits the mechanical automation of calculations using logarithms

smart card: a credit-card style card that has a microcomputer embedded within it; it carries more information to assist the owner or user

smart devices: devices and appliances that host an embedded computer system that offers greater control and flexibility

smart matter: materials, machines, and systems whose physical properties depend on the computing that is embedded within them

social informatics: a field of study that centers on the social aspects of computing technology

softlifting: the act of stealing software, usually for personal use (piracy)

software-defined networks (SDNs): the same as virtual private networks (VPNs), where the subscriber can set up and maintain a communications system using management software, on a public network

sonar: the science and engineering of sound propagation in water

SONET: the acronym for Synchronous Optical NETwork, a published standard for networks based on fiber optic communications technology

sound card: a plug-in card for a computer that contains hardware devices for sound processing, conversion, and generation

source code: the human-readable programs that are compiled or interpreted so that they can be executed by a computing machine

speech recognition: the science and engineering of decoding and interpreting audible speech, usually using a computer system

spider: a computer program that travels the Internet to locate web documents and FTP resources, then indexes the documents in a database, which are then searched using software that the search engine provides

spreadsheet: an accounting or business tool that details numerical data in columns for tabulation purposes

static: without movement; stationary

stellar: pertaining to the stars

subnet: a logical section of a large network that simplifies the management of machine addresses

supercomputer: a very high performance computer, usually comprised of many processors and used for modeling and simulation of complex phenomena, like meteorology

superconductivity: the property of a material to pass an electric current with almost no losses; most metals are superconductive only at temperatures near absolute zero

swap files: files used by an operating system to support a virtual memory system, in which the user appears to have access to more memory than is physically available

syllogistic statements: the essential tenets of western philosophical thought, based on hypotheses and categories

synchronization: the time domain ordering of events; often applied when events repeatedly occur simultaneously

synchronized: events occurring at specific points in time with respect to one another

synchronous: synchronized behavior

synergistic: relating to synergism, which is the phenomenon whereby the action of a group of elements is greater than their individual actions

syntactic analyzer: a part of a compiler that scans program source code ensuring that the code meets essential language rules with regard to structure or organization

syntax: a set of rules that a computing language incorporates regarding structure, punctuation, and formatting

tangible: of a nature that is real, as opposed to something that is imaginary or abstract

task partitioning: the act of dividing up work to be done so that it can be separated into distinct tasks, processes, or phases

taxonomy: the classification of elements or objects based on their characteristics

TCP: the acronym for Transmission Control Protocol; a fundamental protocol used in the networks that support the Internet (ARPANET)

TCP/IP networks: interconnected computer networks that use Transmission Control Protocol/Internet Protocol

TCP/IP protocol suite: Transmission Control Protocol/Internet Protocol; a range of functions that can be used to facilitate applications working on the Internet

telegraph: a communication channel that uses cables to convey encoded low bandwidth electrical signals

telemedicine: the technology that permits remote diagnosis and treatment of patients by a medical practitioner; usually interactive bi-directional audio and video signals

telemetry: the science of taking measurements of something and transmitting the data to a distant receiver

teleoperation: any operation that can be carried out remotely by a communications system that enables interactive audio and video signals

teletype: a machine that sends and receives telephonic signals

terabyte: one million million (one trillion, or 1012) bytes

thermal ignition: the combustion of a substance caused by heating it to the point that its particles have enough energy to commence burning without an externally applied flame

thermodynamic: relating to heat energy

three-body problem: an intractable problem in mechanics that involves the attempts to predict the behavior of three bodies under gravitational effects

thumbnail: an image which is a scaled down copy of a much larger image; used to assist in the management of a large catalog of images

time lapse mode: to show a sequence of events occurring at a higher than natural speed so it looks like it is happening rapidly rather than in real time

title bar: the top horizontal border of a rectangular region owned by a program running in a graphical user interface (GUI); it usually contains the program name and can be used to move the region around

tomography: the process of capturing and analyzing X-ray images

T1 digital circuitry: a type of digital network technology that can handle separate voice and/or digital communications lines

topographic: pertaining to the features of a terrain or surface

topology: a method of describing the structure of a system that emphasizes its logical nature rather than its physical characteristics

trademark rights: a trademark is a name, symbol, or phrase that identifies a trading organization and is owned by that organization

trafficking: transporting and selling; especially with regard to illegal merchandise

training data: data used in the creation of a classifier

transaction processing: operations between client and server computers that are made up of many small exchanges that must all be completed for the transaction to proceed

transducers: devices that sense a physical quantity, such as temperature or pressure, and convert that measurement into an electrical signal

transistor: a contraction of TRANSfer resISTOR; a semiconductor device, invented by John Bardeen, Walter Brattain, and William Shockley, which has three terminals; can be used for switching and amplifying electrical signals

translational bridges: special network devices that convert low-level protocols from one type to another

Transmission Control Protocol (TCP): a stream-orientated protocol that uses Internet Protocol (IP); it is responsible for splitting data into packets, transferring it, and reassembling it at the receiver

transmutation: the act of converting one thing into another

trigonometry: a branch of mathematics founded upon the geometry of triangles

triodes: nearly obsolete electronic devices constructed of sealed glass tubes containing metal elements in a vacuum; triodes were used to control electrical signals

Trojan horse: potentially destructive computer program that masquerades as something benign; named after the wooden horse employed by the Acheans to conquer Troy

tunneling: a way of handling different communication protocols, by taking packets of a foreign protocol and changing them so that they appear to be a locally known type

Turing machine: a proposed type of computing machine that takes inputs off paper tape and then moves through a sequence of states under the control of an algorithm; identified by Alan Turing (1912-1954)

1200-baud: a measure of data transmission; in this case the rate of 1200 symbols (usually bits) per second

twisted pair: an inexpensive, medium bandwidth communication channel commonly used in local area networks

ubiquitous: to be commonly available everywhere

ultrasonic: the transmission and reception of sound waves that are at frequencies higher than those audible to humans

Uniform Resource Locator (URL): a reference to a document or a document container using the Hypertext Transfer Protocol (HTTP); consists of a hostname and path to the document

Universal Product Code (UPC): the first barcode standard developed in 1973 and adopted widely since

UNIX: operating system that was originally developed at Bell Laboratories in the early 1970s

uplinks: connections from a client machine to a large network; frequently used when information is being sent to a communications satellite

vacuum tube: an electronic device constructed of a sealed glass tube containing metal elements in a vacuum; used to control electrical signals

valence: a measure of the reactive nature of a chemical element or compound in relation to hydrogen

variable: a symbol, such as a string of letters, which may assume any one of a set of values known as the domain

vector graphics: graphics output systems whereby pairs of coordinates are passed to the graphics controller, which are interpreted as end points of vectors to be drawn on the screen

vector processing: an approach to computing machine architecture that involves the manipulation of vectors (sequences of numbers) in single steps, rather than one number at a time

vector supercomputer: a highly optimized computing machine that provides high performance using a vector processing architecture

velocities: vector quantities that have a magnitude or speed and a direction

Venn diagrams: diagrams used to demonstrate the relationships between sets of objects, named after John Venn, a British logician

venture capitalists: persons or agencies that speculate by providing financial resources to enable product development, in the expectation of larger returns with product maturity

video capture cards: plug-in cards for a computer that accepts video input from devices like televisions and video cameras, allowing the user to record video data onto the computer

video compression algorithms: special algorithms applied to remove certain unnecessary parts of video images in an attempt to reduce their storage size

virtual channel connection: an abstraction of a physical connection between two or more elements (or computers); the complex details of the physical connection are hidden

virtual circuit: like a virtual channel connection, a virtual circuit appears to be a direct path between two elements, but is actually a managed collection of physical connections

Virtual Private Networks (VPNs): a commercial approach to network management where privately owned voice and data networks are set up on public network infrastructure

virtual reality (VR): the use of elaborate input/output devices to create the illusion that the user is in a different environment

virtualization: as if it were real; making something seem real, e.g. a virtual environment

visible speech: a set of symbols, comprising an alphabet, that "spell" sounds instead of words

visualization: a technique whereby complex systems are portrayed in a meaningful way using sophisticated computer graphics systems; e.g., chemical molecules

volatile: subject to rapid change; describes the character of data when current no longer flows to a device (that is, electrical power is switched off)

waveform: an abstraction used in the physical sciences to model energy transmission in the form of longitudinal or transverse waves

web surfers: people who "surf" (search) the Internet frequently

wide area network (WAN): an interconnected network of computers that spans upward from several buildings to whole cities or entire countries and across countries

wireless lavaliere microphones: small microphones worn around the speakers' necks, which attach to their shirts

wireless local area network (WLAN): an interconnected network of computers that uses radio and/or infrared communication channels, rather than cables

workstations: computers (usually within a network) that interact directly with human users (much the same as "client computers")

xerography: a printing process that uses electrostatic elements derived from a photographic image to deposit the ink

XML: the acronym for eXtensible Markup Language; a method of applying structure to data so that documents can be represented

Topic Outline

APPLICATIONS

Agriculture
Aircraft Flight Control
Aircraft Traffic Management
Airline Reservations
Architecture
Art
Astronomy
Biology
Chemistry
Chess Playing
Computerized Manufacturing
Data Mining
Data Processing
Data Warehousing
Decision Support Systems
Desktop Publishing
Digital Images
Digital Libraries
Distance Learning
Document Processing
Economic Modeling
Educational Software
Electronic Campus
Electronic Markets
Expert Systems
Fashion Design
Film and Video Editing
Games
Geographic Information Systems
Home Entertainment
Home System Software
Image Analysis: Medicine

Information Retrieval
Information Systems
Integrated Software
Journalism
Legal Systems
Library Applications
Mathematics
Medical Systems
Molecular Biology
Music
Music Composition
Music, Computer
Navigation
Office Automation Systems
Optical Technology
Pattern Recognition
Photography
Physics
Political Applications
Process Control
Project Management
Railroad Applications
Robotics
Security
Security Applications
Simulators
Space Travel and Exploration
Speech Recognition
System Analysis
Systems Design
Technology of Desktop Publishing
Telephony
Virtual Private Network

Weather Forecasting
World Wide Web

BUSINESS

Accounting Software
ATM Machines
Chip Manufacturing
Computer Professional
Computer Supported Cooperative Work
  (CSCW)
Computerized Manufacturing
Credit Online
Data Mining
Data Processing
Data Warehousing
Database Management Software
Decision Support Systems
Document Processing
E-banking
E-commerce
E-commerce: Economic and Social Aspects
Economic Modeling
Electronic Markets
Office Automation Systems
Process Control
Productivity Software
Project Management
Spreadsheets
SQL
SQL: Databases
Word Processors

CODES

Binary Number System
Codes
Coding Techniques
Cryptography
Information Theory

COMPUTING TECHNIQUES

Analog Computing
Digital Computing
Digital Logic Design

CORPORATIONS AND ORGANIZATIONS

Apple Computer, Inc.
Association for Computing Machinery
Bell Labs
Census Bureau
IBM Corporation
Institute of Electrical and Electronics
  Engineers (IEEE)
Intel Corporation
Microsoft Corporation
Minitel
National Aeronautics and Space Administra-
  tion (NASA)
Xerox Corporation

DECISION SUPPORT

Artificial Intelligence
Decision Support Systems
Expert Systems
Knowledge-Based Systems

EDUCATION

Computer Assisted Instruction
Digital Libraries
Distance Learning
E-books
E-journals and E-publishing
E-mail
Educational Software
Electronic Campus
Virtual Reality in Education

ENTERTAINMENT

Animation
Chess Playing
Computer Vision
Fiction, Computers in
Film and Video Editing
Game Controllers
Games
Home Entertainment
Home System Software
Hypermedia and Multimedia
Music

Music Composition
Music, Computer
Photography

FILM, VIDEO AND PHOTOGRAPHY

Animation
Digital Images
Film and Video Editing
Hypermedia and Multimedia
JPEG, MPEG
Photography

GOVERNMENT

Census Bureau
Computer Fraud and Abuse Act of 1986
Copyright
Government Funding, Research
Information Technology Standards
Minitel
National Aeronautics and Space Administration (NASA)
Patents
Political Applications
Privacy

HARDWARE, COMPUTERS

Analytical Engine
Cache Memory
CAD/CAM, CA Engineering
Central Processing Unit
Chip Manufacturing
Computer System Interfaces
Digital Logic Design
Integrated Circuits
Mainframes
Memory
Memory Devices
Microchip
Microcomputers
Minicomputers
Storage Devices
Supercomputers
Tabulating Machines
Vacuum Tubes
Virtual Memory

HARDWARE, TELECOMMUNICATIONS

Bandwidth
Bridging Devices
Cache Memory
Cell Phones
Cellular Technology
Communication Devices
Fiber Optics
Firewalls
Information Technology Standards
Laser Technology
Networks
Optical Technology
Telecommunications
Telephony
Transmission Media
Wireless Technology

HISTORY, COMPUTERS

Analytical Engine
Babbage, Charles
Early Computers
Early Pioneers
Generations, Computers
Hollerith, Herman
Internet
Jacquard's Loom
Mainframes
Microchip
Microcomputers
Minicomputers
Pascal, Blaise
Supercomputers
Tabulating Machines
Turing Machine
Vacuum Tubes
Virtual Memory

HISTORY, LANGUAGES

Algol-60 Report
Assembly Language and Architecture
Compilers
Generations, Languages
Java Applets

JavaScript
LISP
Logo
Markup Languages
Object-Oriented Languages
Procedural Languages
Programming
SQL
SQL: Databases
Visual Basic

HUMAN INTERACTION

Computer System Interfaces
Human Factors: User Interfaces
Hypertext
Integrated Software
Interactive Systems
Speech Recognition
User Interfaces
Window Interfaces

INFORMATION RELATED TOPICS

Information Access
Information Overload
Information Retrieval
Information Systems
Information Theory
Library Applications
Search Engines
System Analysis
Systems Design

INNOVATION

Artificial Intelligence
Artificial Life
Data Mining
Data Visualization
Data Warehousing
Desktop Publishing
Digital Images
Digital Libraries
Embedded Technology (Ubiquitous
    Computing)
Fiber Optics
Global Positioning Systems

Laser Technology
Mobile Computing
Molecular Computing
Nanocomputing
Optical Character Recognition
Optical Technology
Pattern Recognition
Personal Digital Assistants
Robotics
Robots
Satellite Technology
Scientific Visualization

INPUT AND OUTPUT DEVICES

Display Devices
Game Controllers
Graphic Devices
Input Devices
Keyboard
Magnetic Stripe Cards
Mouse
Pointing Devices
Printing Devices
Reading Tools
Sound Devices
Touch Screens
Video Devices
Word Processors

INTERNET

Authentication
Browsers
Credit Online
Cybercafe
E-banking
E-commerce
E-commerce: Economic and Social Aspects
E-journals and E-publishing
E-mail
Electronic Markets
Entrepreneurs
Internet
Internet: Applications
Internet: Backbone

Internet: History
Intranet
Search Engines
Virtual Private Network
Wireless Technology
World Wide Web

LIBRARIES

Digital Libraries
Distance Learning
E-books
E-journals and E-publishing
E-mail
Electronic Campus
Library Applications

MATHEMATICS

Binary Number System
Boolean Algebra
Codes
Coding Techniques
Cryptography
Information Theory

MEDICINE

Artificial Life
Biology
Cybernetics
Digital Images
Image Analysis: Medicine
Knowledge-Based Systems
Laser Technology
Medical Systems
Molecular Biology
Molecular Computing
Neural Networks
Pattern Recognition
Scientific Visualization

MUSIC

JPEG, MPEG
Music
Music Composition
Music, Computer
Sound Devices

NETWORKS

Asynchronous and Synchronous Transmission
Asynchronous Transfer Mode (ATM)
ATM Transmission
Bandwidth
Boolean Algebra
Bridging Devices
Communication Devices
Embedded Technology (Ubiquitous
    Computing)
Fiber Optics
Firewalls
FTP
Global Positioning Systems
Information Technology Standards
Information Theory
Intranet
Network Design
Network Protocols
Network Topologies
Networks
Routing
Satellite Technology
Security
Security Applications
Security Hardware
Security Software
Serial and Parallel Transmission
Service Providers
TCP/IP
Telecommunications
Telephony
Telnet
Transmission Media
Virtual Private Network
Wireless Technology

PEOPLE

Amdahl, Gene Myron
Asimov, Isaac
Babbage, Charles
Bardeen, John (See entry: Bardeen, John,
    Brattain, Walter H., and Shockley, William
    B.)
Bell, Alexander Graham

Boole, George

Brattain, Walter H. (See entry: Bardeen, John, Brattain, Walter H., and Shockley, William B.)

Computer Professional

Computer Scientists

Cormack, Allan (See entry: Cormack, Allan, and Hounsfield, Godfrey Newbold)

Cray, Seymour

Eckert, J. Presper, Jr. (See entry: Eckert, J. Presper, Jr., and Mauchly, John W.)

Early Pioneers

Entrepreneurs

Feynman, Richard P.

Glushkov, Victor M.

Gross, Alfred J.

Hewlett, William

Hollerith, Herman

Hopper, Grace

Hounsfield, Godfrey Newbold (See entry: Cormack, Allan, and Hounsfield, Godfrey Newbold)

Kemeny, John G.

Lovelace, Ada Byron King, Countess of

Marconi, Guglielmo

Mauchly, John W. (See entry: Eckert, J. Presper, Jr., and Mauchly, John W.)

Morse, Samuel

Newell, Allen

Nyquist, Harry

Organick, Elliot

Pascal, Blaise

Péter, Rózsa

Shannon, Claude E.

Shockley, William B. (See entry: Bardeen, John, Brattain, Walter H., and Shockley, William B.)

Simon, Herbert A.

Turing, Alan M.

Wang, An

Watson, Thomas J., Sr.

von Neumann, John

Zuse, Konrad

PRECURSORS TO COMPUTERS

Abacus

Jacquard's Loom

Napier's Bones

Slide Rule

PROGRAMMING

Algorithms

Binary Number System

Boolean Algebra

Design Tools

Procedural Languages

Programming

PUBLISHING

Desktop Publishing

Hypertext

Markup Languages

Technology of Desktop Publishing

SECURITY

Authentication

Cookies

Digital Signatures

Firewalls

Global Surveillance

Hackers

Hacking

Invasive Programs

Privacy

Security

Security Applications

Security Hardware

Security Software

Social Impact

Software Piracy

Urban Myths

Virtual Private Network

Viruses

SOCIAL ISSUES

Assistive Computer Technology for Persons with Disabilities

Authentication

Censorship: National, International

Computer Fraud and Abuse Act of 1986

Computer Professional

Compatibility (Open Systems Design)
Computer Scientists
Cookies
Copyright
Credit Online
Cybercafe
Digital Libraries
Digital Signatures
Distance Learning
E-banking
E-books
E-commerce
E-commerce: Economic and Social Aspects
E-journals and E-publishing
E-mail
Electronic Campus
Electronic Markets
Entrepreneurs
Ergonomics
Ethics
Fiction, Computers in
Global Surveillance
Government Funding, Research
Home Entertainment
Information Access
Information Overload
Journalism
Library Applications
Medical Systems
Mobile Computing
Open Source
Patents
Personal Digital Assistants
Political Applications
Privacy
Service Providers
Social Impact
Software Piracy
Technology of Desktop Publishing
Telephony
Urban Myths
Virtual Private Network
Virtual Reality in Education
World Wide Web

SOFTWARE

Agents
Browsers
Compilers
Database Management Software
Geographic Information Systems
Human Factors: User Interfaces
Integrated Software
Office Automation Systems
Open Source
Operating Systems
Procedural Languages
Productivity Software
Search Engines
Simulation
Spreadsheets
User Interfaces
Window Interfaces

STUDY AREAS

Artificial Intelligence
Artificial Life
Expert Systems
Information Theory
Molecular Computing
Nanocomputing

TECHNOLOGY, DEVICES

Abacus
Analytical Engine
ATM Machines
Bandwidth
Bridging Devices
Cache Memory
CAD/CAM, CA Engineering
Cell Phones
Cellular Technology
Central Processing Unit
Communication Devices
Computer System Interfaces
Display Devices
Game Controllers
Global Positioning Systems
Graphic Devices

Input Devices
Integrated Circuits
Jacquard's Loom
Keyboard
Magnetic Stripe Cards
Mainframes
Memory
Memory Devices
Microchip
Microcomputers
Minicomputers
Minitel
Mouse
Napier's Bones
Networks
Optical Technology
Personal Digital Assistants
Pointing Devices
Printing Devices
Reading Tools
Robots
Security Hardware
Simulators
Slide Rule
Sound Devices
Storage Devices
Supercomputers
Tabulating Machines
Telecommunications
Touch Screens
Transistors
Transmission Media
Turing Machine
Vacuum Tubes
Video Devices
Virtual Memory
Wireless Technology
Word Processors

TECHNOLOGY, TECHNIQUES

Agents
Analog Computing
Animation
Artificial Intelligence

Artificial Life
Assembly Language and Architecture
Asynchronous and Synchronous Transmission
Asynchronous Transfer Mode (ATM)
ATM Transmission
Authentication
Binary Number System
Boolean Algebra
Browsers
CAD/CAM, CA Engineering
Cellular Technology
Chip Manufacturing
Client/Server Technology
Codes
Coding Techniques
Compatibility (Open Systems Design)
Computer Supported Cooperative Work
  (CSCW)
Computerized Manufacturing
Cookies
Cryptography
Cybernetics
Data Mining
Data Visualization
Data Warehousing
Design Tools
Digital Computing
Digital Images
Digital Logic Design
Digital Signatures
E-banking
Embedded Technology (Ubiquitous
  Computing)
Ergonomics
Expert Systems
Fiber Optics
Firewalls
FTP
Games
Global Positioning Systems
Guru
Hackers
Hacking
Human Factors: User Interfaces
Hypermedia and Multimedia
Hypertext

Image Analysis: Medicine
Information Technology Standards
Information Theory
Interactive Systems
Invasive Programs
JPEG, MPEG
Knowledge-Based Systems
Laser Technology
Magnetic Stripe Cards
Mobile Computing
Molecular Computing
Nanocomputing
Network Design
Network Protocols
Network Topologies
Neural Networks
Operating Systems
Optical Technology
Parallel Processing
Pattern Recognition
Process Control
Routing
Satellite Technology
Scientific Visualization
Search Engines
Security
Security Applications
Security Software
Serial and Parallel Transmission
Simulation
TCP/IP
Telnet
Transmission Media
User Interfaces
Virtual Private Network
Virtual Reality
Viruses
Weather Forecasting
Window Interfaces
Wireless Technology

TELECOMMUNICATIONS, PEOPLE AND ORGANIZATIONS

Bardeen, John (See entry: Bardeen, John, Brattain, Walter H., and Shockley, William B.)

Bell, Alexander Graham
Bell Labs
Brattain, Walter H. (See entry: Bardeen, John, Brattain, Walter H., and Shockley, William B.)
Gross, Alfred J.
Institute of Electrical and Electronics Engineers (IEEE)
Marconi, Guglielmo
Morse, Samuel
Nyquist, Harry
Shannon, Claude E.
Shockley, William B. (See entry: Bardeen, John, Brattain, Walter H., and Shockley, William B.)

TELECOMMUNICATIONS, TECHNOLOGY AND DEVICES

Asynchronous and Synchronous Transmission
Asynchronous Transfer Mode (ATM)
ATM Transmission
Authentication
Bandwidth
Bridging Devices
Cell Phones
Cellular Technology
Coding Techniques
Communication Devices
Cookies
Cryptography
Digital Libraries
Digital Signatures
Distance Learning
Electronic Campus
Electronic Markets
Embedded Technology (Ubiquitous Computing)
Fiber Optics
Firewalls
FTP
Global Positioning Systems
Information Technology Standards
Information Theory
Internet
Internet: Applications

Internet: Backbone

Internet: History

Intranet

Mobile Computing

Network Design

Network Protocols

Network Topologies

Networks

Optical Technology

Routing

Satellite Technology

Security

Serial and Parallel Transmission

Service Providers

Supercomputers

TCP/IP

Telecommunications

Telephony

Telnet

Transistors

Transmission Media

Virtual Private Network

Wireless Technology

World Wide Web

Cumulative Index

Note: Page numbers in **boldface type** indicate article titles; those in italic type indicate illustrations. The number preceding the colon indicates the volume number; the number after a colon indicates the page number.

A

A-Train game, 1:70

AAL (ATM adaptation layer), 2:11–12, 4:18, 4:20

Abacuses, 1:**1–2**, 1:*1*, 1:41, 1:53, 2:87

ABC (Atanasoff-Berry computer), 1:42, 1:53, 1:60, 1:61

ABR (available bit rate) service, 2:11

Académie, of France, 1:165

Academy of Sciences of Ukraine, Computer Center, 4:119

Accelerated graphics ports (AGPs), 2:54–55

Access software, 3:60, 3:66, 3:169

Accounting software, 3:**1–3**
  accounts payable, 3:1
  accounts receivable, 3:1–2
  for agriculture, 3:3–6
  budgeting, 3:3
  criteria for selecting, 3:3
  depreciation tracking, 3:2–3
  for early computers, 1:134
  fixed asset tracking, 3:2–3
  general ledger, 3:1
  inventory, 3:2
  job cost estimating, 3:2
  payroll, 3:2
  personal finance, 3:60, 3:110
  sales order tracking, 3:3
  spreadsheets, 1:135, 1:137
  tax preparation, 3:1
  See also specific software applications; Spreadsheets

ACE (Automatic Computing Engine), 1:198

ACM (Association for Computing Machinery), 1:**21–24**
  ALGOL–60 report, 2:**1–3**, 2:155, 3:159
  code of ethics, 1:24, 4:99, 4:100
  Computer Sciences Accreditation Board, 1:22
  curriculum recommendations, 1:21–22
  Digital Library, 1:22, 1:23, 4:69, 4:84
  Eckert-Mauchly award, 4:5
  Elliot Organick and, 3:159
  events and services, 1:23
  Fellows Program, 1:24
  history, 1:21
  publications, 1:23
  student activities, 1:22–23
  Turing award, 1:21, 1:198, 4:173, 4:198
  volunteerism and SIGs, 1:23–24

ACM/IEEE-Software Engineering Code of Ethics, 4:99, 4:100

Acrobat Reader, 3:112, 4:28

Active Accessibility software, 4:16

Active Buddy software agent, 4:*2*

Active matrix LCDs (AMLCDs), 2:66–67, 2:68

Activision, 1:68

Actuators, hydraulic or pneumatic, 2:166

Acuity, defined, 1:112

Ada Joint Program Office, 1:124

Ada programming language, 1:80, 1:124, 2:158–159

Adaptive differential pulse code modulation, 2:184

ADCs (analog to digital converters), 1:30–31, 1:42, 1:148, 4:175

Adding machines, 1:3
  See also Calculating devices

Additive sound synthesis, 3:147

Address buses, 2:8, 2:27

Addressing protocols, 2:37, 2:120
  See also IP (Internet Protocol)

Addressing rewriteable CDs (CD-RWs), 3:113, 4:127

Adleman, Leonard, 4:52

Administrative Behavior, 4:197

Adobe Systems
  Acrobat Reader, 3:112, 4:28
  e-book Reader, 3:112
  Electronic Book Exchange, 3:112
  Illustrator, 3:169
  PageMaker, 1:157, 3:70, 3:74, 3:169, 3:197, 4:160
  PDF, 2:105, 2:149, 3:112, 4:28, 4:77, 4:83–84
  Photoshop, 3:18, 3:169, 4:6, 4:67, 4:160, 4:181
  See also Postscript page description language

ADR (advanced digital recording) tapes, 2:188

ADSL (asymmetric DSL), 2:47, 4:26

Advance phase, of hacking, 3:105

Advanced Computing Systems Laboratory, 4:4

Advanced Encryption Standard algorithm Rijndael, 4:52

Advanced Micro Devices, 1:107, 1:181

Advanced mobile phone system (AMPS), 2:30, 2:31–32

Advanced Networks and Services (ANS), 4:144

Advanced Research Projects Agency. *See* ARPA

Advanced Research Projects Agency Network. *See* ARPANET

Advanced Streaming Format, 2:184

Advertising. *See* Marketing

Aerial Experiment Association (AEA), 2:17–18

Aerodynamics, defined, 3:32

Aether medium, 2:201

Aetna Life and Casualty Company, punched cards, 1:186

Agents, intelligent software, 4:**1–4**
  Active Buddy, 4:*2*
  agent-location directories, 4:3
  for artificial life models, 4:10–11
  for commodity trading, 4:3
  database linking tools, 4:1–2
  defined, 1:114
  direct manipulation, 4:129
  distributed systems, 4:2–3
  enterprise information systems, 4:3
  information aggregating agents, 4:1
  personal assistants, 4:1
  security and, 4:2–3

"Agents on the Web," 4:3

Aggregate, defined, 2:213

AGPs (accelerated graphics ports), 2:54–55

Agricultural Adjustment Administration, punched-card checks, 1:188

Agriculture, 3:**3–6**
  CANs, 3:5–6
  computerized research, 3:6
  decision-making software, 3:4–5
  expert systems tools, 3:88
  image analysis tools, 3:117
  IPM models, 3:4–5
  landscape software, 3:5
  pest control software, 3:4–5
  PLC applications, 3:6
  precision, 3:4
  recordkeeping software, 3:4
  seeding rate calculations, 3:6
  simulation models, 3:4, 3:5, 3:6
  weed management software, 3:*5*

AI (Artificial intelligence), 1:**18–21**
  Allen Newell's contributions, 4:172–173
  Bolt Beranek and Newman research, 2:101
  chess strategies, 3:36
  Claude Shannon's contributions, 4:196
  computer "thoughts," 4:6
  cybernetic applications, 4:57
  data mining techniques, 4:60
  decision-making applications, 3:67, 3:69
  defined, 1:21, 2:87, 3:36, 4:10
  distinguished from artificial life, 4:10–11
  distinguished from neural networks, 3:152
  for embedded technologies, 3:86

expert systems and, 2:87, 2:88–89, 3:53, 3:87
  game applications, 1:67
  GIS tools, 3:101
  Herbert Simon's contributions, 4:197
  heuristic-based searches, 1:20
  history, 1:18
  information retrieval research, 1:96
  knowledge manipulation, 1:19–20
  knowledge representation, 1:18–19
  legal applications, 3:128
  LISP and, 2:99–100
  nanocomputing for, 4:170
  natural language processing, 1:20
  pattern recognition, 1:114
  for personalized search engines, 4:135
  political event simulations, 4:184
  programming languages, 4:174
  prototypes, 2:100
  railroad applications, 3:176
  robotics and, 1:170, 3:53
  social and moral consequences, 1:20
  Turing Test, 1:21, 1:198
  See also Agents, intelligent software; Artificial life; Neural networks; Pattern recognition; Robotics/robots

AIBO robotic dog, 4:124, 4:*125*

AIEE (American Institute of Electrical Engineers), 1:102, 1:*103*

Aiken, Howard H., 1:51, 1:59–60, 1:212, 2:222, 3:206

Aiken Industries, 1:60

Ailerons, defined, 3:7

AIMACO programming language, 2:156

Air bag deployment, embedded systems, 1:114

Air Force, U.S., 2:73

Air quality, DSS tools, 3:68

Aircraft design
  Alexander Graham Bell and, 2:17–18
  CAD-CAM tools, 3:*30*, 3:31
  ergonomics, 1:64
  FEDs, 2:68
  process control, 3:164

Aircraft flight control, 3:**6–10**
  Apollo spacecraft, 1:151, 1:*152*, 1:153, 3:186–187
  auto-pilots, 3:7–9
  expert systems, 3:88
  FAA certification, 3:8–9

fly-by-wire systems, 1:151, 2:216
  FMSs, 3:7, 3:9
  Freedom 7 spacecraft, 1:151
  navigation systems, 3:149–150
  of space reconnaissance satellites, 4:117
  See also Simulators, aircraft flight training

Aircraft traffic control (ATC)
  computers for, 3:11–12
  distinguished from aircraft traffic management, 3:12
  handing off, 3:11
  history, 3:10
  radar, 3:10–11, 3:*11*
  TRACONs, 3:11

Aircraft traffic management (ATM), 1:42, 3:**10–12**, 3:*11*

Airline passengers, security measures, 3:15

Airline reservations, 3:**13–16**
  airline deregulation and, 3:14
  computerized reservation systems, 3:13–15, 3:*13*
  database software, 1:27
  electronic tickets, 3:15
  EPSS applications, 3:43
  expanded customer services, 3:15
  Orbitz.com, 3:15, 4:81
  passenger tracking, 3:14, 3:15
  reservation systems, history, 3:13–14
  through Internet, 3:15
  Travelocity.com, 3:15, 4:80, 4:81, 4:128

Airline tickets, printing, 2:150

AITP (Association for Information Technology Professionals), code of ethics, 4:99, 4:101

Akers, John, 1:91

Aladdin, 1:13

Alaska Railroad, PTC project, 3:176

Alcom, Al, 1:67–68

Aldus PageMaker. *See* Adobe Systems: PageMaker

ALGOL programming language, 2:1–2
  Backus-Naur form, 2:2
  begin-end delimiters, 2:155
  for computer music, 2:114
  defined, 3:161
  MAD and, 3:159
  for minicomputers, 1:141
  Niklaus Wirth and, 2:157
  version 58, 2:155
  version 60, 2:1, 2:155
  version 68, 2:1, 2:155, 2:159

Algol-60 report, **2:1–3**, 2:155, 3:159

Algorithmic Language. *See* ALGOL programming language

Algorithmic music composition, 3:147

Algorithms, 2:**3–5**
  and AI programming, 2:100
  in Algol-60 report, 2:1
  Analytical Engine's use of, 1:80
  and artificial intelligence, 1:19–20
  in assembly and machine languages, 2:153
  for astronomy, 3:23
  for CAD systems, 3:17
  for code breaking, 1:54
  compression/decompression, 2:97, 3:112
  conflict probe, 3:12
  convex hulls, 3:101
  defined, 1:54, 2:1, 3:6, 4:11
  definiteness, 2:3
  in digital computers, 2:4
  for DNA sequencing, 3:142
  for DSSs, 3:67
  effectiveness, 2:3, 2:4
  encryption, 2:173
  Euclid's contributions, 2:4
  evolutionary, 4:11
  finiteness, 2:3
  for gene sequencing, 3:27–28
  for information retrieval, 1:96
  input, 2:3
  line sweeping, 3:101
  minimax, 3:36
  for neural networks, 3:155
  non-numerical, 2:101
  origin of term, 2:3
  output, 2:3, 2:4, 2:52
  parallel, 2:137
  Rijndael encryption, 4:52
  routing, 4:187, 4:203
  for scientific visualization, 3:178
  search engines as, 2:4
  serial, 2:137
  software, patents on, 4:177–178
  tools for defining, 2:55–58
  transposition, 4:49
  Turing's contributions, 1:200, 2:4
  video compression, 4:88
  Voronoi diagrams, 3:101

Alice Comedies, 1:12

Alice in Wonderland, 1:12

ALife. *See* Artificial life

All-points-addressable mode, 3:198

All the Web search engine, 4:191

Allen Newell Award (ACM), 1:21

Allen, Paul, 1:137, 1:138, 4:94

Alliance for Telecommunications Industry Solutions, 1:100

Alpha beta pruning, defined, 3:36

ALPHA format, 3:136

Alphabet
  as information standard, 1:97
  source, 2:42
  use in cryptography, 4:50–51

Alphanumeric, defined, 2:81

Altair 8800, 1:137

AltaVista search engine, 1:219, 4:189, 4:*190*, 4:191

Alternative Museum, 4:8

Alto workstation, 4:147

ALUs (arithmetic and logic units), 2:6, 2:32, 2:33, 2:34

Amadeus Global Travel Distribution reservation system, 3:14

Amazon.com, 1:45, 4:*64*, 4:79, 4:93–94

Ambient, defined, 3:84

Ambiguity
  defined, 2:139
  in pattern recognition, 2:*139*
  in programming, 2:161

Amdahl Corporation, 4:4–5

Amdahl, Gene Myron, 4:**4–6**, 4:*4*

America Online. *See* AOL

American Airlines
  computerized reservation systems, 3:13–14
  DSS tools, 3:68
  online reservations, 3:15

American Association for the Promotion of the Teaching of Speech to the Deaf, 2:17

American Bankers Association, 1:100

American Cash Register Company, 1:211

American Chemical Society, online conferences, 4:36

American Civil Liberties Union, 1:168, 4:34

American Express, data mining, 1:167, 4:59

American Folklore, 4:206

American Institute of Electrical Engineers, 1:102, 1:*103*

American Mathematical Society Journals, 4:84

American Memory project, 4:70

American National Standards Institute. *See* ANSI

American Standard Code for Information Interchange. *See* ASCII

American Standards Association, 2:41

Americans with Disabilities Act, 4:12, 4:16

Ameritech, 1:28

Amino acids, 3:142

AMLCDs (active matrix LCDs), 2:66–67, 2:68

Amortized, defined, 2:208

Amplification, discovery, 1:202

Amplifiers
  in audio equipment, 1:132, 4:126
  for hearing impaired persons, 4:14
  inverters, 2:59
  negative feedback, 4:175
  transistors as, 1:106, 1:196
  for transmission lines, 2:201

Amplitude modulation of lasers, 3:127

AMPS (advanced mobile phone system), 2:30, 2:31–32

AMR corporation, 3:15

Amtrak, PTC project, 3:176

Analog computing, 1:**2–5**
  current status, 1:5
  differential analyzers, 1:3–5, 1:50, 3:162
  distinguished from digital computing, 1:2, 1:40, 1:131–132
  dominance, 1:3
  early auto-pilots, 3:9
  early calculators, 1:3–4, 1:41–42, 1:*41*, 1:60
  early video games, 1:68
  electronics, 1:4–5
  IBM tabulator, 1:60
  linear integrated circuits, 1:106
  Lord Kelvin's computer, 3:162
  mechanical computers, 1:4–5
  process control applications, 1:5
  programming, 1:132
  slide rules, 1:2, 1:3, 1:*4*, 1:**181–182**, 3:162
  speed vs. accuracy, 1:40, 1:42

Analog (continuous) simulations, 1:179–180

Analog, defined, 1:30, 2:76, 3:9, 4:39

Analog signals
  bandwidth, 4:24–25
  optical fiber transmission, 2:76
  sound transmission, 2:*182*
  video image transmission, 2:204, 4:39

Analog sound synthesis and recording, 1:147–148

Analog to digital converters. *See* ADCs

Analogous, defined, 2:145

Analysis-oriented music models, 3:146

ANALYTIC programming language, 4:120

Analytic simulation, defined, 3:32

Analytical Engine, 1:**5–8**, 2:115, 2:159, 2:222, 3:162
  Ada Lovelace on, 1:123–124, 1:149
  application of concept, 1:51, 1:52
  defined, 1:149
  invention, 1:24–25
  as mechanical, 1:131
  number system of, 1:42
  punched cards, 1:7, 1:25, 1:80, 1:186

Analytical Society, 1:25

And-gates, 1:27, 2:19–20, 2:59–60

AND operators, 2:22, 4:189

Andor Systems, 4:5

Andreessen, Marc, 1:219, 4:30

Andrew Project, 4:121

Andy Capp's bar, 1:67–68

Anechoic chambers, 1:*28*

Angle modulation of lasers, 3:127

Animation, 1:**8–15**
  defined, 1:8
  by Disney Studios, 1:10, 1:*11*, 1:12–13
  distinguished from VR, 2:214, 2:216
  for games, 1:12, 1:14–15
  history, 1:12–13
  kinetics and kinematics, 2:216
  by MGM, 1:13
  parallel processing for, 2:135
  plug-in programs, 4:28
  principles, 1:13–14
  for scientific visualization, 3:177–178
  for simulations, 1:180–181
  software for creating, 1:13, 1:15
  story creation, 1:8–10
  techniques, 1:11–12
  types, 1:10–11
  for visual effects, 1:*9*, 1:13
  for weather maps, 3:209
  Web, 1:14

Animatronics, 1:10, 1:11

Annan, Kofi, 4:132–133

Anodes, defined, 1:201

Anonymizer software, 1:168

Anonymous reposting servers, 1:177

ANS (Advanced Networks and Services), 4:144

ANSI (American National Standards Institute), 1:100, 2:105, 2:128, 2:159, 3:136

ANSNET, 4:144–145

Antarctic ice flow, GIS tracking, 4:117

Anthrax, and bioterrorism, 3:27

Anthropology, genetics research and, 3:142

Anthropomorphic, defined, 2:166

Anti-aliasing, defined, 1:69

Anti-trust suits
  against American Cash Register, 1:211
  against IBM, 1:90
  against Intel Corporation, 1:109
  against Microsoft, 1:138–139, 4:140
  Sherman Antitrust Act, 1:138, 1:211

Anti-virus software, 1:209–210, 2:96, 3:105–106, 3:112, 3:180–181

Anti-viruses, 1:208, 2:95

Anticipation animation principle, 1:13

Antonelli, Jean Kathleen McNulty Mauchly, 1:63

AOL (America Online), 1:70, 1:218–219, 3:113, 4:28, 4:98
  Instant Messenger, 4:140, 4:193

AOL Time Warner, suit against Microsoft, 4:140

Apache Project, 3:156, 3:157

Apogee of satellite orbits, 2:169–170

Apollo Reservation System, 3:14

Apollo spacecraft, 1:151, 1:*152*, 1:153, 3:185, 3:186

Appeal animation principle, 1:14

Apple Computer, Inc., 1:**15–18**
  agreement with Microsoft, 1:17, 1:138
  beginnings, 1:15, 4:94–95
  challenged by IBM-PCs, 1:17
  game simulations, 1:181
  Jobs, Steven, 1:15–17, 1:*16*, 1:69
  lack of open architecture, 1:17, 1:36
  suit against Microsoft, 1:138
  Wozniak, Stephen, 1:15–17, 1:69

Apple computers and software
  AIFF sound format, 2:183
  Apple I, 1:15, 4:95
  Apple II, 1:16–17, 1:36, 1:138, 1:218–219, 4:95
  Apple III, 1:17
  compatibility issues, 2:48–50
  G3 laptop, 1:17
  G4 series, 3:58

HyperCard, 1:88
iMac, 1:17
Lisa, 1:17, 1:111
Newton MessagePad, 2:142
PowerBook, 1:17
PowerMac G4, 1:17
Unicode supported by, 2:42
window manager, 1:112, 1:217
See also Macintosh computers

Apple Laserwriter printers, 3:70, 3:72, 3:74, 3:198

Applets
  defined, 2:128, 4:82
  invasive programs and, 4:109
  Java, 2:128, 4:82, 4:**152–155**

Application-neutral languages, 2:105

Application Service Providers (ASPs), 4:193

Application viruses, 1:207

Application wizards, 1:216

Applications. *See* Software

Approximation, defined, 3:162

Arbiters. *See* I/O controllers

Arc tangent, defined, 1:85

Archie index and search tool, 4:149

Architecture, 3:**16–19**
  of assembly languages, 2:**5–7**
  CAD, history, 3:16
  CAD tools, 3:17–19, 3:*17*
  computational tools, 3:18
  decision support systems, 3:18
  defined, 2:5, 3:16
  early use of computers, 3:16
  new technologies, 3:18
  Von Neumann, 2:217
  See also Network architecture; Parallel architecture

Archives, of e-journals, 4:82

Archiving utilities, 3:112

Arcs animation principle, 1:14

Area codes, introduction, 3:200

Argonne National Laboratory, DSS tools, 3:68

ARINC 429 serial buses, 2:181

Aristotle, on vacuums, 1:166

Arithmetic. *See* Mathematics

Arithmetic and logic units. *See* ALUs

Army, U.S.
  Ballistics Research Laboratory, 1:51, 1:55, 1:202
  ENIAC programming, 1:51, 2:73
  firing tables, 1:59, 2:74

Around the World in Eighty Days, 3:20

ARPA (Advanced Research Projects Agency), 1:115, 4:146, 4:203–204

ARPANET
  government research grants, 1:81
  as origin of Internet, 1:115,
    1:218, 2:90, 3:133, 4:144, 4:147
  PLI encryption devices, 2:213
  security, 1:175, 1:176
  TCP/IP and, 4:203–204
Array processors, 2:136
Arsenic, as silicon doping element,
  3:39
Art, 4:**6–9**
  computerized databases, 4:8
  digital images as, 4:6, 4:8
  digital photography, 4:7
  Janet Zweig, 4:6
  museums, 4:7–8
  See also Digital images; Graphics
Art Abstracts, 4:8
Art Dink, A-Train game, 1:70
The Art of 3-D Computer Animation,
  1:13
The Art of Computer Programming,
  1:21
Art restoration, Sistine Chapel, 4:6,
  4:7
Arthasastra, on cryptanalysis, 4:49
Artificial intelligence (AI). *See* AI
  (Artificial Intelligence).
Artificial Intelligence: AI, 1:20
Artificial life, 4:**9–11**
  agents, 4:10–11
  cellular automata, 4:9
  distinguished from artificial intel-
    ligence, 4:10–11
  Game of Life, 4:9–11
  neural networks and, 4:11
  and robots, 4:11
  simulation models, 4:*10*
Artistic licenses, 3:156
Artzt, Russ, 4:96
ASA (American Standards Association), 2:41
ASCII (American Standard Code for
  Information Interchange)
  attributes, 2:41
  as block code, 2:42, 2:*43*
  coding schemes, 2:109
  defined, 1:93, 2:109, 4:137
  for e-books, 4:77
  introduction, 2:41
  query format, 1:93
  as standard, 1:101
ASes (Autonomous Systems), 4:143
Asheim, Lester, 4:31
Asimov, Isaac, 1:14, 1:173, 3:**19–21**,
  3:*19*, 4:104
ASK Computer Systems Inc., 4:96

Ask Jeeves search engine, 4:128
AskA services, 4:131
ASPs (Application Service
  Providers), 4:193
Assembler programs, 1:77, 2:7
Assembly language and architecture,
  1:76–77, 1:77, 2:**5–8**, 2:125
  for Altair 8800, 1:137
  assemblers, 2:7
  compilers, 2:51
  distinguished from high-level
    languages, 2:7
  machine code instructions, 2:6–7
  for microprocessor autopilots, 3:9
  mnemonic codes, 2:7, 2:51
  uses, 2:125
  V2 Operating System, 2:6
Assets, illiquid, 4:91
Assistive computer technology for
  persons with disabilities, 4:**11–17**
  Americans with Disabilities Act,
    4:12, 4:16
  Disabilities Discrimination Act,
    4:12, 4:16
  e-mail, 4:12
  GPS applications, 4:117
  hearing impairments, 4:14–15
  instant messaging, 4:12
  Internet resources, 4:12
  LCD panels, 4:87
  learning disabilities, 4:13, 4:15
  motor impairments, 4:13–14
  operating system adaptations,
    4:12, 4:16
  PC adaptations, 4:11–12
  Rehabilitation Act, 4:16
  speech recognition technology,
    3:204–205
  user interfaces, 4:129
  visual impairments, 4:12–13,
    4:30, 4:31, 4:117
Association for Computing Machinery. *See* ACM
Association for Information Technology Professionals (AITP),
  code of ethics, 4:99, 4:101
Association Francais de Normalization (AFNOR), 1:100
Association models, 4:62
Asteroids game, 1:67
Astronauts, simulators for, 1:*179*,
  2:181
Astronomy, 3:**21–24**
  computer applications, history,
    3:22
  cosmology studies, 3:22
  defined, 3:21
  knowledge representation, 1:18

scientific visualization, 3:177
SETI@home, 3:22
stellar structure studies, 3:22
supercomputers as tools, 3:23
telescopes, 3:22, 3:*23*
three-body problems, 3:22
three-dimensional models, 3:22,
  3:23
Astrophysics, computational, 3:23
Asymmetric DSL (ADSL), 2:47,
  4:26
Asynchronous and synchronous
  transmission, 2:**8–10**
  asynchronous signals, 2:8
  bandwidth use, 2:9
  examples, 2:8
  HDLC, 2:9
  and information access, 4:132
  protocols, 2:8–9
  synchronous signals, 2:8
@ sign, 4:146
Atanasoff-Berry computer. *See* ABC
Atanasoff, John Vincent, 1:42, 1:53,
  1:59, 1:*60*, 1:61, 2:74
AT&T
  acceptance of ASCII, 2:41
  ASA role, 2:41
  Bell Labs, 1:27–28, 2:12–13
  frequency division multiplexing,
    3:33
  Harry Nyquist and, 4:174–175
  peering agreements, 4:145
  SDNs, 2:213
  switching systems, history, 3:*200*
Atari
  Blockbuster game, 1:69
  game controllers, 2:79
  4-bit VCS console, 1:69
  I, Robot game, 1:14
  Nolan Bushnell and, 4:98, 4:126
  Pong machines, 1:67–68, 4:126
  ST computer series, 1:14
ATC. *See* Aircraft traffic control
ATI series video cards, 1:15
ATIS (Alliance for Telecommunica-
  tions Industry Solutions), 1:100
Atlantis, 1:13
ATM adaptation layer. *See* AAL
ATM (Asynchronous Transfer
  Mode) transmission, 2:**10–12**,
  4:**17–20**
  ABR service, 2:11
  advantages, 2:10, 4:17, 4:20
  ATM layer, 4:19–20
  CBR service, 2:11–12
  cells, 1:155–156, 2:10–11, 4:17,
    4:18

ATM (Asynchronous Transfer Mode) transmission (continued)
CLP connections, 4:18
development of, 2:10
GFC connections, 4:18, 4:20
HEC connections, 4:18
for ITV, 4:88
multiplexing, 4:20
as network architecture, 1:155–156, 2:118–119, 4:17, 4:19, 4:20
parameter specification, 2:11
physical layer, 4:19
protocols, 2:12, 4:17
PT connections, 4:18
UBR service, 2:11–12
VBR-NRT service, 2:11
VBR-RT service, 2:11–12
VCCs and VCs, 2:10–11
VCI connections, 4:18, 4:20
VPI connections, 4:18, 4:20
ATM Forum, 2:11, 4:18
ATMs (Automatic Teller Machines), 3:24–26, 3:24
bandwidth use, 4:17
as command-line systems, 1:111
in convenience stores, 3:26
cryptography and, 4:49
vs. debit cards, 3:26
history, 3:25
ISO-owned machines, 3:26
MAC Network, 4:74
mainframe computers, 1:126
new features, 3:26
operating systems, 3:25
PINs, 4:22–23
as proprietary, 3:25
receipt printing, 2:150
security, 2:140, 3:25, 3:26, 4:22–23
service fees, 3:26
statistics, 3:26
user interfaces, 2:146, 2:198, 3:25, 4:128
See also Magnetic stripe cards and readers; Smart cards
Atom bombs
Cuban Missile Crisis, 4:115
in Dr. Strangelove, 4:105
Manhattan Project, 2:217–218, 3:121, 3:158, 4:102–103
physics research, 3:162
Atomic clocks, 3:151
Atomic Energy Commission, 1:93, 3:57
Attenuation
of electrical technologies, 2:75
of fiber optics, 2:76–77

ATTNET, 4:193
Attributes, in object-oriented languages, 2:126
ATV space craft, 1:135
AU format, 1:101
Auctions, online. See eBay
Audio file formats, 1:101, 3:113
Audio oscillator, invention, 3:108
Audio recognition techniques, 3:147
Audiometer, invention, 2:17
Audion vacuum tube, 1:201
Augment system, 1:87
Authentication, 4:21–24
to access e-journals, 4:82–83
defined, 2:173, 4:80
digital certificates, 2:213, 4:23–24, 4:80, 4:83
digital signatures, 1:175, 4:52, 4:71–73
for e-banking, 4:74
encrypted information, 4:21, 4:22
facial scans, 4:21
fingerprint scans, 2:96, 2:138, 4:21, 4:22, 4:23
FTP servers, 4:110
Kerberos, 4:83
one-factor methods, 4:21
by operating systems, 4:24
PINs, 2:174, 3:25, 4:22–23
to prevent unauthorized copying, 4:46
public-key cryptosystems, 1:176, 4:52
retinal scans, 2:140, 4:21, 4:22
two-factor methods, 4:21
userids, 2:175, 4:21, 4:74, 4:107, 4:109
See also Passwords (passcodes)
Authentication servers, 1:176
Authentication tokens, 2:173, 4:21–23
Authorization, in security systems, 2:173, 2:175
Auto-pilots
for aircraft, 3:7–9
analog vs. digital, 3:9
FAA certification, 3:8–9
FMCs, 3:7
FMSs, 3:7, 3:9
gyros, 3:7
how they work, 3:7
microprocessors in, 3:7–9
ROM, 3:9
for ships, 3:6–7
software, 3:8–9
AutoCAD software, 3:31

AutoDesk 3D Studio Viz software, 3:18
AutoDesSys Inc. software, 3:18
"Automata," 4:105
Automata theory, 1:27, 4:119
Automatic Computing Engine (ACE), 1:198
Automatic object recognition. See Computer vision
Automatic Teller Machines. See ATMs
Automation
and process control, 3:164–166
for railroads, 3:173
Automatons, 1:169, 4:104
Automobiles
CAD-CAM tools, 3:31
diagnostic software, 3:43
DSS tools, 3:68
embedded technologies, 1:114, 3:87
ergonomic designs, 1:64
expert systems, 3:88, 3:89
navigation systems, 3:150
process control, 3:164
robots in manufacturing, 3:53
sales and leasing software, 3:43
Autonomous, defined, 1:169, 2:166
Autonomous Systems (ASes), 4:143
Available bit rate (ABR) service, 2:11
Axioms, defined, 4:173
Aztecs, abacus of, 1:1

B

Babbage, Charles, 1:24–26, 1:25
Ada Lovelace and, 1:26, 1:80, 1:122, 1:123–124, 2:115, 2:159
awards, 3:22
government research grants, 1:80
inventions, 1:26
Konrad Zuse and, 2:222
as physicist, 3:161–162
publications, 1:26
See also Analytical Engine; Difference Engine
Baby monitors, wireless, 2:219
Back end of compiler, 2:52
Back pain, preventing, 1:65–66
Back-up copies, distinguished from piracy, 3:182
Backing stores, for VM systems, 2:210, 2:211
Backus, John, 2:2, 2:125, 2:154, 2:155
Backus-Naur form (BNF), 2:2
Bacteria, bioinformatic studies, 3:28, 3:142–143

Bacteriorhodopsin, as silicon chip replacement, 3:144

Baer, Ralph, 1:67

Bakelite, 1:53

Ballard, Robert, 3:115

Ballistics
    computer calculations, 1:50, 1:55, 1:71, 1:202, 2:73, 3:59
    defined, 1:50, 3:186
    firing tables, 1:59, 2:74

Ballistics Research Laboratory, U.S. Army, 1:51, 1:55, 1:202

Bambi, 1:10, 1:12

Bandwidth, 4:**24–27**
    for analog signals, 4:24–25
    for ATM transmissions, 4:17
    broadband, 1:161, 2:47, 4:25–26
    for cell phones, 3:32–33
    for client/server systems, 2:39
    compression to conserve, 2:97
    for data transfer, 2:9
    defined, 1:125, 2:9, 3:32
    for digital signals, 4:25
    for electrical technologies, 2:75
    for fiber optics, 2:77
    high, defined, 4:88
    for Internet, 2:105, 2:212, 4:24, 4:162
    for Internet browsers, 4:141–142
    for ITV, 3:75
    limitations, 4:24, 4:204, 4:205
    for mainframes, 1:125
    narrowband, 4:25
    for networks, 2:86, 2:123, 3:114
    research, history, 4:27
    for telecommunications, 4:24
    for telephone signals, 2:47, 4:192
    for television signals, 1:161, 2:47, 4:25
    upload vs. download, 4:26–27

Banks and financial institutions
    consumer credit ratings, 4:48–49
    data integrity, 4:62
    data mining, 4:59
    DSS tools, 3:68
    e-banking, 1:46, 4:**73–75**, 4:91–92
    electronic market, 4:89–90
    MICR technology, 2:134, 2:164
    online access to, 1:46
    privacy and security, 1:168, 1:*176*, 2:140, 3:105–107
    See also ATMs (Automatic Teller Machines)

Bao, Zhenan, 4:*168*

Bar charts (histograms), 3:61, 3:*62*

Bar code scanners, 2:92, 2:132–133, 2:*133*, 2:144, 2:163, 3:127

Bar code sorters (BCSs), 2:163

Bar codes
    as binary digits, 2:163
    defined, 2:144, 3:29
    history, 2:163
    UGPIC, 2:163
    UPC, 2:133, 2:163
    uses, 2:133, 2:163–164, 3:28, 3:174

Baran, Paul, 4:146

Barbera, Joseph, 1:13

Bardeen, John, 2:**12–15**, 2:*13*
    superconductivity research, 1:106
    transistor research, 1:63, 1:72, 1:104, 1:106, 1:192

Barnard, Dr. Christiaan, 3:56–57

Barnstorming, early aircraft, 3:10

Barometers, 1:166, 3:208

Barron, C.B., 1:211

Barry, Hank, 4:*44*

Bartik, Jennings, 1:63

Base-2 number system. *See* Binary number system

Base-8 number systems. *See* Octal number system

Base-10 number system. *See* Decimal number system

Base-16 number system. *See* Hexadecimal number system

Base+offset addressing model, 2:*206*, 2:*207*, 2:209

Base stations, for cell phones, 3:33

Basic Input Output System (BIOS), 1:130, 2:111

BASIC programming language, 1:78
    for computer music, 2:114
    development, 2:2, 2:125, 3:120–121
    dialects, 2:157
    interpreting, 2:153
    learned by children, 2:157
    Microsoft and, 1:137, 1:138, 4:94, 4:208
    ROM storage, 2:111
    SBASIC, 2:157
    Visual BASIC, 2:95, 2:128, 2:157, 4:74, 4:**208–212**

Batch processing, 1:93, 1:126, 1:141, 3:14, 3:71, 3:198

Batteries
    for CMOS, 1:130
    for display devices, 2:67
    for transistor radios, 1:192

Baud, defined, 1:153, 2:46

Baud rates, 1:69, 2:46–47, 4:25

Baudot, Jean-Maurice Émile, 2:40, 2:*46*

Bauer, Fritz, 2:155

Baughman, Ernest, 4:206

Baum, L. Frank, 4:104

Bayesian networks, defined, 3:69

BBB (Better Business Bureau), 4:48

BBN, first PLI, 2:213

BCD (binary coded decimal), 3:136

BCDIC (Binary Coded Decimal Interchange Code), 2:41

BCSs (bar code sorters), 2:163

Bear, Greg, 4:106

Beardsley, Richard K., 4:206

Beauty and the Beast, 1:13

Beginners' All-purpose Symbolic Instruction Code. *See* BASIC programming language

Beinn Bhreagh, 2:17

Bell, Alexander Graham, 1:102, 1:189, 2:**15–18**, 2:*16*, 3:199

Bell Atlantic, 1:28

Bell Communications Research (Bellcore), 1:28

Bell Labs, 1:**27–29**
    C programming language, 2:158, 2:202
    cellular technology, 2:30
    compiler-compilers, 2:2
    computer-generated sound, 1:149, 2:115–116
    famous employees, 1:27, 1:198, 2:13–15, 4:175–176
    government research grants, 1:81
    manufacturing branch, 1:27, 1:141
    Model 1 computer, 1:51
    organic transistors, 1:195
    research and development, 1:27–28, 3:202
    transistor invention, 1:27, 1:72, 1:89, 1:106, 1:192, 2:12–15, 4:126, 4:*168*

Bell South, 1:28

Bell Telephone Company (Bell System), 1:28, 2:17, 3:200, 4:192

Bennett, Gillian, 4:207

Bentley Inc., ProjectBank, 3:18

Berliner, Emil, 1:*98*

Berne Convention, international copyright standards, 4:46

Berners-Lee, Tim, 1:218, 4:29–30, 4:*93*, 4:121, 4:140, 4:149

Bernoulli numbers, 1:26, 1:124

Berry, Clifford, 1:42, 1:53, 1:60

Berson, Tom, 2:173

Berzelius, J.J., 2:111

Betamax VCRs, 2:204

Better Business Bureau (BBB), 4:48

Bezos, Jeff, 4:93–94

The Bibliography of the History of Art, 4:8

"Big Brother" (*1984*), 4:118

Bill and Melinda Gates Foundation, 3:131, 4:94

Billington, James, 4:*70*

Billions of floating point operations per second (GigaFLOPS), 2:137, 3:58

Bina, Eric, 4:30

BINAC (Binary Automatic Computer), 1:*85*, 2:74

Binary (base-2) number system, 1:**29–31**

  for ABC, 1:42

  defined, 1:7, 2:117, 4:179

  for digital data, 1:30–31, 1:40, 1:60, 2:108–109

  for EDSAC, 1:42

  for EDVAC, 1:56

  flip-flop relays, 1:51, 1:106–107, 2:5–6

  for machine-language programs, 1:76

  operations, 1:30

  origin, 1:30

  overview, 1:29

  positional notation, 1:29–30

  translating, 1:86, 1:120

  for Z machines, 1:52–53, 1:62

Binary code

  bar codes as, 2:163

  defined, 2:42

  machine language as, 2:51

Binary coded decimal (BCD), 3:136

Binary Coded Decimal Interchange Code (BCDIC), 2:41

Binary, defined, 1:60, 2:5

Binary digits. *See* Bits

Binomial theorem, 1:165

Bioengineering, 3:28

Bioinformatics, 3:27–28, 3:45, 3:143–144

Biology, 3:**26–29**

  artificial life, 4:**9–11**

  bioengineering, 3:28

  bioinformatics, 3:27–28, 3:45, 3:143–144

  biomedical engineering, 3:28–29

  disease control applications, 3:27

  environmental, 3:28

  expert systems, 3:88

  image analysis tools, 3:117

  mathematical, 3:137

  mechanized lab tests, 3:28

  molecular, 3:**142–145**

teaching tools, 3:164

  See also Medical systems; Molecular biology

Biomedical engineering, 3:28–29

Biometrics, 2:140

  facial scans, 4:21, 4:67, 4:114

  fingerprint scans, 2:96, 2:138, 4:21, 4:22, 4:*23*, 4:68

  retinal scans, 2:140, 4:21, 4:*22*

BIOS (Basic Input Output System), 1:130, 2:111

Bioterrorism, 1:49, 3:27

Bipolar Junction Transistors (BJTs), 1:196

Bit mapped display (raster scan display), 2:82, 3:49

Bit maps, defined, 2:149

Bit rates, 2:11, 2:98

BITNET, 4:144, 4:148

Bits

  in coding schemes, 1:77, 2:108–109

  defined, 1:2, 2:9, 4:67

  in *Gulliver's Travels*, 4:104

  Morse Code symbols as, 2:40

  overview, 1:29–31

Bitstream, defined, 2:117

Black Hat hackers, 4:123

Blackboard course management system, 3:76

The Blair Witch Project, 3:95

Blindness. *See* Visual impairments, assistive technologies

Block codes, 2:42, 2:*43*, 2:44

Blockbuster Entertainment Corporation, data mining, 1:167, 4:59

Blockbuster game, 1:69

Blood Music, 4:106

Blue Box, hacking tool, 4:123

Blue Horizon computer, 1:184

Blue Storm computer, 1:185

Bluetooth wireless technology, 2:220, 4:166

BNF (Backus-Naur form), 2:2

Boeing, CAD applications, 3:*30*, 3:31

Bolt Beranek and Newman, 2:101

Bombardier Aerospace CRJ700, 3:*8*

The Bombe decoder, 1:54

Bonaparte, Marie, 4:206

Bongo programming language, 2:104

Book hacker attack, 1:177

Book sellers

  Amazon.com, 1:45, 4:*64*, 4:79, 4:93–94

  Bookscan, 4:79

  e-books and, 4:77

  Soundscan, 4:79

Bookkeeping. *See* Accounting software; spreadsheets

Bookscan, 4:79

Boole, George, 1:18, 2:**18–20**, 2:*18*

Boole, Mary (Everest), 2:18–19

Boolean algebra, 2:**20–24**

  ALU operations and, 2:33

  computer design and, 2:22–23

  defined, 2:18, 4:195

  information theory and, 2:23

  network design and, 2:117–118

  role of, 1:41

  syllogistic statements, 2:19

  truth tables, 2:20–22, 2:*21*, 2:*22*

  Venn diagrams, 2:19

Boolean information retrieval, 1:93–96, 2:23

Boolean logic and operators, 1:219, 2:19–20, 2:22–23, 3:128, 4:171, 4:189

Boot viruses, 1:207

Boron, as doping element, 1:105, 3:39

Bosnia-Herzegovina, cybercafes, 4:54

Boston

  An Wang's contributions, 3:207

Boston School for Deaf Mutes (Horace Mann School), 2:16

Botkin, B.A., 4:206

Botvinnik, Mikhail, 3:37

Boulez, Pierre, 3:146

Bounded rationality, 4:198

Bowles, Kenneth, 2:157

Braille screen readers, 4:13

"The Brain," 4:105

Brain research

  cybernetic applications, 4:57

  neural modeling, 4:57

  supercomputers as tool, 1:185

Brattain, Walter H., 1:63, 1:72, 1:106, 1:192, 2:**12–15**, 2:*13*

Braun, Karl Ferdinand, 4:164

Bricklin, Daniel, 1:135, 3:167, 3:193, 4:98

Bridging devices, 2:**24–27**

  bridges, 2:24–26, 2:*25*

  distinguished from routers, 2:26

  gateways, 2:26–27

  network function, 2:24–26, 2:*25*

  repeaters, 2:24

  translational, 4:205

A Brief History of Time, 4:*15*

British Association for the Advancement of Science, 1:26

British Open University, distance learning, 3:75

British Standards Institute (BSI), 1:100

British Telecommunications, Soul Catcher, 4:57

Britton, Lionel, 4:105

Broadband access, 3:113, 4:204

Broadband signals, 1:161, 2:47, 4:25, 4:25–26

Broadcast communications
    access infrastructure, 2:78
    networks, 1:154, 1:190–191
    wireless, 2:219
    See also Radio; Television

Brotherhood of Locomotive Engineers, 3:176

Browsers. *See* Internet browsers

Brunel wide-gauge railway track, 1:26

BSA (Business Software Alliance), 3:183, 3:184

BSD UNIX, 4:204

Buchanan, Bruce, 3:88

Budgeting software, 3:3

Buffers, in CPUs, 2:6

Bunny suits, for chip manufacturing, 3:*39*, 4:167

Burroughs, mainframe computers, 1:89, 1:125

Bursty, defined, 4:17

Buses
    address, 2:8, 2:27
    ARINC, 2:181
    defined, 2:5
    function, 2:5, 2:32, 2:52, 2:200–201
    for parallel transmission, 2:176–177
    PCI, 2:54
    topologies, 1:155, 1:156, 2:123–124
    transmission media, 2:200–201
    USB, 2:54, 2:178

Bush, George H., 1:87

Bush, George W., 4:101, 4:183

Bush, Vannevar, 1:*58*
    Claude Shannon and, 4:195
    Differential Analyzer, 3:162
    early computer contributions, 1:50, 1:58–59, 1:87
    hypertext, 4:29

Bushnell, Nolan, 1:67–68, 4:98, 4:126

Busicom, Intel and, 1:107–108

Business Software Alliance (BSA), 3:183, 3:184

Business-to-business e-commerce, 1:43

Business-to-consumer e-commerce, 1:43

Busy tones, long-distance calls, 3:201

Byron, Lord (George Gordon), 1:122, 1:123, 2:159

Bytes
    in coding schemes, 1:77, 1:101, 2:109
    defined, 1:29, 2:9
    multiples, 1:129
    synchronization, 2:9

C

C programming language, 1:78
    development, 2:1, 2:158
    grammar, 2:51
    for parallel architecture, 2:137
    register variables, 2:158
    UNIX and, 2:158
    uses, 1:141, 1:179, 1:208, 2:158, 3:138

C++ programming language, 1:80, 1:179, 1:208, 2:95, 2:128, 4:74

Cable & Wireless, peering agreements, 4:145

Cable modems, 3:113, 4:26–28

Cable systems, 1:191–192, 2:220, 4:166

Cable television, 2:47, 4:25–26, 4:*26*

Cables, conditioned, 2:178

Cache controllers, 2:27–28

Cache memory, 2:**27–29**
    defined, 1:74
    how it works, 2:27–29
    in Madison Itanium processor, 2:28
    problems, 2:28
    and program execution speed, 2:28
    VM and, 2:209–210, 2:*210*

CAD (computer-aided design)
    for agriculture, 3:4
    for architects, 3:16–19, 3:*17*
    automatic layout generation, 3:17
    cost estimates, 3:17
    to create CNC/NC codes, 3:31
    to create prototypes, 3:18
    defined, 2:168
    digitizing, 3:31
    for engineers, 3:16
    for fashion design, 3:91–94, 3:*92*
    H.L. Hunley recovery, 3:32
    history, 3:16
    interfaces and input devices, 3:16, 3:18, 3:30–31, 3:91
    invention, 3:30

for landscapers, 3:5
    manufacturing applications, 3:31, 3:51
    orthogonal projections, 3:93
    for scientific visualization, 3:177–178
    specification documentation, 3:17
    structure and mechanical calculations, 3:17
    supervisory computers for, 2:168
    three-dimensional models, 3:18
    virtual bodies, 3:94

CAD-CAM (computer-aided design-computer-aided manufacture)
    for aircraft design, 3:*30*
    CA engineering, 3:**29–32**
    CNC/NC codes, 3:31
    computerized manufacturing applications, 3:51–52
    as interactive systems, 1:110

CAD (computer-aided design) software
    Adobe Photoshop, 3:18
    AutoCAD, 3:31
    AutoDesk 3D Studio Viz, 3:18
    AutoDesSys Inc., 3:18
    FormZ, 3:18
    IntCAD, 3:32
    Microstation, 3:31
    ProjectBank, 3:18

CADD (computer-aided design and drafting). *See* CAD

CAE (computer-aided engineering), 3:30, 3:32, 3:51

Caesar cipher, 4:50

CAI. *See* Computer-assisted instruction

Calculating devices
    abacuses, 1:**1–2**, 1:*1*, 1:41, 1:53, 2:87
    adding machines, 1:3
    analog computers, 1:2, 1:3–4, 1:41–42, 1:*41*
    differential analyzers, 1:3–5, 1:50–51, 3:162, 4:195
    EAM, 1:187–188
    early, by Intel, 1:134–135
    hand-held, 1:192, 2:34, 4:102
    Hollerith's tabulating machine, 1:84, 1:186, 1:*187*, 1:211, 3:1, 3:59
    Howard Aiken's contributions, 1:59
    HP Model 2116 controller, 3:109
    LOCI, 3:207
    Marchand hand calculators, 4:102
    mechanical, 1:131

Calculating devices (continued)

Napier's bones, 1:**150**

in *Paris in the Twentieth Century*, 4:105

Pascal's contributions, 1:41–42, 1:*41*, 1:165–166, 4:199

slide rules, 1:2, 1:3, 1:*4*, 1:**181–182**

Turing Machine, 1:59, 1:**199–201**, 4:9, 4:11, 4:55

Vannevar Bush's contributions, 1:58

See also Analytical Engine; Difference Engine; ENIAC

Calculus

defined, 1:165

differential equations, 1:3, 1:132

lambda, 1:19, 2:99

Leibnitz's contributions, 1:165

Pascal's contributions, 1:165

predicate, 1:19

California Digital Library, 4:70

California Institute of Technology, JPL, 3:187, 3:188, 4:178

Callback modems, 1:176

Calm computing, 3:84–86

CAM (computer-aided manufacturing), 3:30, 3:31, 3:51–52, 3:93

Cambridge Journals Online, 4:84

Cambridge University

EDSAC project, 1:56–57, 1:62, 1:72

Multiple Access System, 1:175

Camcorders, 2:204, 4:*66*

Cameras

document, 4:86

to record ATM transactions, 3:25, 3:26

television, for computer vision, 4:38–39

Cameras, digital

distinguished from 35-mm cameras, 4:178–179

how they work, 4:179

as input devices, 2:91

Kodak's instructional guides, 4:179

for mobile computing devices, 4:166

multimedia applications, 2:83, 2:85

for PDAs, 2:142

resolution, 4:179

Sony Mavica, 4:178

video, 2:204

See also Digital images; Photography

Campbell, John, 3:20

Cancer, and cell phone use, 3:33, 3:35

Cancer diagnosis and treatment

data mining techniques, 4:60

expert systems tools, 3:88

genetics research, 3:142

imaging tools, 3:117

neural network tools, 3:154–155

pattern recognition tools, 2:139–140, 2:*140*

Canonic and-or implementation, 2:60–61

CANs (controller area networks), 3:5–6

Capacitive sensors, 2:148

Capacitive touch-screen panels, 2:146, 2:200

Capacitors, 1:53, 1:104, 1:129, 2:80, 2:111

CAPP (computer-aided process planning), 3:53–54

Capture Lab, 3:49

Card, Stuart, 4:174

Carlos, Juan, 4:*70*

Carlson, Chester, 1:220, 1:*221*

Carmen San Diego software, 3:82

Carnegie Institute of Technology, decision-making studies, 3:67

Carnegie Mellon University

CERT, 3:*181*, 4:72, 4:148

electronic commerce degree, 4:*78*

Carpal tunnel syndrome (CTS), 1:65, 1:121–122

Carriers, signal, 2:46

Carter, Tom, 2:30

Carterfone decision, 2:30

Cartography, defined, 3:101

CAs (Certificates of Authority), 2:213, 4:24

Cascading Style Sheets (CSS), 2:107, 4:140

Case-based decision-making tools, 3:18

Case-management tools, legal applications, 3:129–130

Case, Steven, 4:98

CASE (computer-aided software engineering) tools, 2:58

Casio

Cassiopeia E-125 PDA, 2:143–144

EM-500 PDA, 2:143–144

GPS wristwatch, 4:*113*

Cassidy, Air Vice-Marshall, 3:56

Castle Wolfenstein, 1:15

CAT (computer-assisted tomography), 3:55–56, 3:57, 3:115, 3:177, 3:*178*

Cat bonds and options, 4:91

Catastrophe insurance, online, 4:91

Catastrophe Risk Exchange (CATEX), 4:91

Catchword, RealPage, 4:83

Cathode ray tubes. *See* CRTs

Cathodes, defined, 1:201

CATV (Community Antenna Television) systems, 1:191–192

CAVE Automated Virtual Environment, 1:204–206

The Caves of Steel, 3:21

CBR (constant bit rate service) service, 2:11–12

CCITT (Consultative Committee for International Telegraphy and Telephony), 1:99–100

CCTV (Closed Circuit Television), 4:118

CD (compact disc) drives, 3:113

CD-R (compact disc-recordable) technology, 2:190

CD-ROMs (compact disc-read only memory)

access to memory, 2:206

for desktop publishing, 3:199

for educational software, 3:83, 4:36

library applications, 3:133

for multimedia, 1:14

for personal computers, 1:137

for reference tools, 3:112–113

SCSI for, 2:54

as storage devices, 2:85, 2:111, 2:190

transistors for, 1:196

WORM technology, 2:190

CD-RWs (addressing rewriteable CDs), 3:113, 4:127

CDC (Centers for Disease Control and Prevention), 3:27

CDC (Control Data Corporation), 1604 and 6600 computers, 3:57

CDCM Computer Music Series, 1:149

CDMA (code division multiple access) standard, 2:32, 3:34

CDPD (cellular digital packet data), 4:166

CDs (compact discs)

for distance learning, 3:77

invention, 1:164

as multimedia, 2:83

mylar for, 2:189

sound compression, 2:183

CDS2000E Enterprise Server, 4:5

Cedeno, Judy, 4:96

Cell addresses, 1:*131*

Cell Delay Variation (CDV), 2:12

Cell Loss Priority (CLP) connections, 4:18

Cell phones, 3:**32–35**
  code division multiplexing, 3:34
  combined with PDAs, 3:*34*, 3:*35*, 4:166
  digital standards, 3:33–34
  first generation, 3:33
  frequency division multiplexing, 3:33
  frequency reuse, 3:32–33
  GSM standard, 2:32, 3:33–34, 4:49
  hackers' access to, 4:123
  health risks, 3:33, 3:35
  HLRs, 3:33, 3:201–202
  and information overload, 4:133
  instant messaging, 3:34–35, 4:193
  microbrowsers, 3:34
  mobility management, 3:33
  as PCs, 2:32
  personalization techniques, 4:135
  second generation, 3:33–34
  sub-bands, 3:33
  telephony, 3:201–202
  third generation (3G), 2:47, 3:34, 3:87
  VLRs, 3:201–202
  web-enabled, 4:131
  See also Telephones/telephone systems

Cells, ATM transmission, 1:155–156, 2:10–11, 4:17

Cellular automata, 4:9

Cellular digital packet data (CDPD), 4:166

Cellular neural networks (CNNs), 4:171

Cellular technology, 2:**29–32**
  algorithms for handoff process, 2:30
  AMPS, 2:30, 2:31–32
  Bell Labs' contributions, 2:30
  cell system interconnections, 2:30
  communication channels, 2:30
  digital, 2:31–32
  FCC rulings, 2:30
  invention, 1:190
  microwave links, 2:*203*
  MPS, 2:29–30
  for PDAs, 2:142
  PSTN, 2:29–30
  regulations, 2:31
  simplex and duplex systems, 2:29–30
  SMART system, 2:*31*

standards, 2:32
  telephone display lighting, 2:67
  as wireless, 2:219, 2:221
  See also Wireless technology

CEN (Council on European Normalization), 1:100

Censorship, 4:**31–34**
  arguments for and against, 4:32, 4:34
  distinguished from selection, 4:31–32
  vs. free speech, 4:32, 4:33–34, 4:101–102, 4:132
  hate speech, 4:*33*, 4:101–102
  host blocking, 4:32
  intent of, 4:31–32
  international, 4:33–34, 4:101–102
  keyword blocking, 4:32
  organizations to monitor, 4:34
  protocol filtering, 4:32

CenStats system, 1:32–33

Census Bureau (U.S.), 1:**31–34**, 1:*33*
  data analysis tools, 1:32–34, 1:211
  history, 1:31, 1:32
  information on Internet, 1:32–34
  punched cards, 1:32, 1:81, 1:83, 1:84, 1:88, 1:186, 2:93, 3:1, 3:59, 4:126
  2000 census, 1:84
  UNIVAC purchaser, 2:73

Center for Democracy and Technology, 1:168, 4:34

Center for Molecular Modeling, 4:36–37

Centers for Disease Control and Prevention (CDC), 3:27

Central Intelligence Agency. *See* CIA

Central processing units. *See* CPUs

Centre for English Cultural Tradition and Language, 4:207

CENTREX service, 2:213

Centronics connectors, 2:178

Cerf, Vinton, 4:*203*

CERN (European Organization for Nuclear Research)
  Enquire program, 4:92
  web server software, 3:157

CERT (Computer Emergency Response Team), 3:*181*, 4:72, 4:148

Certificates, defined, 4:83

Certificates of Authority (CAs), 2:213, 4:24

CESAR body research study, 1:*82*

Chads, hanging, 4:183

Challenger space shuttle, 3:187, 4:103–104

Channel Tunnel, Ada programming, 2:159

Channels, mainframe, 1:127

Chaos theory, defined, 4:57

Character-based interfaces, 3:203

Charting data, 3:192–193, 3:*192*

Chat rooms
  client/server models, 2:38
  for distance learning, 3:77
  as home entertainment, 4:124
  instant messaging, 4:140
  political applications, 4:182

Check scanning, MICR technology, 2:134

Checksum, defined, 2:120, 3:180

Chemdex, 4:80

Chemistry, 4:**34–37**
  computational, 4:36, 4:37
  computer sciences training, 4:35–37
  database management, 4:36–37
  DENDRAL, 3:88, 3:124
  equation engines, 4:35
  Internet resources, 4:36–37
  mass spectrometry analyses, 3:88, 4:36
  mathematical principles, 4:34–35
  molecular modeling, 4:*35*, 4:36
  nanocomputing, 4:**169–172**
  online conferences, 4:36
  periodic table and comic book history, 4:37
  physics principles, 4:34–35
  teaching tools, 3:164, 4:35–36
  thermodynamic calculations, 3:158
  user interfaces, 3:205

Chemometrics, 4:36

Chen, Steven, 3:58

Chernikov, S.N., 4:119

Chess playing, computerized, 3:**35–38**
  Alan Turing and, 3:37
  Allen Newell and, 4:173
  Claude Shannon and, 3:37, 4:196
  heuristic-based searches, 1:20
  history, 3:37
  how it works, 3:35–36, 3:*36*
  ICCA, 3:37
  on Internet, 3:37–38
  KAISSA, 3:37
  Kasparov vs. IBM Deep Blue, 1:23, 1:*70*, 2:*89*, 3:37
  Konrad Zuse's and, 2:222
  variables, 3:35–36

Chess playing, traditional, 3:35

Chicago Mercantile Exchange, 4:*89*

Children
BASIC programming language, 2:157
deaf, teaching, 2:17
e-books for, 4:77
expert systems tools, 3:88
language learning, 1:20
Logo programming language, 2:101–104
See also Education

China
abacus, 1:1–2, 1:*1*, 2:87
binary number system, 1:30
early automatons, 1:169
ISP registration, 4:33
national intranet, 4:152
software piracy, 3:184

Chip manufacturing, 3:**38–41**
"bunny suits," 3:*39*, 4:167
economics, 2:61, 3:40–41
manufacturing process, 2:15
micro-wire bonding, 2:*62*
molecular computing, 4:**167–169**
nanocomputing, 4:**169–172**
parallel vs. serial processes, 4:171–172
photomask processing, 3:38–39, 4:45
silicon processing, 1:105–106, 1:133, 1:194–195, 3:38, 3:39
sterile environments, 3:*39*, 4:167
transistor gate fabrication, 3:39–40
See also Microchips/microprocessors

Cholesteric displays, 2:66, 2:67, 2:68
Chomsky, Noam, 2:2
Chowning, John, 1:149, 2:116, 3:146
CHRISTMA EXEC worm, 1:208
A Christmas Carol, 3:59
Chromatic dispersion, 2:76, 2:77
Church, Alonzo, 1:197, 1:200, 2:99, 3:121
CIA (Central Intelligence Agency)
global surveillance, 4:117
magnetic tape storage, 2:*92*
network design, 2:*118*
CICS (Customer Information Control System), 1:127
Cigarette consumption, economic modeling example, 3:78–80
CIM (computer integrated manufacturing), 3:54
Cinderella, 1:12
CinemaScope, 1:12
Ciphers
Caesar, 4:50

defined, 4:50
polyalphabetic, 4:50–51
transposition, 4:49, 4:51
Circle-of operations paradigms, in system analysis, 2:194
Circuit board manufacturing, CAD-CAM application, 3:31
Circuit level firewalls. See Transport layer firewalls
Circuit-switched networks, 1:154, 2:10
Circuits design, Boolean algebra and, 2:22–23, 2:*22*, 2:*23*
Cirrus ATM network, 3:25
Cisco Systems, 3:45, 4:152
Citizens' Band radio, 3:103
Citizens Radio Corporation, 3:103
CIX (Commercial Internet Exchange), 4:145, 4:149
Cladding, of optical fiber, 2:75–76
Claris Works, 3:119
Clark, Joan, 1:199
Clarke, Arthur C., 3:21, 4:92
Class vs. object, in object-oriented languages, 2:126
Classifiers
defined, 2:138
labeled and training data, 2:139–140
Claymation, 1:10
Client/server technology, 2:**35–39**
for chat rooms, 2:38
concurrent models, 2:37–38
design issues, 2:39
distributed computing systems, 2:35–36, 2:39
for electronic library catalogs, 3:132
iterative models, 2:36–37
protocols, 2:36–37, 2:38–39
server process, 2:36
three-tier systems, 2:38
for web servers, 2:38
Clients
DBMS, 2:186
defined, 2:36, 4:27
Clinton, Bill, 1:50, 2:*175*, 4:182
CLIs. See Command-line systems
A Close Shave, 1:10
Closed Circuit Television (CCTV), 4:118
Clothing design. See Fashion design
CLP (Cell Loss Priority) connections, 4:18
Cluster analysis, 4:60
CMN (Common Music Notation), 3:145

CMOS (complementary metal oxide semiconductor)
function, 1:130
how it works, 3:38
for mainframes, 1:125
manufacturing process, 3:38–39
size reductions, 4:170
for spacecraft computers, 1:153, 3:187
CMYK color gamut, 2:151, 4:66
CNC/NC (computer numeric control/numeric control) codes, 3:31
CNet search engine, 1:219
CNNs (cellular neural networks), defined, 4:171
Co-located applications. See Synchronous/co-located applications
Coaxial cables (co-ax), 2:75, 2:201, 4:25, 4:*26*
COBOL programming language
characters in ASCII, 2:41
DATA division, 2:156
development, 2:156
ENVIRONMENT division, 2:156
Frances Holberton and, 1:63
Grace Hopper and, 1:85, 1:86, 2:156
IDENTIFICATION division, 2:156
ISAM, 2:156
for mainframes, 1:127
Microsoft and, 1:137
for music, 2:114
object-oriented features, 2:156
PROCEDURE division, 2:156
for second-generation computers, 1:72
for third-generation computers, 1:78
version 74, 2:156
Code-breaking. See Cryptography
Code division multiple access (CDMA) standard, 2:32, 3:34
Code Red worm, 3:*181*, 4:*108*
Codes, 2:**40–42**
ASCII, 2:41, 2:42
Baudot's, 2:40–41, 2:*46*
BCDIC, 2:41
binary, 2:42, 2:108–109
block, 2:42, 2:*43*, 2:44
C-10, 1:85
copyrights for, 4:45
EBCDIC, 1:*131*, 2:41, 2:109
Enigma, 1:54, 4:51
error-correcting, 1:27, 2:44–45, 2:*44*

event-handling functions, 1:112–113

FIELDATA, 2:41

Hamming, 2:45

Hollerith, 2:92

ITA₂, 2:41

machine-dependent, 2:51

machine-independent, 2:52

malicious, 4:72

mnemonic, 1:76, 2:51

operation, 1:77

pseudo-random, 4:113

pseudocode, 2:57, 2:162

scanning, 1:120, 2:91

symbol probabilities, 2:42–44

uniquely decodeable, 2:44

universal, 2:42

variable length, 2:43–44

See also Bar codes; DNA; DNA computers; Morse Code

Coding techniques, 2:**42–45**

code efficiency, 2:42–44

code robustness, 2:44–45

mathematical principles, 3:138

Cognitive, defined, 3:151

CoLab project, 3:49

Cold War

computer applications, 1:57

and economy, 3:58

Collaborative work systems, 1:158–159

Collating machines, 1:185

Collation services, 4:193

College of William and Mary, computer technologies, 3:*131*

Color printing. *See* Printing, color

Colorado, cybercafes, 4:55

Colossus (Colossus—The Forbin Project), 4:105

Colossus computer, 1:54–55, 1:59, 1:71, 4:51

Columbia School of Mines, 1:84

Columbia University, sound synthesis research, 2:116

Columbine School massacre, 1:68

COM (computer output microfilm) devices, 2:152

Command and Conquer game, 1:70

Command-line systems (CLIs), 1:110–112, 2:130, 3:130, 4:128, 4:205

Commerce (traditional), vs. e-commerce, 1:45–47

Commercial Data Servers, 4:5

Commercial Internet Exchange (CIX), 4:145, 4:149

Commercial Translator programming language, 2:156

Committee on Women in Computing, 1:23

Commodities, defined, 3:137, 4:3

Commodities markets, 4:88

Commodore

Amiga, 1:14

PET, 1:36

Common Business Oriented Language. *See* COBOL programming language

Common Music Notation (CMN), 3:145

Common Object Request Broker Architecture (CORBA) model, 2:39

Communication channels

defined, 4:136

encoding techniques, 4:137–138

for mobile telephones, 2:30

noise and errors, 4:136–137

See also Bandwidth

Communication devices, 2:**45–48**

See also Cellular technology; Internet; Modems; Satellite technology; Telephones/telephone systems

Communications Act (1995 and 1996), 4:192

Communications privacy, 1:166

Community Antenna Television (CATV) systems, 1:191–192

Compact disc-read only memory. *See* CD-ROMs

Compact disc-recordable (CD-R) technology, 2:190

Compact discs. *See* CDs

Companding, to digitize sound, 2:182–183, 2:*183*

Compaq, compatibility issues, 2:50

Compatibility

defined, 2:48

of electrical interfaces, 2:48–49, 2:53

Compatibility (open systems design), 2:**48–50**

Apple computers' lack of, 1:17, 1:36

computer system interfaces, 2:48–50, 2:**52–55**

infrastructures, 2:*49*

standards, 1:89–90, 2:48–49

types of, 2:49

upgradability and portability, 2:49–50

Wang computers' lack of, 3:207

Compatible Time Sharing System, 1:175

Compiled, defined, 4:*155*

Compiled executable code, defined, 4:208

Compiler compilers, 2:2

Compiler theory, 2:2–3

Compilers, 2:**50–52**

A-0, 1:86

B-0 (Flow-Matic), 1:86

defined, 1:141, 2:2

front and back ends, 2:51–52

lexical analyzer, 2:50–51

machine-dependent and -independent phases, 2:51–52

for minicomputers, 1:141

programming languages, 1:78–79, 2:2, 2:128, 2:153, 2:154, 2:158

role of registers, 2:51

syntactic analyzer, 2:50–51

Complementary metal oxide semiconductor. *See* CMOS

Complex Number Computer, 1:51

Components, in object-oriented languages, 2:127

Composition houses, function, 3:71

Composition, music. *See* Music composition

Compound documents, 3:119–120

Compression

of digital images, 4:67

mathematical principles, 3:138

MP3, 2:184

of sound signals, 2:183–184

utilities, 3:112

of video images, 2:204, 3:96–97, 4:88

Compression standards. *See* JPEG; MPEG

CompuServe

e-mail communications, 1:218

Internet browser, 4:28

routing, 4:*186*

Computational astrophysics, 3:23

Computational chemistry, 4:36, 4:37

Computational steering, 3:177

Computer-aided design (drafting). *See* CAD

Computer-aided design-computer-aided manufacture. *See* CAD-CAM

Computer-aided engineering (CAE), 3:30, 3:32, 3:51

Computer-aided manufacturing. *See* CAM

Computer-aided process planning (CAPP), 3:53–54

Computer-aided software engineering (CASE) tools, 2:58

Computer-assisted instruction (CAI), 3:**41–44**
  in biology, 3:164
  in chemistry, 3:164
  e-learning, 3:41
  educational software, 3:**80–83**
  electronic books, 3:43
  for engineers, 3:159
  EPSS, 3:43–44
  history of, 3:41
  integrated with traditional curriculum, 3:*42*
  LMSs, 3:41
  in mathematics, 3:138
  in physics, 3:164
  SCORM standard, 3:42
  See also Distance learning
Computer-assisted reporting, 4:161
Computer-assisted tomography (computed tomography). *See* CAT
Computer Associates, 4:96
Computer bugs
  debugging, 1:78, 1:203, 2:39, 2:101, 2:162, 4:100
  defined, 2:161
  origin of term, 1:53, 1:85, 1:*86*
Computer Cantata, 3:145
Computer consultants, 1:39
Computer Emergency Response Team (CERT), 3:*181*, 4:72, 4:148
Computer Fraud and Abuse Act of 1986, 1:**34–38**
  1984 Act, 1:34–35
  Morris worm, 1:35, 1:37
  necessity for, 1:34, 1:36–37
  offenses and penalties, 1:35–36
  Robert Morris, 1:*35*
Computer integrated manufacturing (CIM), 3:54
Computer magazine, 1:104
Computer Music Series, 1:149
Computer numeric control/numeric control codes (CNC/NC), 3:31
Computer output microfilm (COM) devices, 2:152
Computer ownership, statistics, 1:33
Computer professionals, 1:**38–40**, 3:**44–47**, 3:*46*
  ACM's support, 1:**21–24**
  background for, 1:38, 1:39
  in bioinformatics, 3:45
  characteristics of good, 2:161–163, 2:*161*
  as computer security consultants, 4:124
  and current economy, 3:44–45

  in distance learning technologies, 3:77
  educational requirements, 1:39, 3:45
  ethics, 4:**99–102**
  hacking by, 4:121–122
  as hardware engineers, 3:45–46
  as IT specialists, 3:47
  job outlook, 1:40
  multimedia development careers, 2:84
  as programmers, 3:46–47
  as software developers, 3:47
  specialties, 1:38–39
  women as, 1:63
  See also specific computer scientists and programmers
Computer Professionals for Social Responsibility, 4:34
Computer-related crimes, 1:34–37, 1:49–50
  See also Hacking/hackers
Computer Scale Company, 1:186
Computer Science: A First Course, 3:159
Computer science academic programs
  Cisco Systems, 3:45
  curriculum recommendations, 1:21–22, 1:103
  electronic teaching aids, 4:86, 4:88
  ethics education, 4:**99–102**
  Harvard Computational Laboratory, 1:60
  MIT, 3:45
  study materials, 3:159
Computer Sciences Accreditation Board, 1:22
Computer Security Act (1987), 1:168
Computer security and privacy. *See* Privacy; Security
Computer Society (IEEE). *See* IEEE: Computer Society
Computer Space game, 1:67
Computer supported cooperative work (CSCW), 3:**47–50**
  application domains, 3:48–49
  evolution of, 3:47–48
  synchronous/co-located applications, 3:49–50
  technologies, 3:49
Computer system interfaces, 2:**52–55**
  AGP, 2:54–55
  Centronics connectors, 2:178
  compatibility, 2:48–50
  computer-based systems, 2:48–50

  Cyberspace Data Monitoring System, 2:*53*
  DB-25, 2:178
  with I/O devices, 2:52–54
  parallel-to-serial conversion, 2:177
  protocols, 2:54
  SCSI, 2:54
  serial-to-parallel conversions, 2:177
  standards, 2:53–54
  UARTs, 2:177
  USB, 2:54
Computer vision, 4:**37–40**
  depth perception, 4:38
  digitizing images, 4:38–39, 4:67–68
  edge-detection, 4:39
  frame grabbers, 4:39
  image extraction and recognition, 4:39–40
  image pre-processors, 4:39
  image segmentation, 4:39
  lens adjustment, 4:38
  light-sensing capabilities, 4:38
  manufacturing applications, 4:40
  and pattern recognition, 4:40
  training templates, 4:40
  for visually impaired persons, 4:40
  See also Robotics/robots
Computerized manufacturing, 3:**50–55**, 3:*52*
  CAD, 3:51
  CAE, 3:51
  CAPP, 3:53–54
  CIM, 3:54
  embedded computers, 3:52, 3:53
  flexible manufacturing systems, 3:52–53
  minicomputers for, 1:140
  robots for, 1:170, 1:171–172, 2:166, 3:53
  simulator applications, 1:180
Computerized reservation systems. *See* CRSs
Computing Scale Company of America, 1:88
Computing-Tabulating-Recording Company (CTR), 1:84, 1:88, 1:186, 1:211
Computing time, selling, 2:45–46
Concatenates, defined, 4:156
Concentric, 2:75, 2:189
Conceptualization, defined, 2:194
Concurrency control, of databases, 2:186–187

Concurrent client server models, 2:37–38

Concurrent, defined, 2:37

Conductors, properties of, 1:132
See also Semiconductors

Cones
of eyes, 4:38
in sound devices, 2:181–182

Confidentiality. *See* Privacy

Configuration files, 1:175

Conflict probe algorithms, 3:12

Conforming negatives, video editing, 3:97–98

Confucianism, and binary number system, 1:30

Connection Machine, 2:136

Connection-oriented technologies, 2:10

Conservation. *See* Environmental sciences/protection

Consolidated Rail Corporation, computer conversion, 3:174–175

Constant bit rate (CBR) service, 2:11–12

Constitution (U.S.)
on censorship, 4:32, 4:101, 4:132
Commerce Clause, 1:35

Consultative Committee for International Telegraphy and Telephony (CCITT), 1:99–100

Contemporary Legend, 4:207

Continental Airlines, online reservations, 3:15

Control Data Corporation (CDC), 1604 and 6600 computers, 3:57

Control units, role in CPU, 2:6, 2:32

Control Video Corp., Gameline game, 1:69–70

Controller area networks (CANs), 3:5–6

Convergence, Internet strategy, 4:149

Convergence Sublayer (CS), 4:20

Conversational programming language, 2:101

Conversions (computer), problems created by, 3:174–175

Convex hull algorithms, 3:101

Conway, John, 4:9–10

Cookies, 4:**40–43**
disabling, 1:168, 4:42
and e-commerce, 4:40–41
passwords in, 4:42
privacy issues, 4:42
and search engines, 4:42
and web pages, 4:41–42, 4:156

"Cool factor," of computer learning systems, 3:42, 3:83

Copernicus, Earth-centric model, 1:18

COPS security software, 3:181

Copy machines, Xerox, 1:220–221, 1:*221*

Copying tools, integrated software, 3:119

Copyrights, 4:**43–46**
Apple vs. Microsoft, 1:138
on bioinformatics software, 3:143–144
copy distinguished from work, 4:45–46
defined, 4:176
and digital art, 4:8
digital copying, 4:43–44, 4:127
and digital libraries, 3:132, 4:71
establishing, 4:44–45
ethical principles, 4:*100*
fair dealing privileges, 4:44
fair use privileges, 4:43–44
Free BSD, 3:156
illegal sound recordings, 2:184–185, 4:43, 4:*44*, 4:205
information access and, 4:132
as intellectual property, 1:36, 4:46
international, Berne Convention, 4:46
materials covered/not covered, 4:45
periods of control, 4:43
preventing unauthorized use, 4:46
registering, 4:45
rights of reproduction, 4:43
and software piracy, 3:183–185
SPCA, 4:45
unfixed works, 4:45
See also Intellectual property; Patents

CORBA (Common Object Request Broker Architecture) model, 2:39

Core memory
An Wang's contributions, 3:207
government research grants, 1:82
invention, 1:57

Corel software
Draw, 3:169
Photopaint, 3:169, 4:67
VENTURA, 1:157, 3:169, 3:197
WordPerfect, 3:167
WordPerfect Office, 3:110
WordPerfect Works, 3:170

Cormack, Alan, 3:**55–57**, 3:*55*

Corn, genetically engineered, 3:143

Cornell University, in Internet history, 4:142

"The Corpse in the Car," 4:206

Corpus programs, 1:37

Correlation analyses, 4:60–61

Correspondence courses. *See* Distance learning

Cosine functions, 1:96, 2:46

Cosmology, supercomputers to study, 3:22

Council on European Normalization (CEN), 1:100

Counterfeit Access Device and Computer Fraud and Abuse Act of 1984 (1984 Act), 1:34–35

Counterfeit software, 3:183–184

Course, in aircraft navigation, 3:7

Courtroom proceedings
electronic transcripts, 3:130
paperless trials, 3:130–131

Covering tracks, by hackers, 3:105

Cowcatchers, invention of, 1:26

CPUs (central processing units), 2:**32–35**
access to ROM data, 2:111
ALUs, 2:6, 2:32
and animation technology, 1:14
buffers, 2:6
cache memory, 2:**27–29**
computational steering and, 3:177
control units, 2:6, 2:32
defined, 1:141, 2:5, 3:41, 4:5
differences among, 2:7
for games, 1:181
graphic devices' use of, 2:82
integrated circuit technology, 1:74
for Intel microprocessors, 2:34–35
interaction with RAM, 2:32
machine code instructions, 2:6–7
of Madison Itanium processor, 2:28
for mainframes, 1:127
memory managers, 2:111–112
processor managers, 2:129
registers, 2:5–6, 2:32, 2:33, 2:51
role in computer, 2:5, 2:32
for security hardware, 2:172–173
silicon chips, 1:74
speed vs. I/O device speed, 2:52
for supercomputers, 1:182
synchronization, 2:33
transistor-based, 2:33
vacuum tubes in, 2:33
for video editing, 3:96

CRACK security software, 3:181, 3:182

Crackers, distinguished from hackers, 3:104, 4:123
Cratchit, Bob, 3:59
Crawls, defined, 3:209
Cray computers
    Cray-1, 1:*183*, 3:57–58
    Cray-2, 3:58
    Cray-3, 3:58
    Cray-X MP, 3:58
    parallel processors, 2:135
Cray Research, 3:57–58
Cray, Seymour, 3:**57–59**
CRC (cyclical redundancy check) coder, 2:120
Creature Comforts, 1:10
Credit cards
    fraud, 4:48
    hackers' access to, 3:104, 3:105
    for Internet shopping, 3:26
    magnetic stripe technology, 3:**134–136**
    online applications for, 4:48–49
    pattern recognition to prevent fraud, 2:141
    receipt printing, 2:150
    smart cards, 2:*165*
Credit, defined, 4:47
Credit information
    1984 Act provisions, 1:34
    access to credit reports, 4:48–49
    ratings of consumers, 4:48–49
Credit online, 4:**46–49**
    BBB endorsements, 4:48
    eBay's reputation system, 4:47–48
    fraud, statistics, 4:48
    ratings of online retailers, 4:47–48
Crik, Francis, 4:36
Crookes, Sir William, 1:201
Crop production software, 3:4–5
Cross-platform, defined, 3:49
Crossbar switching, 4:171
Crossroads magazine, 1:23
CRSs (computerized reservation systems), 3:14–15
CRT-based word processors, 3:211
CRTs (cathode ray tubes)
    vs. AMLCDs, 2:68
    for ATM displays, 3:25
    color, 2:63–64
    defined, 1:56, 3:25
    for digitizing tablets, 2:198
    disadvantages, 2:64
    how they work, 2:63
    interlace scanning, 2:63
    invention, 1:188

for memory systems, 1:56, 1:62
for minicomputers, 1:141
monochrome, 2:63
for PPIs, 3:12
progressive scanning, 2:63
shadow mask, 2:63–64
in Sketchpad display, 3:30
vacuum tubes in, 1:203
Cryptanalysis, defined, 4:49
Crypto iButton, 2:173–174
Cryptographic machines, 1:54, 1:59, 1:71, 4:*50*
Cryptography, 4:**49–53**
    Alan Turing's contributions, 1:54, 1:59, 1:198
    as authentication tool, 4:21, 4:22, 4:127
    automatic, 4:51
    ciphers, 1:175, 4:49, 4:50–51
    cryptosystems, 1:176, 2:173–174
    decoding machines, 1:53–55, 1:71
    defined, 1:43, 2:213, 3:138
    DES, 4:51–52
    digital signatures, 1:175, 4:52, 4:**71–73**
    for e-banking, 4:74
    for e-books, 4:76
    for e-commerce, 1:44–45
    encryption, 4:21, 4:72, 4:127
    end-to-end, 2:213
    Enigma, 1:54, 4:51
    to ensure privacy, 1:168, 2:213
    history, 4:49–51
    Internet and, 4:49
    keys, 4:49–50
    magnetic stripe cards, 3:134
    military applications, 4:*50*, 4:51
    Navajo Code Talkers, 4:51
    one-time pads, 4:51
    PLI, 2:213
    polyalphabetic ciphers, 4:50–51
    polyalphabetic substitution systems, 4:51
    private key cryptosystems, 4:52
    public key cryptosystems, 1:175, 1:176, 2:174, 4:52
    Purple cryptosystem, 4:51
    radio communications and, 4:51
    Rijndael algorithm, 4:52
    rotor machines, 4:51
    transformation algorithms, 4:49
    tunnel mode, 2:213
Crystal graphics software, 3:169
CS (Convergence Sublayer), 4:20
CSCWs. *See* Computer Supported Cooperative Works
CSNET, 4:144, 4:148

CSOUND, 3:146
CSS (Cascading Style Sheets), 2:107, 4:140
CT-scanning, 3:56
CTR. *See* Computing-Tabulating-Recording Company
CTS (carpal tunnel syndrome), 1:65, 1:121–122
Cuban Missile Crisis, 4:115
Cuneiform, defined, 4:49
Cursors, pointing and position-indicator, 2:144–145
CUseeMe software, 3:77
Customer Information Control System (CICS), 1:127
Cut (work) prints, 1:10
Cute FTP, 4:205
Cutout animation, 1:10
Cutting tools, integrated software, 3:119
CXS Railroad, GPS technology, 3:174
Cybercafes, 4:**53–55**, 4:*54*, 4:*139*
Cyberia cybercafe, 4:53
Cybernetics, 4:**55–58**
    artificial intelligence and, 4:57
    benefits of, 4:57–58
    defined, 3:160
    distinguished from Newtonian view, 4:56–57
    history, 4:55
    human body as machine, 4:57
    Institute of Cybernetics, 4:119
    neural modeling, 4:57
    Norbert Wiener and, 4:55–56, 4:*56*
    origin of term, 4:56
    recursive functions, 3:160
    and robots, 4:58
    Soul Catcher, 4:57
    Victor Glushkov and, 4:119
CyberPatrol filter, 4:32
Cyberpunk, 4:106
CyberSitter filter, 4:32
Cyberspace Data Monitoring System, 2:*53*
Cybertherapy, 3:140
Cyclical redundancy check coder (CRC), 2:120
Cycloids, Pascal's contributions, 1:165
Cyclotrons, Harvard, 3:55

D

Da Vinci Surgical System, 2:168
DACs (digital to analog conversions), 1:42, 1:148, 2:114–115, 3:146

Daguerreotypes, Samuel Morse and, 2:114

Daisywheel printers, 2:152

Dalai Lama, 1:*116*

D'Albe, Fournier, 2:132

Dallas Semiconductor, Crypto iButton, 2:173–174

Dangling string network monitors, 3:84–86

Dante II telerobot, 1:*172*

Dark fiber, for fiber optics, 2:76, 2:78

DARPA (Defense Advanced Research Projects Agency), 1:81, 1:115, 1:218

Dartmouth University
BASIC programming language, 2:2
John Kemeny and, 3:121

DAT (digital audio tape), 2:188, 2:190

Data
defined, 4:58
integrity of, 4:62
meta, 4:58
nonoperational, 4:58
operational (transactional), 4:58

Data acquisition, minicomputers for, 1:140

Data Definition Language (DDL), 2:185

Data Encryption Standard (DES), 4:51–52

Data entry systems. *See* Input devices

Data Extraction System (DES), 1:32

Data flow diagrams (DFDs), 2:197

Data General, minicomputer manufacturing, 1:141

Data gloves, for multimedia systems, 2:85

Data hiding, in object-oriented languages, 2:126

Data-link layer frames, 2:26–27

Data manipulation instructions, 2:32–33

Data Manipulation Language (DML), 2:185–186

Data mining, 4:**58–63**
by American Express, 1:167, 4:59
artificial intelligence and, 4:60
association models, 4:62
by Blockbuster, 1:167, 4:59
cluster analysis, 4:60
of computerized reservation systems, 3:15
correlation, 4:60–61
costs, 4:62
data integrity and, 4:62

for data warehouse systems, 4:65
decision trees, 4:61
defined, 1:113, 2:135, 3:64
factor analysis, 4:61
internal and external factors, 4:59
linear regression, 4:60
mailing lists, 4:148
Market Basket, 4:62
marketing applications, 4:59–60, 4:62
by National Basketball Association, 4:62
neural network tools, 4:62
pattern recognition tools, 2:141
vs. privacy, 1:167–168, 4:62, 4:79
scientific and medical applications, 4:60
and scientific visualization, 3:178
by supercomputers, 1:184–185, 2:135
by WalMart, 4:60
See also Statistical analyses

Data partitioning, defined, 2:39

Data processing, 3:**59–61**
analog-digital conversions, 1:42
automatic, 2:69
batch, 3:14
by Census Bureau, 1:31–34, 3:59
history, 3:59
IBM's early contributions, 1:89
political information, 4:183–184
punched cards for, 1:83–84
Sabre system, 3:14–15
software for, 3:60
transaction, 3:14
for weather forecasting, 3:59, 3:*60*

Data recorders, 1:188

Data reduction techniques, 4:60, 4:61

Data sampling, for scientific visualization, 3:179

Data scanners. *See* Scanners

Data structures, 2:125

Data transfer instructions, 2:32–33

Data visualization, 3:**61–64**
filter queries, 3:62
histograms (bar charts), 3:61, 3:*62*
history, 3:61
maps, geographical, 3:61
mathematical principles, 3:138–139
multidimensional (VIBE), 3:62–63
for online presentations, 3:62
pie charts, 3:61, 3:63

pitfalls in using, 3:63–64
scatterplots, 3:61
spreadsheet data, 3:61
time series, 3:61
See also Scientific visualization

Data warehousing, 4:**63–65**
Amazon.com, 4:*64*
applications, 4:63
data mining and, 4:65
defined, 3:67
distinguished from on-demand approaches, 4:63
for distributed, closed systems, 4:64–65
for monolithic systems, 4:64
multi-tier architecture, 4:65
online analytic processing, 4:65
software tools, 4:65
for unrelated sources, 4:65
updating database, 4:63–64

Database administrators, role of, 3:66

Database management software, 3:**64–67**
Access, 3:60, 3:66, 3:169
FileMaker Pro, 3:66, 3:169
Informix, 3:194
Ingres, 3:194
MySQL, 3:60
Oracle, 2:42, 3:60, 3:66, 3:132, 3:169, 3:194
RDB, 3:194
SQL Server, 3:66, 3:169
Sybase, 3:194

Database management systems (DBMSs)
for chemistry, 4:36–37
concurrency control, 2:186
for e-banking, 4:74
function, 2:185–186, 3:60, 3:169
for GIS, 3:99, 3:101
locking, 2:186–187
lost update problems, 2:186
online credit information, 4:48
SCHOOL, example, 3:194–195, 3:*194*
SQL, 1:79, 2:**185–187**, 3:65, 3:**194–196**
to track students, 3:169, 3:194
for video editing, 3:97

Databases
art-related, 4:8
of astronomic data, 3:22–23
authentication to access, 4:21
compatibility issues, 2:49
data partitioning, 2:39
DB/2 subsystem, 1:127

Databases (continued)
defined, 3:60
DIALOG, 1:93
document processing, 2:69
for DSSs, 3:69
functions, 2:185, 3:194, 3:196
for GPS receivers, 3:151
for groupware, 3:170
IMS subsystems, 1:127
information privacy and,
1:166–168
information retrieval, 1:**92–97**,
2:88
Internet access to, 3:64
LEXIS-NEXIS, 1:93
library applications, 3:132–133
linking agents, 4:1–2
medical applications, 3:27, 3:140,
3:144
MEDLARS, 1:93
MEDLINE, 1:93
micromarketing software, 1:167
railroad applications, 3:173–174
relational, 3:60, 3:65, 3:101,
3:132, 3:194, 4:63, 4:151–152
relational organization, 2:86
and scientific visualization, 3:179
security and privacy issues,
3:66–67, 3:140
spatial, 3:101
spreadsheet functions, 3:192–193
structure, 3:65
uses, 3:64
See also Knowledge-based systems
Day traders, 4:90
DB/2 subsystem, 1:127
DB-25 interface standard, 2:178
DBMSs. *See* Database management
systems
DCOM (Distributed Component
Object Model), 2:39
DDL (Data Definition Language),
2:185
DDoS (Distributed Denial of Ser-
vice), 3:180
De facto, defined, 1:99, 2:37, 3:112
De Forest, Lee, 1:71, 1:*201*, 1:202
De jure, defined, 1:99
De Morgan, Augustus, 1:123
Dead Reckoning, 1:15
Deafness, Alexander Graham Bell
and, 2:16–17
Death Race game, 1:68
Deathtrap Dungeon, 1:15
Debit cards, vs. ATM use, 3:26
Debugging, 1:53
defined, 1:203, 2:101

high-level languages, 1:78
modules, 2:162
parallel processing, 2:39
of software, ethics, 4:100
tools, lack of, 2:101
See also Computer bugs
DEC. *See* Digital Equipment Corporation
Decibel, origin of term, 2:17
Decimal (base-10) number system,
1:29–30, 1:42, 1:55
Decision support systems (DSS),
2:88, 3:**67–70**
active mode, 3:68–69
applications, 3:67, 3:70
for architects, 3:18
for business and finance, 3:68
-case based, 3:18
for crop production, 3:4–5
decision models, 2:196–197
DXplain, 3:68
as equipment selection tools, 3:5
fuzzy logic, 3:4, 3:90
generative, 3:18
GIS tools, 3:101
Herbert Simon's contributions,
4:197–198
history, 3:67
inference engines, 3:69
knowledge bases, 3:69, 3:123–124
for livestock and poultry production, 3:4–5
manufacturing applications, 3:68
medical applications, 3:68–69,
3:69
passive mode, 3:68–69
performance analysis, 3:18
under certainty and under uncertainty, 3:69
user interfaces, 3:69
See also Expert systems
Decision trees, 2:141, 2:196, 4:61
*The Decline and Fall of the Roman
Empire*, 3:19
Decoding machines. *See* Cryptogra-
phy
Decompression utilities, 2:204,
3:112
Dede, Chris, 1:205
Defense Advanced Research Projects
Agency. *See* DARPA
Defined document type definition
(DTD), 2:105–106, 2:107
Definiteness of algorithms, 2:3
Deformations, defined, 3:51
Degrade, defined, 3:89, 4:178
Degrees of freedom, of aircraft, 3:7
Delay-line storage, 1:56

Delimiters, defined, 2:155
DELPHI programming language,
2:128
Delta Airlines, online reservations,
3:15
DeMarco, Tom, 2:197
Demodulation of signals, 2:46
Demographics
customer, data mining, 4:59
defined, 4:59
information on employees, 3:2
of voters, 4:183–184
DENDRAL expert system, 3:88,
3:124
Denial of Service (DoS) and Distrib-
uted Denial of Service (DDoS),
2:96, 3:104, 3:180
Denning, Peter J., 4:121
Densities, defined, 2:188
Dentistry, image analysis tools,
3:117
Deoxyribonucleic acid. *See* DNA
Department of Defense (U.S.)
Ada Joint Program Office, 1:124
Ada programming language,
2:158
ARPA (Advanced Research Pro-
jects Agency), 1:81, 1:115,
1:218, 4:146, 4:203–204
global surveillance, 4:117
government research grants, 1:81
HOLWG, 2:159
programming aims, 2:158–159
programming costs, 2:156
SCORM standard, 3:82
See also ARPANET;
Military/warfare
Department of Energy (U.S.), ES-
NET and HEPNET, 4:144
Department of Transportation
(U.S.)
and airline reservation practices,
3:14–15
Federal Railroad Administration,
3:175
Depreciation tracking software,
3:2–3
Depth perception, ultrasonic and
radar techniques, 4:38
Deregulation
of airline industry, 3:14
of telecommunications, 4:192
DES (Data Extraction System), 1:32
DES (Data Encryption Standard),
4:51–52
Desargues, Girard, 1:165
Descartes, René, 1:165
Design tools, 2:**55–58**

CASE tools, 2:58
  flowcharts, 2:55–57, 2:56, 2:57
  Nassi-Shneiderman diagrams, 2:57–58, 2:57
  pseudocode, 2:57
  See also CAD
Desktop computers. *See* Personal computers
Desktop publishing (DTP), 3:**70–74**
  digital images, 4:67
  history, 3:70
  information management concerns, 3:73–74
  OAS applications, 1:157
  printed copies, 2:149
  quality concerns, 3:73, 3:197–198
  as revolutionary, 3:70, 3:72, 3:73
  by word processors, 3:197, 3:213
Desktop publishing software
  Corel VENTURA, 1:157, 3:169, 3:197
  FrameMaker, 3:197
  InDesign, 4:160
  Interleaf, 3:197
  Microsoft Publisher, 1:157, 3:169
  PageMaker, 1:157, 3:70, 3:74, 3:169, 3:197, 4:160
  Quark Xpress, 3:169, 3:197, 4:160
  WYSIWYG, 3:70, 3:72, 3:74, 3:196–197
  XML for, 3:74
Desktop publishing technology, 3:**196–199**
  Apple Laserwriter printers, 3:70, 3:72, 3:74, 3:198
  for CD-ROMs, 3:199
  DTP computers, 3:196–197
  high-resolution printing, 3:197–199
  Macintosh computers, 3:70, 3:72, 3:74, 3:196–197
  PARC's contributions, 3:70
  for World Wide Web, 3:199
  See also Postscript page description language
Desktop video, impact on journalism, 4:162
Desktop videoconferencing, OAS applications, 1:158
Destruction Derby, 1:15
Dethloff, Jürgen, 2:165
Deutsch Institute fur Normung (DIN), 1:100
Device drivers, and system software, 3:167
Device managers, 2:129
Devol, George C., Jr., 1:170

DFDs (data flow diagrams), 2:197
DHTML (Dynamic Hypertext Markup Language), 1:14
Diacritical marks, Morse Code translations, 2:114
Diagnostic tools
  bacterial infection detectors, 3:144
  CAT, 3:55–56, 3:57, 3:115, 3:177, 3:*178*
  decision support systems, 3:**67–70**
  EPSS, for auto mechanics, 3:43
  expert systems, 3:88–89
  knowledge bases, 3:123–124
  mechanized lab tests, 3:28
  MRI, 3:116–117, 3:*116*
  neural networks, 3:154–155
  nuclear medicine, 3:115–116
  radiology, 2:139–140, 2:*140*, 3:55–56, 3:114
  scientific visualization, 3:177
  ultrasound, 3:114–115, 4:66
  See also Image analysis, medicine; Medical systems
Dialects of programming languages, 2:154, 2:157
Dialog-based systems, 1:111
DIALOG information system, 1:93
Dick Tracy comic books, 3:103
Dickens, Charles, 3:59
Dielectric, defined, 2:146
Difference Engine, 1:*6*, 1:18, 1:25, 1:80, 1:123, 3:162
Differential analyzers, 1:3–5, 1:50–51, 3:162, 4:195
Differential equations, 1:3–5, 1:132
Differential measurements, for GPS, 4:114
Differential pulse code modulation, 2:184
Diffie, Whitfield, 4:52
Digital-analog systems, for sound synthesis, 2:114
Digital art, copyrights, 4:8
Digital audio, for radio news, 4:161
Digital audio tape (DAT), 2:188, 2:190
Digital cash. *See* Electronic cash
Digital certificates, 2:213, 4:23–24, 4:80, 4:83
Digital checks. *See* Electronic checks
Digital computing, 1:**40–43**
  abacuses for, 1:**1–2**, 1:41, 1:53, 2:87
  Atanasoff's contributions, 1:60
  binary number system and, 1:29–31, 1:40, 2:108–109

Boolean arithmetic and logic, 1:41
  distinguished from analog computing, 1:2–3, 1:40, 1:131–132
  floating-point numbers, conversions, 1:40
  image processing, 1:160
  integrated circuit technology, 1:106–107
  music-related, 1:147, 1:148
  physics applications, 3:162–163
  size of machines and, 1:42–43
  space applications, 1:151
  speed vs. accuracy, 1:40, 1:42–43
  tabulating machines, 1:185
  telephony, 1:189–190
Digital, defined, 1:148, 3:162
Digital design, 1:27
Digital divide, 3:131, 4:130–131
Digital Equipment Corporation (DEC)
  Grace Hopper at, 1:86
  PDP and VAX computers, 1:13, 1:14, 1:36, 1:141–142, 2:51, 2:116
Digital filters, for sound cards, 2:184
Digital fish finders, 4:*134*
Digital images, 4:**65–68**
  advantages, 4:67
  as art, 4:6, 4:8
  black and white, 4:66
  color, 4:66, 4:67
  compression, 2:97, 4:67
  and computer vision, 4:38–39, 4:67–68
  concerns and advantages, 4:6
  editing, 4:181
  for electronic classrooms, 4:86
  formats, 4:67
  Gimp, 4:67
  JPEG format, 4:179
  medical applications, 4:67
  in museums, 4:7–8
  photography, 4:7, 4:**178–181**
  Photopaint, 4:67
  Photoshop, 3:18, 3:169, 4:6, 4:67, 4:160, 4:181
  pixilation, 4:7
  resolution, 4:66–67
  scanning, 4:180–181
  security applications, 4:21, 4:67
  software, 4:181
  for television, 4:160–161
  ultrasound, 3:114–115, 4:66
  X-rays, 4:66
  See also Cameras, digital; Graphics; Image analysis, medicine

Digital Landfill, 4:6–7

Digital libraries. *See* Libraries, digital

Digital Library Federation, 4:69

Digital Library Initiatives, 4:69

Digital linear tape (DLT), 2:188

Digital logic design, 2:**58–62**
  and-gates, 2:59–60
  canonic and-or implementation, 2:60–61
  and chip manufacturing costs, 2:61
  integrated circuits, 2:61–62
  inverters, 2:59
  logical descriptions, 2:61
  not-gates, 2:58–59
  or-gates, 2:59

Digital Millennium Copyright Act (DMCA), 3:185

Digital signatures, 4:**71–73**
  defined, 4:52
  E-Signature Act, 4:71–72
  integrity compromised, 4:72–73
  malicious codes, 4:72
  PKIs, 4:52, 4:72
  sending, 4:72
  tools for creating, 4:72
  uses, 4:71

Digital sound signals
  companding, 2:182–183, 2:*183*
  quantizing, 2:182, 2:*183*

Digital sound synthesis and recording, 1:148–149

Digital standards for cell phones, 3:33–34

Digital subscriber loop. *See* DSL system

Digital Theft Deterrence and Copyright Damages Improvement Act, 3:185

Digital to analog conversions. *See* DACs

Digital versatile disc-read only memory. *See* DVD-ROM

Digital versatile discs. *See* DVDs

Digital video images, 2:204

Digital video recorders, 4:124

Digital wallets. *See* Electronic cash

Digital watermarks, 4:71, 4:127

Digitize, defined, 1:30–31, 4:86

Digitizing tablets, 2:198, 3:30–31

Dijkstra, Edsger W., 2:162

Diode tubes, 1:196, 1:201

Diodes
  defined, 1:161
  photo, 3:127
  semiconductor laser, 2:75, 2:77, 3:127

DIPs (dual in-line pins), 2:109

Direct Hit search engine, 4:191

Direct manipulation systems, 1:111, 1:112–113, 4:129

Direction buttons, 1:215–216, 1:*215*, 1:*217*

Director software, 1:14

Directories
  for intelligent agents, 4:3
  search engine, 4:191

Directory Name Server (DNS), 1:176

Disabilities. *See* Assistive computer technology for persons with disabilities

Disabilities Discrimination Act, 4:12, 4:16

Discrete events, simulating, 1:179

Discrete numbers, defined, 1:31

Disease control
  Bill and Melinda Gates Foundation, 4:94
  CDC's role, 3:27
  genetic studies, 3:142–143
  mathematical models, 3:137

Disintermediation, defined, 1:45

Disk controllers, encryption hardware for, 2:173

Disk drives, encryption hardware for, 2:173

Disk management tools, 3:111

Disk operating system. *See* MS-DOS

Diskettes, introduced, 1:188

Disney Brother Studios, 1:12

Disney, Roy O., 1:12

Disney Studios
  animated films, 1:10, 1:*11*, 1:12–13, 3:108
  collaboration with Hewlett-Packard, 3:108

Disney, Walt, 1:10, 1:12–13

Display devices, 2:**62–68**
  AMLCDs vs. CRTs, 2:68
  for ATMs, 3:25
  for CAD systems, 3:31
  for cell phones, 4:133
  for classroom VCRs, 4:86
  color gamuts, 2:151
  CRTs, 1:203, 2:63–64
  current technologies, 1:203
  for DSSs, 2:88
  electronic white boards, 3:49–50, 3:77
  ergonomically correct, 1:65
  FEDs, 2:68
  flat screen monitors, 2:*65*
  HDTV, 2:66
  history, 2:62–63

human interactions with, 4:128
  interactive graphics for, 2:69
  LCDs, 2:64–68
  lighting sources, 2:67–68
  magnification software, 4:12–13
  for multimedia applications, 2:85, 2:86
  for PDAs, 2:141, 4:133
  PPIs, 3:10–11
  reflective vs. transmissive modes, 2:67
  resolution, 4:66–67
  SmartBoards, 3:76, 4:86
  with speech output, 4:13
  for television, 2:63–64, 2:66
  terminals, 2:63
  touch-sensitive panels, 4:86
  for video editing, 3:97
  See also Graphic devices

Distance learning, 3:**75–77**
  Blackboard course management system, 3:76
  CUseeMe software, 3:77
  digital resources for, 3:134
  distant/asynchronous, 3:76–77, 3:76
  distant/synchronous, 3:76, 3:77
  distinguished from distributed learning, 3:75
  groupware, 3:76
  history, 3:75
  ITV, 3:75, 3:76–77
  jobs for instructional professionals, 3:77
  local/asynchronous, 3:76, 3:77
  local/synchronous, 3:76
  multimedia applications, 2:84, 2:85
  NetMeeting software, 3:77
  online educational courses, 1:46, 1:220, 3:75–77, 3:80–82, 4:36–37
  real-time support, 4:88
  smart classrooms, 3:76
  statistics, 3:41
  via radio and television, 3:75
  WebCT course management system, 3:76

Distant/asynchronous learning model, 3:76–77, 3:76

Distant/synchronous learning model, 3:76, 3:77

Distributed application servers, 2:39

Distributed Component Object Model (DCOM), 2:39

Distributed computing systems
  client/server model, 2:36

distinguished from parallel systems, 2:35

how they work, 2:35–36

interconnection bandwidth, 2:39

Distributed learning. *See* Distance learning

Distributed systems, 4:2–3

Division of Computational Bioscience, Center for Informational Technology, 4:36–37

Division of Parasitic Diseases (DPD), 3:27

DLT (digital linear tape), 2:188

DMCA (Digital Millennium Copyright Act), 3:185

DML (Data Manipulation Language), 2:185–186

DNA (deoxyribonucleic acid), 3:28, 3:142, 3:*143*

DNA computers, 4:167–169, 4:170–171

DNS (Directory Name Server), 1:176

Document cameras, for electronic classrooms, 4:86

Document Object Model

of JavaScript, 4:157–158

of XML, 2:107

Document processing, 2:**68–72**

automatic data processing, 2:69

document structures and formats, 2:71

e-mail, 2:71

intelligent agents, 2:72

interactive graphics, 2:69–70

multimedia documents, 2:70

OCR technology, 2:92, 2:**132–134**

reprographics, 2:69

role of, 2:68–69

telecommunications, 2:70–71

typographics, 2:69

Documentation

of building specifications, 3:17

Linux Documentation Project, 3:157–158

of software, ethics, 4:100

in system analysis, 2:195

DoD (Department of Defense) model. *See* TCP/IP protocol suite

Dodge, Charles, 1:149

Domain naming system, security, 1:176

Domains, application, 3:48–49

Domesday Book, 1:166

Donkey Kong game, 1:69

Dope sheets, 1:9

Doping of silicon, 1:105, 1:133, 3:39

Dorson, Richard M., 4:206

DOS. *See* MS-DOS

DoS (Denial of Service) attacks, 2:96, 3:104

Dot matrix printers, 2:149–150

Dot.coms

defined, 1:45, 4:80

stock price fluctuations, 3:44, 4:193

successful, 4:81

DoubleClick, 4:79

Download bandwidth, 4:26–27

DPD (Division of Parasitic Diseases), 3:27

Dr. Strangelove, 4:105

Dragging, defined, 1:213

DragonBall EZ, 2:142

DRAM (dynamic random-access memory), 2:109, 2:111, 2:209

Dreamcast game, 2:80, 4:126

Dreamweaver software, 1:14, 3:110

Drexel Institute of Technology, bar code technology, 2:163

Drive failures, repairing, 1:127

Drivers, defined, 1:121, 2:145

Droids. *See* Robotics/robots

Drop-down menus, 1:215, 1:*216*

DSL (digital subscriber loop) system, 2:47, 3:113, 4:130, 4:193

DSS. *See* Decision support systems

DTD (defined document type definition), 2:105–106, 2:107

DTP. *See* Desktop publishing

Dual in-line pins (DIPs), 2:109

Dudley Observatory, 3:162

Dumb terminals, 1:128, 1:142, 2:106, 4:165

Dumbo, 1:12

Dungeon Hack, 1:15

Duplex communication systems, defined, 2:29

Dutch Railways, Nederlandse Spoorwegen, 3:176

DVD-ROM (digital versatile disc-read only memory), 2:204, 3:113

DVDs (digital versatile discs), 3:113

access to memory, 2:205–206

for distance learning, 3:76, 3:77

for electronic classrooms, 4:86

MPEG-2, 2:98

for rental movies, 2:190

as storage devices, 2:111, 2:190–191, 2:*205*

viewing devices, 2:204–205

Dvorak, August, 1:120

Dvorak keyboards, 1:120–121

DXplain system, 3:68

DX7 synthesizer, 3:148

Dye sublimation printers, 2:152

Dynabook computers, 1:80, 1:216–217

Dynamic, defined, 2:110

Dynamic Hypertext Markup Language (dHTML), 1:14

Dynamic links, defined, 4:82

Dynamic random-access memory (DRAM), 2:109, 2:111, 2:209

Dynamic routing, 4:187

Dynatech Newstar, 4:160

E

E-banking, 4:**73–75**, 4:91–92

authentication, 4:74

Citibank, 4:74

to complement traditional banks, 4:73–74

electronic cash, 4:75

electronic signatures, 4:*75*

encryption, 4:74

firewalls, 4:74–75

how it works, 4:74

Internet-only, 4:74

NationsBank, 4:74

NetBank, 4:74

smart cards, 4:75

E-benefits, 4:96

E-book readers, 4:76–77, 4:*76*

Acrobat Reader, 3:112

Gemstar, 4:77

in libraries, 3:134

Rocket eBooks, 4:77

SoftBooks, 4:77

software for, 3:112

E-books, 3:43, 4:**76–78**

ASCII and PDF standards, 4:77

encryption, 4:76

future of, 4:77

in libraries, 3:134

pros and cons, 4:77

Riding the Bullet, 4:77

uses, 4:77

E-commerce, 1:**43–46**

academic degrees in, 4:*78*

vs. ATM use, 3:26

cookies, 1:168, 4:**40–43**

credit card applications, 4:48–49

digital signatures, 1:175, 4:52, 4:**71–73**

document processing applications, 2:71

dot.coms, 1:45, 3:44, 4:80, 4:81, 4:193

electronic checks, 4:*75*, 4:91

electronic market, 4:**88–92**

E-commerce (continued)
    encryption, 1:43, 1:44–45, 4:49, 4:52
    future, 1:46
    investigating online retailers, 4:46–48
    marketing, 1:45
    micropayments, 1:44
    overview, 1:43
    protocols, 1:43
    security, 1:43, 2:176, 4:49
    shopping carts, 1:43
    vs. traditional commerce, 1:45–46
    XML for, 4:79
E-commerce, economic and social aspects, 1:46, 1:115–116, 4:**78–81**
    business supply chains, 4:79
    competition among sellers, 1:45–46, 4:81
    dot.com businesses, 1:45, 4:80–81, 4:193
    infrastructure costs, 4:80
    privacy, 1:167–168, 4:79
    sales statistics, 1:47
    security, 1:43, 1:45, 2:176, 4:80
    transaction costs, 4:78–79
E-commerce, specific web sites
    Amazon.com, 1:45, 4:64, 4:79, 4:93–94
    Chemdex, 4:80
    eBay, 1:44, 4:47–48, 4:81, 4:90, 4:97
    Land's End, 4:80
    Orbitz.com, 3:15, 4:81
    Travelocity.com, 4:80, 4:81, 4:128
    WebVan, 4:80
E-Expo, Internet access, 4:131
E-journals and e-publishing, 4:**81–84**
    access to, 4:81–82
    advantages, 4:81
    authentication and verification, 4:82–83
    changing URLs, 4:82
    computer science publications, 4:84
    dynamic links, 4:82
    e-newspaper readers, 1:91
    formats, 4:83–84
    library applications, 3:134
    multimedia applications, 4:82
    proxy servers, 4:83
    scholarly publications, 4:82
    server crashes, 4:82
    software, 1:157
    SPARC, 4:82

E-learning. See Computer-assisted instruction; Distance learning
E-mail, 1:**47–50**
    attachments, 1:47, 1:49, 2:94, 4:138
    and bioterrorism, 1:49
    business use, 1:49–50, 1:158, 4:139
    digital signatures, 4:**71–73**
    for disabled persons, 4:12, 4:14, 4:15–16
    discussion groups, 1:47, 1:49
    distinguished from snail mail, 1:47
    distinguished from voice communication, 1:48–49
    document processing role, 2:71
    gopher, 3:118
    history, 1:47, 1:218, 4:146
    ISPs, 1:47, 1:49, 2:213
    MIME, 4:138–139
    retrieval centers, 1:48, 4:53
    Russia, Cafemax, 4:139
    security/privacy, 1:49, 1:168, 1:175–177, 3:181
    sendmail, 3:157
    sent by Queen Elizabeth II, 4:148
    spam, 1:49
    standards, 1:100
    user interfaces, 3:205
    voice-driven, 4:140
    See also Internet; Invasive programs; ISPs
E-mail software
    Eudora, 1:158
    from ISPs, 1:47, 3:113
    Lotus Notes, 1:158, 4:139–140
    Microsoft Outlook, 1:158
E-Signature Act, 4:71–72
EAM (electromechanical accounting machine), 1:187–188
EAPROM (electrically alterable programmable read-only memory), 2:109, 2:111
Early computers, 1:**50–57**
    ABC, 1:53
    for ballistics computations, 1:50, 1:55, 1:59, 1:71, 1:202
    Bell Labs' contributions, 1:27, 1:51
    BINAC, 1:85
    the Bombe, 1:54
    CDC 1604, 3:57
    Colossus, 1:54–55, 1:59, 1:71, 4:51
    differential analyzers, 1:3–5, 1:50–51, 3:162, 4:195

EDSAC, 1:42, 1:56–57, 1:62, 1:72
EDVAC, 1:55–56, 1:72, 2:74
EMIDEC 1100, 3:56
ENIAC, 2:33, 2:34, 2:72–74, 2:218
ERA, 3:57
ergonomic designs, 1:65
Harvard Mark series, 1:51–53, 1:52, 1:59–60, 1:84–85, 1:89, 1:212
IAS machine, 1:72
IBM 701, 1:72, 1:89, 4:4
IBM 7090, 1:72
IBM System/360, 1:74, 1:89–90, 1:125, 1:126–127, 4:4, 4:5
information retrieval, 1:93, 1:94
keyboard commands, 2:145
Manchester Mark I, 1:56, 1:61–62
as mechanical, 1:131
MIR, 4:120
MITS Altair, 4:94
programming, 1:63, 1:72–73, 1:75–79, 1:134, 2:41
RAMAC 305, 1:89
regulations lacking, 1:34, 1:36–37
software for, 1:56
terminals, 2:45, 2:63, 3:48
Turing Machine, 1:59, 1:197–198, 1:**199–201**
Whirlwind, 1:57
WISC, 4:4
Xanadu, 1:88
Z machines, 1:52–53, 1:62
See also Analytical Engine; ENIAC; Generations, computers; UNIVAC
Early pioneers, 1:**58–64**
    Aiken, Howard, 1:51, 1:59–60, 1:212, 2:222, 3:206
    Antonelli, Jean, 1:63
    Atanasoff, John, 1:42, 1:53, 1:59, 1:60, 1:61, 2:74
    Bardeen, John, 1:63, 1:72, 1:104, 1:106, 1:192, 2:**12–14**
    Bartik, Jennings, 1:63
    Brattain, Walter, 1:63, 1:72, 1:106, 1:192, 2:**12–14**
    Bush, Vannevar, 1:50, 1:58–59, 1:58, 1:87, 4:29, 4:195
    gurus, 4:**120–121**
    Holberton, Frances, 1:63
    Meltzer, Marlyn, 1:63
    Newman, Maxwell, 1:56, 1:61–62, 1:199
    von Neumann, John, 2:74, 2:**217–218**

Wilkes, Maurice, 1:42, 1:56–57, 1:62, 1:72, 1:198

Williams, Frederic, 1:56, 1:61, 1:62

Zuse, Konrad, 1:52–53, 1:59, 1:62, 2:**221–223**

See also Eckert, J. Presper, Jr.; Mauchly, John W.; Shockley, William; Turing, Alan M.

EARN (European Academic and Research Network), 4:144

Earth-centered coordinates, GPS, 4:114

Earth-fixed coordinates, GPS, 4:114

Earthworms, genetically engineered, 3:143

EBay, 1:*44*, 4:47–48, 4:81, 4:90, 4:97

EBCDIC (Extended Binary Coded Decimal Interchange Code), 1:*131*, 2:41, 2:109

EBONE (European backbone networks), 4:143, 4:145

ECHO communication satellite, 2:170

Eckert, J. Presper, Jr., 1:60–61, 2:**72–75**, 2:*73*

ENIAC project, 1:42, 1:55, 1:60, 1:71, 1:72, 3:59

UNIVAC project, 1:32, 1:72, 1:188

Eckert-Mauchly Award, 4:5

Eckert-Mauchly Corporation, 1:85, 2:73–74

ECMA (European Computer Manufacturers Association), 1:100

ECMAScript, 4:159

Econometrics, 3:78

Economic data, gathered by Census Bureau, 1:31, 1:33

Economic modeling, 3:**78–80**

healthcare applications, 3:*79*

neural networks for, 3:154, 3:155

regression analysis, 3:78

simulations, 3:79–80

supercomputers for, 3:80

Economic modeling software

GAMS, 3:79–80

Gauss, 3:79

Limdep, 3:79

Mathematica, 3:79

Matlab, 3:79

Microsoft Excel, 3:78

RATS, 3:79

SAS, 3:78

SPSS, 3:78

STATA, 3:79

TSP, 3:79

Economics

of chip manufacturing, 3:40–41

of dot.com market, 3:44, 4:193

of DSL providers, 4:193

Grosch's Law, 4:120–121

impact of Cold War, 3:58

impact of computer technology, 4:200

Economics of Manufactures and Machinery, 1:26

Edge-detection, for computer vision, 4:39

EDI (Electronic Data Interchange), 1:43, 1:99

Edison, Thomas

AIEE founder, 1:102, 1:*103*

on debugging, 1:53

electrical research, 1:201

as entertainment system inventor, 4:126

Edit decision lists, video editing, 3:97

EDS, Ross Perot and, 4:98

EDSAC (Electronic Delay Storage Automatic Calculator), 1:42, 1:*56*–57, 1:62, 1:72

Education, 4:**99–102**

application domains, 3:48–49

in biology, 3:164

in chemistry, 3:164, 4:35–37

for computer professionals, 1:39, 3:45, 4:99

data warehousing applications, 4:63

electronic campus, 4:**84–88**

in engineering, 3:159

information access and, 4:132

in law, 3:*131*

library applications, 3:**131–134**

Logo applications, 2:101–104

in mathematics, 3:138, 3:159, 3:161

OMR applications, 2:133, 2:164

online courses, 1:46, 1:220, 2:84, 2:85

PASCAL as teaching tool, 2:157–158

in physics, 3:164

role of e-books, 4:77

South Dakota, technology, 4:149

student tracking software, 3:169, 3:194

training simulators, 1:178, 1:*179*, 1:*204*, 2:178–181

virtual reality in, 1:**203–206**, 2:216

See also Computer-assisted instruction; Computer science academic programs; Distance learning

Educational software, 3:**80–83**

for chemistry students, 4:36

computer environment, 3:83

computer requirements, 3:81

costs, 3:82

effectiveness, 3:*81*, 3:83

LMSs, 3:80–82

marketing issues, 3:82–83

for musicians, 1:147, 1:*148*

standards for evaluating, 3:81–82

and teacher preparedness, 3:82, 3:83

upgradability, 3:81

user interfaces, 4:127

EduCommerce, 1:46

EDVAC (Electronic Discrete Variable Automatic Computer), 1:55–56, 2:74

EEPROM (electronic erasable programmable read only memory), 1:130

EFF (Electronic Frontier Foundation), 1:168, 4:34, 4:52, 4:149

Effectiveness, of algorithms, 2:3–4

Effector cells, in nervous system, 3:153

EGP (Exterior Gateway Protocol), 4:143

Egress, defined, 2:201

EIA (Engineering Industries Association), 1:100, 2:9

Eich, Brendan, 4:158

800-calls, 3:201

Einstein, Albert, 2:218, 3:121

Eisenhower, Dwight, 1:72

Elections

computer predictions, 1:72, 4:183

computerized voting and vote counting, 4:183, 4:*184*

hanging chads, 4:183

punch cards for voting, 1:*94*, 4:183

touch-screen voting machines, 2:*199*

See also Political applications

Electrical appliances, compatibility, 2:48–49

Electrical circuits

expert systems tools, 3:88

gates, 2:58–60

oscilloscopes to monitor, 1:2, 1:40

Electrically alterable programmable read-only memory (EAPROM), 2:109, 2:111

Electro-acoustic music, 1:147

Electro-optics, 3:127

Electrocardiography (ECG), expert systems tools, 3:88

Electroluminescent panels, 2:67

Electromagnetic energy
  for cell phones, 3:32–33
  in laser technology, 3:125–126
  of light vs. radio waves,
    1:160–161
  for networks, 1:155
  for wireless transmission, 2:202,
    2:219

Electromagnetic relays, for Z computers, 2:222

Electromagnetic spectrum, defined,
  2:220

Electromechanical accounting machine (EAM), 1:187–188

Electromechanical computer mice,
  2:146

Electron guns, 1:203, 2:63

Electronic Book Exchange (EBX),
  3:112

The Electronic Brain. *See* Neural
  networks

Electronic campus, 3:76, 4:**84–88**
  assistive technologies for disabled
    persons, 4:*87*
  audio needs, 4:85–86
  classrooms, 4:*85*, 4:86–87
  electronic tally systems, 4:88
  film projectors, 4:85
  interactive television, 4:88
  media centers, 4:86
  multimedia applications, 4:84–85,
    4:86
  networked laptops and peripherals, 4:88
  VCRs, 4:86

Electronic cash, 1:44, 1:176, 4:75,
  4:90, 4:91

Electronic checks, 4:**73–75**, 4:*75*,
  4:91

Electronic collaboration, 1:158–159

Electronic Commerce, 4:26

Electronic Communications Privacy
  Act (1986), 1:168

Electronic Data Interchange (EDI),
  1:43, 1:99

Electronic Data Systems, Capture
  Lab, 3:49

Electronic Delay Storage Automatic
  Calculator (EDSAC), 1:42,
  1:56–57, 1:62, 1:72

Electronic Discrete Variable Automatic Computer (EDVAC),
  1:55–56, 2:74

Electronic docking of legal proceedings, 3:130

Electronic erasable programmable
  read only memory (EEPROM),
  1:130

Electronic Forums, ACM, 1:23–24

Electronic Frontier Foundation
  (EFF), 1:168, 4:34, 4:52, 4:149

Electronic libraries. *See* Libraries,
  digital; Libraries, electronic catalogs

Electronic markets, 4:**88–92**
  catastrophe insurance, 4:91
  Chicago Mercantile Exchange,
    4:*89*
  electronic banking, 1:46,
    4:**73–75**, 4:91–92
  stock and commodities, 4:89–90
  World Wide Web and, 4:89–90

Electronic meeting rooms, 3:*50*
  Capture Lab, 3:49
  electronic meeting systems, 3:49,
    3:170
  See also Electronic campus

Electronic Numerical Integrator and
  Computer. *See* ENIAC

Electronic Performance Support
  Systems (EPSS), 3:43–44

Electronic Privacy Information Center, 1:168

Electronic signatures, 4:*75*

Electronic Signatures in Global and
  National Commerce Act. *See* E-
  Signature Act

Electronic toys, 4:124, 4:*125*

Electronic wallets. *See* Electronic
  cash

Electronic white boards, 3:49–50,
  3:77

Elements, 2:4

Elite hackers, 4:123

Ellison, Harlan, 4:105

Ellison, Larry, 4:98

Elographics (EloTouch Systems),
  2:198

Elsevier Science Direct, e-journal,
  4:84

Elxsi, Ltd., 4:5

Embedded objects, integrated software, 3:119–120

Embedded technology (ubiquitous
  computing), 3:**83–87**
  artificial intelligence and, 3:86
  calm computing, 3:84–86
  defined, 1:114
  infrastructure needs, 3:84,
    3:86–87
  manufacturing applications, 3:52,
    3:53
  medical applications, 3:139
  origin of term, 3:84
  pervasive computing, 3:84
  portable computing, 3:84
  programming languages, 2:7
  related technologies, 3:86–87

  security issues, 3:87
  smart cards, 2:164–165, 2:*165*,
    3:136, 3:139
  smart devices and buildings, 3:87
  space applications, 1:151–152
  wearable computing, 3:*85*, 3:86

EMIDEC 1100 computer, 3:56

Emoticons, 1:49, 4:148

Employment, impact of robots on,
  1:171–172, 4:*201*

Encapsulation, in object-oriented
  languages, 2:126

Encarta encyclopedia, 3:113

Encoders, 1:119–120, 1:145

Encryption. *See* Cryptography

Encyclopedia of Cybernetics, 4:119

Encyclopedias, on CD-ROMs,
  3:112–113

End effectors, defined, 2:166

Endeavor Information Systems,
  Voyager software, 3:133

Enemy of the State, 4:105–106

Energy industry, process control,
  3:164

Engelbart, Douglas, 1:21, 1:87,
  1:145, 2:146

Engelberger, Joseph, 1:170, 1:171

Engineering
  application domains, 3:49
  biomedical, 3:28
  CAD tools, 3:16
  CAE tools, 3:30, 3:32, 3:51
  computer education, 3:159
  hardware, 3:45–46
  knowledge bases, 3:124

Engineering Industries Association
  (EIA), 1:100, 2:9

ENIAC (Electronic Numerical Integrator and Computer)
  ballistics tests, 2:73
  invention, 1:7, 1:42, 1:55,
    1:60–61, 1:71, 2:*34*, 2:72–74,
    2:218, 3:59
  patents, 1:60, 1:61
  programming, 1:63
  security issues, 1:174
  stored program concept, 1:72
  vacuum tubes, 1:202–203, 2:33,
    4:126

ENIAC-on-a-chip, 1:202

Enigma cryptographic machine and
  code, 1:54, 4:51

Enquire program, 4:92

Enterprise information systems, defined, 4:3

Enterprise resource planning (ERP)
  programs, 4:97

Entrepreneurs, 4:**92–99**

Berners-Lee, Tim, 4:29–30, 4:92–93, 4:*93*, 4:121, 4:140

Bezos, Jeff, 4:93–94

Bricklin, Daniel, 3:167, 3:193, 4:98

Bushnell, Nolan, 1:67–68, 4:98, 4:126

Case, Steven, 4:98

Ellison, Larry, 4:98

Filo, David, 1:219, 4:98

Frankston, Robert, 3:193, 4:98

Gates, Bill, 1:137, 1:138, 3:131, 4:94, 4:*95*

Jobs, Steven, 1:15–17, 1:*16*, 1:69, 3:108–109, 4:30, 4:94

Kapor, Mitchell, 4:96

Kurtzig, Sandra, 4:96

Lopker, Pamela, 4:97

Omidyar, Pierre, 1:*44*, 4:97

Perot, Ross, 4:98

Thompson, John W., 4:97–98

Wang, An, 3:**206–208**, 3:*206*, 3:212

Wozniak, Stephen, 1:15–17, 1:69, 4:94–95

Yang, Jerry, 1:219, 4:98

Entscheidungsproblem, Alan Turing's contributions, 1:199, 1:200

Enumeration phase, of hacking, 3:105

Environmental Protection Agency (EPA), standards, 1:99

Environmental sciences/protection

  bioengineering tools, 3:28

  bioinformatics tools, 3:27–28

  computer applications, 3:137

  DSS tools, 3:68

  GIS tools, 3:101

  global surveillance tools, 4:118

  technologies, 3:28

  William Hewlett's contributions, 3:109

Ephemeris data, GPS, 4:113–114

EPROM (erasable programmable read-only memory), 1:130, 2:109, 2:111

EPSS (Electronic Performance Support Systems), 3:43–44

Equation engines, 4:35

Equifax, 4:48–49

ERA computer, 3:57

Eraserhead pointing devices, 2:148

Ergonomics, 1:**64–67**

  and carpal tunnel syndrome, 1:65, 1:121–122

  defined, 2:91

  early computers, 1:65

  flexibility principles, 1:64, 1:66

  human-machine interactions, 1:64–65

  of joysticks, 2:79

  keyboards, 1:121–122, 1:*121*

  of keyboards, 2:91

  repetitive stress, 1:*66*, 1:121–122

  of user interfaces, 3:205

  workplace guidelines, 1:65–67, 1:*66*

Ericsson, cell phone/PDA unit, 3:*34*

ERP (enterprise resource planning) programs, 4:97

Error control functions, serial transmission, 2:120

Error correcting codes, 2:44–45

Erwise browser, 4:30

ESA (European Space Agency), 1:135

EsAC model, 3:146

EShop, 4:97

ESNET, 4:144

Esoteric

  defined, 1:132

  microcomputer programs as, 1:134

  optical switching materials as, 1:162

E'Speak, 2:39

Estridge, Phil, 1:90–91

Ethernets, 1:*156*

  availability, 2:10

  defined, 4:136

  LAN standard, 2:124, 4:147

  PARC's contributions, 1:222

Ethical hackers, 4:123

Ethics, 4:**99–102**

  ACM code, 1:24, 4:99, 4:100

  ACM/IEEE-CS Code, 4:100

  AITP code, 4:99, 4:101

  downloading pornography, 4:101

  freedom of speech, 4:32, 4:33–34, 4:101–102

  IEEE-CS code, 4:99

  intellectual property protection, 4:100

  missile defense systems, 4:101

  privacy issues, 4:101

  of software development, 4:100–101

  whistle-blowing responsibility, 4:99

  World Wide Web and, 1:220

Euclid, 2:*4*

Euclidean geometry, defined, 1:165

Eudora software, 1:158

Europe, software piracy, 3:184

European backbone networks (EBONE), 4:143, 4:145

European Centre for Medium-Range Weather Forecasts, 1:185

European Computer Manufacturers Association (ECMA), 1:100

European Space Agency (ESA), 1:135

Event analysis, 2:194

Event-handling functions, 1:112–113

Evolution

  and biologically inspired robots, 4:11

  genetics research and, 3:142–143

Exaggeration animation principle, 1:14

Excel software, 3:60, 3:78, 3:169, 3:193

Exidy, Death Race game, 1:68

Expansion slots, for handheld computers, 4:166

Expedia.com, 3:15

Expert systems (ES), 3:**87–91**

  for agricultural decision making, 3:4, 3:5

  AI as, 2:88

  applications, 3:88

  and artificial intelligence, 3:53, 3:87

  for automotive systems analysis, 3:*89*

  costs, 3:88

  current research, 3:91

  defined, 2:87

  DENDRAL, 3:88, 3:124

  frame systems, 3:90

  history, 3:87–88

  inference engines, 3:89–90, 3:91, 3:123, 3:124

  for information retrieval, 1:96

  as IT, 2:87

  knowledge bases for, 3:89–90, 3:91

  political applications, 4:184

  programming, 3:88–89

  robots as, 2:89

  semantic nets, 3:90

  shells, 3:90

  structured systems, 3:90

  VR as, 2:88–89

  See also Knowledge-based systems

Expert Systems Catalog of Applications, 3:88

ExploreZip worm, 1:208

Extended Binary Coded Decimal Interchange Code (EBCDIC), 1:*131*, 2:41, 2:109

Extended markup language. *See* XML

Exterior Gateway Protocol (EGP), 4:143
Extraterrestrial life, SETI@home, 3:22
Extreme Ultraviolet Explorer, 2:169
Eye motion tracking systems, 2:85
Eye strain, preventing, 1:65–66, 4:38
Eyes (human)
    anatomy, 4:38
    retinal scans, 2:140, 4:21, 4:22

F

FAA (Federal Aviation Administration), 3:8–9, 3:68
Facial scans, 4:21, 4:114
Facsimile transmission machines. *See* FAXs
Factor analysis, 4:61
Fail-safe, defined, 3:9
Fair dealing privileges, 4:44
Fair use privileges, 4:43–44
Fairchild Camera and Instrument, 1:68
Fairchild Semiconductor, 1:73, 1:106, 1:107, 2:15, 2:34, 3:40
Fairlight, 1:149
"Falling Through the Net: Toward Digital Inclusion," 4:130
Famicom video game console, 1:14
Fantasia, 1:*11*, 1:12, 3:108
Fashion design, 3:**91–94**
    CAD tools, 3:91–94, 3:*92*
    CAM tools, 3:93
    cost-analysis tools, 3:92
    fabric-utilization tools, 3:93
    patternmaking, 3:92–93
"The Fatal Initiation," 4:206
FAX-modems, 1:158
FAXs (facsimile transmission machines)
    Harry Nyquist's contributions, 4:175
    as input device, 2:87, 3:203
    OAS applications, 1:158
    in *Paris in the Twentieth Century*, 4:105
FBI (Federal Bureau of Investigation)
    fingerprint identification, 4:68
    hacker attacks, 3:105
    NCIC, 1:167
    security at 2002 Winter Olympics, 4:114
    statistics on hackers, 4:123
FCC (Federal Communications Commission), 2:30, 3:103
FDDI (Fiber Distributed Data Interface), 2:118

Federal Aviation Administration (FAA), 3:8–9, 3:68
Federal Communications Commission (FCC), 2:30, 3:103
Federal interest computer, 1:35–36
Federal Railroad Administration (FRA), 3:175
FEDs (field emission displays), 2:68
Feedback
    and robot movements, 2:168
    in VR, 2:214
Feedback circuits, 1:4–5
Feeding systems, for livestock and poultry, 3:6
Feiertag, Rich, 2:173
Feigenbaum, Edward, 3:124
Fermat, Pierre de, 1:165
Ferromagnetic storage media, 1:163–164
FETs (Field Effect Transistors), 1:196
Feurzeig, Wallace, 2:101
The Feynman Lectures on Physics, 4:103
Feynman, Richard P., 4:**102–104**, 4:*103*
Fiber Distributed Data Interface (FDDI), 2:118
Fiber optic rings, 4:194
Fiber optics, 2:**75–78**
    attenuation, 2:76–77
    bandwidth, 2:77
    for broadband signals, 1:161, 4:25
    cables, splicing, 2:77, 2:78
    chromatic dispersion, 2:76, 2:77
    cost, 2:76, 2:77–78
    dark fiber, 2:76, 2:78
    for data transfer, 2:47
    defined, 1:156, 2:17, 4:25
    vs. electrical transmission, 2:75
    for electronic classrooms, 4:86
    for frame relay, 1:156
    FTH, 2:47
    how it works, 2:75–76
    infrastructure, 2:78
    internal reflection, 1:161
    LEDs, 1:161–162, 2:75, 2:76
    for long-distance transmissions, 2:178, 2:201–202
    for mainframes, 1:127
    mode velocities, 2:76
    multi- and single-mode fibers, 2:76, 2:77
    for networks, 1:155
    as nonlinear, 2:76, 2:78
    photodiodes, 2:75
    photonic switching, 2:78

    semiconductor diode lasers, 2:75, 2:77, 3:127
    for sensors, 2:75
    SNR at receiver, 2:76–77
    solitons, 2:78
    for telecommunications, 2:75, 4:192, 4:194–195
    for telephone systems, 1:190, 2:17
    time-division multiplexing, 2:76
    ultimate capacity, 2:77
    for VR gloves, 2:214
    wavelengths used, 1:161–162
    WDM, 2:76
    See also Optical technology
Fiber to the desktop, 2:78
Fiber to the home (FTH), 2:47, 2:78
Fiction, computers in, 4:**104–107**
    cyberpunk, 4:106
    hacker portrayals, 4:106
    urban myths, 4:**206–208**
    See also Movies; *specific books*
FIDONET, 4:144, 4:148
Field Effect Transistors (FETs), 1:196
Field emission displays (FEDs), 2:68
Field searching, by search engines, 4:189
FIELDATA code, 2:41
Filaments, of vacuum tubes, 1:202
File access controls, 1:175
File managers, 2:130, 4:141
File Transfer Protocol. *See* FTP
Film
    vs. digital photographic systems, 4:179
    photographic, history, 3:94
    projectors, educational applications, 4:85
    vs. videotape, 3:94–95, 3:99
    wet vs. digital darkrooms, 4:160
Film and video editing, 3:**94–99**
    film editing, 3:95–96
    videotape editing, 3:*95*, 3:96–99, 4:160–161
Filo, David, 1:219, 4:98
Filter queries, for data visualization, 3:62
Finale software, 3:146
Financial institutions. *See* Banks and financial institutions
FindLaw search engine, 4:189
Fine, Sara, 4:31
Fingerprint scanning
    for authentication, 4:21, 4:22, 4:*23*, 4:68
    pattern recognition tools, 2:138
    software, 2:96

Finite state control, 1:199

Finiteness of algorithms, 2:3

Fire hydrants, standardization, 1:99

Firewalls, 1:177, 4:**107–110**

    application layer, 4:109

    defined, 4:74

    for e-banking, 4:74–75

    for e-commerce, 4:80

    as hacking prevention, 3:105

    hardware and software tools, 4:109

    for intranets, 4:150, 4:151

    and invasive programs, 3:182, 4:*108*, 4:109

    network layer, 4:107–108, 4:109

    port IDs, 4:107

    security policies, 4:107

    transport layer, 4:108–109

Firewire (IEEE-1394), 2:178

Firing tables (ballistics), 1:59, 2:74

Firmware. *See* ROM

First Warning Systems, in weather forecasts, 3:209

Fish and Wildlife Service (U.S.), environmental efforts, 3:28

Fish cryptographic machine, 1:54

Fish finders, digital, 4:*134*

Fisher, Anna, 1:*179*

Fixed asset tracking software, 3:2–3

Fixed base aircraft simulators, 2:180

Flash software, 1:14

Fleming, Ambrose, 1:201

Fleming, John, 4:163

Flexible manufacturing systems, 3:52–53

Flight management computers (FMCs), 3:7

Flight management systems (FMSs), 3:7, 3:9

Flight Simulator game, 4:127

Flight simulators. *See* Simulators, aircraft flight training

Flint, Charles R., 1:211

The Flintstones, 1:13

Flip-flop relays

    in buffers, 2:6

    in CPUs, 2:5–6, 2:33

    function, 1:51, 1:106–107

    manufacturing, 2:61

    in minicomputers, 1:141

Floating-point numbers, conversion, 1:40

Floating-point operations, 2:137, 3:57

Floppy disks (diskettes), 2:189–190, 2:206

FLOPS (floating point operations per second), 2:137, 3:57

Flow control functions, serial transmission, 2:120

Flow-Matic compiler, 1:86

Flowcharts, 2:55–57

    defined, 2:162

    graphics software, 3:169

    macro, 2:56

    micro (detail), 2:56–57, 2:*56*

    role of, 2:55–56

    structured, 2:57–58, 2:*57*, 2:162

    symbols, 2:55, 2:*56*, 2:197

    in systems design, 2:197

Flowers and Trees, 1:12

FLOWMATIC programming language, 2:156

Fluid dynamics, defined, 3:32

Fluorinert as coolant, 3:58

Fluxions, invention, 1:3

Fly-by-wire systems, 1:151, 2:216

Flynn, Michael, 2:135

FM (frequency modulation), 2:29, 2:31–32, 2:116

FM synthesis sound cards, 2:184

FMCs (flight management computers), 3:7

FMSs (flight management systems), 3:7, 3:9

FOAFtale (Friend of a Friend Tale) *News*, 4:207

Focus windows, 1:215

FOIA (Freedom of Information Act), 4:182

Follow-through animation principle, 1:13

Foot pedals, for multimedia systems, 2:85

Footprinting (reconnaissance) by hackers, 3:104

Force feedback controllers, 2:80–81

Ford Foundation, engineering education, 3:159

Ford Motor Company

    CAD applications, 3:31

    DSS tools, 3:68

Forethought, Inc., 1:137

Form-based systems, 1:111

Forms, dot matrix printers for, 2:150

Formula Translator. *See* FORTRAN programming language

Formulas, in spreadsheets, 3:192

FormZ software, 3:18

Forrester, Jay W., 1:57, 2:109

Forster, E.M., 4:105

Forsythe, A.I., 3:159

FORTH programming language, 1:78

FORTRAN programming language

    ASCII characters, 2:41

    attributes, 1:78, 1:137

    compilers, 1:141, 2:153, 2:154

    for computer music, 2:114

    development, 1:63, 1:72, 2:1–2, 2:125, 2:154

    for flight simulators, 2:181

    for mathematical software, 3:138

    version 77, 2:154–155

    version 90, 2:155

    version 95, 2:155

    version 2000x, 2:155

    version I, 2:154

    version II, 2:125, 2:154

    version III, 2:154

    version IV, 2:154

4GLs. *See* Languages, very-high-level

Fractals, 3:*137*

Frame grabbers, 4:39

Frame relay, 1:156

Frame systems, for expert systems, 3:90

FrameMaker software, 3:197

France

    cybercafes, 4:54

    early automatons, 1:169

    Minitel network, 1:**142–145**, 4:54

    software piracy, 3:184

    TGV rail system, 2:159

France Télécom, 1:142–144, 2:165

Frankel, Stanley, 4:102–103

Franklin, Benjamin, 4:118

Frankston, Robert, 3:193, 4:98

Free BSD copyrights, 3:156

Free Software Foundation (FSF), 3:155–157

Free speech

    vs. censorship, 4:32, 4:33–34, 4:132

    ethical principles, 4:101–102

    invasive programs as, 2:96

Free trade, information technology standards, 1:101

Freedom of Information Act (FOIA), 4:182

Freedom 7 spacecraft, 1:151

Freespace loss, 2:220

Frege, Gottlob, 1:18

Frend, William, 1:122–123

Freon, defined, 3:57

Frequency bands, 2:220

Frequency division multiplexing, 3:33

Frequency modulation. *See* FM

Frequency Modulation Synthesis, 3:148

Frequency reuse, 3:32–33

Frequent flyer mileage, recordkeeping, 3:15

Frisch, Otto, 3:55

Frogs, genetically engineered, 3:143

Front end of compiler, 2:52

FSF (Free Software Foundation), 3:155–157

FSK (frequency shifting key), 2:46

FTH (fiber to the home) systems, 2:47, 2:78

FTP (File Transfer Protocol), 4:**110–112**
  aborting transfer, 4:111
  authentication, 4:110
  client/server technology, 2:37
  close command, 4:111
  control information connections, 4:111
  Cute, 4:205
  data transfer connections, 4:111
  defined, 4:32
  ease of use, 4:206
  firewalls, 4:108
  functions, 4:205–206
  GET command, 4:111
  history, 4:149, 4:205
  initiate session command, 4:111
  objectives, 4:110
  PUT command, 4:111
  vs. Telnet, 4:111, 4:205

Fujitsu
  as Amdahl competitor, 4:5
  as IBM competitor, 1:90
  parallel processors, 2:135

Full-text indexing, by search engines, 4:188

Functional programming, 2:99

Functions, in spreadsheets, 3:192

Funding a Revolution, 1:178

Fuzzy logic, 3:4, 3:90, 3:166

Fylstra, Daniel, 3:193

G

Galaxies, astronomical studies, 3:21–22

Gale, Leonard, 2:113

Galileo (astronomer), 1:165, 3:178, 3:179

Galileo International Inc. reservation system, 3:14

Galileo Jupiter probe, 3:188

Galleys, desktop publishing, 3:72

Gallium arsenide, 3:58

Gallup Organization, 4:183

Game controllers, 2:**79–81**
  force feedback, 2:80–81

history, 1:14–15, 1:69, 2:79–80
joysticks, 1:67, 2:79–80, 2:85, 2:146–147, 3:203
for multimedia systems, 2:85
RAM, 2:81
ROM, 2:81
yokes, two-handed, 2:79, 2:80

Game of Life, 4:9–11

GameBoy video game units, 1:69, 2:80

GameCube, 1:15

Gameline game, 1:69–70

Games, computer, 1:**67–71**
  access to, 1:67–68
  analog systems, 1:68
  animation technology, 1:12, 1:14–15
  business applications, 1:70, 1:180
  in cybercafes, 4:54
  cybernetic applications, 4:57
  estimated number of, 3:37
  graphic devices, 2:83
  history, 1:67, 4:126
  home system software for, 3:114
  how they work, 2:80
  interactive, 1:68, 1:110, 1:*110*, 2:84, 2:85
  Internet gaming, 1:68, 2:80, 3:37–38, 3:48, 3:114
  Japanese contributions, 1:69
  LSI circuits, 1:68
  modem transmission, 1:69–70
  multimedia applications, 4:127
  simulation, 1:70–71, 1:181
  user interfaces, 4:127
  violence and, 1:68, 1:70
  virtual reality, 1:67
  See also specific games

The Games Factory, 1:15

Games, traditional
  chess, 1:20
  electronic versions, 1:15
  Monte Carlo casinos, 1:180

GAMS (General Algebraic Modeling System), 3:79–80

Gamuts, color, 2:151–152, 4:66, 4:67

Gantt charts, 3:172, 3:*173*

Garage door openers, wireless, 2:219

Gardiner Foundation Award, 3:57

Garrison, Bruce, 4:161

Gates
  and, 2:19–20, 2:22, 2:59–60
  defined, 2:58
  nand, 2:60
  nor, 2:59

not, 2:19, 2:*22*, 2:23, 2:58–59
  or, 2:19, 2:*23*, 2:59

Gates, Bill, 1:137, 1:138, 3:131, 4:94, 4:*95*

Gateway bridging devices, 2:26–27, 4:148

Gattaca, 4:167–169

Gauss software, 3:79

Gaussian classifier pattern recognition, 2:141

Gbps, defined, 4:143

Gemini Program, 3:186

Gemstar, 4:77

Gene Amdahl's Law, 2:138

Gene sequencing. *See* Bioinformatics

Gene therapy (genetic engineering), 3:143, 4:167

Genealogies, printing, 2:152

General Algebraic Modeling System (GAMS), 3:79–80

General ledger software, 3:1

General Motors
  DSS tools, 3:68
  OnStar navigation system, 3:151
  robotics technologies, 1:170

General Public License (GPL), 3:156

Generalized Markup Language (GML), 2:105

Generations, computers, 1:**71–75**
  first, 1:71–72
  fourth, 1:74–75
  increasing size, 1:130
  second, 1:72–73
  third, 1:73–74

Generations, languages, 1:**75–80**
  first (machine), 1:75–76
  fourth (very high-level), 1:79–80
  object-oriented, 1:80
  second (assembly), 1:76–77, 1:137
  third (high-level), 1:78–79
  See also Languages; *specific languages*

Generative CAPP systems, 3:54

Generative decision-making tools, 3:18

Generic Flow Control (GFC) connections, 4:18, 4:20

Genesis game, 1:69

Genetic engineering (gene therapy), 3:143, 4:167

Genetic studies
  benefits, 3:142–143
  bioinformatics, 3:27–28, 3:45, 3:143–144
  DNA, 3:28, 3:142, 3:*143*

DNA computers, 4:167–169, 4:170–171

Watson and Crik, 4:36

Genuity, peering agreements, 4:145

GEO (Geostationary Orbit) satellites, 2:*202*

Geographic information systems (GIS), 3:**99–102**

agricultural applications, 3:6

attribute components, 3:99

data-sharing standards, 3:99–100

database management systems, 3:99, 3:101

databases for, 3:196

decision support functions, 3:101

distance calculations, 3:100–101

geometry components, 3:99

for global surveillance, 4:117

GPS and, 3:99

information sharing, 3:101

map reclassification operations, 3:100

overlays, 3:99, 3:100

remotely sensed images, 3:99, 3:*100*

spatial query processing, 3:101

thematic mapping, 3:101

tracking ice flow changes, 4:117

virtual advisors, 4:132

web-based, 3:101

Geography

computer applications, 3:137–138

maps, 3:28, 3:61, 3:101

Geometry

defined, 1:180

Euclidean, 1:165

fractals, 3:*137*

in GIS, 3:99

George Mason University, Space-Science World, 1:205

Geostationary Operational Environmental Satellites (GOES), 2:170

Geostationary orbit (GSO), 2:170, 4:117

German Aeronautics Research Institute, 2:222

Germanium, 1:105, 1:132, 1:133, 2:13

Germany

Internet censorship, 4:34

software piracy, 3:184

Gerrity, Tom, 3:67

Gerstner, Louis V., Jr., 1:91–92

Gery, Gloria, 3:43

Getty Institute, digital research facilities, 4:8

GFC (Generic Flow Control) connections, 4:18, 4:20

Gibbons, Edward, 3:19

Gibson, William, 4:106

GIF (Graphic Interchange Format), 1:8, 1:14, 4:67

GIF89 software, 1:14

Gigabit networking, 2:135

Gigabytes, defined, 4:170

GigaFLOPS (billions of floating point operations per second), 2:137, 3:58

Gigahertz (GHz), 2:220

Giles, C. L., 4:190

Gilliam, Terry, 1:10

Gimp software, 4:67

GIS. *See* Geographic Information Systems

Gladiator, pirated, 4:*100*

Glass, for fiber optics, 1:161

Glenn, John, 3:186

Glidden, Carlos, 1:120

Global Internet Liberty Campaign, 4:34

Global positioning systems (GPS), 4:**112–114**

Ada programming, 2:159

agricultural applications, 3:6

basic principle, 4:112

Casio wristwatch, 4:*113*

control segment (OCS), 4:113

differential measurements, 4:114

as GIS tool, 3:99, 4:132

GLOSNASS, 4:114

measurement coordinates, 4:114

for mobile computing devices, 4:166

for navigation, 4:117

NAVSTAR, 2:172

OnStar, 3:151

post-processing data, 4:114

precision farming, 4:117

railroad applications, 3:174

real-time data processing, 4:114

receivers, 4:114

satellite constellations, 2:170, 2:202, 3:151, 4:112–113, 4:114

signal weakness, 4:114

space segment, 4:112–113

user segment, 4:113–114

vehicle tracking, 4:117

at Winter Olympics, 4:114

Global surveillance, 4:**115–118**

CCTV, 4:118

Cuban Missile Crisis, 4:115

IKONOS satellite, 4:*115*

impact on society, 4:118

Landsat 7 satellite, 4:*116*

NRO, 4:117

See also Geographic information systems; Global positioning systems

Global system for mobile (GSM) standard, 2:32, 3:33–34, 4:49

Global warming, system analysis, 2:*193*

GLOSNASS GPS, 4:114

Glushkov, Victor M., 4:**119–120**

GML (Generalized Markup Language), 2:105

GMT (Greenwich Mean Time), 3:149

GNOME Office, 3:110

GNOME open source project, 3:157

Gnomons, of sundials, 3:149

GNU Linus operating system, 1:135

GNU project, 3:156, 3:157

Goals, Operators, Methods, and Selection (GOMS) system, 4:174

GOES (Geostationary Operational Environmental Satellites), 2:170

Goldberg, Emmanuel, 2:132

Goldfarb, Charles, 2:105

Goldstine, Herman H., 2:74

Goodlet, B.L., 3:55

Google search engine, 1:219, 4:189, 4:191

Gopher, 3:118, 4:149

Gordon, George (Lord Byron), 1:122, 1:123

Gore, Al, 4:183

Gosling, James, 4:121

Gould, Chester, 3:103

Government Code and Cypher School, 1:53–54, 1:198

Government funding, research, 1:**80–82**

Alan Turing, 1:81

CESAR body research study, 1:*82*

Charles Babbage, 1:80

collaboration with industry/universities, 1:81–82

Department of Defense, 1:81

expenditure statistics, 1:81

on information retrieval, 1:93

NSF, 1:81

Government, U.S., data on private citizens, 1:166–167

See also specific governmental agencies

GPL (General Public License), 3:156

GPS. *See* Global positioning systems

Graam-Leach-Blilely Act (1999), 1:168

Graduate Management Aptitude Test (GMAT), OMR scoring, 2:133

Graduate Records Examination (GRE), OMR scoring, 2:164

Grammar of programming languages, 2:2–3, 2:51

A Grand Day Out, 1:10

Granholm, Jackson, 4:120

Granularity of translations, 2:208

Graphic devices, 2:**81–83**
  AGP interfaces, 2:54–55
  bitmapped display, 2:82
  for consumer electronics, 2:83
  graphic display properties, 2:81–82
  hidden surface removal, 2:83
  vector graphics display, 2:82–83
  video co-processors, 2:82
  wearable, 2:82
  wire frame forms, 2:83
  See also Display devices

Graphic Interchange Format (GIF), 1:8, 1:14, 4:67

Graphic primitives, 3:30, 3:198

Graphical-based interfaces, 3:203

Graphical instrument editors, 1:149

Graphical user interfaces. *See* GUIs

Graphics
  anti-aliasing, 1:69
  bit maps, 2:149
  for computer games, 1:68, 1:69
  computer-generated, 1:160
  for desktop publishing, 3:198–199
  flowcharts, 2:55–57, 2:*56*
  GIS tools, 3:101
  government research grants, 1:82
  interactive, 2:69–70
  JPEG format, 1:101, 2:**96–99**, 4:67, 4:179
  legal applications, 3:130
  object linking and embedding, 3:119–120
  SIGGRAPH computer graphics show, 1:23
  for simulations, 1:180, 3:16
  vs. text mode output, 2:81
  TIFF format, 1:101
  turtle, 2:101
  vector, 2:82
  for VR applications, 1:205
  for weather maps, 3:209, 3:*210*
  for window-based interfaces, 1:217
  See also Digital images; Display devices; Hypermedia; Multimedia; Printing devices

Graphics accelerator cards, 1:14–15

Graphics computers
  Silicon Graphics, 3:209
  for weather maps, 3:209

Graphics controllers, 2:82

Graphics software
  Adobe Illustrator, 3:169
  Corel Draw, 3:169
  Crystal graphics, 3:169
  Gimp, 4:67
  Harvard graphics, 3:169
  Macro Media Flash, 3:169
  Painter, 3:169
  Photopaint, 3:169, 4:67
  Photoshop, 3:18, 3:169, 4:6, 4:67, 4:160, 4:181
  Picture It, 3:169
  presentation software, 3:169–170
  Smart Draw, 3:169
  Visio, 3:169

Graphics tablets, 2:*147*, 2:148

Graphs. *See* Data visualization

Gray, Elisha, 2:17

Great Britain. *See* United Kingdom

Greenwich Mean Time (GMT), 3:149

Grocery stores
  bar codes, 2:163
  checkout stations, 4:*59*
  smart cards, 2:165
  WebVan, 4:80

Groote Schuur Hospital, 3:56–57

Groove machine, 3:147

Grosch, H.R.J., 4:120–121

Grosch's Law, 4:120–121

Gross, Alfred J., 3:**102–103**, 3:*102*

Gross Electronics, 3:103

Grötrupp, Helmut, 2:165

Groupware
  defined, 3:48
  for distance learning, 3:76
  Lotus Notes, 3:170, 4:139–140
  for OAS, 1:158

Grove, Andy (Gróf, Adras), 1:107, 1:108, 1:109

Groves, General Leslie, 2:218, 4:103

GSM (global system for mobile) standard, 2:32, 3:33–34, 4:49

GSO (geostationary orbit) satellites, 4:117

G3 laptop computer, 1:17

Guardbands, 4:25

GUIs (graphical user interfaces)
  for Alto workstation, 4:147
  for ATMs, 3:25
  for browsers, 4:30

vs. command-line systems, 4:205
  defined, 1:81, 2:91, 3:25, 4:208
  for DOS, 3:203–204
  for DTP computers, 3:196–197
  for Excel, 3:193
  government research grants on, 1:81
  HTML for, 2:106, 4:151
  invention, 1:218
  for Macintosh computers, 2:130
  mouse as, 1:145, 2:91
  PARC contributions, 1:222
  pointing cursors and, 2:145
  for sound synthesis, 1:149
  for UNIX and Linux, 2:130, 3:203
  WIMP interfaces, 1:111
  for window-based interfaces, 3:203–204
  World Wide Web as, 1:218

Gulliver's Travels, 4:104

Gunfight game, 1:68

Gunter, Edmund, 1:182

Gurus, 4:**120–121**
  Berners-Lee, Tim, 1:218, 4:29–30, 4:121, 4:140, 4:149
  Denning, Peter J., 4:121
  Gosling, James, 4:121
  Granholm, Jackson, 4:120
  Grosch, H.R.J., 4:120–121
  Moore, Gordon, 1:107, 1:108, 2:15, 2:33, 3:40, 4:121
  origin of term, 4:120
  Torvalds, Linus, 2:131, 3:157, 4:*120*, 4:121
  web site use of term, 4:121
  See also Early pioneers; Entrepreneurs

Gutenberg, Johannes, 2:87

Gutenberg Project, 3:134, 4:76

Gyros (gyroscopes), defined, 3:7

H

Hacking/hackers, 3:**104–107**, 4:**121–124**
  defined, 4:121
  descriptions of, 1:206–207, 2:93, 2:96, 3:104
  economic damage, 4:123–124
  ex-employees as, 4:123
  and illegal sound recordings, 2:185
  intent of, 1:206–207, 2:93–94, 3:104, 3:106, 4:123
  media portrayal of, 3:104, 4:106
  targets, 1:36–37, 1:45, 1:49, 2:213, 4:123–124

types of, 4:123
and Y2K, 3:105
See also Invasive programs; Trojan horses; Viruses; Worms
Hacking/hackers, countermeasures, 3:105–106
  computer security consultants, 4:124
  firewalls, 4:**107–110**
  intelligent agents, 4:2–3
  pattern recognition tools, 2:141
  prosecution, 1:176, 1:210, 3:107
  security software, 3:**179–182**, 4:97–98
  vulnerability assessment tools, 3:105–106
Hacking/hackers, specific
  Book attack, 1:177
  Kevin Mitnick, 4:*122*
  Maxim, 3:105
  Wily hacker attack, 1:177
Hacking/hackers, strategies
  advance, 3:105
  avoiding detection, 1:209–210, 3:105
  covering tracks, 3:105
  disabling unauthorized copying devices, 4:46
  DoS and DDoS attacks, 3:2:96, 3:104, 3:180
  enumeration, 3:105
  footprinting, 3:104
  illegal entry, 4:123
  illegal possession of passwords, 4:122–123
  malicious codes in digital signatures, 4:72
  penetration, 3:105
  scanning, 3:104
  tools of, 3:*106*
Haddock, John, 4:7
HAL, fictional supercomputer, 4:105
Half-tone printing, 2:149, 2:151
Haloid Xerox, Inc., 1:220–221
Ham radios, 3:102
Hamilton, Edmond, 4:105
Hamming code, 2:45
Hamming, Richard, 1:27, 2:45
Hand-drawn (cel) animation, 1:10, 1:*11*
Handheld computers
  architectural applications, 3:18
  Asimov's prediction, 3:20
  e-book readers, 3:112, 3:134, 4:76–77, 4:*76*
  expansion slots, 4:166
  memory cards, 4:166
  for mobile computing, 4:165–166

scanners, 2:92, 2:134
  ubiquitous computing and, 3:84
  See also PDAs
Handoff process
  in air traffic management, 3:11
  for cell phones, 2:30, 3:33
Handshaking signals, 2:8–9
Handwritten documents
  graphic tablets and, 2:148–149
  OCR to digitize, 2:133–134
  pattern recognition tools, 2:138–139
  PDAs to digitize, 2:144
Hankey, Rosalie, 4:206
Hanna, William, 1:13
Happy (CIA magnetic tape storage arm), 2:*92*
Haptic, defined, 2:214
Hard-disk loading of software, 3:184
Hard disks, 2:188–190, 2:205–206
Hard drives
  disk management utilities, 3:110–111
  for early computers, 2:93
  for personal computers, 1:137
  SCSI for, 2:54
  for supercomputers, 1:182–183
Hard vs. soft copies, 2:69, 2:71
Hardware representation, in Algol-60 report, 2:1
Harvard graphics software, 3:169
Harvard Mark I computer, 1:51–53, 1:*52*, 1:59, 1:84–85, 1:89, 1:212
Harvard Mark II computer, 1:53, 1:60, 1:84–85
Harvard Mark III computer, 1:84–85
Harvard Mark IV computer, 3:206
Harvard University
  An Wang at, 3:206–207
  Computational Laboratory, 1:60
  Cyclotron, 3:55
  Grace Hopper at, 1:85
Hate speech, censorship, 4:*33*, 4:101–102
Hawking, Stephen, 4:*15*
Hazardous materials/environments
  computer vision tools, 4:67
  expert systems tools, 3:88
  robotics technologies for, 1:170, 2:166, 3:53
Hazen, Harold Locke, 1:50
HDLC (High-level Data Link Control), 2:9
HDTV (high definition television), 2:66, 4:124, 4:126
Head crashes, 2:190

Head-mounted displays (HMDs), 1:204, 1:205, 2:214, 3:*85*, 3:86
Head-related transfer functions, 2:184
Header Error Control (HEC), 4:18, 4:19
Headers, packet protocols, 2:120
Heading, in aircraft navigation, 3:7
Headphones, wireless, 2:220
Heal, Laird, 1:205
Health care. *See* Medical systems
Health Insurance Portability and Accountability Act (1996), 1:168
Hearing impairments, assistive technologies
  amplification systems, 4:14
  e-mail, 4:14
  TTYs, 4:14
Heart transplants, 3:56–57
Hearts, artificial, 3:28
Hearts game, electronic version, 1:15
Heath Robinson decoder, 1:54
Hebb, Donald, 3:154
HEC (Header Error Control) connections, 4:18, 4:19
Heilig, Mort, 2:214
Heinz Nixdorf Museums Forum, 4:38
Helium-6 research, 3:55
Hellman, Martin, 4:52
Help features, agents for, 1:114
Helsinki University, browser research, 4:30
Henry, Joseph, 2:113
Henschel Aircraft Company, 2:221
HEPNET, 4:144
Herodotus, on cryptography, 4:49
Herschel, John, 1:25
Hertz (Hz), defined, 2:220
Hertz, Heinrich, 2:219
Heuristic-based searches, 3:90
Heuristic knowledge, 3:123, 3:124, 3:154
Heuristics, defined, 1:20, 3:90
Hewlett-Packard Company (HP), 3:107–109
  collaboration with Disney Studios, 3:108
  employee-oriented policies, 3:108
  initial products, 3:108
  inkjet printers, 3:198
  minicomputer manufacturing, 1:141
  Model 2116 controller, 3:109
  Sandra Kurtzig and, 4:96
  Steven Jobs and, 3:108–109, 4:94
  Unicode supported by, 2:42

Hewlett, William, 3:**107–109**, 3:*108*

Hexadecimal (base-16) number system
  for Analytical Engine, 1:42
  converting binary numbers to, 1:30
  defined, 1:29
  for machine language, 1:76

Hidden Markov Models (HMMs), 3:189

Hidden surface removal, 2:83

Hierarchical networks, 1:115

Hierarchical paradigms in system analysis, 2:194

Higgins, Professor Henry, 2:15–16

High-bandwidth, defined, 4:88

High definition television (HDTV), 2:66, 4:124, 4:126

High-definition video, 3:98–99

High-level Data Link Control (HDLC), 2:9

High-level (third generation) languages. *See* Languages, high-level

High-Order Language Working Group (HOLWG), 2:159

High-Performance Computing and Communications program (HPCC), 2:135

High-precision/high recall, 4:189

High-precision/low recall, 4:189

High pressure, barometric reading, 3:208

High-speed data links, for radar data, 3:12

High-speed memory. *See* RAM

Hilbert, David, 1:199–200

Hiller, Lejaren, 1:149, 3:145

Hillis, W. Daniel, 2:160

Histograms (bar charts), 3:61, 3:*62*

Hitachi
  as IBM competitor, 1:90
  parallel processors, 2:135

The Hitchhiker's Guide to the Galaxy, 1:15

H.L. Hunley recovery, CA engineering tools, 3:32

HLRs (home location registers), 3:33, 3:201–202

HMDs (head-mounted displays), 1:204, 1:205, 1:206, 2:214, 3:*85*, 3:86
  defined, 1:204

HMMs (Hidden Markov Models), 3:189

Hoaxes, defined, 4:206

Hoff, Marcian, 1:108

Hoffman, E.T.A., 4:104

Holberton, Frances Snyder, 1:63

Holistic, defined, 3:4

Holland, Dutch Railways, 3:176

Holler, F. James, 4:37

Hollerith cards, 4:125–126

Hollerith code, 2:92

Hollerith Electrical Tabulating Machine, 1:84, 1:186, 1:*187*, 1:211

Hollerith, Herman, 1:**83–84**, 1:*83*
  and Census Bureau, 1:32, 1:81, 3:1
  punched cards, 1:32, 1:83–84, 1:88, 1:186, 1:*187*, 2:41, 2:92, 2:93, 3:59
  Tabulating Machine Company, 1:88, 1:186

Holograms, 3:127

HOLWG (High Order Language Working Group), 2:159

Home entertainment, 4:**124–127**
  CDs, 1:164, 2:83, 2:183, 2:189, 3:77, 4:124
  copyright issues, 4:127
  digital video recorders, 4:124
  DVDs, 2:204–205, 2:*205*, 4:124
  electronic toys, 4:124, 4:*125*
  HDTV, 2:66, 4:124, 4:126
  history, 4:125–126
  impact of computing technologies, 4:126–127
  impact of electricity, 4:126
  Internet gaming, 1:68, 2:80, 3:37–38, 3:48, 3:114, 4:124
  MP3, 4:126–127
  music keyboards and synthesizers, 4:124
  streaming audio and video software, 4:126–127
  TiVo digital video recorders, 4:124, 4:126, 4:127
  writeable CD and DVD players, 4:126
  See also Cameras, digital; Games, computer; Radio; Television

Home location registers (HLRs), 3:33, 3:201–202

Home system software, 3:**109–114**
  Adobe Acrobat Reader, 3:112
  anti-virus software, 3:105–106, 3:112
  archiving and compression utilities, 3:112
  categories, 3:110
  CD-Rs and CD-RW, 3:113
  DVDs, 3:76, 3:77, 3:113
  e-book readers, 3:112
  future applications, 3:114
  games, 3:**35–38**, 3:48, 3:114
  Internet connectivity tools, 3:113
  office suites, 3:110, 3:118–120, 3:170, 3:184

reference tools, 3:112–113
streaming audio and video, 3:113
system and disk management utilities, 3:110–111

Homer, robot descriptions, 1:172

Homing beacons, as navigation tools, 3:149–150

Honeywell
  minicomputer manufacturing, 1:141
  suit against Sperry-Rand, 2:74

Hopkins Beast, 1:169

Hopper, Grace Murray, 1:**84–87**, 1:*86*
  award (ACM), 1:21
  COBOL work, 1:85, 1:86
  coined "computer bug," 1:53, 1:85
  compiler research, 1:86
  FORTRAN work, 2:156
  Harvard Mark I-series computers, 1:84–85

Horty, John, 3:128

Host blocking, 4:32

Hot type, 3:71

HotBot search engine, 4:189

Hotel reservations, through CRS, 3:15

Hotmail.com, 1:47

HotSync Manager software, 2:142

Hounsfield, Godfrey Newbold, 3:**55–57**, 3:*56*

HP. *See* Hewlett-Packard Company

HP UX operating system, 2:129

HPCC (High Performance Computing and Communications) program, 2:135

HTML (Hypertext Markup Language)
  for automatic documentation, 2:127
  browsers and, 4:28–29
  coding, example, 2:*105*
  defined, 3:118, 4:28
  development, 4:30, 4:92, 4:121
  distinguished from XML, 2:107
  for e-banking, 4:74
  for e-journals, 4:83
  for e-mail, 1:47
  embedded JavaScript programs, 4:155–156
  for GUIs, 2:106, 4:151
  for online credit information, 4:48
  syntax, 2:106, 4:153
  for World Wide Web, 1:101, 1:218, 2:71, 2:105–106, 4:30, 4:151

HTML composer/editors, 3:110
HTTP (hypertext transfer protocol)
    cookies and, 4:40
    defined, 4:27
    development, 4:29, 4:92, 4:121
    for servers, 2:71
    Trojan horses and, 4:109
    for World Wide Web, 1:101,
        1:218, 2:37
Hubbard, Gardiner, 2:17
Hubbard, Mabel, 2:16–17
Huffman Codes, 2:44
Hughes, Thomas, 1:178
Human behavior
    GOMS system, 4:174
    Herbert Simon and, 4:197–198
Human body, as machine, 4:57
*Human Factors in Engineering and
    Design*, 1:64
Human factors, user interfaces,
    3:202–203, 4:**127–130**
    agents, 4:129
    aircraft, 1:64
    assistive technologies for disabled
        persons, 4:**11–16**, 4:*87*
    automobiles, 1:64
    for computer games, 4:127
    display devices, 4:128–129
    for educational software, 4:127
    Ernest McCormick's contribu-
        tions, 1:64–65
    fill-in forms, 4:128
    hardware for, 4:129
    multiple tasks, 4:128–129
    psychological issues, 4:200–201
    role of, 4:127
    software for, 4:129
    software tutorials, 4:129
    spreadsheets, 4:128
    standards, 1:100
    3-D (virtual reality), 4:129
    See also Ergonomics; Interactive
        systems
Human resources
    database linking agents, 4:1–2
    E-benefits, 4:96
    employee demographics, 3:2
    payroll software, 3:2
Human Rights Watch, 4:33
Humdrum model, 3:146
Hurricane Andrew, catastrophe in-
    surance, 4:91
Hurst, G. Sam, 2:198
Hydraulic, defined, 2:166
Hydrofoil HD4, 2:18
Hydrologic, defined, 3:99
HyperCard, 1:88

Hyperlinks
    browsers and, 4:27
    in compound documents, 3:120
    defined, 4:188
    for e-books, 4:76
    e-journals, 4:81
    function, 4:30
    search engines and, 1:96
Hypermedia, 2:**83–86**
    defined, 2:84
    distinguished from multimedia,
        2:83
    early demonstrations, 1:87
    examples, 2:83
    information retrieval, 1:92
    OAS applications, 1:159–160
    technology, 2:86
Hypertext, 1:**87–88**, 2:84, 4:29, 4:30,
    4:92
Hypertext Markup Language. *See*
    HTML
Hypertext transfer protocol. *See*
    HTTP

I

"I Have No Mouth, and I Must
    Scream," 4:105
I-Minitel, 1:144
I-mode cell phones, 3:34
I/O channels, in networks, 2:35
I/O controllers (arbiters), 2:54
I/O (Input/Output) devices
    defined, 2:35
    of early computers, 2:45
    interfaces with computer,
        2:52–54
    of minicomputers, 1:141
    for multimedia applications, 2:85
    See also Input devices
I, Robot, 1:14, 1:173, 3:20
IAS machine, 1:72
IBM card readers, 1:55
IBM cards, 1:186, 1:187
    See also Punched cards
IBM clones (IBM-compatible),
    1:137, 4:4–5
IBM computers
    701 model, 1:72, 1:89, 1:212, 4:4
    704 model, 2:154
    1401 model, 2:93
    1500-series workstations, 3:41
    7090 model, 1:27, 1:72
    AP-101, 3:187
    ASCI White supercomputer,
        2:136
    Blue Storm, 1:185
    compatibility issues, 2:48–50

Deep Blue, 1:23, 1:*70*, 2:*89*, 3:36,
    3:37
    for early spacecraft, 3:186
    FORTRAN for, 2:155
    parallel processors, 2:135
    System/360 series, 1:74, 1:89–90,
        1:125, 1:126–127, 4:4, 4:5
    See also IBM-PCs
IBM Corporation, 1:**88–92**
    ASA role, 2:41
    beginnings, 1:84, 1:88, 1:186,
        1:211–212, 3:59
    Bill Gates and, 4:94
    competitors, 1:90
    e-newspaper readers, 1:*91*
    economic downturn, 1:91
    Lotus Development purchase,
        3:193, 4:96
    standards, 1:89–90
    THINK signs, 1:89, 1:211
    Thomas J. Watson, Jr., 1:89–90,
        1:212
    Thomas J. Watson Sr., 1:88–89,
        1:210, 1:211–212, 1:*211*
    Unicode supported by, 2:42
IBM Corporation, legal issues
    anti-trust suits, 1:90
    conflicts with Microsoft, 1:138
    intellectual property rights, 1:91
    privacy policies, 4:79
    source code sharing, 3:155,
        3:156–157
IBM Corporation, research
    Advanced Computing Systems
        Laboratory, 4:4
    database system development,
        3:60
    EBCDIC, 2:41
    first CRS, 3:24
    FORTRAN development, 2:154
    Gene Amdahl and, 4:4–6
    government research grants, 1:81
    Harvard Mark I computer, 1:52,
        1:*52*, 1:53, 1:89
    Internet backbone funding, 4:144
    John von Neumann and, 2:218
    John W. Thompson and, 4:97
    mainframe computers, 1:125
    microcomputers, 1:135–136
    NASA and, 1:153
    optical microchips, 1:134
    SGML development, 2:105
    Stretch Project, 4:4
    TCP/IP intranet, 4:152
IBM equipment
    650 data recorder, 1:188
    3740 device, 1:188

IBM equipment (continued)
  e-newspaper readers, 1:*91*
  MTST, 3:210–211
  RS/4000 routers, 4:143
  SNA routers, 2:27
  tabulators, 1:60, 4:102
IBM OS/2, 1:138, 3:25
IBM OS/390, 2:129
IBM OS/400, 2:129
IBM-PCs
  8086/8088, 1:142
  browsers for, 4:30
  compatibility issues, 2:49
  i-Minitel for, 1:144
  Intel microprocessors, 1:17, 1:74, 1:90, 1:107, 1:108, 1:137, 3:193
  introduction, 1:17, 1:90–92
  microcomputers, 1:135–136, 1:*136*
  open architecture, 1:36, 1:91
  palm-sized, 2:142
  space applications, 1:135
  Web access, 1:218
ICCA (International Computer Chess Association), 3:37
ICL DAP (Distributed Array Processor), 2:136
Icons, 1:213, 1:*215*, 2:127, 2:145
ICs. *See* Integrated circuits
IDEAL, e-journal, 4:84
Identification. *See* Authentication; Userids and IDs
Identification cards, smart cards as, 2:165
Identification indicators, 2:175
IDEs (Integrated Development Environments), 1:110
IDS (intrusion detection systems)
  anomaly-based, 3:180
  host-based, 3:180
  network-based, 3:180
  signature-based, 3:180
IDSA (Interactive Digital Software Association), 1:181
IEC (International ElectroMechanical Commission), 1:99, 1:100
IEEE (Institute of Electrical and Electronics Engineers), 1:**102–104**
  Computer Society, 1:102–104, 4:5, 4:99
  curriculum recommendations, 1:103
  history, 1:102, 1:*103*
  Joint Conference on Digital Libraries, 4:69
  membership statistics, 1:102
  publications, 1:102, 1:104

  standards, 1:100, 1:102, 1:103, 3:138, 4:166
  Xplore, e-journal, 4:84
IEEE-1394 (Firewire), 2:178
IEEE Internet Computing Online magazine, 4:3
IETF (Internet Engineering Task Force), 1:100, 2:11
If-then statements, 3:90, 3:123
Igor software, 3:146
Illiac Suite, 1:149, 3:145
Illiad, descriptions of robots, 1:172
Illiquid, defined, 4:91
Illustrator software, 3:169
ILOVEYOU virus, 1:*209*
IMac computer, 1:17
Image analysis, medicine, 3:**114–117**
  applications, 3:117
  CAT, 3:55–56, 3:57, 3:114–115, 3:177, 3:*178*
  computers for, 3:117
  MRI, 3:116–117, 3:*116*
  radiology, 2:139–140, 2:*140*
  radiology (nuclear medicine), 3:55–56, 3:114, 3:115–116
  ultrasound, 3:114–115, 4:66
Image extraction and recognition, for computer vision, 4:39–40
Image pre-processors, 4:39
Image processing systems
  for e-banking, 4:74
  OAS applications, 1:159–160
  parallel processing, 2:134–135
  pattern recognition tools, 2:**138–141**
  for scientific visualization, 3:177–178
  See also Digital images
Image segmentation, for computer vision, 4:39
ImmersaDesks, 1:204, 1:205–206
  defined, 1:204
ImmersaWalls, 1:204, 1:205
  defined, 1:204
Immersive, defined, 1:181
Impact printers, 1:128
Implementing repeaters, 2:178
IMS subsystem, 1:127
In-betweening animation technique, 1:11–12
"In the Deep of Time," 4:105
Inclination of satellite orbits, 2:169–170
Independent service organizations (ISOs), as ATM owners, 3:26
InDesign software, 4:160
Index terms
  for digital libraries, 4:70

  for information retrieval, 1:96
  for search engines, 4:134, 4:190
Indexed Sequential Access Method (ISAM), 2:156
Indiana Folklore, 4:206–207
Indiana University, sound synthesis research, 2:116
Industrial Revolution, and home entertainment, 4:125
Inference, defined, 3:124
Inference (reasoning) engines
  brute-force searches, 3:90
  current research, 3:91
  for DSS applications, 3:69
  for expert systems, 3:89
  heuristic-based searches, 3:90
  for knowledge-based systems, 3:123–124
Information access, 4:**130–133**
  asynchronous and synchronous applications, 4:132
  digital divide, 3:131, 4:130–131
  impact on education, 4:132
  impact on society, 4:132–133
  Internet browsers, 4:132
  modes, 4:131
  multilingual concerns, 4:131
  political information, 4:181–182
  search engines, 4:130
  worldwide, 4:*131*
Information aggregating agents, 4:1
Information, defined, 2:86–87, 4:135, 4:137
Information overload, 4:**133–136**
  impact of mobile computing devices, 4:133
  personalization techniques, 4:135
  search engine usefulness, 4:134–135
  statistics, 4:133
Information privacy. *See* Privacy
Information processing languages (IPLs), 4:174
Information retrieval (IR), 1:**92–97**
  agents, intelligent software, 4:**1–4**
  Archie, 4:149
  Boolean searches, 1:93–95, 2:19–20, 2:23
  cache memory and, 2:27–28
  data warehousing, 3:67, 4:**63–65**
  e-books and, 4:76–77
  e-journals, 4:81–82
  for GIS, 3:101
  history, 1:93
  hypermedia and, 2:83
  hypertext and, 1:87–88
  index terms, 1:95–96

information overload and, 4:**133–136**

library applications, 3:**131–134**, 4:69

personalization techniques, 4:135

smart cards, 2:165

Smart system, 1:95

TREC research, 1:96

vector space models, 1:95

See also Database management systems; Internet browsers; Memory managers; Search engines

Information retrieval systems (IRS), 2:88

Information systems, 2:**86–90**

database linking agents, 4:1–2

decision support, 2:88

expert, 2:87, 2:88–89

information retrieval, 2:88

Internet as, 2:90

IT, 2:87

management information, 2:89–90

personal information managers, 2:141–142, *2:143*, 4:1

See also Databases

Information systems managers, *1:39*

Information technology (IT)

AI as, 2:87

expert systems as, 2:87

jobs for computer professionals, 3:47

Information technology standards, 1:**97–101**

for CAIs, 3:42

for cell phone system, 2:32

compatibility (open systems design), 2:**48–50**

for compression, 2:97

for computer interfaces, 2:48–50, 2:53–54

for computer software, 1:100–101

for copyright protection, international, 4:46

current issues, 1:101

for digital libraries, 4:69, 4:71

for e-books, 4:77

for educational software, 3:81–82

for GIS data sharing, 3:99–100

history, 1:100

IBM-established, 1:89–90

for Internet interfaces, 2:49

for JavaScript, 4:159

networking protocols as, 2:37

overview, 1:97–99

for telecommunications, *1:98*, 1:99

for World Wide Web, 2:71

See also Protocols

Information technology standards, specific

AAL, 2:11–12

Advanced Encryption Standard algorithm Rijndael, 4:52

AGP interfaces, 2:54–55

ASA code, 2:41

ATIS, 1:100

CCITT, 1:99–100

DES, 4:51–52

EBCDIC, 2:109

ECMA, 1:100

EIA, 1:100

GSM, 2:32, 3:33–34, 4:49

IEC, 1:99, 1:100

IEEE, 1:100, 1:102, 1:103, 4:166

IETF, 1:100, 2:11

IS-95, 3:33–34

IS-136, 3:33–34

ISO, 1:99, 1:100

NCITS, 1:100

NISO, 1:100

OSI Reference Model, 2:120–121

PCI, 2:54

SCSI, 2:54

SGML, 2:105

TDMA, 3:34

UNICODE, 1:101

USB, 2:54

W3C, 1:100

*.zip extension, 3:112

See also ANSI; ASCII; JPEG format; MPEG format; TCP/IP

Information theory, 4:**136–138**

Boolean algebra and, 2:23

Claude Shannon and, 1:27, 4:137, 4:175, 4:195–196

encoding techniques, 4:137–138

noise and errors, 4:136–137

Informix databases, 3:132, 3:194

Infrared ports, for PDAs, 2:143

Infrared touch-screen panels, 2:200

Infrared (IR) waves, 2:202–203, 2:218–219, 2:220

Infrastructure

for computer industry, *2:49*, 3:45–46

defined, 1:181, 2:49, 3:45, 4:80

for educational software systems, 3:82

for embedded technologies, 3:84, 3:86–87

for fiber optics, 2:78

for high-speed data transmission, 2:46–47

for mobile computing, 4:164

for railroads, 3:173

for telecommunications, 4:192

Ingots (silicon), defined, 1:105

Ingres databases, 3:194

Ingress, defined, 2:201

Inheritance, in object-oriented languages, 2:126–127

Ink Development Corp., 4:97

Inkjet printers

color, 2:151

for desktop publishing, 3:198

how they work, 2:150–151

resolution, 2:150–151

Inks, colored, 2:151–152

Innovative Interfaces Inc., Millennium system, 3:133

Input

of algorithms, 2:3, 2:4

in system analysis, 2:194

Input devices, 2:**90–93**

ATM card readers, 3:25

for CAD systems, 3:16, 3:18, 3:30–31, 3:91

digitizing tablets, 2:198, 3:30–31

for DTP computers, 3:196–197

graphics tablets, *2:147*, 2:148

hands-free wireless infrared, 2:93

I/O devices, 2:35, 2:45, 2:52–54, 2:85

innovations, 2:54

magnetic stripe readers, 2:91

for music composition, 3:146–147

paper tape, 2:91

pen, 2:148

role of, 2:90–91

sub-atomic particle scanners, 3:163

touch pads, 2:146

trackballs, 2:148

typewriters, 3:202, 3:210–211

for voice recognition, 2:92–93

See also Cameras, digital; Joysticks; Keyboards; Light pens; Mouse, computer; OCR; Punched cards; Scanners; Touch screens

Input/Output devices. *See* I/O devices

Inquisition, impact on scientific research, 1:165

Instant messaging

AOL Instant Messenger, 4:140

for disabled persons, 4:12, 4:15–16

Instant messaging (continued)
SMS, 3:34–35
for teenagers, 4:193
Windows Messenger, 4:140
Institute de Recherche et de Coordination Acoustique/Musique, 2:116
Institute for Advanced Studies, 2:217
Institute for Advanced Study machine (IAS machine), 1:72
Institute for Social Inventions, International Internet-free Day, 1:115
Institute of Cybernetics (U.S.S.R.), 4:119
Institute of Electrical and Electronics Engineers. *See* IEEE
Institute of Museum and Library Services, 4:69
Institute of Radio Engineers (IRE), 1:102
Instituut voor Sonologie, 2:116
Insulators, 1:132
Insurance
catastrophe, online, 4:91
computer applications, 3:137
E-benefits, 4:96
Intangible, defined, 4:45
IntCAD (intelligent computer-aided design), 3:32
Integrated circuits (ICs), 1:**104–107**, 1:*105*
advantages, 1:162
ALU functions, 2:34
in Cray-1 computer, 3:58
defined, 1:73, 2:58, 3:58, 4:121
DIPs, 2:109
for early spacecraft computers, 3:187
fiber optics for, 1:161–163
invention, 1:104, 1:141, 2:33–34, 2:*110*
light-sensing capabilities, 3:127
linear, 1:106
for minicomputers, 1:141
for NASA, 1:153
patents, 1:107
PGAs, 2:109
SECs, 2:109
SIMMs, 2:109
size reductions, 1:105–106, 1:107, 1:108
in third-generation computers, 1:73–74
See also Microchips/microprocessors; Semiconductors; Transistors
Integrated circuits, construction and manufacturing
Fairchild Semiconductor, 2:34

large-scale integration, 2:61–62
medium-scale integration, 2:61
molecular computing, 4:**167–169**
nanocomputing, 4:**169–172**
small-scale integration, 2:61
very-large-scale integration, 2:62
See also Chip manufacturing
Integrated Development Environments (IDEs), 1:110
Integrated pest management (IPM), 3:4–5
Integrated Service Digital Network (ISDN), 2:10, 2:11, 3:75, 4:26, 4:88
Integrated software, 3:**117–120**
compound documents, 3:119–120
cut and paste tools, 3:119
history, 3:118–119
hyperlinks, 3:120
Lotus SmartSuite 97, 3:119
Lotus Works, 3:170
Microsoft Office 97, 3:119
Microsoft Works, 3:170
object linking and embedding, 3:119–120
office suites, 3:110, 3:118–120, 3:170, 3:184
productivity software packages, 3:170
uses, 3:117–118
WordPerfect Works, 3:170
See also Spreadsheets
Integration, defined, 2:61
Intel Corporation, 1:**107–109**
anti-trust suits, 1:109
beginnings, 2:15
and Busicom, 1:107–108
compatibility issues, 2:48, 2:50
founding, 1:107–108
game simulations, 1:181
intellectual property rights, 1:91
market share, 1:109
Robert Noyce and, 2:*110*
Intel microprocessors
4004, 1:74, 1:107, 1:108, 1:134–135, 2:34
8008, 1:108
8060, 1:74
8080, 1:15, 1:68
8086, 2:34–35
8088, 1:108
80486, 1:107
for ATMs, 3:25
CPUs, 2:35
for IBM-PCs, 1:17, 1:74, 1:90, 1:107, 1:108, 1:137, 3:193

list of key, 1:109
Madison Itanium, 2:28
manufacturing process, 1:108–109
patents, 1:108
Pentium (586), 2:35
Pentium III Xeon, 1:107
Pentium IV, 1:107, 1:108, 2:35
Pentium Pro PC, 1:74
x86 series, 2:35
Intellectual property
Computer Fraud and Abuse Act, 1:37
defined, 1:36, 4:46
and digital libraries, 4:71
ethical principles, 4:100
IBM-PCs as, 1:91
and illegal sound recordings, 2:184–185, 4:*43*, 4:*44*, 4:205
information access and, 4:132
software as, 3:155–156, 3:184–185, 4:177–178
See also Copyrights; Patents
Intelligence, definitions, 1:20–21
Intelligent agents, 2:72
Intelligent computer-aided design (IntCAD), 3:32
Intelligent Network (IN), telephony, 3:201
Intelligent software agents. *See* Agents, intelligent software
Interactive Digital Software Association (IDSA), 1:181
Interactive systems, 1:**109–115**
agents, 1:111, 4:**1–4**, 4:129
CAD-CAM systems, 1:110, 3:**29–32**
command-line systems, 1:110
direct manipulation, 1:111, 1:112–113, 4:129
display devices, 2:63
embedded systems, 1:111, 1:114
games and simulations, 1:*110*, 2:84
graphics, 2:69–70
hypermedia, 2:86
IDEs, 1:110
Minitel network, 1:**142–145**
MIT research, 3:67
multimedia, 1:87, 2:84–86
online newspapers, 2:85, 4:*162*
for scientific visualization, 3:177–178
Sketchpad, 3:16, 3:30
Vannevar Bush's contributions, 1:87
virtualization/visualization, 1:111, 1:113

window interfaces, 1:**212–218**

Xerox Star, 1:111

See also GUIs; Internet browsers; Search engines; User interfaces

Interactive television (ITV), 3:75, 3:76–77, 4:88

Interconnectivity

Bluetooth cable system, 2:220, 4:166

data warehousing, 3:67, 4:**63–65**

defined, 1:34

hypertext and, 1:88

information theory, 4:**136–138**

intelligent agents and, 4:2–4

Internet backbone, 4:**142–146**

of nanoscale devices, 4:171

parallel transmission, 2:119

serial vs. parallel transmission, 2:119

See also Buses; Compatibility (open systems design); Networks

Interfaces

defined, 2:48, 3:25, 4:89

electrical, standards, 2:48–49

See also Computer system interfaces; Human factors, user interfaces; User interfaces; Window interfaces

Interlace scanning, 2:63

Interleaf software, 3:197

Internal factors, in data mining, 4:59

Internal reflection, for fiber optics, 1:161

Internal Revenue Service (U.S.). *See* IRS

Internal storage. *See* Memory/memory devices

International Association for Cybercafes, 4:53

International Business Machines Corporation. *See* IBM Corporation

International Collegiate Programming Contest, 1:23

International Computer Chess Association (ICCA), 3:37

International Conference on Computer Communications, 1:218

International ElectroMechanical Commission (IEC), 1:99, 1:100

International Electrotechnical Commission, 2:96

International Honor Society for the Computing Sciences (Upsilon Pi Epsilon), 1:104

International Internet-free Day, 1:115

International Journal of Geographical Information Science, 3:101

International Organization for Standardization. *See* ISO

International Society for Folk Narrative Research, 4:207

International Space Station, 1:135

International Time Recording Company, 1:88, 1:186

Internet, 1:**115–117**

bandwidth, 2:105, 2:212, 4:24, 4:162, 4:204

censorship protocols, 4:32–34

Census Bureau information on, 1:32–34

communication protocols, 1:116, 1:218

as communication system, 2:47

copyrights and, 4:43

and CSCWs, 3:48

dangling string network monitors, 3:84–86

distinguished from Minitel, 1:144–145

distinguished from telephone networks, 1:116–117

distinguished from World Wide Web, 1:218, 2:71

document processing role, 2:71

domain naming systems, 1:176

economic and social impact, 1:115–116, 1:*116*, 4:200

federal interest computer laws, 1:35

information overload, 4:**133–136**

as information system, 2:90

intelligent agents, 2:72

International Internet-free Day, 1:115

as LAN, 1:191

MP3 audio, 2:98

multimedia applications, 3:204

music transmission, 1:147

as network, 1:157, 2:24

Norton Internet Security, 4:98

as packet-switched network, 1:116–117, 4:146

programming languages, 2:128

public access sites, 4:131

QoS difficulties, 2:213–214

software, 1:218

telephony and, 3:202

See also E-commerce; FTP; World Wide Web

Internet, applications, 4:**138–142**

peer-to-peer networking, 1:115, 4:138, 4:141

See also E-mail; Internet browsers

Internet, backbone, 4:**142–146**

ANSNET, 4:144–145

ASes, routing, 4:143

backbone, defined, 4:142

EBONE, 4:143, 4:145

EGP, 4:143

history, 4:142

NAPs, 4:145

NSFNET, 4:142–145

peering agreements, 4:145–146

peering points, 4:143

SONET, 4:143

T1 and T3 lines, 4:26–27, 4:143

TCP/IP network organization, 4:142–143

technology, 4:143

transit agreements, 4:145–146

Internet browsers, 4:**27–31**

applets, 2:128, 4:82, 4:109, 4:152–155

automatic documentation and, 2:127

bandwidths, 4:141–142

cookies, 1:168, 4:**40–43**

defined, 2:71

for disabled persons, 4:16, 4:30, 4:31

document processing role, 2:71

free, 1:45, 1:138, 4:28, 4:30

functions, 4:28, 4:*29*

GUIs, 4:30

history, 4:29–30

information aggregating agents, 4:1

integrated with file managers, 4:141

as interactive systems, 1:110

JavaScript interpretation, 4:155–158

microbrowsers for cell phones, 3:34

open source model, 4:141

RDF, 4:31

specialized, 4:28

SSLs, 1:43, 4:49, 4:74

user interfaces, 4:132

via intranets, 4:150

VR for, 2:214

W3C and, 4:140

as Web clients, 4:27

See also HTML; HTTP; URLs; XML

Internet browsers, specific

America Online, 1:218–219, 4:28, 4:140

CompuServe, 4:28

Erwise, 4:30

Lynx, 4:30

Mosaic, 1:218, 4:30, 4:149

Internet browsers, specific (continued)
Netscape Communicator, 3:113
Netscape vs. Microsoft, litigation, 4:140
Nexus, 1:218, 4:30
role of Microsoft and Netscape, 4:140
Shockwave, 1:14
Viola-WWW, 4:30
See also Internet Explorer; Netscape Navigator
Internet cafes. *See* Cybercafes
Internet connections
access speed, 4:24
ADSL, 2:47, 4:26
bandwidth, 2:105, 2:212, 4:24
bridging devices for, 2:24
broadband communications, 4:25–26
cable modems, 3:113, 4:26–28
fiber optics for, 2:78
interface standards, 2:49
ISDN, 2:10, 2:11, 4:26
mainframe connections, 1:126, 1:128
for mobile computing devices, 4:166
modem speeds, 2:46–47
routers, 1:117
TCP, 2:37
wireless access, 2:47, 2:220
See also ISPs; Routing/routers
Internet Engineering Task Force (IETF), 1:100, 2:11
Internet Explorer
cookie storage, 4:42
dominance, 1:219, 3:113
features, 4:28
introduction, 4:30–31
for Macintosh computers, 1:138
unfair competition suit, 4:140
user interfaces, 4:132
Web animation, 1:14
Internet, history, 4:**146–150**
Alto workstation, 4:147
ARPANET, 1:115, 1:218, 2:90, 4:144, 4:147
commercial use, 4:149
convergence, 4:149
EFF, 4:149
FTP introduced, 4:149
gopher, 3:118, 4:149
legal issues, 4:149–150
NCP standard, 4:146
packet-switched networks, 1:116–117, 4:146, 4:*147*

privatization, 4:149
South Dakota, technology, 4:149
TCP proposal, 4:147–148
Internet piracy, 3:183
Internet Protocol. *See* IP
Internet resources
"Agents on the Web," 4:3
airline reservations, 3:15
animation technology, 1:14
astronomic data, 3:23
CCTV monitoring and control, 4:118
chat rooms, 2:38, 4:124
chemistry, 4:36–37
chess playing, 3:37–38
for conservation groups, 3:28
cybercafes, 4:**53–55**, 4:*54*, 4:*139*
cybertherapy, 3:140
databases, 3:64
Digital Landfill, 4:6–7
digital libraries, 4:69, 4:*70*
for disabled persons, 4:12, 4:14, 4:15–16
downloading software, 1:44, 1:46
e-banking, 1:46, 4:**73–75**
e-journals and e-publishing, 4:**81–84**
educational courses, 1:46, 1:220, 2:84, 2:85, 3:75–77, 3:80–82, 4:36–37
free e-mail providers, 1:47, 1:49
games, 1:68, 1:181, 2:80, 2:84, 2:85, 3:37–38, 3:48, 3:114, 4:124
government research grants, 1:81
information access, 4:**130–133**
for journalists, 4:161
legal applications, 3:129, 3:130
library applications, 3:131–134
mathematical software, 3:138
open source software, 3:155–156
parasitic disease information, 3:27
political information, 4:182, 4:183
stock trading, 4:89–90
video editing via, 3:98–99
weather forecasting information, 3:209
See also E-commerce
Internet routers, 2:12
Internet Service Providers. *See* ISPs
Internet Society, 1:168
Interpolation
in animation, 1:12
of digital images, 4:181

Interpress page description language, 3:199
Intranets, 4:**150–152**
benefits, 4:150
database connections, 4:63
defined, 1:43, 4:63
for disabled persons, 4:15–16
EDI, 1:43
examples, 4:152
firewalls, 4:151
functions, 4:150
library applications, 3:133
Navy Marine Corps, 4:*151*
as networks, 1:157
TCP/IP, 4:150
tracking user access, 4:151
web servers, 4:150
Introduction to Cybernetics, 4:119
Introduction to Finite Mathematics, 3:121
Introduction to Mathematical Logic, 1:200
The Intruders: The Invasion of Privacy by Government and Industry, 1:168
Intrusion detection systems (IDS)
anomaly-based, 3:180
host-based, 3:180
network-based, 3:180
signature-based, 3:180
Intuitive Surgical, Da Vinci Surgical System, 2:168
Invasive programs, 2:**93–96**
anti-virus software, 2:96, 3:112
authors of, 1:207, 2:93, 2:96
Computer Fraud and Abuse Act, 1:**34–38**
Corpus programs, 1:37
damage caused by, 2:93, 2:94
DoS and DDoS attacks, 2:96, 3:104, 3:180
intent of, 1:206–207, 2:93–94
legality of writing, 1:210, 2:96
payloads, 2:93
probe programs, 1:37
protection from, 3:105–106
security software, 3:**179–182**, 4:97–98
trigger conditions, 2:93
See also Hacking/hackers; Privacy; Security; Trojan horses; Viruses; Worms
Inventory software, 3:2
Inverters, role in logic design, 2:59
An Investigation of the Laws of Thought, 2:18
The Invisible Man, 3:20
Ionosphere, defined, 4:114

IP (Internet Protocol)
  to access e-journals, 4:82–83
  address availability, 2:122
  datagrams, 2:12
  defined, 2:11, 4:82
  dominance of, 2:37
  function, 1:116, 4:202
  reliability, 2:121–122, 4:203
  for routers, 2:26–27, 4:203
  for ubiquitous computing, 3:87
  See also TCP/IP
IPLs (information processing languages), 4:174
IPv6, 2:122
IR. *See* Information retrieval
IRE (Institute of Radio Engineers), 1:102
Iridium system, 2:202
IRIX operating system, 2:129
IRS (information retrieval systems), 2:88
IRS (Internal Revenue Service)
  DSS tools, 3:68
  tax preparation software, 3:1, 3:43, 3:60
IS-95 and -96 standards for cell phones, 3:33–34
Isaacson, Leonard, 1:149
ISAM (Indexed Sequential Access Method), 2:156
ISDN (Integrated Service Digital Network), 2:10, 2:11, 3:75, 4:26, 4:88
ISO (International Organization for Standardization), 1:99, 1:100, 2:42
  JavaScript, 4:159
  JPEG and MPEG standards, 2:96
  magnetic stripe cards, 3:136
  SGML standard, 2:105
ISOs (independent service organizations), as ATM owners, 3:26
Isosceles triangle, defined, 4:38
ISPs (Internet service providers)
  ASPs, 4:193
  censorship and, 4:33–34
  connection software, 3:113
  cost of service, 4:130
  defined, 1:47, 2:213, 4:33
  free e-mail providers, 1:47, 1:49
  and FTP, 4:205
  and increased e-mail volume, 4:138
  Internet backbone, 4:142–143
  SLAs with corporations, 2:213–214
  spam filters, 1:49

  technical support, 4:*194*
  telephony and, 3:202
  uplinks, 4:193
  upload vs. download transmission, 4:26–27
ISPs, specific
  America Online, 1:70, 1:218–219, 3:113
  ATTNET, 4:193
  CIX, 4:149
  PSINET, 4:145, 4:149, 4:193
  UUNET, 4:193
IT. *See* Information technology
ITA₂ code, 2:41
Iterative client server models, 2:36–37
Iterative, defined, 2:37
ITV (interactive television), 3:75, 3:76–77, 4:88
Iwatami, Toru, 1:69
*IX, defined, 4:143

J
Jacquard, Joseph-Marie, 1:83, 1:117, 1:119, 1:169, 4:199
Jacquard's loom, 1:**117–119**, 1:*118*
  Ada Lovelace on, 1:124
  punched cards, 1:7, 1:83, 1:169, 1:186
  social impact, 4:199
JANET, 4:144
Japan
  cybercafes, 4:55
  I-mode cell phones, 3:34
  Nippon Telephone and Telegraph Corporation, 4:*23*
  Purple cryptosystem, 4:51
  Shinkansen (bullet trains), 3:174, 3:*175*
  software piracy, 3:184
  video game technology, 1:69
Java applets, 4:**152–155**
  class library, 4:154
  destroy method, 4:153
  for e-journals, 4:82
  examples, 4:154, 4:*155*
  function, 2:128, 4:152
  help in learning, 4:153
  how they work, 4:152–153
  init method, 4:153
  paint method, 4:153
  start method, 4:153
  stop method, 4:153
Java programming language
  for e-banking, 4:74
  for Internet game tools, 3:114
  James Gosling and, 4:121

  for Java applets, 4:151, 4:154
  JINI model, 2:39, 3:86
  for mainframe servers, 1:128
  as object-oriented, 1:80
  security problems, 1:177, 1:208, 2:95
  smart card standards, 2:174
Java Virtual Machine (JVM), 2:128, 4:152
JavaScript programming language, 4:**155–159**
  Brendan Eich and, 4:158
  DOM, 4:157–158
  ECMAScript, 4:159
  examples, 4:156–157, 4:*156*, 4:*157*, 4:158, 4:*159*
  functions, 4:155–156
  for invasive programs, 2:95
  as loosely typed, 4:156
JavaSpaces, 2:39
Jaws, 1:11, 1:68
JCL (Job Control Language), 1:127
Jeopardy!, electronic version, 1:15
Jerry's Guide to the World Wide Web, 1:219, 4:98
Jet Propulsion Laboratory (JPL), 3:187, 3:188, 4:178
Jetsons, 1:13
JFIF (JPEG File Interchange Format), 2:97
JINI model, 2:39, 3:86
Joan/Eleanor project, 3:102
Job cost estimating software
  accounting, 3:2
  for architects, 3:17
  for fashion industry, 3:92
Job-entry computers, Bell Labs' Model 1, 1:51
Jobs, Steven, 1:15–17, 1:*16*, 1:69, 3:108–109, 4:30, 4:94–96
Jogging memory, 1:53
Johns Hopkins University, Hopkins Beast, 1:169
Johnson, A., 1:206
Johnson, J.B., 4:175
Johnson, Lyndon, 3:109
Joint Conference on Digital Libraries (IEEE), 4:69
Jones, D.F., 4:105
Journalism, 4:**159–162**
  computer-assisted reporting, 4:161
  desktop video and, 4:162
  digital graphics and audio, 4:160–161
  e-journals and e-publishing, 3:134, 4:**81–84**

Journalism (continued)
   history of computer use, 4:159–160
   Internet resources, 4:161
   multimedia applications, 4:160
   online newspapers, 4:161–162, 4:162
   television newsroom hardware and software, 4:160, 4:183
Joysticks, 1:67, 2:79–80, 2:85, 2:146–147, 3:203
   See also Game controllers
JPEG format, 2:96–99
   defined, 2:85, 4:179
   file extensions, 2:97
   JFIF, 2:97
   lossy compression, 2:97, 4:67
   as standard, 1:101, 2:96–97
   2000, 2:97
   uses, 2:97
JPL (Jet Propulsion Laboratory), 3:187, 3:188, 4:178
JSTOR, e-journal, 4:84
Julia, Gaston, 3:138
Juno.com, 1:47
Jupiter Media Metrix, 1:46
Jurassic Park, 1:11
JVM. See Java Virtual Machine

K

K-nearest-neighbors pattern recognition, 2:141
Kahn, Robert, 4:146–147, 4:148, 4:203
KAISSA chess-playing program, 3:37
Kapek, Karel, 1:172–173, 3:20
Kapor Enterprises, Inc., 4:96
Kapor, Mitchell, 3:193, 4:96, 4:149
Karlstrom, Karl V., Outstanding Educator award, 1:21
Karpov, Anatoly, 3:37
Kasparov, Garry, 1:23, 1:70, 2:89, 3:37
Katz, Phil, 3:112
Kay, Alan, 1:80
Kbps, defined, 2:178
KDE open source project, 3:157
Keller, Helen, 2:17
Kelvin, Lord (William Thomson), 3:162
Kemeny, John G., 2:2, 2:157, 3:120–122, 3:122, 4:208
Kempelen, Baron Wolfgang von, 3:37
Kennedy, John F., 3:186
Kerberos authentication technique, 4:83

Kerlow, Isaac Victor, 1:13
Kernighan, Brian, 1:27
Key sets, keyboard, 1:119
Keyboard controllers, 2:91
Keyboards, 1:119–122
   adaptations for disabled persons, 4:13
   for desktop publishing, 3:197
   Dvorak, 1:120–121
   ergonomics, 1:65, 1:121–122, 1:121, 2:91
   how they work, 1:119–120, 2:91
   innovations, 2:54
   key arrangements, 1:120
   multilingual, 1:121
   for music composition, 3:146–147
   in Paris in the Twentieth Century, 4:105
   for PDAs, 2:141, 2:144
   programmable, 3:204–205
   QWERTY, 1:120
   scan codes, 2:91
   typewriters, 1:120
   window interfaces, 1:215
   wireless, 2:220
Keyframing animation technique, 1:11–12
Keypunch machines, 1:185, 1:186
Keys, cryptographic, 4:49–50
Keyword blocking, 4:32
Keywords
   for programming languages, 2:153–154
   for speech recognition, 3:190
Kholodenko, Elena, 4:78
Kilby, Jack, 1:73, 1:74, 1:106, 1:107
Killer Instinct, 1:15
Kilobytes, 1:29, 1:129
Kilohertz (kHz), defined, 2:220
Kinematics, defined, 2:216
Kinetics, defined, 2:216
King, Ada Byron, Countess of Lovelace. See Lovelace, Ada Byron King, Countess of
King, Martin Luther, Jr., 4:7
King, Stephen, 4:77
King, William, 1:123
Kittredge, Jeannett, 1:211
Kleinrock, Leonard, 4:146, 4:147
Kludge, defined, 4:120
Kluwer Online, e-journal, 4:84
Knowledge-based systems, 3:122–124
   applications, 3:124
   current challenges and research, 3:91, 3:124

databases as, 1:96
   decision-making, 3:123–124
   diagnostic, 3:123–124
   expert system shells, 3:90
   factual knowledge, 3:123, 3:124
   GIS tools, 3:101
   heuristic knowledge, 3:123, 3:124
   if-then statements, 3:90, 3:123
   inference engines, 3:123–124
   Joshua Lederberg and, 3:124
   knowledge base creation, 3:89–90, 3:123–124
   predictions, 3:123–124
   troubleshooting, 3:90
   user interfaces, 3:123
   See also Databases; Expert systems
Knowledge discovery. See Data mining
Knowledge manipulation, 1:19–20
Knowledge representation, 1:18–19
Knowledge workers, for document processing, 2:69
Knuth, Donald, 1:21, 1:22
Kodak, instructional guides, 4:179
KPMG, KWorld intranet, 4:152
Kubrick, Stanley, 4:105
Kurosh, A.S., 4:119
Kurtz, Thomas, 2:2, 2:157, 3:120–121, 4:208
Kurtzig, Sandra, 4:96
Kurzwell scanners, 2:164

L

Lab tests, mechanized, 3:28
Labeled data, in pattern recognition, 2:139–140
Laboratorio Permanente per l'Informatica Musicale, 2:116
Lady and the Tramp, 1:12
LaGrange, Joseph, 2:18
Laird, John E., 4:173
Lakeside Programming Group, 1:138
Lambda calculus, defined, 2:99
LAN standard Ethernet, 2:124
LAN standard Token Ring, 2:124
Land's End, 4:80
Landsat satellites, 2:170–171, 4:116
Landscape design and construction software, 3:5
Langton, Christopher, 4:9
Language models, for speech recognition, 3:189
Language theory, programming languages and, 2:2–3

Languages, assembly. *See* Assembly language and architecture

Languages, business
AIMACO, 2:156
Commercial Translator, 2:156
FLOWMATIC, 2:156
See also BASIC programming language; COBOL

Languages, generations, 1:**75–80**
See also Languages: assembly, high-level, machine, object-oriented, and very-high-level

Languages, high-level (third generation), 1:78–79, 2:7, 2:125, 2:153
See also BASIC; C, COBOL, FORTH, FORTRAN, and PASCAL programming languages

Languages, information processing (IPLs), 4:174

Languages, machine, 1:75–76, 1:78, 2:6–7, 2:50–52, 2:114

Languages, markup, 2:**104–108**
application-neutral, 2:105
attributes, 2:69, 2:104
dHTML, 1:14
economics, 2:105
GML, 2:105
history, 2:104–105
MathML, 2:107–108
SMIL, 2:108
VRML, 1:10–11
XHTML, 2:107
See also HTML; SGML; XML

Languages, meta, 2:107

Languages, music modeling, 3:146

Languages, natural
as communication standards, 1:97
Morse Code translation, 2:114
multilingual keyboards, 1:121
processing, 1:20, 1:96
symbolic representation of information, 2:42, 2:45
translation tools, 2:101

Languages, object-oriented, 2:**124–128**
Ada, 1:80, 1:124, 2:158–159
attributes and members, 2:126
Bongo, 2:104
client/server models for, 2:39
components, 2:127
data structures, 2:125–126
DELPHI, 2:128
encapsulation and data hiding, 2:126
icons, 2:127
inheritance, 2:126–127
Logo versions, 2:104

object vs. class, 2:126
polymorphism, 2:127
RMI, 2:39
Smalltalk, 1:80, 1:216–217, 2:125–126, 2:128
syntax, 2:127
uses, 2:125–126
See also C++, Java, JavaScript, and Visual BASIC programming languages

Languages, page description
Interpress, 3:199
PDF, 2:105, 2:149, 3:112, 4:77, 4:83–84
Postscript, 2:149, 3:70, 3:72, 3:74, 3:198–199, 4:67

Languages, procedural, 2:**153–160**
compatibility issues, 2:158
compiling, 2:153
function, 2:153
interpreting, 2:153
RPC for, 2:39
See also Ada; ALGOL; BASIC; C; COBOL; FORTRAN; PASCAL

Languages, programming
for AI programming, 2:99–100
Bernoulli numbers, 1:26
for calculating devices, 1:141
comparative linguistic analysis, 3:159
compilers to translate, 2:50–52
conversational, 2:101
dialects, 2:154
for embedded systems, 2:7
evolution of, 2:125–126
functional, 2:99
grammar and symbols, 2:2–3
for invasive programs, 1:207–209, 2:95, 2:96
JCL, 1:127
keywords, 2:153–154
for mainframes, 1:128
meta symbols, 2:2–3
for microcomputers, 1:135
for music synthesis, 1:149
nonterminal symbols, 2:2–3
object-oriented, 1:80
parallel, 2:135
parse trees, 2:2
for personal computers, 2:7
predicate calculus, 1:19
prolog, 1:19
for real-time systems, 2:159
source, 2:50
standards, 1:100
structured, 2:125, 2:157

syntax, 2:1–3, 2:101, 2:154
system software and, 3:167
terminal symbols, 2:2
universal, 2:154, 2:155
utility for specific tasks, 2:154
See also specific languages

Languages, scripting, 3:118

Languages, very-high-level (4GLs), 1:79–80

LANs (local area networks), 2:119–122
ATM for, 2:10, 4:17
bridges, 2:24–26, 2:25
for CIA, 2:118
communication channels, 4:138
defined, 1:115, 2:24, 3:47, 4:1
firewalls for, 4:107
function, 1:156
history, 4:147
Internet backbone, 4:143
IR transmission media, 2:202–203
Kmart, and PDA technology, 2:144
for mainframes, 1:128
for mobile computing, 4:166
network architecture and, 2:117–118
for OAS, 1:157
repeaters, 2:24
role in CSCWs, 3:47–48, 3:50
security software for, 2:176
technology, defined, 2:10
telecommunications role, 1:191
twisted-pair transmission lines, 2:201
Wang's contributions, 3:207
wireless (WLAN), 2:221

Laplace, Pierre-Simon, 2:18

Laptop/notebook computers
Apple G3, 1:17
Dynabook, 1:80, 1:216–217
early portable computers, 2:64
electroluminescent panels, 2:67
for electronic books, 3:43
graphic devices, 2:83
keyboards, 1:119
networked, for electronic classrooms, 4:88
provided by schools, 3:83
touchpads, 2:146
trackballs, 1:147, 2:148
ubiquitous computing and, 3:84
wearable, 3:85
wireless, 2:221
See also PDAs

Large-scale integrated circuits (LSI), 1:68, 1:74, 1:141, 2:61–62

Larson, Lance Stafford, Outstanding Student Scholarship, 1:104

Laser disc players, for electronic classrooms, 4:86

Laser printers, 3:*125*
    Apple Laserwriter, 3:70, 3:72, 3:74, 3:198
    color, 2:*70*, 2:152
    how they work, 2:151, 3:127
    impact on document processing, 2:69
    for mainframes, 1:128
    PARC's contributions, 1:222
    Xerox 4045 CP, 2:*150*
    Xerox 9700, 3:198

Laser technology, 3:**125–128**, 3:*125*
    amplitude modulation, 3:127
    angle modulation, 3:127
    for bar code scanners, 3:127
    for flatbed scanners, 4:180–181
    how it works, 3:125–126
    light shows and holograms, 3:127
    medical applications, 3:125, 3:127–128
    metastable states, 3:126
    military applications, 3:125, 3:128
    monochromatic light beams, 3:126–127
    optical discs, 3:127
    photon population inversions, 3:126
    semiconductor diodes, 2:75, 2:77, 3:127

Lasker Award, 3:57

Lasseter, John, 1:13

Latent variables, in data mining, 4:61

Lathrop, George Parsons, 4:105

Laugh-O-Gram films, 1:12

Law enforcement
    ATM card thievery, 3:26
    electronic theft, 1:*176*
    vs. privacy issues, 1:167
    prosecution of hackers, 1:210, 2:96, 3:107
    radio communications for, 2:29
    SMART system for, 2:*31*
    for software piracy, 3:184–185
    See also Security

Lawrence Berkeley Laboratory, hacking attacks, 1:177

Lawrence, Steve, 4:190

LCDs (liquid crystal displays)
    cholesteric, 2:66, 2:67, 2:68
    construction, 2:64–65
    defined, 2:198

    display panels, 4:87
    how they work, 2:64
    lighting sources, 2:67–68
    projection technology, 4:86
    reflective vs. transmissive modes, 2:67
    TFTAM (AMLCD), 2:66–67, 2:68
    for touch screens, 2:198–199
    yield, 2:67

LDP (Linux Documentation Project), 3:157–158

Learning Company
    Carmen San Diego, 3:82
    Reader Rabbit, 3:82

Learning disabilities, assistive technologies, 4:13

Learning management systems. *See* LMSs

Learning Research and Development Center (LDRC), 3:41

Learning the Sciences of the 21st Century, 1:205

Lecture, origin of term, 4:84

Lederberg, Joshua, 3:*124*

LEDs (light emitting diodes)
    defined, 2:67
    for display devices, 2:67
    for fiber optics, 1:161, 2:75, 2:76
    for joysticks, 2:80
    for optical computer mice, 2:145–146

Lee, J.A.N., 3:158

Legal research software
    Boolean logic and operators, 3:128
    FindLaw search engine, 4:189
    Internet access, 3:129
    Lexis, 3:128–129
    Westlaw, 3:129

Legal systems, 3:**128–131**
    artificial intelligence and, 3:128
    case management, 3:129–130
    computer technologies for law students, 3:*131*
    courtroom proceedings, 3:130–131, 3:*131*
    document assembly, 3:129
    electronic docking, 3:130
    electronic file filing and retrieval, 3:130
    graphics tools, 3:130
    legal research, 3:128–129
    litigation support, 3:130

LEGO-Logo, 2:103

Leibnitz, Gottfried Wilhelm von, 1:18, 1:165, 2:18, 4:55, 4:199

Leica the space dog, 2:170

Leitz Camera, 2:222

LEO (Low Earth Orbit) satellites, 2:170, 2:202, 4:117

Lesser General Public License (LGPL), 3:156

Levin, Ira, 4:104

Lexical analyzers, 2:2, 2:50–51

Lexis legal research system, 3:128–129

LEXIS-NEXIS information system, 1:93

Libraries, censorship, 4:31–32

Libraries, digital, 4:**68–71**
    access to, 4:68–69
    ACM, 1:23, 4:69, 4:84
    advantages, 4:69
    American Memory project, 4:70
    characteristics, 4:68, 4:71
    Digital Library Federation, 4:69
    e-journals, 4:82
    hypermedia for, 2:86
    IEEE Joint Conference, 4:69
    Institute of Museum and Library Services, 4:69
    metadata, 4:68
    political information, 4:181
    resources for, 3:134
    social, legal, ethical issues, 4:69, 4:71, 4:132
    Spain/U.S. joint project, 4:*70*
    standards, protocols, interfaces, 4:69, 4:71
    technology, 4:70–71

Libraries, electronic catalogs, 3:*133*
    client/server technology, 3:132
    database management systems, 3:132–133
    Millennium system, 3:133
    OCLC, 3:132
    OPACs, 3:132–133
    operating systems, 3:132
    UNICORN, 3:133
    Voyager system, 3:133

Library applications, 3:**131–134**
    data warehousing, 4:63
    digital resources, 3:134
    electronic catalogs, 3:132–133, 3:*133*
    history, 3:131–132
    information retrieval systems for, 2:88
    Library of Congress Classification, 4:68
    MARC, 3:132
    networks, 3:133
    OPACs, 3:132–133
    See also Digital Libraries

Library of Congress (LC)
American Memory project, 4:70
automation study, 3:132
collaboration with National Library of Spain, 4:70
Library of Congress Classification, 4:68
Licensing agreements
GPL, 3:156
for open source software, 3:156
for software, 3:182–183
Licklider, Joseph, 4:146
Light Amplification by Stimulated Emission of Radiation. *See* Laser technology
Light pens, 2:91, 2:147, 2:148
for CAD systems, 3:16
for music composition, 3:146
for PDAs, 2:141, 2:144
Light shows, laser, 3:127
Limdep software, 3:79
Line printers, for mainframes, 1:128
Line sweeping algorithms, 3:101
Linear, defined, 2:138
Linear Pulse Coding Modulation, 2:182–183
Linear regression, 4:60
Linear vs. non-linear video editors, 3:96, 4:161
Link, Edwin, 1:178
Link Trainer, 1:178
Linked applications, integrated software, 3:119–120
Links. *See* Hyperlinks; URLs
Linux Documentation Project (LDP), 3:157–158
Linux operating system
applications, 2:129
bioinformatics use, 3:144
defined, 3:144
distinguished from UNIX, 2:131
history, 2:130–131
JVM for, 2:128
Linus Torvalds and, 2:131, 3:157, 4:120, 4:121
for mobile computing, 4:166
as open source, 3:157
user interfaces, 2:130
X-Windows, 1:217
The Lion King, 1:13
Liquid crystal displays. *See* LCDs
Lisa computer, 1:17, 1:111
LISP (List Processing) programming language, 2:99–100
artificial intelligence and, 1:19
interpretive environment, 2:100
John McCarthy and, 1:21

lists, 2:99–100
Logo as dialect, 2:100
object system and function overloading, 2:100
for parallel architecture, 2:137
run-time type checking, 2:100
syntax, 2:100
Litigation support tools, 3:130
The Little Mermaid, 1:13
LiveScript programming language, 4:158
Livestock and poultry production
computer-based feeding systems, 3:6
decision-making software, 3:4–5
recordkeeping software, 3:4
LMDS (local multipoint distribution service), 2:221
LMSs (learning management systems)
advantages/disadvantages, 3:42
"cool factor," 3:42, 3:83
developers, marketing issues, 3:82–83
evaluating, 3:81–82
how they work, 3:41–42
for non-traditional students, 3:43, 3:80
Local area networks. *See* LANs
Local/asynchronous learning model, 3:76, 3:77
Local loops, 2:221, 4:25
Local multipoint distribution service. *See* LMDS
Local/synchronous learning model, 3:76
Locales, multilingual keyboard layouts, 1:121
LOCI desktop calculators, 3:207
LOCK security systems, 2:172–173
Locking, of databases, 2:186–187
Logan Airport, aircraft flight simulation, 2:179
Logarithmic calculators, 3:206
Logarithms
defined, 1:2, 3:206
Difference Engine tables, 1:25
John Napier and, 1:150, 1:182
slide rules and, 1:2, 1:182
Logic
defined, 1:79
for expert systems, 3:90
fuzzy, 3:4, 3:90, 3:166
predicate, 3:90
for process control, 3:164
propositional, 3:138–139
Turing Machine as tool, 1:199–200

Logic, Boolean. *See* Boolean logic and operators
Logic chips, Intel designs, 1:107–108
Logic Theorem Machine (Logic Theorist), 4:172, 4:173, 4:198
Logical descriptions, 2:61
Logicon, Inc., UGPIC, 2:163
Logo Laboratory, 2:101
Logo programming language, 2:100–104
Bongo, 2:104
for elementary school education, 2:101
history, 2:100–101
learning activities, 2:101–102
LEGO-Logo, 2:103
MicroWorlds interpreter, 2:103
music, 2:103
object-oriented versions, 2:104
primitives, 2:102, 2:103
procedures, 2:102–103, 2:102, 2:103
as recursive, 2:102, 2:103
requirements, 2:101
StarLogo, 2:103–104
turtles, 2:101
variables, 2:102
Long-distance telephone calls, 3:200, 3:201
Long, Sen. Edward, 1:168
Loosely-typed languages, 4:156
Lopker, Pamela, 4:97
LORAN and LORAN-C navigation systems, 3:9, 3:151
Lorraine Motel, 4:7
Los Alamos Scientific Laboratory, 4:102–103
Lossy compression, 2:97, 2:184, 4:67
Lost update problems, databases, 2:186
Lotus Development Corporation, 3:193, 4:96
Lotus software
Freelance Graphics, 1:160, 3:169–170
Lotus 1-2-3, 3:1, 3:60, 3:118, 3:169, 3:193, 4:96
Notes, 1:158, 3:170, 4:139–140
SmartSuite, 3:119, 3:170
Word Pro, 3:167
Works, 3:170
Lovelace, Ada Byron King, Countess of, 1:122–124, 1:122
Ada programming language, 1:80, 1:124, 2:159
Analytical Engine for music, 1:149, 2:115

Lovelace, Ada Byron King, Countess of (continued)
  on artificial intelligence, 1:18
  collaboration with Charles Babbage, 1:26, 1:80, 1:123–124, 2:159
  as first programmer, 1:7, 1:80, 1:122, 1:124, 2:159
  on Jacquard's loom, 1:124
LoveLetter worm, 1:208, 2:93, 2:95
Low Earth Orbit satellites. *See* LEO satellites
Low-level languages. *See* Assembly language and architecture
Low precision/high recall, 4:188–189
Low pressure, barometric reading, 3:208
LSI (large-scale integrated) circuits, 1:68, 1:74, 1:141, 2:61–62
Lucent, 1:28
Lumens, defined, 4:86
Lycos search engine, 1:219, 4:191
Lynx browser, 4:30

M

MAC (Media Access Control), 2:24, 2:118–119, 3:159
MAC ATM Network, 4:74
Machine-dependent codes, 2:51
Machine-independent codes, 2:52
Machine language. *See* Languages, machine
Machine readable cataloging (MARC), 3:134
"The Machine Stops," 4:105
Machines, cybernetic studies, 4:55–58
Macintosh computers
  browsers for, 4:28, 4:30
  desktop publishing and, 3:70, 3:72, 3:196–197
  development, 1:17, 4:95
  Excel spreadsheet for, 3:193
  File Maker Pro for, 3:66
  i-Minitel for, 1:144
  Microsoft contributions, 1:138
  mouse introduced, 2:91
  web access, 1:218–219
  X-Windows, 1:217
Macintosh operating systems
  for microcomputers, 2:129
  OS X, 2:209
  point-and-click interfaces, 2:145
  virtual addressing, 2:209
  window interfaces, 1:111, 1:217, 2:49, 2:130
Macro Media Flash software, 3:169

Macro viruses, 1:207
Macromedia software, 1:14, 3:110
Macros, in spreadsheets, 3:192–193
MAD (Michigan Algorithm Decoder) programming language, 3:159
The MAD Primer, 3:159
Madison Itanium processor, 2:28
MAE (Metropolitan Area Exchange), 4:145
Maezal Chess Automaton (the Turk), 3:37
Magellan spacecraft, *2:53*
Magnavox, Odyssey game, 1:68
Magnetic core storage, 2:109
Magnetic disks
  access speed, 2:189
  advantages, 2:189–190
  costs, 2:190
  for document processing, 2:69
  failures, 2:190
  floppy, 2:189–190, 2:206
  hard, 2:188–190, 2:205–206
  for mainframe storage, 1:127
  for microcomputers, 2:189
  mylar for, 2:187, 2:189
  for secondary storage, 1:129, 1:163–164, 2:111
  for VM, 1:131
Magnetic drums, 2:187, *2:188*
Magnetic ink character recognition (MICR), 2:92, 2:134, 2:164
Magnetic resonance imaging (MRI), 3:116–117, *3:116*
Magnetic sensors, 2:148
Magnetic stripe cards and readers, 2:91, 3:**134–136**
  for ATMs, 3:*25*, 3:134
  as authentication tokens, 4:22–23
  coding formats, 3:136
  credit cards, 3:136
  how they work, 3:134–136, 3:*135*, 3:*136*
  membership cards, 3:134
  for removable storage, 1:163–164
  smart cards, 2:164–165, 3:136
Magnetic Tape Selectric Typewriter (MTST), 3:210–211
Magnetic tapes
  cartridge, 2:91, 2:188
  defined, 1:72, 3:186
  densities, 2:188
  for document processing, 2:69
  Happy, CIA storage area, 2:*92*
  history, 1:188, 2:93, 2:187
  for information retrieval systems, 1:93, 2:188

  for mainframes, 2:91
  mylar for, 2:187, 2:189
  NASA's use of, 1:153
  railroad applications, 3:174
  reel-to-reel, 2:91, 2:188
  for secondary storage, 1:129, 1:163–164, 2:91, 2:93, 2:111
  for tape backups, 2:188
Magnification software, for visually impared persons, 4:12–13
Mail trap doors, security issues, 1:175
Mailing lists. *See* Data mining
Main storage. *See* Memory/memory devices
Mainframe computers, 1:**125–128**
  accounting software for, 3:3
  for airline reservations, 3:15
  Amdahl's contributions, 4:4–5
  An Wang's contributions, 3:206
  channels, 1:127
  CMOS technology, 1:125
  communication controllers, 1:128
  CPUs, 1:127
  data bandwidth, 1:125
  defined, 1:17, 2:41, 3:3, 4:4
  for desktop publishing, 3:197
  early user interfaces, 3:47
  games played on, 1:67
  IBM's contributions, 1:89–90
  as Internet servers, 1:126, 1:128
  for journalism, 4:160
  line printers, 1:128
  Logo for, 2:101
  magnetic tape drives for, 2:91
  mass storage devices, 1:127
  for medical image analyses, 3:117
  operating systems, 1:125, 1:126–127, 2:129
  vs. personal computers, 1:125–126, 1:134
  and "priesthood" of computers, 1:65
  programming languages, 1:78
  size and cost reduction, 1:125, 1:*126*
  source code, 3:155
  telecommunications, 1:191
  terminals, 2:45
  time-sharing, 1:126
  twisted pair connections for, 2:45
Malaria, CDC and, 3:27
Malaysia, cybercafes, 4:54
Malicious codes, defined, 4:72
Mammography, pattern recognition tools, 2:139–140, 2:*140*
Management information systems (MIS), 2:89–90

Manchester Mark I computer, 1:56, 1:61–62, 1:198

Mandelbrot, Benoit B., 3:138

Mandelbrot sets, 3:138

Manhattan Project, 2:217–218, 3:121, 3:158, 4:102–103

Manipulation robotics technology, 1:171

MANs (metropolitan area networks), 1:156, 1:157, 2:117–118

Manufacturing
computer-aided (CAM), 3:30, 3:31, 3:51–52, 3:93
computer vision applications, 4:68
computerized, 3:**50–55**
document processing, 2:68
DSS tools, 3:68
e-commerce applications, 4:79
ERP programs, 4:97
expert systems tools, 3:88
of LCDs, yield, 2:67
mathematics of, 1:26
MFG/PRO software, 4:97
of microprocessors, 2:15
process control, 3:**164–166**
robotics technologies, 4:40
standardization, 1:97–99

Map overlay operations, with GIS, 3:100

Map reclassification operations, with GIS, 3:100

Maps, geographical
coloring problem, 4:168–169
computer cartography, 3:101
GPS applications, 4:117
history, 3:61
telemetry as tool, 3:28
See also Geographic information systems

Maps, weather, 3:209

MARC (machine readable cataloging), 3:134

Marchand hand calculators, 4:102

Marconi, Guglielmo, 2:201, 2:219, 4:126, 4:**163–164**, 4:*163*

Marino, Roland, 2:165

Mario Bros. game, 1:69

Mark I computer. See Harvard Mark I computer; Manchester Mark I computer

Mark II computer. See Harvard Mark II computer

Mark sense technology. See OMR (optical mark recognition)

Marker computers, 1:27

Market Basket analyses, 4:62

Marketing
cookies and, 1:168, 4:40–42, 4:156

in cybercafes, 4:55
DoubleClick, 4:79
of educational software, 3:82–83
"learning" user preferences, 4:1
vs. privacy issues, 1:167–168, 4:42
through CRS databases, 3:15
through e-mail messages, 4:139
See also Data mining; E-commerce

Markup languages. See Languages, markup

Mars Pathfinder Mission, 2:167–168

Marsh's supermarket, bar code scanners, 2:163

Mary Poppins, 1:13

Maser (Microwave Amplification by Stimulated Emission of Radiation), 3:125

Mass spectrometry analyses, 3:88, 4:36

Massachusetts Institute of Technology. See MIT

Massively parallel architecture (processors), 1:162, 2:103–104, 3:58

MasterCard, SET, 1:43

Mathematica software, 3:79

Mathematical Markup Language (MathML), 2:107–108

The Mathematical Theory of Communication, 4:196

Mathematicians
Boole, George, 1:18, 2:**18–20**
Boole, Mary, 2:19
Euclid, 2:4
Glushkov, Victor M., 4:**119–120**
Julia, Gaston, 3:138
Kemeny, John G., 2:2, 2:157, 3:**120–122**, 4:208
Leibnitz, Gottfried Wilhelm von, 1:18, 1:165, 4:55
Mandelbrot, Benoit B., 3:138
McCarthy, John, 2:99
Mohammed al-Khowarizmi, 2:3
Napier, John, 1:2, 1:150, 1:182
Newell, Allen, 4:**172–174**, 4:*173*
Newton, Isaac, 1:3, 1:25
Pascal, Blaise, 1:41–42, 1:**164–166**, 1:*165*, 4:55
Péter, Rózsa, 3:**160–161**
Stott, Alicia Boole, 2:19
See also Babbage, Charles; Lovelace, Ada Byron King, Countess of; Shannon, Claude E.; Turing, Alan M.

Mathematics, 3:**137–139**
application software, 3:138
and astronomy, 3:22, 3:23, 3:162

binomial theorem, 1:165
and biology, 3:137
calculus, 1:3–5, 1:132, 1:165, 2:99
and chemistry, 4:34–35
and cryptography, 3:138
cycloids, 1:165
and ecology, 3:137
education and teaching tools, 2:101–102, 3:138, 3:159, 3:161
and environmental issues, 3:137
Euclidean geometry, 1:165
and geography, 3:137–138
IEEE standards, 3:138
impact of Inquisition on, 1:165
John von Neumann on, 2:218
Julia and Mandelbrot sets, 3:138
knowledge representation, 1:18
and life insurance, 3:137
logarithms, 1:2, 1:25, 1:150, 1:182
of manufacturing processes, 1:26
medical applications, 3:137
microprocessors as logic, 3:138–139
modeling, 1:180
Napier's bones, 1:**150**
as navigation tool, 3:148–149
and physics, 3:138, 3:162–163
recursive functions, 3:160
software, 3:138
trigonometry, 1:3
Turing Machine as tool, 1:199–200
wavelet, for JPEG, 2:97
See also Algorithms; Binary number system; Boolean algebra

Mathews, Max, 1:149, 2:*115*

MathML (Mathematical Markup Language), 2:107–108

Matlab software, 3:79

The Matrix, 4:107

Mauchly, John W., 1:61, 2:*34*, 2:**72–75**, 2:*73*
ACM founder, 1:21
ENIAC project, 1:42, 1:55, 1:60–61, 1:71, 1:72, 3:59
UNIVAC project, 1:32, 1:72, 1:188

Mavica digital cameras, 4:178

Max Headroom, 4:106–107

Maxim, hacker, 3:105

Maxis, Sim games, 1:70, 4:7

MaxwellWorld, 1:205

McCarthy, John, 1:21, 2:99, 4:173

McCormick, Ernest J., 1:64–65

McGuinn, Roger, 4:*44*

MCI, Internet backbone funding, 4:144

Mechanical computers, 1:4–5, 1:41–42, 1:*41*, 1:131
See also Analytical Engine; Difference Engine

Media Access Control (MAC), 2:24, 2:118–119, 3:159

Medical records, 3:140

Medical robotics, 1:170

Medical systems, 3:**139–142**
  bar code scanners, 2:*133*
  biomedical engineering, 3:28–29
  brain research, 1:185
  data mining, 4:60
  data warehousing, 4:63
  databases, 3:139–140
  to detect bacterial infection, 3:144
  disease tracking and prevention, 3:27
  DSS tools, 3:68–69, 3:*69*
  DXplain, 3:68
  economic modeling, 3:*79*
  education, VR applications, 1:*204*
  embedded, 3:139
  expert systems/knowledge bases, 3:88, 3:124
  health care policy simulations, 1:70
  health statistics tracking, 1:32
  laser technology, 3:125, 3:127–128
  mechanized lab tests, 3:28
  neural network tools, 3:154–155
  pattern recognition tools, 2:138–140, 2:*140*
  PDAs for, 2:142
  prescription drug information, 3:139, 3:140
  robots, 1:170, 1:171, 2:168, 3:141–142
  scientific visualization, 3:177
  simulated surgeries, 2:216
  smart cards, 2:165, 3:139
  surgery, 3:*141*, 3:*205*
  tele-health, 3:140–142
  telemedicine, 1:113
  Therac-25 radiation therapy machine failure, 4:100–101
  user interfaces, 3:205
  See also CAT (computer-assisted tomography); Image analysis, medicine; specific diseases

Medium-scale integrated (MSI) circuits, 1:141, 2:61

MEDLARS information system, 1:93

MEDLINE information systems, 1:93

Megabytes, defined, 1:129

Megahertz (MHz), defined, 2:220

Meissner, L.P., 3:159

Meitner, Lise, 3:55

Melissa worm, 1:208, 2:95

Meltzer, Marlyn Wecoff, 1:63

Members, in object-oriented languages, 2:126

Memex devices, 1:58–59, 1:87

Memory extender. See Memex device

Memory management units (MMUs), 2:208

Memory managers
  base+offset addressing model, 2:*206*, 2:*207*, 2:209
  function, 2:129
  and information retrieval, 2:111–112
  physical addressing model, 2:206–207, 2:*206*, 2:*207*, 2:208–209
  See also Virtual memory

Memory/memory devices, 1:**128–131**, 2:**108–112**
  ABC computer, 1:53
  access to, 2:33
  cache, 2:**27–29**, 2:209, 2:210
  capacitors for, 2:111
  cell storage, 1:*131*
  Colossus computer, 1:54
  core, 1:57, 1:82
  cost of, 2:112
  CRT-based, 1:56, 1:62
  deallocation, 2:112
  DRAM, 2:109, 2:111, 2:209
  graphic devices' use of, 2:82
  Harvard Mark I computer, 1:51–52
  history, 2:108–109
  IBM AP-101 computer, 3:187
  increasing size, 1:130
  for minicomputers, 1:141, 1:142
  for mobile computing devices, 4:166
  in printing devices, 2:149
  protection hardware, 1:174–175, 2:173
  role in computer, 2:5
  semiconductor memory, 2:109
  single-chip, 4:170
  SRAM, 2:109, 2:110–111
  synonyms, 1:128
  transistors for, 2:109, 2:111
  vacuum tubes for, 2:109
  volatility of, 2:109, 2:111, 2:187

Z machines, 1:52–53
See also CMOS; RAM; ROM; Virtual memory

Menabrea, Luigi Federico, 1:123

Menu bars, 1:215, 1:*216*

Menu-based systems, 1:111, 2:130

Menu labels, 1:215, 1:*216*

Mercury-Atlas rocket, 3:186

Mercury man-in-space program, 1:153

MERIT, Internet backbone funding, 4:144

Merwin, Richard E., Scholarship, 1:104

Mesh topology, 1:155, 2:123, 2:124

Meta languages, 2:107

Meta symbols, 2:2–3

MetaCrawler search engine, 4:189, 4:191

Metadata, 4:58, 4:68

"The Metal Giants," 4:105

Metallica vs. Napster, 4:*44*

Metasearch engines, 4:189

Metasearch sites, 1:219

Metastable states, in laser technology, 3:126

Meteorologists, defined, 3:208

Metric system prefixes, 2:77

Metropolitan Area Exchange (MAE), 4:145

Metropolitan area networks. See MANs

Mexico, cybercafes, 4:55

MFENET, 4:144

MFG/PRO software, 4:97

MGM (Metro-Goldwyn-Mayer), animated films by, 1:13

Michelangelo, Sistine Chapel, 4:6, 4:7

Michie, Donald, 1:198

Michigan Algorithm Decoder (MAD) programming language, 3:159

Mickey Mouse, 1:*11*, 1:12

MICR (magnetic ink character recognition), 2:92, 2:134, 2:164

Micro Instrumentation and Telemetry Systems (MITS), 1:137

Microamperes, defined, 4:170

Microchips/microprocessors, 1:**131–134**, 1:*133*
  access to memory, 2:205
  in auto-pilots, 3:7–9
  defined, 1:89, 3:139
  for fourth-generation computers, 1:74–75
  for game controllers, 2:81
  government research grants, 1:81

MMUs, 2:208
optical, 1:134
for RAM, 1:129
replaced by organic computers, 1:195, 4:106
for ROM, 1:129–130
silicon chips, 1:74
size reduction, 1:107, 1:108–109, 4:167
in smart cards, 2:164–165
speed, 3:39–40
treatment processes, 1:105–106
William Shockley's contributions, 2:15
See also Chip manufacturing; Integrated circuits; Intel microprocessors; Semiconductors

Microchips/microprocessors, specific
Advanced Micro Devices, 1:107
F8, 1:68
IBM, 1:137
Motorola, 1:16, 1:107
6502 MOS Technologies, 1:15
SLT, 1:89–90
Texas Instruments, 1:107, 2:33

Microcomputers, 1:**134–137**
for classroom use, 4:86, 4:88
defined, 3:207
ergonomic designs, 1:65
hardware limitations, 1:136
history, 1:134–135
IBM, 1:135–136, 1:*136*
Logo and, 2:101
magnetic disks, 2:189
operating systems, 1:136, 2:129, 2:157
origin of term, 1:135
programming, 1:135
RAM requirements, 1:136
size reductions, 1:136
space applications, 1:135, 1:151
spreadsheets for, 3:193
tape cartridges for, 2:188
for telecommuting, 1:159
video games for, 1:68
Wang VS, 3:207

Microfilm, COM devices, 2:152
Micromarketing, 1:167–168
See also Data mining
Micropayments, 1:44
Microphones
for CCTV, 4:118
for voice recognition, 2:92, 4:14
wireless lavaliere, 4:85
Microprose, Transport Tycoon game, 1:70
Microsoft Corporation, 1:**137–139**

agreements with Apple, 1:17, 1:138
anti-trust suits, 1:138–139
compatibility issues, 2:48–50
conflicts with IBM, 1:138
corporate headquarters, 1:*139*
free browsers, 1:45
Gates, Bill, 1:137, 1:138, 3:131, 4:94, 4:*95*
history, 1:137, 4:94
intellectual property rights, 1:91
software development, 1:137
sued by Apple, 1:138
sued by Netscape, 4:140
Unicode supported by, 2:42

Microsoft Disk Operating System. *See* MS-DOS

Microsoft Office
dominance, 1:137, 3:110
help feature, 1:114
integration, 3:119, 3:170
for Macintosh computers, 1:138
piracy, 3:182, 3:184
XP, 3:*111*
zip disks, 2:189

Microsoft Sidewinder Force Feedback Pro Joystick, 2:81

Microsoft software
Access, 3:60, 3:66, 3:169
Active Accessibility, 4:16
Advanced Streaming Format, 2:184
Bookshelf, 1:137
CE operating system, 2:128
Clippy, 4:1, 4:3
Encarta, 3:113
Excel, 1:137, 3:60, 3:78, 3:169, 3:193
Flight Simulator game, 4:127
FrontPage, 3:110
for home systems, 3:114
open source software, 3:156–157
Outlook, 1:158
Picture It, 3:169
piracy of, 3:182–184
PowerPoint, 1:137, 1:160, 3:169–170
Publisher, 1:157, 3:169
Reader, 3:112
SQL Server, 3:66, 3:169
Visio, 3:169
WAVE, 2:183, 3:113
Word, 1:137, 1:157, 3:110, 3:167, 4:1
Works, 3:110, 3:119, 3:170
See also Internet Explorer; Microsoft Office

Microsoft VBA programming language, 1:208, 2:95

Microsoft Windows, 1:137–138
browsers for, 4:28, 4:30–31
compatibility issues, 2:49
free browsers with, 1:45, 1:138
GUIs, 2:48, 2:130, 3:193, 3:203–204
interfaces, 1:217
JVM for, 2:128
keyboard locales, 1:121
Media Player, 3:113
Messenger, 4:140
for palm-sized PCs, 2:142
version 95, 1:138, 1:217, 2:130
version 98, 1:138, 1:217, 2:129, 2:130
version 2000, 1:138, 1:217, 2:129, 2:130, 2:209
version NT, 1:138, 1:217, 2:128, 2:209
version XP, 1:138
WinCE, 2:143, 3:35

Microsoft X-Cube game, 1:15
Microsoft Xbox game, 2:80
Microstation software, 3:31
Microwave Amplification by Stimulated Emission of Radiation (maser), 3:*125*
Microwave links, 2:202, 2:*203*, 4:25, 4:136
MicroWorlds Logo interpreter, 2:103

Middle Ages
markets, 4:88
printing technology, 3:71

Middle East, software piracy, 3:184
MIDI (Musical Instrument Digital Interface), 1:149–150, 2:184, 3:146, 3:147
Midway, Gunfight game, 1:68

Military/warfare
ballistics computations, 1:50, 1:55, 1:71, 1:202, 2:73, 3:59
computer applications, 1:4, 1:58
computerized manufacturing, 3:50–51
cryptography, 1:53–55, 1:59, 1:71, 1:198, 4:*50*, 4:51, 4:196
Cuban Missile Crisis, 4:115
Cyberspace Data Monitoring System, 2:*53*
electromechanical feedback systems, 4:175
ENIAC programming, 2:73
ergonomically designed aircraft, 1:64
and fictional computers, 4:105–106

Military/warfare (continued)
FIELDATA code, 2:41
firing tables, 1:59, 2:74
global surveillance, 4:115–118
GPS applications, 4:117
IBM AP-101 computers, 3:187
knowledge bases, 3:124
and Konrad Zuse's research, 2:222
laser technology, 3:125, 3:128
Manhattan Project, 2:217–218, 3:121, 3:158, 4:102–103
missile defense systems, 1:153, 4:101
navigation systems, 3:150
neural network applications, 3:155
punched card applications, 1:186–187
robotics technologies, 1:170
simulator applications, 2:179
SONAR, 3:114–115
video games and, 1:67, 1:68, 1:70
walkie-talkies, 3:102
See also Department of Defense (U.S.)
Milky Way, 3:21–22
Millennium information system, 3:133
Miller, Joan, 2:115
Millisecond, defined, 1:55
Milliwatts, defined, 3:126
MIMD (Multiple Instruction, Multiple Data), 2:135, 2:136, 2:137
MIME (Multipurpose Internet Mail Extensions), 4:138–139
Mind over Matter, 4:6
Mindspring/Earthlink, spam filters, 1:49
Minicomputers, 1:**139–142**, 1:*140*
applications, 1:140, 1:141
batch processing, 1:141
for CAI, 3:41
compilers, 1:141
CRTs, 1:141
defined, 1:135, 3:41, 4:199–200
distinguished from personal computers, 1:141
I/O devices, 1:141
ICs for, 1:141
library applications, 3:132
Logo for, 2:101
memory, 1:141
operating systems, 2:129, 2:157
PDP and VAX, 1:13, 1:14, 1:36, 1:141–142, 2:116
programming languages, 1:141
railroad applications, 3:173–174

register numbers, 1:141
rugged-ized, 1:140
size and cost, 1:139–140
for telecommunications, 1:191
Wang VS, 3:207
Minimax algorithm, defined, 3:36
Minitel network, 1:**142–145**
vs. cybercafes, 4:54
distinguished from Internet, 1:144–145
history, 1:142–143
i-Minitel, 1:144
rates, 1:144
security/privacy, 1:145
service statistics, 1:144
services provided, 1:144
Videotex terminals, 1:*143*
Minix operating system, 2:131
Minsky, Marvin, 4:173
Minuteman Missile, integrated circuit technology, 1:153
MIR computer, 4:120
MIS (management information systems), 2:89–90
MISD (Multiple Instruction, Single Data), 2:135–136
Missile defense systems, ethics, 4:101
MIT (Massachusetts Institute of Technology)
AI research, 2:101
Claude Shannon at, 4:195
computer security research, 1:175
decision-making studies, 3:67
Elliot Organick and, 3:159
flight simulators, 1:*179*
game research, 1:67
Herman Hollerith and, 1:83
Kerberos authentication technique, 4:83
Laboratory for Computer Science, 4:29
Logo Laboratory, 2:101
magnetic core storage, 2:109
MUSIC XI, 2:116
Sketchpad development, 3:16
Technologies Instrumentation Lab, 3:187
technology-related training, 3:45
VisiCalc, 3:193
X-Windows, 1:217
MIT Journals Online, 4:84
Mitnick, Kevin, 4:*122*
MITS Altair home computer, 1:137, 4:94
MMUs (memory management units), 2:208

Mnemonic codes, 1:76, 2:7, 2:51
Mnemonics, defined, 2:7
Mobile computing, 4:**164–167**
expansion slot approach, 4:166
handheld computers for, 4:165–166
information overload and, 4:133
LANs, 4:166
PalmOS, 3:35
technical challenges, 4:164–165
uses, 4:164, 4:*165*, 4:166
wireless connections, 4:165, 4:166
See also Cellular technology; PDAs
Mobile phone systems (MPS), 2:29–30
Mobile phones. *See* Cell phones
Mobile robotics technology, 1:171
Mobility management, for cell phones
handoffs, 3:33
home and visitor location registers, 3:33
mobile switching centers, 3:33
Mobitex wireless services, 4:166
Modalities, defined, 3:86
Model animation, 1:10
Model 1 computer, Bell Labs, 1:51
Models
agent-based and individual-based, 4:11
algebraic, automated, 4:120
artificial life, 4:**9–11**
association, 4:62
computer, 1:180
economic, 3:**78–80**, 3:154, 3:155
mathematical, 3:137–138
molecular, 4:*35*
neural, 4:57
of political events, 4:184
of problem-solving, 4:198
to represent artificial intelligence, 1:18
See also Simulation models
Modems
asynchronous operation, 2:8
baud rates, 2:46–47
cable, 3:113, 4:26–28
callback, 1:176
CDPD, 2:220
defined, 2:46, 3:202, 4:25
DSL, 2:47
FAX-modems, 1:158
fiber optic links, 2:47
FSK, 2:46
function, 4:25

high-speed, 2:47
integrated, 2:142
interconnectivity of computers, 1:34
invention, 2:46
RS-232 protocols, 2:178
for telecommuting, 1:159
telephony and, 3:202
1200-baud, 1:69–70
wireless, 2:47, 2:202, 2:220
Modulation of signals, 2:46, 3:147
Modulator Demodulators. *See* Modems
Modules, defined, 2:162
Mohammed al-Khowarizmi, 2:3
Mohawk Data Sciences, first data recorder, 1:188
Molecular biology, 3:**142–145**
bacteriorhodopsin research, 3:144
bioengineering as tool, 3:28
bioinformatics, 3:27–28, 3:45, 3:142–143, 3:*143*
computer simulations of experiments, 4:36
genetic engineering, 3:143
image analysis tools, 3:117
medical applications, 3:144
NCBI, 3:144
supercomputers to study, 1:184–185
See also Biology
Molecular computing, 4:**167–169**
coloring problem, 4:168–169
DNA computers, 4:167–169, 4:170–171
how it works, 4:167–168
microbial robots, 4:167
nanocomputing, 4:**169–172**
organic transistors, 1:195, 4:106, 4:*168*
supercomputers for, 4:169
Molecular dynamics, supercomputers to study, 2:134–135
Molecular modeling, 4:*35*, 4:36
Monarch Marking, bar code scanners, 2:163
Money software, 3:60
Monitor screens. *See* Display devices
Monochromatic light beams, 3:126–127
Monopoly, electronic version, 1:15
Monroe calculator, 1:60
Monte Carlo simulations, 1:180
Monty Python's Flying Circus, 1:10
MOODS system, 3:147
Moon, space explorations, 3:186–187

Moore, Ed, 1:27
Moore, Gordon, 1:107, 1:108, 2:15, 2:33, 3:40, 4:121
Moore School of Electrical Engineering
differential analyzers, 1:51, 3:162
ENIAC project, 1:55, 1:60–61, 1:71–73, 1:202, 2:72, 2:74
Moore's Law, 1:107, 1:108, 2:33, 3:40, 4:121
Moran, Thomas, 4:174
Morris, Robert T., 1:*35*, 1:37
Morse Code, 2:*43*
American version, 2:113
applications, 2:*40*
attributes, 2:40, 2:42–43
Guglielmo Marconi and, 4:163
International version, 2:113, 2:114
Samuel Morse and, 2:112–113, 2:*112*
translation problems, 2:114
Morse, Samuel, 1:161, 2:40, 2:**112–114**, 2:*112*, 2:219
Mortal Kombat game, 1:68
MOS Technologies 6502 chips, 1:15
Mosaic browser, 1:218, 4:30, 4:149
Motherboards, defined, 1:15
Motion-base aircraft simulators, 2:180–181
Motion Picture Association of America, copyright laws, 4:*100*
Motor controllers, for process control, 3:164
Motor impairments, assistive technologies
alternative communication systems, 4:14
keyboard adaptations, 4:13
mouse, 1:*146*
OCR software, 4:13
pointing tools, 1:*146*
voice synthesizers, 4:*15*
Motorola
DragonBall EZ, 2:142
microprocessors, 1:16, 1:107
Mouse, computer, 1:**145–147**, 2:145–146
attributes, 1:145
for desktop publishing, 3:197
direct manipulation systems, 1:112
for disabled persons, 1:*146*
electromechanical, 2:146
government research grants, 1:81, 1:82
how they work, 1:145–146, 2:91, 2:145
invention, 1:21, 1:145, 2:146

optical, 2:145
origin of term, 1:145
serial communications, 2:146
software drive communication, 2:145
trackballs, 1:145–146
as user interface, 3:203
window interfaces and, 1:213–214
wireless, 1:147, 2:220
Mouse pads, 2:145–146
Movies
educational applications, 4:85
MPEG format, 1:101
VCRs, 1:164
See also Film and video editing
Movies, computers in
Colossus—The Forbin Project, 4:105
Dr. Strangelove, 4:105
Enemy of the State, 4:105–106
Fantastic Voyage, 4:105
Gattaca, 4:167
The Matrix, 4:107
Max Headroom, 4:106–107
The Net, 4:106
pixilated *Titanic*, 4:7
robots, 1:173
The Stepford Wives, 4:104
Tron, 4:106
2001: A Space Odyssey, 3:21, 4:105
WarGames, 4:*106*
Moving Picture Expert Group. *See* MPEG format
Mozilla Public License, 3:156
MPEG format, 2:**96–99**
file extensions, 2:98
MP3 audio, 2:98
MPEG-1, 2:96
MPEG-2, 2:98
MPEG-4, 2:98
MPEG-7, 2:99
MPEG-21, 2:99
as standard, 1:101, 2:11, 2:96–97
for streaming audio and video, 3:113
uses, 2:86, 2:97–98
MPPs (massively parallel processors), 3:58
MPS (mobile phone system), 2:29–30
MP3 (MPEG-2 Layer III) format, 2:184, 2:185, 4:126–127, 4:166
MRI (magnetic resonance imaging), 3:116–117, 3:*116*
MS-DOS (Microsoft Disk Operating System)
BASIC programming language, 4:208

MS-DOS (Microsoft Disk Operating System) (continued)
for IBM-PCs, 1:17, 1:90, 1:110–111, 1:217, 2:129, 2:157
user interfaces, 2:130, 3:203–204
MSI (medium-scale integration) circuits, 1:141, 2:61
MSN search engine, 4:191
MSS (multi-spectral scanner), Landsat, 2:170–171
MTST (Magnetic Tape Selectric Typewriter), 3:210–211
Muffett, Alec, 3:182
Mulan, 1:13
Multi-dimensional reporting. *See* Online analytic processing
Multi-spectral scanner (MSS), Landsat, 2:170–171
Multi-User Domain (MUD), 4:148
Multi-user dungeons (MUDs), 3:48
Multics security kernel (systems), 1:175, 2:172, 3:159
Multilingual character codes, 2:42
Multimedia, 2:**83–86**
CD-ROMs for, 2:85, 2:190
database applications, 3:196
defined, 2:84
development careers, 2:84
for digital libraries, 4:70
for distance education, 2:84, 2:85
distinguished from hypermedia, 2:83
documents, 2:70
for e-books, 4:77
for e-journals, 2:84, 2:85, 4:82
educational applications, 4:84–85, 4:86
encyclopedias, 3:113
examples, 2:83
for games, 2:84, 2:85, 4:127
I/O devices, 2:85
information retrieval, 1:92
JPEG format, 2:85
MPEG formats, 2:86, 2:99
OAS applications, 1:159–160
PDA access to, 2:142
presentations, 2:*84*
for television newsrooms, 4:160
user interfaces, 3:204
Multimedia Content Description Interface. *See* MPEG-7
Multimedia Framework. *See* MPEG-21
Multimedia indexing, and speech recognition, 3:190
Multiplane animation camera, 1:12
Multiple Access System, 1:175

Multiple Instruction, Multiple Data (MIMD), 2:135, 2:136, 2:137
Multiple Instruction, Single Data (MISD), 2:135–136
Multiple Virtual Systems (MVS), 1:126–127
Multiplexing
ATM transmission, 4:20
binary, logic design, 2:60–61
computer data on telephone lines, 2:47
defined, 2:60
time-division, 2:76
Multipurpose Internet Mail Extensions (MIME), 4:138–139
Multitasking (multiprogramming), 1:136, 2:37–38, 2:134
Multivac, fictional computer, 3:20
Museums
Alternative, 4:8
censorship, 4:31–32
computer vision demonstrations, 4:38
digital art, 4:7–8
Getty Institute, 4:8
Institute of Museum and Library Services, 4:69
political information, 4:181
Music boxes, mechanical, 4:125–126
Music composition, 1:147, 1:149, 2:116, 3:**145–148**
algorithmic, 3:147
audio, 3:147–148
audio recognition, 3:147
CMN, 3:145
direct audio synthesis, 3:145–146
functions and techniques, 3:147–148
MIDI, 1:149–150, 2:184, 3:146, 3:147
MOODS system, 3:147
music score production, 3:145
notational, 3:146–147
optical music recognition, 3:147
paths, composer to listener, 3:*145*
signals played through DACs, 3:146
Music, computer, 1:**147–150**, 2:**114–116**
Analytical Engine application, 2:115
concerts, 1:149
devices for creating, 2:*115*
digital-analog hybrid systems, 2:114
digital to analog conversions, 2:114–115

digitizing, 1:31, 2:116
history, 1:149–150, 2:115
illegal copying, 2:184–185
keyboards and synthesizers, 4:124
Logo and, 2:103
modeling, 3:146
programming languages, 2:114
sign-bit extraction technique, 2:114
storage devices, 1:164
training hardware and software, 1:147, 1:*148*
See also Sound synthesis and recording
MUSIC III, 1:149
MUSIC V, 2:115–116
MUSIC XI, 2:116
Music XML modeling language, 3:146
Musical Instrument Digital Interface. *See* MIDI
Musical instruments
Fairlight, 1:149
Synclavier, 1:149
MusicData model, 3:146
MVS (Multiple Virtual Systems), 1:126–127
Mylar, 2:187, 2:189
MySQL software, 3:60
Myst, 1:12, 1:15

N

N- and P-type transistor regions, 1:195–196
NACA (National Advisory Committee on Aeronautics), 1:151
Namco, Pac-Man game, 1:14, 1:15, 1:69
Nand-gates, 2:60
Nanocomputing, 4:**169–172**
benefits, 4:170, 4:*171*
Boolean logic, 4:171
CNN architecture, 4:171
crossbar switching, 4:171
defined, 4:167
DNA computers, 4:167–169, 4:170–171
fabrication techniques, 4:171–172
molecular computing, 4:**167–169**
QCA, 4:171
quantum dots, 4:170
self assembly, 4:172
single electron devices, 4:170
size, 4:*171*
Nanometers, defined, 1:161, 3:127
Nanoscale, defined, 4:169

Nanoseconds, defined, 1:162, 2:109, 3:127

Nanotechnology, defined, 2:168

Napier, John, 1:2, 1:*150*, 1:182

Napier, Mark, 4:6–7

Napier's bones, 1:**150**

NAPs (Network Access Points), 4:145

Napster vs. copyright law, 2:185, 4:43, 4:*44*, 4:205

Narrowband, defined, 4:25

NASA (National Aeronautics and Space Administration), 1:**151–154**
  CMOS technology, 1:153
  computer technologies used by, 1:153, 3:185–187
  digital imaging technology, 4:178
  embedded real-time systems, 1:151–152
  Extreme Ultraviolet Explorer, 2:169
  history, 1:151
  impact on computer industry, 1:154
  information retrieval, 1:93
  integrated circuit technology, 1:153
  networks, 1:153
  PSAs, 1:173, 2:*171*
  redundancy and backup systems, 1:152–153
  Science Internet, 4:144
  self-replicating systems, 2:218
  Sojourner robot, 2:167–168, 2:*167*
  SPAN, 4:144
  Web site, Sputnik signals, 2:169
  See also Space travel and exploration

NASD, EPSS applications, 3:43

Nasdaq stock market, 4:88

Nassi, Isaac, 2:57

Nassi-Shneiderman diagrams, 2:57–58, 2:*57*

NAT (Network Address Translation), 4:109

National Advisory Committee on Aeronautics (NACA), 1:151

National Aeronautics and Space Administration. *See* NASA (National Aeronautics and Space Administration)

National Archives, satellite reconnaissance photos, 4:117

National Basketball Association (NBA), 4:62

National Bureau of Standards, 1:32, 1:99

National Cash Register. *See* NCR

National Center for Biotechnology Information (NCBI), 3:27, 3:144

National Center for Supercomputing Applications (NCSA), 1:218, 4:30, 4:142

National Committee for Information Technology Standards (NCITS), 1:100

National Computer Security Center (NCSC), 2:172, 2:173

National Crime Information Center (NCIC), 1:167

National Electronic Disease Surveillance System, 3:27

National Information Infrastructure Protection Act of 1996, 1:36

National Information Standards Organization (NISO), 1:100

National Institute for Standards and Technology, 1:96, 1:99, 4:52

National Institutes of Health (NIH), 3:27, 3:144, 4:36

National Library of Medicine (NLM), 1:93, 3:144

National Physical Laboratory, 4:146

National Reconnaissance Office (NRO), 4:117

National Science Foundation. *See* NSF

National Weather Service (NWS), 3:208

NationsBank, 4:74

Natural language interfaces, 4:128

Naur, Peter, 2:1, 2:155

Navajo Code Talkers, 4:51

NAVDAC (Naval Data Automation Command), 1:86

Navigation, 3:**148–151**
  of aircraft, 3:6–9, 3:*8*, 3:88, 3:149–150, 3:186–187
  GPS, 2:159, 2:172, 3:6, 3:9, 3:99, 3:151
  IBM AP-101 computers, 3:187
  LORAN systems, 3:9, 3:151
  mathematics of, 3:148–149
  Omega systems, 3:151
  of ships, 3:6–7, 3:149–150
  systems for automobiles, 3:*150*
  time zones, 3:149
  as universal skill, 3:149

Navigation Satellite Timing and Ranging (NAVSTAR), 4:112

Navigation satellites, 2:171–172

Navy (U.S.)
  battery-operated weather stations, 3:103
  Cyberspace Data Monitoring System, 2:*53*
  Whirlpool project, 3:16

Navy Marine Corps Intranet (NMCI), 4:*151*

NBA (National Basketball Association), 4:62

NCBI (National Center for Biotechnology Information), 3:27, 3:144

NCIC (National Crime Information Center), database privacy, 1:167

NCITS (National Committee for Information Technology Standards), 1:100

NCP (Network Control Protocol), 4:146, 4:148

NCR (National Cash Register)
  bar code scanners, 2:163
  mainframe computers, 1:125
  Thomas J. Watson Sr., 1:88, 1:*211*

NCSA (National Center for Supercomputing Applications), 1:218, 4:30, 4:142

NCSC (National Computer Security Center), Orange Book ratings, 2:172, 2:173

Nederlandse Spoorwegen, 3:176

Negative cut lists, video editing, 3:97

Neilson, A.C., 2:73

Nelson, Ted, 4:29, 4:92

Nelson, Theodor, 1:87, 1:88

Neon light technology, 3:125–126

NES (Nintendo Entertainment System), 1:69

NESSY, visual learning, 4:38

The Net, 4:106

NET (No Internet Theft) Act, 3:185

NetBank, 4:74

NetMeeting software, 3:77

NetNanny filter, 4:32

Netscape Communications, 3:113, 4:30–31, 4:140, 4:158

Netscape Navigator
  cookies, 4:40, 4:42
  dominance, 1:219, 4:140
  features, 4:28
  introduction, 4:30–31
  open source versions, 4:141
  user interfaces, 4:132
  Web animation, 1:14

Netscape Public License, 3:156

Network Access Points (NAPs), 4:145

Network Address Translation (NAT), 4:109

Network architecture
  Ethernet, 2:10, 2:118–119
  FDDI, 2:118
  LAN and, 2:117–118

Network architecture (continued)
  MAC protocols, 2:24, 2:118–119
  MAN and, 2:117–118
  OSI Reference Model, 2:120
  selecting, 2:118–119
  Token Ring, 2:118, 2:124
  WAN and, 2:117–118
Network Control Protocol (NCP), 4:146, 4:148
Network design, 2:**117–119**
  AGP interfaces, 2:54–55
  asynchronous operation, 2:8
  bridging devices, 2:**24–27**
  client/server protocols, 2:36–37
  client/server technology, 2:**35–39**
  network analysis, 2:117
  objectives, 2:117
  operating systems, 2:129
  redundancy, 2:26
  role of, 2:*118*
  systems design and, 2:195
  TCP/IP, 2:119
  WAN, 2:117
  WLAN, 2:221
Network engineering, 2:119
Network interfaces, 2:49
Network managers, 2:130
Network news, 4:148
Network protocols, 2:**119–122**
  See also IP; TCP; TCP/IP
Network sniffing, 1:177
Network topologies, 1:154–155, 2:**122–124**
  bus, 1:155, 2:123–124
  criteria for selecting, 2:123
  links, 1:154
  mesh, 1:155, 2:123, 2:124
  nodes, 1:154–155, 2:123
  protocols, 2:124
  ring, 1:155, 2:124
  role in network design, 2:118
  star, 1:155, 2:123, 2:124
  transmission links, 2:122–123
  tree, 1:155, 2:123, 2:124
Networked windows (NeWs), 1:217, 4:121
Networks, 1:**154–157**
  ATM transmission, 1:155–156
  of ATMs, 3:25–26
  broadcast, 1:154
  circuit-switched, 1:154, 2:10
  computing power, 2:35
  copper cabling for, 1:155
  dangling string monitors, 3:84–86
  data interchange, for railroads, 3:174

data warehousing, 3:67, 4:**63–65**
  digital libraries, 4:70–71
  electromagnetic energy use, 1:155
  entry by hackers, 3:104
  fiber optics for, 1:155, 2:78
  firewalls, 1:177, 3:105, 4:74–75, 4:80, 4:**107–110**
  frame relay, 1:156
  gateway bridging devices, 2:26–27, 4:148
  HDLC, 2:9
  high-bandwidth access, 2:86
  hypertext and design, 1:88
  intelligent agent management tools, 4:2–3
  Internet/intranets as, 1:157
  library applications, 3:133
  PARC contributions, 1:222
  peer-to-peer vs. hierarchical, 1:115
  personal area networking, 4:166
  site licenses for software, 3:182
  subnets, 3:181
  window interfaces, 1:217
  See also Internet; LANs; MANs; Packet-switched networks; Routing/routers; Virtual private networks; WANs; World Wide Web
Networks, specific
  ANSNET, 4:144–145
  BITNET, 4:144, 4:148
  Cirrus, 3:25
  CSNET, 4:144, 4:148
  EARN, 4:144
  ESNET, 4:144
  Ethernet, 1:*156*, 1:222
  FIDONET, 4:144, 4:148
  HEPNET, 4:144
  ISDN, 2:10
  JANET, 4:144
  MFENET, 4:144
  NASA-developed, 1:153
  NASA Science Internet, 4:144
  Plus, 3:25
  SPAN, 4:144
  USAN, 4:144
  USENET, 4:144
  UUNET, 4:145, 4:148
Neural modeling, defined, 4:57
Neural network pattern recognition, defined, 2:141
Neural networks, 3:**151–155**, 3:*152*
  and artificial life, 4:11
  cellular (CNNs), 4:171
  for data mining, 4:62

decision-making applications, 3:69
  defined, 3:69, 4:11
  distinguished from artificial intelligence, 3:152
  hard-wired, 3:153–154
  vs. heuristic techniques, 3:154
  how they work, 3:153
  medical applications, 3:155
  military applications, 3:155
  NP complete problems, 3:154
  to predict stock market trends, 3:154
  principles, 3:152–153
  process control applications, 3:166
  training, 3:154–155
  truth values, 3:154
  TSP problems, 3:154
Neurobiology, neural network principles, 3:152–153
Neurology, supercomputers as tool, 1:185
Neutrally coded text, 2:105
New York City, terrorist attacks, 3:15, 4:*116*
Newell, Allen, 4:**172–174**, 4:*173*, 4:198
Newman, Lyn, 1:199
Newman, Maxwell, 1:56, 1:61–62, 1:199
NeWs (networked windows), 1:217, 4:121
News online, 4:161–162
Newspapers, online, 2:84, 2:85, 4:161–162, 4:*162*
Newton, Isaac, 1:3, 1:25, 2:18
Newton MessagePad, 2:142
Newtonian view, vs. cybernetics, 4:56–57
NewtonWorld, 1:205
NeXT computers, 1:16, 2:183, 4:30, 4:95–96
Nexus browser, 1:218, 4:30
NIH (National Institutes of Health), 3:27, 3:144, 4:36
1984, 4:118
1984 Act, 1:34–35
Nintendo
  Donkey Kong game, 1:69
  Entertainment System (NES), 1:14, 1:69
  Famicom, 1:14
  GameBoy, 1:69, 2:80
  GameCube, 1:15
  Mario Bros. game, 1:69
  revenues from games, 1:181
  64, 4:126
  user interfaces, 4:127

The Ninth Bridgewater Treatise, 1:26

Nippon Telephone and Telegraph Corporation, fingerprint scans, 4:*23*

NISO (National Information Standards Organization), 1:100

NLEs (non-linear editors), 3:96–98, 4:161

NLM (National Library of Medicine), 1:93, 3:144

NMAP security software, 3:181

No Internet Theft Act. *See* NET Act

No. 1 Electronic Switching System (1E), 1:27, 3:200

Nobel prizes
  Bell Labs employees, 1:27
  CAT inventors, 3:55, 3:57
  decision-making research, 4:198
  quantum electrodynamics, 4:103
  radio transmitters, 4:164
  superconductivity research, 1:106
  transistor inventors, 1:63, 1:106, 1:192, 2:13, 2:14

Nodes, network, 2:123

Noël (contemporary of Pascal), 1:166

Noise, in communication channels, 4:136–137

Non-linear editors (NLEs), 3:96–98, 4:161

Non-linear, fiber optics as, 2:76, 2:78

Non-linear quantization, 2:183

Nonoperational data, 4:58

Nonterminal symbols, 2:2–3

Nor-gates, 2:59

Norfolk Southern Railroad, computer conversion, 3:174–175

Norman, Donald, 1:111

Northrop Aircraft, UNIVAC purchaser, 2:73

Northwest Airlines, online reservations, 3:15

Norton security systems, 4:98

Not-gates, 2:58–59

NOT operators, 2:19, 2:*22*, 2:23, 4:189

Notation-oriented music models, 3:146

Notebook computers. *See* Laptop computers

Notions, in fashion industry, 3:92

Novell NetWare operating system, 2:128

Noyce, Robert, 1:73, 1:74, 1:106, 1:107, 2:15, 2:*110*

NP complete (difficult) problems, 3:154

NPN transistors, 1:196

NRO (National Reconnaissance Office), 4:117

NSF (National Science Foundation)
  Acceptable Use Policy, 4:148, 4:149
  computer research funding, 1:81
  CSNET, 4:144, 4:148
  Digital Library Initiatives, 4:69
  Elliot Organick and, 3:159
  Internet backbone funding, 4:144–145
  USAN, 4:144
  vBNS, 4:149

NSFNET, 1:115, 4:142–145, 4:148, 4:149

N² transistors, 1:194–195

Nuclear medicine (radiology), 3:115–116

Nuclear power plants
  John Kemeny and, 3:*122*
  robotics applications, 1:170
  simulator applications, 2:181, 2:216

Nucleotides, 3:142

Numerical cosmology, 3:22

Nutrition, livestock and poultry feeding systems, 3:6

Nutt, Roy, 2:154

NWS (National Weather Service), 3:208

Nynex, 1:28

Nyquist, Harry, 4:27, 4:**174–176**

Nyquist Intersymbol Interference Theorem, 4:27

O

O-rings, of Challenger space shuttle, 4:103

OAS. *See* Office automation systems

Object-based/object oriented-programming environments, 1:112–113

Object linking and embedding (OLE), 3:119–120

Object-oriented languages. *See* Languages, object-oriented

Object-oriented software development, 2:197

Object system and function overloading, 2:100

Object vs. class, in object-oriented languages, 2:126

Occupational Health and Safety Administration (OSHA), 1:99

OCLC (Online Computer Library Center), 3:132

OCR (optical character recognition), 2:**132–134**

bar code scanners, 2:92, 2:*133*, 2:163

data scanners, 2:92, 2:132–133, 2:164

defined, 4:13

for disabled persons, 4:13

handwritten characters, 2:133–134

history, 2:132, 2:164

how it works, 2:164

for legal documents, 3:130

MICR, 2:134, 2:164

uses, 2:164, 4:68

See also Pattern recognition

OCS (Operational Control System), 4:113

Octal (base-8) number system
  defined, 1:76
  for digital data, 1:42
  for machine language, 1:76

Octophones, 2:132

Odyssey game, 1:68

OEM (original equipment manufacturer), 3:183, 3:184

Office automation systems (OAS), 1:**157–160**

computer system architecture, 2:5

document processing, 2:**69–72**

Douglas Engelbart's contributions, 1:87

electronic collaboration, 1:157, 1:158–159

electronic communication, 1:157, 1:158

high-tech meeting rooms, 1:*159*

image processing, 1:157, 1:159–160

LAN's role, 1:157

office management, 1:157, 1:160

Xerox Star, 1:111

See also Desktop publishing; Office suite software; Word processors

Office of Strategic Services (OSS), 3:102

Office suite software
  for business use, 3:118–120
  GNOME Office, 3:110
  HTML composer/editor, 3:110
  integrated, 3:118, 3:119
  Lotus SmartSuite, 3:170
  Microsoft Works, 3:110
  OEM unbundling, 3:183, 3:184
  OpenOffice, 3:110
  personal finance, 3:110
  piracy, statistics, 3:184
  for software developers, 3:118

Office suite software (continued)
StarOffice, 3:110
WordPerfect Office, 3:110
See also Microsoft Office
Offline, defined, 1:93
OGAS (Statewide Automated System for Data Collection and Processing), 4:120
Oil refining, process control, 3:164
OLAP (online analytic processing), 4:60, 4:65
OLE (object linking and embedding), 3:119–120
Olympia, in "The Sandman," 4:104
Olympics, computerized security, 4:114
Oman, software piracy, 3:184
Omega navigation systems, 3:151
Omidyar, Pierre, 1:44, 4:97
OMR (optical mark recognition), 2:92, 2:133, 2:164
On-board memory. See Cache memory
ON Technology, 4:96
1E (No. 1 Electronic Switching System), 1:27, 3:200
101 Dalmations, 1:12
One-time pads, telegraph, 4:51
Online analytic processing (OLAP), 4:60, 4:65
Online Computer Library Center (OCLC), 3:132
Online operating systems, government research grants, 1:81
Online Public Access Catalogs (OPACs), 3:132–133
OnStar navigation system, 3:151
OOP (object-oriented programming). See Languages, object-oriented
Opel, John R., 1:90
Open architecture, of IBM-PCs, 1:36, 1:91
Open computer systems
compatibility issues, 2:48–50
Internet as, 2:49
Open Port Technology, patent, 4:177
Open source, 3:155–158
Apache project, 3:157
development models, 3:156–157
documentation, 3:157–158
FSF, 3:155
GNOME, 3:157
GNU project, 3:156, 3:157
GPLs, 3:156
vs. intellectual property, 3:155–156

Internet browsers, 4:141
KDE, 3:157
Linux operating system, 3:156–157, 4:120, 4:166
Open Source Certification Program, 3:156
Open Source Definition, 3:156
Open Source Initiative, 3:156
Open systems design. See Compatibility (open systems design)
Open Systems Interconnection Reference Model. See OSI Reference Model
Open VMS Alpha operating system, 2:129
Operands, 1:77
Operating systems, 2:128–132
adaptations for disabled persons, 4:12, 4:16
authentication mechanisms, 4:24
Bell Labs' contributions, 1:27
BIOS, 1:130, 2:111
compatibility issues, 2:48–50
defined, 3:25
device managers, 2:129
direct-manipulation systems, 1:112–113
for electronic library catalogs, 3:132
file access policies, 2:131
file managers, 2:130
function, 2:128–129
for graphics applications, 3:209
and GUIs, 2:130
JVMs, 2:128
for mainframes, 1:126–127
memory management, 2:111–112, 2:129, 2:131
menu-, form-, and dialog-based, 1:111
for microcomputers, 1:136
for minicomputers, 1:142
network managers, 2:130
open source, 3:155–158
printer policies, 2:131
processor managers, 2:129, 2:131
programming languages, 2:7
for specific platforms, 2:129
standards, 1:100
stealth viruses and, 1:210
swap files, 2:173
system management utilities, 3:110–111
system resources policies, 2:131
system software and, 3:167
user access policies, 2:131
Operating systems, specific
GNU Linus, 1:135

HP-UX, 2:129
IBM OS/2, 1:138, 3:25
IBM OS/390, 2:129
IBM OS/400, 2:129
IRIX, 2:129
Linux, 2:129–131, 3:144, 3:157–158
Microsoft CE, 2:128
Minix, 2:131
Novell NetWare, 2:128
Open VMS Alpha, 2:129
OS/360 series, 1:89–90, 1:125, 1:126–127
Palm OS, 2:128, 2:142, 3:35, 4:165–166
PocketPC, 4:165–166
Sun Solaris, 2:129
UNICOS, 2:129
V2, 2:6
See also Linux operating system; Macintosh operating system; Microsoft Windows; MS-DOS; UNIX
Operation codes, for assembly language, 1:77
Operational amplifiers, 1:4–5
Operational Control System (OCS), 4:113
Operational (transactional) data, 4:58
Oppenheimer, J. Robert, 2:218, 4:103
OPS languages, 4:174
Optical character recognition. See OCR
Optical computer mice, 2:145
Optical computing, 2:78
Optical disc-read only memory (OD-ROM). See CD-ROMs
Optical discs
laser technology, 3:127
for secondary storage, 1:129, 1:164, 2:190
for video storage, 2:66
See also CD-ROMs; DVDs
Optical mark recognition (OMR), 2:92, 2:133, 2:164
Optical microchips, 1:134
Optical music recognition techniques, 3:147
Optical technology, 1:160–164
adaptations for speed, 1:162
electro-optics, 3:127
electromagnetic energy, 1:160–161, 1:164
fiber optics for, 1:161–162
for graphics tablets, 2:147–148

for high-density data storage, 1:164

for ICs, 1:161–163

for mass storage, 1:163

massively parallel architecture, 1:162

semiconductor diode lasers, 2:75, 2:77

switching light signals, 1:162–163

for telephone systems, 1:190

WORM, 1:*163*

Optically readable marks, 2:132–133

Or-gates, 1:27, 2:59

OR operators, 2:19, 2:*23*

Oracle database management system, 3:60, 3:66, 3:169

electronic library catalogs, 3:132

Larry Ellison and, 4:98

SQL, 3:194

Unicode supported by, 2:42

Orange Book (TCSEC) ratings, 2:172, 2:173

Orbital Science Corporation, 3:103

Orbiting Astronomical Observatory flight series, 3:186

Orbits

of satellites, 2:169–170, 2:172, 4:112–113

of spacecraft, 3:186

Orbitz.com, 3:15, 4:81

Organic transistors (computers), 4:*168*

Bell Labs, 1:195

fictional, 4:106

molecular computing, 4:**167–169**

nanocomputing, 4:**169–172**

Organick, Elliot, 3:**158–160**

The Organization of Behavior, 3:154

Organizational memory, and process control, 3:164, 3:166

Original equipment manufacturer (OEM), 3:183, 3:184

Orthogonal, defined, 2:145, 3:93

Orthogonal projections, in pattern-making, 3:93

Orwell, George, 4:118

OS/360-series operating systems, 1:89–90, 1:125, 1:126–127

Oscillators

audio, 3:108, 3:148

defined, 1:147, 2:200

Oscilloscopes, 1:2, 1:40, 2:53

OSHA (Occupational Health and Safety Administration), standards, 1:99

OSI (Open Systems Interconnection) Reference Model

defined, 4:19

layers and functions, 2:*121*

to organize protocol functions, 2:120

vs. TCP/IP, 2:121–122

Oughtred, William, 1:182

Out-of-band, defined, 4:111

Output

of algorithms, 2:3, 2:4

in system analysis, 2:194

Overhead, defined, 1:45, 4:77

Overlapping Action animation principle, 1:13

Overlapping windows, 1:212, 1:*213*, 1:217

Overlays, in GIS, 3:99

Oxford University Press Journals, 4:84

Ozma of OZ, 4:104

P

Pac-Man game, 1:14, 1:15, 1:69

Packard, David, 3:107–108, 3:109

Packet filtering (network layer) firewalls, 4:107–108, 4:109, 4:151

Packet Radio, 4:203

Packet Satellite, 4:203

Packet spoofing, 1:177

Packet-switched networks

ATM transmission, 1:155, 2:10, 4:17

defined, 1:154, 4:146, 4:203

distinguished from telephone networks, 4:146

government research grants, 1:82

Internet as, 1:116–117, 4:146

Leonard Kleinrock and, 4:*147*

library applications, 3:133

Packets

CRC coder, 2:120

defined, 2:120, 3:180, 4:139

intranet filtering, 4:151

network protocols, 2:*120*

for telephony, 3:201

PacTel, 1:28

Page description languages. *See* Languages, page description

Page scanners, 2:92, 2:134

Page tables, for VM systems, 2:*210*, 2:211

PageMaker software, 1:157, 3:70, 3:74, 3:169, 4:160

Pagers, invention, 3:103

Painter software, 3:169

Pakistani Brain boot virus, 1:207, 2:94

Palm computers

distinguished from PDAs, 2:142

LCDs for, 2:67

Palm, Inc.

Palm m100, 2:142

Palm VIIx, 2:142, 2:*143*

Palm OS, 2:128, 2:142, 3:35

PalmPilot, 2:142

Palo Alto Research Center, Xerox Corporation. *See* PARC

Paper

increased consumption, 2:148–149

for specific printing tasks, 2:151–152

Paper tape, 2:91, 3:31

Paperless trials, 3:130–131

Papert, Seymour, 2:101

Paradigms, defined, 1:112, 2:36, 4:63–64

Parallel algorithms, 2:137

Parallel architecture

asynchronous operation, 2:137

Michael Flynn's taxonomy, 2:135–136

MIMD, 2:135, 2:136, 2:137

MISD, 2:135–136

performance, 2:137–138

selection criteria, 2:136

SIMD, 2:135, 2:136, 2:137

SISD, 2:135

speedup, 2:137–138

SPMD, 2:136

vector processing, 2:136

Parallel computing systems. *See* Parallel processing

Parallel debugging, defined, 2:39

Parallel processing, 2:**134–138**

Ada programming language for, 2:159

animations and simulations, 2:135

array processors, 2:136

and artificial life, 4:11

barriers to, 2:137

computing power, 2:35

data mining, 2:135

defined, 1:153, 2:159

distinguished from distributed systems, 2:35

distinguished from multitasking, 2:134

DNA computers, 4:167, 4:169

fastest computers, 2:135

in fourth-generation computers, 1:74–75

functions, 2:134–135

gigabit networking, 2:135

HPCC, 2:135

interconnection bandwidth, 2:39

Parallel processing (continued)
  manufacturers, 2:135
  for NASA, 1:153
  programming, 2:135, 2:137
  SETI@home, 3:22
  for supercomputers, 1:183
  synchronous operation, 2:136
  weather forecasting, 2:135
  See also Supercomputers
Parallel-to-serial conversion, 2:177
Parallel transmission, 2:**176–178**
  applications, 2:177–178
  Boolean algebra and, *2:23*
  buses, 2:176–177
  distinguished from serial, 2:119
  fiber optics for, 2:178
  interface standards, 2:178
  limitations, 2:178
  synchronization, 2:177
  UARTs, 2:177
Parametric, defined, 3:152
PARC (Palo Alto Research Center)
  Alto computer, 1:216–217, 1:222, 4:147
  CoLab project, 3:49
  computer worms, 1:208, 2:95
  desktop publishing contributions, 3:70, 3:197, 3:199
  funding for computer research, 1:81
  Smalltalk, 1:80
  ubiquitous computing, 3:84
Paris in the Twentieth Century, 4:105
Parity method, for drive repairs, 1:127
Parker, Trey, 1:10
Parks, Nick, 1:10
Parnas, David, 1:151
Parse trees, 2:2
Partitioning, of memory, 1:174
Pascal, Blaise, 1:**164–166**, 1:*165*
  contributions to mathematics, 1:165
  mechanical calculating machines, 1:41–42, 1:*41*, 1:165–166, 4:199
  on nature of computing machinery, 4:55
  philosophical and religious writings, 1:166
  on Torricelli's hypothesis, 1:166
PASCAL programming language
  Ada programming and, 2:159
  for computer music, 2:114
  development, 2:1, 2:2, 2:157
  functions, 1:78
  grammar, 2:51
  operating systems, 2:157

  as structured language, 2:125, 2:157
  UCSD Pascal, 2:157–158
Pascaline, 1:165–166
Pascal's theorem, 1:165
Pascal's triangle, 1:165
Passwords (passcodes)
  to access e-journals, 4:82
  for authentication systems, 2:173, 2:175–176, 4:21–22
  for censorship protocols, 4:33
  in cookies, 4:42
  and CRACK security software, 3:182
  for e-banking, 4:74
  illegal possession/trafficking, 1:36, 3:104, 4:122–123
  to prevent unauthorized copying, 4:46
  protecting, 1:175, 1:176
  used by Trojan Horses, 2:95–96
Paste-up boards (mechanicals), 3:72
Pasting tools, integrated software, 3:119
Patent Office, U.S., 4:176–178
Patents, 4:**176–178**
  disclosures, 4:176
  as intellectual property, 1:36, 4:176
  international, 4:176–177
  invalidating, 4:176
  periods of control, 4:176
  protection vs. trade secrets, 4:177
  recent rulings, 4:178
  rights of owners, 4:176
  on software, 4:177–178
Patents, on specific technologies
  ABC, 1:60, 1:61
  Alfred Gross' inventions, 3:103
  early telephone, 2:17
  ENIAC, 1:60, 1:61
  Guglielmo Marconi's inventions, 4:163–164
  Harry Nyquist's inventions, 4:175
  Hollerith's tabulating machine, 1:83
  hydrofoil HD4, 2:18
  integrated circuits, 1:107
  Open Port Technology, 4:*177*
  robotics technologies, 1:170
  telegraph, 2:17, 2:40
  transistors, 1:192
Pattern recognition, 2:**138–141**
  ambiguity, 2:*139*
  classifiers, 2:138–139

  by computers vs. humans, 2:138–139
  decision trees, 2:141
  defined, 1:114, 3:56, 4:172
  Gaussian classifiers, 2:141
  Glushkov's contributions, 4:120
  k-nearest-neighbors, 2:141
  labeled data, 2:139–140
  neural networks, 2:141
  statistical techniques, 2:140–141
  structural techniques, 2:141
  training data, 2:139–140
Pattern recognition applications
  biometrics, 2:140
  CAT tools, 3:55–56, 3:57
  computer vision, 4:40
  cybernetics, 4:57
  data mining, 2:141
  fingerprint analysis, 2:138
  optical music recognition, 3:147
  PDAs, 2:144
  robotics, 2:141
  speech recognition, 2:138
  See also OCR
Patterson, John H., 1:211
PaulingWorld, 1:205
Payload Type (PT) connections, 4:18
Payloads
  of invasive programs, 1:207
  robot capabilities, 2:166–167
Payroll software, 3:2, 4:1–2
PCI (peripheral components interconnect), 2:54
PCs. *See* IBM-PCs; Personal computers
PDAs (personal digital assistants), 2:**141–144**
  browsers for, 4:28
  combined with cell phones, 3:*34*, 3:35, 4:166
  criteria for selecting, 2:142
  defined, 2:198, 3:35, 4:28
  distinguished from palm computers, 2:142
  graphic devices, 2:83
  handwriting recognition, 2:144
  and information overload, 4:138
  infrared ports, 2:143
  integrated modems, 2:142
  keyboards, 2:141, 2:144
  light pens, 2:141, 2:144
  operating systems, 2:129, 2:142
  personalization techniques, 4:135
  RAM, 2:142
  reducing information overload, 4:133

ROM, 2:142–143

speakers, 2:143

synchronized with microcomputers, 2:142–143

touch screens, 2:141, 2:142, 2:198

voice recorders, 2:141

web-enabled, 4:131

wireless, 2:142, 2:144, 2:220–221

PDAs, hardware and software

ActiveSync 3.1, 2:143

Cassio, 2:143–144

DragonBall EZ, 2:142

HotSync Manager, 2:142

Newton MessagePad, 2:142

Palm m100, 2:142

Palm VIIx, 2:142, 2:143

PalmOS, 3:35

PalmPilot, 2:142

PDT 6840 wireless, 2:144

Pocket Mirror, 2:142

PDAs, uses

bar code scanning, 2:144

Kmart applications, 2:144

medical applications, 2:143, 3:139

as PIMs, 2:141–142, 2:143

PDF (Portable Document Format), 2:105, 2:149, 3:112, 4:77, 4:83–84

PDP-series computers, 1:13, 1:14, 1:36, 1:141–142, 2:116

PDT 6840 wireless PDAs, 2:144

Peacock, George, 1:25

Peer-to-peer networking (P2P), 1:115, 4:138, 4:141

Peerce, Sir William, 4:163

Peering agreements, among Internet backbones, 4:145–146

Peering points, switching networks, 4:143

PEM (Privacy-enhanced Electronic Mail), 1:168, 1:177

Pen input devices, 2:148

Pencil tests, 1:8

Penetration phase, of hacking, 3:105

Pennsylvania State University, CAI research, 3:41

The Pensés, 1:166

Pentagon, terrorist attacks, 4:115

The Perfect Storm, 1:9

Performance analysis decision-making tools, 3:18

Perigee of satellite orbits, 2:169–170

Peripheral components interconnect (PCI), 2:54

Peripherals, defined, 2:198

Perl programming language, 1:208

Perlis, Alan, 2:155

Permanent virtual channels (PVCs), 2:10, 2:11

Permutations, defined, 4:6

Perot, Ross, 4:98

Perry, James T., 4:26

Personal area networking, defined, 4:166

Personal assistants, Microsoft Clippy, 4:1, 4:3

Personal computers (PCs)

Altair 8800, 1:137

animation software, 1:13

CD-ROMs for, 1:137

as computing standard, 1:99

distinguished from minicomputers, 1:141

Dynabook, 1:80

embedded systems and, 3:139

graphic devices, 2:83

home system software for, 3:109–114

internal hard drives, 1:137

vs. mainframes, 1:125–126

mobile phones, 2:32

modems, 3:202

personalization techniques, 4:135

pre-loaded software, 3:184

programming languages, 1:137, 2:7

regulating, 1:34–37

security issues, 1:174–178

size and cost reductions, 1:193

user interfaces, 3:48

video cards, 1:14–15

Xerox Alto, 1:216–217, 1:222, 4:147

See also Apple computers; Compatibility (open systems design); IBM-PCs; Macintosh computers

Personal computers, uses

ATMs, 3:25

desktop publishing, 3:70, 3:74, 3:196–197

disabled persons, 4:11–12

i-Minitel for, 1:144

legal documents, 3:129

medical image analyses, 3:117

photography, 4:179–180, 4:180

television newsrooms, 4:160

video editing, 3:96

weather forecasting, 3:208–209

Personal digital assistants. See PDAs

Personal finance software. See Accounting software

Personal identification numbers (PINs), 2:173, 3:25, 4:22–23

Personal information managers (PIMs), 2:141–142, 2:143, 4:1

Personal satellite assistants (PSAs), 1:173, 2:171

Personalization techniques

information overload and, 4:135

for search engines, 4:135

for television, 4:135

PERT (Program Evaluation and Revue Technique) charts, 3:171–172, 3:172

Pervasive computing, 3:84

Pest control

computer tools, 3:6

IPM models, 3:4–5

Pesticides, application rate calculations, 3:6

Peter Pan, 1:12

Péter, Rózsa (Politzer), 3:160–161

PGAs (pin-grid arrays), 2:109

PGP (Pretty Good Privacy) software, 1:168, 1:177

Philanthropy

An Wang, 3:207

Bill and Melinda Gates Foundation, 3:131, 4:94

William and Flora Hewlett Foundation, 3:109

Philco Corporation, Transac S-2000, 1:72

Philips, TiVo, 4:124, 4:126, 4:127

A Philosopher Looks at Science, 3:121

Phonographs, invention, 4:126

Phosphorous, as doping element, 1:105, 3:39

Phosphors, 1:203, 2:63

Photo diodes, 3:127

Photography, 4:178–181

analog vs. digital, 4:178–179

Daguerreotypes, 2:114

digital, as art, 4:7

digitizing, 1:31, 1:159–160

fax machines and, 4:175

image editing, 4:181

Jason Salavon's work, 4:7

John Haddock's work, 4:7

JPEG format, 4:179

JPL's contributions, 4:178

Kodak's instructional guides, 4:179

NASA's contributions, 4:178

OCR technology, 2:134

and personal computers, 4:179–180, 4:180

printing technology, 2:152

scanners and, 4:180–181

software for manipulating, 3:169

wet vs. digital darkrooms, 4:160

See also Cameras, digital; Digital images; Film

Photolithography, 1:193, 1:194–195

Photomask processing, 3:38–39, 4:45

Photonic switching, fiber optics and, 2:78

Photons
defined, 2:78
in laser technology, 3:125–126

Photopaint software, 3:169, 4:67

Photosensitivity, of computer visual devices, 4:38

Photoshop software, 3:18, 3:169, 4:6, 4:67, 4:160, 4:181

Phototypesetting, 3:71

Phreakers, 4:123

Physical addressing model, 2:206–207, 2:*206*, 2:*207*, 2:208–209

Physical layer, ATM transmission, 4:19

Physical medium (PM) sublayer, ATM transmission, 4:19

Physical modeling synthesis (PhM), 3:148

Physics, 3:**161–164**
approximations, 3:162
and chemistry, 4:34–35
computational astrophysics, 3:23
computer applications, 3:138
early analog computers, 3:162
early digital computers, 3:162
Internet resources, 3:164
nanocomputing, 4:**169–172**
Nyquist's Theorem, 4:27
Shannon's Theorem, 4:27
sub-atomic particle photographs, 3:163
teaching tools, 3:164
visualization, 3:162–164, 3:*163*

Picoseconds, defined, 1:162

PICS (Platform for Internet Content Selection), 4:140

Picture It software, 3:169

Picture lock, video editing, 3:97

PID (proportional-integral-derivative) controllers, 3:165

PIE 3D Game Creation, 1:15

Pie charts, 3:61, 3:63

Pierce, John, 2:115

Piezoelectric crystals, 2:150, 3:115

Pigs Is Pigs, 1:13

PIMs (personal information managers), 2:141–142, 2:*143*, 4:1

Pin-grid arrays (PGAs), 2:109

Ping sweeps, defined, 3:104

Pinocchio, 1:12, 1:13

PINs (personal identification numbers), 2:173, 3:26, 4:22–23

Piracy
punched cards, 1:119
software, 1:36, 3:**182–185**, 4:123

Pitch, of aircraft, 3:7

Pixar, Inc., 1:16

Pixels
in computer displays vs. printer output, 2:149
defined, 1:31, 2:63, 3:115, 4:39
in digital images, 1:113, 2:81–82, 4:65–66, 4:179
vs. picture quality, 2:66
sub, for LCDs, 2:66

Pixilation, defined, 4:7

PKI. *See* Public key infrastructure

PL/1 programming language, 2:114, 2:159

Plane-polarized light, for LCDs, 2:65–66

Plane position indicators (PPIs), 3:12

Plankalkül programming language, 2:222

Platform for Internet Content Selection (PICS), 4:140

Playing with Infinity: Mathematical Explorations and Excursions, 3:160, 3:161

PlayStation video game units, 1:15, 1:69, 2:80, 4:126

PLCs (programmable logic controllers), agricultural applications, 3:6

Plessey Telecommunications, bar code scanners, 2:163

PLI (Private Line Interface), 2:213

Plotter printing devices, 2:152

Plotting techniques and devices
physics applications, 3:162–163
scatterplots, 3:61
for spreadsheets, 3:192–193, 3:*192*, 4:96

Plug-and-play devices, 2:26, 4:5

Plug-in programs, defined, 4:28

Plummer, R.P., 3:159

Plus ATM network, 3:25

PN semiconductor chips, 1:195–196

Pneumatic, defined, 1:178, 2:166, 3:53

Pneumatic training simulators, 1:178

Pneumonia, electronic detection, 3:144

PNG format, 4:67

PNP transistors, 1:196

Pocahontas, 1:13

Pocket Mirror software, 2:142

PocketPC, 4:165–166

Point-and-click interfaces, 2:145

Pointing devices, 2:**144–148**
data gloves, 2:85
for disabled persons, 3:205, 4:*87*
eraserhead, 2:148
eye-motion tracking systems, 2:85
foot pedals, 2:85
graphics tablets, 2:*147*, 2:148
light pens, 2:91, 2:141, 2:144, 2:*147*, 2:148
pen input devices, 2:148
touch pads, 2:146
touch screens, 2:141, 2:142, 2:146, 2:**197–200**
trackballs, 2:148
See also Joysticks; Mouse, computer

Points of interest (POI), in multidimensional displays, 3:*63*

"The Poison Dress," 4:206

Polar orbits, 2:170

Polarity, defined, 2:109

Polarizers, defined, 2:65–66

Political applications, 4:**181–185**
administration tools, 4:184
computer predictions, 1:72, 4:183
computerization information resources, 4:181–182
direct-mail communications, 4:182
event simulations, 4:184
Internet communications, 4:182
polling and statistical analysis, 4:183
presentation materials, 4:182
voting and vote counting, 4:183
voting district boundaries, 4:183

Polonius security system, 2:173

Polyalphabetic ciphers, 4:50–51

Polyalphabetic substitution systems, 4:51

Polygonal, defined, 2:83, 3:99

Polymorphic viruses, 1:209–210

Polymorphism, in object-oriented languages, 2:127

Polynomials, 1:18, 1:25

Polypeptides, defined, 4:36

Polyphony, sound cards, 2:184

Pong machines, 1:67–68, 4:126

Population inversions, defined, 3:126

Population migration patterns, 3:137–138

Pornography
censorship and, 4:**31–34**, 4:132
downloading, ethics, 4:101

Port IDs, 4:107

Port scans, defined, 3:104

Portability, of computers and software, 2:49, 3:84

Portable computers. *See* Handheld computers; Laptop/notebook computers; PDAs

Portable Document Format. *See* PDF

Ports (input/output), defined, 3:9

Pose-to-pose Action animation principle, 1:14

Positional notation, 1:29–30

Positive Train Control (PTC) project, 3:175–176

Post, E.L., 2:2

Postal system (U.S.)
  bar codes, 2:163
  e-mail vs. snail mail, 1:47, 2:90
  OCR tools, 4:68
  routing, 4:185
  uniform postal rates, 1:26

Postscript page description language, 2:149, 3:70, 3:72, 3:74, 3:198–199, 4:67

Potentiometers, defined, 2:80

PowerBook computer, 1:17

PowerMac G4 computer, 1:17

PowerPoint software, 1:137, 1:160, 3:169–170

PPIs (plane position indicators), 3:12

Precision agriculture (site-specific farming), 3:4, 4:117

Predicate logic systems, 3:90

Predictions, of knowledge-based systems, 3:123–124

Prescription drugs
  computer-based research, 3:140
  genetics research and, 3:142
  harmful interactions, 3:140
  PDAs to investigate, 3:139

Presentation software
  Lotus Freelance Graphics, 1:160, 3:169–170
  OAS applications, 1:159–160
  PowerPoint, 1:137, 1:160, 3:169–170
  SPC Harvard Graphics, 1:160
  uses, 3:169

Presentations
  CSCW for, 3:49–50
  data visualization for, 3:**61–64**
  multimedia for, 2:*84*, 2:86

President's Commission on the Space Shuttle Challenger Accident, 4:103–104

Pressure-sensitive sensors, 2:148

Pretty Good Privacy (PGP) software, 1:168, 1:177

Price, Mark, 4:62

Primary storage. *See* Memory/memory devices

Primitives, graphic
  in CAD systems, 3:30
  in Logo, 2:102, 2:103
  for scientific visualization, 3:179

Princeton University
  IAS machine, 1:72
  Institute for Advanced Studies, 2:217
  in Internet history, 4:142
  John Kemeny and, 3:121

Printing
  publishing technology, 3:70–72, 3:197–198
  See also Desktop publishing

Printing, color
  color gamuts, 2:151–152, 4:66, 4:67
  half-tone, 2:149, 2:151
  inks, 2:151–152
  paper for, 2:151–152

Printing devices, 2:**148–153**
  compatibility, 2:49
  connection to computers, 2:177–178
  for desktop publishing, 3:70, 3:72, 3:74, 3:197–199
  function, 2:149
  memory, 2:149
  and paper consumption, 2:148–149
  paper types, 2:151–152
  resolution, 2:149, 4:66–67
  See also Page description languages

Printing devices, types
  daisywheel, 2:152
  Diablo, 3:212
  dot matrix, 2:149–150
  dye sublimation, 2:152
  impact, 1:128
  inkjet, 2:150–151, 3:198
  line printers, 1:128
  plotters, 2:152
  printing presses, 2:87, 3:197–198
  solid ink, 2:151
  thermal wax, color, 2:152
  Xerox 9700, 3:198
  See also Laser printers

Privacy, 1:**166–169**
  BBB program to confirm, 4:48
  of census information, 1:33
  Computer Fraud and Abuse Act, 1:**34–38**
  Computer Security Act, 1:168
  cookies and, 4:42

cryptography to ensure, 1:168, 2:213, 4:**49–53**
vs. data mining, 1:167–168, 4:62, 4:79
of e-mail, 1:49–50
of early computers, 1:36–37
efforts to ensure, 1:168
Electronic Communications Privacy Act, 1:168
of financial institutes, 1:168, 1:*176*
vs. global surveillance, 4:118
Graam-Leach-Blilely Act, 1:168
Health Insurance Portability and Accountability Act, 1:168
historical invasions of, 1:166–167
IBM's policies on, 4:79
information vs. communications, 1:166
vs. law enforcement, 1:167
of medical records, 3:140
vs. micromarketing, 1:167–168, 4:62
Multics security kernel, 1:175
organizations and publications, 1:168–169
PGP and PEM software, 1:168, 1:177
protecting, in ethics code, 4:101
of VPNs, 2:213, 3:180
World Wide Web, 1:220
See also Hacking/hackers; Security

Privacy and American Business, 1:168

Privacy-enhanced Electronic Mail (PEM), 1:168, 1:177

Privacy Forum, 1:168

Privacy Journal, 1:169

The Privacy Rights Clearinghouse, 1:168

Privacy Times, 1:169

Private-key (symmetric) cryptography, 4:52, 4:72

Private Line Interface (PLI), 2:213

Privatized, defined, 1:115

Probability distribution, of code symbols, 2:42–44

Probe programs, 1:37

Problem-solving, organizational, 4:197–198

Procedural languages. *See* Languages, procedural

Procedural (standard) programming, 2:99

Process control, 3:**164–166**
  analog computing for, 1:5
  applications, 3:164

Process control (continued)
  field, process, and control nets, 3:*164*
  fuzzy logic, 3:166
  interconnectivity, 3:164–165
  interlocking and basic logic, 3:164
  minicomputers for, 1:140
  motor controllers, 3:164
  and neural networks, 3:166
  organizational memory, 3:164, 3:166
  PID controllers, 3:165
  recovering from disturbances, 3:166
  software, for 1E switching system, 1:27
  system architecture, 3:164, 3:*165*
  See also Manufacturing
Processor managers, 2:129
Processors. *See* CPUs; Microchips/microprocessors
Productivity software, 3:**166–170**, 3:*168*
  See also Database management software; Desktop publishing software; Graphics software; Integrated software; Presentation software; Spreadsheets; Word processors
Progenitor, defined, 4:106
Program control, telephony, 3:200–201
Program Evaluation and Revue Technique. *See* PERT charts
Programmable logic controllers (PLCs), 3:6
Programmable read-only memory (PROM), 1:130, 2:109, 2:111
Programmers. *See* Computer professionals; Early pioneers
Programming, 2:**160–163**
  ambiguity, avoiding, 2:161
  analog computers, 1:132
  attributes, 2:159
  client/server design issues, 2:39
  computer scientists in, 1:38
  costs, 2:154, 2:156
  debugging, 2:39, 2:101, 2:162
  design tools, 2:**55–58**
  early computers, 1:36–37, 1:63, 1:72
  for embedded technologies, 3:86
  event-driven, 2:126
  for expert systems, 3:88–89
  flowcharts, 2:162
  functional vs. procedural, 2:99
  International Collegiate Programming Contest, 1:23

Mark I-series computers, 1:85
  for object oriented environments, 1:112–113
  for parallel architecture, 2:137
  process- vs. event-driven approaches, 1:112–113
  pseudocode, 2:162
  robotics technologies, 2:168
  structured, 2:162
  subroutines, 1:57
  tabulating machines vs. computers, 1:188
  techniques, 2:160–163
  See also Codes
Programming Language Structures, 3:*159*
Programming languages. *See* Languages, programming
Programs. *See* Software; *specific computer programs*
Progressive scanning, 2:63
Project Gemini, 1:151
Project management and planning, 3:**170–173**
  defining and organizing tasks, 3:171–172
  Gantt charts, 3:172, 3:*173*
  goal setting, 3:171
  PERT charts, 3:171–173, 3:*172*
  time scheduling, 3:172
  tracking, 3:172
Project Mercury, 1:151
Project Whirlwind, 1:178
ProjectBank software, 3:18
Projectors
  computer, 2:67
  movie, 4:126
  overhead, 4:85, 4:86
Projects, defined, 3:170–171
Prolog, 1:19
PROM (programmable read-only memory), 1:130, 2:109, 2:111
Proportional-integral-derivative (PID) controllers, 3:165
Propositional logic, microprocessors as, 3:138–139
Proprietary information, 1:96, 1:174, 2:41, 2:104, 3:25
Protein Data Bank, 1:184–185
Protocol filtering, 4:32–43
Protocols
  to access main memory, 2:205–206
  addressing, 2:37
  for asynchronous and synchronous transmission, 2:8–9, 2:12
  checksums, 2:120
  for client/server systems, 2:36–37

defined, 1:43, 2:8, 4:32
  for digital libraries, 4:71
  for document processing, 2:71
  functions, 2:120–121, 4:202–203
  for inter-satellite communications, 2:170
  for interface management, 2:54
  packet format, 2:120
  security-related, 1:176–177
  signaling, 4:17
  standards, 1:100
  for Web interactions, 4:141
Protocols, specific
  EDI, 1:43
  MAC, 2:24, 2:118–119, 3:159
  MIDI, 1:149–150, 2:184, 3:146, 3:147
  NCP, 4:146, 4:148
  OSI Reference Model, 2:120–121
  PCI, 2:54
  RPC, 2:38–39
  RS-232, 2:9, 2:178
  RS-232/232-C, 2:9, 2:178
  RS-449, 2:178
  SMTP, 2:37, 4:108
  SNA, 4:152
  SOAP, 4:141
  TCP, 1:116, 2:37, 2:121–122, 4:110, 4:147–148
  Telnet, 4:**204–206**
  WAP, 3:34
  See also FTP; HTTP; IP; Network protocols; TCP/IP
Prototypes
  of bar codes, 2:163
  CAD to create, 3:18
  CAE to create, 3:32, 3:51
  of CAT, 3:56
  defined, 2:100, 3:18
  of smart devices, 3:84
  in system analysis and design, 2:194, 2:196
The Provincial Letters, 1:166
Proxy firewalls. *See* Transport layer firewalls
Proxy port IDs, 4:109
Proxy servers, 4:83
Prudential, UNIVAC purchaser, 2:73
PSAs (personal satellite assistants), 1:173, 2:*171*
Pseudo-random code, 4:113
Pseudocode, 2:*57*, 2:162
PSINET, 4:145, 4:149, 4:193
PSTN (public switched telephone network), 2:29–30
Psychology, cybertherapy, 3:140

PT (Payload Type) connections, 4:18

PTC (Positive Train Control) project, 3:175–176

PTV, personalized television listings, 4:135

P2P (peer-to-peer networking), 1:115, 4:138, 4:141

Public access Internet sites, 4:131

Public computer systems, touch screens, 2:198

Public-key cryptosystems, 1:176, 4:52

Public key infrastructure (PKI), 2:174, 3:87, 4:72, 4:83

Public Policy Institute of California, 3:109

Public switched telephone network (PSTN), 2:29–30

Publication languages, in Algol-60 report, 2:1

Publisher software, 3:169

Publishing technology
    vs. e-books, 4:76–77
    mid-twentieth century, 3:71–72, 3:197–198
    printing press, 2:87
    through Middle ages, 3:70–71
    See also Desktop publishing; E-journals and e-publishing

Pucks, as CAD tool, 3:30–31

Punched cards
    Analytical Engine, 1:7, 1:25, 1:80, 1:186
    business applications, 1:186–188
    census applications, 1:32, 1:81, 1:83–84, 1:88, 1:186, 2:93
    character code, 2:41
    defined, 1:7, 2:41, 4:126
    for document processing, 2:69
    EAM, 1:187–188
    for early computers, 3:48
    ENIAC, 1:71
    Herman Hollerith and, 1:32, 1:83–84, 1:88, 1:186, 1:187, 2:41, 2:92, 2:93, 3:59
    IBM cards, 1:186, 1:187
    for information retrieval systems, 1:93, 1:94
    as input devices, 2:92
    Jacquard's loom, 1:7, 1:83, 1:**117–119**, 1:124, 1:169, 1:186
    keypunch machines, 1:185, 1:187
    Mark series computers, 1:85
    for mass storage, 1:163
    for mechanical music boxes, 4:125–126
    piracy, 1:119
    readers, 1:55, 2:92

tabulating machines, 1:**185–189**
    in textile industry, 1:83
    as voting tool, 1:94, 4:183
    for Z computers, 2:222

Puppet animation, 1:10

Purdue University, COPS, 3:181

Purple cryptosystem, 4:51

PVC plastic, for insulators, 1:132

PVCs (permanent virtual channels), 2:10, 2:11

Q

QAD Inc., 4:97

QIC (quarter-inch cartridges), 2:188

QoS (quality of service)
    of ATM, 2:10
    defined, 2:213
    of Internet, 2:213–214

QSpace, 4:48–49

Quadtrees, 3:101

Quantizing, to digitize sound, 2:182, 2:183

Quantum Computer Services, 1:70

Quantum-dot cellular automata (QCA), 4:171

Quantum dots, 4:170

Quantum electrodynamics, 4:103

Quantum mechanics, defined, 4:170

Quark Xpress software, 3:169, 3:197, 4:160

Quarter-inch cartridges (QIC), 2:188

Quatro Pro software, 3:60, 3:169

Queen Elizabeth II, e-mail, 4:148

Queens College, sound synthesis research, 2:116

Queries
    Boolean searches, 1:93–95, 2:19–20
    in expert systems, 3:88, 3:90
    for information retrieval, 1:92–93
    in vector space models, 1:96
    XML, 2:107

Query language, 1:79

Queues, routing, 4:187

Quicken software, 3:1, 3:60, 3:169

Quicktime VR, 1:10–11

QWERTY keyboards, 1:120

R

R-trees, 3:101

RACF subsystem, 1:127

Radar
    for ATC systems, 3:10–11, 3:11
    defined, 2:191, 3:10, 4:38

Doppler, 3:209
    high-speed data links, 3:12

Radio
    Alfred Gross and, 3:102–103
    broadcast telecommunications, 1:190–191
    Citizens' Band, 3:103
    cryptography and, 4:51
    for distance learning, 3:75
    early wireless, 2:29–30, 2:219
    electromagnetic energy use, 1:160–161
    Guglielmo Marconi and, 2:201, 2:219, 4:126, 4:**163–164**
    ham, 3:102
    journalism, 4:161
    police, 2:29
    rectification operation, 1:201
    transistors, 1:192
    transmission lines, 2:201
    WDM, 1:162

Radio frequency (RF) communications, 2:201, 2:218–219, 2:220

Radio navigation, 3:7, 3:149–150, 3:151

Radio Shack TRS-80, 1:36

Radio telescopes, 3:22, 3:23

Radio transmitters, for cell phones, 3:33

Radio waves, for MRI, 3:116–117

Radiology
    pattern recognition tools, 2:139–140, 2:140, 3:55–56
    radioactive materials, 3:115–116
    Therac-25 failure, 4:100–101

RAID (random array of inexpensive disks), 1:127

Railroad applications, 3:**173–176**
    bar code tracking systems, 3:174
    communication technologies, 3:173
    computer conversion difficulties, 3:174–175
    GPS technology, 3:174
    history, 3:173–174
    infrastructures, 3:173
    linked databases, 3:173–174
    PTC project, 3:175–176
    punched cards, 1:83, 1:186
    satellite tracking, 3:174
    transponders, 3:174

Railroads
    French TGV, 2:159
    Shinkansen (bullet trains), 3:174, 3:175
    standardization, 1:97–99
    studied by Charles Babbage, 1:26

RAM (random access memory)
defined, 1:74, 2:5
DRAM, 2:109, 2:111, 2:209
ferromagnetic storage media,
1:163
in fourth-generation computers,
1:74
for game controllers, 2:81
interaction with CPU, 2:32
for mainframes, 1:127
memory managers, 2:111–112,
2:129
for microcomputers, 1:136
for PDAs, 2:142
role in computer, 2:110, 2:187
SRAM, 2:109, 2:110–111
storage capacity, 1:129
for supercomputers, 1:182
for video editing, 3:96
volatility, 1:129, 2:111, 2:187
See also Memory/memory devices
RAMAC 305 computer, 1:89
Random array of inexpensive disks
(RAID), 1:127
*Random Essays on Mathematics, Edu-
cation and Computers*, 3:121
Ranger lunar impact probes, 3:186
Rasmussen, Steen, 4:*10*
Raster, defined, 3:31
Raster image processing (RIP),
3:199
Raster scan patterns (bitmapped dis-
play), 1:203, 2:82
RATS software, 3:79
Raven, 1:15
RCA
early radios, 4:126
mainframe computers, 1:89,
1:125
RDB databases, 3:194
RDBMSs (relational database man-
agement systems), 3:59
RDF (Resource Description Frame-
work), 4:31
Read only memory. *See* ROM
Read only mode, for database users,
3:66
Reader Rabbit educational software,
3:82
Reading tools, 2:**163–166**
OMR, 2:92, 2:133, 2:164
smart cards, 2:164–165, 2:*165*,
2:174
for visually impared persons,
4:12–13, 4:30, 4:31, 4:117
See also Bar codes; OCR; Scanners
Reagan, Ronald, 3:103, 3:109, 4:101
Real Networks, Real Player, 3:113

Real-time strategy (RTS), computer
games, 4:*128*
Real-time systems
computerized reservation systems, 3:14
defined, 4:88
distance learning support, 4:88
programming languages for,
2:159
space applications, 1:151–152,
2:168
RealAudio format, 2:184
RealNetworks, 2:184
Reaver, J. Russell, 4:206
Recognition vocabularies, 3:189
Recordkeeping software. *See* Accounting software
Rectification, defined, 1:201
*Recursive Functions in Computer The-
ory*, 3:161
Recursive functions/procedures,
2:102, 2:*103*, 3:160–161
Red Alert game, 4:127, 4:*128*
Red Hat, open source software,
3:156–157
Reddy, Raj, 1:21
Redundant systems
airline reservation hardware and
software, 3:15
error-correcting codes, 2:*44*
networks, 2:26
space applications, 1:152–153,
3:186–187
Reel-to-reel tapes, 2:91
Reference languages, in Algol-60 report, 2:1
Reflective displays, 2:67
Registers
addressing models and,
2:206–209
C programming variables, 2:158
for minicomputers, 1:141
role in CPU, 2:5–6, 2:32, 2:33,
2:51
special and general-purpose, 2:6
Regression analysis, 3:78
Rehabilitation Act, Section 508, 4:16
Relational database management
systems (RDBMSs), 3:59
Relational databases
defined, 3:60, 4:63
function, 3:65
GIS tools, 3:101
Informix, 3:132
for intranet security, 4:151–152
library applications, 3:132
Oracle, 2:42, 3:60, 3:66, 3:132
SQL and, 3:194

Relay contact systems, defined,
3:160
Relay satellite, 2:170
Relevance feedback, 1:96
Relevancy scores, for information
retrieval, 4:134
Religion
Blaise Pascal on, 1:166
Charles Babbage on, 1:26
Inquisition vs. science, 1:165
Remington-Rand Corporation,
1:188, 2:74, 2:222
Remote control devices, IR trans-
mission, 2:202–203
Remote Method Invocation (RMI),
2:39
Remote Procedure Call (RPC) protocol, 2:38–39
Repeaters
as bridging devices, 2:24
for transmission lines, 2:201
for wireless technology, 2:202
Repetitive stress injuries, preventing,
1:*66*, 1:121–122
Répons, 3:146
Reproducer tabulating machines,
1:185, 1:188
Reprographics, 2:69
Requests for Comments (RFCs),
2:11, 4:110
Research, computer-based
agriculture, 3:6
architecture, 3:18
art and art history, 4:8
astronomy, 3:22–23
biology, 3:28
chemistry, 4:36–37
digitized full-text documents,
4:132
e-books, 4:77
e-journals, 4:82
gene sequencing, 3:27–28
legal applications, 3:128–129,
4:189
medicine, 3:140
virtual reference desks,
4:130–131
See also Data mining; Libraries,
digital
Research, Government funding for,
1:**80–82**, 1:93
Resistive touch-screen panels, 2:146,
2:199
Resistors, 1:104, 2:54
Resolution
of computer monitors, 4:66–67
of digital cameras, 4:179

of printing devices, 2:149, 2:150–151, 3:197–199, 4:66–67

Resource Description Framework (RDF), 4:31

Retail businesses

traditional, vs. e-commerce, 1:45–47

See also E-commerce

Retinal (iris) scans, 2:140, 4:21, 4:*22*

Retroviruses, 1:209, 1:210

RF (radio frequency) communications, 2:201, 2:218–219, 2:220

RFCs (Requests for Comments), 2:11, 4:110

RGB color gamut, 2:151, 4:66, 4:67

Rice, genetically engineered, 3:143

Riding the Bullet, 4:77

Rifkin, Stanley Mark, 1:*176*

Rights of reproduction, 4:43

Rijndael encryption algorithm, 4:52

Ring topology, 1:155, 2:124

RIP (raster image processing), 3:199

Risks, and catastrophe insurance, 4:91

Risks forum, 1:23

Ritchie, Dennis, 1:21, 1:27, 2:158

Rivest, Ronald, 4:52

RMI (Remote Method Invocation), 2:39

Roberval, Gilles Personier de, 1:165

Robotics/robots, 1:**169–173**, 2:**166–168**

AIBO robotic dog, 4:124, 4:*125*

in ancient China, 1:169

anthropomorphism, 1:171, 2:166, 4:104–105

artificial intelligence and, 1:170, 3:53

and artificial life, 4:11

automatons, 1:169, 4:104

computer scientists' role, 1:38–39

Dante II, 1:*172*

and cybernetics, 4:57–58

defined, 1:38, 2:111, 4:37

Devol's contributions, 1:170

EPROM for, 2:111

as expert systems, 2:89

feedback, 2:168

Glushkov's contributions, 4:120

Hopkins Beast, 1:169

manipulation technology, 1:171

manipulator arms, 2:166

microbial, 4:167

movement, 1:171, 2:166, 2:167–168, 2:*167*

multifunctionality, 3:53

NESSY, 4:38

origin of term, 1:173

pattern recognition tools, 2:141

payload capability, 2:166–167

pneumatic mechanisms, 3:53

power sources, 2:168

process control, 3:164

programming languages, 2:159

purpose, 2:166

real-time control systems, 2:168

in search engines, 4:188

Shakey (robot), 1:170

social implications, 1:171–172, 4:*201*

vision and sensor technologies, 1:171, 4:37–40, 4:67–68

Walters' contributions, 1:169

Robotics/robots, applications

bomb diffusion, 1:*19*

Happy magnetic tape storage area, 2:*92*

hazardous environments, 1:170, 1:171, 1:*172*, 2:166, 3:53

manufacturing, 1:108–109, 1:170, 1:171, 2:166, 3:53

medicine, 1:170, 1:171, 2:168, 3:141–142, 3:168

military, 1:170

nanotechnology, 2:168

space exploration, 1:170, 1:171, 2:167–168, 2:*167*

supervisory roles, 2:168

telemetry equipment, 2:167

transportation applications, 1:170

Robotics/robots, fictional

Artificial Intelligence: AI, 1:20

Asimov's Three Laws of Robotics, 3:20–21, 4:104

"droids" on film, 1:173

I, Robot, 1:14, 1:173, 3:20

Illiad, 1:172

"In the Deep of Time," 4:105

"The Metal Giants," 4:105

Olympia, in "The Sandman," 4:104

Rossum's Robots, 1:172–173, 3:20

"Runabout," 1:173, 4:104

Star Wars, 3:20

Tik-Tok of Oz, 4:104

Westworld, 4:104

Rocket eBooks, 4:77

Rodman, Dennis, 1:205

Rods, of eyes, 4:38

Rogers, Lawrence, 4:146

Roll, of aircraft, 3:7

ROM (read only memory), 1:129–130, 2:109

of auto-pilots, 3:9

defined, 2:5

EAPROM, 2:109, 2:111

EEPROM, 1:130

EPROM, 1:130, 2:109, 2:111

for game controllers, 2:81

for PDAs, 2:142–143

PROM, 1:130, 2:109, 2:111

role in computer, 2:111

volatility, 2:111

See also Memory/memory devices

Roman numerals, to represent knowledge, 1:18

Roosevelt, Franklin, 1:87, 2:218

Rosenbloom, Paul S., 4:173

Ross, Sheldon, 1:178

Rossum's Robots, 1:172–173, 3:20

Rotor machines, 4:51

Round Earth Project, 1:205–206

Routing/routers, 4:**185–187**

in ASes, 4:143

for CIA, 2:*118*

at CompuServe, 4:*186*

defined, 1:117, 2:119

distinguished from bridges, 2:26

dynamic, 4:187

function, 2:26, 4:185–186, 4:203

IBM RS/4000, 4:143

IBM SNA, 2:27

IPs, 2:26–27

in network design, 2:119

static, 4:186–187

Routing tables, 2:26

Royal Astronomical Society, 3:22

RPC (Remote Procedure Call) protocol, 2:38–39

RPG programming language, 1:141

RS-232/232-C protocols, 2:9, 2:178

RS-449 protocol, 2:178

RSA public-key cryptosystem, 1:176, 4:52

RTS (real-time strategy), computer games, 4:*128*

Rudolph the Red-Nosed Reindeer, 1:10

Rule-based systems. *See* Expert systems

Rules of Restoration and Reduction, 2:3

Run-time type checking, 2:100

Rusch, Frank, 1:205

Russell, Steve, 1:67

Russia (U.S.S.R.)

Academy of Sciences of Ukraine, Computer Center, 4:119

Cybercafes in, 4:*139*

Cold War, 1:57, 4:115

e-mail use, 4:*139*

Institute of Cybernetics, 4:119

software piracy, 3:184

Russia (U.S.S.R.) (continued)
  space program, 2:169, 2:170,
    3:187
  Sputnik, 2:*169*, 2:170, 3:104,
    4:115

S

Sabre (Semi-Automated Business
    Research Environment) system,
    3:14–15
Sachs, Jonathan, 4:96
SafeSurf filter, 4:32
Safety
  CAVE educational materials,
    1:205
  of cell phones, 3:33, 3:35
Safety-critical software, ethical con-
    cerns, 4:100–101
SAGE (Semi-Automatic Ground
    Environment), 3:14
Salavon, Jason, 4:7
Sales order tracking software, 3:3
Salton, Gerard, 1:95
Sampling, to digitize sound, 1:31,
    1:148–149, 1:*149*, 2:*182*
San Diego Supercomputer Center,
    1:184
Sanders Associates, 1:67
"The Sandman," 4:104
SAR (Segmentation and Reassembly)
    sublayer, 4:20
SARIN, computer generated molec-
    ular model, 4:*35*
Sarnoff, David, 4:126
SAS software, 3:78
SATAN security software, 3:181
Satellite technology, 2:**169–172**
  for distance learning, 3:76–77
  flight control, 4:117
  for global surveillance,
    4:**115–118**
  as IT, 2:87
  for navigation, 2:171–172
  protocols, 2:170
  remote sensing, 3:28
  as sensors, 2:191
  statistics, 2:169
  for telephone systems, 1:190,
    2:170
  for television, 2:78, 2:170
  to track railroad trains, 3:174
  to transmit video images, 3:99
  to transmit weather forecasts,
    3:208
Satellites
  constellations, 2:170, 2:202,
    3:151, 4:112–113, 4:114
  Cuban Missile Crisis, 4:115

defined, 2:169
Extreme Ultraviolet Explorer,
    2:169
GEO, 2:170–171, 2:202
GSO, 4:117
IKONOS, 4:*115*
Iridium system, 2:202
Landsat, 2:170–171, 4:*116*
LEO, 2:170, 2:202, 4:117
NAVSTAR, 2:172
orbits, 2:169–170, 2:172
PSAs, 1:173, 2:*171*
Relay, 2:170
Sputnik, 2:*169*, 2:170, 3:104,
    4:115
  See also Global positioning sys-
    tems
Satisficing, 4:198
Saudi Arabia, Internet censorship,
    4:33–34
SAW (surface acoustic wave)
    screens, 2:146, 2:200
Sayre, David, 2:154
SBASIC programming language,
    2:157
Scaler processors, 3:58
Scanners
  bar code, 2:92, 2:132–133, 2:*133*,
    2:144, 2:163, 3:127
  biometric, 4:21–23, 4:*22*, 4:*23*
  in CAD systems, 3:31
  for image processing, 1:160
  as input devices, 3:203
  Kurzwell, 2:164
  measuring quality of, 4:181
  MICR, 2:92
  multimedia applications, 2:85
  OMR, 2:92, 2:133, 2:164
  page and hand-held, 2:92
  for photographs, 2:152,
    4:180–181
  physics applications, 3:163
  for visually impared persons, 4:13
  See also OCR
Scanning, by CRTs, 2:63–64
Scanning, by hackers, 3:104
Scanning code, 1:120, 2:91
Scatterplots, 3:61
Schematic, defined, 3:31
Schlumberger SEED (Science Ex-
    cellence in Education Develop-
    ment), 4:37
Schneider, Gary P., 4:26
Scholarly Publishing and Academic
    Resources Coalition (SPARC),
    4:82
Scholastic Aptitude Test (SAT),
    OMR scoring, 2:133, 2:164

Schon, Hendrik, 4:*168*
Science fiction. *See* Fiction, comput-
    ers in; Robotics/robots, fictional;
    specific authors
Scientific visualization, 3:**176–179**
  animation, 3:177–178
  applications, 3:162–164, 3:*163*,
    3:176–177
  CAT, 3:55–56, 3:57, 3:115,
    3:177, 3:*178*
  chemistry applications, 4:*35*, 4:36
  computational steering, 3:177
  data mining, 3:178
  data sampling, 3:179
  function, 3:177
  graphical primitives, 3:179
  new uses, 3:179
  software tools, 3:178–179
Scooby Doo, 1:13
Score software, 3:146
SCORM (Shared Content Object
    Reference Model), 3:42, 3:82
SCPA (Semiconductor Chip Protec-
    tion Act), 4:45
Screen readers, for disabled persons,
    4:13, 4:15
Script Kiddies, hackers, 4:123
Script viruses, 1:207
Scripting languages, defined, 3:118
Scriptoria, 3:71
Scroll bars, 1:215–216, 1:*217*
Scrooge, Ebenezer, 3:59
SCSI (small computer system inter-
    face standard), 2:54
SCSL (Sun Community Source Li-
    cense), 3:156
Scullin, Frederick J., Jr., 1:37
SDNs (software-defined networks),
    2:213
Search engines, 4:**188–191**
  as algorithms, 2:4
  Boolean operators, 1:219, 2:23,
    4:189
  cookies and, 4:42
  directories, 4:191
  evaluating information,
    4:190–191
  field searching, 4:189
  hyperlinks, 1:96, 4:188
  indexes for, 4:134, 4:188,
    4:189–190
  and information access, 4:130
  invisible web, 4:190
  metasearches, 1:219, 4:189
  personalization techniques, 4:135
  precision and recall characteris-
    tics, 4:134–135, 4:188–189
  proprietary information, 1:96

relevancy scores, 4:134, 4:188, 4:189

search expression, 4:188

spiders (robots), 4:188, 4:189–190

user interfaces, 4:128

vocabulary mismatches, 4:134

See also Internet browsers

Search engines, specific

All the Web, 4:191

AltaVista, 1:219, 4:189, 4:*190*, 4:191

Ask Jeeves, 4:128

Direct Hit, 4:191

FindLaw, 4:189

Google, 1:219, 4:189, 4:191

HotBot, 4:189

Lycos, 1:219, 4:191

Metacrawler, 4:189, 4:191

MSN, 4:191

Search.com, 4:189, 4:191

Vivisimo, 4:189, 4:191

Yahoo!, 1:219

Search expressions, 4:188

Search for ExtraTerrestrial Intelligence (SETI@home), 3:22

Search.com search, 4:189, 4:191

Seaton, Col. Charles W., 1:31

Seattle Computer Products, 1:137

Seavey, Barbara, 3:55

Secondary Action animation principle, 1:14

SECs (single edge contacts), 2:109

Secure Computing Corporation, LOCK, 2:172–173

Secure Electronic Transactions. *See* SET

Secure Sockets Layer. *See* SSL

Security, 1:**174–178**

asset value factors, 2:174

authentication, 1:174, 1:176, 2:173, 2:175, 4:**21–24**

authorization, 1:174, 2:173, 2:175

biometrics, 2:140

Computer Fraud and Abuse Act of 1986, 1:**34–37**

computer security consultants, 4:124

domain naming system, 1:176

of early computers, 1:36–37

facial scans, 4:21, 4:67, 4:114

file access controls, 1:175

history, 1:174

intelligent agents and, 4:2–3

Java, problems, 1:177

1984 Act provisions, 1:34–35

password protection, 1:175, 1:176, 2:95–96, 2:173

threat factors, 2:174

of VPNs, 2:213, 3:180

vulnerability factors, 2:174

See also Hacking/hackers; Invasive programs; Privacy

Security applications (software), 2:**174–176**, 3:**179–182**

anonymous reposting servers, 1:177

COPS, 3:181

CRACK, 3:181, 3:182

digital signatures, 1:175

function, 3:179

history, 2:176

identification, 1:174, 2:175

intrusion detection systems, 3:180

network sniffing, 1:177

NMAP, 3:181

Norton security systems, 4:98

packet spoofing, 1:177

pattern recognition tools, 2:140, 2:141

PGP and PEM, 1:168, 1:177

SATAN, 3:181

selecting, 2:176

Symantec, 4:97–98

Tripwire, 3:180

virus detection systems, 3:180–181

See also Firewalls

Security, for specific systems

airline reservations, 3:15

ARPANET, 1:175, 1:176

banks and financial institutions, 1:168, 1:*176*, 3:25

credit information, 4:46–48

databases, 3:66–67

e-banking, 4:74–75

e-commerce, 1:43, 1:45, 2:176, 4:80

e-mail, 1:49

electronic cash, 1:176

electronic signatures, 4:*75*

embedded technologies, 3:87

Internet, 2:174–176, 2:*175*, 2:212

intranets, 4:151–152

LANs, 2:176

Minitel network, 1:145

Telnet, 4:205

UUCP, 1:175

Security hardware, 2:**172–174**

authentication tokens, 2:173, 4:21–23

callback modems, 1:176

CCTV, 4:118

Crypto iButton, 2:173–174

cryptosystems, 2:173–174, 4:**49–53**

cryptosystems, public-key, 1:175, 1:176, 2:174

LOCK, 2:172–173

magnetic stripe cards, 3:134–135

for memory protection, 1:174–175, 2:173

Multics, 1:175, 2:172, 3:159

PKI, 2:174, 3:87, 4:72, 4:83

Polonius, 2:173

RACF subsystem, 1:127

SET, 1:43, 3:87

smart cards, 1:176, 2:174

SSL, 1:43, 3:180, 4:49, 4:74, 4:80

Security software. *See* Security applications

Sega, Dreamcast, 2:80, 4:126

Sega, Genesis game console, 1:69

Selection, distinguished from censorship, 4:31–32

Selegue, John P., 4:37

Self assembly, of nanoscale particles, 4:172

Self-replicating systems, 2:218

Semantic nets, for expert systems, 3:90

Semantics, defined, 2:106

Semi-Automated Business Research Environment (Sabre system), 3:14–15

Semi-Automatic Ground Environment (SAGE), 3:14

Semiconductor Chip Protection Act (SCPA), 4:45

Semiconductor diode lasers, 2:75, 2:77, 3:127

Semiconductor memory, 2:109

Semiconductors, 2:*110*

defined, 1:131

diffusion, 1:195

economics, 3:40–41

forward and negative biases, 1:195–196

germanium, 1:106, 1:132, 1:133

invention, 2:13

manufacturing process, 1:105–106, 1:132–133

properties of, 1:132, 1:133, 1:193–194

See also Integrated circuits; Silicon; Transistors

Sendmail, 3:157

Sensors

defined, 1:40, 2:75

fiber optics for, 2:75

Sensors (continued)
  for graphics tablets, 2:147–148
  for joysticks, 2:147
  smart, wireless, 2:220
  as system components, 2:191
SEQUEL (Structured English Query Language), 3:194
Sequential, defined, 2:177
Sequential processing, 1:56, 2:177
Serial algorithms, 2:137
Serial-to-parallel conversions, 2:177
Serial transmission, 2:**176–178**
  addressing function, 2:120
  applications, 2:177, 2:178
  ARINC 429 buses, 2:181
  bit serial mode, 2:177
  Boolean algebra and, 2:22
  distinguished from parallel, 2:119
  error-control function, 2:120
  fiber optics for, 2:178
  flow control function, 2:120
  IEEE-1394 (Firewire), 2:178
  limitations, 2:178
  mice to computer, 2:146
  protocols, 2:119–122
  RS-232 protocol, 2:178
  RS-449, 2:178
  synchronous/asynchronous, 2:177
  UARTs, 2:177
  USB, 2:178
Servers
  in client/server systems, 2:36
  crashes, in e-journals, 4:82
  DBMS, 2:186
  defined, 2:36, 4:82
  document processing role, 2:71
  for mobile computing, 4:165
  proxy, 4:83
  and TCP/IP networks, 2:122
  Web, 4:27, 4:40–42, 4:48, 4:150
Service Level Agreements (SLAs), 2:213–214
Service providers, 4:**191–195**
  ASPs, 4:193
  future of, 4:194–195
  storage devices, 4:193
  See also ISPs; Telecommunications; Telegraph; Telephones/telephone systems
SET (Secure Electronic Transactions), 1:43, 3:87
SETI@home (Search for ExtraTerrestrial Intelligence), 3:22
Sexually explicit material, censorship, 4:**31–34**
SGI
  Nintendo 64, 4:126
  parallel processors, 2:135

SGML (Standard Generalized Markup Language), 2:105–106, 2:107, 4:65, 4:83
SGML DTD, 2:106
Shadow mask CRTs, 2:63–64
Shakey (robot), 1:170
Shamir, Adi, 4:52
Shannon, Claude E., 4:**195–197**, 4:*195*
  Alan Turing and, 1:198, 4:196
  Boolean algebra, 2:19, 4:196
  chess-playing computers, 3:37, 4:196
  digital design and, 1:27
  information theory, 4:27, 4:137, 4:175
Shannon's Theorem, 4:27
Shared Content Object Reference Model (SCORM), 3:42, 3:82
Shareware
  Cute FTP, 4:205–206
  mathematical software, 3:138
Shaw, John Clifford, 4:173, 4:174, 4:198
Sheridan, Peter, 2:154
Sherman Antitrust Act, 1:138, 1:211
Sherman, John, 1:211
Shielded twisted pairs (STP), 2:201
Shielded wires, for noise immunity, 2:178
Shinkansen (bullet trains), 3:174, 3:*175*
Ships
  auto-pilots, 3:6–7
  navigation systems, 3:149–150
Shneiderman, Ben, 2:57
Shockley Semiconductor, 1:106, 2:15
Shockley, William, 1:63, 1:72, 1:106, 1:132, 1:192, 2:**12–15**, 2:*13*
Shockware, 3:114
Shockwave Internet Browser, 1:14
Sholes, Christopher Latham, 1:120
Shopping carts, electronic, 1:43, 4:40–42
Short-messaging services (SMSs), 3:34–35
Shrimp boats, in ATC systems, 3:11
Shuttleworth, Mark, 3:187
Sibelius software, 3:146
Sidewalks of America, 4:206
Siemens Corporation, 2:198
Sierra Monolithics Inc., 1:134
SIGGRAPH computer graphics show, 1:23
Sign-bit extraction technique, 2:114
Signal-to-noise ratio (SNR), of transmission links, 2:76–77

Signaling protocols, 4:17
Signaling System 7, 3:201
SIGs (Special Interest Groups), 1:23
Silicon
  defined, 1:74, 2:15, 3:38, 4:167
  doping, 1:105–106, 1:133
  limitations, 1:108
  mining, 2:111
  properties, 1:104–105, 1:132–133, 1:193–194, 2:109, 2:111
Silicon chips
  alternatives to, 1:195, 3:144, 4:106, 4:167, 4:170–172
  N-type, 1:105
  P-type, 1:106
  See also Chip manufacturing; Microchips/microprocessors
Silicon Graphics computers, 3:209
Silicon Valley, 1:75, 1:106, 1:133, 2:15, 2:111, 3:108, 4:96
Silly Symphonies, 1:12
Silver, Bernard, 2:163
Silver halide, 4:179
SimCity game, 1:70, 4:7
SIMD (Single Instruction, Multiple Data), 2:135, 2:136, 2:137
SimHealth, 1:70
SIMMs (single in-line memory modules), 2:109
Simon, Herbert A., 4:173, 4:174, 4:**197–198**, 4:*197*
Simple Mail Transfer Protocol (SMTP), 4:108
Simple Object Access Protocol (SOAP), 4:141
Simplex communication systems, defined, 2:29
Simputers, defined, 4:166
SimRefinery, 1:70
Simulation models
  agricultural applications, 3:4, 3:5, 3:6
  of biochemistry experiments, 4:36
  computer modeling, 1:180
  computerized manufacturing applications, 3:51
  data visualization techniques, 3:62
  of disease organisms, 3:*28*
  economic modeling, 3:**79–80**
  economic value, 1:178–179
  GAMS, 3:79
  health care policies, 1:70
  legal applications, 3:130
  Mathematica, 3:79
  molecular modeling, 4:*35*

Monte Carlo, 1:180
physics applications, 3:162–164
of political events, 4:184
for supertanker designs, 2:216–217
three-dimensional building models, 3:18
wind tunnel aerodynamics, 3:32
Simulators, 2:**178–181**
for air traffic controllers, 2:181
amusement park robots, 1:170
analog (continuous), 1:179–180
animation technology, 1:180–181
artificial life, 4:**9–11**
Dead Reckoning, 1:15
defined, 1:178
discrete, 1:179
game technology, 1:70–71, 2:80–81
graphics techniques, 1:180
history, 1:178
as interactive systems, 1:110
for nuclear reactor operators, 2:181, 2:216
parallel processing for, 2:135
realism in multimedia, 4:127
Sim Art, 1:15
Sim City, 1:15
SOAR project, 4:172, 4:173, 4:174
social situations, 1:181
supercomputers for, 1:*183*, 1:184
for surgeons, 2:216
user interfaces, 3:205
See also Virtual reality
Simulators, aircraft flight training, 1:180, 2:*179*, 3:*8*
advantages, 2:179–181, 2:216
applications, 2:178–179
ARINC 429 buses, 2:181
for astronauts, 1:*179*, 2:181
computer systems, 2:181
fixed-base, 2:180
graphics for, 3:16
Link Trainer, 1:178
motion-base, 2:180–181
programming, 2:181
Sinatra, Frank, 1:68
Sine waves, 2:46, 4:24
Singapore, Internet censorship, 4:34
Single-chip memory, 4:170
Single edge contacts (SECs), 2:109
Single electron devices, 4:170
Single in-line memory modules (SIMMs), 2:109
Single Instruction, Multiple Data (SIMD), 2:135, 2:136, 2:137

Single Program, Multiple Data (SPMD), 2:136
Sirsi Corporation, UNICORN, 3:133
SISD (Single Instruction, Single Data), 2:135
SISL (Sun Industry Standards License), 3:156
Sistine Chapel, 4:6, 4:7
Site licenses, for software, 3:182
Site-specific farming (precision agriculture), 3:4
Sketchpad systems, 3:16, 3:30
Ski resorts, bar codes, 2:163–164
SLAs (Service Level Agreements), between ISPs and corporations, 2:213–214
Sleeping Beauty, 1:12
Slide rules, 1:2, 1:3, 1:*4*, 1:**181–182**, 3:109, 3:162
Slow In and Out animation principle, 1:14
SLT (Solid Logic Technology), 1:89–90
Small computer system interface standard (SCSI), 2:54
Small-scale integration circuit fabrication, 2:61
Smallpox, and bioterrorism, 3:27
Smalltalk programming language, 1:80, 1:216–217, 2:125–126, 2:128
Smart buildings, 3:84, 3:87
Smart cards, 2:*165*
defined, 1:176, 2:174, 4:75
distinguished from magnetic swipe cards, 2:164–165, 3:136
history, 2:165
Java standards, 2:174
medical applications, 3:139
uses, 2:165, 4:75
Smart classrooms. *See* Electronic campus
Smart devices, 3:84
Smart Draw software, 3:169
Smart information retrieval system, 1:95
Smart matter, 1:222
SMART system, 2:*31*
Smart Technology, SmartBoard, 3:76, 4:86
SMDL modeling language, 3:146
SMIL (Synchronized Multimedia Integration Language), 2:108
Smith, F.O., 2:113
Smith, Paul, 4:207
SMSs (short-messaging services), 3:34–35

SMTP (Simple Mail Transfer Protocol), 2:37, 4:108
Smurfs, 1:13
SNA (Systems Network Architecture), 4:152
Snail mail, distinguished from e-mail, 1:47
Snow White and the Seven Dwarfs, 1:10, 1:12
SNR (signal-to-noise ratio), of transmission links, 2:76–77
SOAP (Simple Object Access Protocol), 4:141
SOAR project, 4:172, 4:173, 4:174
Social impact, 4:**198–202**
of computer technology, Asimov's views, 3:21
of computers on work, 4:199–200
of digital libraries, 4:69, 4:71
ethics and computing, 4:101–102
of global surveillance, 4:118
history of computing technology, 4:199
of information access, 4:130–131, 4:132–133
information gathered by Census Bureau, 1:31, 1:33
of Internet, 1:115–116, 1:219–220, 2:90, 4:200
of robotics, 1:171–172
social informatics, 4:199
of telecommuting, 1:159
of video games, 1:68, 1:70–71
Social informatics, 4:199
Social Security Administration
data processing contract to IBM, 1:89
punched card use, 1:188
SoftBooks, 4:77
Softlifting. *See* Software piracy
Software
compatibility issues, 2:48–50
copyrights on, 4:**43–46**
database, for micromarketing, 1:167
downloading, 1:44, 1:46
for early computers, 1:56, 1:134
groupware, 1:158–159, 3:48, 3:76, 3:170, 4:139–140
home system, 3:**109–114**
IEEE standards, 1:103
integrated, 3:**117–120**
as intellectual property, 3:184–185
licensing agreements, 3:182–183
open source, 3:**155–158**
patent protections, 4:177–178
promoted in cybercafes, 4:55

Software (continued)
redundancy, 3:15
site licenses, 3:182
system, 3:166–167
upgradability and portability, 2:49
See also specific types of software and software names
Software and Information Industry Association (SIIA), 3:184
Software defined networks (SDNs), 2:213
Software development
computer programmers for, 3:47
ethical principles, 4:100–101
integrated office suites for, 3:118
object-oriented, 2:125–128, 2:197
programming languages, 2:104, 2:197
systems design and, 2:195
Therac-25 failure, 4:100–101
Software drivers, 1:121, 2:145
Software inertia, defined, 2:137
Software piracy, 3:**182–185**
Computer Fraud and Abuse Act, 1:36
counterfeiting and Internet piracy, 3:183–184
Digital Theft Deterrence and Copyright Damages Improvement Act, 3:185
DMCA, 3:185
hard-disk loading, 3:184
NET Act, 3:185
OEM unbundling, 3:183, 3:184
perpetrators, 3:185
rates, calculating, 3:184
softlifting, 3:183
Software Police Ltd., 3:*183*
statistics, 3:183, 3:184
unauthorized renting, 3:184
Warez Dudez hackers, 4:123
what constitutes, 3:182–183
Software Police Ltd., 3:*183*
Sojourner robot, 2:167–168, 2:*167*
Solid ink printers, 2:151
Solid Logic Technology (SLT), 1:89–90
Solitaire, electronic version, 1:15
Solitons, defined, 2:78
Sonar, 2:191, 3:114–115
SONET, 4:143
Song of the South, 1:12
Sony
AIBO robotic dog, 4:124, 4:*125*
Betamax VCRs, 2:204
Mavica digital camera, 4:178

PlayStation, 1:15, 1:69, 2:80, 4:126
revenues from games, 1:181
Sorting machines, 1:185, 1:187
Soul Catcher, 4:57
Soulé, Samuel W., 1:120
Sound cards, 2:184, 4:13, 4:14, 4:28
Sound devices, 2:**181–185**
analog sound signals, 2:*182*
audio files, 1:101
Bell Labs' contributions, 1:*28*
companding, 2:182–183, 2:*183*
compression, 2:183–184
for computer games, 1:14–15, 1:68
for electronic classrooms, 4:85–86
encoding, 2:183
to generate music, 2:115
how they work, 2:181–182
illegal copying, 2:184–185
multimedia applications, 2:85
Napster, 2:185, 4:205
non-linear quantization, 2:183
plug-in programs, 4:28
quantizing, 2:182, 2:*183*
sampling, 2:182–183, 2:*182*
Sound formats, 2:183
Sound synthesis and recording, 1:147–149, 2:114–116
additive, 3:147
audio music composition, 3:147–148
FM, 3:148
physical modeling, 3:148
sound editing with NLEs, 3:98
subtractive, 3:148
for television, 4:160–161
SoundBlaster sound cards, 1:15
Soundscan, 4:79
Source code
compilers to translate, 2:50
defined, 3:155
open source, 3:**155–158**, 4:*120*, 4:141, 4:166
South Dakota, most "wired" state, 4:149
South Park, 1:10
Southwest Bell, 1:28
Space debris, 2:169
Space Imaging, IKONOS satellite, 4:*115*
The Space Race, 2:169
Space travel and exploration, 3:**185–188**
Apollo, 1:151, 1:*152*, 1:153, 3:185, 3:186

Challenger, 3:187, 4:103–104
computers for early spacecraft, 3:186–187
Cyberspace Data Monitoring System, 2:*53*
Endeavor, 3:*100*
expert systems tools, 3:88
Extreme Ultraviolet Explorer, 2:169
flight simulators, 1:178, 1:*179*, 2:181
Galileo Jupiter probe, 3:188
Gemini Program, 3:186
IBM AP-101 computers, 3:187
JPL's contributions, 3:187, 3:188
Mercury-Atlas rocket, 3:186
microcomputers and, 1:135
minicomputers and, 1:141
Orbiting Astronomical Observatory flight series, 3:186
Ranger lunar impact probes, 3:186
redundancy and backup systems, 1:153
robotics technologies, 1:170, 1:171, 1:173, 2:167–168, 2:*167*
Russian, 2:169–170, 2:*169*, 3:187, 4:115
self-replicating systems, 2:218
Sojourner robot, 2:*167*
supercomputers to study, 1:183–184
tourists, 3:187
unpiloted spacecraft, 3:187–188
Viking, 3:187
Voyager probes, 1:153, 2:*53*, 3:187–188, 3:*188*
See also National Aeronautics and Space Administration
SpaceScience World, 1:205
Spacewar! game, 1:14, 1:67
Spain, digital libraries, 4:*70*
Spaminator, 1:49
Spamming, 1:49
SPAN, 4:144
SPARC (Scholarly Publishing and Academic Resources Coalition), 4:82
Spartans, transposition algorithms, 4:49
Spatial databases, 3:101
Spatial query processing, with GIS, 3:101
SPC Harvard Graphics, 1:160
Speakers, wireless, 2:220
Special Interest Groups (SIGs), 1:23
Speech indexing systems, 3:190
Speech output software, for visually impared persons, 4:13

Speech (voice) recognition, 3:**188–191**
  agents for, 1:114
  cybernetic applications, 4:57
  defined, 1:82
  dictation applications, 3:189–190
  for disabled persons, 3:204, 4:14
  HMMs, 3:189
  input devices, 2:92–93, 3:190, 3:203, 3:204, 3:205
  keywords, 3:190
  multimedia indexing applications, 3:190
  octophones, 2:132
  pattern recognition tools, 2:138
  recognition vocabularies, 3:189
  research grants, 1:82
  training the software, 4:14
  transactional applications, 3:190
  word lattice representation, 3:189
Speech, visible, 2:16
Speedup, as performance measure, 2:137–138
Spellchecking, agents for, 1:114
Sperry Rand, 1:89, 1:125, 2:74
Spider silk, genetically engineered, 3:143
Spiders, search engine, 4:188, 4:189–190
Spielberg, Steven, 1:20
Spiral paradigm, in systems design, 2:196
SPMD (Single Program, Multiple Data), 2:136
Spoofing
  packet, 1:177
  protection from, 1:176
Spreadsheet software
  Excel, 1:137, 3:60, 3:169, 3:193
  Lotus 1-2-3, 3:1, 3:60, 3:118, 3:169, 3:193, 4:96
  Quatro Pro, 3:60, 3:169
  Quicken, 3:169
  VisiCalc, 3:167, 3:193, 4:95, 4:98
  VisiPlot, 4:96
Spreadsheets, 3:**191–194**
  cells, 3:*191*
  charting and plotting, 3:192–193, 3:*192*
  chemistry applications, 4:35
  data visualization techniques, 3:61
  database functions, 3:192–193
  distinguished from worksheets, 3:191
  early, lack of integration, 3:119
  formulas and functions, 3:192
  history, 1:135, 3:193

  how to use, 3:168–169
  integration, 3:*118*
  labels, 3:192
  for legal documents, 3:129
  macros, 3:192–193
  nonelectric, 3:167
  object linking and embedding, 3:119–120
  user interfaces, 4:128
  uses, 3:167–168
  what-if analyses, 3:169, 3:192
Springer LINK, e-journal, 4:84
Sprint, peering agreements, 4:145
SPSS software, 3:78
Sputnik, 2:*169*, 2:170, 3:104, 4:115
SQL programming language, 2:**185–187**, 3:**194–196**
  applications, 3:196
  commands, 3:195–196
  for database management systems, 3:65, 3:66–67
  MySQL, 3:60
  SCHOOL, example, 3:194–195, 3:*194*
  syntax and logic, 1:79
SQL Server, 3:66
Squash and Stretch animation principle, 1:13
SRAM (static random-access memory), 2:109, 2:110–111
SRC Computers, 3:58
SSL (Secure Sockets Layer), 1:43, 3:180, 4:49, 4:74, 4:80
Staging animation principle, 1:13
Stallman, Richard, 3:*157*
Stamps (postage), from ATMs, 3:26
Standard Generalized Markup Language. *See* SGML
Standardized tests
  and educational software, 3:83
  OMR scoring, 2:133, 2:164
Standards
  de facto, 1:99
  de jure, 1:99
  defined, 1:97
  for electrical interfaces, 2:48–49
  examples and categories, 1:97
  for fire hydrants, 1:99
  ISO, 2:42, 3:42
  for manufacturing, 1:97–99
  for mathematical formats, 3:138
  organizations responsible for, 1:99–100
  for railroads, 1:97–99
  See also Information technology standards

Stanford Research Institute (SRI)
  artificial intelligence research, 1:170
  Internet history, 4:146
  invention of mouse, 1:145
  office automation research, 1:87
  sound synthesis research, 2:116
Stanford University
  DENDRAL expert system, 3:88, 3:124
  DSS tools, 3:68
Star topology, 1:155, 2:123, 2:124
Star Wars, 1:11, 1:68, 1:173
Star Wars missile defense system, 4:101
StarLogo, 2:103–104
StarOffice, 3:110
STATA software, 3:79
State University of New York, sound synthesis research, 2:116
Stateful Packet Filtering (application layer) firewalls, 4:109
Statewide Automated System for Data Collection and Processing (OGAS), 4:120
Static, defined, 2:110
Static random-access memory (SRAM), 2:109, 2:110–111
Static routing, 4:186–187
Statistical analyses
  of agricultural data, 3:6
  Bayesian networks, 3:69
  chemistry applications, 4:36
  economic modeling, 3:**78–80**
  GIS tools, 3:101
  Pascal's contributions, 1:165
  of political topics, 4:183
  regression analyses, 3:78
  to track diseases, 3:27
  visualization tools, 3:176–177
  See also Census Bureau (U.S.); Data mining
Statistical multiplexing, defined, 2:11
Statistical pattern recognition tools, 2:140–141
Statistical Society, British Association, 1:26
Stealth viruses, 1:209, 1:210
Steamboat Willie, 1:12
Steiner Trees (STs), 2:123
Stellar, defined, 3:22
Stenberg, W., 3:159
The Stepford Wives, 4:104
Stereoscopes, 2:91
stereotactic radiosurgery, 3:*205*
Stevenson, Adlai, 1:72
Stibitz, George R., 1:51

Stock and commodities markets
Cat bonds and options, 4:91
Chicago Mercantile Exchange, 4:*89*
data warehousing applications, 4:63–64
day traders, 4:90
dot.coms, 3:44, 4:80
electronic, 4:89–90
electronic payment systems, 4:91–92
electronic vs. traditional investing, 4:89–90
intelligent agents and, 4:3
knowledge bases, 3:124
Nasdaq, 4:88
neural network tools, 3:154, 3:155
online brokerage firms, 4:90
trading through ATMs, 3:26
Stoll, Cliff, 1:177
Stone, Matt, 1:10
Storage devices, 2:**187–191**
buffers in CPUs, 2:6
cache memory, 2:**27–29**, 2:209, 2:210, 2:*210*
CD-ROMs, 2:85, 2:111
CDs, 1:164
CMOS, 1:130
cost, 2:190
delay-line, 1:56
document processing, 2:**68–72**
DVDs, 2:111, 2:190–191
IBM 650, 1:188
IBM 3740, 1:188
magnetic, 1:72, 1:93, 1:163–164
magnetic cores, 2:109
magnetic disks, 2:111, 2:188–190
magnetic drums, 2:187, 2:*188*
magnetic tapes, 2:91, 2:93, 2:111, 2:187–188
mass, for mainframes, 1:127
for NASA, 1:153
OCR technology, 2:134
optical discs, 2:66, 2:190
optical technology for, 1:163, 1:164
paper tape, 2:91
punched cards, 1:163
RAM as, 2:110
role in computer, 2:5
for ROM, 1:130
SCSI for, 2:54
secondary, 1:129, 2:187–191
for supercomputers, 1:182–183
tape drives, 1:127
transistors, 2:109

vacuum tubes as, 2:109
VCRs as, 1:164
VM, 1:128, 1:131
See also Memory/memory devices
Storch, Randy, 4:*177*
Stored program computers, 1:56, 1:61–62, 1:72, 1:75, 2:74, 2:93
Stored value cards, 2:165
Story treatments, 1:8
Storyboards, 1:8–9
Stott, Alicia Boole, 2:18–19
STP (shielded twisted pairs), 2:201
Straight-ahead animation principle, 1:14
The Strange Theory of Light and Matter, 4:103
Streaming audio and video software, 3:113, 4:126–127
Street Fighter, 1:15
Stretch Project, IBM, 4:4
Strict, XHTML, 2:107
Structural pattern recognition tools, 2:141
Structured Analysis and System Specification, 2:197
Structured English Query Language (SEQUEL), 3:194
Structured objects, for expert systems, 3:90
Structured programming, 2:162
Structured Query Language. *See* SQL programming language
Stucken, Harro, 2:222
Styluses, for touch screens, 2:198, 2:200
Suan-pan (2/5 abacus), 1:1–2
Sub-bands, for cell phones, 3:33
Subnet, defined, 3:181
Subroutines, 1:57, 3:162
Subtractive sound synthesis, 3:148
Suhh al-a 'sha, on cryptography, 4:49
Sun Community Source License (SCSL), 3:156
Sun Industry Standards License (SISL), 3:156
Sun Microsystems
compatibility issues, 2:48
and home system software, 3:114
Java development, 2:128
μ-Law sound format, 2:183
NeWS windowing system, 4:121
servers, 2:*36*
StarOffice, 3:110
Unicode supported by, 2:42
window interfaces, 1:217
Sun Solaris
JVM for, 2:128
operating systems, 2:129

Sundials, 3:149
Supercomputers, 1:**182–185**
astronomic applications, 3:22, 3:23
astrophysics applications, 1:183–184
brain research, 1:185
components, 1:182–183
computing power, 2:35
data mining, 1:184–185, 2:135
defined, 1:202, 2:35, 3:23, 4:4
economic modeling applications, 3:80
in fiction, 4:105
future applications, 1:185
hardware engineers to build, 3:45
IBM Stretch Project, 4:4
Internet backbone for, 4:142
vs. mainframes, 1:125
for molecular computing, 4:169
molecular dynamics studies, 2:134–135
NSFNET to connect, 4:142, 4:148
operating systems, 2:129
parallel processing, 1:183
parallel processors as, 2:134
requirements for, 1:141
Seymour Cray and, 3:57–58
simulations, 1:184
speed, 1:202
Top 500, 2:135
vector processing, 2:136
von Neumann Architecture, 2:217
for weather forecasting, 2:135, 3:80, 3:208
See also Parallel processing
Supercomputers, specific
ASCI White, 2:*136*
Blue Horizon, 1:184
Blue Storm, 1:185
Cray, 1:183, 1:*184*
Deep Blue, 1:23, 1:*70*, 2:*89*, 3:36, 3:37
HAL, fictional, 4:105
Superconductivity, defined, 2:14
Superscalers, 1:74–75
Supertribalization, and satellite communication, 2:219
Surely You're Joking, Mr. Feynman!, 4:102, 4:103
Surface acoustic wave (SAW) screens, 2:146, 2:200
SurfWatch filter, 4:32
Surgery
computer-assisted, 3:*141*, 3:*205*

robotic, 2:168, 3:141–142

simulated, 2:216

Sutherland, Ivan, 1:21, 2:214, 3:16, 3:30

SVCs (switched virtual channels), 2:10, 2:11

Swap files, defined, 2:173

Swift, Jonathan, 4:104

Switchboards, 3:*200*

Switches, transistors as, 1:106

Switching offices, for telephone service. *See* Telephony

Sybase databases, 3:194

Syllogistic statements, defined, 2:19

Symantec, 4:97–98

Symbol Technologies, Inc., Kmart PDAs, 2:144

Symbolic notation

for AI programming, 2:99–100

for machine language, 1:76

Synchronization

of client/server systems, 2:39

computer interfaces and, 2:53

defined, 2:39

parallel transmission, 2:177

PDAs with microcomputers, 2:142–143

Synchronization bytes, flags, preambles, 2:9

Synchronized Multimedia Integration Language (SMIL), 2:108

Synchronous/co-located applications, electronic meeting rooms, 3:49–50, 3:*50*

Synchronous transmission. *See* Asynchronous and synchronous transmission

Synclavier, 1:149

Synergistically, defined, 3:54

Syntactic analyzers, role in compilers, 2:50–51

Syntactic structure of languages, 1:20

Syntax

of assembly languages, 2:7

defined, 1:79, 2:1, 4:40

of HTML, 2:106, 4:153

of LISP, 2:100

of Logo, 2:102

of object-oriented languages, 2:127

of programming languages, 2:1–3, 2:101, 2:154

search expression, 4:188

of Visual Basic, 4:208, 4:212

Synthesis language programs, 1:149

Synthesis of Computing Automata, 4:119

Syracuse University, bacteriorhodopsin research, 3:144

System Administration, Networking, and Security Institute, 4:124

System analysis, 2:**191–195**

circle-of operations paradigms, 2:194

conceptual stage, 2:194

distinguished from systems design, 2:192

documentation, 2:195

event analysis, 2:194

of global warming, 2:*193*

hierarchical paradigms, 2:194

input, throughput, output, 2:194

of needs and requirements, 2:192–193

prototype creation, 2:194

retrofitting functions, 2:191–192

system creation function, 2:191–192

timeline paradigms, 2:194

trouble-shooting functions, 2:191–192

waterfall paradigms, 2:194

System software, defined, 3:166–167

Systems, defined, 2:86–87

Systems design, 2:**195–197**

decision models, 2:196–197

DFDs, 2:197

distinguished from system analysis, 2:192

flowcharts, 2:197

implementation, 2:196

prototype creation, 2:194, 2:196

role of, 2:195

sequence of tasks, 2:196

spiral paradigm, 2:196

waterfall paradigms, 2:195–196, 2:197

Systems engineering, 2:195–197

Systems Network Architecture (SNA), 4:152

Sytek, Inc., Polonius security system, 2:173

T

Tabulating Machine Company, 1:84, 1:88, 1:186, 3:59

Tabulating machines, 1:**185–189**

business applications, 1:186–188

collators, 1:185, 1:187

distinguished from computers, 1:188

EAM, 1:187–188

government research grants, 1:81

Hollerith Electrical Tabulating Machine, 1:83–84, 1:186, 1:*187*, 1:211, 3:1

keypunch machines, 1:185, 1:186, 1:187

reproducers, 1:185, 1:188

sorters, 1:185

voting tools, 4:183, 4:*184*

Talcott, Lucia, 1:84

Tally systems, electronic, 4:88

Tangible, defined, 4:45

Tape backups, 2:188

Tape cartridges, 2:91, 2:188–190

Tape drives, 1:127, 2:54

Tarski, Alfred, 1:18

Task partitioning, 2:39

Tasks, concurrently executable, 2:159

Tax preparation software

EPSS, 3:43

Lotus, 3:1

Quicken, 3:1, 3:60

TurboTax, 3:43

Taxonomy, defined, 2:135

TCP (Transmission Control Protocol), 1:116, 2:37, 2:121–122, 4:110, 4:148, 4:202–203

TCP/IP, 4:**202–204**

advantages, 2:122

conversion from NCP, 4:148

future of, 2:122

history, 4:203–204

how it works, 1:116, 2:121–122, 4:202–203

for intranets, 4:150

in network design, 1:128, 1:157, 2:119, 4:142–143

vs. OSI protocols, 2:121–122

as standard, 4:203

UBR for, 2:11

See also IP

TCP/IP protocol suite, 2:212–213, 4:107

TDMA (time division multiple access) standard, 2:32, 3:34

Teachers, computer science training, 3:82, 3:83

Tech News digest, 1:23

Technicolor, in animation, 1:12

Technology of desktop publishing. *See* Desktop publishing technology

Technology scaling, in chip manufacturing, 3:40

TekGear, 2:82

Telcordia, 1:28

Tele-health, 3:140–142

Telecommunications, 1:**189–192**

Telecommunications (continued)
ATIS, 1:100
bandwidth, 4:24
beginnings, 1:189
Bell Labs' research, 1:27–28
broadcast, 1:190–191
communication devices, 2:**45–48**
competing technologies, 1:191–192
computer-based, 1:191
deregulation, 4:192
digital telephony, 1:189–190
document processing role, 2:70–71
fiber optics for, 2:75, 4:192, 4:194–195
future of, 4:194–195
infrastructure, 4:192
origin of term, 1:189
service providers, 4:**191–195**
user interfaces, 3:205
VTAM subsystem, 1:127
Telecommunications Act (1996), 4:149
Telecommuting, 1:158–159, 2:90, 4:200
Teleconferencing. *See* Video conferencing
Telegraph
Charles Wheatstone and, 1:123, 2:91
cryptography and, 4:51
defined, 1:189, 4:192
Guglielmo Marconi and, 4:163
Harry Nyquist and, 4:175
history, 1:189, 2:40, 2:*46*, 2:113–114, 4:192
impact on railroads, 3:173
multiple, 2:16–17
as OCR prototype, 2:132
optical technology, 1:161
paper tape for, 2:91
Samuel Morse and, 2:**112–114**, 2:219
wireless, 2:219
See also Morse Code
Telemedicine, 1:113
Telemetry, 2:167, 3:28
Teleoperation, 1:170, 1:171
Telephone companies, micromarketing, 1:167
Telephone directories, for Minitel network, 1:142–144
Telephone switching systems. *See* Telephony
Telephones/telephone systems
Alexander Graham Bell and, 2:**15–18**, 3:199

bandwidth, 1:161, 2:47, 4:25, 4:192
CENTREX service, 2:213
communication satellites, 2:170
for decision support systems, 2:88
deregulation, 4:192
distinguished from Internet, 1:116–117
distinguished from packet-switched networks, 4:146
DSL system, 2:47
fiber optics for, 1:190, 2:17, 2:78
hackers' access to, 4:123
Harry Nyquist's contributions, 4:175
history, 1:189, 1:*190*, 2:15–17, 2:29–30, 4:192
impact on information retrieval, 1:93
impact on railroads, 3:173
information technology standards, 1:*98*, 1:99
Minitel network, 1:**142–145**
multiplexing, 2:47
network topologies, 2:123
optical technology, 1:161
smart cards, 2:165
switchboards, 1:*190*
switching systems, 2:14
third generation (3G), 2:47, 3:87
transistors for, 2:12–13
to transmit computer data, 2:46–47
TTYs, 4:14
voice mail, 1:48–49, 1:158
WLLs, 2:221
See also Cell phones; Telecommunications
Telephony, 3:**199–202**
Bell System innovations, 3:200, 3:202
cell phone roaming, 3:201–202
defined, 3:199
digital, 1:189–190
800-calls, 3:201
history, 3:200–201, 3:*200*
HLRs, 3:33, 3:201–202
Intelligent Network (IN), 3:201
long distance calls, 3:200, 3:201
modems, 3:202
1E processor, 3:200
Signaling System 7, 3:201
switching offices, 3:199
switching systems, history, 1:27, 1:51, 1:189–190
synergy with computing, 3:199
VLRs, 3:201–202

wired vs. program control, 3:200–201
Telerobotics, 1:171, 1:*172*
Telescopes
radio, 3:22
VLA, 3:*23*
Teletype Corporation, ASA role, 2:41
Teletype machines (teleprinters), 2:40–41, 2:*62*, 3:48
Teletypewriter for the Deaf (TTY), 4:14
Television
access infrastructure, 2:78
bandwidth, 1:161, 2:47
broadcast telecommunications, 1:191
cable, 2:47, 4:25–26, 4:*26*
CCTV, 4:118
communication satellites, 2:78, 2:170
compression encoding, 3:138
digital, MPEG-2, 2:98
display devices, 2:63–64
for distance learning, 3:75
as game display, 2:*79*
HDTV, 2:66, 4:124, 4:126
head-mounted stereoscopic, 2:214
for high-speed data transmission, 2:47
interactive, 3:75
news online, 4:161–162
newsroom computers, 4:160, 4:183
optical technology, 1:161, 1:164
PTV, personalized listings, 4:135
smart cards to access, 2:165
as system, 2:87
UHF channels, reassigned, 2:30
weather forecasts, 3:**208–210**
wireless, 2:219
Television cameras, for computer vision, 4:38–39
Telnet, 4:**204–206**
ease of use, 4:206
FTP and, 4:111, 4:205–206
function, 4:204
security concerns, 4:205
user interface concerns, 4:205
Telstar communication satellite, 2:170
Temple Institute, Jerusalem, 3:*17*
Terabytes, defined, 1:125, 4:60
TeraFLOPS, 2:137
Terminal radar control centers (TRACONs), 3:11
Terminal symbols, 2:2

Terminals, computer, 2:63
Terrorist attacks
   bioterrorism, 3:27
   facial scans to prevent, 4:21,
      4:114
   Flight Simulator game alter-
      ations, 4:127
   global surveillance and, 4:*114*,
      4:*116*, 4:118
   on New York City, 4:*116*
   on Pentagon, 4:*115*
   September 11, 2001, impact on
      airlines, 3:15
   2002 Winter Olympics security,
      4:114
   and Y2K, 3:105
Tetris, 1:15
Tetrodes, 1:202
Texas Instruments
   integrated circuit technology,
      1:73, 1:106, 1:107, 2:33
   microprocessors, 1:107
   minicomputer manufacturing,
      1:141
Text Retrieval Evaluation Conference (TREC), 1:96
Textile industry
   computerized manufacturing,
      3:*52*
   fabrics for fashion industry,
      3:92–93
   See also Jacquard's loom
Textiles, for embedded technologies,
   3:86
Textual information
   distinguished from graphic dis-
      plays, 2:81
   in electronic format, 1:93
   hypermedia to access, 2:84
   markup languages for, 2:**104–108**
   See also Document processing;
      OCR; Word processors
TFTAM (thin film transistor active
   matrix) LCDs, 2:66–67
Tfxidf values, 1:95
Thakkar, Umesh, 1:205
Thematic mapping, 2:170–171,
   3:101
Therac-25 radiation therapy ma-
   chine failure, 4:100–101
Thermal ignition, 1:60
Thermal wax transfer printers, 2:152
Thermodynamic, defined, 3:158
Thin film transistor active matrix
   (TFTAM) LCDs, 2:66–67
THINK signs, 1:89, 1:211
Thinking Machines Corporation,
   Connection Machine, 2:136
Thompson, John W., 4:97–98

Thompson, Ken, 1:21, 1:27, 2:158
Thomson, William (Lord Kelvin),
   3:162
Three-body problems, defined, 3:22
3-D animation, 1:10
3-D interfaces, 4:129
3-D visualization, 3:62–63, 3:*63*
   See also Simulators; Virtual real-
      ity
3Com Palm Computing, 2:142
3G telephone systems, 2:47, 3:34,
   3:87
Throughput, in system analysis,
   2:194
Thumbnails, 1:216, 1:*217*
Tickets
   airline, printing, 2:150
   airline reservations, 3:**13–16**
   from ATMs, 3:26
   e-mail marketing messages, 4:139
Tide predictions, computer applica-
   tions, 1:3
Tier 1 ISPs, 4:193
TIFF format, 1:101, 4:67
TIGER system, 1:32
Tik-Tok of Oz, 4:104
Tiling windows, 1:212–213, 1:*214*
Time division multiple access
   (TDMA) standard, 2:32, 3:34
Time division multiplexing, 2:76
Time lapse mode weather maps,
   3:209
The Time Machine, 3:20
Time series charts, 3:61
Time-sharing computers
   Bell Labs' Model 1, 1:51
   file access controls, 1:175
   government research grants, 1:82
   Kemeny and Kurtz's contribu-
      tions, 2:157
   Logo and, 2:101
   mainframe connections, 1:126
   minicomputers as, 1:140, 1:142
Time-Sharing Option (TSO), 1:127
Time zones, 1:*98*, 3:149
Timeline paradigms, in system
   analysis, 2:194
Timing animation principle, 1:13
Titanic, pixilated reproduction, 4:7
Titchmarsh, E.C., 1:198
Title bars, 1:213, 1:*215*
Tito, Dennis, 3:187
TiVo digital video recorders, 4:124,
   4:126, 4:127
Token Ring, 2:118
Tokens. *See* Authentication tokens
Tom and Jerry, 1:13

Tomb Raider, 1:12, 1:15
Tomography, defined, 3:177
T1 and T3 lines, 4:26, 4:143, 4:174,
   4:175, 4:193
Top Grossing Film of All Time, 4:7
Topographic, defined, 4:178
Topology, defined, 1:154
Torricelli, Evangelista, 1:166
Torricelli's hypothesis, 1:166
Torvalds, Linus, 2:131, 3:157, 4:*120*,
   4:121
Touch pads, 2:146
Touch screens, 2:**197–200**
   advantages, 2:198
   applications, 2:146, 2:197–198,
      2:*199*
   capacitive panels, 2:146, 2:200
   development, 2:198
   for e-book readers, 4:77
   how they work, 2:198–199
   infrared panels, 2:200
   for PDAs, 2:141, 2:142, 2:198
   resistive panels, 2:146, 2:199
   SAW panels, 2:146, 2:200
   styluses, 2:198, 2:200
   surface wave, 2:146
   wave interruption panels, 2:200
   on wearable computers, 3:*85*
Touch-sensitive display panels,
   4:86
Toy Story, 1:10, 1:16
Toyota, CAD applications, 3:31
Track, in aircraft navigation, 3:7
Trackballs, 1:146–147, 2:148
TRACONs (terminal radar control
   centers), 3:11
Trade secrets, as intellectual prop-
   erty, 1:36, 4:177
Trademarks, 1:36, 4:176
Traf-O-Data, 1:138, 4:94
Trafficking, software piracy as,
   3:184
Trailers, packet protocols, 2:120
Training
   of computer visual devices,
      4:39–40
   job, EPSS applications, 3:43–44
   of neural networks, 3:154–155
   of voice recognition software,
      4:14
   See also Education
Training data, in pattern recogni-
   tion, 2:139–140
Transac S-2000 computer, 1:72
Transaction costs, e-commerce vs.
   traditional businesses, 4:78–79
Transaction processing systems, de-
   fined, 3:14

Transactional speech recognition, 3:190

Transducers, defined, 2:145

Transistor gates, 3:39–40

Transistors, 1:**192–197**
 as amplifiers vs. switches, 1:106, 1:196
 in Bardeen's garage door, 2:14
 BJT, 1:196
 in CDC 1604, 3:57
 defined, 1:27, 2:14, 3:38
 FET, 1:196
 for flip-flops, 2:61
 for gates, 2:61
 invention, 1:27, 1:63, 1:72, 1:89, 1:106, 1:132, 2:12–13, 3:132, 4:126
 manufacturing process, 1:193, 1:194–195
 for memory devices, 2:109, 2:111
 Moore's law, 1:108, 2:33, 3:40, 4:121
 organic, 1:195, 4:106, 4:**167–169**, 4:*168*
 patents, 1:192
 physical principals, 1:193–194
 in second-generation computers, 1:72–73
 size, 1:*193*, 1:195
 speed vs. gate length, 3:39–40
 in UNIVAC, 2:33
 See also CMOS; Integrated circuits; Semiconductors

Transit agreements, among Internet backbones, 4:145–146

Transitional, XHTML, 2:107

Translational bridges, 4:205

Translators
 ADCs, 1:30–31, 1:42, 1:148, 4:175
 for assembly languages, 1:77, 2:51
 DACs, 1:42, 1:148, 2:114–115, 3:146
 drivers, 1:121
 gateways as, 2:26–27
 granularity, 2:208
 graphics controllers, 2:82
 for high-level languages, 1:78–79
 interpreters, 2:153
 MicroWorlds Logo interpreter, 2:103
 music to machine language, 2:114
 scanning to binary codes, 1:120
 VM systems, 2:207–208, 2:209–211, 2:*210*
 See also Compilers

Transmission Control Protocol. *See* TCP

Transmission Convergence (TC) sublayer, ATM transmission, 4:19

Transmission lines, 1:161

Transmission links, 2:122–123

Transmission media, 2:**200–203**
 aether, 2:201
 amplifiers and repeaters, 2:201
 coaxial cables, 2:201, 4:25, 4:*26*
 data transfer within computers, 2:200
 ethernets, 4:136
 fiber optic cables, 4:136, 4:192
 infrared radiation, 2:202–203
 ingress and egress, 2:201
 for Internet connection, 4:26–27
 microwave links, 2:202, 2:*203*, 3:199, 4:25
 for mobile computing, 4:165
 for RF communications, 2:201
 twisted pair cables, 2:201
 See also Buses; Fiber optics; Satellite technology; Wireless technology

Transmissive displays, 2:67

Transmutation, defined, 1:8

Transponders, for train tracking, 3:174

Transport layer firewalls, 4:108–109

Transport Tycoon game, 1:70

Transportation
 robotics technologies, 1:170
 simulator applications, 1:180
 as system, 2:87

Transposition algorithms (ciphers), 4:49, 4:51

Travan tape cartridges, 2:188

Travel
 airline reservations, 3:**13–16**
 data warehousing applications, 4:63
 role of e-books, 4:77

Travel agencies
 computerized reservation systems, 3:14–15
 EPSS applications, 3:43
 vs. online services, 4:81

Traveling salesperson problem (TSP), 3:79, 3:154

Travelocity.com, 3:15, 4:80, 4:81, 4:128

Treatise on the Calculus of Finite Differences, 2:18

TREC (Text Retrieval Evaluation Conference), 1:96

Tree topologies, 1:155, 2:123, 2:124

Trigonometry, 1:3, 1:25

Trillions of floating point operations per second (TeraFLOPS), 2:137

Trilogy Systems Corporation, 4:5

Triodes, 1:132

Tripwire, 3:180

Trojan horses, 1:208–209
 defined, 1:177, 3:105, 4:123
 DoS attacks, 2:96
 firewalls to thwart, 4:109
 intent of, 1:207, 2:93–94, 2:95–96
 Internet-enabled, 2:95–96
 programming languages, 2:96
 protection from, 3:106, 3:*181*
 released by hackers, 4:123
 Zombie, 2:96
 See also Invasive programs

Tron, 4:106

Trusted Computer Systems Evaluation Criteria. *See* Orange Book ratings

Truth tables, in Boolean algebra, 2:20–22, 2:*21*, 2:*22*

Truth values of hypothesis, 3:154

TSO (Time-Sharing Option), 1:127

TSP (traveling salesperson problem), 3:79, 3:154

TTY (Teletypewriter for the Deaf), 4:14

Tunnel mode encryption, 2:213

Tunneling, in VPNs, 2:213

TurboTax software, 3:43

Turenas, 3:146

Turing, Alan M., 1:**197–199**, 1:*197*
 algorithm definitions, 2:4
 Alonzo Church and, 1:197, 1:200
 chess-playing computers, 3:37
 Claude Shannon and, 4:196
 code-breaking research, 1:54, 1:59, 1:198
 early computer research, 1:198
 government research grants, 1:81

Turing Machine, 1:59, 1:197–198, 1:**199–201**, 4:11
 and artificial life, 4:9
 and cybernetics, 4:55
 defined, 4:9

Turing Test, 1:20–21, 1:198

Turtles, Logo, 2:101

1200-baud data transmission, 1:69

Twenty Thousand Leagues Under the Sea, 3:20

Twisted pair cables
 defined, 2:45
 for LAN, 2:201
 shielded (STP), 2:201
 unshielded (UTP), 2:201

Two-key cryptography. *See* Public-key cryptosystems

2001: A Space Odyssey, 3:21, 4:105

Typefaces, for desktop publishing, 3:197–198

Typewriter keyboards, history, 1:120

Typewriters
as display device prototype, 2:62
as input devices, 3:202, 3:210–211

Typing
agents to monitor, 1:114
keyboards, 1:**119–122**
Typographics, 2:69

U

UARTs (universal asynchronous receiver transmitters), 2:177

Ub Iwerks, 1:12

Ubiquitous
defined, 1:3, 2:35, 3:83, 4:165
Internet as, 1:191
microprocessors as, 1:151
slide rules as, 1:3

Ubiquitous computing. *See* Embedded technology

Ubiquity forum, 1:23

UBR (unspecified bit rate) service, 2:11–12

UCSD Pascal, 2:157–158

UGPIC (Universal Grocery Products Identification Code), 2:163

UHF (ultra-high frequency) channels, 2:30

Ulrich, Lars, 4:*44*

Ultrasonic, 4:38

Ultrasound, 3:114–115, 4:66

Unauthorized renting of software, 3:184

Under certainty and under uncertainty, 3:69

Unfixed works, copyrights, 4:45

UNICODE standard, 1:101, 2:42

UNICORN information system, 3:133

UNICOS operating system, 2:129

Unified Modeling Language (UML), 2:197

Uniform Resource Locators. *See* URLs

Unimation Corporation, 1:170

Uniprocessors vs. parallel processors, 1:75

Uniquely decodeable codes, 2:44

United Airlines
computerized reservation systems, 3:14, 3:15

United Kingdom (Great Britain)
British Association for the Advancement of Science, 1:26

British Standards Institute, 1:100

Centre for English Cultural Tradition and Language, 4:207

cybercafes, 4:54

Disabilities Discrimination Act, 4:12, 4:16

early computer research, 1:53–55

Government Code and Cypher School, 1:53–55, 1:198

JANET, 4:144

software piracy, 3:184

Statistical Society, British Association, 1:26

United Nations, on information access, 4:132–133

United States Postal Service (USPS), 2:163

United States, software piracy, 3:184

UNIVAC (Universal Automatic Computer), 1:*73*
for census tabulations, 1:32
compilers, 1:86
government research grants, 1:81
invention, 1:72, 1:188, 2:33, 2:73, 3:59
security issues, 1:174
Seymour Cray and, 3:57

Universal asynchronous receiver transmitters (UARTs), 2:177

Universal computers, 2:218

Universal constructors, 2:218

Universal Grocery Products Identification Code (UGPIC), 2:163

Universal Product Code (UPC), 2:133, 2:163

Universal serial bus (USB), 2:54, 2:178

Universities
digital libraries, 4:70
e-journals, 4:82

University College, London, Internet history, 4:146–147

University of Alberta (Canada), CAI research, 3:41

University of Arizona, Electronic Meeting Systems, 3:49

University of Bielefeld, NESSY, 4:38

University of California
BSD UNIX, 4:204
California Digital Library, 4:70
in Internet history, 4:142, 4:146
UCSD Pascal, 2:157–158
Viola-WWW browser, 4:30

University of Houston, Computing Center, 3:158

University of Illinois
in Internet history, 4:142

Mosaic browser, 4:30
Round Earth Project, 1:205–206
sound synthesis research, 2:116
virtual reality in education, 1:205

University of Iowa, punched card use, 1:188

University of Kansas, Lynx browser, 4:30

University of Massachusetts, chemistry courses on CD-ROM, 4:36

University of Michigan, Elliot Organick and, 3:159

University of Michigan, sound synthesis research, 2:116

University of Pittsburgh
electronic classrooms, 4:*85*
LCD panels, 4:87
Learning Research and Development Center, 3:41

University of Sheffield, Centre for English Cultural Tradition and Language, 4:207

University of Utah, Internet history, 4:146

UNIX C library, 2:158

UNIX operating system
Bell Labs and, 3:202
browsers for, 4:28, 4:30
BSD, 4:204
and C programming language, 2:158
COPS security software, 3:181
CRACK security software, 3:181, 3:182
distinguished from Linux, 2:131, 3:157
for electronic library catalogs, 3:132
as interactive system, 1:110–111
inventors, 1:21, 1:27
JVM for, 2:128
for mainframes, 1:128, 2:129
for minicomputers, 1:141, 2:129
user interfaces, 2:130, 3:203
virtual addressing, 2:209
for workstations, 2:129
X-Windows for, 1:112, 1:217

Unix-Unix System Mail (UUCP), 1:175

Unshielded twisted pairs (UTPs), 2:201

Unspecified bit rate (UBR) service, 2:11–12

UPC (Universal Product Code), 2:133, 2:163

Upgradability of computers and software (upward compatibility), 2:49, 4:5

Uplinks, by Tier 1 ISPs, 4:193

Upload bandwidth, 4:26–27

Upsilon Pi Epsilon (International Honor Society for the Computing Sciences), 1:104

Urban myths (legends), 4:**206–208**
  American Folklore, 4:206
  Centre for English Cultural Tradition and Language, 4:207
  computer-related, examples, 4:207
  Contemporary Legend, 4:207
  "The Corpse in the Car," 4:206
  "The Fatal Initiation," 4:206
  hoaxes, 4:206
  Indiana Folklore, 4:206–207
  International Society for Folk Narrative Research, 4:207
  "The Poison Dress," 4:206
  Sidewalks of America, 4:206
  "The Vanishing Hitchhiker," 4:206
  web sites to combat, 4:207
  While Rome Burns, 4:206
  World Trade Center, last photo, 4:207

URLs (Uniform Resource Locators)
  browsers and, 4:27
  changing, in e-journals, 4:82
  cookies used by, 4:42
  defined, 4:40
  development, 4:30, 4:92, 4:121
  and e-banking authentication, 4:74
  function, 1:220, 4:31

US West, 1:28

USAN, 4:144

USB (universal serial bus), 2:54, 2:178

USENET, 4:144

Usenet filter, 4:32

User interfaces, 3:**202–206**
  for ATMs, 3:25, 4:128
  for CAD systems, 3:16, 3:18, 3:30–31, 3:91
  character-based, 3:203
  command-based, 2:130
  command-line, 4:128
  dangling string network monitors, 3:84–86
  DBMS, 2:185–187
  for digital libraries, 4:71
  for disabled persons, 1:*146*, 3:204–205, 4:**11–16**, 4:*87*, 4:129
  for DOS, 3:203–204
  for DSSs, 3:69
  for DTP computers, 3:196–197
  of early mainframes, 3:47

for embedded technologies, 3:84–86
ergonomics, 3:205
graphical-based, 3:203
head-mounted displays, 1:204, 1:205, 1:206, 2:214, 3:*85*, 3:86
for health care practitioners, 3:*205*
hypertext, 1:87–88
for Internet browsers, 4:132
for knowledge-based systems, 3:123
menu-based, 2:130
for multimedia systems, 2:85
natural language, 4:128
network, 2:49
and operating system managers, 2:129
for PCs, 3:48
point-and-click, 2:145
programming languages, 4:129
software for, 4:129
speech recognition software, 3:188–190, 3:203, 3:204, 3:205
standards, 1:100
telecommunications, 3:205
for UNIX systems, 3:203
for video editing, 3:97
VR environments, 3:204, 4:129
window interfaces, 1:**212–218**, 3:203–204
See also Display devices; Ergonomics; GUIs; Human factors, user interfaces; Input devices

Userids and IDs, 2:175, 4:21, 4:74, 4:107, 4:109

USS *Grace Hopper*, 1:87

USS *Yorktown*, sonar to locate, 3:115

Utilities
  disk fragmentation tools, 3:111
  disk management tools, 3:111
  system software and, 3:167

UTPs (unshielded twisted pairs), 2:201

UUCP (Unix-Unix System Mail), security, 1:175

UUNET, 4:145, 4:148, 4:193

V

Vacuum tubes, 1:**201–203**
  for Colossus, 1:54
  current applications, 1:203
  defined, 1:51, 2:13, 4:105
  for differential analyzer, 1:51
  for early computers, 1:81, 1:192, 2:109

for early radio amplifiers, 4:126
for electronic equipment, 1:106, 1:192
for ENIAC, 1:202–203, 2:33, 2:72
invention, 1:71, 1:201–202
Lee De Forest's contributions, 1:*201*, 1:202
for UNIVAC, 1:72, 3:57
for Z machines, 2:222
See also CRTs

Vacuums, Torricelli's hypothesis on, 1:166

Valence, defined, 1:193

Valenti, Jack, 4:*100*

"The Vanishing Hitchhiker," 4:206

Variable-length codes, 2:43–44

Variables
  defined, 2:58
  Logo, 2:102

Varian, minicomputer manufacturing, 1:141

Variant CAPP systems, 3:54

VAX-series computers, 1:13, 1:142, 2:51

VBA (Visual BASIC for Applications), 4:210

VBNS (Very-high-speed Backbone Network Service), 4:149

VBR-NRT (variable bit rate-non-real time) service, 2:11

VBR-RT (variable bit rate-real-time) service, 2:11–12

VBScript programming language, 4:74, 4:210

VCCs (virtual channel connections), 2:10

VCI (Virtual Channel Identifier), 4:18, 4:20

VCRs (videocassette recorders), 1:164
  Betamax, 2:204
  digital, 4:124
  for distance learning, 3:76
  for electronic classrooms, 4:86
  MPEG standards, 2:11–12
  role in movie industry, 3:94–99

VCs (virtual circuits), 2:10–11

Vector, defined, 3:31

Vector graphics displays, 2:82–83

Vector processing, 1:183, 2:136, 3:58

Vector space models of information retrieval, 1:95

Velocities, defined, 2:76

Venn diagrams, 2:19

VENTURA software, 1:157, 3:169, 3:197

Venture capitalists, funding for dot.coms, 3:44, 4:80, 4:193

Vercoe, Barry, 2:116

Vernam, Gilbert, 4:51

Verne, Jules, 3:19, 3:20, 4:105

Veronica, Internet tool, 4:149

Very-high-level (fourth generation) languages. *See* Languages, very-high-level

Very-high-speed Backbone Network Service (vBNS), 4:149

Very Large Array (VLA) telescopes, 3:*23*

Very-large-scale integration (VLSI) circuits, 1:74, 1:141, 2:62

VHS, as videotape standard, 1:99

VIBE (Visual Information Browsing Environment), 3:62–63, 3:*63*

Video cameras, digital, 2:204

Video capture cards, 1:14–15, 1:160, 2:203, 2:204

Video co-processors, 2:82

Video compression algorithms, 4:88

Video conferencing
  desktop, 1:158
  early demonstrations, 1:87
  equipment for, 2:204
  fiber optics for, 2:78
  OAS applications, 1:158, 1:*159*

Video devices, 2:**203–205**

Video distribution networks, 4:86

Video editing (film and video editing), 2:204, 3:**94–99**, 3:*95*
  future applications, 3:98–99
  high-speed interconnections, 3:96
  linear vs. non-linear, 3:96, 4:161
  NLEs, 3:96–98
  RAM requirements, 3:96
  sound tracks, 3:98
  speech recognition software, 3:190
  television, 4:160–161
  video masters, 3:97–98
  video switchers, 3:98

Video file formats, 3:113

Video games. *See* Games, computer

Video output cards, 2:203
  decompression, 2:204
  digital to analog conversions, 2:204

Video technology, MPEG standards, 2:11–12, 2:*98*

Videocassette recorders. *See* VCRs

Videotape
  distinguished from film, 3:94–95
  high-definition, 3:95, 3:98–99
  VHS, 1:99

Videotex terminals, 1:*143*

Vietnam
  Internet censorship, 4:33–34
  software piracy, 3:184

Vietnam Conflict, antiwar protests, 3:121

Viking space probe, 3:187–188

Viola-WWW browser, 4:30

Violence, and video games, 1:68, 1:70

Virtual advisors, for GPS, 4:132

Virtual bodies, in fashion design, 3:94

Virtual channel connections (VCCs), 2:10

Virtual Channel Identifier (VCI), 4:18, 4:20

Virtual circuits (VCs), 2:10–11

Virtual communities, 1:46, 4:200

Virtual environments (VEs), 2:214

Virtual libraries. *See* Libraries, digital

Virtual memory (VM), 1:131, 2:112, 2:**205–211**
  addressing model, 2:*206*, 2:207–208, 2:*208*, 2:209
  backing stores, 2:*210*, 2:211
  caching, 2:209, 2:*210*
  current use, 2:209
  MVS, 1:126–127
  page tables, 2:*210*, 2:211
  Peter Denning and, 4:121
  as security tool, 1:174–175
  translating, 2:207–208, 2:209–211, 2:*210*

Virtual Path Identifier (VPI) connections, 4:18, 4:20

Virtual private networks (VPNs), 2:**211–214**
  CENTREX service, 2:213
  defined, 2:212
  digital certificates, 2:213
  global, 2:213, 2:214
  motivations for building, 2:213–214
  PLI, 2:213
  SDNs, 2:213
  security/privacy, 2:213, 3:180
  tunneling, 2:213

Virtual reality (VR), 2:**214–217**
  3-D interfaces, 4:129
  applications, 2:216
  defined, 1:10, 2:88, 4:129
  distinguished from animation, 1:10–11, 2:214, 2:216
  distinguished from wearable computing, 3:86
  expert systems and, 2:88–89

force feedback information, 2:214
  game applications, 1:67
  gloves, 2:214, 2:*215*
  haptic devices, 2:214
  helmets, 2:*215*
  history, 2:214
  immersive interactions, 1:181, 2:216
  mathematical calculations for, 2:216
  for simulations, 1:180–181
  software, research grants, 1:82
  theory, 2:215–216
  user interfaces, 3:204
  visors, 3:*85*
  VRML, 2:214
  See also Simulators

Virtual reality in education, 1:**203–206**, 1:*204*
  CAVEs, 1:204, 1:205–206
  Round Earth Project, 1:205–206
  SpaceScience World, 1:205

Virtual Reality Modeling Language (VRML), 1:10–11, 2:214

Virtual reference desks, 4:130–131

Virtualization, in interactive systems, 1:111, 1:113–114

Viruses (computer), 1:**206–210**
  anti-virus software, 1:209–210, 2:96, 3:105–106, 3:112, 3:180–181
  anti-viruses, 1:208, 2:95
  application-type, 1:207, 2:94
  boot-type, 1:207
  defined, 1:37
  history of, 1:176, 1:207
  how they work, 1:208, 2:94–95
  ILOVEYOU, 1:*209*
  intent of, 2:93–94
  legality of writing, 1:210
  macro-type, 1:207, 2:94
  Pakistani Brain boot, 1:207, 2:94
  polymorphic, 1:209–210
  programming languages, 2:95
  released by hackers, 4:123
  retro-type, 1:209, 1:210
  script-type, 1:207
  statistics, 1:207
  stealth, 1:209, 1:210
  transmission, 1:49, 2:*94*
  See also Invasive programs; Trojan horses; Worms

Viruses (human), computer simulations, 3:*28*

Visa, SET, 1:43

Visible Man, 3:177

Visible speech, defined, 2:16

VisiCalc software, 3:167, 3:193, 4:95, 4:98

Visio software, 3:169

Vision, computer. *See* Computer vision

VisiPlot, 4:96

Visitor location registers (VLRs), 3:201–202

Visual BASIC for Applications (VBA), 4:210

Visual BASIC programming language, 4:**208–212**

    defining control characteristics, 4:209–210, 4:*210*

    examples of code, 4:*211*

    function, 4:208

    history, 4:208

    interface creation, 4:208–209, 4:*209*

    learned by children, 2:157

    as object-oriented, 2:128

    for online banking, 4:74

    for viruses, 1:208, 2:95

    See also BASIC programming language

Visual BASIC Scripting Edition (VBScript), 4:74, 4:210

Visual impairments, assistive technologies

    computer vision tools, 4:40

    GPS applications, 4:117

    Lynx browser, 4:30, 4:31

    magnification software, 4:12–13

    OCR software, 4:13

    screen readers, 4:13

    speech recognition software, 3:204

    See also Assistive computer technology for persons with disabilities

Visual Information Browsing Environment (VIBE), 3:62–63, 3:*63*

Visual interactive simulation. *See* Virtual reality

Visualization, defined, 3:162

Visualization systems and techniques

    data visualization, 3:**61–64**

    defined, 3:51

    interactive systems, 1:113

    scientific visualization, 3:162–164, 3:*163*, 3:**176–179**

    user interfaces, 3:205

    See also Computer vision; Image analysis, medicine; Virtual reality (VR)

Vivisimo search engine, 4:189, 4:191

VLA (Very Large Array) telescopes, 3:*23*

VLRs (visitor location registers), 3:201–202

VLSI (very-large-scale integration) circuits, 1:74, 1:141, 2:62

VM. *See* Virtual memory

Vocabularies, for speech recognition, 3:189

Vocabulary mismatch problems, 4:134

Vocoder, 2:116

Voice coils, in sound devices, 2:181–182

Voice mail systems, 3:205

    vs. e-mail, 1:48–49

    integrated with e-mail, 4:140

    OAS applications, 1:158

Voice recognition. *See* Speech recognition

Voice recorders, for PDAs, 2:141

Voice synthesizers, for disabled persons, 4:*15*

Volatility

    of CMOS, 1:130

    of memory devices, 2:109

    of RAM, 1:129, 2:111, 2:187

    of ROM, 1:129–130, 2:111

    of VM, 1:131

Volcanoes

    studied by Charles Babbage, 1:26

    visualization of eruptions, 3:177

Volta prize/Volta Bureau, 2:17

Volvo, CAD applications, 3:31

Von Neumann Architecture, 2:217

Von Neumann, John, 2:**217–218**, 2:*217*

    Alan Turing and, 1:197

    cellular automata, 4:9, 4:10

    EDVAC project, 1:55–56, 1:61, 2:74

    ENIAC project, 1:72, 2:218

    IAS machine, 1:72

    John Kemeny and, 3:121

    Manhattan Project, 2:217–218

    self-replicating systems, 2:218

Von Neumann machine, 1:56

Voronoi diagrams, 3:101

Voting. *See* Elections; Political applications

Voting, touch screens for, 2:*199*

Voyager space probes, 1:153, 2:*53*, 3:187–188, 3:*188*

VPI (Virtual Path Identifier) connections, 4:18, 4:20

VPNs. *See* Virtual private networks

VR. *See* Virtual reality

VRML (Virtual Reality Modeling Language), 1:10–11, 2:214

VTAM subsystem, 1:127

V2 Operating System, 2:6

Vulnerability assessment tools, 3:105–106

W

Walker, James, 4:*78*

Walkie-talkies, 2:219, 3:102–103

Wallace and Gromit, 1:10

WalMart, data mining, 4:60

Walt Disney's Wonderful World of Color, 1:12–13

Walters, Grey, 1:169

Wang, An, 3:**206–208**, 3:*206*, 3:212

Wang, Charles, 4:96

Wang computers

    1200 computer, 3:212

    VS minicomputers, 3:207

Wang Laboratories, 3:206

Wang Word Processing System, 3:207, 3:*211*, 3:212

Wannabes, hackers, 4:123

WANs (wide area networks)

    ATM for, 4:17

    defined, 1:128, 4:142

    function, 1:156

    network architectures, 2:117–118

    vs. VPNs, 2:211–212, 2:213

WAP (wireless application protocol), 3:34

The War of the Worlds, 3:20

Warcraft game, 1:70

Warez Dudez hackers, 4:123

WarGames, 4:*106*

Warnock, John, 3:199

Waterfall paradigms

    in systems analysis, 2:194

    in systems design, 2:195–196, 2:197

Watson, James, 4:36

Watson, Thomas A., 1:189, 2:17

Watson, Thomas J., Jr., 1:89–90, 1:212

Watson, Thomas J., Sr., 1:88–89, 1:186, 1:**210–212**, 1:*211*

WAV file format, 1:101, 3:113

Wave interruption touch-screen panels, 2:200

WAVE sound format, 2:183

Wave table synthesis, sound cards, 2:184

Waveform, defined, 2:81

Wavelength division multiplexing (WDM), 1:162, 2:76

Wavelet mathematics, 2:97

Waypoints, in aircraft navigation, 3:7, 3:9, 3:150

Wearable computing, 3:*85*, 3:86

Weather forecasting, 3:**208–210**
  crawls, 3:209
  data processing applications, 3:59, 3:*60*
  data reception and delivery, 3:208–209
  Doppler Radar, 3:209
  EDVAC for, 2:74
  expert systems for, 3:88
  First Warning Systems, 3:209
  GOES for, 2:170
  high and low pressure, 3:208
  Internet access, 3:209
  John Mauchly's contributions, 2:74
  knowledge bases, 3:124
  maps, graphics for, 3:209, 3:*210*
  NWS, 3:208
  scientific visualization, 3:177
  soundings, 3:208
  supercomputers for, 1:185, 2:135, 3:80, 3:208
  WSI, 3:208
Weather Services International (WSI), 3:208
Web animation, 1:14
Web application programs, languages for, 4:74
Web-based commerce. *See* E-commerce
Web browsers. *See* Internet browsers
Web design, XML for, 2:106–108
Web servers
  CERN software, 3:157
  cookies and, 4:40–42
  Internet browsers and, 4:27
  for intranets, 4:150
  online credit information, 4:48
Web sites
  authentication to access, 4:21, 4:23–24
  cookies and, 4:40–42, 4:*41*
  damaged by hackers, 3:104
  digital art, 4:7–8
  index terms, 4:134
  Internet browsers and, 4:28–29, 4:*29*
  Java applets, 4:**152–155**, 4:*155*
  LCD projector displays, 4:88
  standards, 4:140
  use of "guru," 4:121
Web sites, specific
  Alternative Museum, 4:8
  Center for Molecular Modeling, 4:36–37
  Digital Landfill, 4:6–7

  periodic table and comic book history, 4:37
  Sputnik signals, 3:104
  urban legend information, 4:207
Web surfers, 1:219
  See also Internet browsers
WebCT course management system, 3:76
Webphone, 1:144, 1:*219*
WebSENSE filter, 4:32
WebVan, 4:80
WEDELMUSIC modeling language, 3:146
Weed management software, 3:*5*
WeedCast software, 3:*5*
Wei, Pei, 4:30
Weiser, Mark, 3:84
Wells Fargo Bank, firewalls, 4:75
Wells, H.G., 3:19, 3:20
Werbos, Paul J., 3:154
West Publishing Company, Westlaw legal research tools, 3:129
Western Electric Company (WECo), 1:27–28
Western Music Notation. *See* Common Music Notation
Westworld, 4:104
What-if analyses, 3:169, 3:192
What-you-see-is-what-you-get. *See* WYSIWYG
Wheatstone, Charles, 1:123, 2:91
While Rome Burns, 4:206
Whirlpool project, 3:16
Whirlwind computer, 1:57
White Hat hackers, 4:123
Whitman, Meg, 1:*44*
Whittle, Capt. Frank, 1:*4*
Wide area networks. *See* WANs
Wiener, Norbert, 4:55–56, 4:*56*
Wiley InterScience, e-journal, 4:84
Wilkes, Maurice V.
  Alan Turing and, 1:198
  EDSAC project, 1:42, 1:56–57, 1:62, 1:72
  Manchester Mark I computer, 1:56
William and Flora Hewlett Foundation, 3:109
William the Conqueror, Domesday Book, 1:166
Williams, Frederic, 1:56, 1:61, 1:62
Williams, John, 4:62
Wily hacker attack, 1:177
WIMP (windows, icon, menu, pointer) interfaces, 1:111, 3:196, 4:128
  See also GUIs

WinCE operating system, 2:143, 3:35
Window interfaces, 1:**212–218**
  application wizards, 1:216
  closing, 1:213, 1:214, 1:*215*, 1:*216*
  customizing, 1:216
  direction buttons, 1:215–216, 1:*217*
  dragging, 1:213–214
  for DTP computers, 3:196
  Focus windows, 1:215
  for graphics and multimedia, 2:70–71
  iconifying, 1:213, 1:214, 1:*215*
  for Macintosh computers, 1:111, 1:217
  menu bars, 1:215
  multiple tasks, 4:128–129
  for networked computers, 1:217
  overlapping, 1:212, 1:*213*, 1:217
  PARC contributions, 1:216–217, 1:222
  programming, 1:216–217
  resizing, 1:213
  restoring, 1:213, 1:214
  scroll bars, 1:215–216, 1:*217*
  Smalltalk programs, 1:80, 1:216–217
  thumbnails, 1:216, 1:*217*
  tiling, 1:212–213, 1:*214*
  title bars, 1:213, 1:*215*
  for World Wide Web, 1:218–219
  See also Microsoft Windows
Window managers, direct manipulation-systems, 1:112–113
Windows Media Player software, 3:113
Wing Commander, 1:15
Wire frame graphic display forms, 2:83
Wired control, telephony, 3:200
Wired technology
  ethernets, 4:136
  fiber optic cables, 4:136
  for networks, 1:155
Wireless application protocol (WAP), 3:34
Wireless lavaliere microphones, 4:85
Wireless local area networks (WLANs), 2:221
Wireless local loops (WLLs), 2:221
Wireless technology, 2:**218–221**
  Alfred Gross and, 3:102–103
  freespace loss, 2:220
  history, 2:219
  infrared waves, 2:218–219, 2:220

Wireless technology (continued)
  Mobitex services, 4:166
  repeaters, 2:202
  RF communications, 2:218–219, 2:220
  signal blockage, 2:219–220
  transmission media, 2:202, 4:136
  See also Cellular technology
Wireless technology, uses
  Bluetooth cable system, 2:220, 4:166
  broadcast communications, 1:190–191, 2:219
  CCTV, 4:118
  early radio receiver, 2:*219*
  hands-free infrared input devices, 2:93
  LMDS, 2:221
  mobile computing, 4:165, 4:166
  modems, 2:47, 2:202, 2:220
  networks, 1:155
  PDAs, 2:142, 2:144, 2:220–221
  telegraph, 2:219
  telephone systems, 1:190, 3:199
  WLLs, 2:221
Wireless Telegraph and Signal Company, 4:163
Wirth, Niklaus, 2:1, 2:155, 2:*157*
Wisconsin Integrally Synchronized Computer (WISC), 4:4
WLANs (wireless local area networks), 2:221
WLLs (wireless local loops), 2:221
Women Accepted for Volunteer Emergency Service (WAVES), 1:85
Women in computer sciences, 1:63
  Antonelli, Jean, 1:63
  Bartik, Jennings, 1:63
  Holberton, Frances Snyder, 1:63
  Hopper, Grace, 1:21, 1:53, 1:**84–87**, 1:*86*, 2:156
  Kurtzig, Sandra, 4:96
  Lopker, Pamela, 4:97
  Meltzer, Marlyn Wecoff, 1:63
  See also Lovelace, Ada Byron King, Countess of
Women in Technology International, 1:63
Wong, Ray, 2:173
Woodland, Joseph, 2:163
Woollcott, Alexander, 4:206
Word lattice representation, 3:189
Word processors, 3:**210–213**
  chemistry applications, 4:35
  CRT-based, 3:211
  cut, copy, and paste tools, 3:119

desktop publishing features, 3:197, 3:213
  early, lack of integration, 3:119
  expanded features, 3:213
  integration, 3:119
  object linking and embedding, 3:119–120
  standards, 1:101
  term coined, 3:210–211
  text editing function, 3:212
  text entering function, 3:212
  text formatting function, 3:212–213
  uses, 3:167
Word processors, specific
  Corel, 1:157
  Lotus Word Pro, 3:167
  MTST, 3:210–211
  Wang Word Processing System, 3:207, 3:*211*, 3:212
Word software (Microsoft), 1:137, 1:157, 3:167
  Clippy, 4:1, 4:3
  for HTML files, 3:110
WordPerfect software, 1:157, 3:119, 3:167
  Office, 3:110
  Works, 3:170
WordStar software, 3:119
Work (cut) prints, 1:10
Worksheets. *See* Spreadsheets
Workstations
  ergonomically correct, 1:65–67, 1:*66*
  IBM 1500-series, 3:41
  operating systems, 2:129
World Trade Center
  Flight Simulator game alterations, 4:127
  terrorist attacks, 4:*116*
  urban myths, last photo (computerized), 4:207
World Wide Web, 1:**218–220**
  animation technology, 1:14
  Apache Project and, 3:157
  cache memory and, 2:28
  cookies, 1:168, 4:**40–43**
  distinguished from Internet, 1:218, 2:71
  document processing role, 2:71
  DTP page layout, 3:199
  ethics of intellectual property, 4:100
  GUIs, 1:218
  history, 2:90, 4:29–30
  hyperlinks, 4:30
  hypermedia and, 2:83, 2:86

hypertext, 4:29, 4:30
  intranet access to, 4:150
  JavaScript, 4:**155–159**
  Jerry's Guide to the World Wide Web, 1:219, 4:98
  multimedia applications, 2:84, 3:204
  physics applications, 3:164
  privacy issues, 1:220
  programming/markup languages, 2:71, 2:104, 2:105, 2:106
  Rehabilitation Act and, 4:16
  social and ethical issues, 1:219–220, 2:90, 4:200
  standards, 1:101, 1:218, 2:71
  URLs, 1:220, 4:30
  web-based GIS, 3:101
  See also HTML; HTTP; Internet; Internet browsers; Search engines; Web servers; Web sites
World Wide Web Consortium (W3C), 2:107, 4:29, 4:31
WorldCom, peering agreements, 4:145
Worldspan LP reservation system, 3:14
WorldWideWeb (WWW), 1:218, 4:30, 4:149
WORM (write once, read many) technology, 1:*163*, 2:190
Worms
  CHRISTMA EXEC, 1:208
  Code Red, 3:*181*, 4:*108*
  defined, 1:37
  e-mail transmission, 1:49, 2:*94*, 2:*95*
  ExploreZip, 1:208
  history, 1:176, 1:208, 4:148
  how they work, 2:95
  intent of, 2:93–94, 2:95
  LoveLetter, 1:208, 2:93, 2:95
  Melissa, 1:208, 2:95
  Morris, 1:37
  payloads, 1:208
  programming languages, 2:95
  protection from, 3:106, 3:*181*
  released by hackers, 4:123
  statistics, 2:95
  at Xerox, 2:95
  See also Invasive programs; Trojan horses; Viruses
Wozniak, Stephen, 1:15–17, 1:69, 4:94–95
Wright Brothers, 2:17–18
Wright, S. Fowler, 4:105
Wrigley's Juicy Fruit gum, bar codes, 2:163

The Wrong Trousers, 1:10

WSI (Weather Services International), 3:208

W3C (World Wide Web Consortium), 1:100, 2:107, 4:29, 4:31, 4:92–93, 4:140

WYSIWYG (what-you-see-is-what-you-get), 1:222, 3:70, 3:72, 3:74, 3:196–197

X

X-Cube, 1:15

X-Files, 3:104

X.509 authentication technique, 4:83

X-rays
  CAT, 3:55–56, 3:57
  CT scanning, 3:115
  digital images, 4:66
  electronic transmission, 3:141

X Window System, 1:112, 1:217

X-Y plotters, 2:63

X, Y, Z coordinates, GPS, 4:114

Xanadu computer, 1:88

Xbox game, 2:80

Xenakis, Iannis, 1:149

Xerography, 1:220, 2:151

Xerox Corporation, 1:**220–223**
  beginnings, 1:220
  computer research, 1:222
  computer worms, 1:208, 2:95
  government research grants, 1:81
  GUIs, 2:130
  Smalltalk, 2:128

window interface research, 1:216–217
  See also PARC (Palo Alto Research Center)

Xerox equipment
  800 computer, 3:212
  4045 CP printer, 2:*150*
  8010 Star computer, 1:111
  9700 printer, 3:198
  Alto computer, 1:222
  copy machines, 1:220–221, 1:*221*
  Dynabook computer, 1:216–217

Xerox technology, animation, 1:12

XHTML, 2:107

XLL (XML linking language), 1:101

XML (Extended Markup Language), 2:106–108
  defined, 4:65
  for desktop publishing, 3:74, 3:199
  development, 4:31
  distinguished from HTML and SGML, 2:107
  Document Object Model, 2:107
  for document processing, 2:71
  for e-commerce, 4:79
  functions, 1:101, 2:107, 4:140
  and GPS, 4:132
  for intelligent agents, 2:72
  MathML, 2:107–108
  Music XML, 3:146
  Query, 2:107
  -RPC, 4:141
  SMIL, 2:108

XPath, 2:107

Xplore, e-journal, 4:84

XSL (XML Stylesheet Language), 1:101, 2:107

Y

Yacc (yet another compiler-compiler), 2:2

Yahoo! (Yet Another Hierarchical Officious Oracle), 1:219, 4:98

Yahoo.com, 1:47

Yamaha DX7 synthesizer, 3:148

Yang, Jerry, 1:219, 4:98

Yaw, of aircraft, 3:7

Y2K problem
  CD2000E tool, 4:5
  and terrorist attacks, 3:105

Z

Z computers, 1:52–53, 1:62, 2:222–223

Zander, Ed, 2:*36*

Zaph, Herman, 1:22

Ziller, Irving, 2:154

Zip drives and disks, 2:189, 2:190

*.zip extension, 3:112

Zip Plus Drive, 2:190

Zombie Trojan horse, 2:96

Zuse Engineering Company, 1:62, 2:222

Zuse, Konrad, 1:52–53, 1:59, 1:62, **2:221–223**

Zweig, Janet, 4:6